DEADPOOL

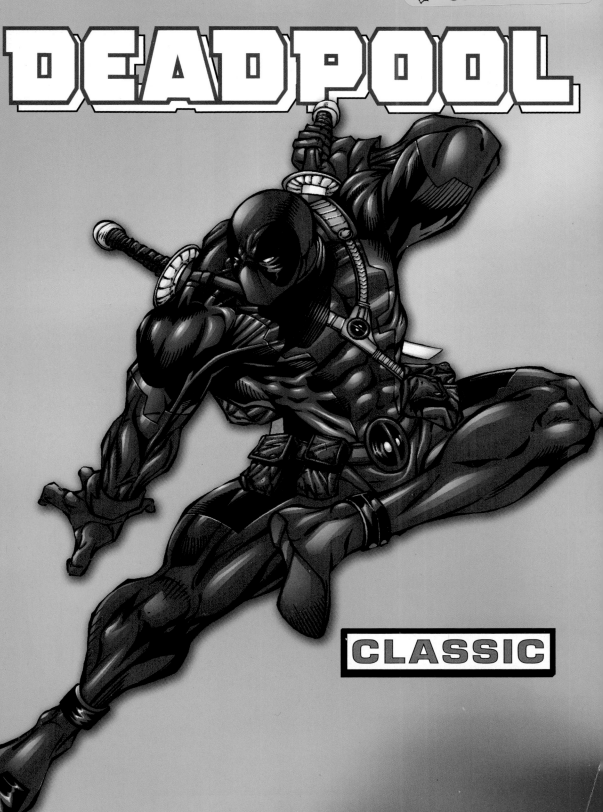

CLASSIC

DEAD·POOL

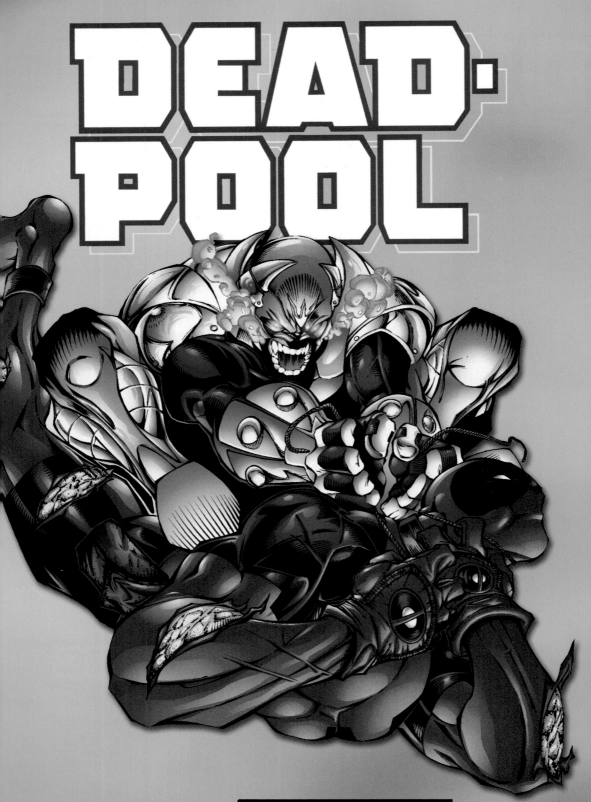

CLASSIC

WRITERS
Joe Kelly with James Felder

PENCILERS
Steve Harris, Walter McDaniel, Pete Woods,
Anthony Williams & Yancey Labat

INKERS
Reggie Jones, John Livesay, Sean Parsons, Walden Wong, Andy Lanning,
Whitney McFarland, Alp Altiner, Rodney Ramos, Scott Elmer & Scott Koblish

COLORISTS
Chris Sotomayor, Shannon Blanchard, Matt Hicks,
Colorgraphix & James Brown

DIGITAL SEPARATIONS
Graphic Colorworks & Digital Chameleon

LETTERERS
Richard Starkings, Comiccraft & Emerson Miranda

ASSISTANT EDITOR
Paul Tutrone

EDITOR
Matt Idelson

EDITOR-IN-CHIEF
Bob Harras

BOOK DESIGNER: Spring Hoteling
PRODUCTION: Ryan Devall
RESEARCH: Jeph York
COLLECTION EDITOR: Mark D. Beazley
EDITORIAL ASSISTANTS: James Emmett & Joe Hochstein
ASSISTANT EDITORS: Nelson Ribeiro & Alex Starbuck
EDITOR, SPECIAL PROJECTS: Jennifer Grünwald
SENIOR EDITOR, SPECIAL PROJECTS: Jeff Youngquist
SENIOR VICE PRESIDENT OF SALES: David Gabriel

EDITOR IN CHIEF: Joe Quesada
PUBLISHER: Dan Buckley
EXECUTIVE PRODUCER: Alan Fine

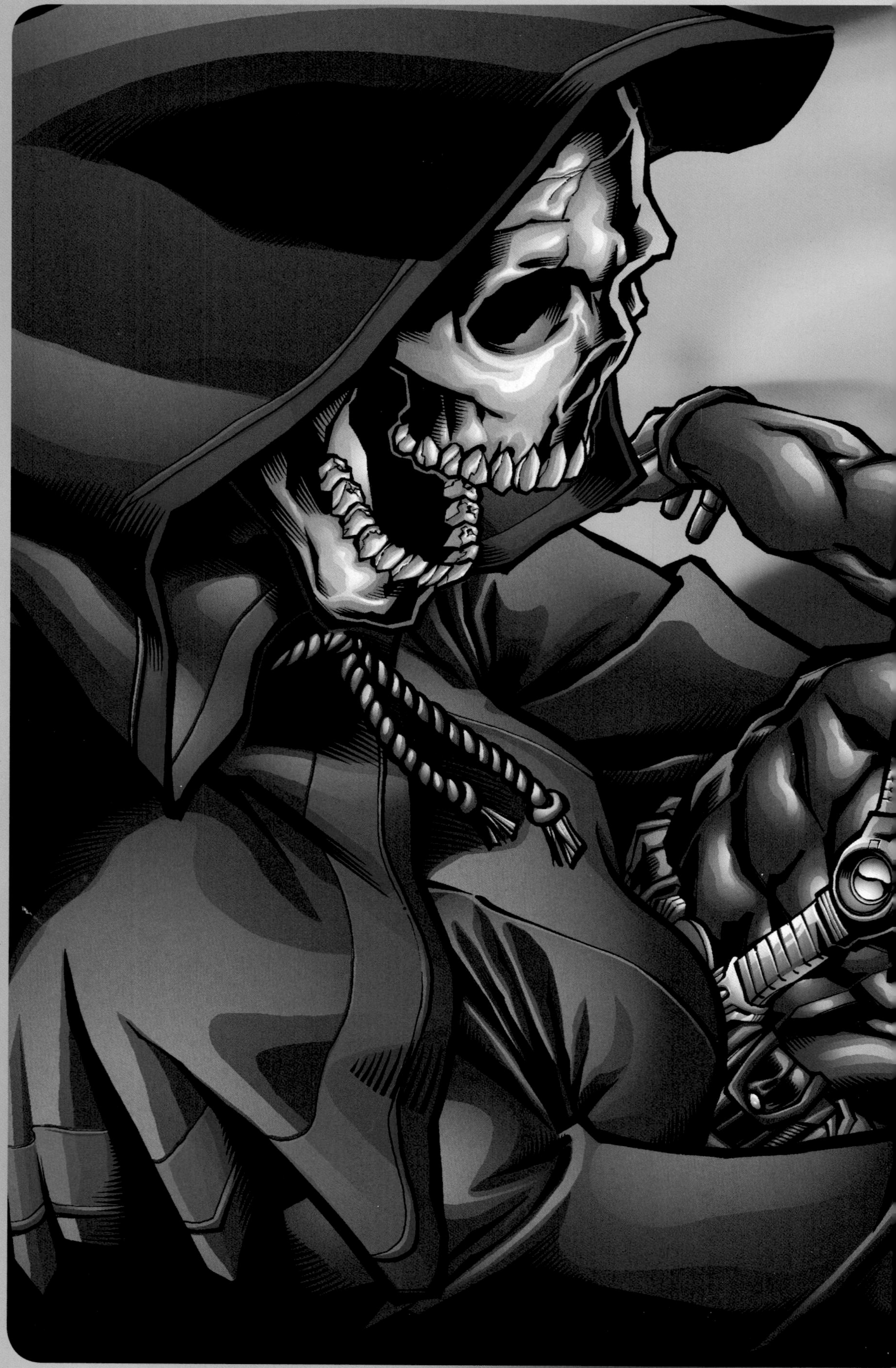

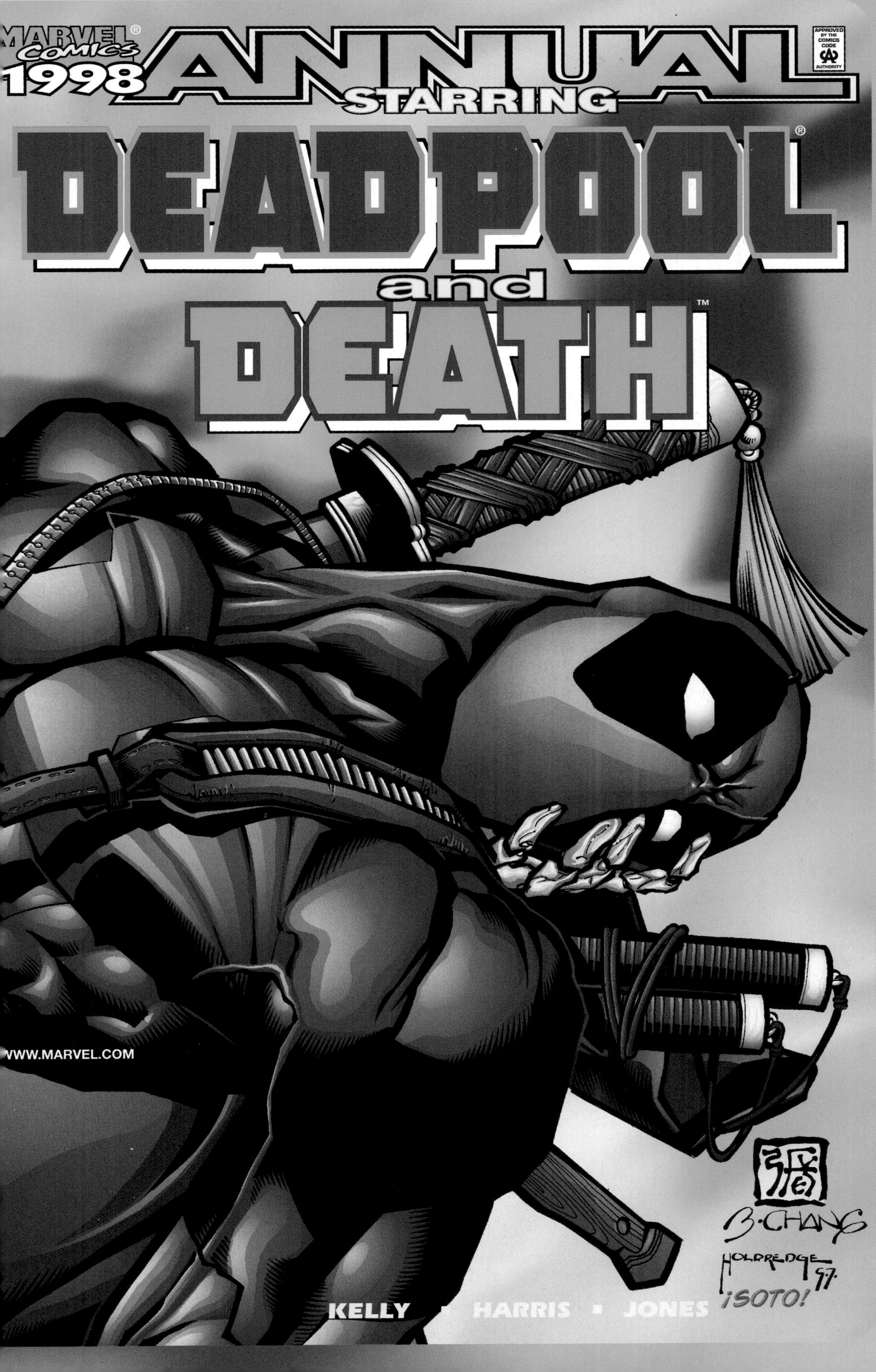
MARVEL COMICS
1998
ANNUAL
STARRING
DEADPOOL
and
DEATH
APPROVED BY THE COMICS CODE AUTHORITY
WWW.MARVEL.COM
B. CHANG
HOLDREDGE 97
¡SOTO!
KELLY • HARRIS • JONES

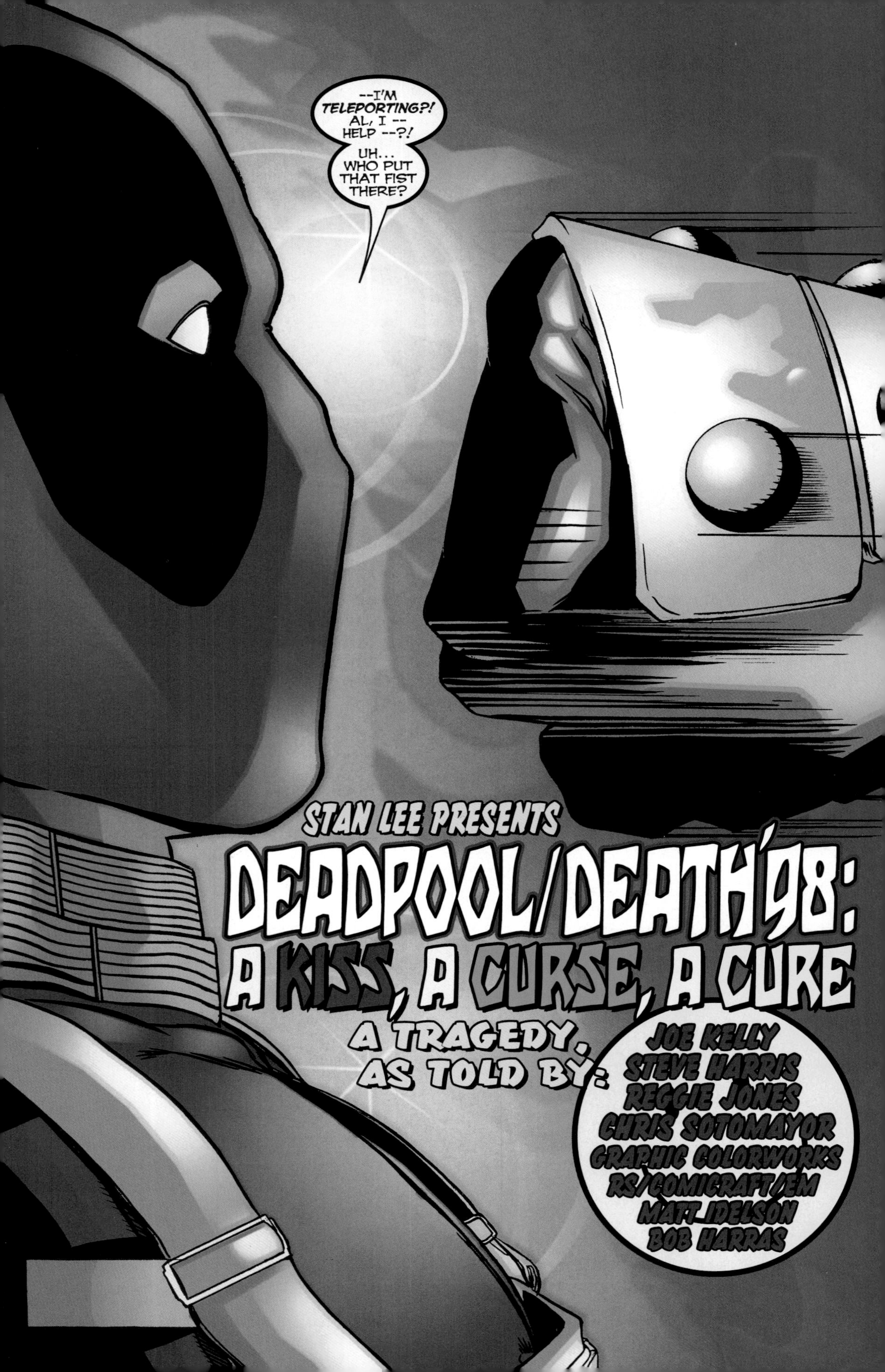
--I'M TELEPORTING?! AL, I -- HELP --?!
UH... WHO PUT THAT FIST THERE?
STAN LEE PRESENTS
DEADPOOL/DEATH '98:
A KISS, A CURSE, A CURE
A TRAGEDY, AS TOLD BY:
JOE KELLY
STEVE HARRIS
REGGIE JONES
CHRIS SOTOMAYOR
GRAPHIC COLORWORKS
RS/COMICRAFT/EM
MATT IDELSON
BOB HARRAS

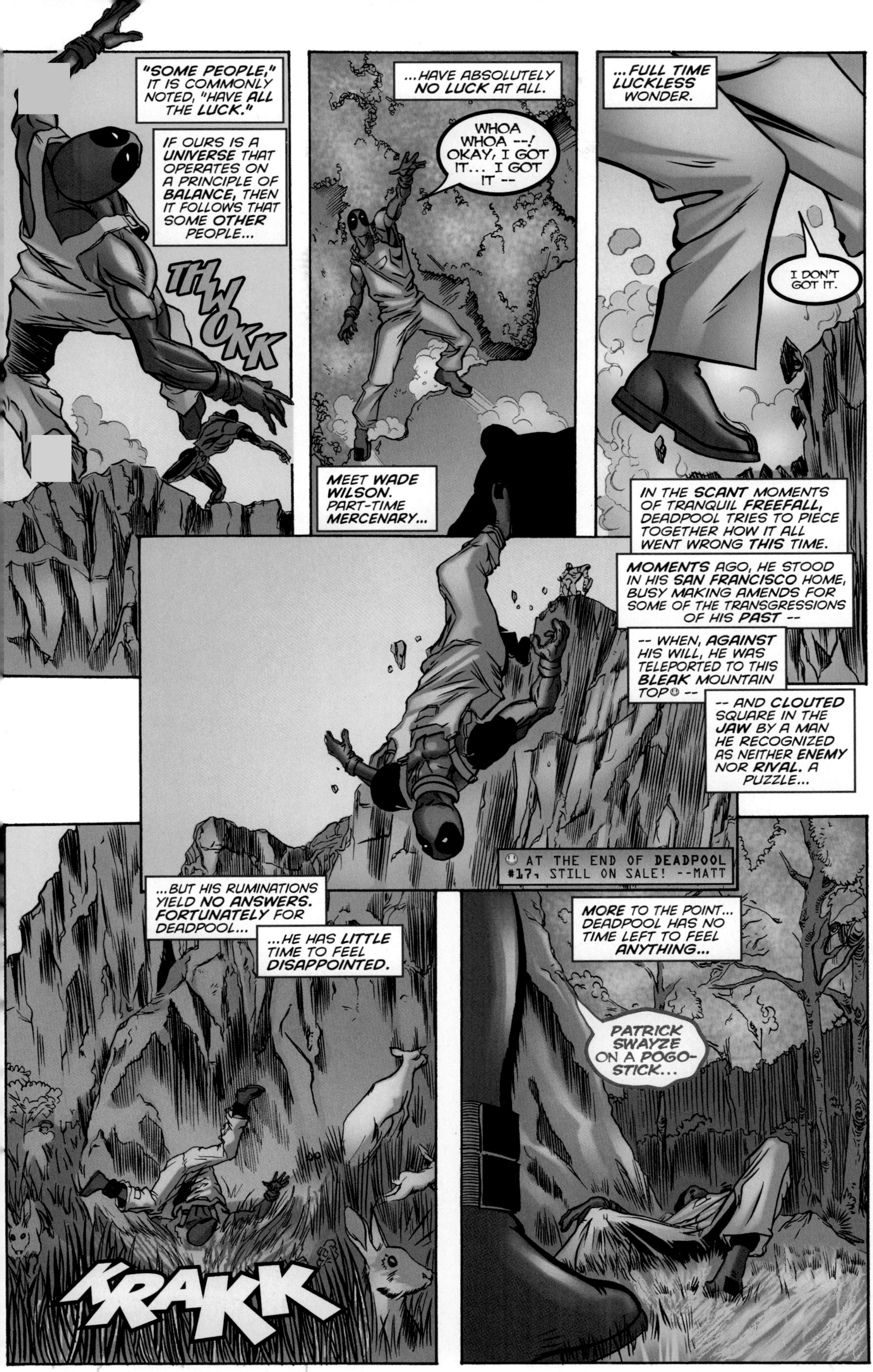
"SOME PEOPLE," IT IS COMMONLY NOTED, "HAVE ALL THE LUCK."
IF OURS IS A UNIVERSE THAT OPERATES ON A PRINCIPLE OF BALANCE, THEN IT FOLLOWS THAT SOME OTHER PEOPLE...
THWOKK
...HAVE ABSOLUTELY NO LUCK AT ALL.
WHOA WHOA --! OKAY, I GOT IT... I GOT IT --
MEET WADE WILSON. PART-TIME MERCENARY...
...FULL TIME LUCKLESS WONDER.
I DON'T GOT IT.
IN THE SCANT MOMENTS OF TRANQUIL FREEFALL, DEADPOOL TRIES TO PIECE TOGETHER HOW IT ALL WENT WRONG THIS TIME.
MOMENTS AGO, HE STOOD IN HIS SAN FRANCISCO HOME, BUSY MAKING AMENDS FOR SOME OF THE TRANSGRESSIONS OF HIS PAST --
-- WHEN, AGAINST HIS WILL, HE WAS TELEPORTED TO THIS BLEAK MOUNTAIN TOP --
-- AND CLOUTED SQUARE IN THE JAW BY A MAN HE RECOGNIZED AS NEITHER ENEMY NOR RIVAL. A PUZZLE...
AT THE END OF DEADPOOL #17, STILL ON SALE! --MATT
...BUT HIS RUMINATIONS YIELD NO ANSWERS. FORTUNATELY FOR DEADPOOL...
...HE HAS LITTLE TIME TO FEEL DISAPPOINTED.
KRAKK
MORE TO THE POINT... DEADPOOL HAS NO TIME LEFT TO FEEL ANYTHING...
PATRICK SWAYZE ON A POGO-STICK...

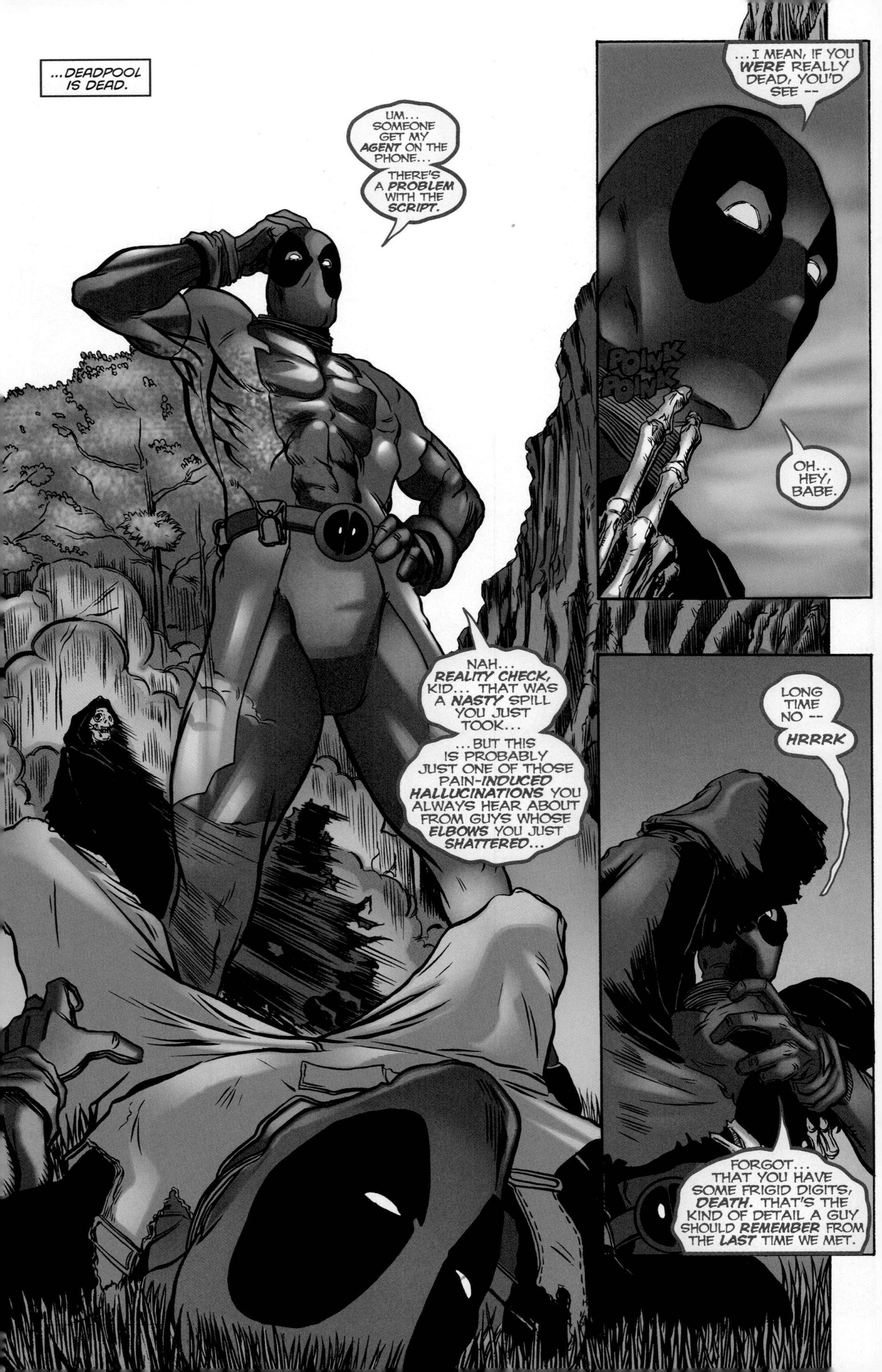
...DEADPOOL IS DEAD.
UM... SOMEONE GET MY AGENT ON THE PHONE...
THERE'S A PROBLEM WITH THE SCRIPT.
...I MEAN, IF YOU WERE REALLY DEAD, YOU'D SEE --
POINK POINK
OH... HEY, BABE.
NAH... REALITY CHECK, KID... THAT WAS A NASTY SPILL YOU JUST TOOK...
...BUT THIS IS PROBABLY JUST ONE OF THOSE PAIN-INDUCED HALLUCINATIONS YOU ALWAYS HEAR ABOUT FROM GUYS WHOSE ELBOWS YOU JUST SHATTERED...
LONG TIME NO -- HRRRK
FORGOT... THAT YOU HAVE SOME FRIGID DIGITS, DEATH. THAT'S THE KIND OF DETAIL A GUY SHOULD REMEMBER FROM THE LAST TIME WE MET.

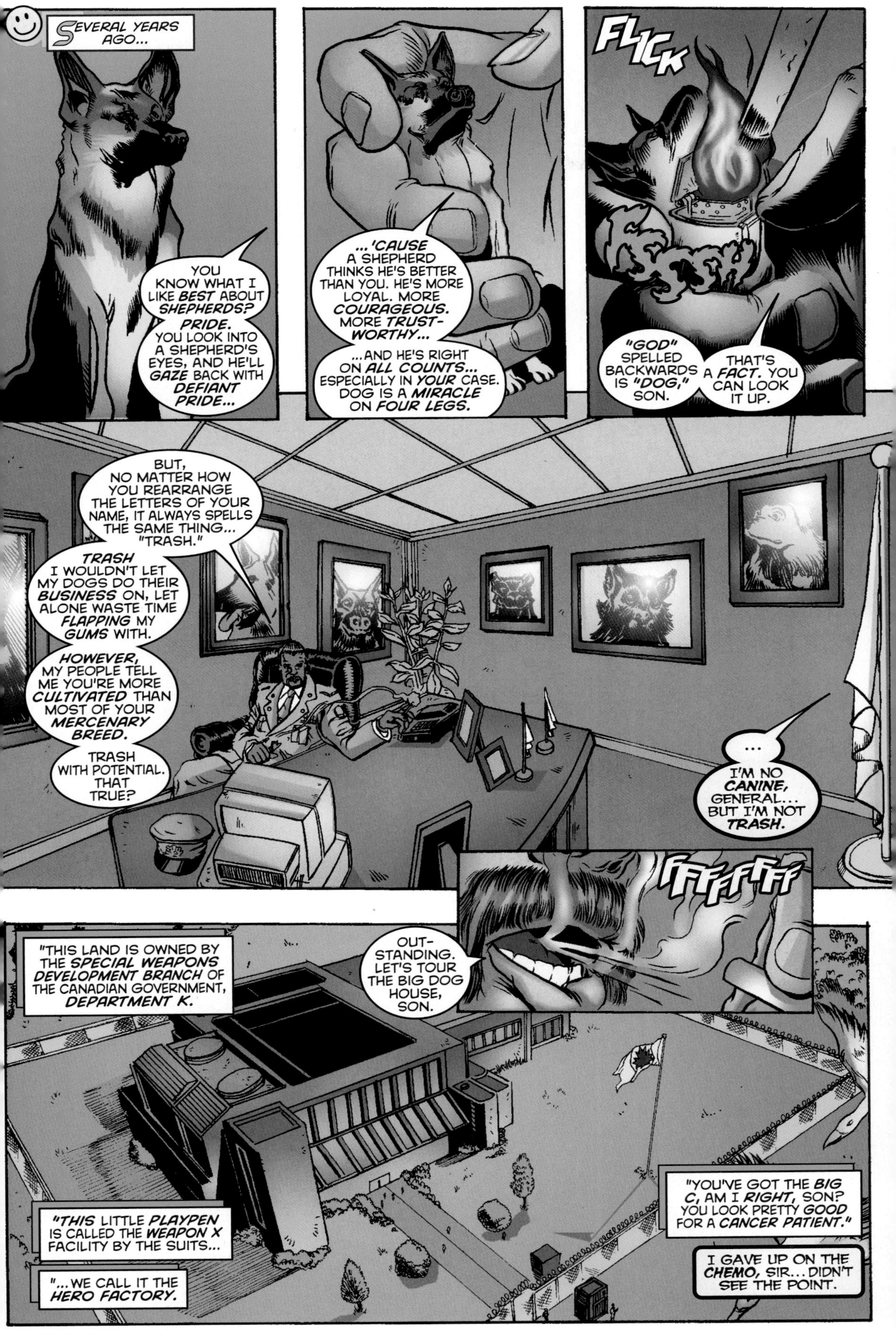
SEVERAL YEARS AGO...
YOU KNOW WHAT I LIKE BEST ABOUT SHEPHERDS? PRIDE.
YOU LOOK INTO A SHEPHERD'S EYES, AND HE'LL GAZE BACK WITH DEFIANT PRIDE...
...'CAUSE A SHEPHERD THINKS HE'S BETTER THAN YOU. HE'S MORE LOYAL. MORE COURAGEOUS. MORE TRUST-WORTHY...
...AND HE'S RIGHT ON ALL COUNTS... ESPECIALLY IN YOUR CASE. DOG IS A MIRACLE ON FOUR LEGS.
FLICK
"GOD" SPELLED BACKWARDS IS "DOG," SON.
THAT'S A FACT. YOU CAN LOOK IT UP.
BUT, NO MATTER HOW YOU REARRANGE THE LETTERS OF YOUR NAME, IT ALWAYS SPELLS THE SAME THING... "TRASH."
TRASH I WOULDN'T LET MY DOGS DO THEIR BUSINESS ON, LET ALONE WASTE TIME FLAPPING MY GUMS WITH.
HOWEVER, MY PEOPLE TELL ME YOU'RE MORE CULTIVATED THAN MOST OF YOUR MERCENARY BREED.
TRASH WITH POTENTIAL. THAT TRUE?
...
I'M NO CANINE, GENERAL... BUT I'M NOT TRASH.
FFFFFFFF
OUT-STANDING. LET'S TOUR THE BIG DOG HOUSE, SON.
"THIS LAND IS OWNED BY THE SPECIAL WEAPONS DEVELOPMENT BRANCH OF THE CANADIAN GOVERNMENT, DEPARTMENT K.
"THIS LITTLE PLAYPEN IS CALLED THE WEAPON X FACILITY BY THE SUITS...
"...WE CALL IT THE HERO FACTORY.
"YOU'VE GOT THE BIG C, AM I RIGHT, SON? YOU LOOK PRETTY GOOD FOR A CANCER PATIENT."
I GAVE UP ON THE CHEMO, SIR... DIDN'T SEE THE POINT.

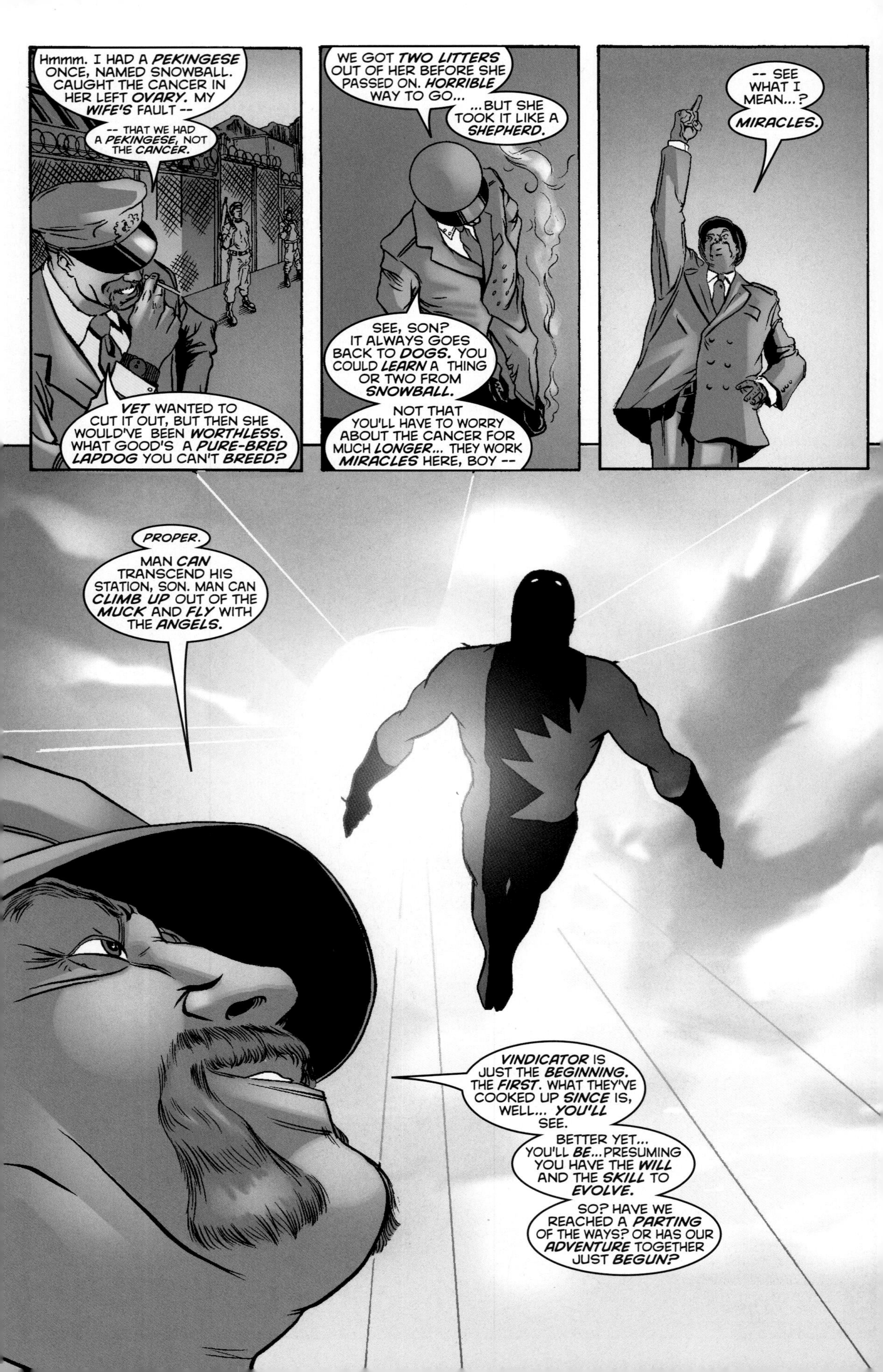
Hmmm. I HAD A PEKINGESE ONCE, NAMED SNOWBALL. CAUGHT THE CANCER IN HER LEFT OVARY. MY WIFE'S FAULT --
-- THAT WE HAD A PEKINGESE, NOT THE CANCER.
VET WANTED TO CUT IT OUT, BUT THEN SHE WOULD'VE BEEN WORTHLESS. WHAT GOOD'S A PURE-BRED LAPDOG YOU CAN'T BREED?
WE GOT TWO LITTERS OUT OF HER BEFORE SHE PASSED ON. HORRIBLE WAY TO GO...
...BUT SHE TOOK IT LIKE A SHEPHERD.
SEE, SON? IT ALWAYS GOES BACK TO DOGS. YOU COULD LEARN A THING OR TWO FROM SNOWBALL.
NOT THAT YOU'LL HAVE TO WORRY ABOUT THE CANCER FOR MUCH LONGER... THEY WORK MIRACLES HERE, BOY --
-- SEE WHAT I MEAN...?
MIRACLES.
PROPER.
MAN CAN TRANSCEND HIS STATION, SON. MAN CAN CLIMB UP OUT OF THE MUCK AND FLY WITH THE ANGELS.
VINDICATOR IS JUST THE BEGINNING. THE FIRST. WHAT THEY'VE COOKED UP SINCE IS, WELL... YOU'LL SEE.
BETTER YET... YOU'LL BE...PRESUMING YOU HAVE THE WILL AND THE SKILL TO EVOLVE.
SO? HAVE WE REACHED A PARTING OF THE WAYS? OR HAS OUR ADVENTURE TOGETHER JUST BEGUN?

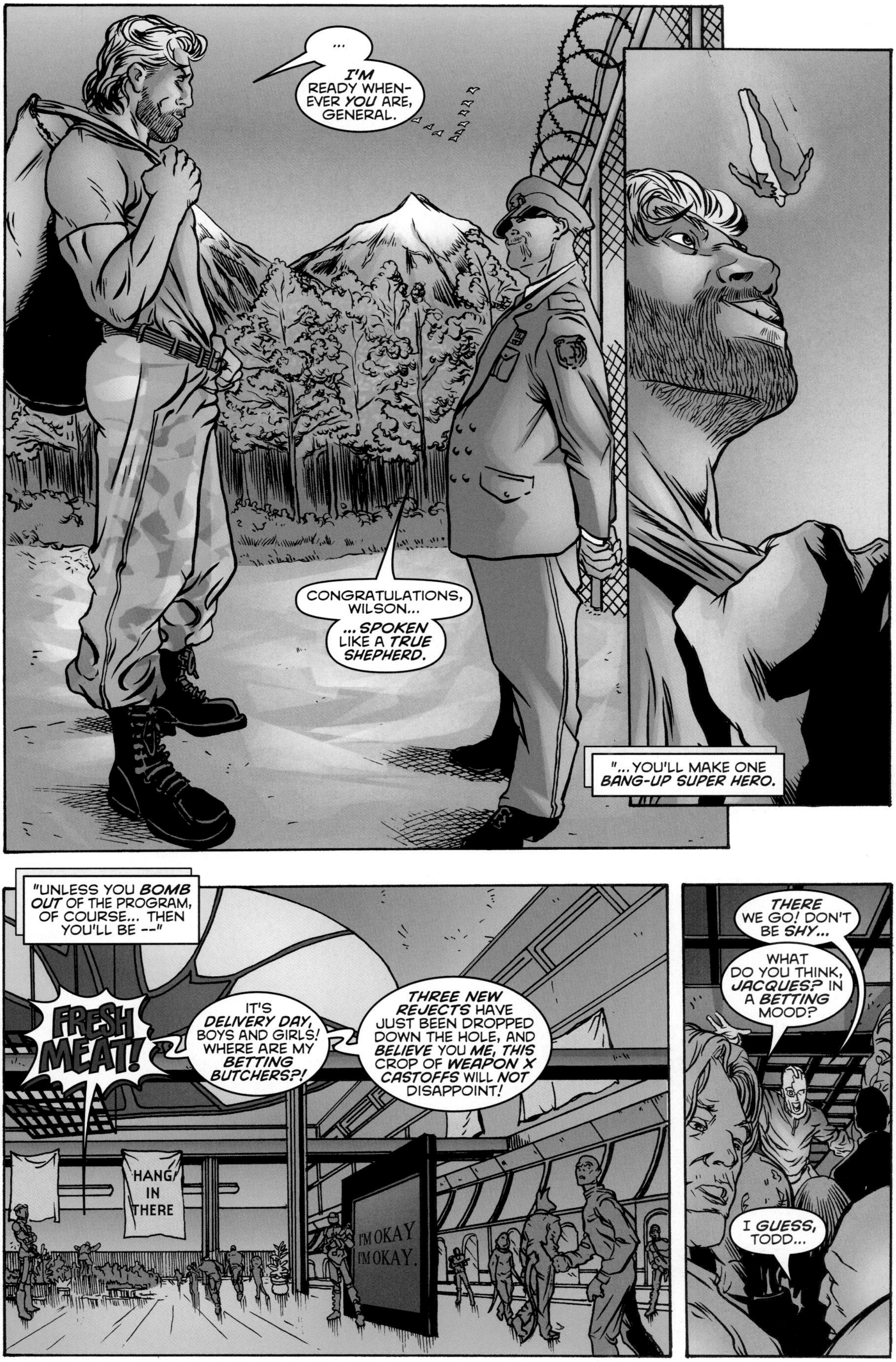
...
I'M READY WHENEVER YOU ARE, GENERAL.
CONGRATULATIONS, WILSON...
...SPOKEN LIKE A TRUE SHEPHERD.
"...YOU'LL MAKE ONE BANG-UP SUPER HERO.
"UNLESS YOU BOMB OUT OF THE PROGRAM, OF COURSE... THEN YOU'LL BE --"
FRESH MEAT!
IT'S DELIVERY DAY, BOYS AND GIRLS! WHERE ARE MY BETTING BUTCHERS?!
THREE NEW REJECTS HAVE JUST BEEN DROPPED DOWN THE HOLE, AND BELIEVE YOU ME, THIS CROP OF WEAPON X CASTOFFS WILL NOT DISAPPOINT!
HANG IN THERE
I'M OKAY I'M OKAY.
THERE WE GO! DON'T BE SHY...
WHAT DO YOU THINK, JACQUES? IN A BETTING MOOD?
I GUESS, TODD...

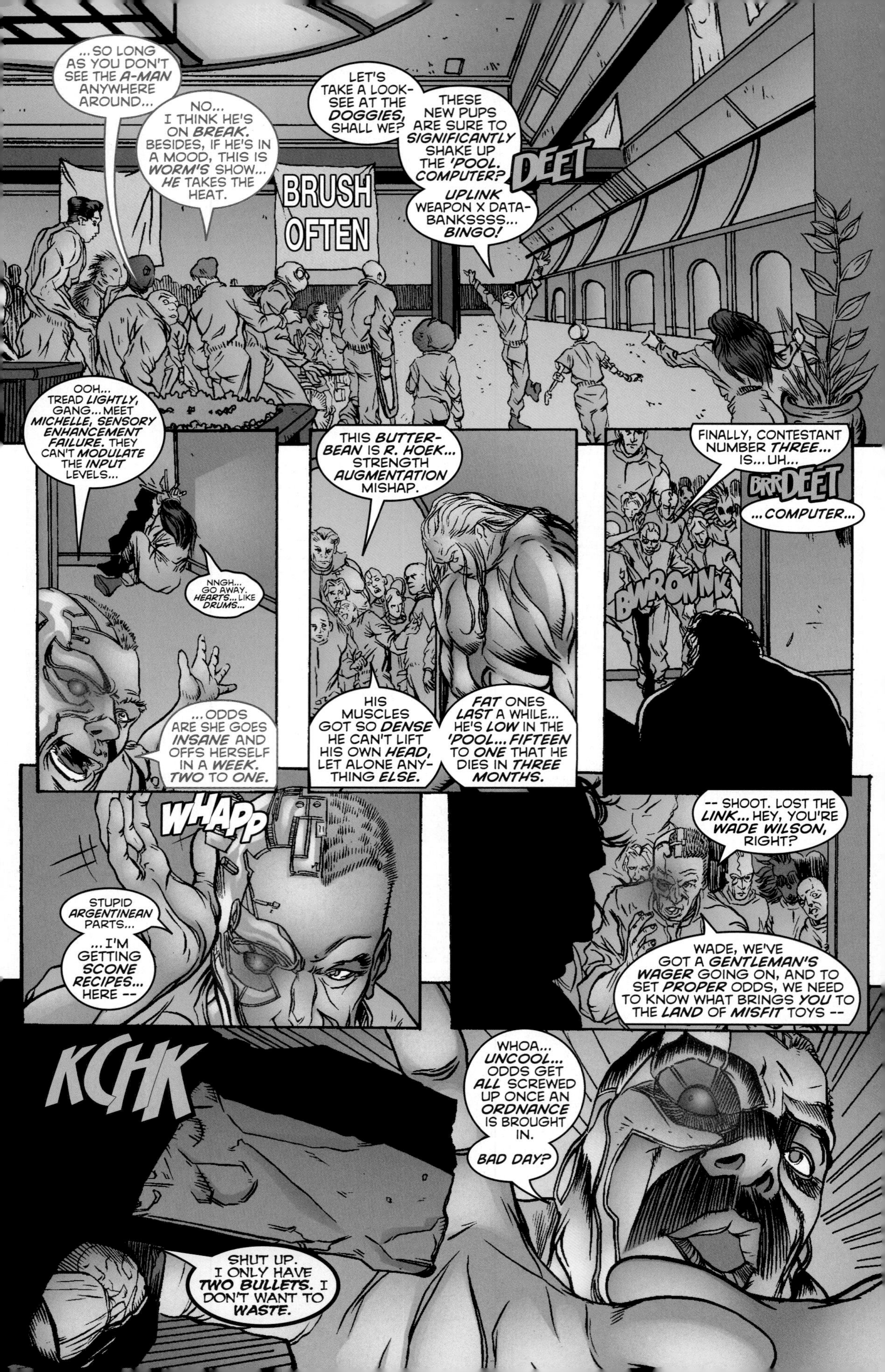
...SO LONG AS YOU DON'T SEE THE A-MAN ANYWHERE AROUND...
NO... I THINK HE'S ON BREAK. BESIDES, IF HE'S IN A MOOD, THIS IS WORM'S SHOW... HE TAKES THE HEAT.
BRUSH OFTEN
LET'S TAKE A LOOK-SEE AT THE DOGGIES, SHALL WE?
THESE NEW PUPS ARE SURE TO SIGNIFICANTLY SHAKE UP THE 'POOL. COMPUTER?
DEET
UPLINK WEAPON X DATA-BANKSSSS... BINGO!
OOH... TREAD LIGHTLY, GANG... MEET MICHELLE, SENSORY ENHANCEMENT FAILURE. THEY CAN'T MODULATE THE INPUT LEVELS...
NNGH... GO AWAY. HEARTS... LIKE DRUMS...
...ODDS ARE SHE GOES INSANE AND OFFS HERSELF IN A WEEK. TWO TO ONE.
THIS BUTTER-BEAN IS R. HOEK... STRENGTH AUGMENTATION MISHAP.
HIS MUSCLES GOT SO DENSE HE CAN'T LIFT HIS OWN HEAD, LET ALONE ANY-THING ELSE.
FAT ONES LAST A WHILE... HE'S LOW IN THE 'POOL... FIFTEEN TO ONE THAT HE DIES IN THREE MONTHS.
FINALLY, CONTESTANT NUMBER THREE... IS... UH...
BRRDEET
...COMPUTER...
BWRONNK
WHAPP
STUPID ARGENTINEAN PARTS...
...I'M GETTING SCONE RECIPES... HERE --
-- SHOOT. LOST THE LINK... HEY, YOU'RE WADE WILSON, RIGHT?
WADE, WE'VE GOT A GENTLEMAN'S WAGER GOING ON, AND TO SET PROPER ODDS, WE NEED TO KNOW WHAT BRINGS YOU TO THE LAND OF MISFIT TOYS --
KCHK
WHOA... UNCOOL... ODDS GET ALL SCREWED UP ONCE AN ORDNANCE IS BROUGHT IN.
BAD DAY?
SHUT UP. I ONLY HAVE TWO BULLETS. I DON'T WANT TO WASTE.

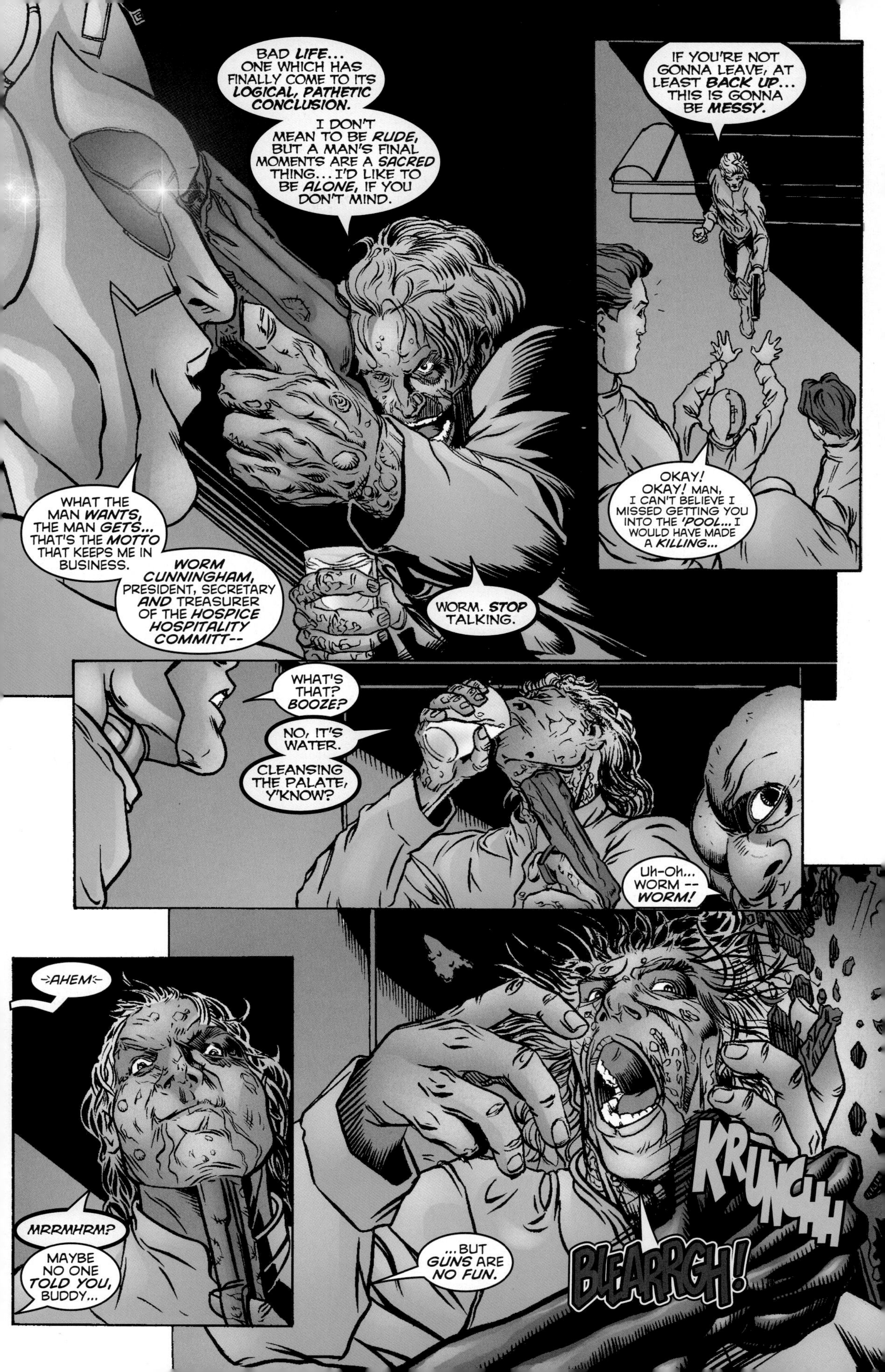
BAD LIFE... ONE WHICH HAS FINALLY COME TO ITS LOGICAL, PATHETIC CONCLUSION.
I DON'T MEAN TO BE RUDE, BUT A MAN'S FINAL MOMENTS ARE A SACRED THING... I'D LIKE TO BE ALONE, IF YOU DON'T MIND.
WHAT THE MAN WANTS, THE MAN GETS... THAT'S THE MOTTO THAT KEEPS ME IN BUSINESS.
WORM CUNNINGHAM, PRESIDENT, SECRETARY AND TREASURER OF THE HOSPICE HOSPITALITY COMMITT--
WORM. STOP TALKING.
IF YOU'RE NOT GONNA LEAVE, AT LEAST BACK UP... THIS IS GONNA BE MESSY.
OKAY! OKAY! MAN, I CAN'T BELIEVE I MISSED GETTING YOU INTO THE 'POOL... I WOULD HAVE MADE A KILLING...
WHAT'S THAT? BOOZE?
NO, IT'S WATER.
CLEANSING THE PALATE, Y'KNOW?
Uh-Oh... WORM -- WORM!
-AHEM-
MRRMHRM?
MAYBE NO ONE TOLD YOU, BUDDY...
...BUT GUNS ARE NO FUN.
KRUNCHH
BLEARRGH!

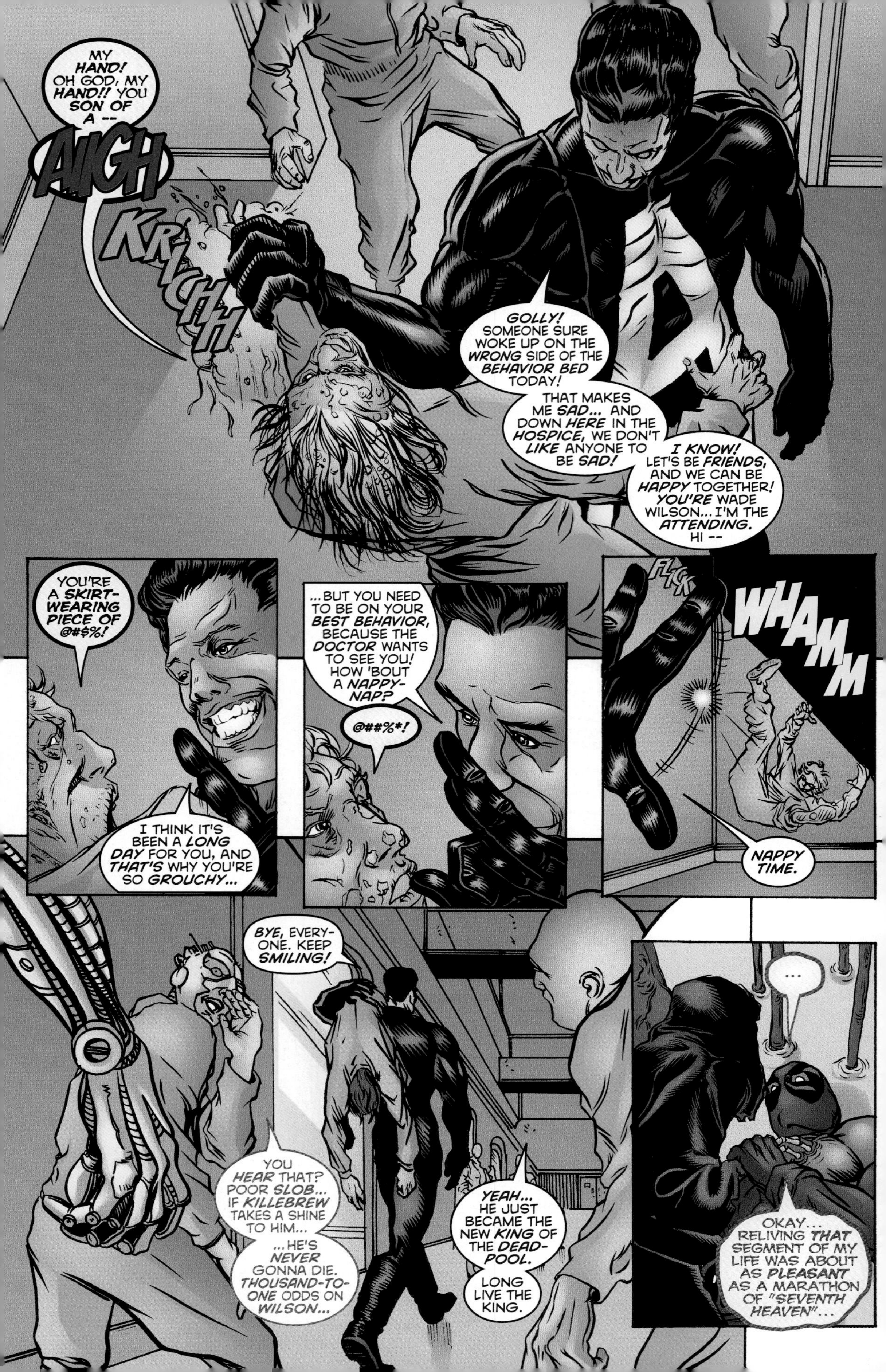
MY HAND! OH GOD, MY HAND!! YOU SON OF A --
AIGH
KRUCHH
GOLLY! SOMEONE SURE WOKE UP ON THE WRONG SIDE OF THE BEHAVIOR BED TODAY!
THAT MAKES ME SAD... AND DOWN HERE IN THE HOSPICE, WE DON'T LIKE ANYONE TO BE SAD!
I KNOW! LET'S BE FRIENDS, AND WE CAN BE HAPPY TOGETHER! YOU'RE WADE WILSON... I'M THE ATTENDING. HI --
YOU'RE A SKIRT-WEARING PIECE OF @#$%!
I THINK IT'S BEEN A LONG DAY FOR YOU, AND THAT'S WHY YOU'RE SO GROUCHY...
...BUT YOU NEED TO BE ON YOUR BEST BEHAVIOR, BECAUSE THE DOCTOR WANTS TO SEE YOU! HOW 'BOUT A NAPPY-NAP?
@##%*!
FLICK
WHAMM
NAPPY TIME.
BYE, EVERY-ONE. KEEP SMILING!
YOU HEAR THAT? POOR SLOB... IF KILLEBREW TAKES A SHINE TO HIM...
...HE'S NEVER GONNA DIE. THOUSAND-TO-ONE ODDS ON WILSON...
YEAH... HE JUST BECAME THE NEW KING OF THE DEAD-POOL.
LONG LIVE THE KING.
...
OKAY... RELIVING THAT SEGMENT OF MY LIFE WAS ABOUT AS PLEASANT AS A MARATHON OF "SEVENTH HEAVEN"...

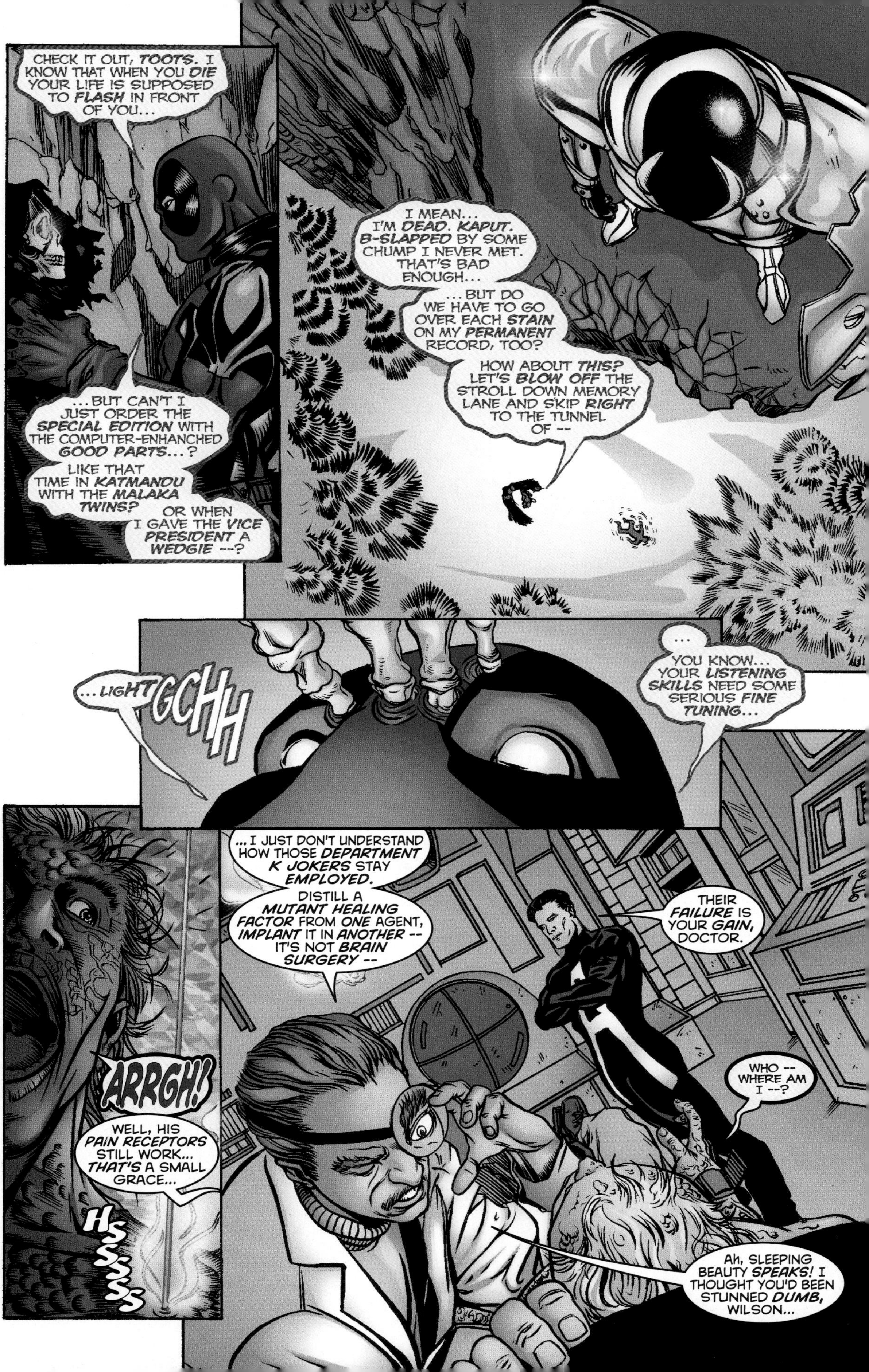
CHECK IT OUT, TOOTS. I KNOW THAT WHEN YOU DIE YOUR LIFE IS SUPPOSED TO FLASH IN FRONT OF YOU...
...BUT CAN'T I JUST ORDER THE SPECIAL EDITION WITH THE COMPUTER-ENHANCHED GOOD PARTS...?
LIKE THAT TIME IN KATMANDU WITH THE MALAKA TWINS?
OR WHEN I GAVE THE VICE PRESIDENT A WEDGIE --?
I MEAN... I'M DEAD. KAPUT. B-SLAPPED BY SOME CHUMP I NEVER MET. THAT'S BAD ENOUGH...
...BUT DO WE HAVE TO GO OVER EACH STAIN ON MY PERMANENT RECORD, TOO?
HOW ABOUT THIS? LET'S BLOW OFF THE STROLL DOWN MEMORY LANE AND SKIP RIGHT TO THE TUNNEL OF --
...LIGHT
GCHH
...
YOU KNOW... YOUR LISTENING SKILLS NEED SOME SERIOUS FINE TUNING...
ARRGH!
WELL, HIS PAIN RECEPTORS STILL WORK... THAT'S A SMALL GRACE...
HSSSSS
...I JUST DON'T UNDERSTAND HOW THOSE DEPARTMENT K JOKERS STAY EMPLOYED.
DISTILL A MUTANT HEALING FACTOR FROM ONE AGENT, IMPLANT IT IN ANOTHER -- IT'S NOT BRAIN SURGERY --
THEIR FAILURE IS YOUR GAIN, DOCTOR.
WHO -- WHERE AM I --?
Ah, SLEEPING BEAUTY SPEAKS! I THOUGHT YOU'D BEEN STUNNED DUMB, WILSON...

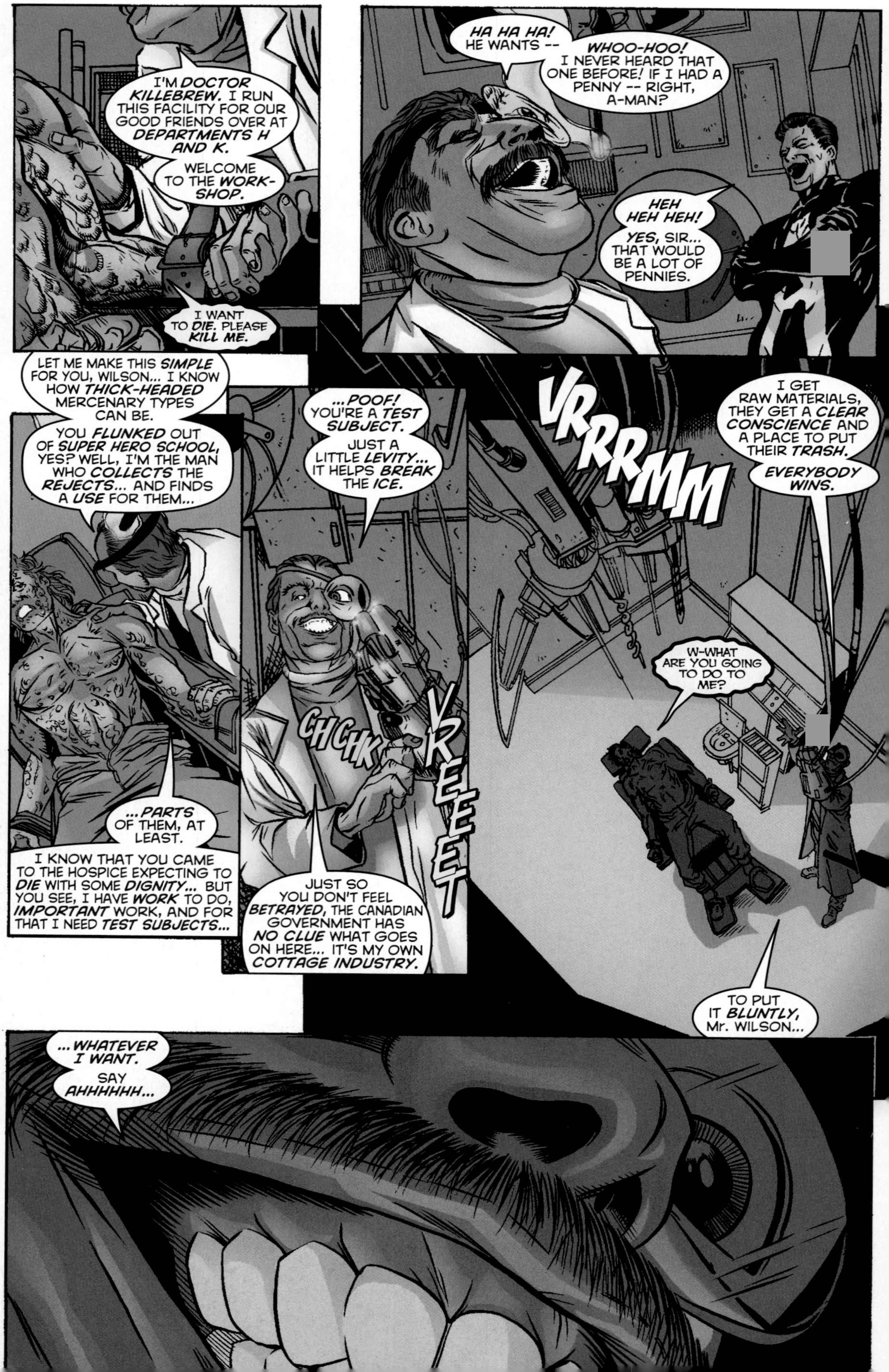

I'M DOCTOR KILLEBREW. I RUN THIS FACILITY FOR OUR GOOD FRIENDS OVER AT DEPARTMENTS H AND K.
WELCOME TO THE WORK-SHOP.
I WANT TO DIE. PLEASE KILL ME.
HA HA HA! HE WANTS --
WHOO-HOO! I NEVER HEARD THAT ONE BEFORE! IF I HAD A PENNY -- RIGHT, A-MAN?
HEH HEH HEH!
YES, SIR... THAT WOULD BE A LOT OF PENNIES.
LET ME MAKE THIS SIMPLE FOR YOU, WILSON... I KNOW HOW THICK-HEADED MERCENARY TYPES CAN BE.
YOU FLUNKED OUT OF SUPER HERO SCHOOL, YES? WELL, I'M THE MAN WHO COLLECTS THE REJECTS... AND FINDS A USE FOR THEM...
...PARTS OF THEM, AT LEAST.
I KNOW THAT YOU CAME TO THE HOSPICE EXPECTING TO DIE WITH SOME DIGNITY... BUT YOU SEE, I HAVE WORK TO DO, IMPORTANT WORK, AND FOR THAT I NEED TEST SUBJECTS...
...POOF! YOU'RE A TEST SUBJECT.
JUST A LITTLE LEVITY... IT HELPS BREAK THE ICE.
CHCHK
VREEEET
JUST SO YOU DON'T FEEL BETRAYED, THE CANADIAN GOVERNMENT HAS NO CLUE WHAT GOES ON HERE... IT'S MY OWN COTTAGE INDUSTRY.
VRRRMMM
I GET RAW MATERIALS, THEY GET A CLEAR CONSCIENCE AND A PLACE TO PUT THEIR TRASH.
EVERYBODY WINS.
W-WHAT ARE YOU GOING TO DO TO ME?
TO PUT IT BLUNTLY, Mr. WILSON...
...WHATEVER I WANT.
SAY AHHHHHH...

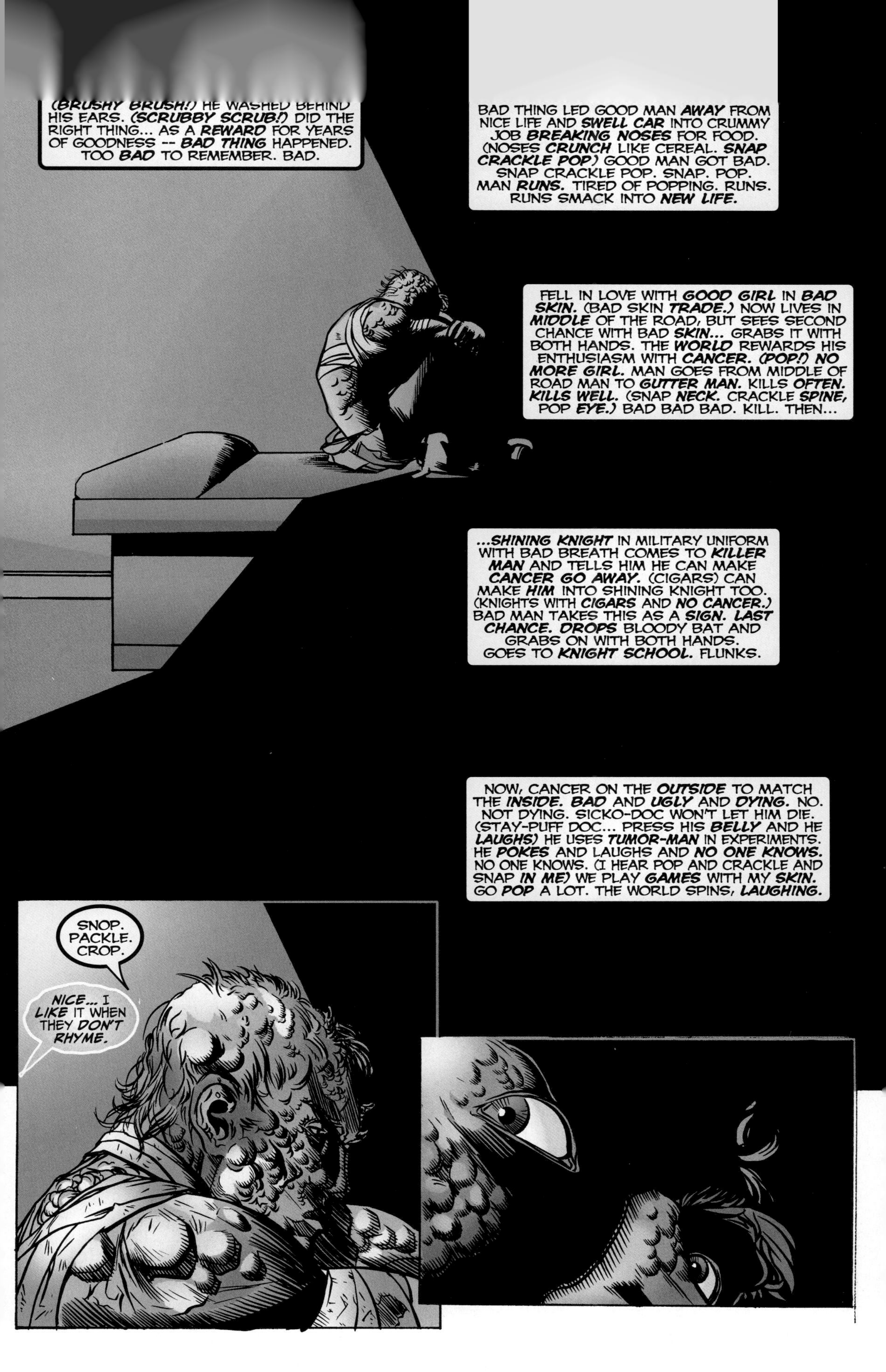
(BRUSHY BRUSH!) HE WASHED BEHIND HIS EARS. (SCRUBBY SCRUB!) DID THE RIGHT THING... AS A REWARD FOR YEARS OF GOODNESS -- BAD THING HAPPENED. TOO BAD TO REMEMBER. BAD.
BAD THING LED GOOD MAN AWAY FROM NICE LIFE AND SWELL CAR INTO CRUMMY JOB BREAKING NOSES FOR FOOD. (NOSES CRUNCH LIKE CEREAL. SNAP CRACKLE POP) GOOD MAN GOT BAD. SNAP CRACKLE POP. SNAP. POP. MAN RUNS. TIRED OF POPPING. RUNS. RUNS SMACK INTO NEW LIFE.
FELL IN LOVE WITH GOOD GIRL IN BAD SKIN. (BAD SKIN TRADE.) NOW LIVES IN MIDDLE OF THE ROAD, BUT SEES SECOND CHANCE WITH BAD SKIN... GRABS IT WITH BOTH HANDS. THE WORLD REWARDS HIS ENTHUSIASM WITH CANCER. (POP!) NO MORE GIRL. MAN GOES FROM MIDDLE OF ROAD MAN TO GUTTER MAN. KILLS OFTEN. KILLS WELL. (SNAP NECK. CRACKLE SPINE, POP EYE.) BAD BAD BAD. KILL. THEN...
...SHINING KNIGHT IN MILITARY UNIFORM WITH BAD BREATH COMES TO KILLER MAN AND TELLS HIM HE CAN MAKE CANCER GO AWAY. (CIGARS) CAN MAKE HIM INTO SHINING KNIGHT TOO. (KNIGHTS WITH CIGARS AND NO CANCER.) BAD MAN TAKES THIS AS A SIGN. LAST CHANCE. DROPS BLOODY BAT AND GRABS ON WITH BOTH HANDS. GOES TO KNIGHT SCHOOL. FLUNKS.
NOW, CANCER ON THE OUTSIDE TO MATCH THE INSIDE. BAD AND UGLY AND DYING. NO. NOT DYING. SICKO-DOC WON'T LET HIM DIE. (STAY-PUFF DOC... PRESS HIS BELLY AND HE LAUGHS) HE USES TUMOR-MAN IN EXPERIMENTS. HE POKES AND LAUGHS AND NO ONE KNOWS. NO ONE KNOWS. (I HEAR POP AND CRACKLE AND SNAP IN ME) WE PLAY GAMES WITH MY SKIN. GO POP A LOT. THE WORLD SPINS, LAUGHING.
SNOP. PACKLE. CROP.
NICE... I LIKE IT WHEN THEY DON'T RHYME.

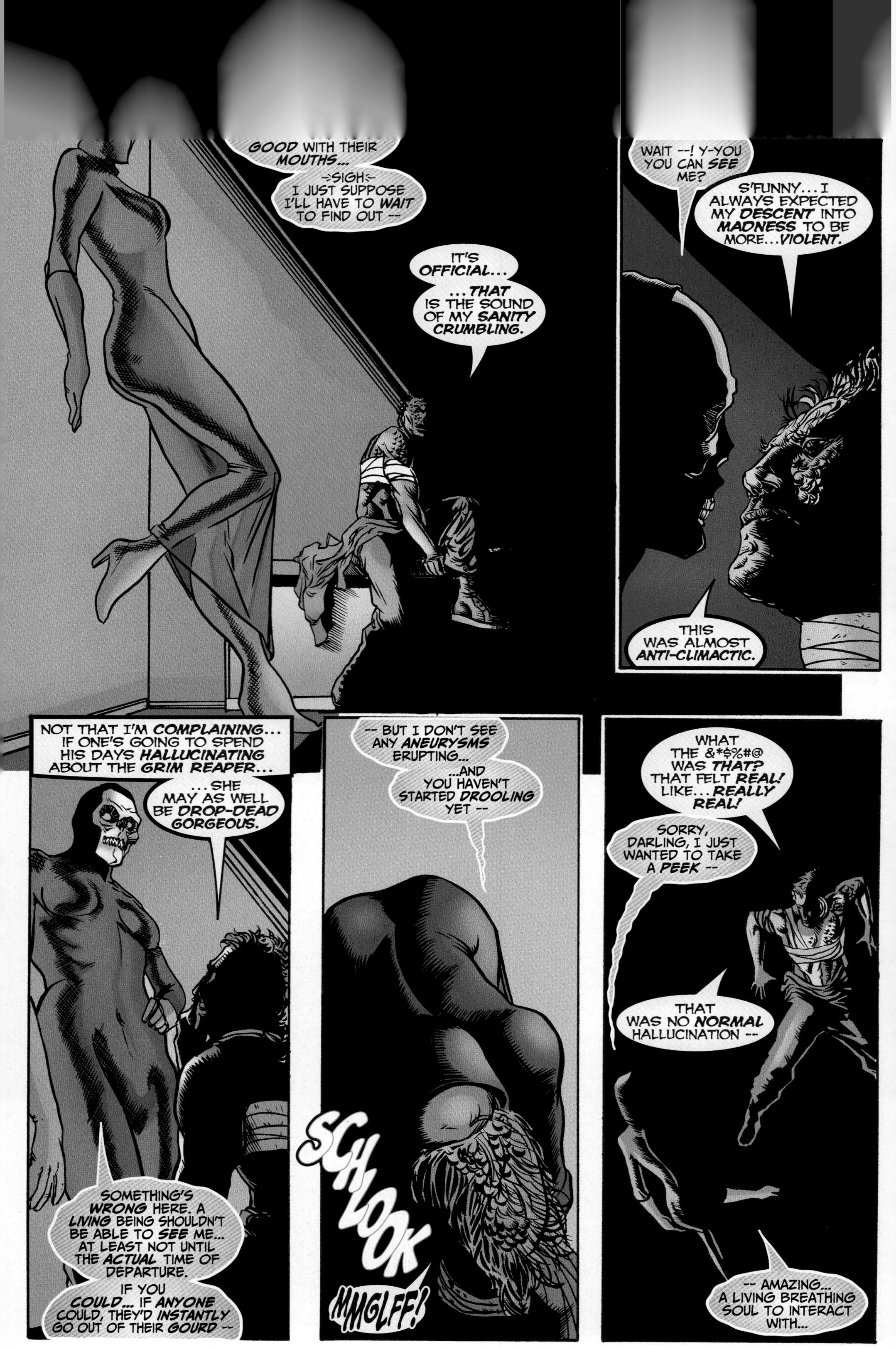

GOOD WITH THEIR MOUTHS...
>SIGH< I JUST SUPPOSE I'LL HAVE TO WAIT TO FIND OUT --
IT'S OFFICIAL...
...THAT IS THE SOUND OF MY SANITY CRUMBLING.
WAIT --! Y-YOU YOU CAN SEE ME?
S'FUNNY... I ALWAYS EXPECTED MY DESCENT INTO MADNESS TO BE MORE... VIOLENT.
THIS WAS ALMOST ANTI-CLIMACTIC.
NOT THAT I'M COMPLAINING... IF ONE'S GOING TO SPEND HIS DAYS HALLUCINATING ABOUT THE GRIM REAPER...
...SHE MAY AS WELL BE DROP-DEAD GORGEOUS.
SOMETHING'S WRONG HERE. A LIVING BEING SHOULDN'T BE ABLE TO SEE ME... AT LEAST NOT UNTIL THE ACTUAL TIME OF DEPARTURE.
IF YOU COULD... IF ANYONE COULD, THEY'D INSTANTLY GO OUT OF THEIR GOURD --
-- BUT I DON'T SEE ANY ANEURYSMS ERUPTING...
...AND YOU HAVEN'T STARTED DROOLING YET --
SCHLOOK
MMGLFF!
WHAT THE &*$%#@ WAS THAT? THAT FELT REAL! LIKE... REALLY REAL!
SORRY, DARLING, I JUST WANTED TO TAKE A PEEK --
THAT WAS NO NORMAL HALLUCINATION --
-- AMAZING... A LIVING BREATHING SOUL TO INTERACT WITH...

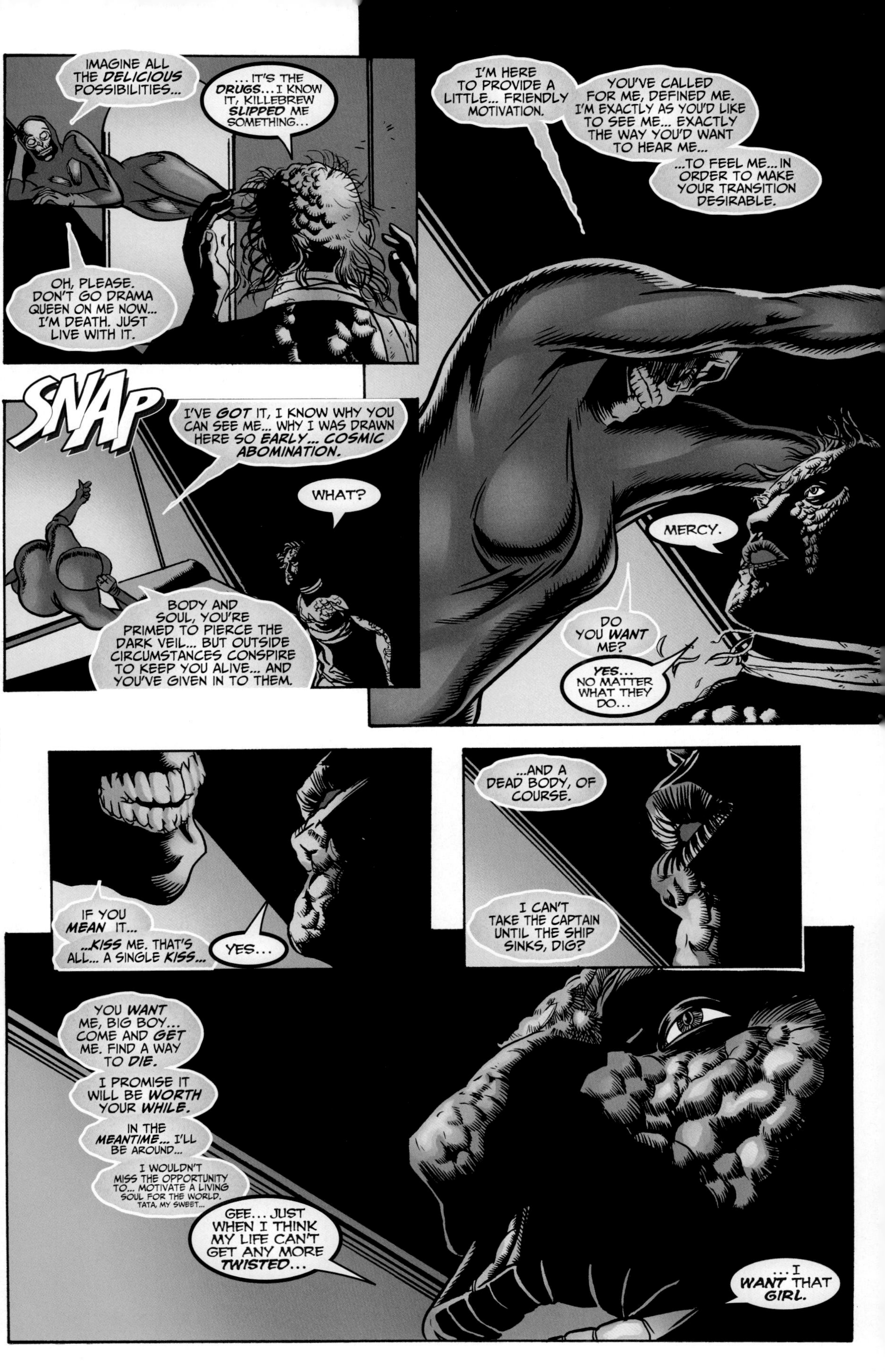
IMAGINE ALL THE DELICIOUS POSSIBILITIES...
...IT'S THE DRUGS... I KNOW IT, KILLEBREW SLIPPED ME SOMETHING...
OH, PLEASE. DON'T GO DRAMA QUEEN ON ME NOW... I'M DEATH. JUST LIVE WITH IT.
I'M HERE TO PROVIDE A LITTLE... FRIENDLY MOTIVATION.
YOU'VE CALLED FOR ME, DEFINED ME. I'M EXACTLY AS YOU'D LIKE TO SEE ME... EXACTLY THE WAY YOU'D WANT TO HEAR ME...
...TO FEEL ME...IN ORDER TO MAKE YOUR TRANSITION DESIRABLE.
SNAP
I'VE GOT IT, I KNOW WHY YOU CAN SEE ME... WHY I WAS DRAWN HERE SO EARLY... COSMIC ABOMINATION.
WHAT?
BODY AND SOUL, YOU'RE PRIMED TO PIERCE THE DARK VEIL... BUT OUTSIDE CIRCUMSTANCES CONSPIRE TO KEEP YOU ALIVE... AND YOU'VE GIVEN IN TO THEM.
MERCY.
DO YOU WANT ME?
YES... NO MATTER WHAT THEY DO...
IF YOU MEAN IT...
...KISS ME. THAT'S ALL... A SINGLE KISS...
YES...
...AND A DEAD BODY, OF COURSE.
I CAN'T TAKE THE CAPTAIN UNTIL THE SHIP SINKS, DIG?
YOU WANT ME, BIG BOY... COME AND GET ME. FIND A WAY TO DIE.
I PROMISE IT WILL BE WORTH YOUR WHILE.
IN THE MEANTIME... I'LL BE AROUND...
I WOULDN'T MISS THE OPPORTUNITY TO... MOTIVATE A LIVING SOUL FOR THE WORLD. TATA, MY SWEET...
GEE... JUST WHEN I THINK MY LIFE CAN'T GET ANY MORE TWISTED...
...I WANT THAT GIRL.

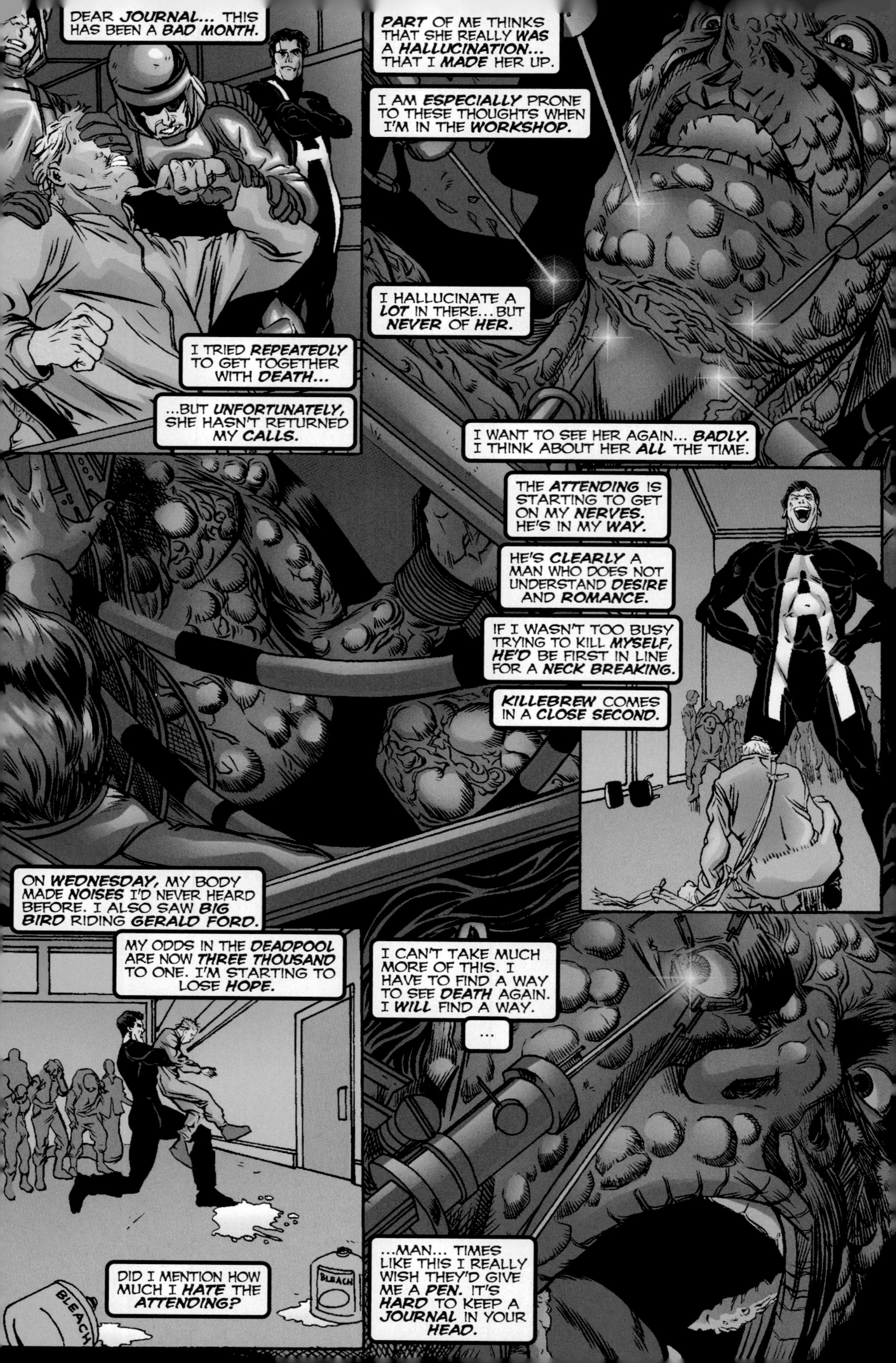
DEAR JOURNAL... THIS HAS BEEN A BAD MONTH.
I TRIED REPEATEDLY TO GET TOGETHER WITH DEATH...
...BUT UNFORTUNATELY, SHE HASN'T RETURNED MY CALLS.
PART OF ME THINKS THAT SHE REALLY WAS A HALLUCINATION... THAT I MADE HER UP.
I AM ESPECIALLY PRONE TO THESE THOUGHTS WHEN I'M IN THE WORKSHOP.
I HALLUCINATE A LOT IN THERE... BUT NEVER OF HER.
I WANT TO SEE HER AGAIN... BADLY. I THINK ABOUT HER ALL THE TIME.
THE ATTENDING IS STARTING TO GET ON MY NERVES. HE'S IN MY WAY.
HE'S CLEARLY A MAN WHO DOES NOT UNDERSTAND DESIRE AND ROMANCE.
IF I WASN'T TOO BUSY TRYING TO KILL MYSELF, HE'D BE FIRST IN LINE FOR A NECK BREAKING.
KILLEBREW COMES IN A CLOSE SECOND.
ON WEDNESDAY, MY BODY MADE NOISES I'D NEVER HEARD BEFORE. I ALSO SAW BIG BIRD RIDING GERALD FORD.
MY ODDS IN THE DEADPOOL ARE NOW THREE THOUSAND TO ONE. I'M STARTING TO LOSE HOPE.
DID I MENTION HOW MUCH I HATE THE ATTENDING?
BLEACH
BLEACH
I CAN'T TAKE MUCH MORE OF THIS. I HAVE TO FIND A WAY TO SEE DEATH AGAIN. I WILL FIND A WAY.
...
...MAN... TIMES LIKE THIS I REALLY WISH THEY'D GIVE ME A PEN. IT'S HARD TO KEEP A JOURNAL IN YOUR HEAD.

THIS IS DEGRADING.

HUG SOMEONE

YOU SHOULD SEE IT FROM OUT *HERE*, FRIEND. IT'S *HYSTERICAL*, TOO. YOUR GO, *TODD*.

CALL. DON'T WORRY, WILSON. THE ATTENDING WILL LET YOU OUT AS SOON AS HE'S FINISHED HIS *ROUNDS*.

YOU GOT ANYTHING, *STEVE*?

I GOT &*#@, *JACQUES*.

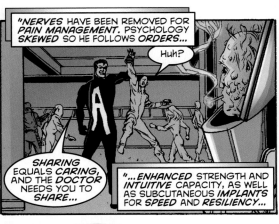

I *FOLD*. LAME HAND.

HA! NEVER IN MY EXPERIENCE AS HOSPITALITY GOD HAVE I MET SOMEONE WITH *SUCH POOR LUCK!* YOU'RE GONNA TOP THE DEADPOOL FOREVER, WILSON. YOU'RE NEVER GONNA BITE IT.

SAYS YOU. I'LL GET THE A-MAN OUT OF MY WAY... SOMEHOW.

RIGHT. A *TUMOR FACTORY* LIKE YOU IS GONNA BEAT THE *PINNACLE* OF *WEAPON X* ENGINEERING? *NOT.* ONLY REASON HE'S NOT OUT *LEAPING BUILDINGS* AND SAVING *BABIES* IS HE'S SUCH A *SADISTIC CREEP.*

EVERYONE HAS A *WEAKNESS.*

NO, NOT *HIM.* COMPUTER?

DEET

"*NERVES* HAVE BEEN REMOVED FOR *PAIN MANAGEMENT. PSYCHOLOGY SKEWED* SO HE FOLLOWS *ORDERS...*

HUH?

SHARING EQUALS *CARING,* AND THE *DOCTOR* NEEDS YOU TO *SHARE...*

"...*ENHANCED* STRENGTH AND *INTUITIVE* CAPACITY, AS WELL AS SUBCUTANEOUS *IMPLANTS* FOR *SPEED* AND *RESILIENCY...*

THANK YOU!

SCHRPPP

AIIGH!

"...AND *TWISTED* AS A *CORKSCREW.* IN *THIS* PLACE, WHATEVER *FRANCIS* WANTS, FRANCIS *GETS.*"

FRANCIS?

OH, SHOOT -- STUPID *UPLINK* -- THAT *SLIPPED, FORGET* I SAID THAT. THE A-MAN *HATES* HIS REAL NAME. *LAST* GUY USED IT WOKE UP ONE DAY WITH HIS *FEET* WHERE HIS *COLON* USED TO BE...

IS THAT SO?

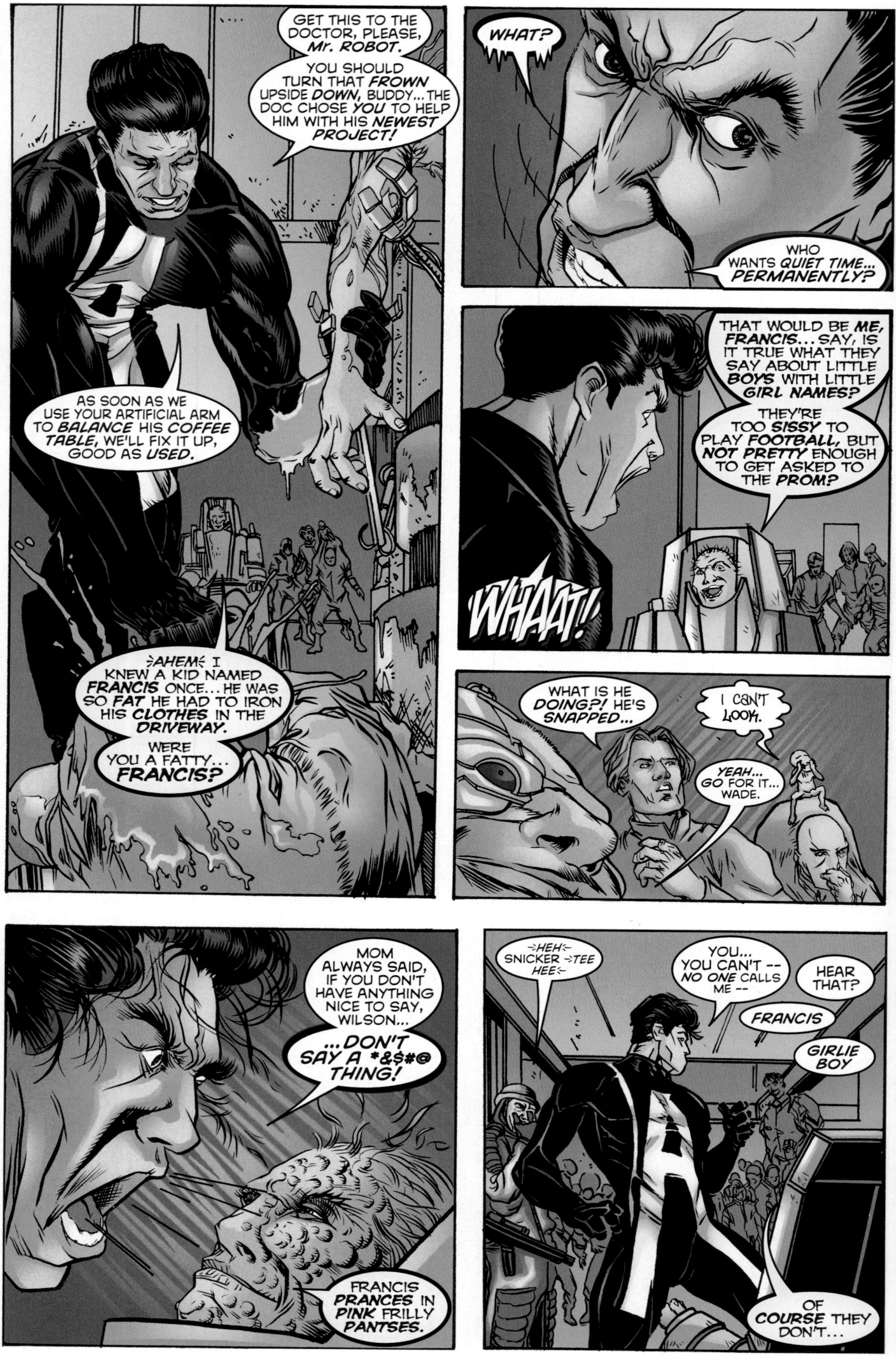
...
GET THIS TO THE DOCTOR, PLEASE, Mr. ROBOT.
YOU SHOULD TURN THAT FROWN UPSIDE DOWN, BUDDY... THE DOC CHOSE YOU TO HELP HIM WITH HIS NEWEST PROJECT!
AS SOON AS WE USE YOUR ARTIFICIAL ARM TO BALANCE HIS COFFEE TABLE, WE'LL FIX IT UP, GOOD AS USED.
AHEM I KNEW A KID NAMED FRANCIS ONCE... HE WAS SO FAT HE HAD TO IRON HIS CLOTHES IN THE DRIVEWAY.
WERE YOU A FATTY... FRANCIS?
WHAT?
WHO WANTS QUIET TIME... PERMANENTLY?
THAT WOULD BE ME, FRANCIS... SAY, IS IT TRUE WHAT THEY SAY ABOUT LITTLE BOYS WITH LITTLE GIRL NAMES?
THEY'RE TOO SISSY TO PLAY FOOTBALL, BUT NOT PRETTY ENOUGH TO GET ASKED TO THE PROM?
WHAAT!
WHAT IS HE DOING?! HE'S SNAPPED...
I CAN'T LOOK.
YEAH... GO FOR IT... WADE.
MOM ALWAYS SAID, IF YOU DON'T HAVE ANYTHING NICE TO SAY, WILSON...
...DON'T SAY A *&$#@ THING!
FRANCIS PRANCES IN PINK FRILLY PANTSES.
HEH SNICKER TEE HEE
YOU... YOU CAN'T -- NO ONE CALLS ME --
HEAR THAT?
FRANCIS
GIRLIE BOY
OF COURSE THEY DON'T...

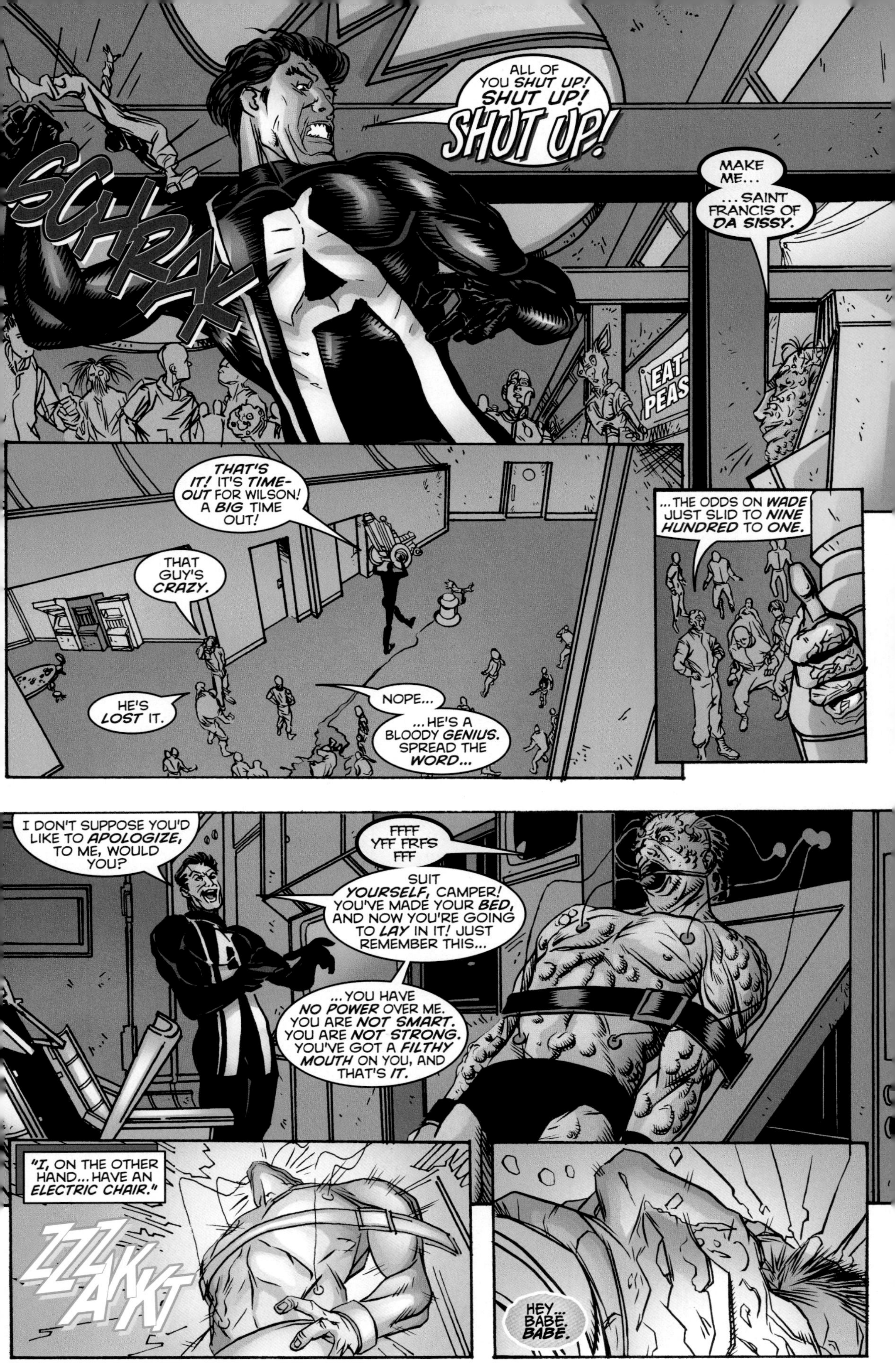
ALL OF YOU SHUT UP! SHUT UP! SHUT UP!
SCHRAK
MAKE ME...
...SAINT FRANCIS OF DA SISSY.
EAT PEAS
THAT'S IT! IT'S TIME-OUT FOR WILSON! A BIG TIME OUT!
THAT GUY'S CRAZY.
HE'S LOST IT.
NOPE...
...HE'S A BLOODY GENIUS. SPREAD THE WORD...
...THE ODDS ON WADE JUST SLID TO NINE HUNDRED TO ONE.
I DON'T SUPPOSE YOU'D LIKE TO APOLOGIZE, TO ME, WOULD YOU?
FFFF YFF FRFS FFF
SUIT YOURSELF, CAMPER! YOU'VE MADE YOUR BED, AND NOW YOU'RE GOING TO LAY IN IT! JUST REMEMBER THIS...
...YOU HAVE NO POWER OVER ME. YOU ARE NOT SMART. YOU ARE NOT STRONG. YOU'VE GOT A FILTHY MOUTH ON YOU, AND THAT'S IT.
"I, ON THE OTHER HAND...HAVE AN ELECTRIC CHAIR."
ZZZAKKT
HEY... BABE. BABE.

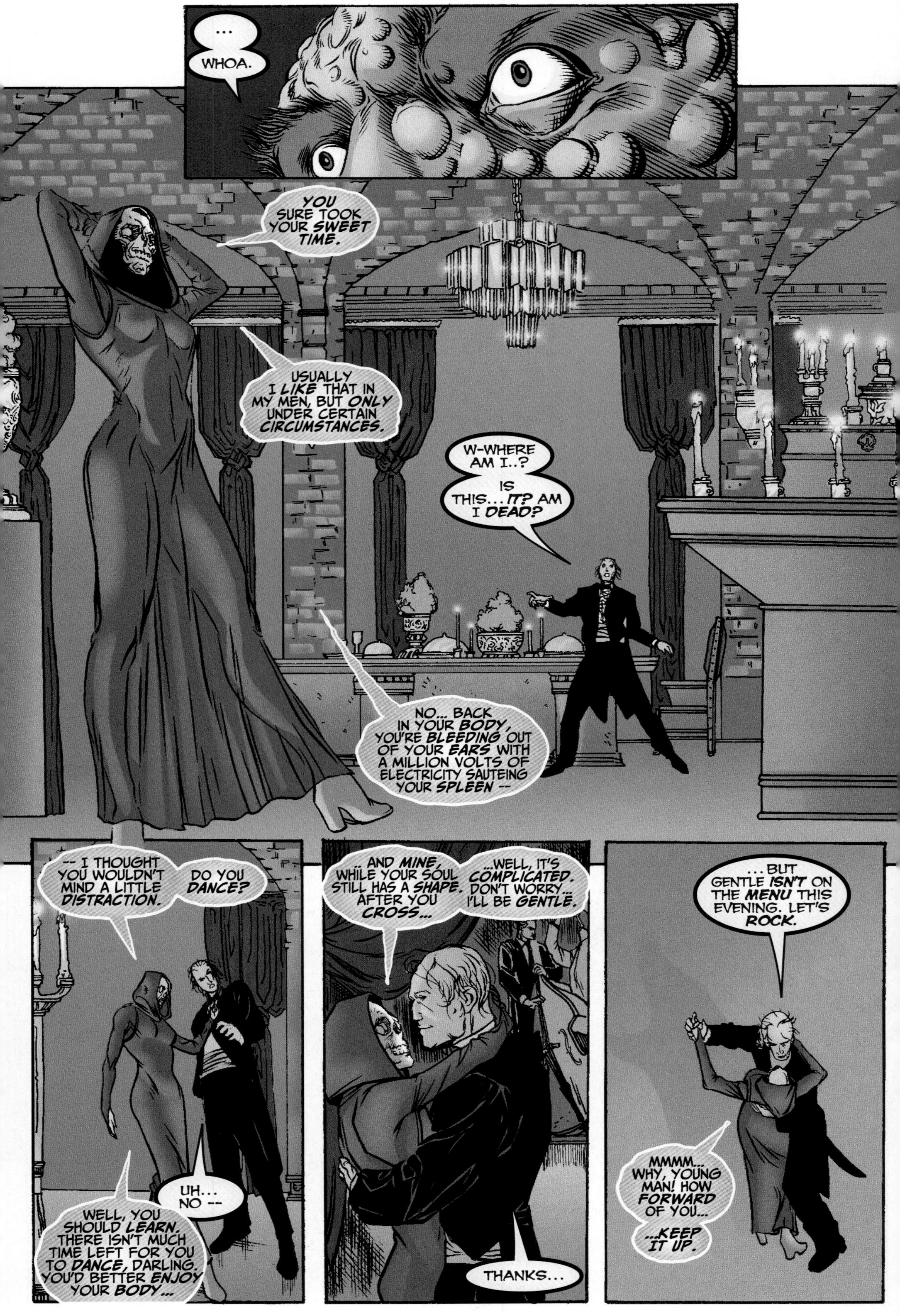
...
WHOA.
YOU SURE TOOK YOUR SWEET TIME.
USUALLY I LIKE THAT IN MY MEN, BUT ONLY UNDER CERTAIN CIRCUMSTANCES.
W-WHERE AM I..?
IS THIS... IT? AM I DEAD?
NO... BACK IN YOUR BODY, YOU'RE BLEEDING OUT OF YOUR EARS WITH A MILLION VOLTS OF ELECTRICITY SAUTEING YOUR SPLEEN --
-- I THOUGHT YOU WOULDN'T MIND A LITTLE DISTRACTION.
DO YOU DANCE?
UH... NO --
WELL, YOU SHOULD LEARN. THERE ISN'T MUCH TIME LEFT FOR YOU TO DANCE, DARLING. YOU'D BETTER ENJOY YOUR BODY...
... AND MINE, WHILE YOUR SOUL STILL HAS A SHAPE. AFTER YOU CROSS...
...WELL, IT'S COMPLICATED. DON'T WORRY... I'LL BE GENTLE.
THANKS...
... BUT GENTLE ISN'T ON THE MENU THIS EVENING. LET'S ROCK.
MMMM... WHY, YOUNG MAN! HOW FORWARD OF YOU...
...KEEP IT UP.

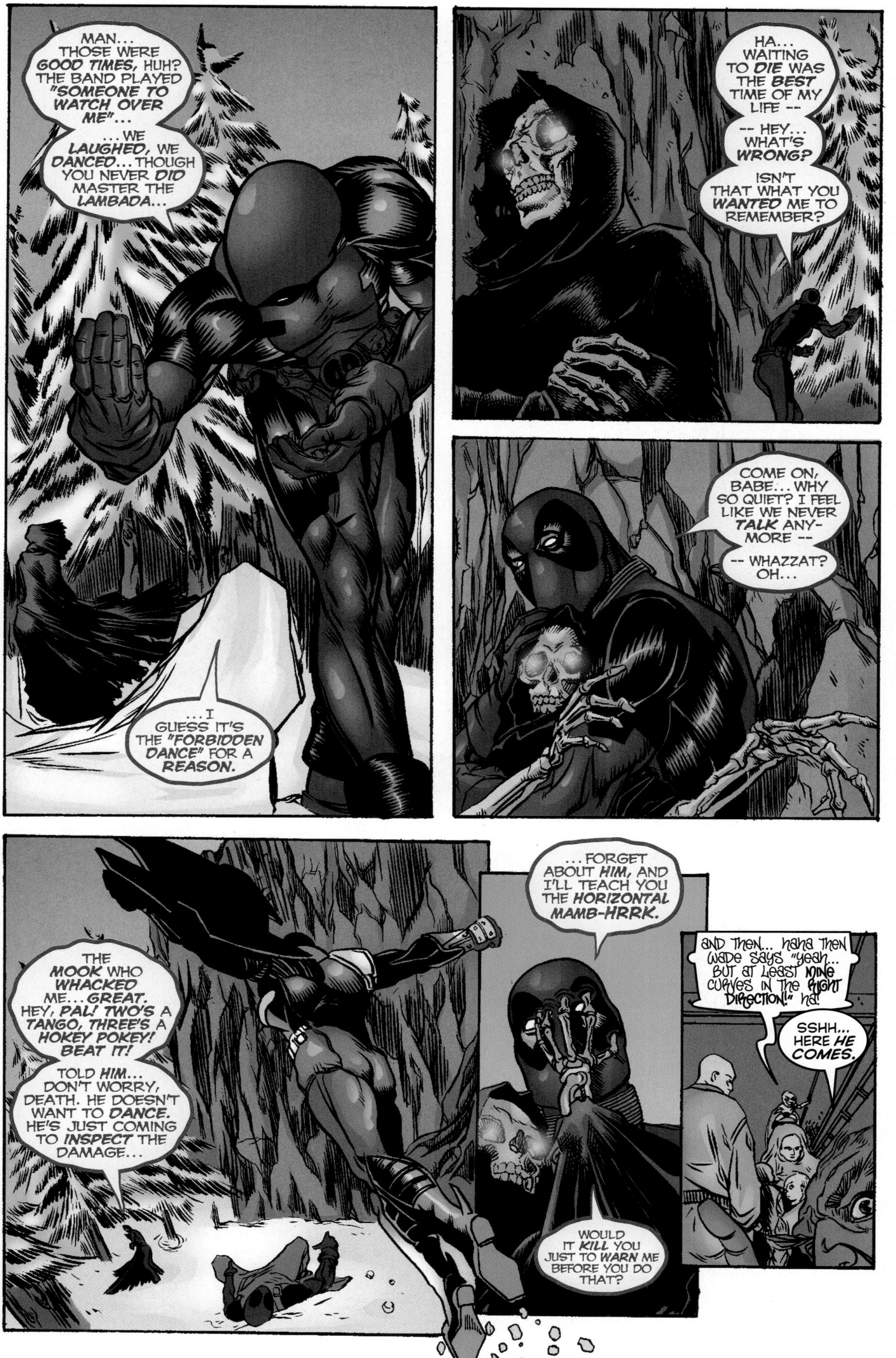

MAN... THOSE WERE *GOOD TIMES*, HUH? THE BAND PLAYED *"SOMEONE TO WATCH OVER ME"*...
...WE *LAUGHED*, WE *DANCED*... THOUGH YOU NEVER *DID* MASTER THE *LAMBADA*...
...I GUESS IT'S THE *"FORBIDDEN DANCE"* FOR A *REASON.*
HA... WAITING TO *DIE* WAS THE *BEST* TIME OF MY LIFE --
-- HEY... WHAT'S *WRONG?*
ISN'T THAT WHAT YOU *WANTED* ME TO REMEMBER?
COME ON, BABE... WHY SO QUIET? I FEEL LIKE WE NEVER *TALK* ANY-MORE --
-- WHAZZAT? OH...
THE *MOOK* WHO *WHACKED* ME... *GREAT.* HEY, *PAL! TWO'S* A *TANGO*, *THREE'S* A *HOKEY POKEY! BEAT IT!*
TOLD *HIM*... DON'T WORRY, DEATH. HE DOESN'T WANT TO *DANCE.* HE'S JUST COMING TO *INSPECT* THE DAMAGE...
...FORGET ABOUT *HIM*, AND I'LL TEACH YOU THE *HORIZONTAL MAMB-HRRK.*
WOULD IT *KILL* YOU JUST TO *WARN* ME BEFORE YOU DO THAT?
AND THEN... haha THEN WADE SAYS "yeah... BUT AT LEAST MINE CURVES IN THE RIGHT DIRECTION!" ha!
SSHH... HERE *HE COMES.*

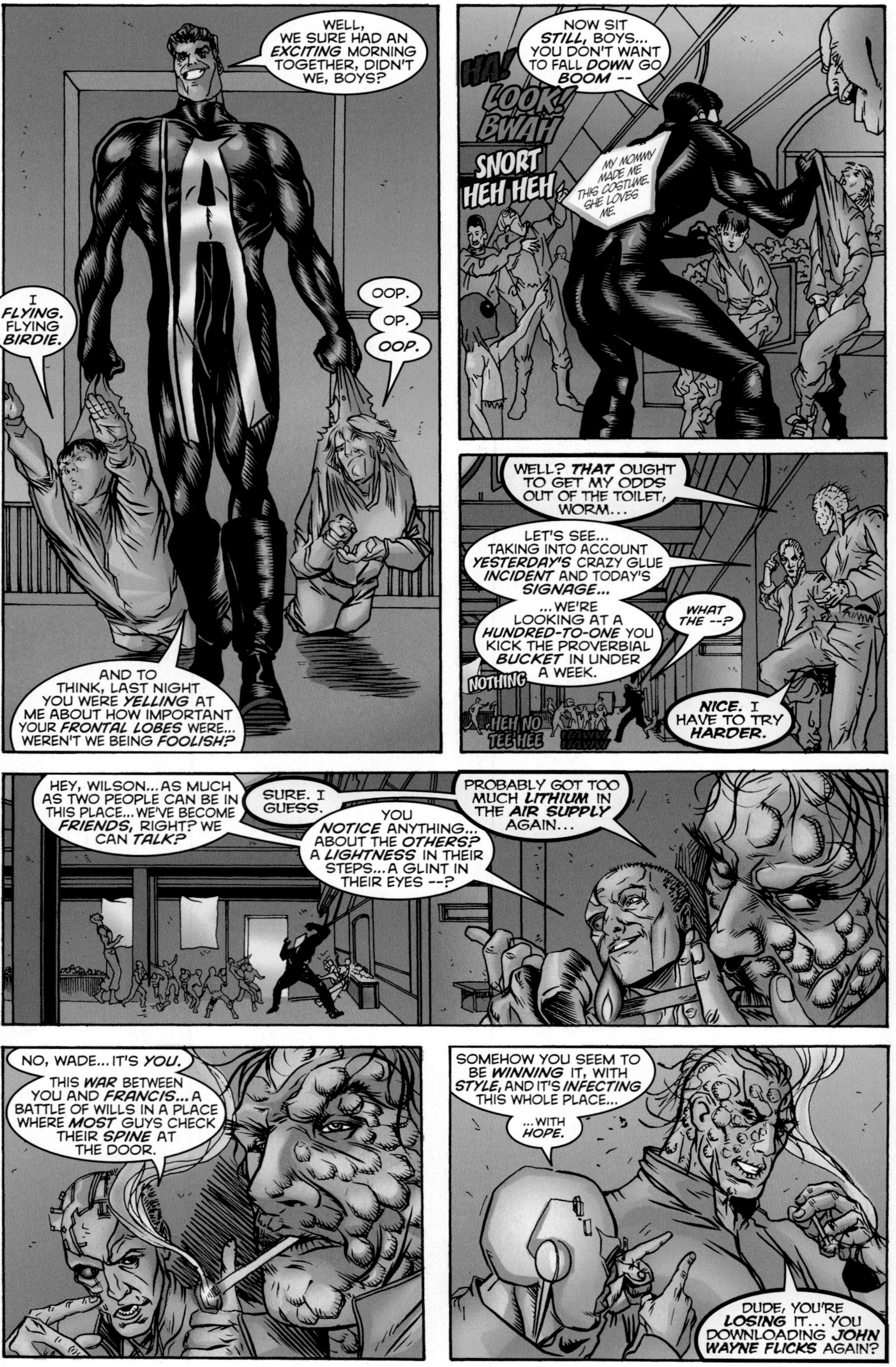
WELL, WE SURE HAD AN EXCITING MORNING TOGETHER, DIDN'T WE, BOYS?
I FLYING. FLYING BIRDIE.
OOP. OP. OOP.
AND TO THINK, LAST NIGHT YOU WERE YELLING AT ME ABOUT HOW IMPORTANT YOUR FRONTAL LOBES WERE... WEREN'T WE BEING FOOLISH?
NOW SIT STILL, BOYS... YOU DON'T WANT TO FALL DOWN GO BOOM --
HA! LOOK! BWAH SNORT HEH HEH
MY MOMMY MADE ME THIS COSTUME. SHE LOVES ME.
WELL? THAT OUGHT TO GET MY ODDS OUT OF THE TOILET, WORM...
LET'S SEE... TAKING INTO ACCOUNT YESTERDAY'S CRAZY GLUE INCIDENT AND TODAY'S SIGNAGE...
...WE'RE LOOKING AT A HUNDRED-TO-ONE YOU KICK THE PROVERBIAL BUCKET IN UNDER A WEEK.
WHAT THE --?
NOTHING
HEH NO TEE HEE
NICE. I HAVE TO TRY HARDER.
HEY, WILSON... AS MUCH AS TWO PEOPLE CAN BE IN THIS PLACE... WE'VE BECOME FRIENDS, RIGHT? WE CAN TALK?
SURE. I GUESS.
YOU NOTICE ANYTHING... ABOUT THE OTHERS? A LIGHTNESS IN THEIR STEPS... A GLINT IN THEIR EYES --?
PROBABLY GOT TOO MUCH LITHIUM IN THE AIR SUPPLY AGAIN...
NO, WADE... IT'S YOU.
THIS WAR BETWEEN YOU AND FRANCIS... A BATTLE OF WILLS IN A PLACE WHERE MOST GUYS CHECK THEIR SPINE AT THE DOOR.
SOMEHOW YOU SEEM TO BE WINNING IT, WITH STYLE, AND IT'S INFECTING THIS WHOLE PLACE...
...WITH HOPE.
DUDE, YOU'RE LOSING IT... YOU DOWNLOADING JOHN WAYNE FLICKS AGAIN?

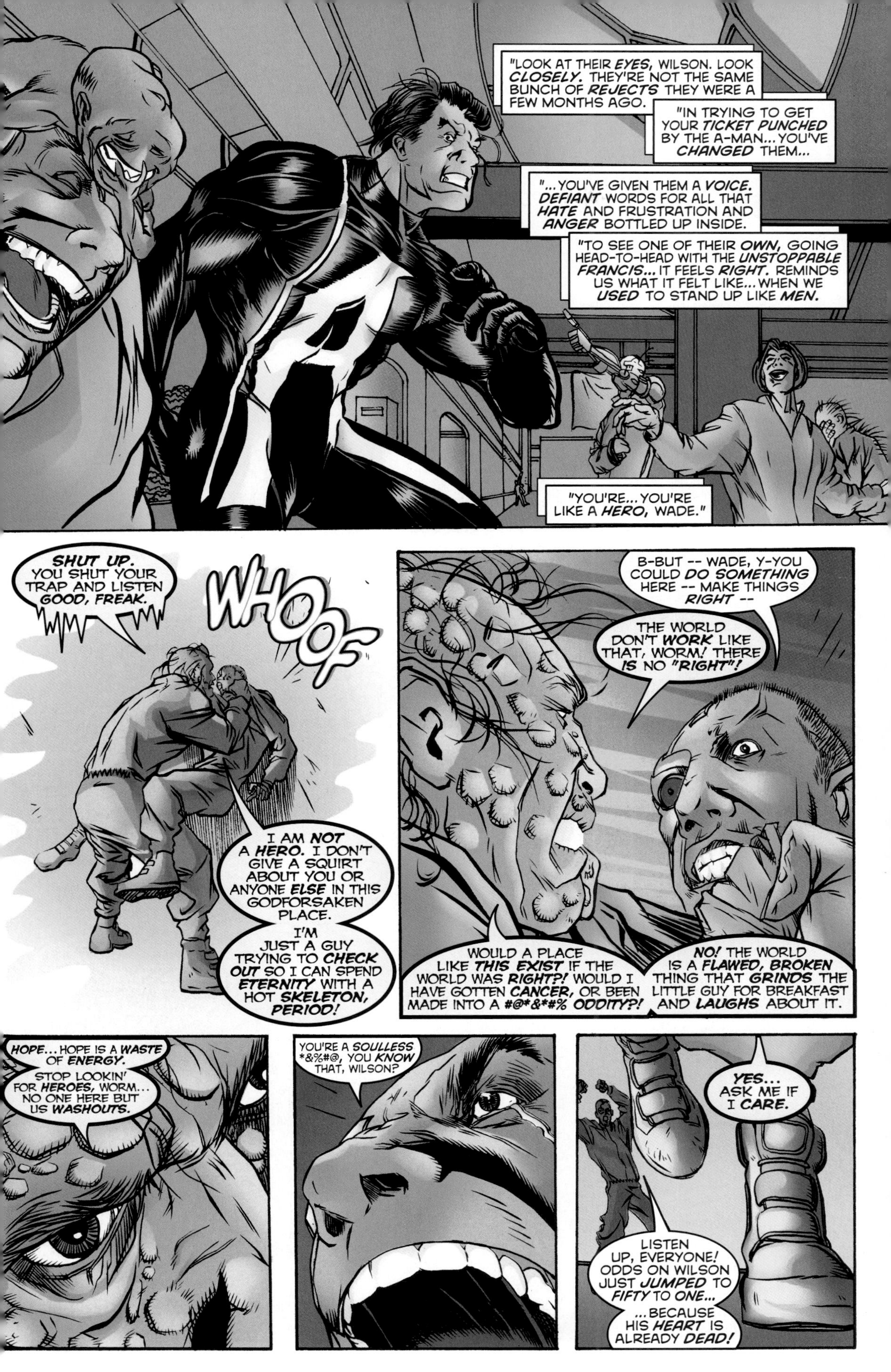

"LOOK AT THEIR EYES, WILSON. LOOK CLOSELY. THEY'RE NOT THE SAME BUNCH OF REJECTS THEY WERE A FEW MONTHS AGO.
"IN TRYING TO GET YOUR TICKET PUNCHED BY THE A-MAN... YOU'VE CHANGED THEM...
"...YOU'VE GIVEN THEM A VOICE. DEFIANT WORDS FOR ALL THAT HATE AND FRUSTRATION AND ANGER BOTTLED UP INSIDE.
"TO SEE ONE OF THEIR OWN, GOING HEAD-TO-HEAD WITH THE UNSTOPPABLE FRANCIS... IT FEELS RIGHT. REMINDS US WHAT IT FELT LIKE... WHEN WE USED TO STAND UP LIKE MEN.
"YOU'RE... YOU'RE LIKE A HERO, WADE."
SHUT UP. YOU SHUT YOUR TRAP AND LISTEN GOOD, FREAK.
WHOOF
I AM NOT A HERO. I DON'T GIVE A SQUIRT ABOUT YOU OR ANYONE ELSE IN THIS GODFORSAKEN PLACE.
I'M JUST A GUY TRYING TO CHECK OUT SO I CAN SPEND ETERNITY WITH A HOT SKELETON, PERIOD!
B-BUT -- WADE, Y-YOU COULD DO SOMETHING HERE -- MAKE THINGS RIGHT --
THE WORLD DON'T WORK LIKE THAT, WORM! THERE IS NO "RIGHT"!
WOULD A PLACE LIKE THIS EXIST IF THE WORLD WAS RIGHT?! WOULD I HAVE GOTTEN CANCER, OR BEEN MADE INTO A #@*&*#% ODDITY?!
NO! THE WORLD IS A FLAWED, BROKEN THING THAT GRINDS THE LITTLE GUY FOR BREAKFAST AND LAUGHS ABOUT IT.
HOPE... HOPE IS A WASTE OF ENERGY.
STOP LOOKIN' FOR HEROES, WORM... NO ONE HERE BUT US WASHOUTS.
YOU'RE A SOULLESS *&%#@, YOU KNOW THAT, WILSON?
YES... ASK ME IF I CARE.
LISTEN UP, EVERYONE! ODDS ON WILSON JUST JUMPED TO FIFTY TO ONE...
...BECAUSE HIS HEART IS ALREADY DEAD!

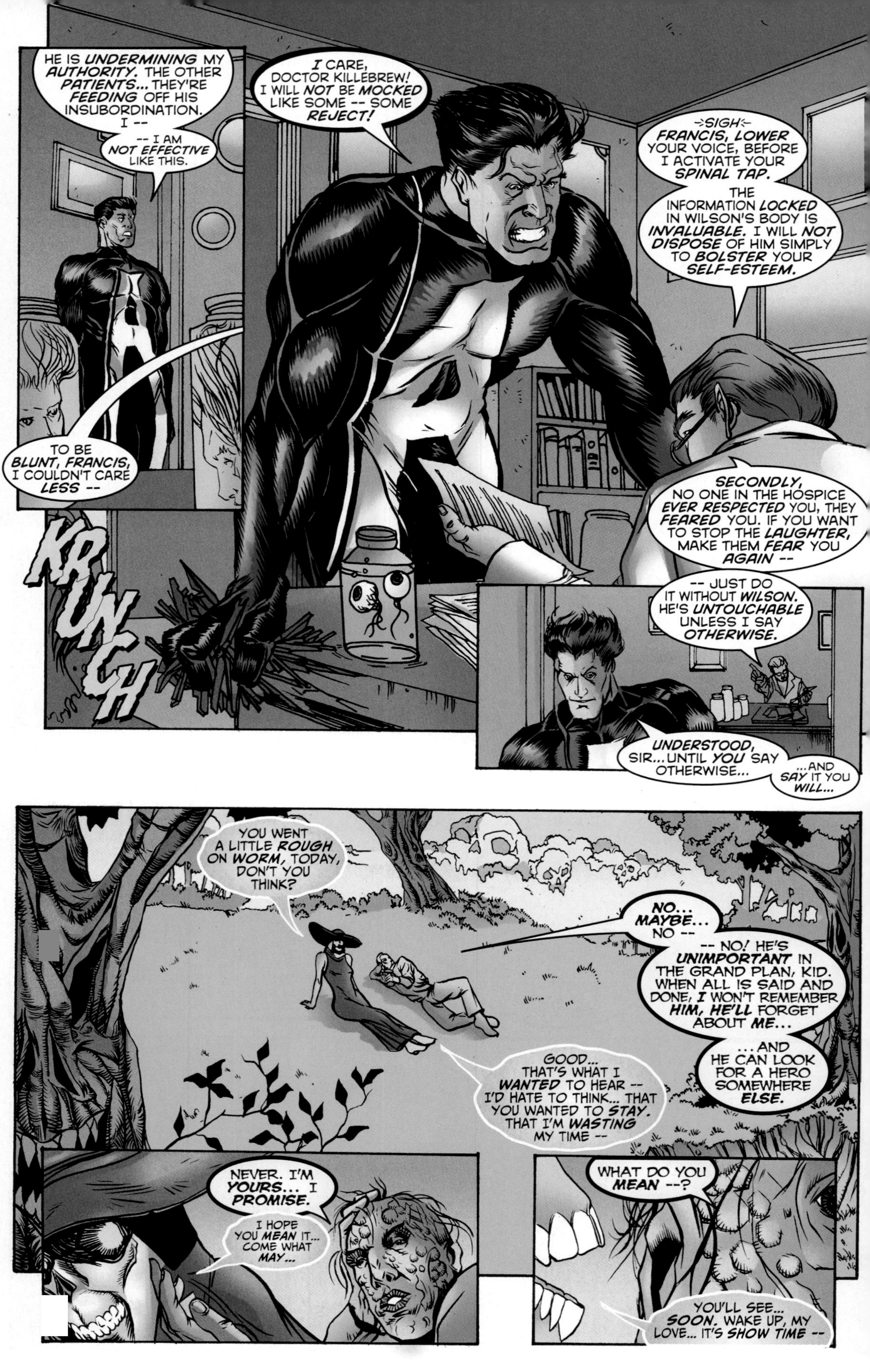
HE IS UNDERMINING MY AUTHORITY. THE OTHER PATIENTS... THEY'RE FEEDING OFF HIS INSUBORDINATION. I --
-- I AM NOT EFFECTIVE LIKE THIS.
TO BE BLUNT, FRANCIS, I COULDN'T CARE LESS --
I CARE, DOCTOR KILLEBREW! I WILL NOT BE MOCKED LIKE SOME -- SOME REJECT!
KRUNCH
-SIGH- FRANCIS, LOWER YOUR VOICE, BEFORE I ACTIVATE YOUR SPINAL TAP.
THE INFORMATION LOCKED IN WILSON'S BODY IS INVALUABLE. I WILL NOT DISPOSE OF HIM SIMPLY TO BOLSTER YOUR SELF-ESTEEM.
SECONDLY, NO ONE IN THE HOSPICE EVER RESPECTED YOU, THEY FEARED YOU. IF YOU WANT TO STOP THE LAUGHTER, MAKE THEM FEAR YOU AGAIN --
-- JUST DO IT WITHOUT WILSON. HE'S UNTOUCHABLE UNLESS I SAY OTHERWISE.
UNDERSTOOD, SIR... UNTIL YOU SAY OTHERWISE...
...AND SAY IT YOU WILL...
YOU WENT A LITTLE ROUGH ON WORM, TODAY, DON'T YOU THINK?
NO... MAYBE... NO --
-- NO! HE'S UNIMPORTANT IN THE GRAND PLAN, KID. WHEN ALL IS SAID AND DONE, I WON'T REMEMBER HIM, HE'LL FORGET ABOUT ME...
...AND HE CAN LOOK FOR A HERO SOMEWHERE ELSE.
GOOD... THAT'S WHAT I WANTED TO HEAR -- I'D HATE TO THINK... THAT YOU WANTED TO STAY. THAT I'M WASTING MY TIME --
NEVER. I'M YOURS... I PROMISE.
I HOPE YOU MEAN IT... COME WHAT MAY...
WHAT DO YOU MEAN --?
YOU'LL SEE... SOON. WAKE UP, MY LOVE... IT'S SHOW TIME --

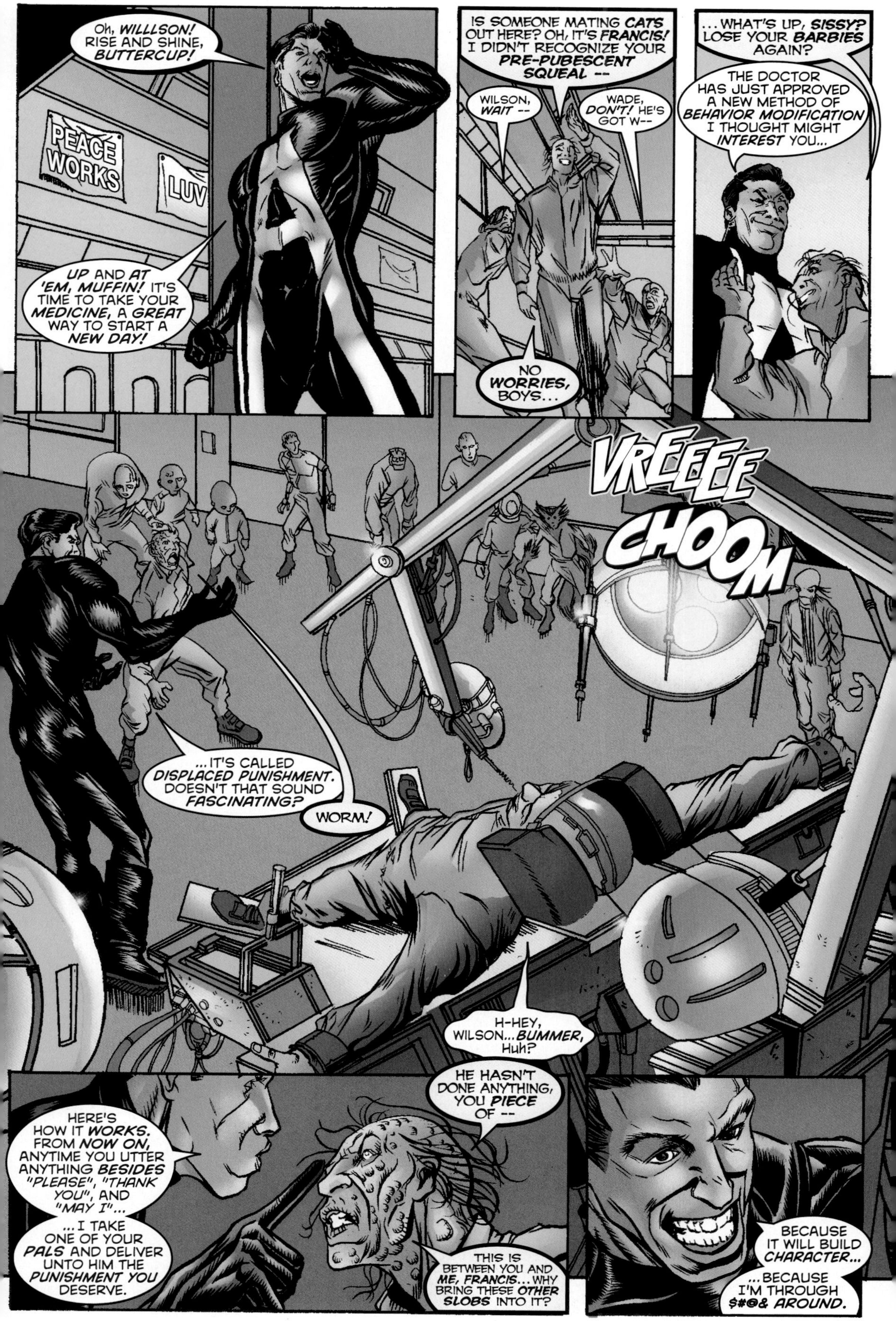
Oh, WILLLSON! RISE AND SHINE, BUTTERCUP!
PEACE WORKS
LUV
UP AND AT 'EM, MUFFIN! IT'S TIME TO TAKE YOUR MEDICINE, A GREAT WAY TO START A NEW DAY!
IS SOMEONE MATING CATS OUT HERE? OH, IT'S FRANCIS! I DIDN'T RECOGNIZE YOUR PRE-PUBESCENT SQUEAL --
WILSON, WAIT --
WADE, DON'T! HE'S GOT W--
NO WORRIES, BOYS...
...WHAT'S UP, SISSY? LOSE YOUR BARBIES AGAIN?
THE DOCTOR HAS JUST APPROVED A NEW METHOD OF BEHAVIOR MODIFICATION I THOUGHT MIGHT INTEREST YOU...
VREEEEE
CHOOM
...IT'S CALLED DISPLACED PUNISHMENT. DOESN'T THAT SOUND FASCINATING?
WORM!
H-HEY, WILSON... BUMMER, HUH?
HERE'S HOW IT WORKS. FROM NOW ON, ANYTIME YOU UTTER ANYTHING BESIDES "PLEASE", "THANK YOU", AND "MAY I"...
...I TAKE ONE OF YOUR PALS AND DELIVER UNTO HIM THE PUNISHMENT YOU DESERVE.
HE HASN'T DONE ANYTHING, YOU PIECE OF --
THIS IS BETWEEN YOU AND ME, FRANCIS... WHY BRING THESE OTHER SLOBS INTO IT?
BECAUSE IT WILL BUILD CHARACTER...
...BECAUSE I'M THROUGH $#@& AROUND.

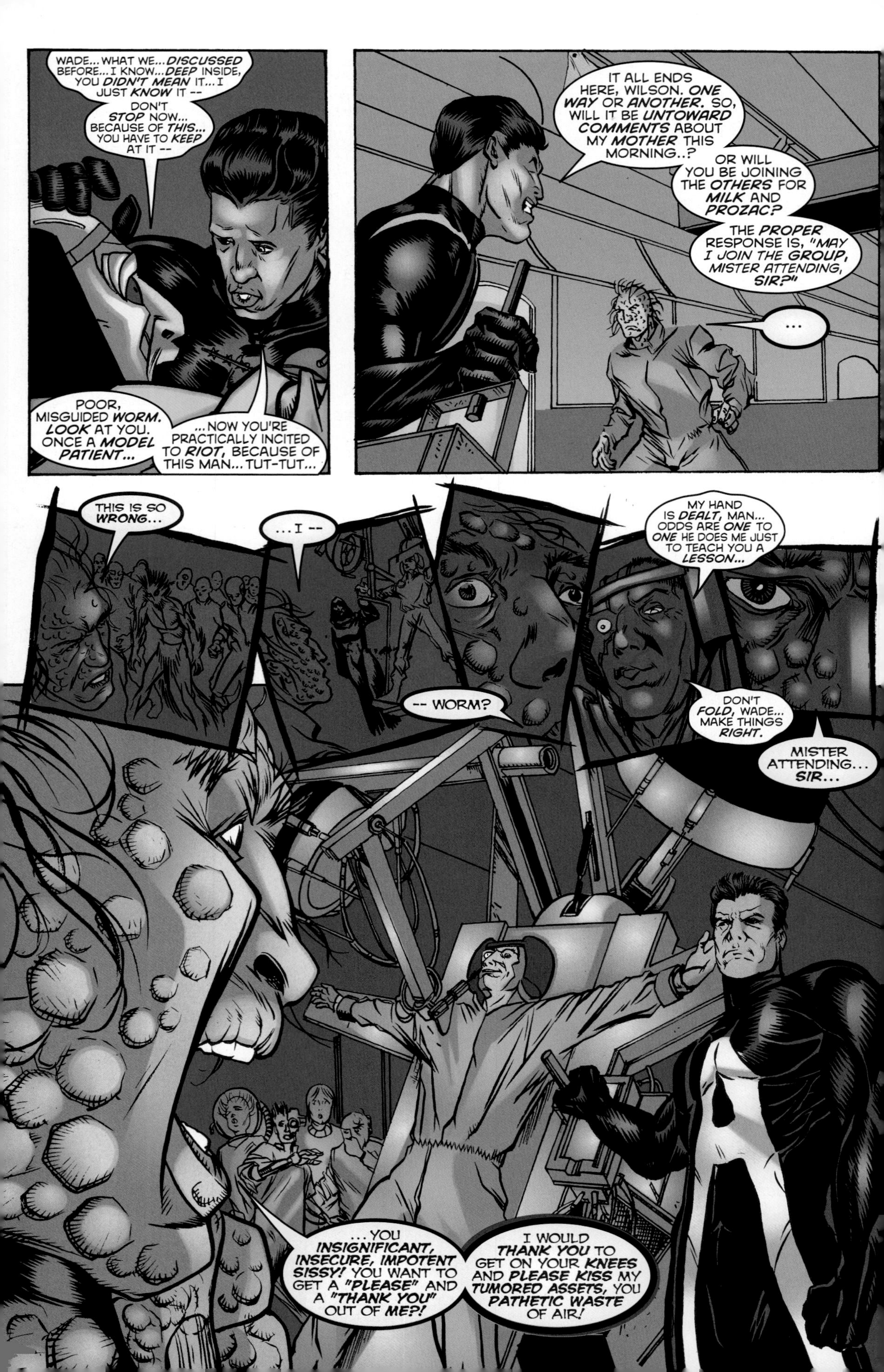
WADE... WHAT WE... DISCUSSED BEFORE... I KNOW... DEEP INSIDE, YOU DIDN'T MEAN IT... I JUST KNOW IT --
DON'T STOP NOW... BECAUSE OF THIS... YOU HAVE TO KEEP AT IT --
POOR, MISGUIDED WORM. LOOK AT YOU. ONCE A MODEL PATIENT...
...NOW YOU'RE PRACTICALLY INCITED TO RIOT, BECAUSE OF THIS MAN... TUT-TUT...
IT ALL ENDS HERE, WILSON. ONE WAY OR ANOTHER. SO, WILL IT BE UNTOWARD COMMENTS ABOUT MY MOTHER THIS MORNING..?
OR WILL YOU BE JOINING THE OTHERS FOR MILK AND PROZAC?
THE PROPER RESPONSE IS, "MAY I JOIN THE GROUP, MISTER ATTENDING, SIR?"
...
THIS IS SO WRONG...
...I --
MY HAND IS DEALT, MAN... ODDS ARE ONE TO ONE HE DOES ME JUST TO TEACH YOU A LESSON...
-- WORM?
DON'T FOLD, WADE... MAKE THINGS RIGHT.
MISTER ATTENDING... SIR...
...YOU INSIGNIFICANT, INSECURE, IMPOTENT SISSY! YOU WANT TO GET A "PLEASE" AND A "THANK YOU" OUT OF ME?!
I WOULD THANK YOU TO GET ON YOUR KNEES AND PLEASE KISS MY TUMORED ASSETS, YOU PATHETIC WASTE OF AIR!

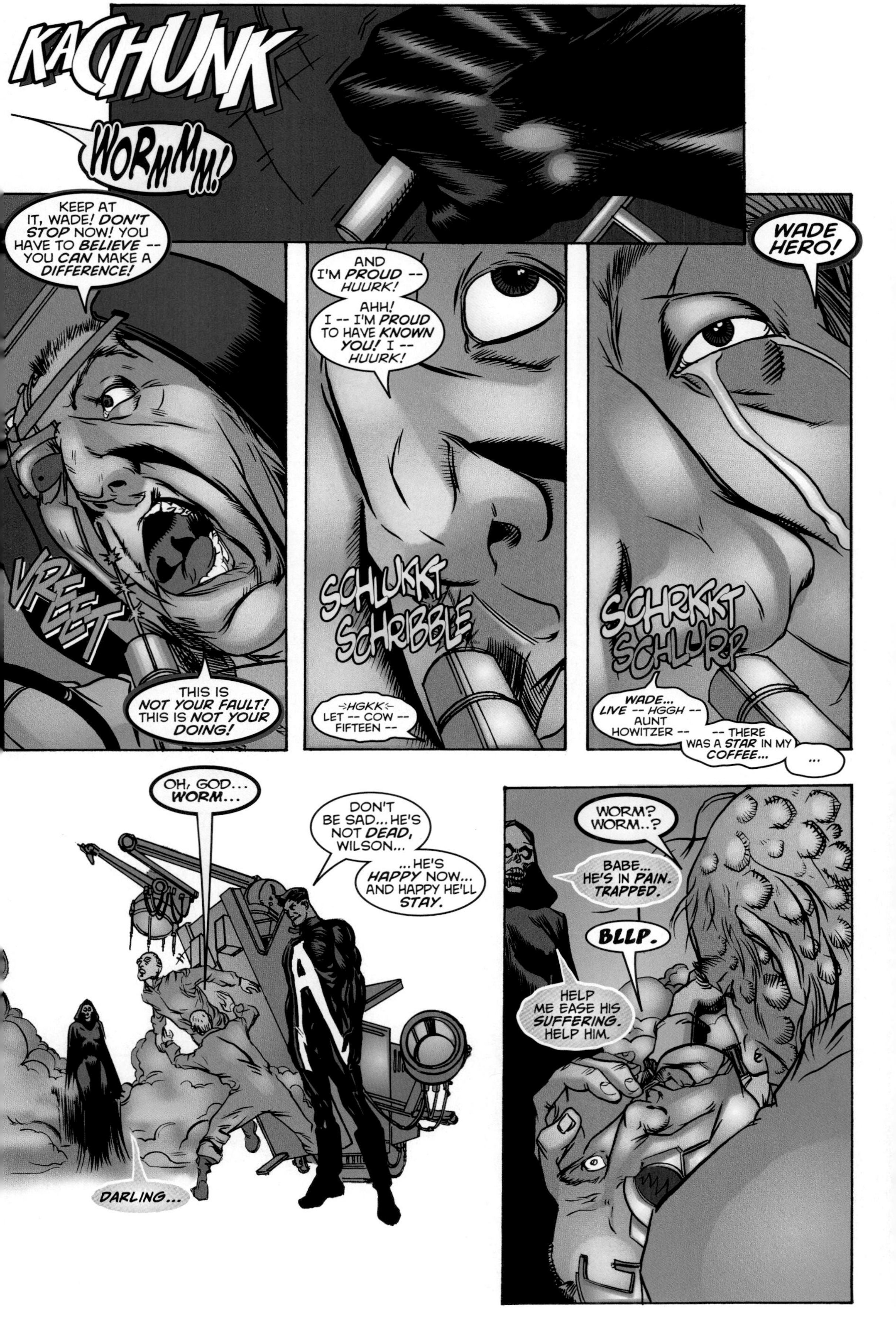
KACHUNK
WORMMM!
KEEP AT IT, WADE! DON'T STOP NOW! YOU HAVE TO BELIEVE -- YOU CAN MAKE A DIFFERENCE!
VREEET
THIS IS NOT YOUR FAULT! THIS IS NOT YOUR DOING!
AND I'M PROUD -- HUURK!
AHH! I -- I'M PROUD TO HAVE KNOWN YOU! I -- HUURK!
SCHLUKKT SCHRIBBLE
HGKK LET -- COW -- FIFTEEN --
WADE HERO!
SCHRKKT SCHLURP
WADE... LIVE -- HGGH -- AUNT HOWITZER --
-- THERE WAS A STAR IN MY COFFEE...
...
OH, GOD... WORM...
DON'T BE SAD... HE'S NOT DEAD, WILSON...
...HE'S HAPPY NOW... AND HAPPY HE'LL STAY.
DARLING...
WORM? WORM..?
BABE... HE'S IN PAIN. TRAPPED.
BLLP.
HELP ME EASE HIS SUFFERING. HELP HIM.

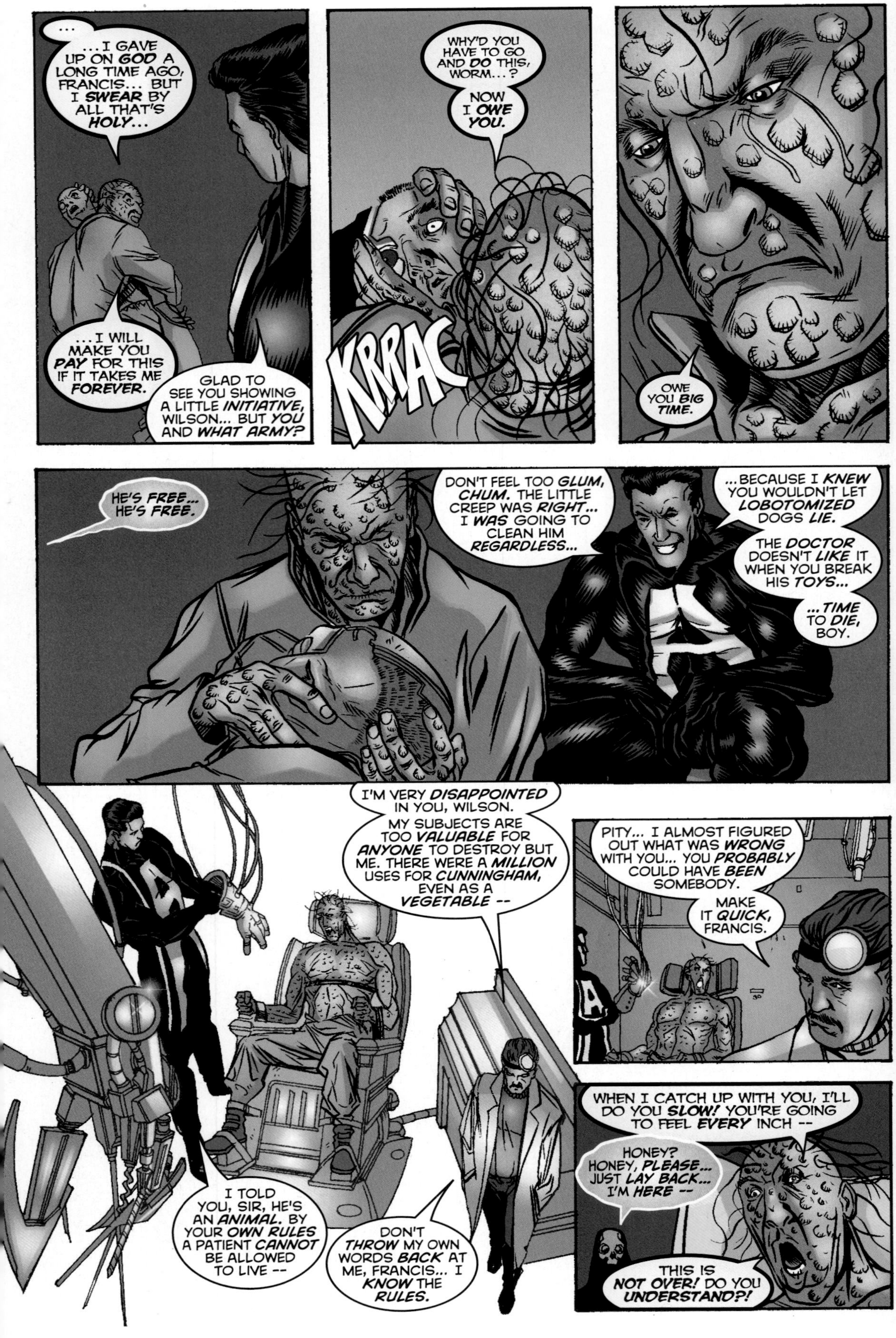
...
...I GAVE UP ON GOD A LONG TIME AGO, FRANCIS... BUT I SWEAR BY ALL THAT'S HOLY...
...I WILL MAKE YOU PAY FOR THIS IF IT TAKES ME FOREVER.
GLAD TO SEE YOU SHOWING A LITTLE INITIATIVE, WILSON... BUT YOU AND WHAT ARMY?
WHY'D YOU HAVE TO GO AND DO THIS, WORM...?
NOW I OWE YOU.
KRRAC
OWE YOU BIG TIME.
HE'S FREE... HE'S FREE.
DON'T FEEL TOO GLUM, CHUM. THE LITTLE CREEP WAS RIGHT... I WAS GOING TO CLEAN HIM REGARDLESS...
...BECAUSE I KNEW YOU WOULDN'T LET LOBOTOMIZED DOGS LIE.
THE DOCTOR DOESN'T LIKE IT WHEN YOU BREAK HIS TOYS...
...TIME TO DIE, BOY.
I'M VERY DISAPPOINTED IN YOU, WILSON.
MY SUBJECTS ARE TOO VALUABLE FOR ANYONE TO DESTROY BUT ME. THERE WERE A MILLION USES FOR CUNNINGHAM, EVEN AS A VEGETABLE --
I TOLD YOU, SIR, HE'S AN ANIMAL. BY YOUR OWN RULES A PATIENT CANNOT BE ALLOWED TO LIVE --
DON'T THROW MY OWN WORDS BACK AT ME, FRANCIS... I KNOW THE RULES.
PITY... I ALMOST FIGURED OUT WHAT WAS WRONG WITH YOU... YOU PROBABLY COULD HAVE BEEN SOMEBODY.
MAKE IT QUICK, FRANCIS.
WHEN I CATCH UP WITH YOU, I'LL DO YOU SLOW! YOU'RE GOING TO FEEL EVERY INCH --
HONEY? HONEY, PLEASE... JUST LAY BACK... I'M HERE --
THIS IS NOT OVER! DO YOU UNDERSTAND?!

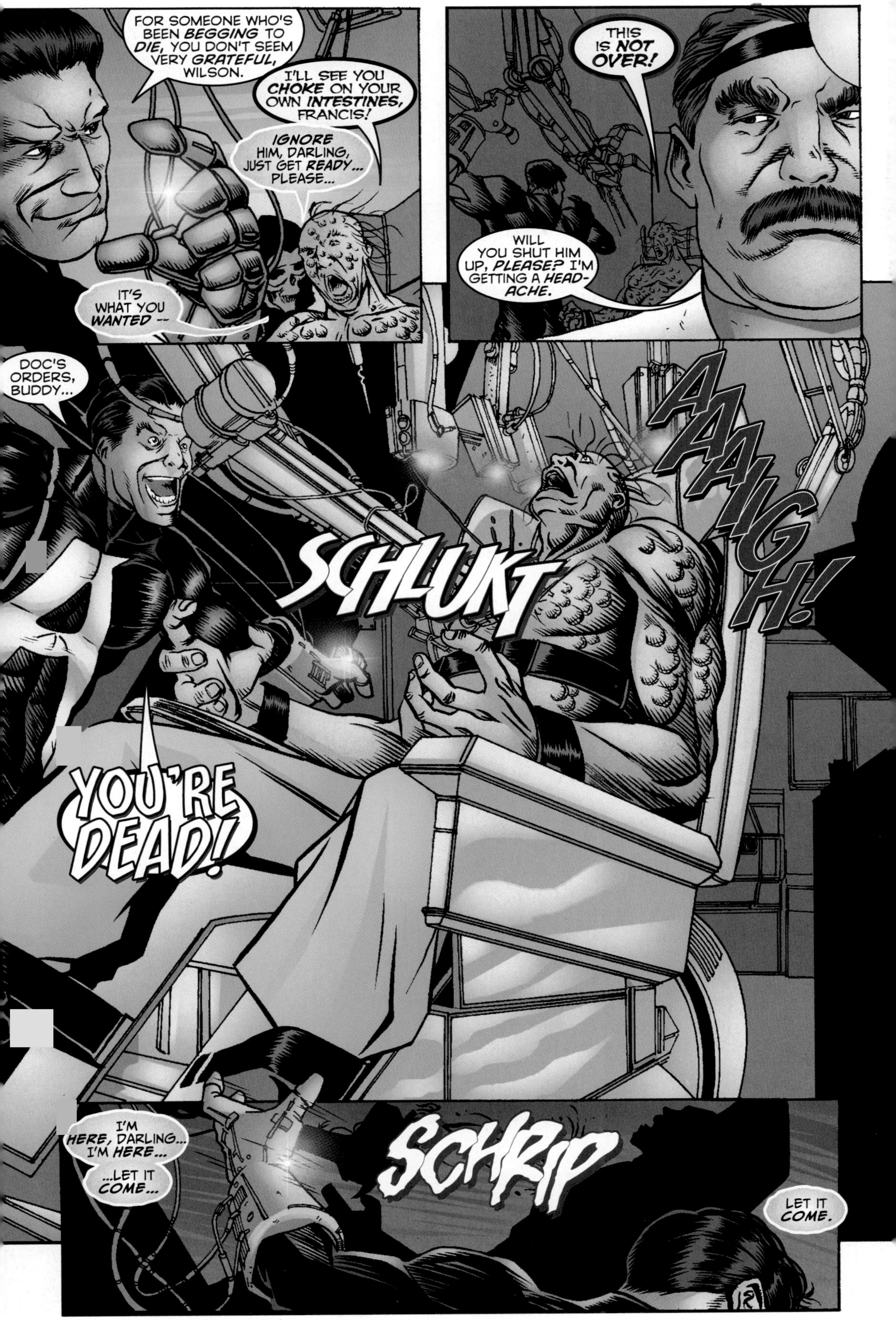
FOR SOMEONE WHO'S BEEN BEGGING TO DIE, YOU DON'T SEEM VERY GRATEFUL, WILSON.
I'LL SEE YOU CHOKE ON YOUR OWN INTESTINES, FRANCIS!
IGNORE HIM, DARLING, JUST GET READY... PLEASE...
IT'S WHAT YOU WANTED --
THIS IS NOT OVER!
WILL YOU SHUT HIM UP, PLEASE? I'M GETTING A HEAD-ACHE.
DOC'S ORDERS, BUDDY...
AAAIGH!
SCHLUKT
YOU'RE DEAD!
I'M HERE, DARLING... I'M HERE...
...LET IT COME...
SCHRIP
LET IT COME.

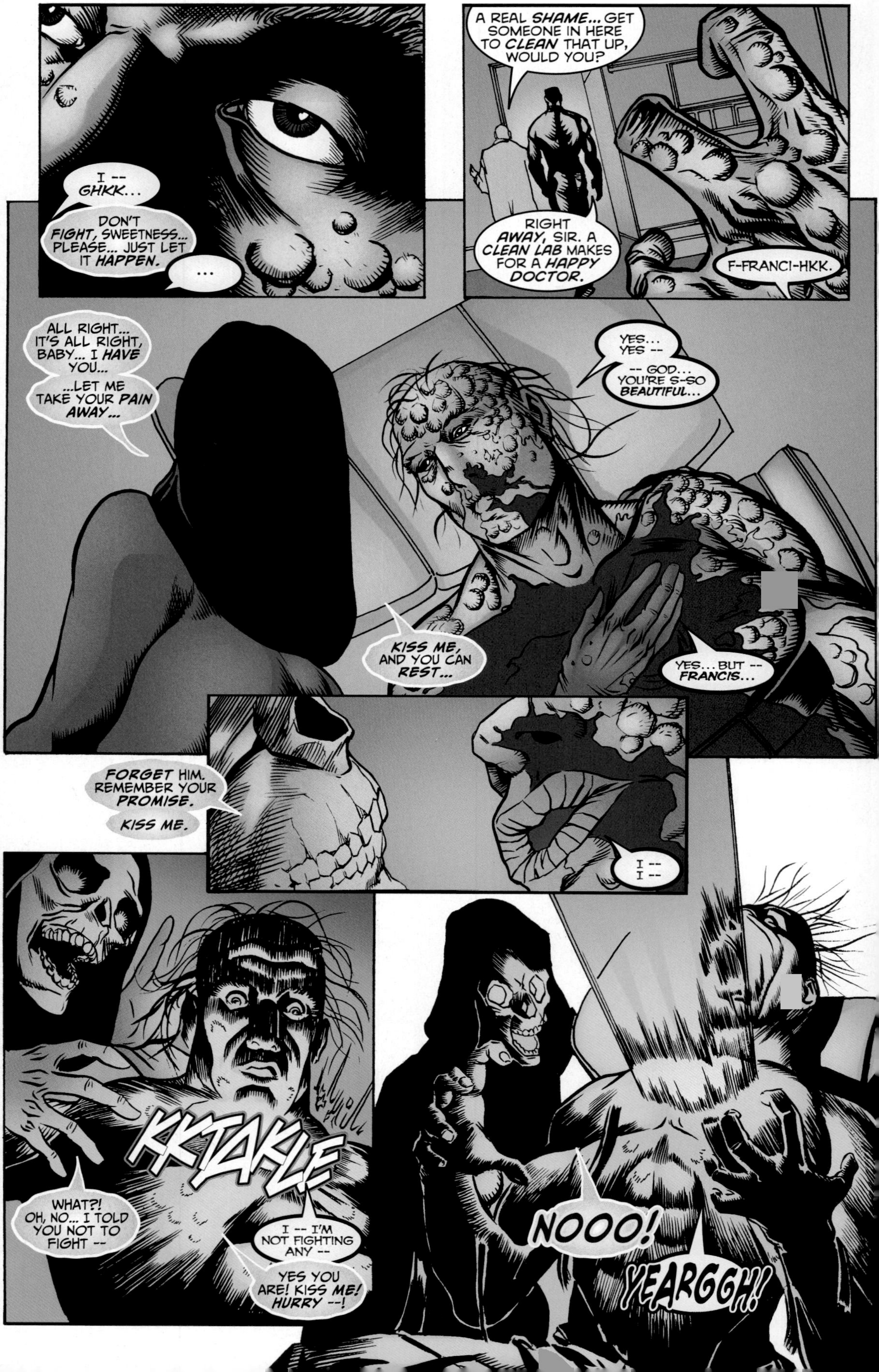

I -- GHKK...
DON'T FIGHT, SWEETNESS... PLEASE... JUST LET IT HAPPEN.
...
A REAL SHAME... GET SOMEONE IN HERE TO CLEAN THAT UP, WOULD YOU?
RIGHT AWAY, SIR. A CLEAN LAB MAKES FOR A HAPPY DOCTOR.
F-FRANCI-HKK.
ALL RIGHT... IT'S ALL RIGHT, BABY... I HAVE YOU...
...LET ME TAKE YOUR PAIN AWAY...
YES... YES --
-- GOD... YOU'RE S-SO BEAUTIFUL...
KISS ME, AND YOU CAN REST...
YES... BUT -- FRANCIS...
FORGET HIM. REMEMBER YOUR PROMISE.
KISS ME.
I -- I --
KKTAKLE
WHAT?! OH, NO... I TOLD YOU NOT TO FIGHT --
I -- I'M NOT FIGHTING ANY --
YES YOU ARE! KISS ME! HURRY --!
NOOO!
YEARGGH!

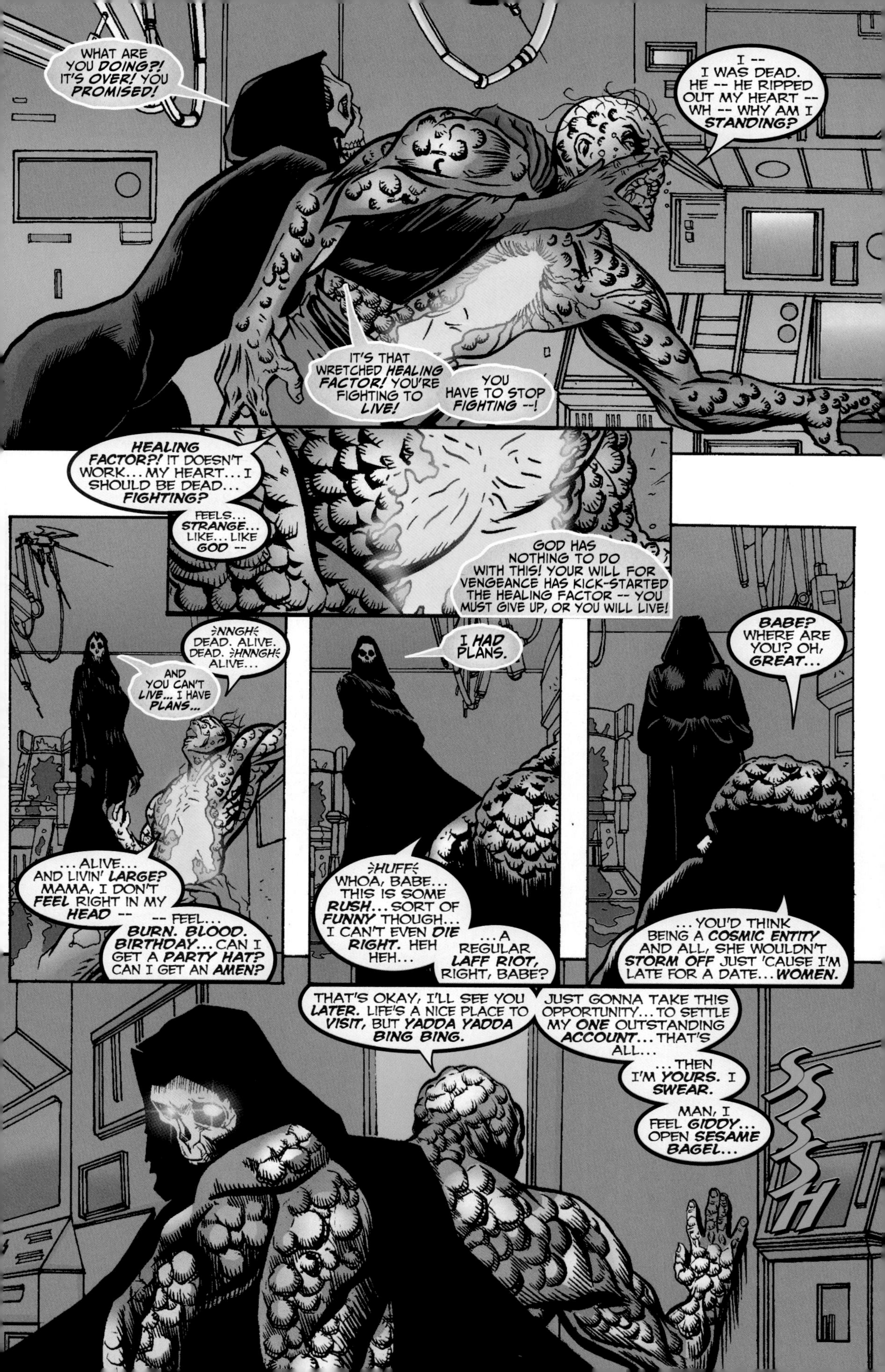
WHAT ARE YOU DOING?! IT'S OVER! YOU PROMISED!
I -- I WAS DEAD. HE -- HE RIPPED OUT MY HEART -- WH -- WHY AM I STANDING?
IT'S THAT WRETCHED HEALING FACTOR! YOU'RE FIGHTING TO LIVE!
YOU HAVE TO STOP FIGHTING --!
HEALING FACTOR?! IT DOESN'T WORK... MY HEART... I SHOULD BE DEAD... FIGHTING?
FEELS... STRANGE... LIKE... LIKE GOD --
GOD HAS NOTHING TO DO WITH THIS! YOUR WILL FOR VENGEANCE HAS KICK-STARTED THE HEALING FACTOR -- YOU MUST GIVE UP, OR YOU WILL LIVE!
NNGH DEAD. ALIVE. DEAD. HNNGH ALIVE...
AND YOU CAN'T LIVE... I HAVE PLANS...
... ALIVE... AND LIVIN' LARGE? MAMA, I DON'T FEEL RIGHT IN MY HEAD --
-- FEEL... BURN. BLOOD. BIRTHDAY... CAN I GET A PARTY HAT? CAN I GET AN AMEN?
I HAD PLANS.
HUFF WHOA, BABE... THIS IS SOME RUSH... SORT OF FUNNY THOUGH... I CAN'T EVEN DIE RIGHT. HEH HEH...
... A REGULAR LAFF RIOT, RIGHT, BABE?
BABE? WHERE ARE YOU? OH, GREAT...
... YOU'D THINK BEING A COSMIC ENTITY AND ALL, SHE WOULDN'T STORM OFF JUST 'CAUSE I'M LATE FOR A DATE... WOMEN.
THAT'S OKAY, I'LL SEE YOU LATER. LIFE'S A NICE PLACE TO VISIT, BUT YADDA YADDA BING BING.
JUST GONNA TAKE THIS OPPORTUNITY... TO SETTLE MY ONE OUTSTANDING ACCOUNT... THAT'S ALL...
... THEN I'M YOURS. I SWEAR.
MAN, I FEEL GIDDY... OPEN SESAME BAGEL...
SSSSHH

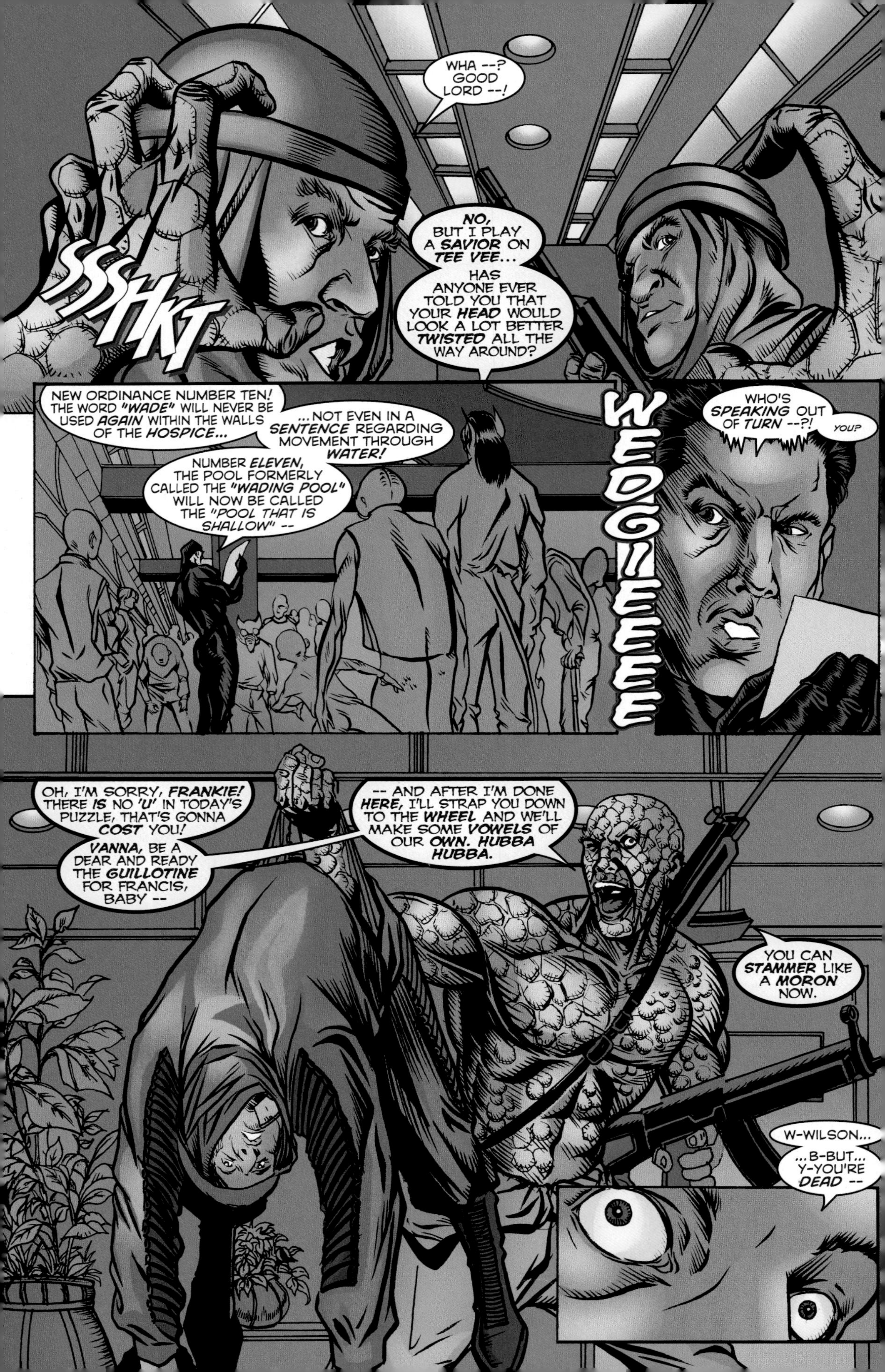
WHA --? GOOD LORD --!
SSSHKT
NO, BUT I PLAY A SAVIOR ON TEE VEE...
HAS ANYONE EVER TOLD YOU THAT YOUR HEAD WOULD LOOK A LOT BETTER TWISTED ALL THE WAY AROUND?
WEDGIEEEE
NEW ORDINANCE NUMBER TEN! THE WORD "WADE" WILL NEVER BE USED AGAIN WITHIN THE WALLS OF THE HOSPICE...
...NOT EVEN IN A SENTENCE REGARDING MOVEMENT THROUGH WATER!
NUMBER ELEVEN, THE POOL FORMERLY CALLED THE "WADING POOL" WILL NOW BE CALLED THE "POOL THAT IS SHALLOW" --
WHO'S SPEAKING OUT OF TURN --?!
YOU?
OH, I'M SORRY, FRANKIE! THERE IS NO 'U' IN TODAY'S PUZZLE, THAT'S GONNA COST YOU!
VANNA, BE A DEAR AND READY THE GUILLOTINE FOR FRANCIS, BABY --
-- AND AFTER I'M DONE HERE, I'LL STRAP YOU DOWN TO THE WHEEL AND WE'LL MAKE SOME VOWELS OF OUR OWN. HUBBA HUBBA.
YOU CAN STAMMER LIKE A MORON NOW.
W-WILSON...
...B-BUT... Y-YOU'RE DEAD --

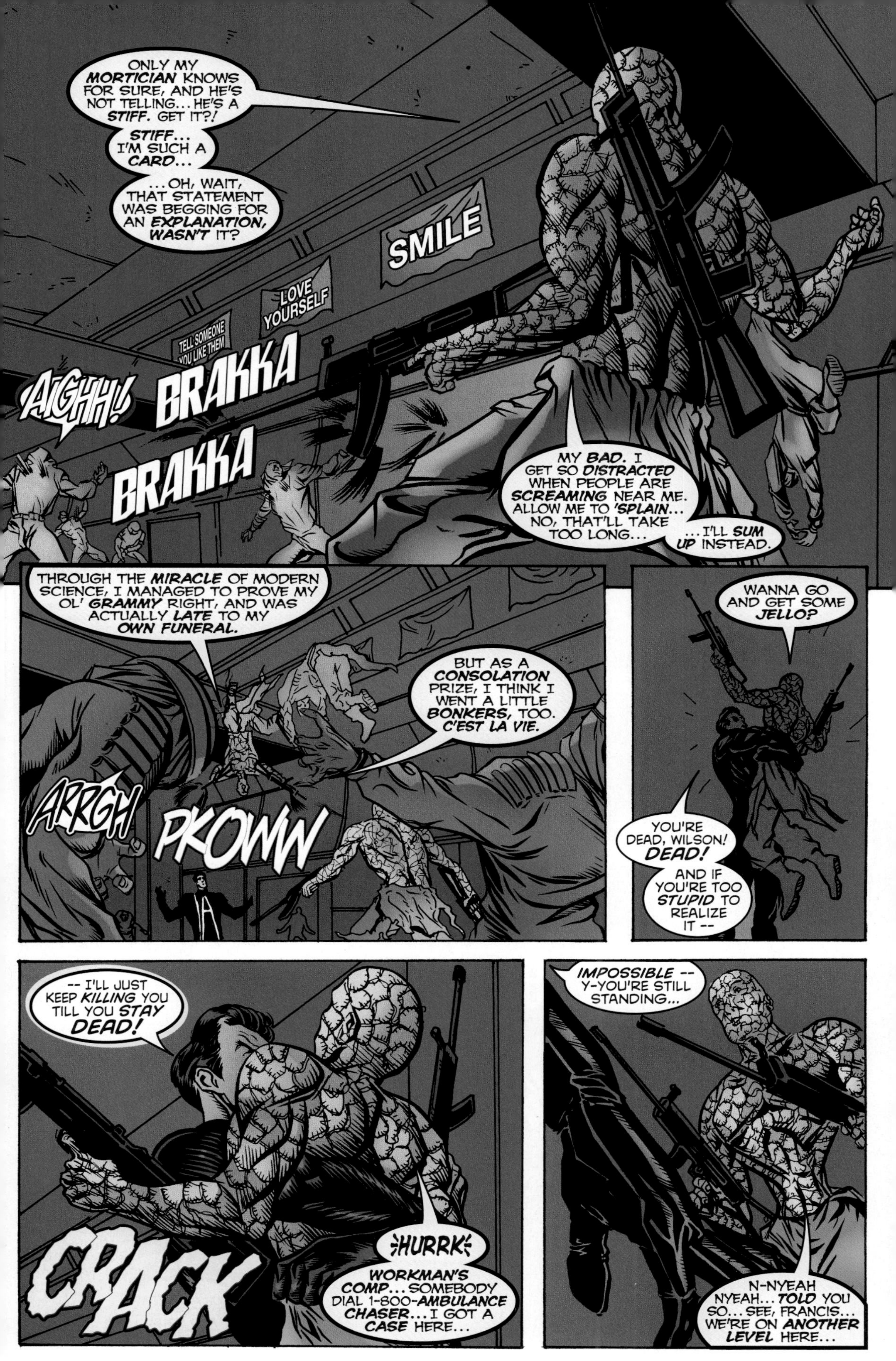

ONLY MY MORTICIAN KNOWS FOR SURE, AND HE'S NOT TELLING... HE'S A STIFF. GET IT?!
STIFF... I'M SUCH A CARD...
...OH, WAIT, THAT STATEMENT WAS BEGGING FOR AN EXPLANATION, WASN'T IT?
SMILE
LOVE YOURSELF
TELL SOMEONE YOU LIKE THEM
AIGHH!
BRAKKA
BRAKKA
MY BAD. I GET SO DISTRACTED WHEN PEOPLE ARE SCREAMING NEAR ME. ALLOW ME TO 'SPLAIN... NO, THAT'LL TAKE TOO LONG...
...I'LL SUM UP INSTEAD.
THROUGH THE MIRACLE OF MODERN SCIENCE, I MANAGED TO PROVE MY OL' GRAMMY RIGHT, AND WAS ACTUALLY LATE TO MY OWN FUNERAL.
BUT AS A CONSOLATION PRIZE, I THINK I WENT A LITTLE BONKERS, TOO. C'EST LA VIE.
ARRGH
PKOWW
WANNA GO AND GET SOME JELLO?
YOU'RE DEAD, WILSON! DEAD!
AND IF YOU'RE TOO STUPID TO REALIZE IT --
-- I'LL JUST KEEP KILLING YOU TILL YOU STAY DEAD!
CRACK
HURRK
WORKMAN'S COMP... SOMEBODY DIAL 1-800-AMBULANCE CHASER... I GOT A CASE HERE...
IMPOSSIBLE -- Y-YOU'RE STILL STANDING...
N-NYEAH NYEAH... TOLD YOU SO... SEE, FRANCIS... WE'RE ON ANOTHER LEVEL HERE...

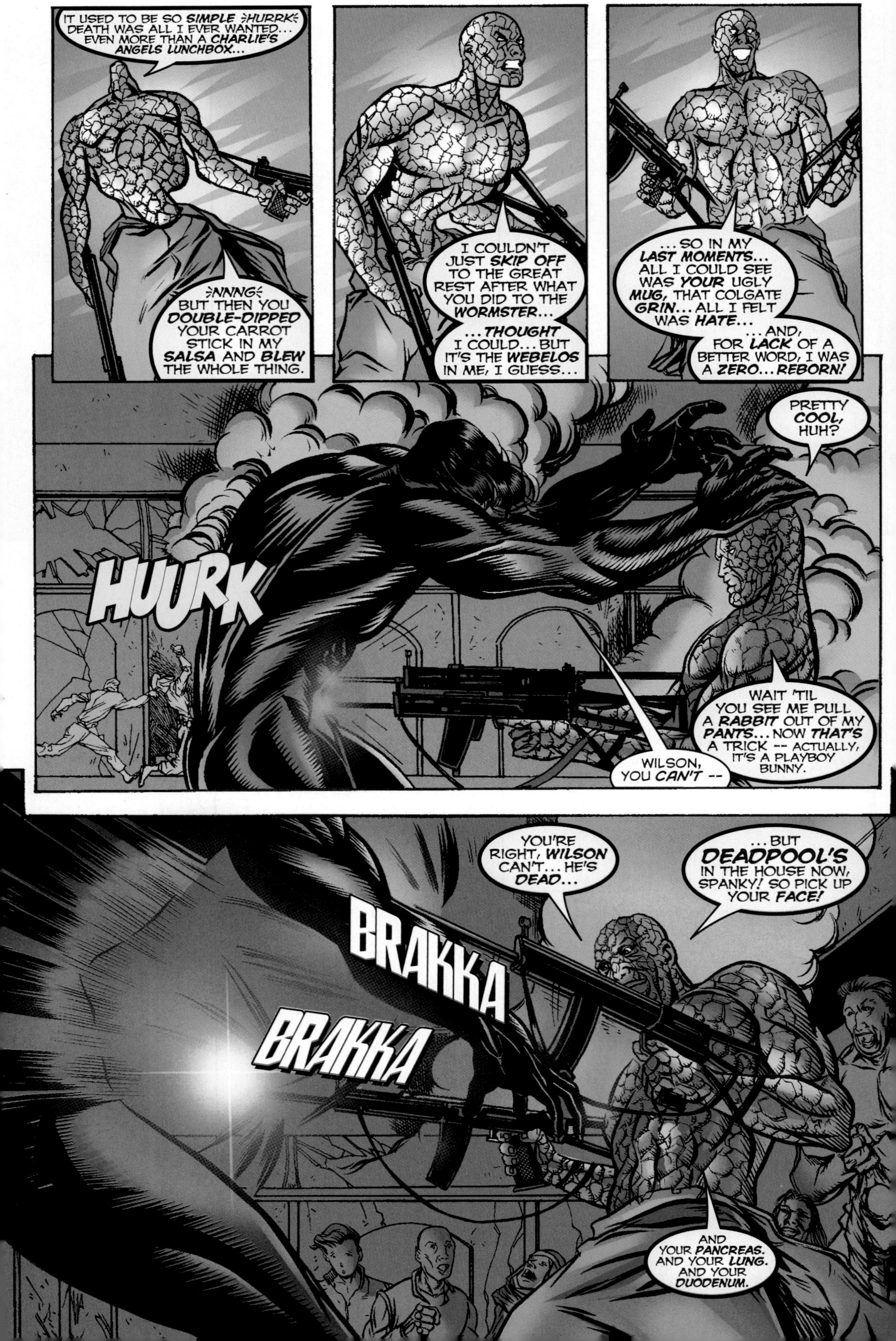
IT USED TO BE SO SIMPLE ≯HURRK≮ DEATH WAS ALL I EVER WANTED... EVEN MORE THAN A CHARLIE'S ANGELS LUNCHBOX...
≯NNNG≮ BUT THEN YOU DOUBLE-DIPPED YOUR CARROT STICK IN MY SALSA AND BLEW THE WHOLE THING.
I COULDN'T JUST SKIP OFF TO THE GREAT REST AFTER WHAT YOU DID TO THE WORMSTER...
...THOUGHT I COULD... BUT IT'S THE WEBELOS IN ME, I GUESS...
...SO IN MY LAST MOMENTS... ALL I COULD SEE WAS YOUR UGLY MUG, THAT COLGATE GRIN... ALL I FELT WAS HATE...
...AND, FOR LACK OF A BETTER WORD, I WAS A ZERO... REBORN!
PRETTY COOL, HUH?
HUURK
WAIT 'TIL YOU SEE ME PULL A RABBIT OUT OF MY PANTS... NOW THAT'S A TRICK -- ACTUALLY, IT'S A PLAYBOY BUNNY.
WILSON, YOU CAN'T --
YOU'RE RIGHT, WILSON CAN'T... HE'S DEAD...
...BUT DEADPOOL'S IN THE HOUSE NOW, SPANKY! SO PICK UP YOUR FACE!
BRAKKA
BRAKKA
AND YOUR PANCREAS. AND YOUR LUNG. AND YOUR DUODENUM.

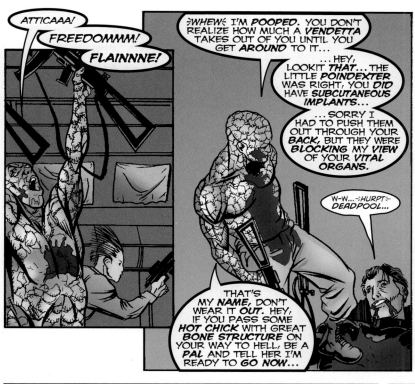

ATTICAAA!

FREEDOMMM!

FLAINNNE!

≳WHEW≲ I'M **POOPED.** YOU DON'T REALIZE HOW MUCH A **VENDETTA** TAKES OUT OF YOU UNTIL YOU GET **AROUND** TO IT...

...HEY, LOOKIT **THAT**...THE LITTLE **POINDEXTER** WAS RIGHT, YOU **DID** HAVE **SUBCUTANEOUS IMPLANTS...**

...SORRY I HAD TO PUSH THEM OUT THROUGH YOUR **BACK,** BUT THEY WERE **BLOCKING** MY **VIEW** OF YOUR **VITAL ORGANS.**

W-W...≳HURPT≲ DEADPOOL...

THAT'S MY **NAME,** DON'T WEAR IT **OUT.** HEY, IF YOU PASS SOME **HOT CHICK** WITH GREAT **BONE STRUCTURE** ON YOUR WAY TO HELL, BE A **PAL** AND TELL HER I'M READY TO **GO NOW...**

Y-YOU'RE SO **UGLY...**YOUR **MAMMA** HAD TO TIE A **STEAK** ON YOU...S-SO THE **DOG** WOULD PLAY WITH YOU... HEH HEH...

UH... OKAY... I HEARD THAT **SHOCK** COULD MESS A GUY UP, BUT THIS IS SAD --

NO...I G-GOT YOU...L-LOOK... S-**SEE,** WILSON... I G-GOT YOU --

"...I GOT YOU **GOOD...** M-MAYBE I D-**DIE** --

WHOA... I'LL BE A **DING-DONG DADDY...** WOULD YOU LOOK AT **THAT?**

"...BUT YOU'LL A-**ALWAYS** BE A **FREAK...**"

I DON'T GET IT...THE **HEALING FACTOR** IS TURNED UP TO **ELEVEN...**MY FACE SHOULD BE --

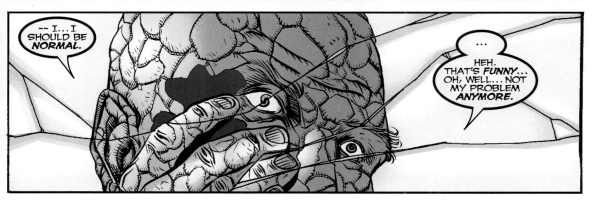

-- I...I SHOULD BE **NORMAL.**

... HEH. THAT'S **FUNNY...** OH, WELL...NOT MY PROBLEM **ANYMORE.**

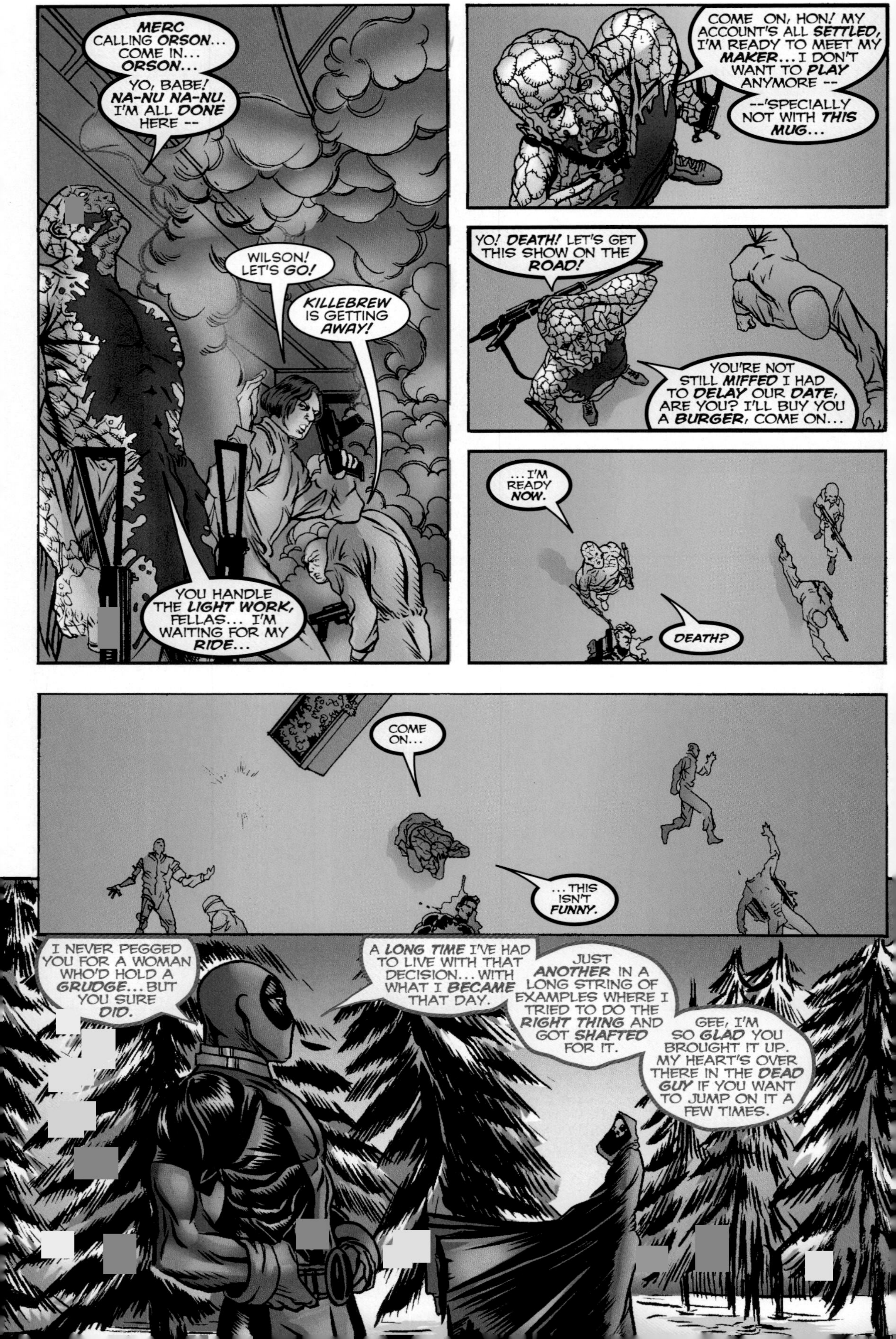
MERC CALLING ORSON... COME IN... ORSON...
YO, BABE! NA-NU NA-NU. I'M ALL DONE HERE --
WILSON! LET'S GO!
KILLEBREW IS GETTING AWAY!
YOU HANDLE THE LIGHT WORK, FELLAS... I'M WAITING FOR MY RIDE...
COME ON, HON! MY ACCOUNT'S ALL SETTLED, I'M READY TO MEET MY MAKER... I DON'T WANT TO PLAY ANYMORE --
--'SPECIALLY NOT WITH THIS MUG...
YO! DEATH! LET'S GET THIS SHOW ON THE ROAD!
YOU'RE NOT STILL MIFFED I HAD TO DELAY OUR DATE, ARE YOU? I'LL BUY YOU A BURGER, COME ON...
...I'M READY NOW.
DEATH?
COME ON...
...THIS ISN'T FUNNY.
I NEVER PEGGED YOU FOR A WOMAN WHO'D HOLD A GRUDGE... BUT YOU SURE DID.
A LONG TIME I'VE HAD TO LIVE WITH THAT DECISION... WITH WHAT I BECAME THAT DAY.
JUST ANOTHER IN A LONG STRING OF EXAMPLES WHERE I TRIED TO DO THE RIGHT THING AND GOT SHAFTED FOR IT.
GEE, I'M SO GLAD YOU BROUGHT IT UP. MY HEART'S OVER THERE IN THE DEAD GUY IF YOU WANT TO JUMP ON IT A FEW TIMES.

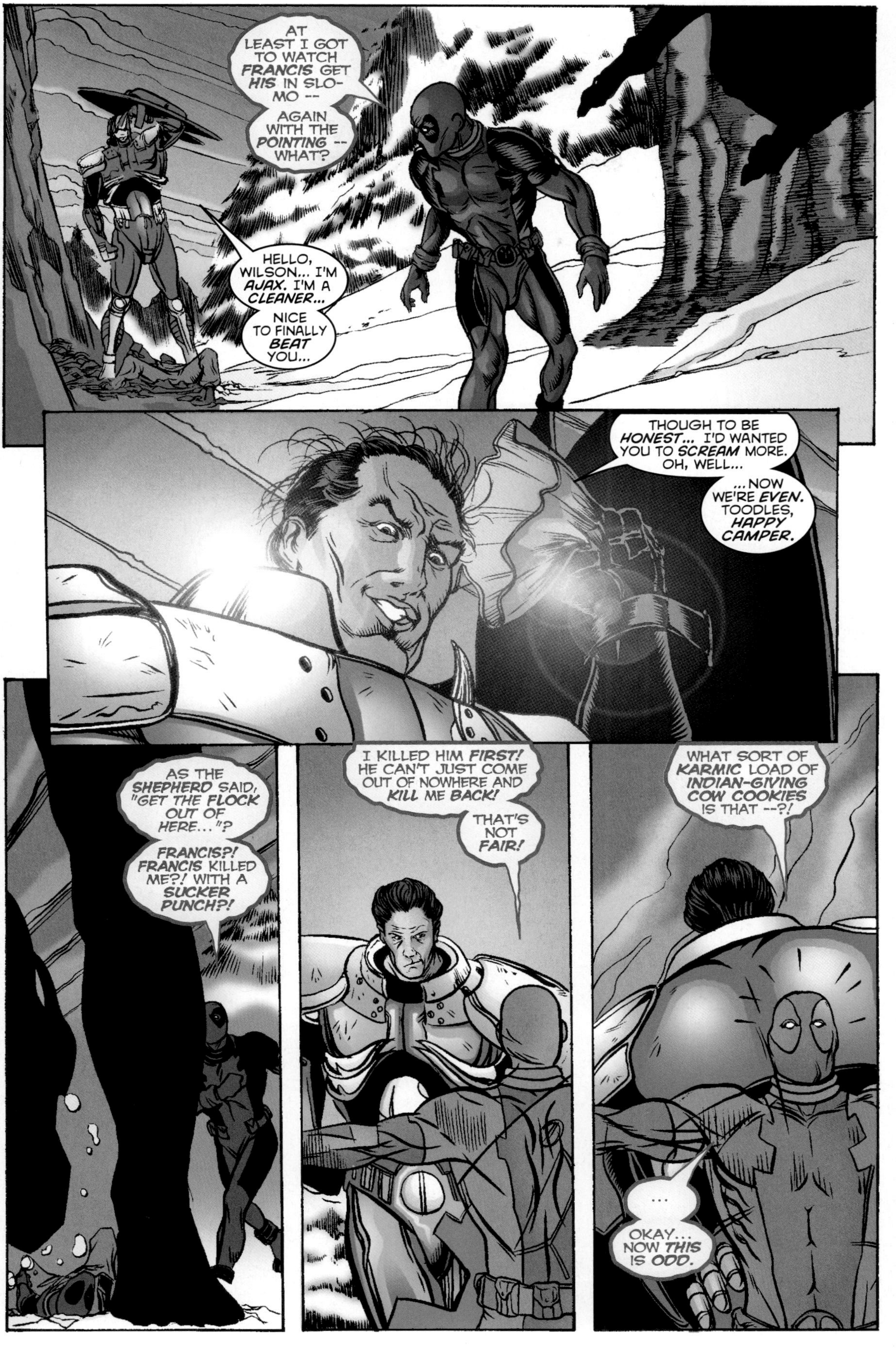

AT LEAST I GOT TO WATCH FRANCIS GET HIS IN SLO-MO --
AGAIN WITH THE POINTING -- WHAT?
HELLO, WILSON... I'M AJAX. I'M A CLEANER...
NICE TO FINALLY BEAT YOU...
THOUGH TO BE HONEST... I'D WANTED YOU TO SCREAM MORE. OH, WELL...
...NOW WE'RE EVEN. TOODLES, HAPPY CAMPER.
AS THE SHEPHERD SAID, "GET THE FLOCK OUT OF HERE..."?
FRANCIS?! FRANCIS KILLED ME?! WITH A SUCKER PUNCH?!
I KILLED HIM FIRST! HE CAN'T JUST COME OUT OF NOWHERE AND KILL ME BACK!
THAT'S NOT FAIR!
WHAT SORT OF KARMIC LOAD OF INDIAN-GIVING COW COOKIES IS THAT --?!
...
OKAY... NOW THIS IS ODD.

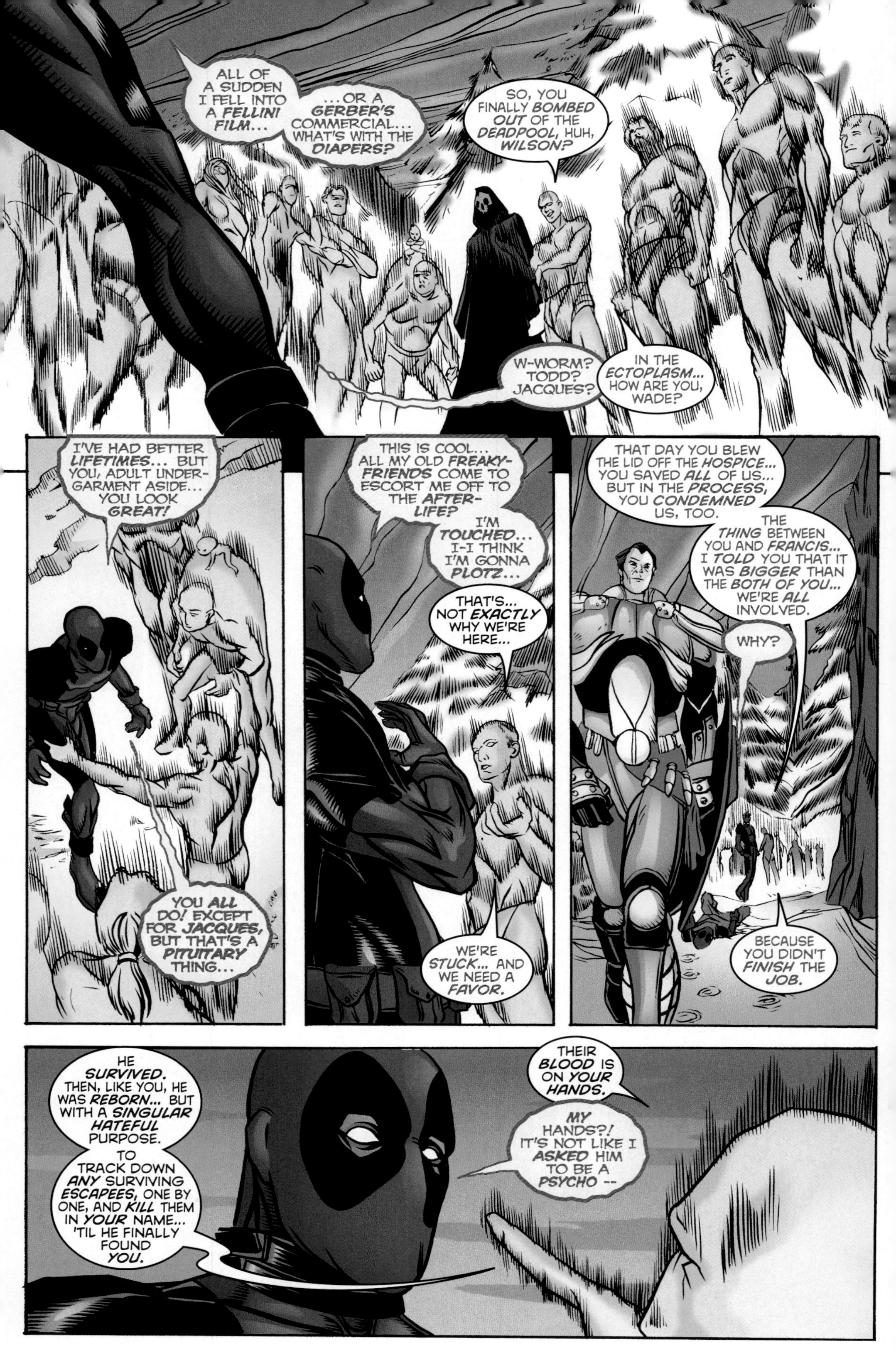

ALL OF A SUDDEN I FELL INTO A FELLINI FILM...
...OR A GERBER'S COMMERCIAL... WHAT'S WITH THE DIAPERS?
SO, YOU FINALLY BOMBED OUT OF THE DEADPOOL, HUH, WILSON?
W-WORM? TODD? JACQUES?
IN THE ECTOPLASM... HOW ARE YOU, WADE?
I'VE HAD BETTER LIFETIMES... BUT YOU, ADULT UNDER-GARMENT ASIDE... YOU LOOK GREAT!
YOU ALL DO! EXCEPT FOR JACQUES, BUT THAT'S A PITUITARY THING...
THIS IS COOL... ALL MY OLD FREAKY-FRIENDS COME TO ESCORT ME OFF TO THE AFTER-LIFE?
I'M TOUCHED... I-I THINK I'M GONNA PLOTZ...
THAT'S... NOT EXACTLY WHY WE'RE HERE...
WE'RE STUCK... AND WE NEED A FAVOR.
THAT DAY YOU BLEW THE LID OFF THE HOSPICE... YOU SAVED ALL OF US... BUT IN THE PROCESS, YOU CONDEMNED US, TOO.
THE THING BETWEEN YOU AND FRANCIS... I TOLD YOU THAT IT WAS BIGGER THAN THE BOTH OF YOU... WE'RE ALL INVOLVED.
WHY?
BECAUSE YOU DIDN'T FINISH THE JOB.
HE SURVIVED. THEN, LIKE YOU, HE WAS REBORN... BUT WITH A SINGULAR HATEFUL PURPOSE.
TO TRACK DOWN ANY SURVIVING ESCAPEES, ONE BY ONE, AND KILL THEM IN YOUR NAME... 'TIL HE FINALLY FOUND YOU.
THEIR BLOOD IS ON YOUR HANDS.
MY HANDS?! IT'S NOT LIKE I ASKED HIM TO BE A PSYCHO --

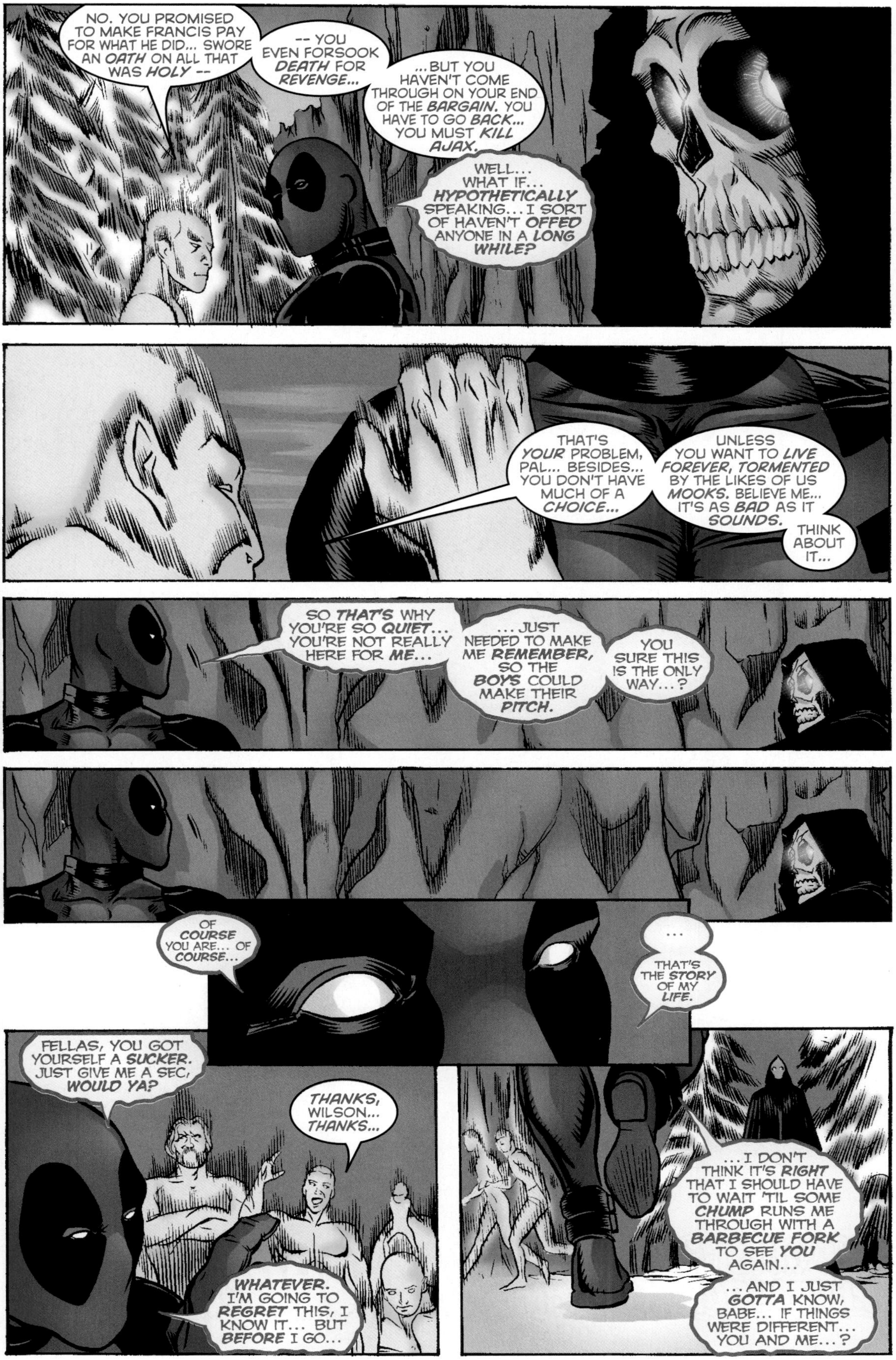

NO. YOU PROMISED TO MAKE FRANCIS PAY FOR WHAT HE DID... SWORE AN OATH ON ALL THAT WAS HOLY --
-- YOU EVEN FORSOOK DEATH FOR REVENGE...
...BUT YOU HAVEN'T COME THROUGH ON YOUR END OF THE BARGAIN. YOU HAVE TO GO BACK... YOU MUST KILL AJAX.
WELL... WHAT IF... HYPOTHETICALLY SPEAKING... I SORT OF HAVEN'T OFFED ANYONE IN A LONG WHILE?
THAT'S YOUR PROBLEM, PAL... BESIDES... YOU DON'T HAVE MUCH OF A CHOICE...
UNLESS YOU WANT TO LIVE FOREVER, TORMENTED BY THE LIKES OF US MOOKS. BELIEVE ME... IT'S AS BAD AS IT SOUNDS.
THINK ABOUT IT...
SO THAT'S WHY YOU'RE SO QUIET... YOU'RE NOT REALLY HERE FOR ME...
... JUST NEEDED TO MAKE ME REMEMBER, SO THE BOYS COULD MAKE THEIR PITCH.
YOU SURE THIS IS THE ONLY WAY...?
OF COURSE YOU ARE... OF COURSE...
...
THAT'S THE STORY OF MY LIFE.
FELLAS, YOU GOT YOURSELF A SUCKER. JUST GIVE ME A SEC, WOULD YA?
THANKS, WILSON... THANKS...
WHATEVER. I'M GOING TO REGRET THIS, I KNOW IT... BUT BEFORE I GO...
...I DON'T THINK IT'S RIGHT THAT I SHOULD HAVE TO WAIT 'TIL SOME CHUMP RUNS ME THROUGH WITH A BARBECUE FORK TO SEE YOU AGAIN...
...AND I JUST GOTTA KNOW, BABE... IF THINGS WERE DIFFERENT... YOU AND ME...?

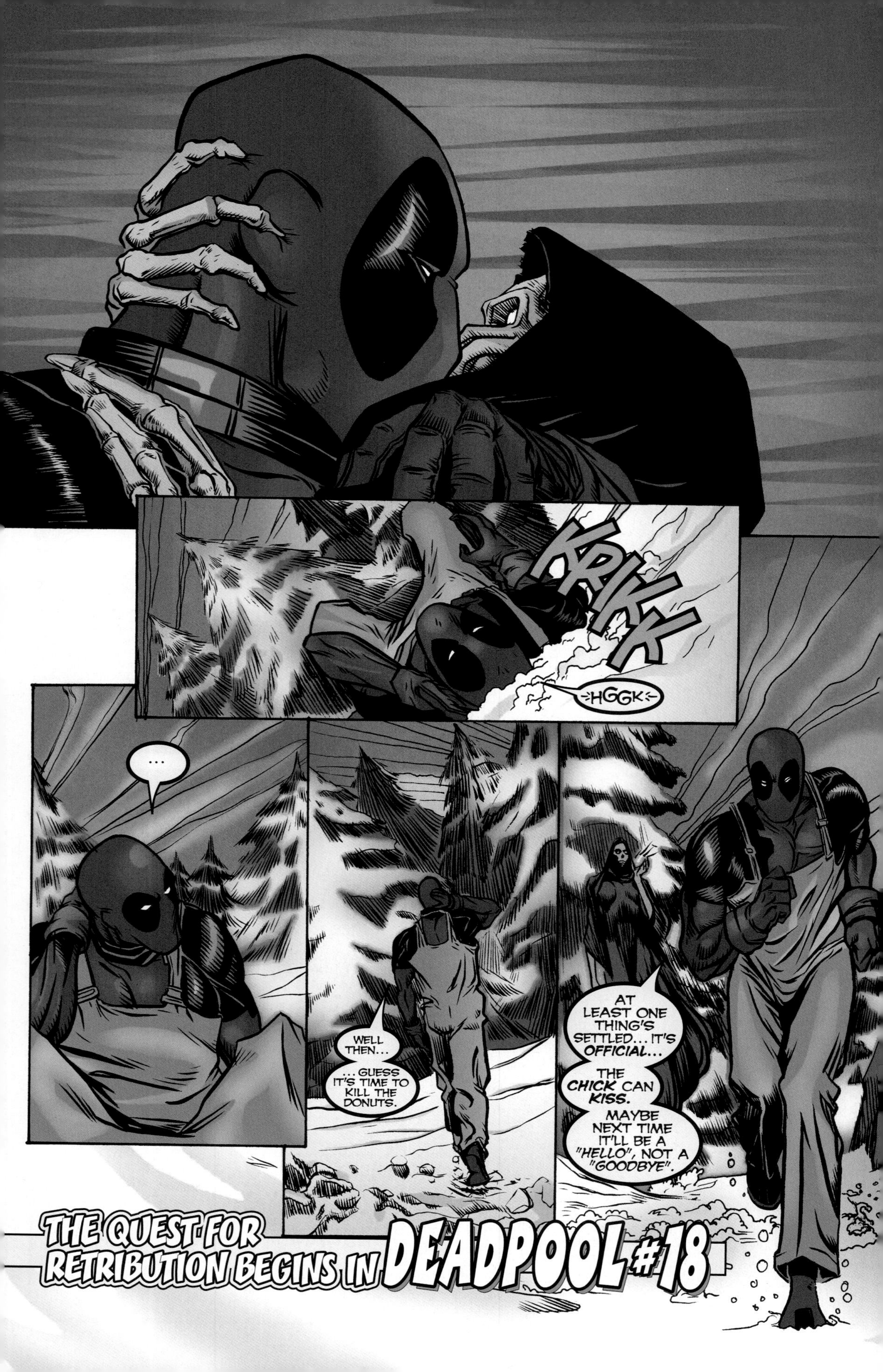
KRIKK
HGGK
...
WELL THEN...
...GUESS IT'S TIME TO KILL THE DONUTS.
AT LEAST ONE THING'S SETTLED... IT'S OFFICIAL...
THE CHICK CAN KISS.
MAYBE NEXT TIME IT'LL BE A "HELLO", NOT A "GOODBYE".
THE QUEST FOR RETRIBUTION BEGINS IN DEADPOOL #18

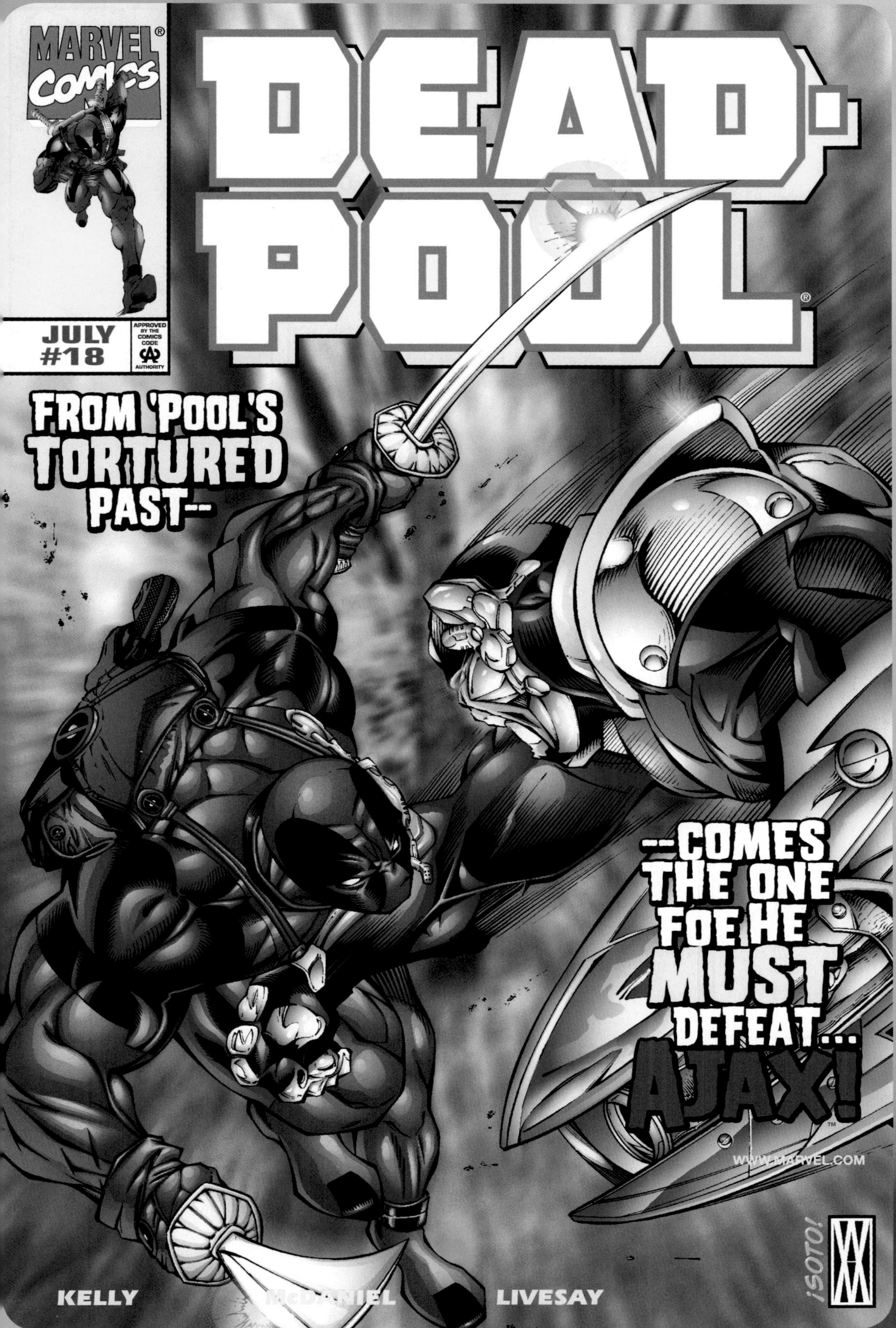
MARVEL COMICS
DEADPOOL
JULY #18
APPROVED BY THE COMICS CODE AUTHORITY
FROM 'POOL'S TORTURED PAST--
--COMES THE ONE FOE HE MUST DEFEAT... AJAX!
WWW.MARVEL.COM
KELLY
McDANIEL
LIVESAY
¡SOTO!

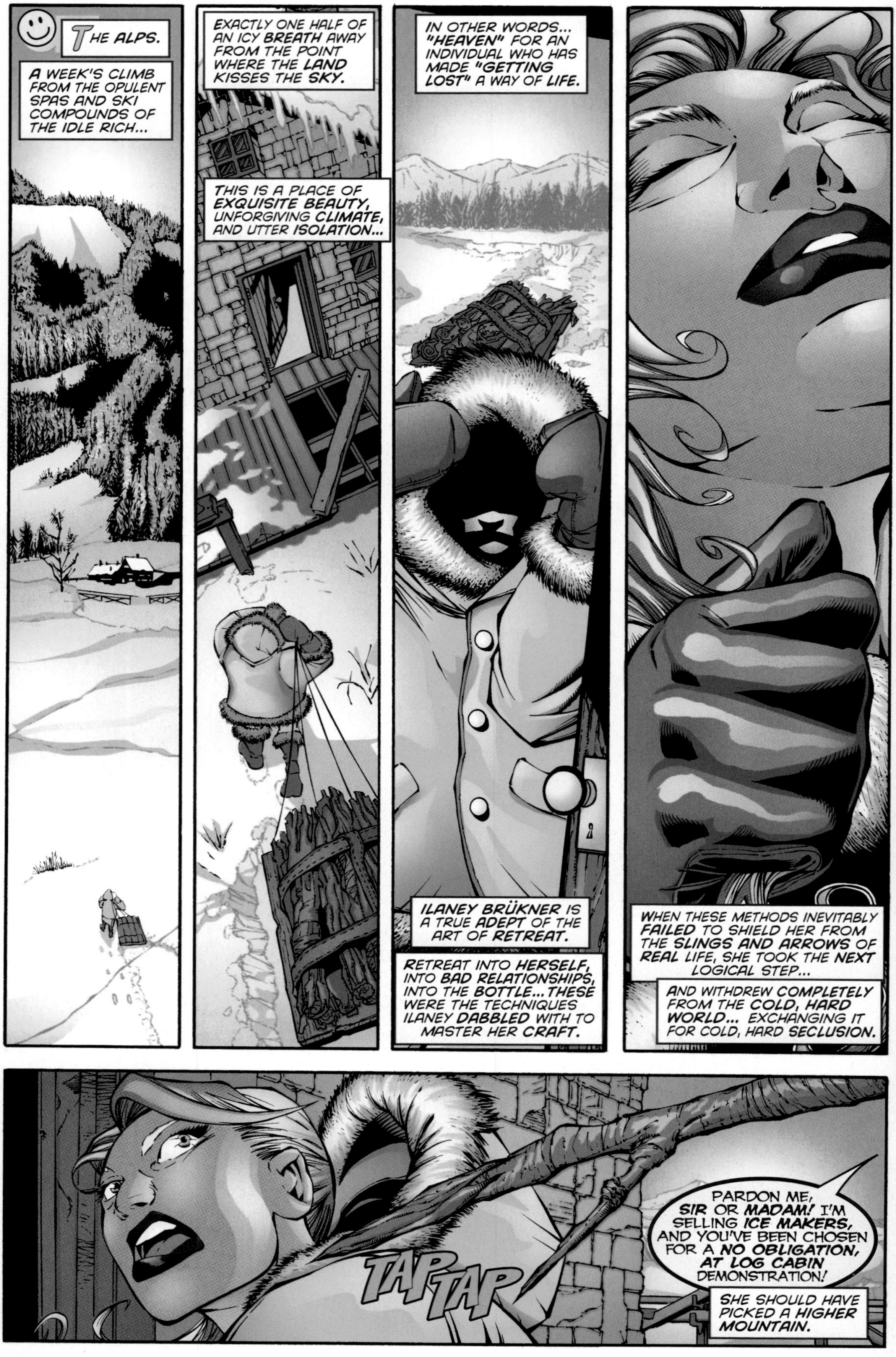
THE ALPS.
A WEEK'S CLIMB FROM THE OPULENT SPAS AND SKI COMPOUNDS OF THE IDLE RICH...
EXACTLY ONE HALF OF AN ICY BREATH AWAY FROM THE POINT WHERE THE LAND KISSES THE SKY.
THIS IS A PLACE OF EXQUISITE BEAUTY, UNFORGIVING CLIMATE, AND UTTER ISOLATION...
IN OTHER WORDS... "HEAVEN" FOR AN INDIVIDUAL WHO HAS MADE "GETTING LOST" A WAY OF LIFE.
ILANEY BRÜKNER IS A TRUE ADEPT OF THE ART OF RETREAT.
RETREAT INTO HERSELF, INTO BAD RELATIONSHIPS, INTO THE BOTTLE...THESE WERE THE TECHNIQUES ILANEY DABBLED WITH TO MASTER HER CRAFT.
WHEN THESE METHODS INEVITABLY FAILED TO SHIELD HER FROM THE SLINGS AND ARROWS OF REAL LIFE, SHE TOOK THE NEXT LOGICAL STEP...
AND WITHDREW COMPLETELY FROM THE COLD, HARD WORLD... EXCHANGING IT FOR COLD, HARD SECLUSION.
TAP TAP
PARDON ME, SIR OR MADAM! I'M SELLING ICE MAKERS, AND YOU'VE BEEN CHOSEN FOR A NO OBLIGATION, AT LOG CABIN DEMONSTRATION!
SHE SHOULD HAVE PICKED A HIGHER MOUNTAIN.

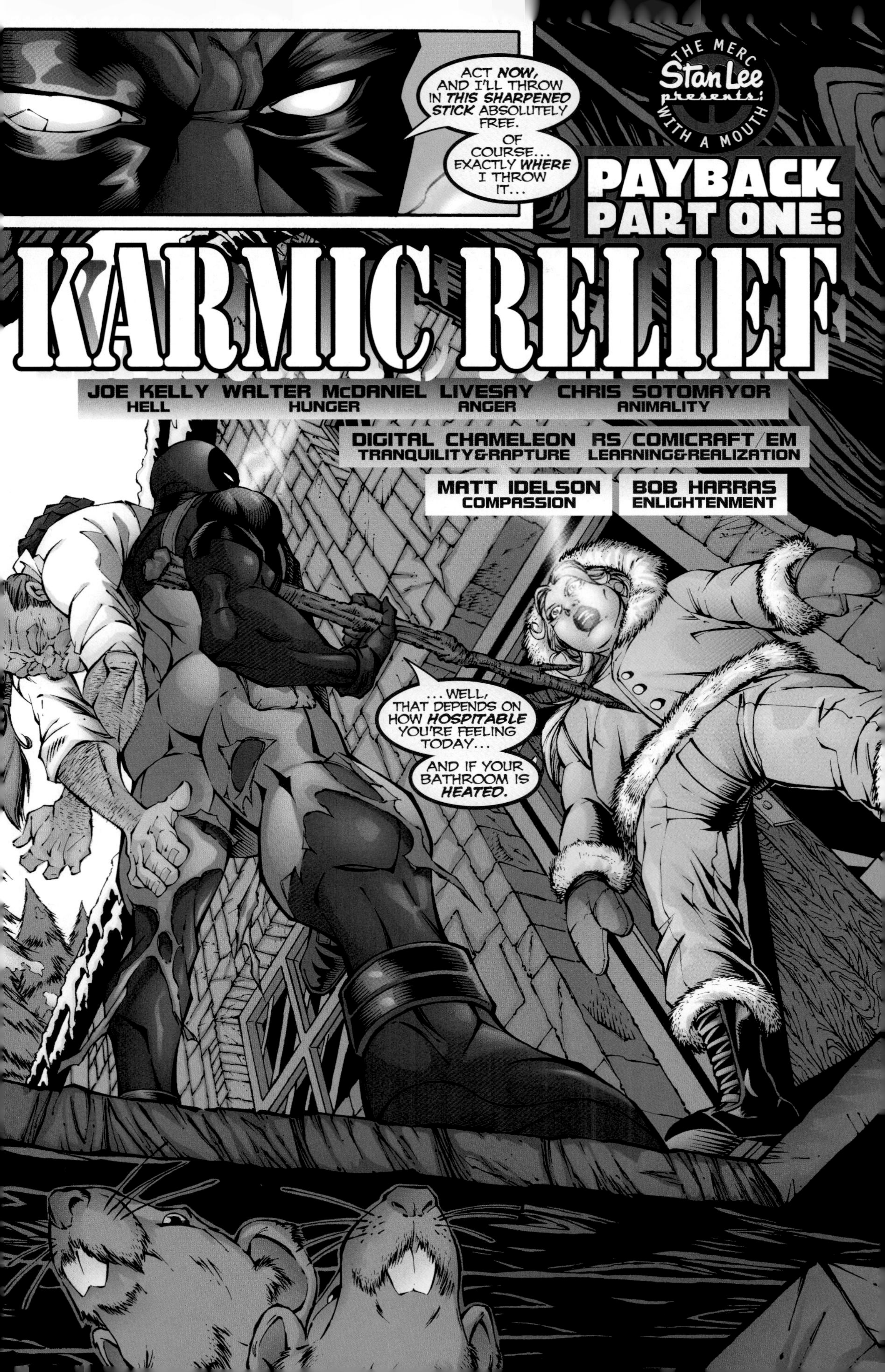

THE MERC WITH A MOUTH
Stan Lee presents:
ACT NOW, AND I'LL THROW IN THIS SHARPENED STICK ABSOLUTELY FREE.
OF COURSE... EXACTLY WHERE I THROW IT...
PAYBACK PART ONE:
KARMIC RELIEF
JOE KELLY HELL
WALTER McDANIEL HUNGER
LIVESAY ANGER
CHRIS SOTOMAYOR ANIMALITY
DIGITAL CHAMELEON TRANQUILITY&RAPTURE
RS/COMICRAFT/EM LEARNING&REALIZATION
MATT IDELSON COMPASSION
BOB HARRAS ENLIGHTENMENT
...WELL, THAT DEPENDS ON HOW HOSPITABLE YOU'RE FEELING TODAY...
AND IF YOUR BATHROOM IS HEATED.

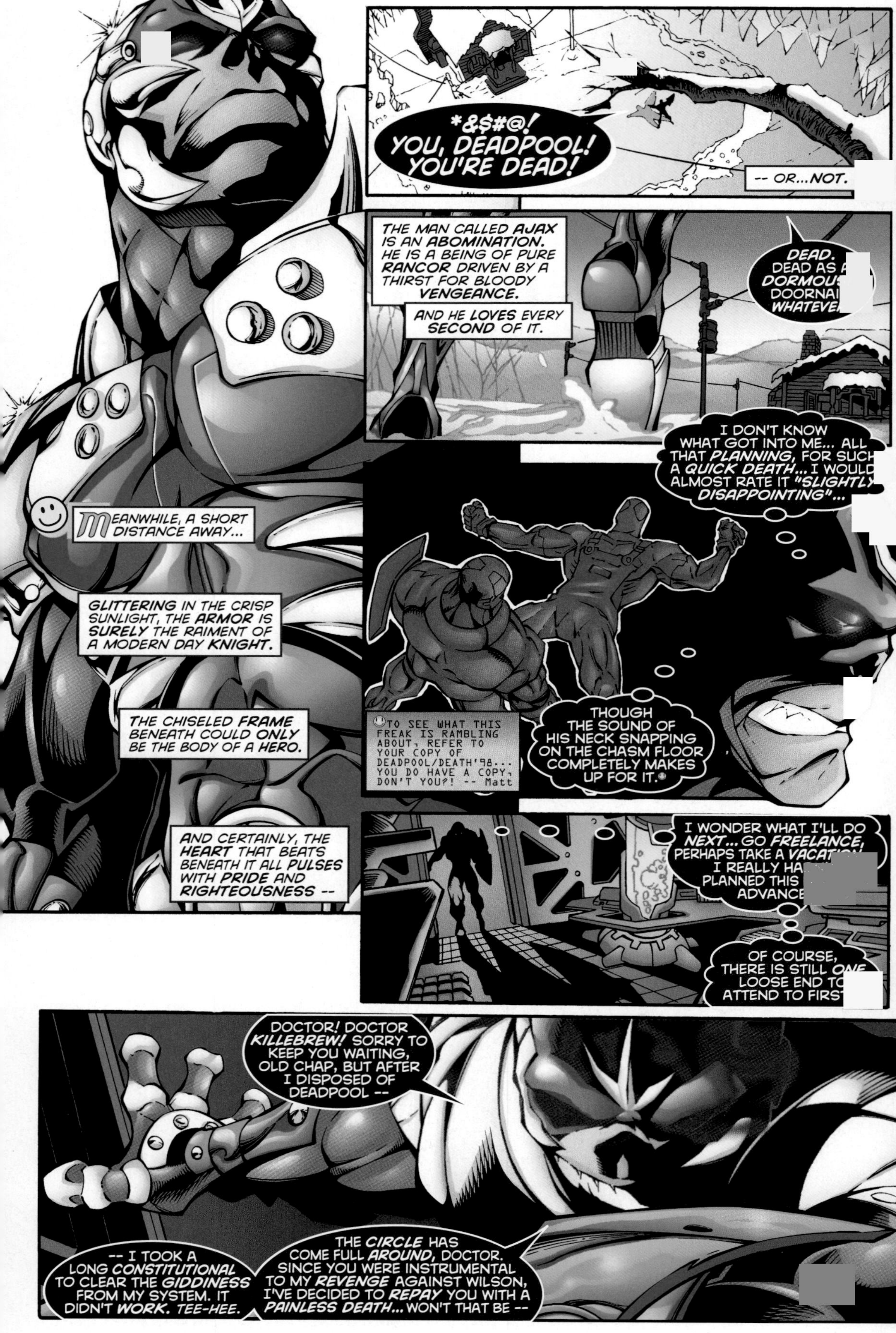
MEANWHILE, A SHORT DISTANCE AWAY...
GLITTERING IN THE CRISP SUNLIGHT, THE ARMOR IS SURELY THE RAIMENT OF A MODERN DAY KNIGHT.
THE CHISELED FRAME BENEATH COULD ONLY BE THE BODY OF A HERO.
AND CERTAINLY, THE HEART THAT BEATS BENEATH IT ALL PULSES WITH PRIDE AND RIGHTEOUSNESS --
*&$#@! YOU, DEADPOOL! YOU'RE DEAD!
-- OR...NOT.
THE MAN CALLED AJAX IS AN ABOMINATION. HE IS A BEING OF PURE RANCOR DRIVEN BY A THIRST FOR BLOODY VENGEANCE.
AND HE LOVES EVERY SECOND OF IT.
DEAD. DEAD AS A DORMOUS DOORNAI WHATEVE
I DON'T KNOW WHAT GOT INTO ME... ALL THAT PLANNING, FOR SUCH A QUICK DEATH... I WOULD ALMOST RATE IT "SLIGHTLY DISAPPOINTING"...
THOUGH THE SOUND OF HIS NECK SNAPPING ON THE CHASM FLOOR COMPLETELY MAKES UP FOR IT.
TO SEE WHAT THIS FREAK IS RAMBLING ABOUT, REFER TO YOUR COPY OF DEADPOOL/DEATH'98... YOU DO HAVE A COPY, DON'T YOU?! -- Matt
I WONDER WHAT I'LL DO NEXT... GO FREELANCE, PERHAPS TAKE A VACATION I REALLY HA PLANNED THIS ADVANCE
OF COURSE, THERE IS STILL ONE LOOSE END TO ATTEND TO FIRST
DOCTOR! DOCTOR KILLEBREW! SORRY TO KEEP YOU WAITING, OLD CHAP, BUT AFTER I DISPOSED OF DEADPOOL --
-- I TOOK A LONG CONSTITUTIONAL TO CLEAR THE GIDDINESS FROM MY SYSTEM. IT DIDN'T WORK. TEE-HEE.
THE CIRCLE HAS COME FULL AROUND, DOCTOR. SINCE YOU WERE INSTRUMENTAL TO MY REVENGE AGAINST WILSON, I'VE DECIDED TO REPAY YOU WITH A PAINLESS DEATH... WON'T THAT BE --

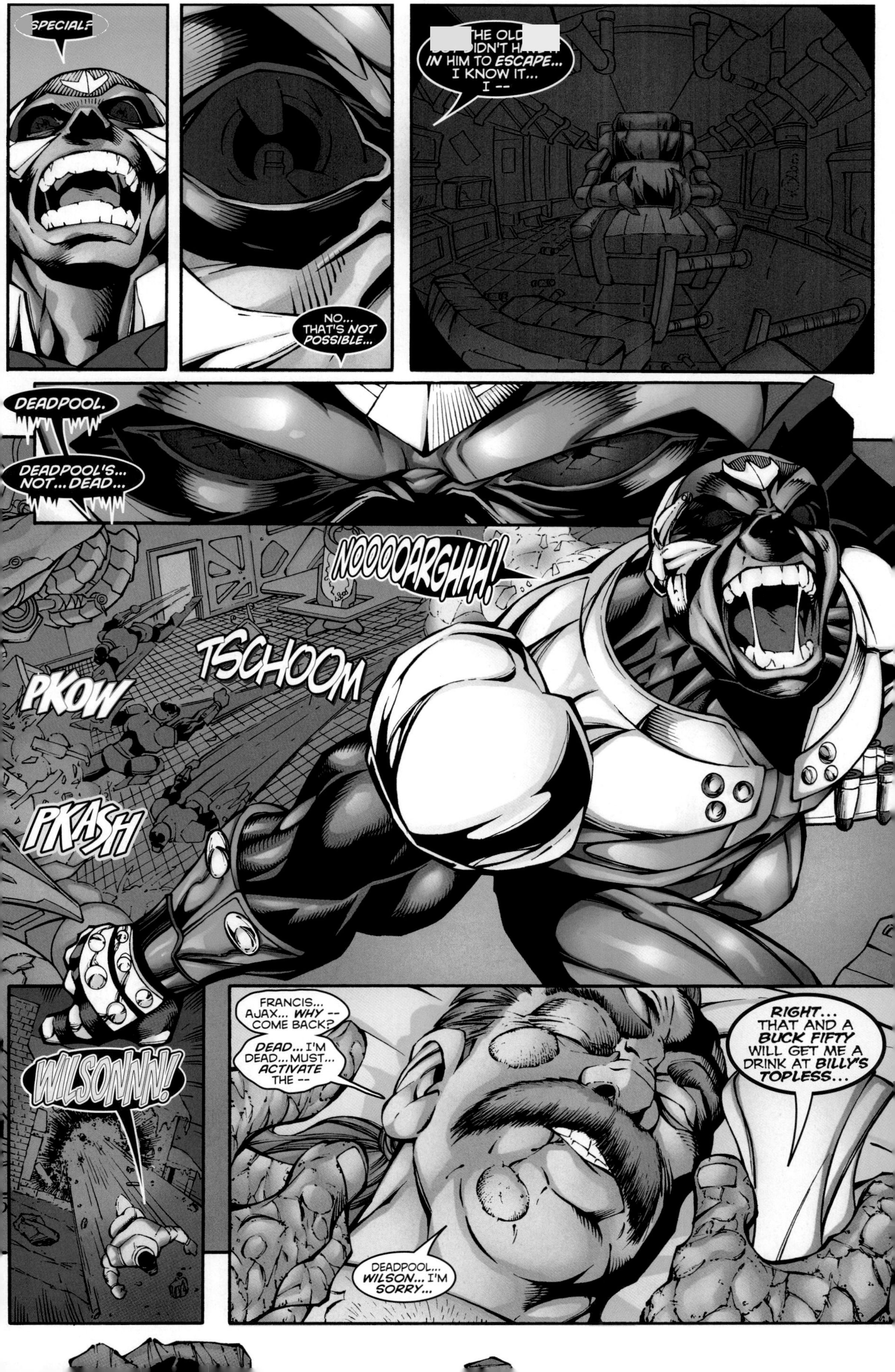
SPECIAL?
NO... THAT'S NOT POSSIBLE...
THE OLD DIDN'T HA IN HIM TO ESCAPE... I KNOW IT... I --
DEADPOOL.
DEADPOOL'S... NOT... DEAD...
NOOOOARGHHH!
TSCHOOM
PKOW
PKASH
WILSONNN!
FRANCIS... AJAX... WHY -- COME BACK?
DEAD... I'M DEAD... MUST... ACTIVATE THE --
RIGHT... THAT AND A BUCK FIFTY WILL GET ME A DRINK AT BILLY'S TOPLESS...
DEADPOOL... WILSON... I'M SORRY...

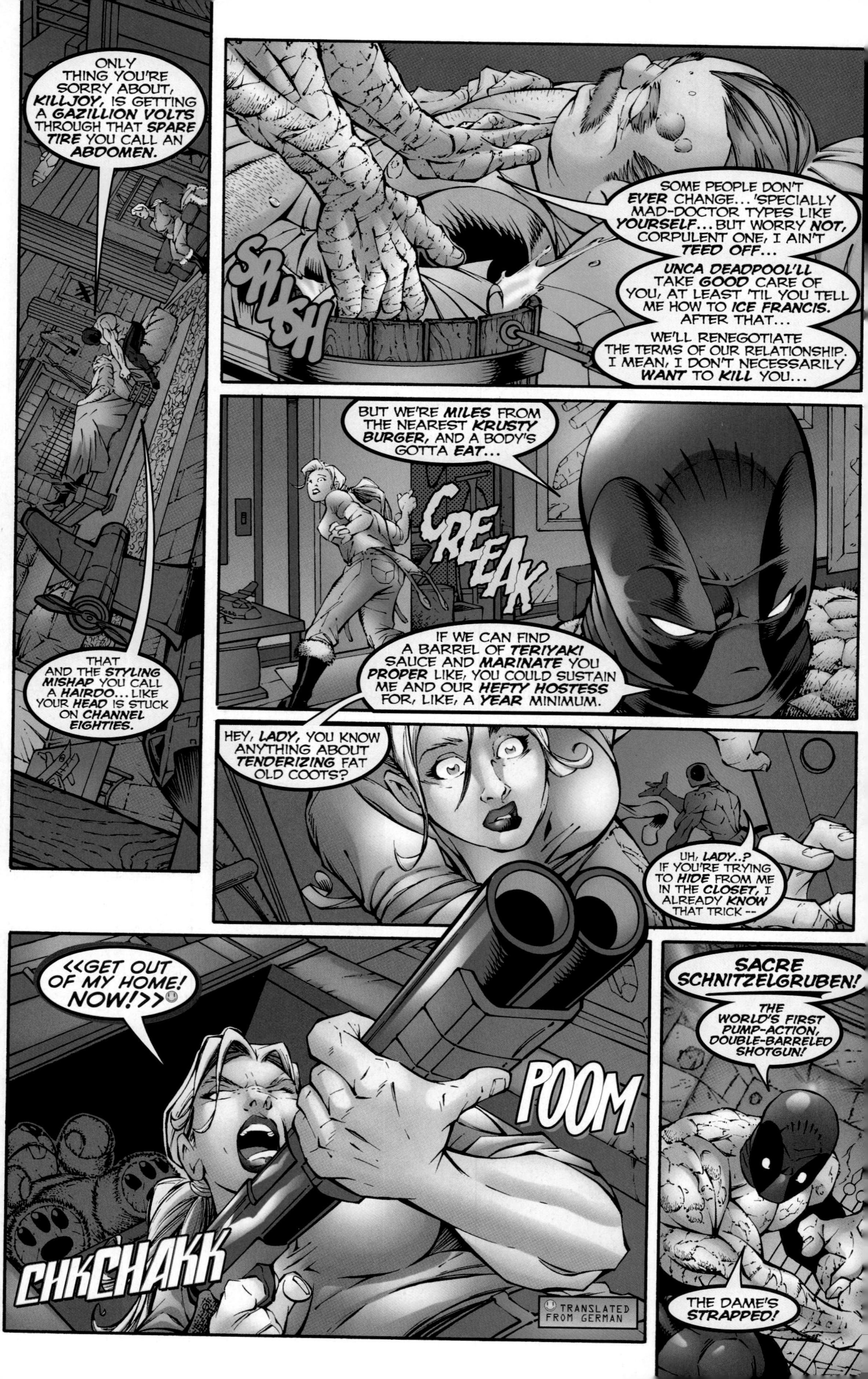
ONLY THING YOU'RE SORRY ABOUT, KILLJOY, IS GETTING A GAZILLION VOLTS THROUGH THAT SPARE TIRE YOU CALL AN ABDOMEN.
THAT AND THE STYLING MISHAP YOU CALL A HAIRDO... LIKE YOUR HEAD IS STUCK ON CHANNEL EIGHTIES.
SPLISH
SOME PEOPLE DON'T EVER CHANGE... 'SPECIALLY MAD-DOCTOR TYPES LIKE YOURSELF... BUT WORRY NOT, CORPULENT ONE, I AIN'T TEED OFF...
UNCA DEADPOOL'LL TAKE GOOD CARE OF YOU, AT LEAST 'TIL YOU TELL ME HOW TO ICE FRANCIS. AFTER THAT...
WE'LL RENEGOTIATE THE TERMS OF OUR RELATIONSHIP. I MEAN, I DON'T NECESSARILY WANT TO KILL YOU...
BUT WE'RE MILES FROM THE NEAREST KRUSTY BURGER, AND A BODY'S GOTTA EAT...
CREEAK
IF WE CAN FIND A BARREL OF TERIYAKI SAUCE AND MARINATE YOU PROPER LIKE, YOU COULD SUSTAIN ME AND OUR HEFTY HOSTESS FOR, LIKE, A YEAR MINIMUM.
HEY, LADY, YOU KNOW ANYTHING ABOUT TENDERIZING FAT OLD COOTS?
UH, LADY..? IF YOU'RE TRYING TO HIDE FROM ME IN THE CLOSET, I ALREADY KNOW THAT TRICK --
<<GET OUT OF MY HOME! NOW!>>
POOM
CHKCHAKK
TRANSLATED FROM GERMAN
SACRE SCHNITZELGRUBEN!
THE WORLD'S FIRST PUMP-ACTION, DOUBLE-BARRELED SHOTGUN!
THE DAME'S STRAPPED!

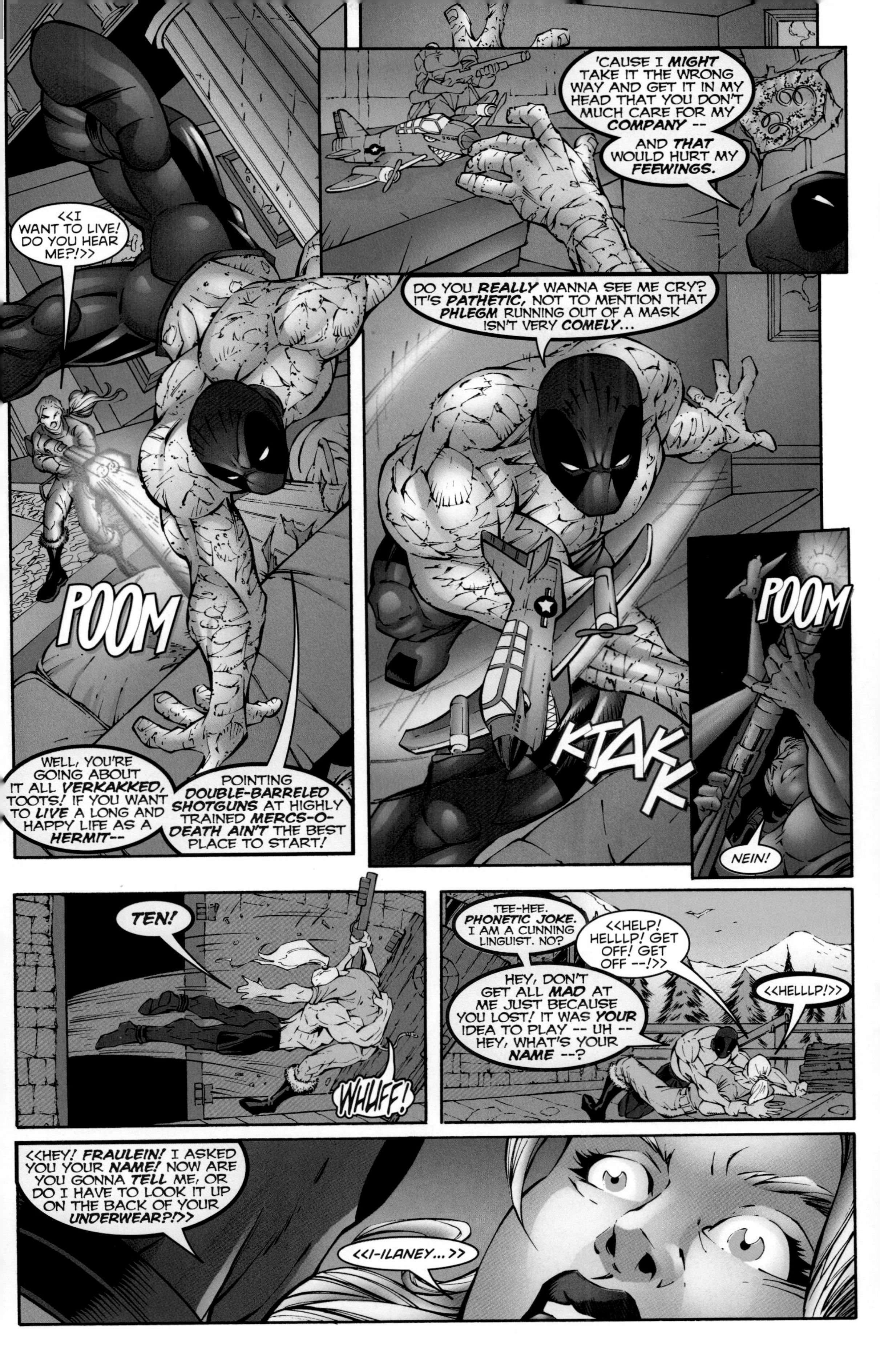
'CAUSE I MIGHT TAKE IT THE WRONG WAY AND GET IT IN MY HEAD THAT YOU DON'T MUCH CARE FOR MY COMPANY --
AND THAT WOULD HURT MY FEEWINGS.
<<I WANT TO LIVE! DO YOU HEAR ME?!>>
DO YOU REALLY WANNA SEE ME CRY? IT'S PATHETIC, NOT TO MENTION THAT PHLEGM RUNNING OUT OF A MASK ISN'T VERY COMELY...
POOM
WELL, YOU'RE GOING ABOUT IT ALL VERKAKKED, TOOTS! IF YOU WANT TO LIVE A LONG AND HAPPY LIFE AS A HERMIT--
POINTING DOUBLE-BARRELED SHOTGUNS AT HIGHLY TRAINED MERCS-O-DEATH AIN'T THE BEST PLACE TO START!
KTAKK
POOM
NEIN!
TEN!
WHUFF!
TEE-HEE. PHONETIC JOKE. I AM A CUNNING LINGUIST. NO?
<<HELP! HELLLP! GET OFF! GET OFF --!>>
HEY, DON'T GET ALL MAD AT ME JUST BECAUSE YOU LOST! IT WAS YOUR IDEA TO PLAY -- UH -- HEY, WHAT'S YOUR NAME --?
<<HELLLP!>>
<<HEY! FRAULEIN! I ASKED YOU YOUR NAME! NOW ARE YOU GONNA TELL ME, OR DO I HAVE TO LOOK IT UP ON THE BACK OF YOUR UNDERWEAR?!?>>
<<I-ILANEY...>>

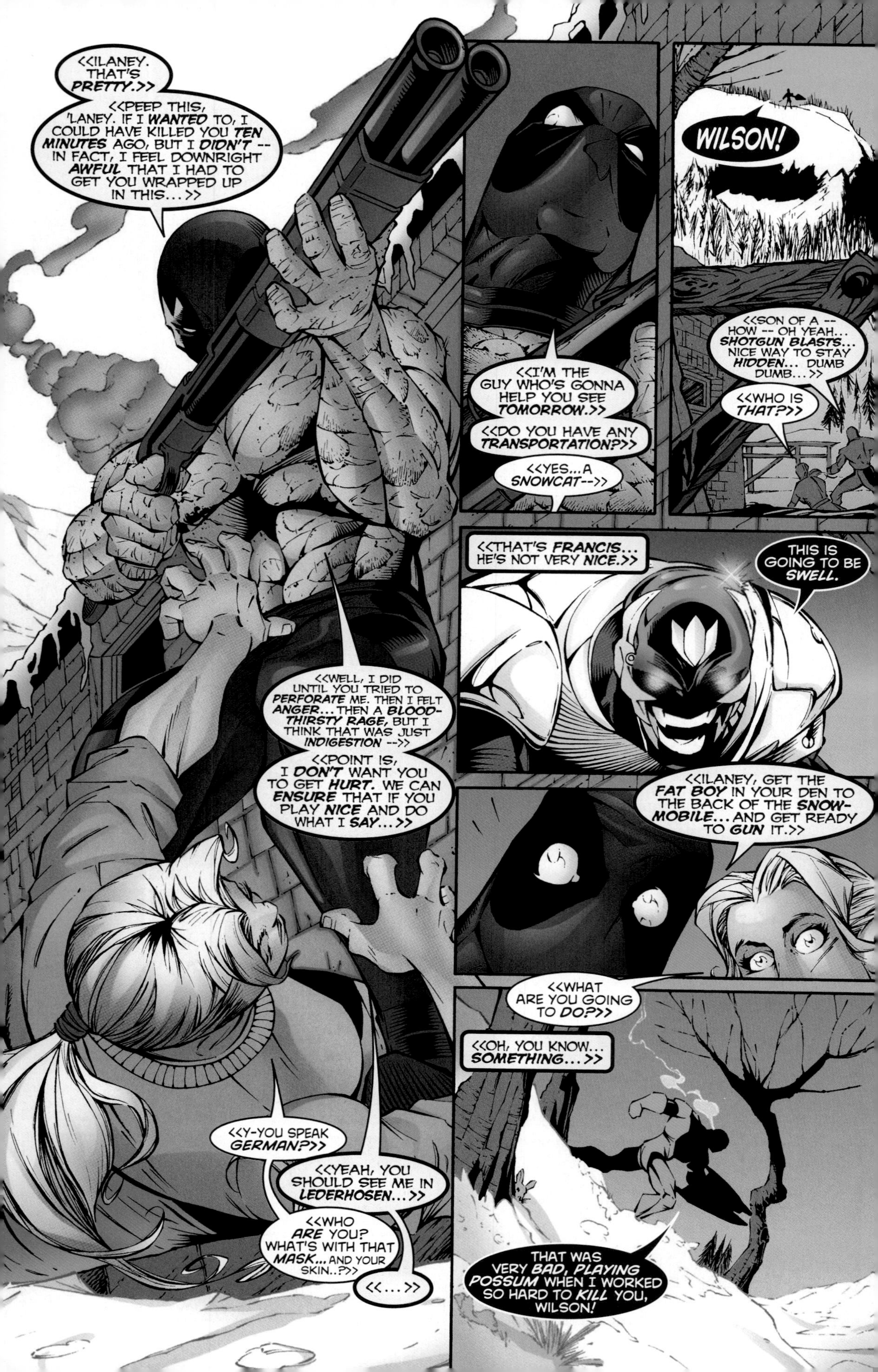

<<ILANEY. THAT'S PRETTY.>>
<<PEEP THIS, 'LANEY. IF I WANTED TO, I COULD HAVE KILLED YOU TEN MINUTES AGO, BUT I DIDN'T -- IN FACT, I FEEL DOWNRIGHT AWFUL THAT I HAD TO GET YOU WRAPPED UP IN THIS...>>
<<WELL, I DID UNTIL YOU TRIED TO PERFORATE ME. THEN I FELT ANGER... THEN A BLOOD-THIRSTY RAGE, BUT I THINK THAT WAS JUST INDIGESTION -->>
<<POINT IS, I DON'T WANT YOU TO GET HURT. WE CAN ENSURE THAT IF YOU PLAY NICE AND DO WHAT I SAY...>>
<<Y-YOU SPEAK GERMAN?>>
<<YEAH, YOU SHOULD SEE ME IN LEDERHOSEN...>>
<<WHO ARE YOU? WHAT'S WITH THAT MASK... AND YOUR SKIN..?>>
<<...>>
<<I'M THE GUY WHO'S GONNA HELP YOU SEE TOMORROW.>>
<<DO YOU HAVE ANY TRANSPORTATION?>>
<<YES...A SNOWCAT-->>
WILSON!
<<SON OF A -- HOW -- OH YEAH... SHOTGUN BLASTS... NICE WAY TO STAY HIDDEN... DUMB DUMB...>>
<<WHO IS THAT?>>
<<THAT'S FRANCIS... HE'S NOT VERY NICE.>>
THIS IS GOING TO BE SWELL.
<<ILANEY, GET THE FAT BOY IN YOUR DEN TO THE BACK OF THE SNOW-MOBILE... AND GET READY TO GUN IT.>>
<<WHAT ARE YOU GOING TO DO?>>
<<OH, YOU KNOW... SOMETHING...>>
THAT WAS VERY BAD, PLAYING POSSUM WHEN I WORKED SO HARD TO KILL YOU, WILSON!

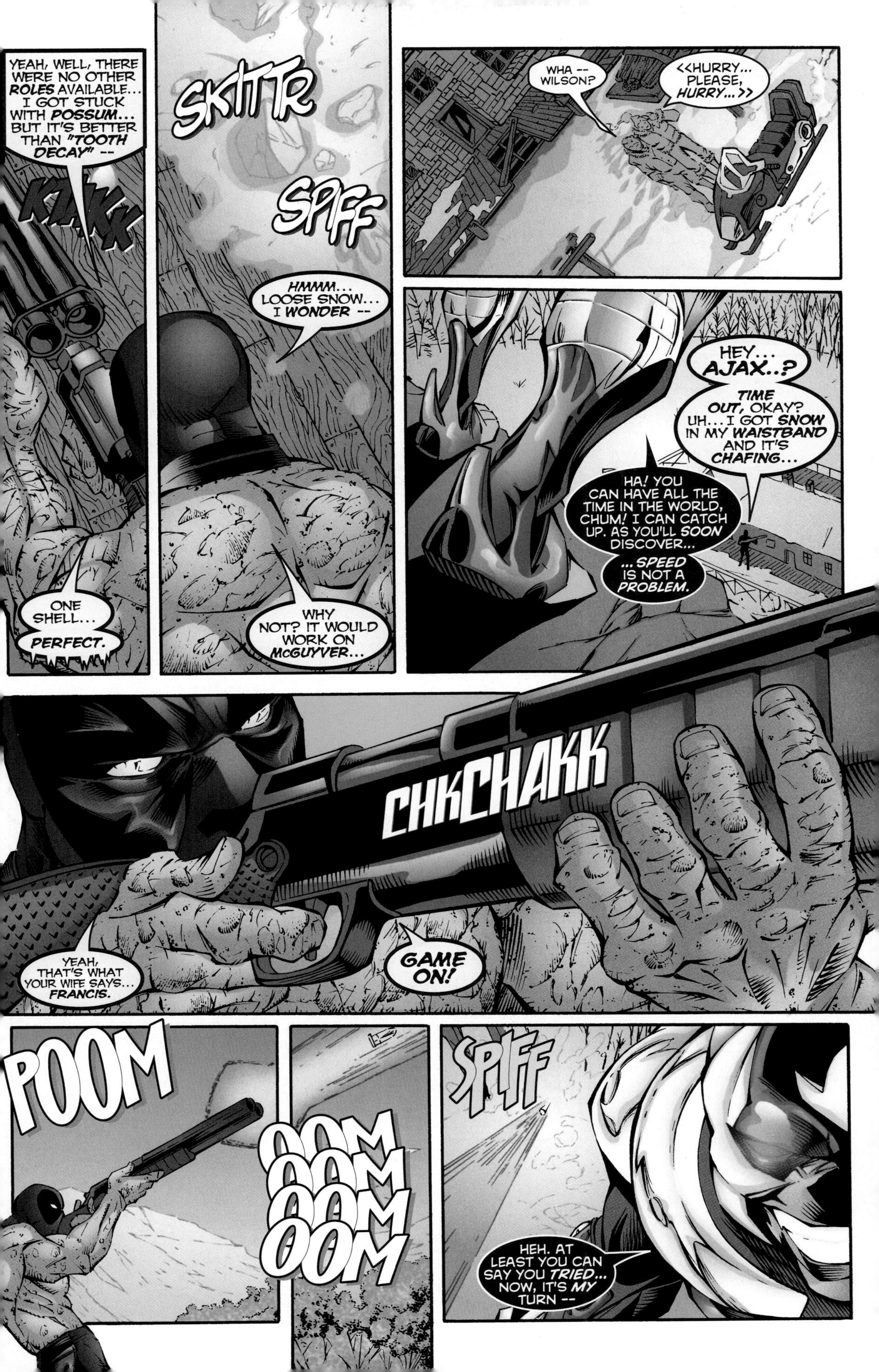

YEAH, WELL, THERE WERE NO OTHER ROLES AVAILABLE... I GOT STUCK WITH POSSUM... BUT IT'S BETTER THAN "TOOTH DECAY" --
KLIKKK
ONE SHELL...
PERFECT.
SKITTR
SPIFF
HMMM... LOOSE SNOW... I WONDER --
WHY NOT? IT WOULD WORK ON McGUYVER...
WHA -- WILSON?
<<HURRY... PLEASE, HURRY...>>
HEY... AJAX..?
TIME OUT, OKAY? UH... I GOT SNOW IN MY WAISTBAND AND IT'S CHAFING...
HA! YOU CAN HAVE ALL THE TIME IN THE WORLD, CHUM! I CAN CATCH UP. AS YOU'LL SOON DISCOVER...
...SPEED IS NOT A PROBLEM.
CHKCHAKK
YEAH, THAT'S WHAT YOUR WIFE SAYS... FRANCIS.
GAME ON!
POOM
OOM
OOM
OOM
OOM
SPIFF
HEH. AT LEAST YOU CAN SAY YOU TRIED... NOW, IT'S MY TURN --

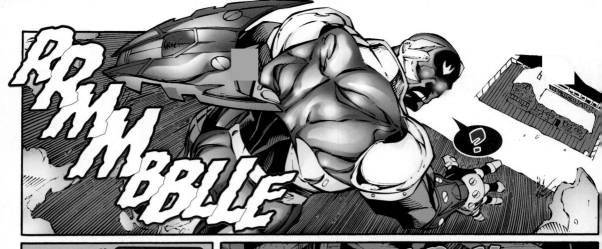

RRMMBBLLE

AVALANCHE!

MGRFFF!

NOW IF ALL GOES ACCORDING TO MY DEVILISHLY SIMPLE PLAN...

...A HUNDRED TONS OF SNOW WILL LOVINGLY SMOTHER AJAX, AND COME TO A STOP BEFORE --

KRUNCH KRAACH

HEY... WAIT... IT'S NOT STOPPING... IT -- YEEK!

♪ I'M SCREAMING 'BOUT A WHIIIITE BLITZ, MISS! JUST LIKE A TIDAL WAVE OF SNOWWW! ♪

ME AN' MY BRIGHT IDEAS...

FLOOSH

<<MY HOUSE!>>

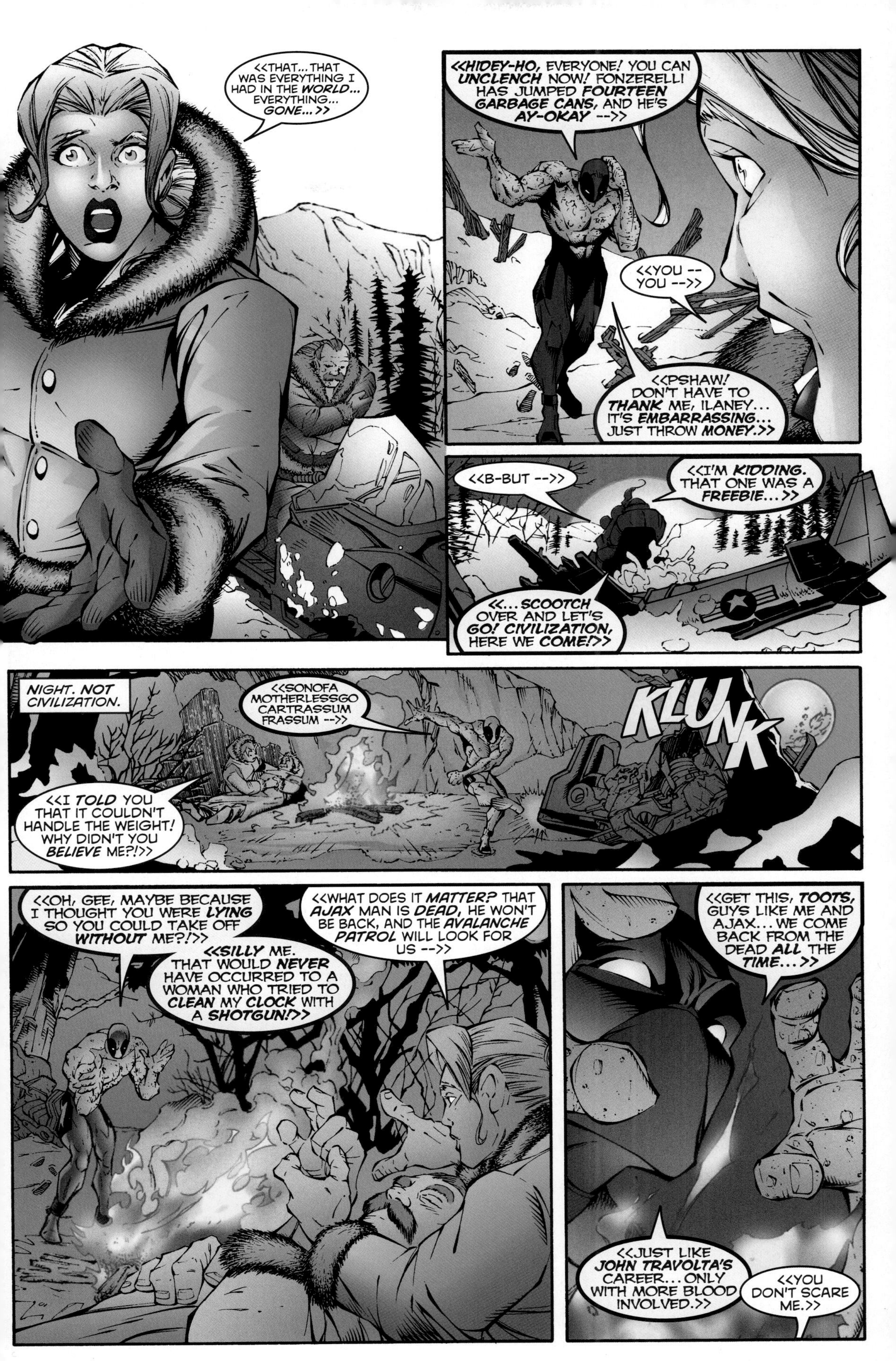

<<THAT... THAT WAS EVERYTHING I HAD IN THE *WORLD*... EVERYTHING... *GONE*...>>
<<*HIDEY-HO*, EVERYONE! YOU CAN *UNCLENCH* NOW! FONZERELLI HAS JUMPED *FOURTEEN GARBAGE CANS*, AND HE'S *AY-OKAY* -->>
<<YOU -- YOU -->>
<<*PSHAW!* DON'T HAVE TO *THANK* ME, ILANEY... IT'S *EMBARRASSING*... JUST THROW *MONEY*.>>
<<B-BUT -->>
<<I'M *KIDDING*. THAT ONE WAS A *FREEBIE*...>>
<<...*SCOOTCH* OVER AND LET'S *GO! CIVILIZATION*, HERE WE *COME!*>>
NIGHT. NOT CIVILIZATION.
<<SONOFA MOTHERLESSGO CARTRASSUM FRASSUM -->>
KLUNK
<<I *TOLD* YOU THAT IT COULDN'T HANDLE THE WEIGHT! WHY DIDN'T YOU *BELIEVE* ME?!>>
<<OH, GEE, MAYBE BECAUSE I THOUGHT YOU WERE *LYING* SO YOU COULD TAKE OFF *WITHOUT* ME?!>>
<<*SILLY* ME. THAT WOULD *NEVER* HAVE OCCURRED TO A WOMAN WHO TRIED TO *CLEAN* MY *CLOCK* WITH A *SHOTGUN!*>>
<<WHAT DOES IT *MATTER?* THAT *AJAX* MAN IS *DEAD*, HE WON'T BE BACK, AND THE *AVALANCHE PATROL* WILL LOOK FOR US -->>
<<GET THIS, *TOOTS*, GUYS LIKE ME AND AJAX... WE COME BACK FROM THE DEAD *ALL* THE *TIME*...>>
<<JUST LIKE *JOHN TRAVOLTA'S* CAREER... ONLY WITH MORE BLOOD INVOLVED.>>
<<YOU DON'T SCARE ME.>>

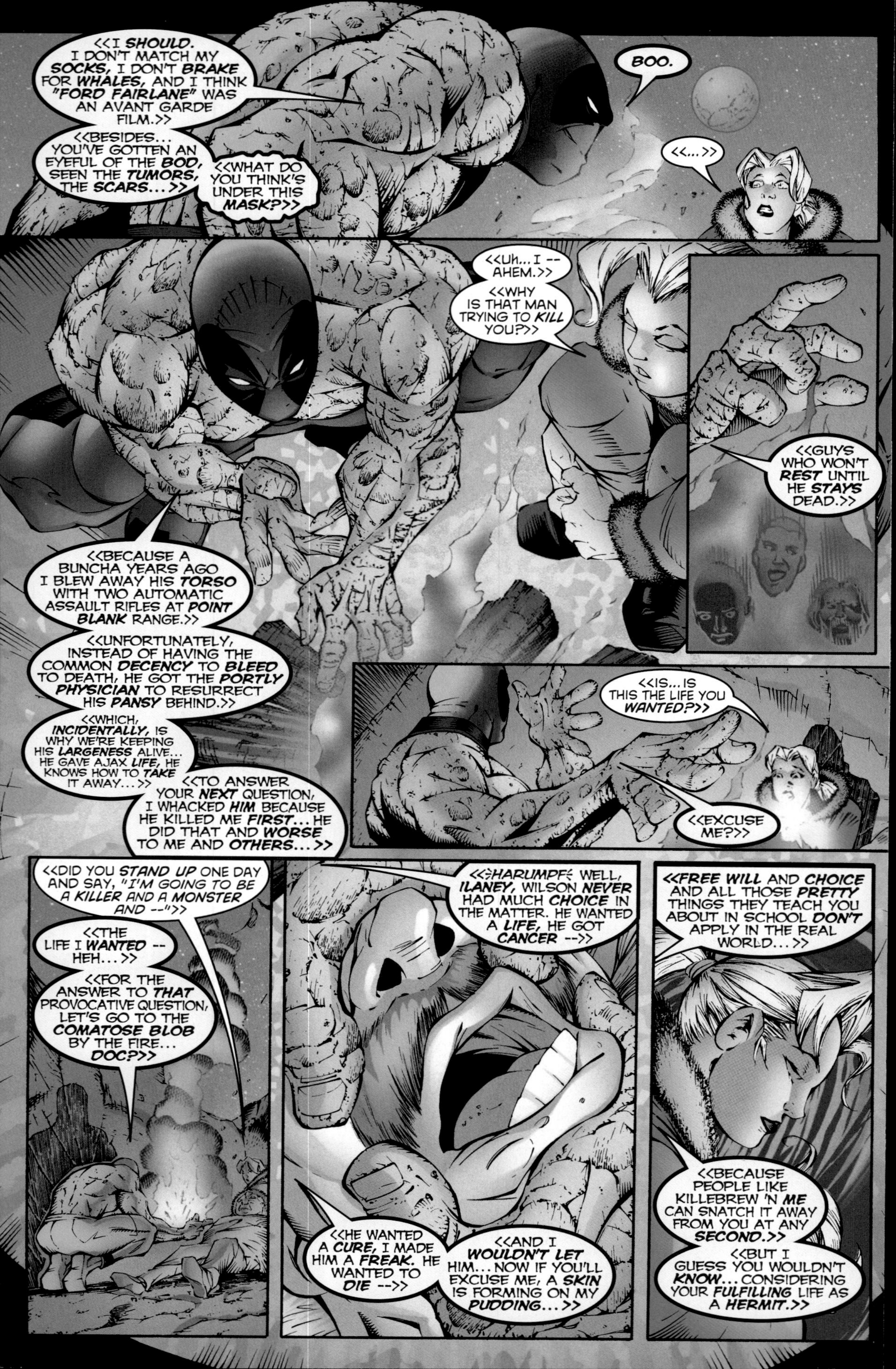

<<I SHOULD. I DON'T MATCH MY SOCKS, I DON'T BRAKE FOR WHALES, AND I THINK "FORD FAIRLANE" WAS AN AVANT GARDE FILM.>>
<<BESIDES... YOU'VE GOTTEN AN EYEFUL OF THE BOD, SEEN THE TUMORS, THE SCARS...>>
<<WHAT DO YOU THINK'S UNDER THIS MASK?>>
BOO.
<<...>>
<<UH... I -- AHEM.>>
<<WHY IS THAT MAN TRYING TO KILL YOU?>>
<<GUYS WHO WON'T REST UNTIL HE STAYS DEAD.>>
<<BECAUSE A BUNCHA YEARS AGO I BLEW AWAY HIS TORSO WITH TWO AUTOMATIC ASSAULT RIFLES AT POINT BLANK RANGE.>>
<<UNFORTUNATELY, INSTEAD OF HAVING THE COMMON DECENCY TO BLEED TO DEATH, HE GOT THE PORTLY PHYSICIAN TO RESURRECT HIS PANSY BEHIND.>>
<<WHICH, INCIDENTALLY, IS WHY WE'RE KEEPING HIS LARGENESS ALIVE... HE GAVE AJAX LIFE, HE KNOWS HOW TO TAKE IT AWAY...>>
<<TO ANSWER YOUR NEXT QUESTION, I WHACKED HIM BECAUSE HE KILLED ME FIRST... HE DID THAT AND WORSE TO ME AND OTHERS...>>
<<IS... IS THIS THE LIFE YOU WANTED?>>
<<EXCUSE ME?>>
<<DID YOU STAND UP ONE DAY AND SAY, "I'M GOING TO BE A KILLER AND A MONSTER AND --">>
<<THE LIFE I WANTED -- HEH...>>
<<FOR THE ANSWER TO THAT PROVOCATIVE QUESTION, LET'S GO TO THE COMATOSE BLOB BY THE FIRE... DOC?>>
<<HARUMPF WELL, ILANEY, WILSON NEVER HAD MUCH CHOICE IN THE MATTER. HE WANTED A LIFE, HE GOT CANCER -->>
<<HE WANTED A CURE, I MADE HIM A FREAK. HE WANTED TO DIE -->>
<<AND I WOULDN'T LET HIM... NOW IF YOU'LL EXCUSE ME, A SKIN IS FORMING ON MY PUDDING...>>
<<FREE WILL AND CHOICE AND ALL THOSE PRETTY THINGS THEY TEACH YOU ABOUT IN SCHOOL DON'T APPLY IN THE REAL WORLD...>>
<<BECAUSE PEOPLE LIKE KILLEBREW 'N ME CAN SNATCH IT AWAY FROM YOU AT ANY SECOND.>>
<<BUT I GUESS YOU WOULDN'T KNOW... CONSIDERING YOUR FULFILLING LIFE AS A HERMIT.>>

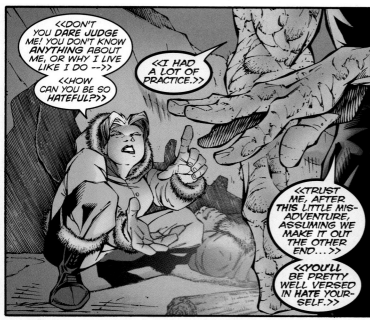

<<DON'T YOU DARE JUDGE ME! YOU DON'T KNOW ANYTHING ABOUT ME, OR WHY I LIVE LIKE I DO --<<

<<HOW CAN YOU BE SO HATEFUL?>>

<<I HAD A LOT OF PRACTICE.>>

<<TRUST ME, AFTER THIS LITTLE MIS-ADVENTURE, ASSUMING WE MAKE IT OUT THE OTHER END...>>

<<YOU'LL BE PRETTY WELL VERSED IN HATE YOUR-SELF.>>

<<I HAVE TO SCARE UP SOME MORE WOOD. SOME OF US WITH A HEALING FACTOR INSTEAD OF A NICE FANCY PARKA ARE STARTING TO CATCH A CHILL...>>

<<DON'T TRY ANYTHING STUPID.>>

<<I'D HATE TO HAVE TO DRAG YOU BOTH TEN MILES THROUGH THE SNOW.>>

<<YOU DON'T KNOW... YOU DON'T KNOW ME...>>

<<...AND I DO KNOW HATE... OH, DO I KNOW HATE --<<

>KAFF< MISS? MISS...

<<MISS, COULD I HAVE SOME WATER --?>>

<<YOU'RE AWAKE!>>

>KAFF< OH... MY GERMAN'S RUSTY -- UNH...

UM... W-WASSER, BITTE?

<<WAIT HERE! I'LL GET YOUR FRIEND! YOU CAN TELL HIM WHAT HE WANTS TO KNOW, AND LEAVE ME BE --<<

NO!

YOU MUSN'T... YOU DON'T UNDER-STAND... NOT YET --

I... I DON'T KNOW HOW TO STOP AJAX... I LIED.

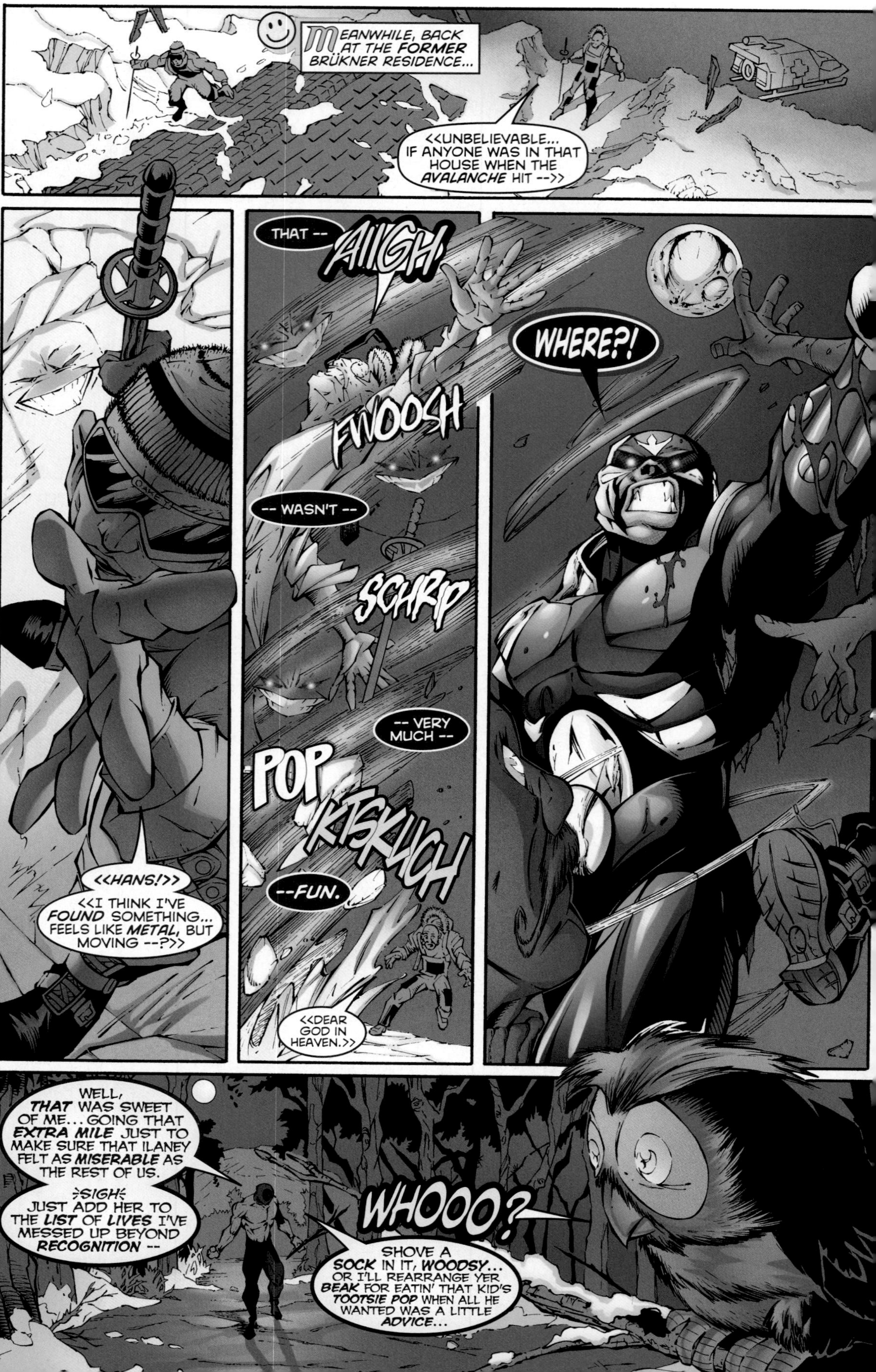
MEANWHILE, BACK AT THE FORMER BRÜKNER RESIDENCE...
<<UNBELIEVABLE... IF ANYONE WAS IN THAT HOUSE WHEN THE AVALANCHE HIT -->>
<<HANS!>>
<<I THINK I'VE FOUND SOMETHING... FEELS LIKE METAL, BUT MOVING --?>>
THAT --
AIIGH
FWOOSH
-- WASN'T --
SCHRIP
-- VERY MUCH --
POP
KTSKLICH
--FUN.
<<DEAR GOD IN HEAVEN.>>
WHERE?!
WELL, THAT WAS SWEET OF ME... GOING THAT EXTRA MILE JUST TO MAKE SURE THAT ILANEY FELT AS MISERABLE AS THE REST OF US.
SIGH
JUST ADD HER TO THE LIST OF LIVES I'VE MESSED UP BEYOND RECOGNITION --
WHOOO?
SHOVE A SOCK IN IT, WOODSY... OR I'LL REARRANGE YER BEAK FOR EATIN' THAT KID'S TOOTSIE POP WHEN ALL HE WANTED WAS A LITTLE ADVICE...

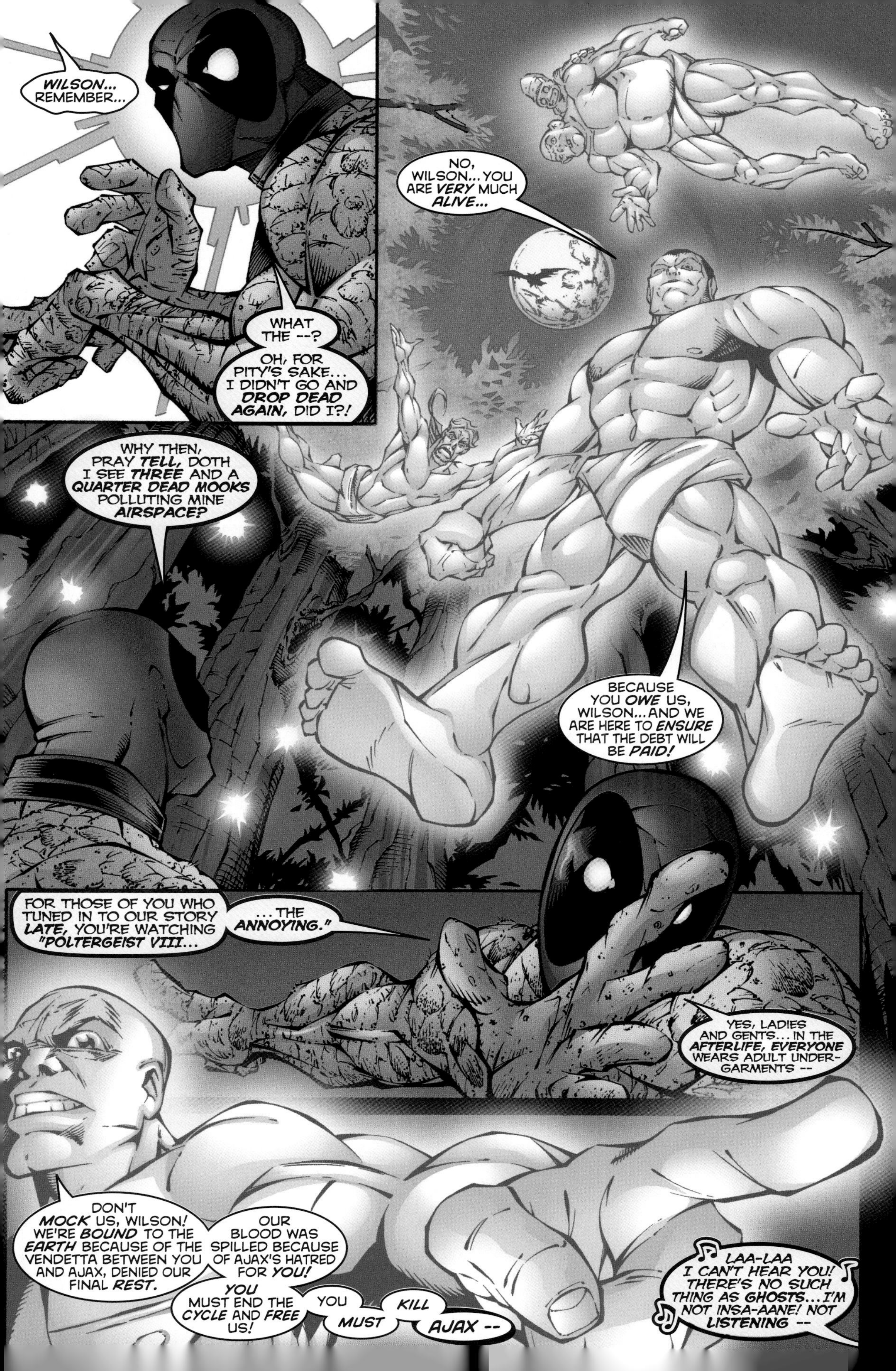
WILSON... REMEMBER...
WHAT THE --?
OH, FOR PITY'S SAKE... I DIDN'T GO AND DROP DEAD AGAIN, DID I?!
NO, WILSON... YOU ARE VERY MUCH ALIVE...
WHY THEN, PRAY TELL, DOTH I SEE THREE AND A QUARTER DEAD MOOKS POLLUTING MINE AIRSPACE?
BECAUSE YOU OWE US, WILSON... AND WE ARE HERE TO ENSURE THAT THE DEBT WILL BE PAID!
FOR THOSE OF YOU WHO TUNED IN TO OUR STORY LATE, YOU'RE WATCHING "POLTERGEIST VIII...
...THE ANNOYING."
YES, LADIES AND GENTS... IN THE AFTERLIFE, EVERYONE WEARS ADULT UNDER-GARMENTS --
DON'T MOCK US, WILSON! WE'RE BOUND TO THE EARTH BECAUSE OF THE VENDETTA BETWEEN YOU AND AJAX, DENIED OUR FINAL REST.
OUR BLOOD WAS SPILLED BECAUSE OF AJAX'S HATRED FOR YOU!
YOU MUST END THE CYCLE AND FREE US!
YOU MUST KILL AJAX --
LAA-LAA I CAN'T HEAR YOU! THERE'S NO SUCH THING AS GHOSTS... I'M NOT INSA-AANE! NOT LISTENING --

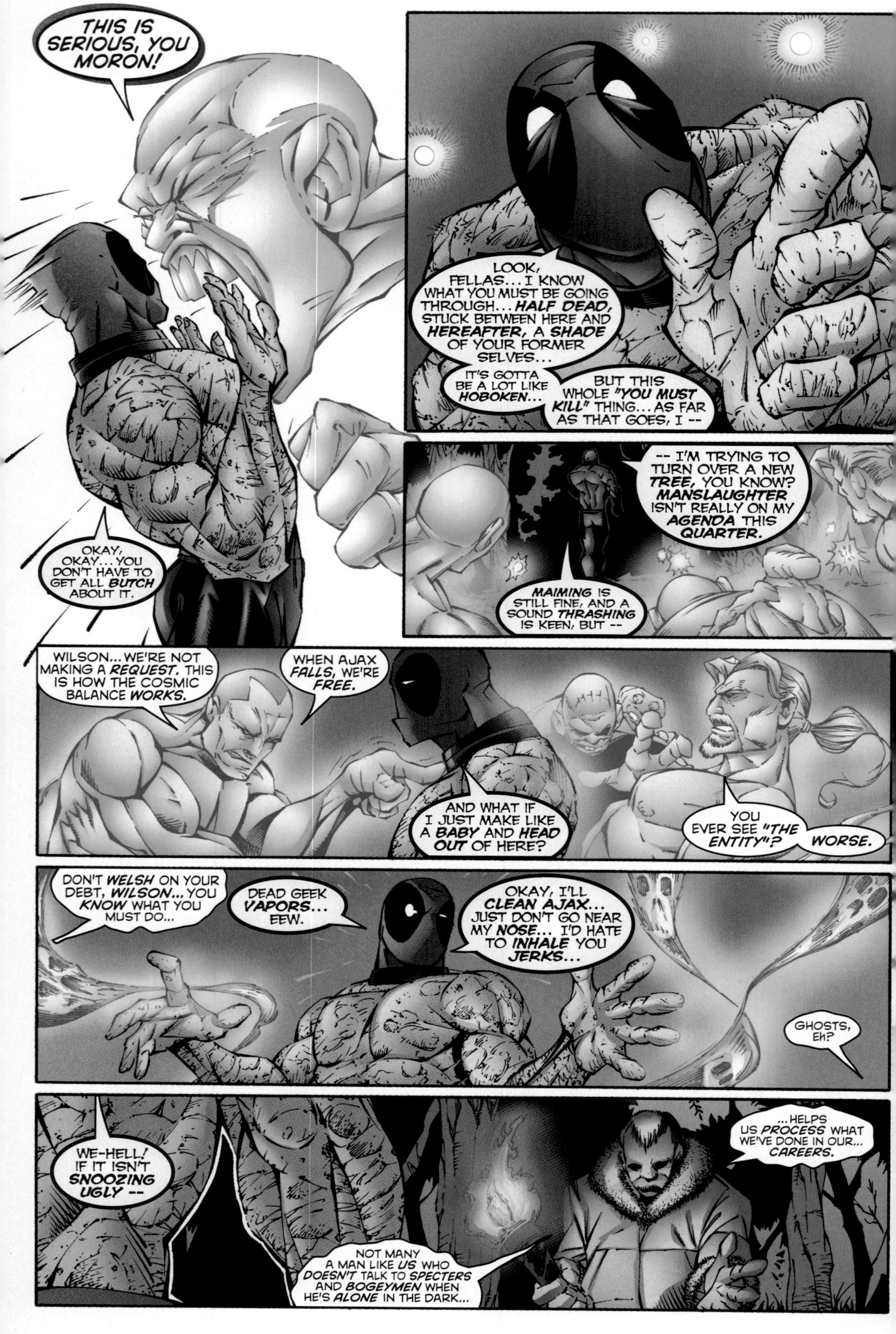
THIS IS SERIOUS, YOU MORON!
OKAY, OKAY... YOU DON'T HAVE TO GET ALL BUTCH ABOUT IT.
LOOK, FELLAS... I KNOW WHAT YOU MUST BE GOING THROUGH... HALF DEAD, STUCK BETWEEN HERE AND HEREAFTER, A SHADE OF YOUR FORMER SELVES...
IT'S GOTTA BE A LOT LIKE HOBOKEN...
BUT THIS WHOLE "YOU MUST KILL" THING... AS FAR AS THAT GOES, I --
-- I'M TRYING TO TURN OVER A NEW TREE, YOU KNOW? MANSLAUGHTER ISN'T REALLY ON MY AGENDA THIS QUARTER.
MAIMING IS STILL FINE, AND A SOUND THRASHING IS KEEN, BUT --
WILSON... WE'RE NOT MAKING A REQUEST. THIS IS HOW THE COSMIC BALANCE WORKS.
WHEN AJAX FALLS, WE'RE FREE.
AND WHAT IF I JUST MAKE LIKE A BABY AND HEAD OUT OF HERE?
YOU EVER SEE "THE ENTITY"?
WORSE.
DON'T WELSH ON YOUR DEBT, WILSON... YOU KNOW WHAT YOU MUST DO...
DEAD GEEK VAPORS... EEW.
OKAY, I'LL CLEAN AJAX... JUST DON'T GO NEAR MY NOSE... I'D HATE TO INHALE YOU JERKS...
GHOSTS, EH?
WE-HELL! IF IT ISN'T SNOOZING UGLY --
...HELPS US PROCESS WHAT WE'VE DONE IN OUR... CAREERS.
NOT MANY A MAN LIKE US WHO DOESN'T TALK TO SPECTERS AND BOGEYMEN WHEN HE'S ALONE IN THE DARK...

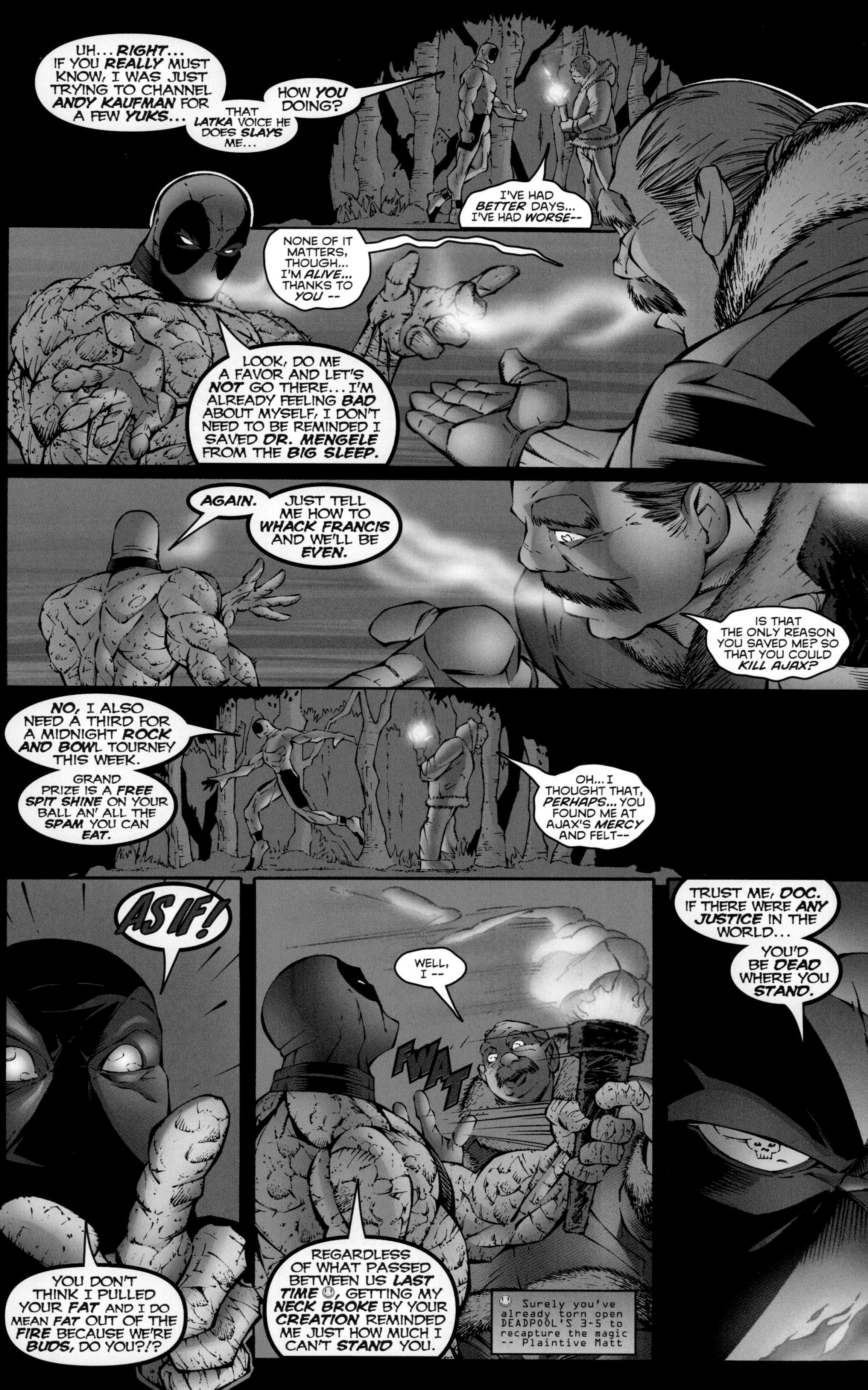

UH... RIGHT... IF YOU REALLY MUST KNOW, I WAS JUST TRYING TO CHANNEL ANDY KAUFMAN FOR A FEW YUKS...
THAT LATKA VOICE HE DOES SLAYS ME...
HOW YOU DOING?
I'VE HAD BETTER DAYS... I'VE HAD WORSE--
NONE OF IT MATTERS, THOUGH... I'M ALIVE... THANKS TO YOU --
LOOK, DO ME A FAVOR AND LET'S NOT GO THERE... I'M ALREADY FEELING BAD ABOUT MYSELF, I DON'T NEED TO BE REMINDED I SAVED DR. MENGELE FROM THE BIG SLEEP.
AGAIN.
JUST TELL ME HOW TO WHACK FRANCIS AND WE'LL BE EVEN.
IS THAT THE ONLY REASON YOU SAVED ME? SO THAT YOU COULD KILL AJAX?
NO, I ALSO NEED A THIRD FOR A MIDNIGHT ROCK AND BOWL TOURNEY THIS WEEK.
GRAND PRIZE IS A FREE SPIT SHINE ON YOUR BALL AN' ALL THE SPAM YOU CAN EAT.
OH... I THOUGHT THAT, PERHAPS... YOU FOUND ME AT AJAX'S MERCY AND FELT--
AS IF!
YOU DON'T THINK I PULLED YOUR FAT AND I DO MEAN FAT OUT OF THE FIRE BECAUSE WE'RE BUDS, DO YOU?!?
WELL, I --
FWAT
REGARDLESS OF WHAT PASSED BETWEEN US LAST TIME ☺, GETTING MY NECK BROKE BY YOUR CREATION REMINDED ME JUST HOW MUCH I CAN'T STAND YOU.
☺ Surely you've already torn open DEADPOOL'S 3-5 to recapture the magic -- Plaintive Matt
TRUST ME, DOC. IF THERE WERE ANY JUSTICE IN THE WORLD...
YOU'D BE DEAD WHERE YOU STAND.

I...I DESERVE THAT...

BUT STILL... CAN'T THERE BE *ANOTHER WAY,* WILSON? ARE WE SO *DEPRAVED...* OR *CURSED* AS THE CASE MAY BE...

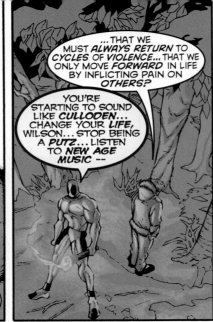

...THAT WE MUST *ALWAYS RETURN* TO *CYCLES OF VIOLENCE...* THAT WE ONLY MOVE *FORWARD* IN LIFE BY INFLICTING PAIN ON *OTHERS?*

YOU'RE STARTING TO SOUND LIKE *CULLODEN...* CHANGE YOUR *LIFE,* WILSON... STOP BEING A *PUTZ...* LISTEN TO *NEW AGE* MUSIC --

WILSON, I'M *SERIOUS...* WE HAVE TO *TRANSCEND* WHO WE *WERE.* I'VE BEEN TRYING TO *BREAK THE CYCLE* AND MAKE UP FOR --

TRYING?! HOW, *EXACTLY,* HAVE YOU BEEN *TRYING?*

IF *MY* FACTS ARE STRAIGHT, YOU WERE *HIDING* IN YOUR LITTLE *TECHNO-CABIN* WHILE *FRANCIS* WAS RUNNING AROUND *KILLING YOUR* EX-PATIENTS!

HIDING FROM YOUR RESPONSIBILITIES IS *NOT* TRANSCENDING *BUPKUS!* SO YOU FEEL GUILTY ABOUT WHAT YOU DID. *BIG DEAL!*

YOU HAVEN'T DONE *JACK* TO MAKE UP FOR *WHO YOU ARE!*

BUT --

WORSE, NOW I HAVE A FLOCK OF *GHOSTS* WHO WON'T STOP BREAKING MY *HUMP* UNTIL I CLEAN UP *YOUR* MESS!

I BEG YOUR --

SO SAVE THE *FRU-FRU PSYCHO BABBLE* FOR THE *ALCOHOLICS* AND *BATTERED HUSBANDS.* THERE'S NO *TWELVE STEP* PROGRAM FOR PEOPLE LIKE US.

YOU CAN'T *TRANSCEND* WHO YOU *WERE* WHEN WHAT YOU *ARE* IS *HUMAN WASTE.* PERIOD.

I -- THAT'S NOT TRUE --

WHATEVER. YOU WANT TO PROVE YOUR *WORTH* AS A BONA FIDE HUMAN BEING, START *SINGING,* BABY --

NAME OF THAT *TUNE* IS, "THIS IS HOW YOU *OBLITERATE* AJAX FOR GOOD..." IN D MINOR.

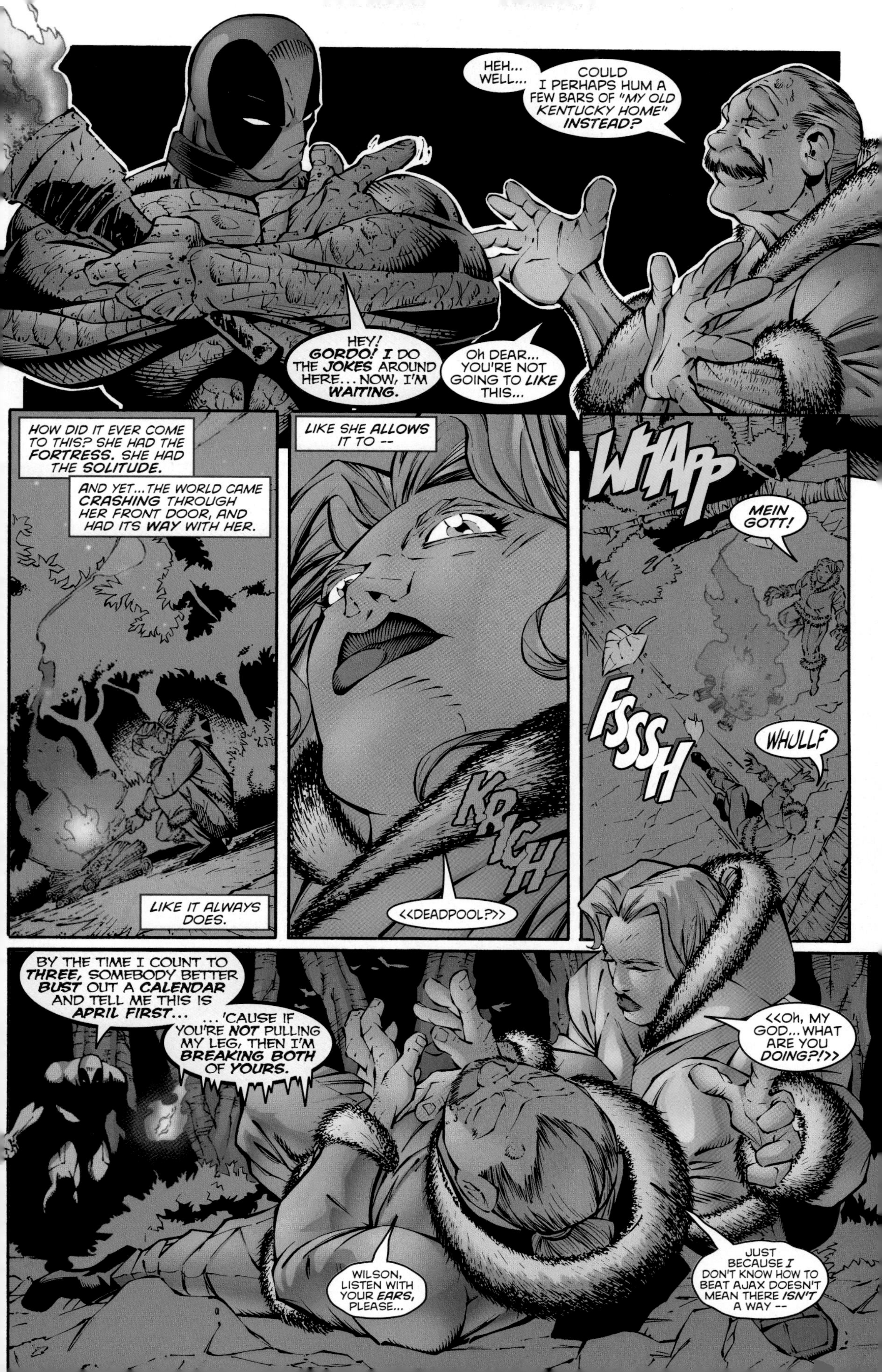

HEH... WELL...
COULD I PERHAPS HUM A FEW BARS OF "MY OLD KENTUCKY HOME" INSTEAD?
HEY! GORDO! I DO THE JOKES AROUND HERE... NOW, I'M WAITING.
Oh DEAR... YOU'RE NOT GOING TO LIKE THIS...
HOW DID IT EVER COME TO THIS? SHE HAD THE FORTRESS. SHE HAD THE SOLITUDE.
AND YET...THE WORLD CAME CRASHING THROUGH HER FRONT DOOR, AND HAD ITS WAY WITH HER.
LIKE IT ALWAYS DOES.
LIKE SHE ALLOWS IT TO --
KRICH
<<DEADPOOL?>>
WHAPP
MEIN GOTT!
FSSSH
WHULLF
BY THE TIME I COUNT TO THREE, SOMEBODY BETTER BUST OUT A CALENDAR AND TELL ME THIS IS APRIL FIRST...
...'CAUSE IF YOU'RE NOT PULLING MY LEG, THEN I'M BREAKING BOTH OF YOURS.
<<Oh, MY GOD... WHAT ARE YOU DOING?!>>
WILSON, LISTEN WITH YOUR EARS, PLEASE...
JUST BECAUSE I DON'T KNOW HOW TO BEAT AJAX DOESN'T MEAN THERE ISN'T A WAY --

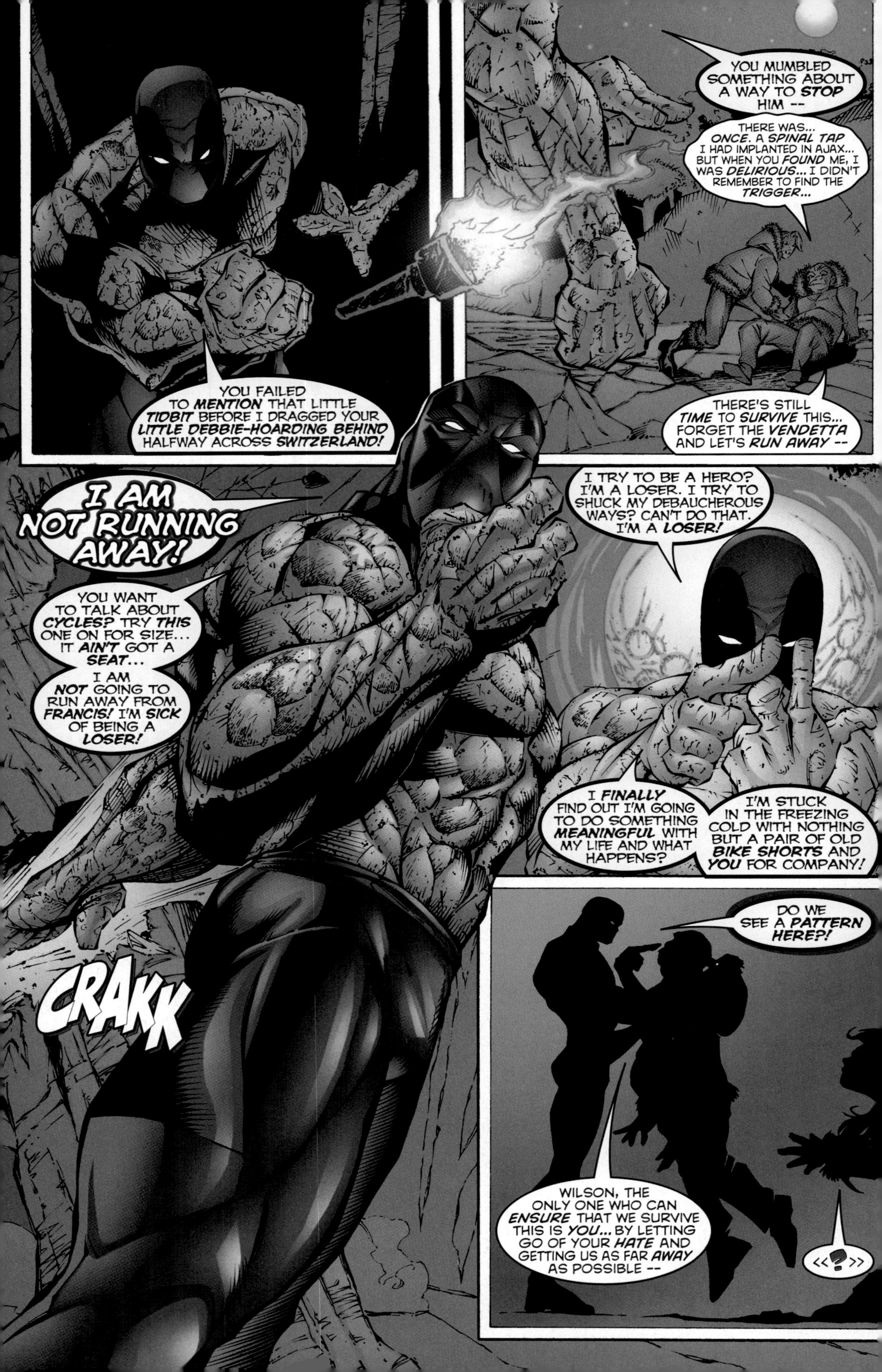
YOU FAILED TO MENTION THAT LITTLE TIOBIT BEFORE I DRAGGED YOUR LITTLE DEBBIE-HOARDING BEHIND HALFWAY ACROSS SWITZERLAND!
YOU MUMBLED SOMETHING ABOUT A WAY TO STOP HIM --
THERE WAS... ONCE. A SPINAL TAP I HAD IMPLANTED IN AJAX... BUT WHEN YOU FOUND ME, I WAS DELIRIOUS... I DIDN'T REMEMBER TO FIND THE TRIGGER...
THERE'S STILL TIME TO SURVIVE THIS... FORGET THE VENDETTA AND LET'S RUN AWAY --
I AM NOT RUNNING AWAY!
YOU WANT TO TALK ABOUT CYCLES? TRY THIS ONE ON FOR SIZE... IT AIN'T GOT A SEAT...
I AM NOT GOING TO RUN AWAY FROM FRANCIS! I'M SICK OF BEING A LOSER!
CRAKK
I TRY TO BE A HERO? I'M A LOSER. I TRY TO SHUCK MY DEBAUCHEROUS WAYS? CAN'T DO THAT. I'M A LOSER!
I FINALLY FIND OUT I'M GOING TO DO SOMETHING MEANINGFUL WITH MY LIFE AND WHAT HAPPENS?
I'M STUCK IN THE FREEZING COLD WITH NOTHING BUT A PAIR OF OLD BIKE SHORTS AND YOU FOR COMPANY!
DO WE SEE A PATTERN HERE?!
WILSON, THE ONLY ONE WHO CAN ENSURE THAT WE SURVIVE THIS IS YOU... BY LETTING GO OF YOUR HATE AND GETTING US AS FAR AWAY AS POSSIBLE --
<<?>>

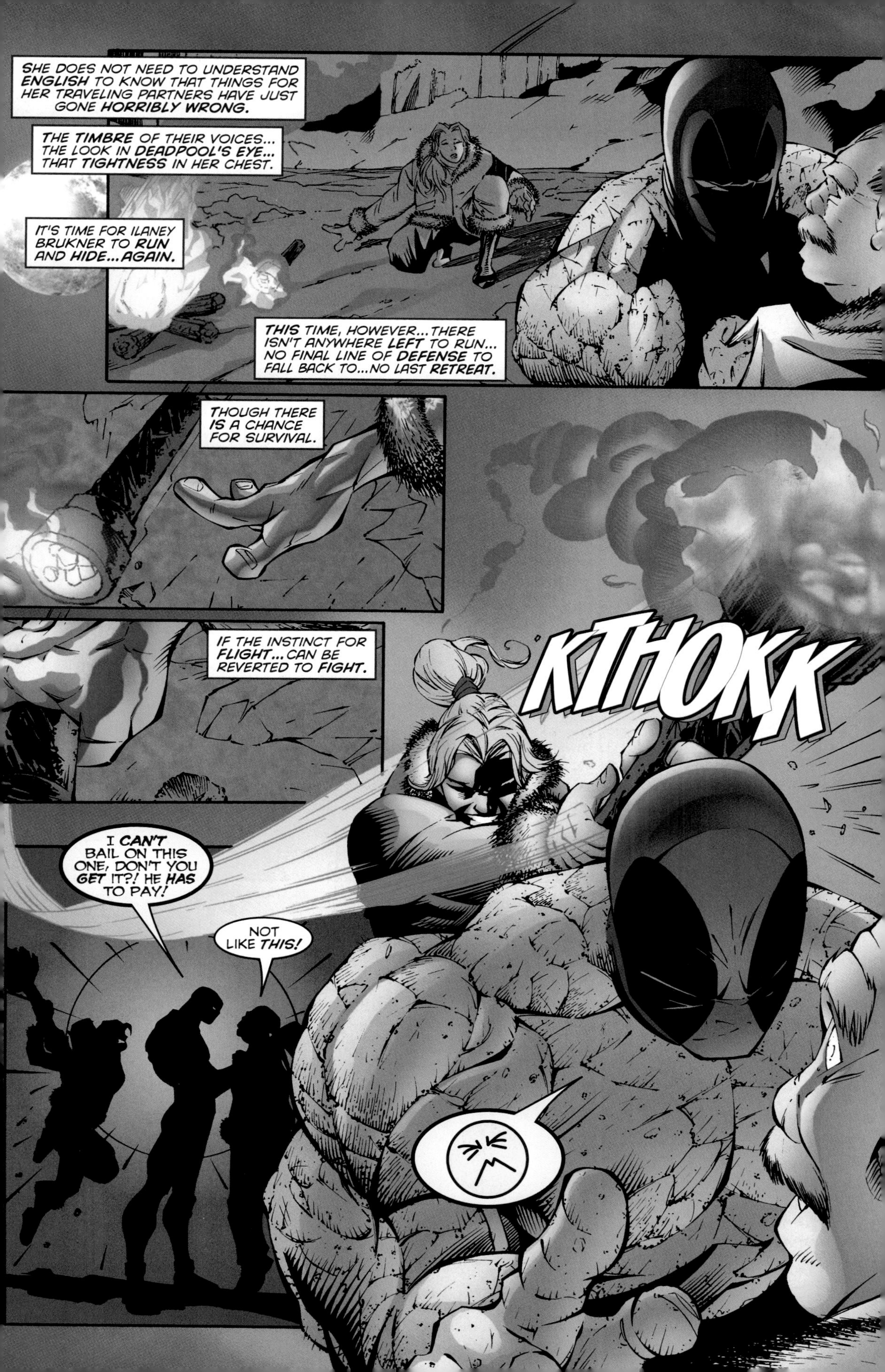

SHE DOES NOT NEED TO UNDERSTAND ENGLISH TO KNOW THAT THINGS FOR HER TRAVELING PARTNERS HAVE JUST GONE HORRIBLY WRONG.
THE TIMBRE OF THEIR VOICES... THE LOOK IN DEADPOOL'S EYE... THAT TIGHTNESS IN HER CHEST.
IT'S TIME FOR ILANEY BRUKNER TO RUN AND HIDE...AGAIN.
THIS TIME, HOWEVER...THERE ISN'T ANYWHERE LEFT TO RUN... NO FINAL LINE OF DEFENSE TO FALL BACK TO...NO LAST RETREAT.
THOUGH THERE IS A CHANCE FOR SURVIVAL.
IF THE INSTINCT FOR FLIGHT...CAN BE REVERTED TO FIGHT.
KTHOKK
I CAN'T BAIL ON THIS ONE, DON'T YOU GET IT?! HE HAS TO PAY!
NOT LIKE THIS!

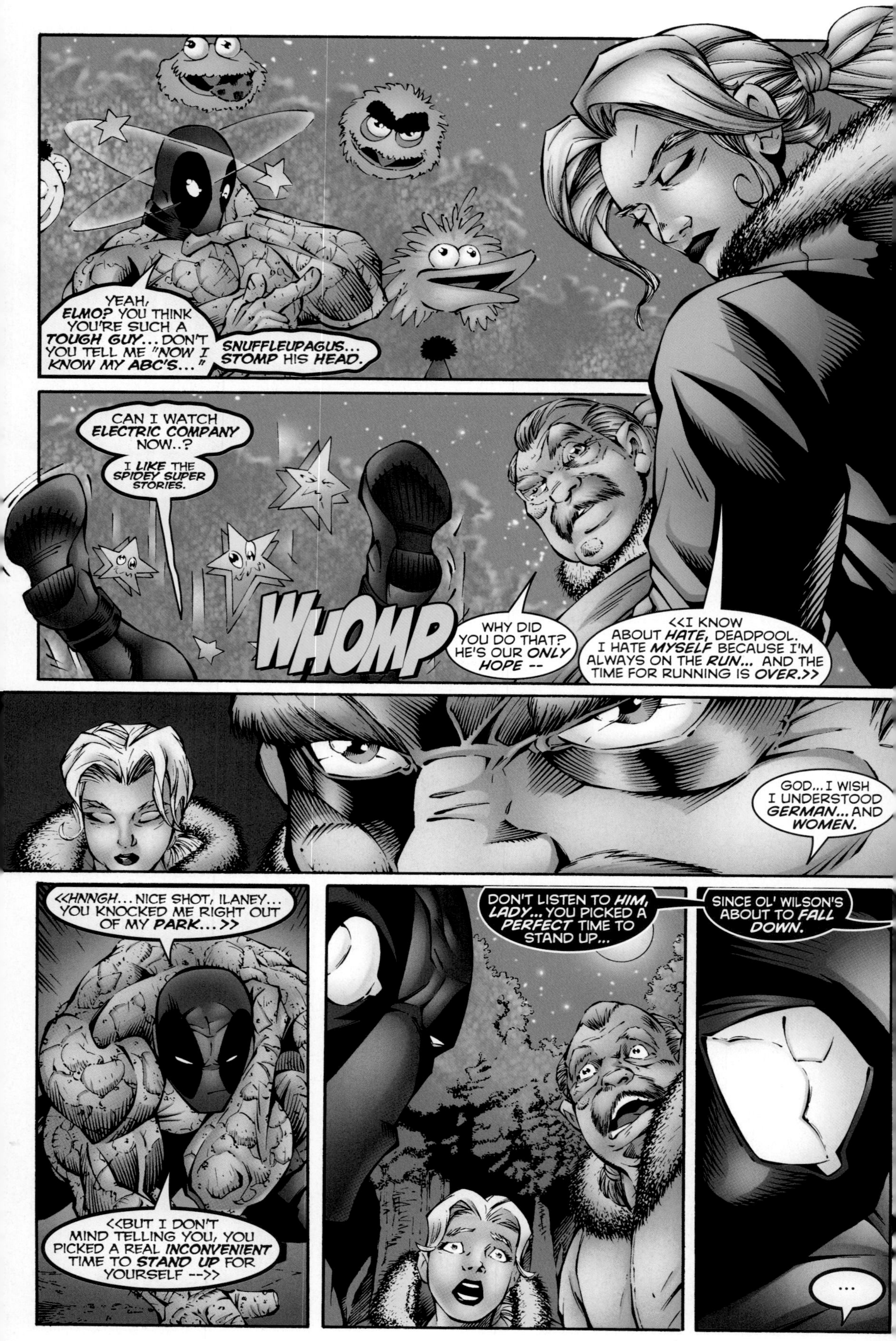

YEAH, ELMO? YOU THINK YOU'RE SUCH A TOUGH GUY... DON'T YOU TELL ME "NOW I KNOW MY ABC'S..."
SNUFFLEUPAGUS... STOMP HIS HEAD.
CAN I WATCH ELECTRIC COMPANY NOW..?
I LIKE THE SPIDEY SUPER STORIES.
WHOMP
WHY DID YOU DO THAT? HE'S OUR ONLY HOPE --
<<I KNOW ABOUT HATE, DEADPOOL. I HATE MYSELF BECAUSE I'M ALWAYS ON THE RUN... AND THE TIME FOR RUNNING IS OVER.>>
GOD... I WISH I UNDERSTOOD GERMAN... AND WOMEN.
<<HNNGH... NICE SHOT, ILANEY... YOU KNOCKED ME RIGHT OUT OF MY PARK...>>
<<BUT I DON'T MIND TELLING YOU, YOU PICKED A REAL INCONVENIENT TIME TO STAND UP FOR YOURSELF -->>
DON'T LISTEN TO HIM, LADY... YOU PICKED A PERFECT TIME TO STAND UP...
SINCE OL' WILSON'S ABOUT TO FALL DOWN.
...

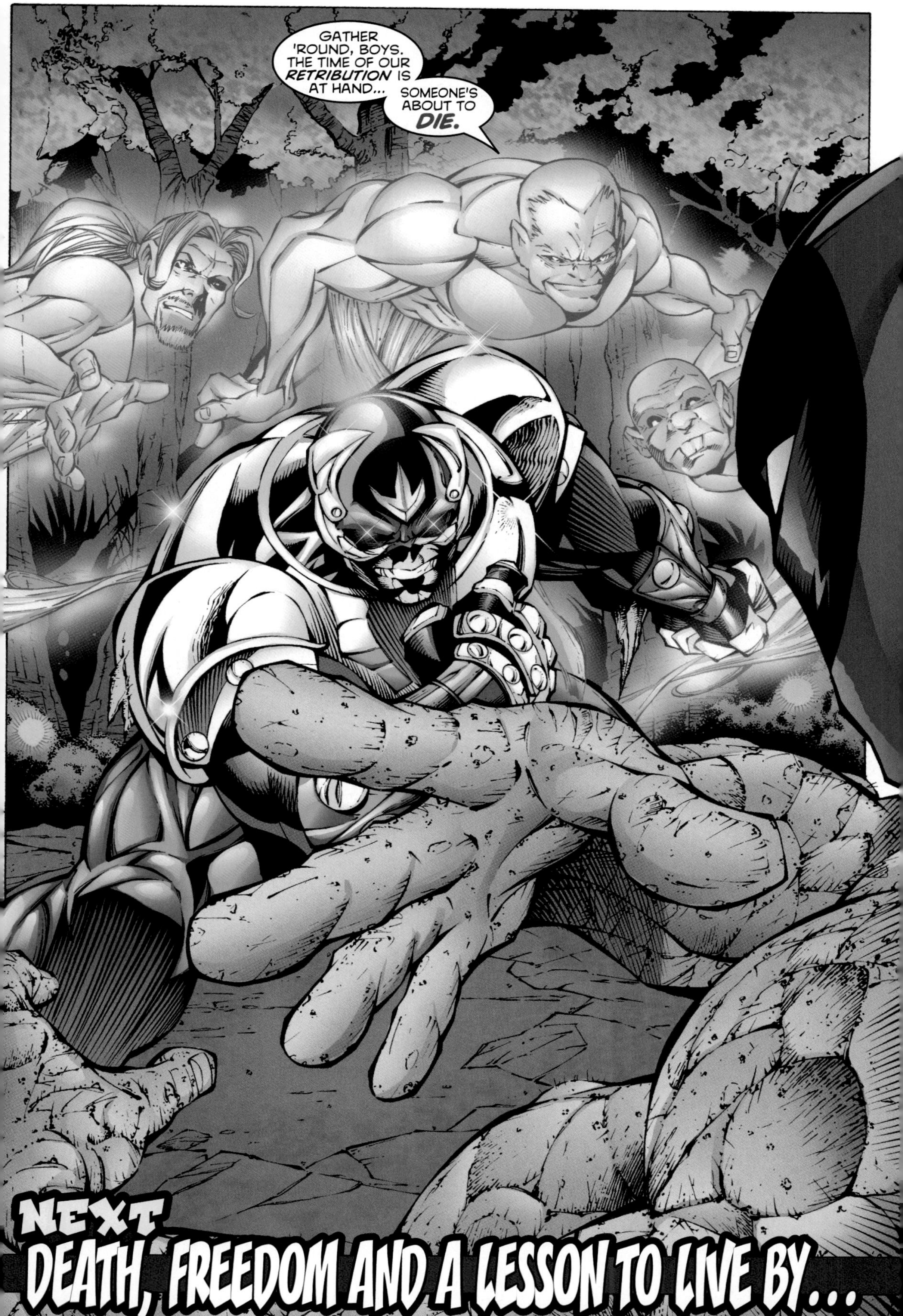
GATHER 'ROUND, BOYS. THE TIME OF OUR RETRIBUTION IS AT HAND...
SOMEONE'S ABOUT TO DIE.
NEXT
DEATH, FREEDOM AND A LESSON TO LIVE BY...

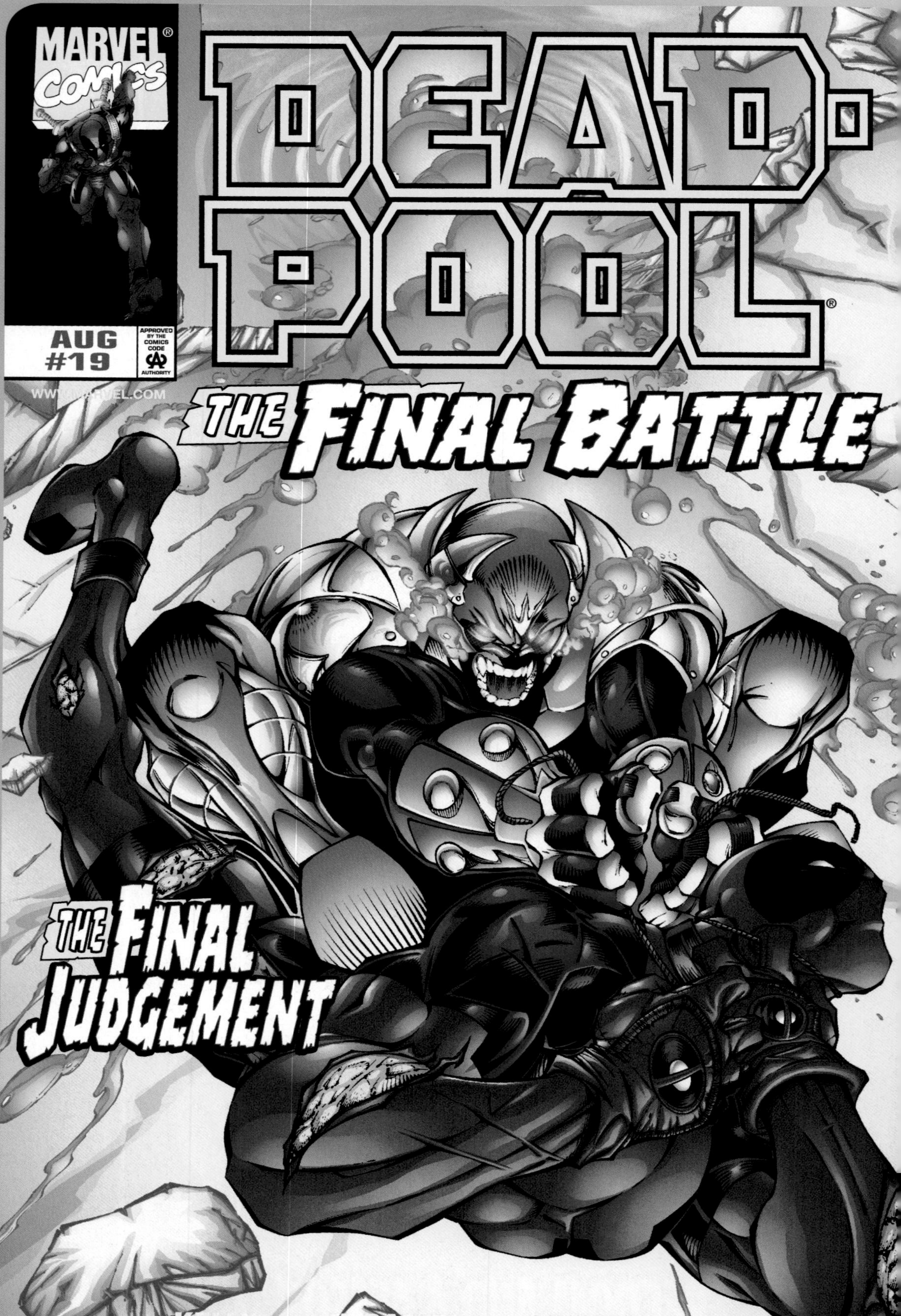
MARVEL® COMICS
DEADPOOL®
AUG #19
APPROVED BY THE COMICS CODE AUTHORITY
WWW.MARVEL.COM
THE FINAL BATTLE
THE FINAL JUDGEMENT
KELLY
MCDANIEL
LIVESAY
PARSONS

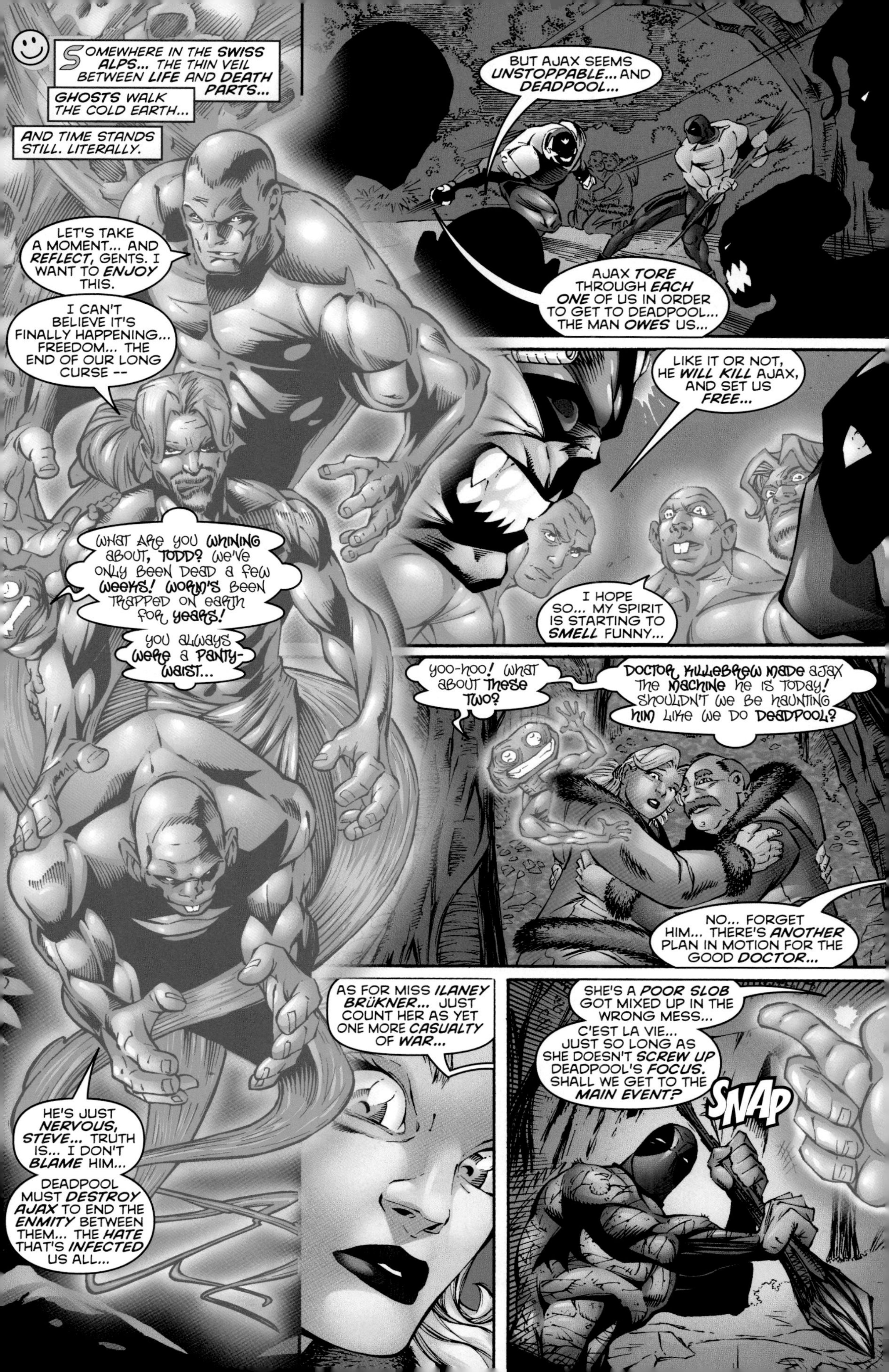

SOMEWHERE IN THE SWISS ALPS... THE THIN VEIL BETWEEN LIFE AND DEATH PARTS...
GHOSTS WALK THE COLD EARTH...
AND TIME STANDS STILL. LITERALLY.
BUT AJAX SEEMS UNSTOPPABLE... AND DEADPOOL...
AJAX TORE THROUGH EACH ONE OF US IN ORDER TO GET TO DEADPOOL... THE MAN OWES US...
LET'S TAKE A MOMENT... AND REFLECT, GENTS. I WANT TO ENJOY THIS.
I CAN'T BELIEVE IT'S FINALLY HAPPENING... FREEDOM... THE END OF OUR LONG CURSE --
LIKE IT OR NOT, HE WILL KILL AJAX, AND SET US FREE...
I HOPE SO... MY SPIRIT IS STARTING TO SMELL FUNNY...
WHAT ARE YOU WHINING ABOUT, TODD? WE'VE ONLY BEEN DEAD A FEW WEEKS! WORM'S BEEN TRAPPED ON EARTH FOR YEARS!
YOU ALWAYS WERE A PANTY-WAIST...
YOO-HOO! WHAT ABOUT THESE TWO?
DOCTOR KILLEBREW MADE AJAX THE MACHINE HE IS TODAY! SHOULDN'T WE BE HAUNTING HIM LIKE WE DO DEADPOOL?
NO... FORGET HIM... THERE'S ANOTHER PLAN IN MOTION FOR THE GOOD DOCTOR...
HE'S JUST NERVOUS, STEVE... TRUTH IS... I DON'T BLAME HIM...
DEADPOOL MUST DESTROY AJAX TO END THE ENMITY BETWEEN THEM... THE HATE THAT'S INFECTED US ALL...
AS FOR MISS ILANEY BRÜKNER... JUST COUNT HER AS YET ONE MORE CASUALTY OF WAR...
SHE'S A POOR SLOB GOT MIXED UP IN THE WRONG MESS...
C'EST LA VIE... JUST SO LONG AS SHE DOESN'T SCREW UP DEADPOOL'S FOCUS. SHALL WE GET TO THE MAIN EVENT?
SNAP

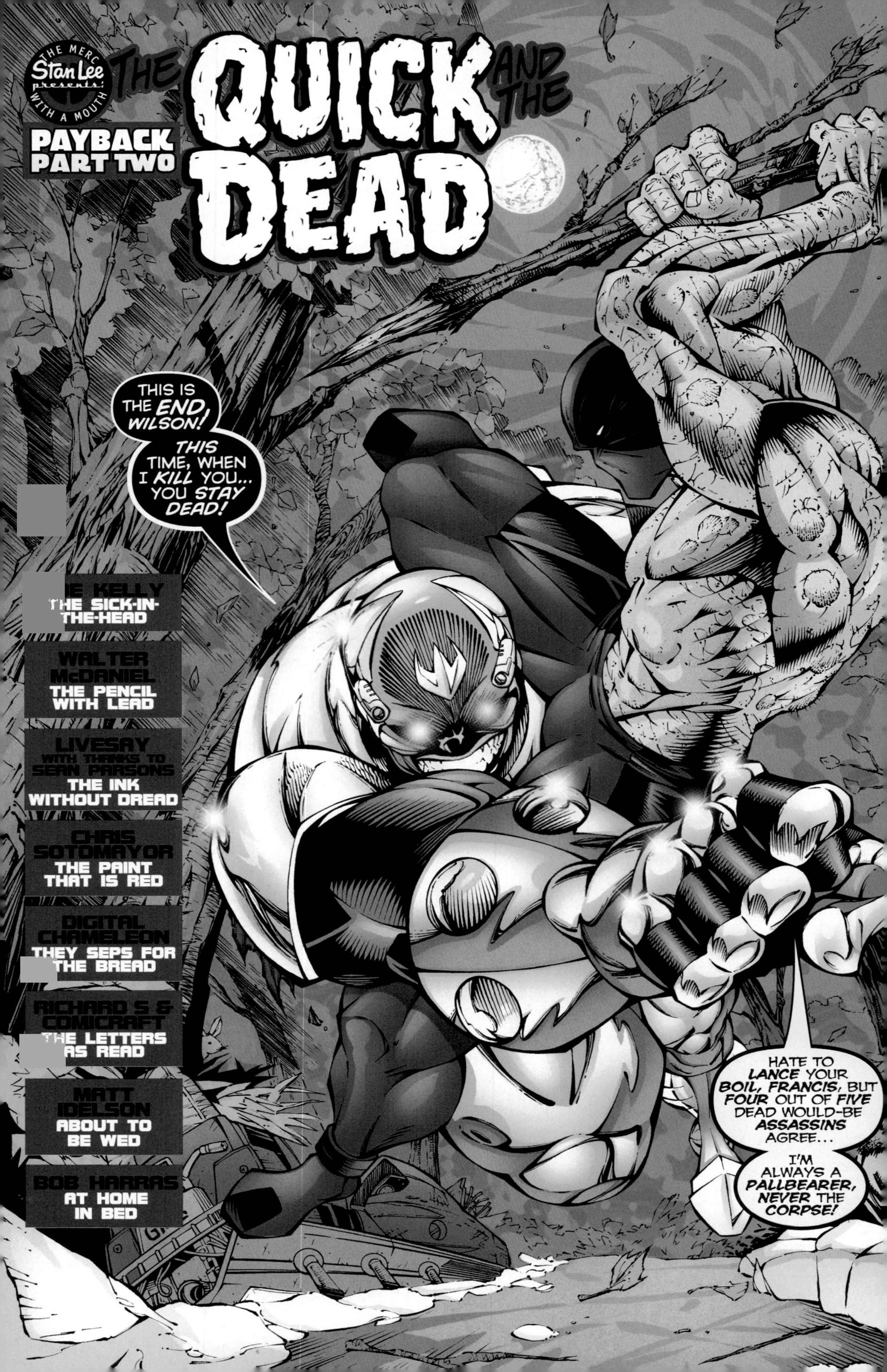

THE MERC WITH A MOUTH
Stan Lee presents!
PAYBACK PART TWO
THE QUICK AND THE DEAD
THIS IS THE END, WILSON! THIS TIME, WHEN I KILL YOU... YOU STAY DEAD!
OE KELLY THE SICK-IN-THE-HEAD
WALTER McDANIEL THE PENCIL WITH LEAD
LIVESAY WITH THANKS TO SEAN PARSONS THE INK WITHOUT DREAD
CHRIS SOTOMAYOR THE PAINT THAT IS RED
DIGITAL CHAMELEON THEY SEPS FOR THE BREAD
RICHARD S & COMICRAFT THE LETTERS AS READ
MATT IDELSON ABOUT TO BE WED
BOB HARRAS AT HOME IN BED
HATE TO LANCE YOUR BOIL, FRANCIS, BUT FOUR OUT OF FIVE DEAD WOULD-BE ASSASSINS AGREE...
I'M ALWAYS A PALLBEARER, NEVER THE CORPSE!

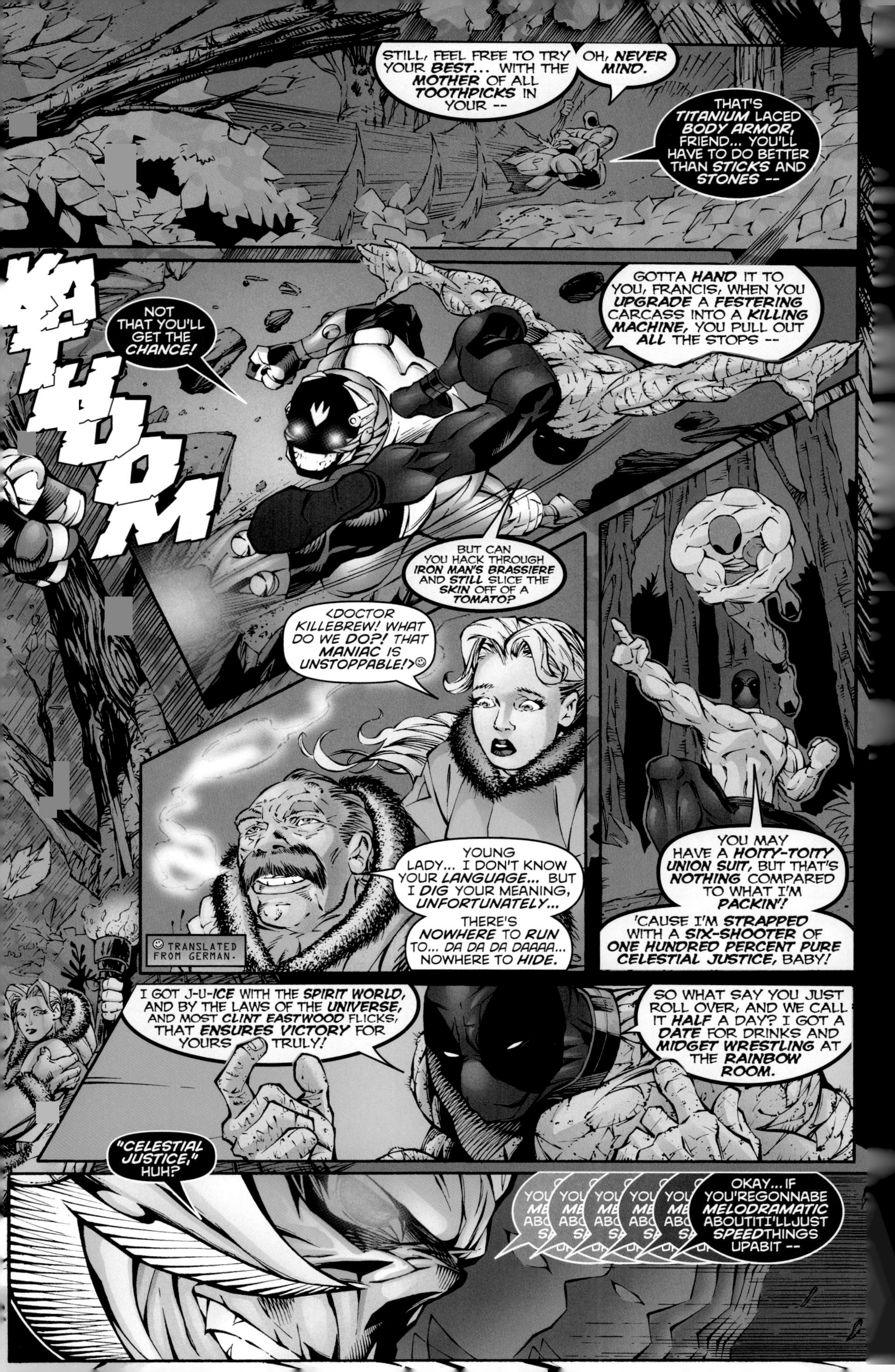
STILL, FEEL FREE TO TRY YOUR BEST... WITH THE MOTHER OF ALL TOOTHPICKS IN YOUR --
OH, NEVER MIND.
THAT'S TITANIUM LACED BODY ARMOR, FRIEND... YOU'LL HAVE TO DO BETTER THAN STICKS AND STONES --
NOT THAT YOU'LL GET THE CHANCE!
GOTTA HAND IT TO YOU, FRANCIS, WHEN YOU UPGRADE A FESTERING CARCASS INTO A KILLING MACHINE, YOU PULL OUT ALL THE STOPS --
BUT CAN YOU HACK THROUGH IRON MAN'S BRASSIERE AND STILL SLICE THE SKIN OFF OF A TOMATO?
<DOCTOR KILLEBREW! WHAT DO WE DO?! THAT MANIAC IS UNSTOPPABLE!>☺
YOUNG LADY... I DON'T KNOW YOUR LANGUAGE... BUT I DIG YOUR MEANING, UNFORTUNATELY...
THERE'S NOWHERE TO RUN TO... DA DA DA DAAAA... NOWHERE TO HIDE.
☺ TRANSLATED FROM GERMAN.
YOU MAY HAVE A HOITY-TOITY UNION SUIT, BUT THAT'S NOTHING COMPARED TO WHAT I'M PACKIN'!
'CAUSE I'M STRAPPED WITH A SIX-SHOOTER OF ONE HUNDRED PERCENT PURE CELESTIAL JUSTICE, BABY!
I GOT J-U-ICE WITH THE SPIRIT WORLD, AND BY THE LAWS OF THE UNIVERSE, AND MOST CLINT EASTWOOD FLICKS, THAT ENSURES VICTORY FOR YOURS TRULY!
SO WHAT SAY YOU JUST ROLL OVER, AND WE CALL IT HALF A DAY? I GOT A DATE FOR DRINKS AND MIDGET WRESTLING AT THE RAINBOW ROOM.
"CELESTIAL JUSTICE," HUH?
OKAY... IF YOU'REGONNABE MELODRAMATIC ABOUTITI'LLJUST SPEEDTHINGS UPABIT --

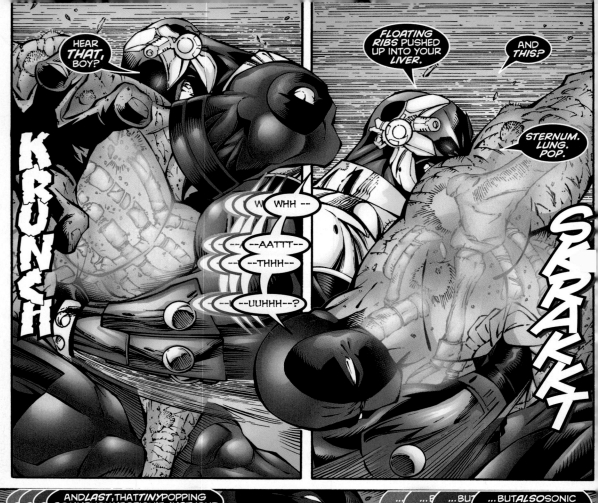

HEAR *THAT*, BOY?

FLOATING *RIBS* PUSHED UP INTO YOUR *LIVER.*

AND *THIS?*

STERNUM. LUNG. POP.

W-- WHH --

-- --AATTT --

-- --THHH --

-- --UUHHH --?

KRUNCH

SKRAKKK

AND *LAST,* THAT *TINY* POPPING SOUND YOU *HEAR* ISN'T *JUST* YOUR *SKULL* FRACTURING...

...BUT ALSO SONIC *MICROBOOMS. IS* SUPERSPEED TH' *COOLEST?*

BAD.

<OH MY GOD -- AJAX IS *KILLING* HIM! HE -- >

<WHAT ARE YOU *DOING?*>

I DON'T *KNOW* IF YOU'RE *SCREAMING* FOR US TO *RUN* FOR THE *HILLS* OR TO WILSON'S *AID...*

IF IT'S THE *FORMER,* I *APOLOGIZE,* BUT I NEED TO *DO* SOMETHING THAT SHOULD HAVE BEEN DONE A *LONG TIME* AGO...

SOMETHING THAT *DEADPOOL,* OF ALL PEOPLE, MADE ME *REALIZE...* ☺

☺ -- LAST ISH! -- REPENTANT MATT

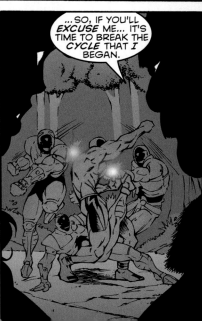

...SO, IF YOU'LL *EXCUSE* ME... IT'S TIME TO BREAK THE *CYCLE* THAT *I* BEGAN.

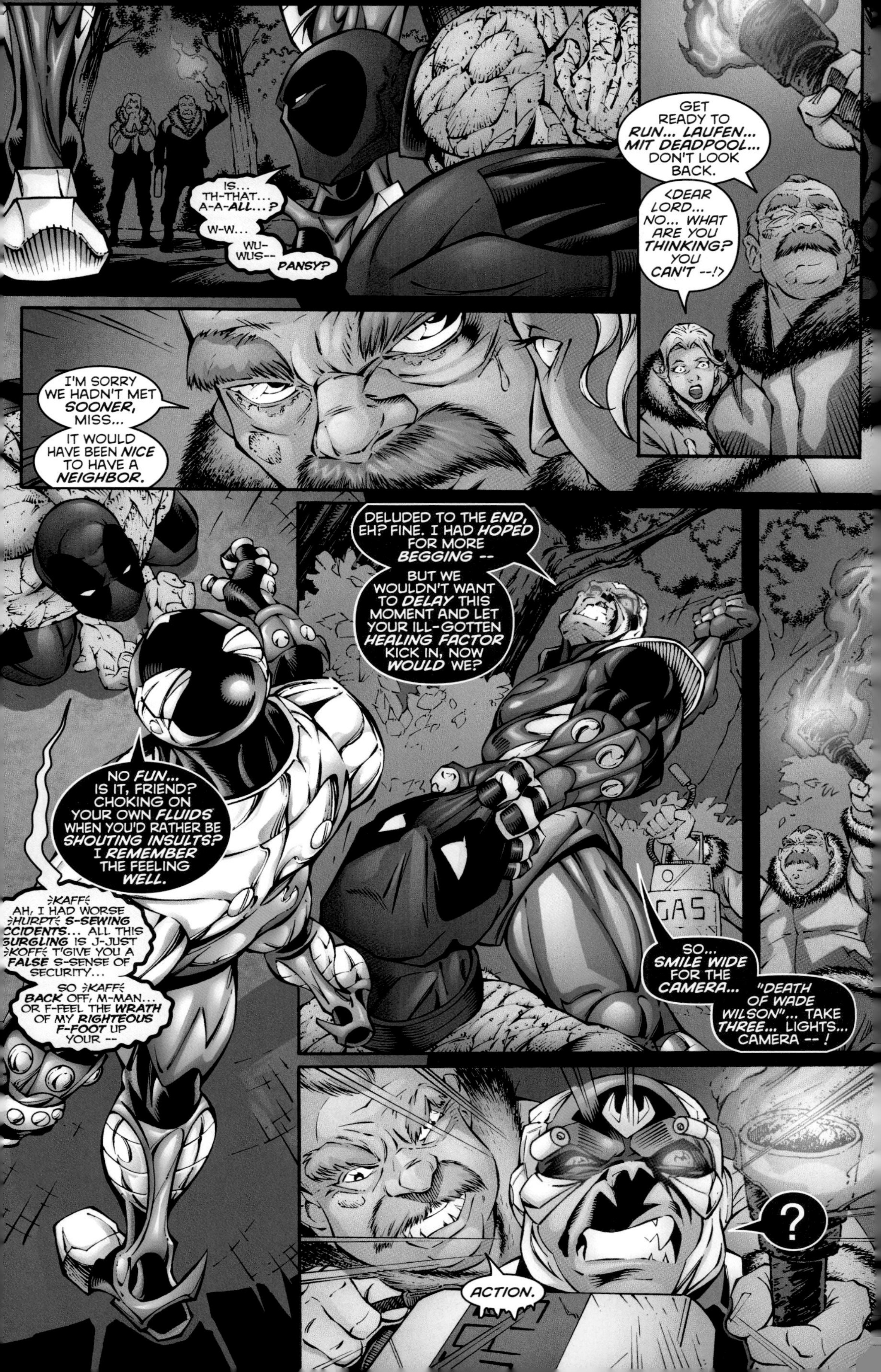

IS... TH-THAT... A-A-ALL...?
W-W...
WU-WUS-- PANSY?
GET READY TO RUN... LAUFEN... MIT DEADPOOL... DON'T LOOK BACK.
<DEAR LORD... NO... WHAT ARE YOU THINKING? YOU CAN'T --!>
I'M SORRY WE HADN'T MET SOONER, MISS... IT WOULD HAVE BEEN NICE TO HAVE A NEIGHBOR.
DELUDED TO THE END, EH? FINE. I HAD HOPED FOR MORE BEGGING --
BUT WE WOULDN'T WANT TO DELAY THIS MOMENT AND LET YOUR ILL-GOTTEN HEALING FACTOR KICK IN, NOW WOULD WE?
NO FUN... IS IT, FRIEND? CHOKING ON YOUR OWN FLUIDS WHEN YOU'D RATHER BE SHOUTING INSULTS? I REMEMBER THE FEELING WELL.
KAFF AH, I HAD WORSE HURPT S-SEWING CCIDENTS... ALL THIS GURGLING IS J-JUST KOFF T'GIVE YOU A FALSE S-SENSE OF SECURITY...
SO KAFF BACK OFF, M-MAN... OR F-FEEL THE WRATH OF MY RIGHTEOUS F-FOOT UP YOUR --
GAS
SO... SMILE WIDE FOR THE CAMERA... "DEATH OF WADE WILSON"... TAKE THREE... LIGHTS... CAMERA -- !
?
ACTION.

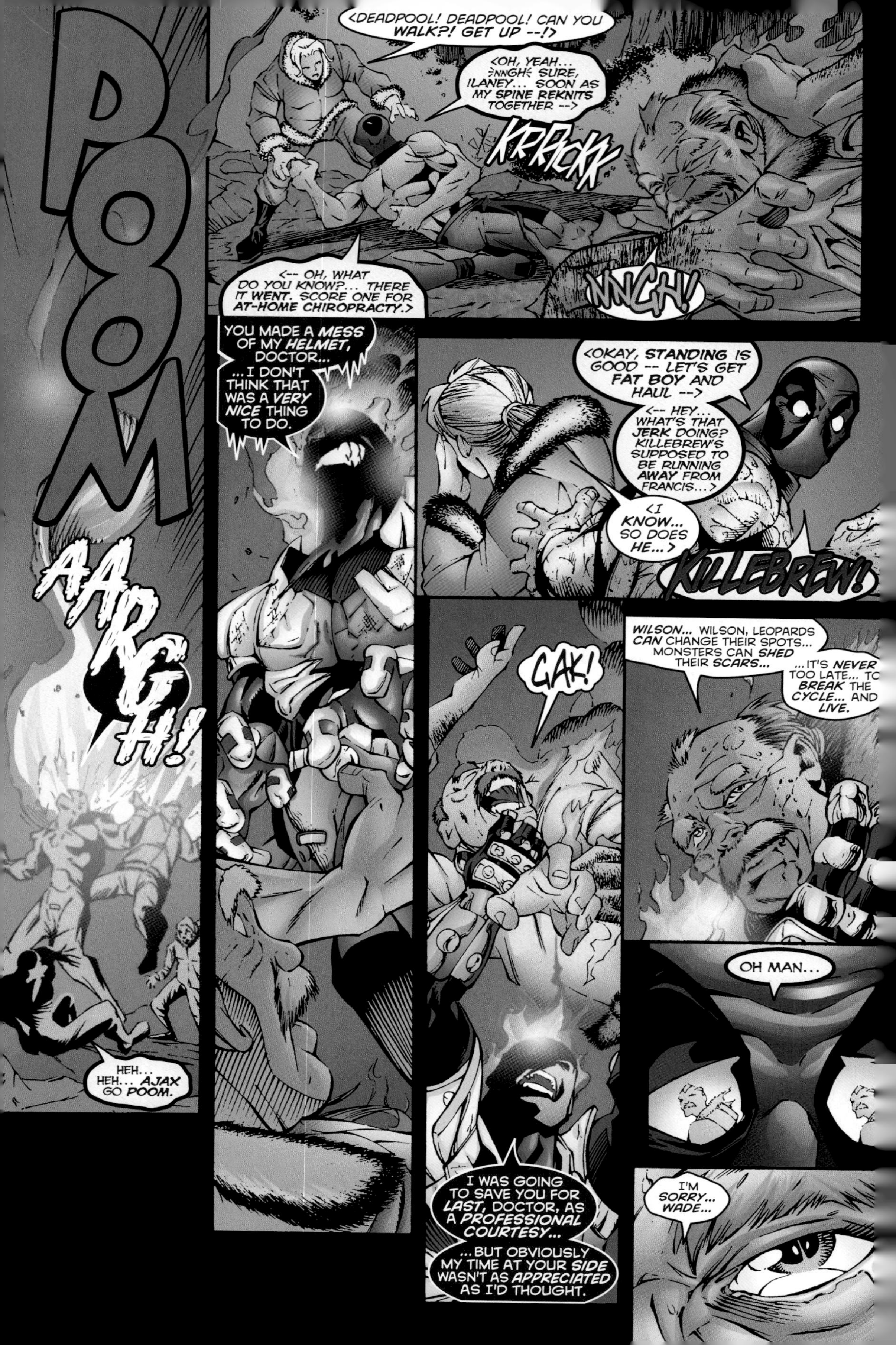
POOM
AARGH!
HEH... HEH... AJAX GO POOM.
<DEADPOOL! DEADPOOL! CAN YOU WALK?! GET UP --!>
<OH, YEAH... NNGH SURE, ILANEY... SOON AS MY SPINE REKNITS TOGETHER -->
KRRACKK
<-- OH, WHAT DO YOU KNOW?... THERE IT WENT. SCORE ONE FOR AT-HOME CHIROPRACTY.>
NNGH!
YOU MADE A MESS OF MY HELMET, DOCTOR...
...I DON'T THINK THAT WAS A VERY NICE THING TO DO.
<OKAY, STANDING IS GOOD -- LET'S GET FAT BOY AND HAUL -->
<-- HEY... WHAT'S THAT JERK DOING? KILLEBREW'S SUPPOSED TO BE RUNNING AWAY FROM FRANCIS...>
<I KNOW... SO DOES HE...>
KILLEBREW!
GAK!
I WAS GOING TO SAVE YOU FOR LAST, DOCTOR, AS A PROFESSIONAL COURTESY...
...BUT OBVIOUSLY MY TIME AT YOUR SIDE WASN'T AS APPRECIATED AS I'D THOUGHT.
WILSON... WILSON, LEOPARDS CAN CHANGE THEIR SPOTS... MONSTERS CAN SHED THEIR SCARS...
...IT'S NEVER TOO LATE... TO BREAK THE CYCLE... AND LIVE.
OH MAN...
I'M SORRY... WADE...

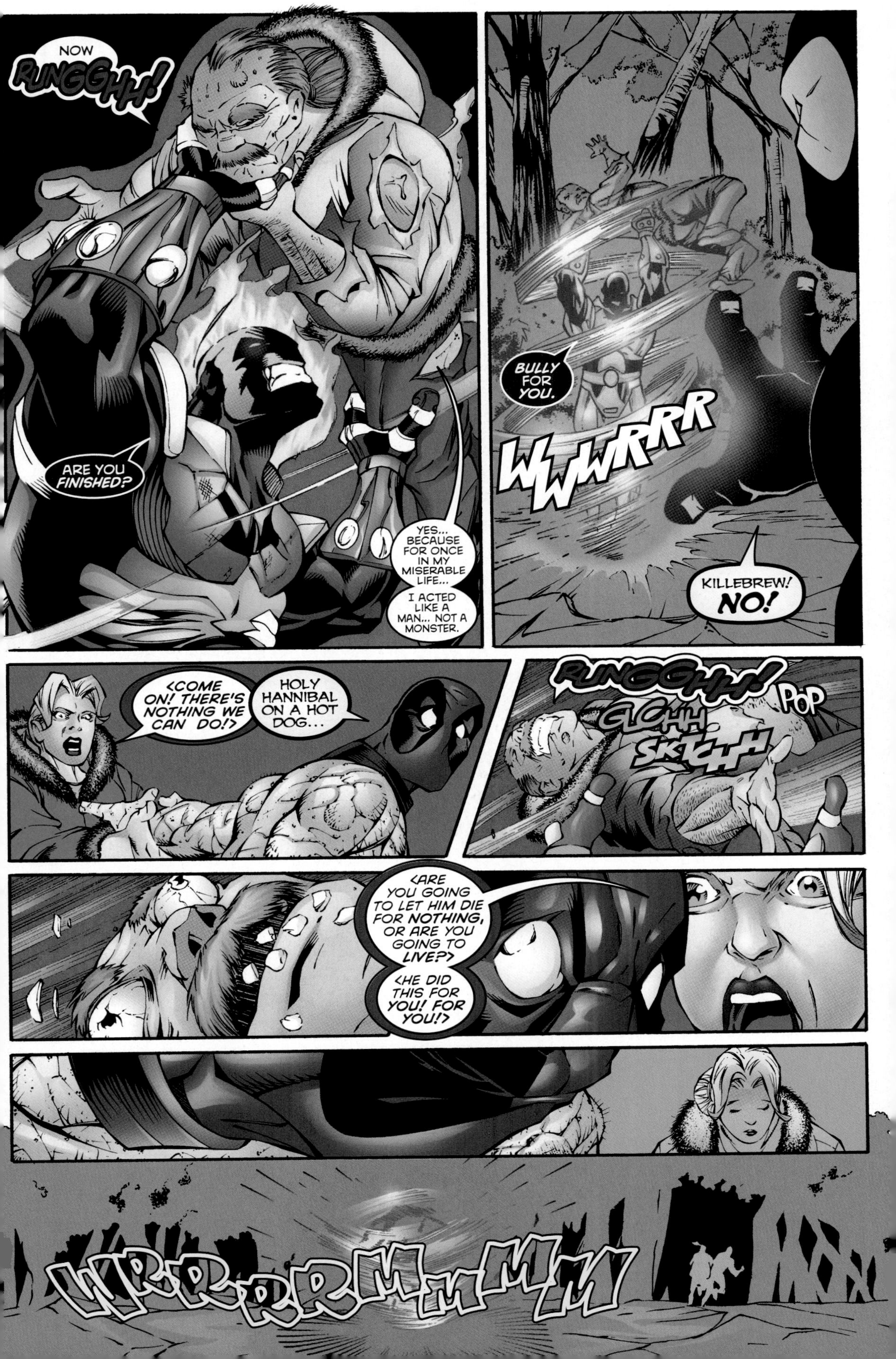
NOW
RUNGGHH!
ARE YOU FINISHED?
YES... BECAUSE FOR ONCE IN MY MISERABLE LIFE...
I ACTED LIKE A MAN... NOT A MONSTER.
BULLY FOR YOU.
WWWRRR
KILLEBREW! NO!
<COME ON! THERE'S NOTHING WE CAN DO!>
HOLY HANNIBAL ON A HOT DOG...
RUNGGHH!
POP
GLGHH
SKTCHH
<ARE YOU GOING TO LET HIM DIE FOR NOTHING, OR ARE YOU GOING TO LIVE?>
<HE DID THIS FOR YOU! FOR YOU!>
WRRRRMMMMM

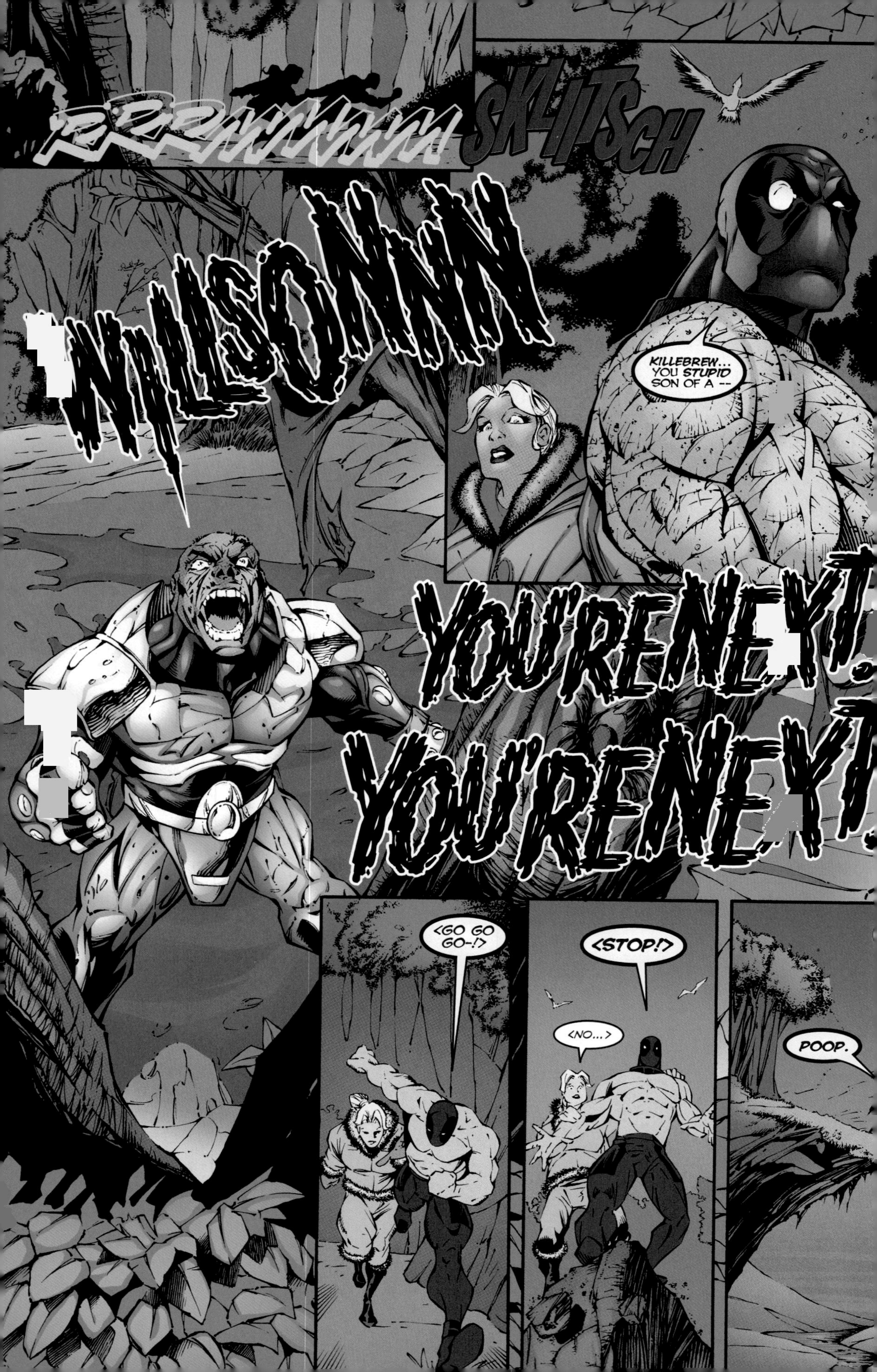
WILLSONNN
KILLEBREW... YOU **STUPID** SON OF A --
YOU'RE NEXT.
YOU'RE NEXT.
<GO GO GO-!>
<STOP!>
<NO...>
POOP.

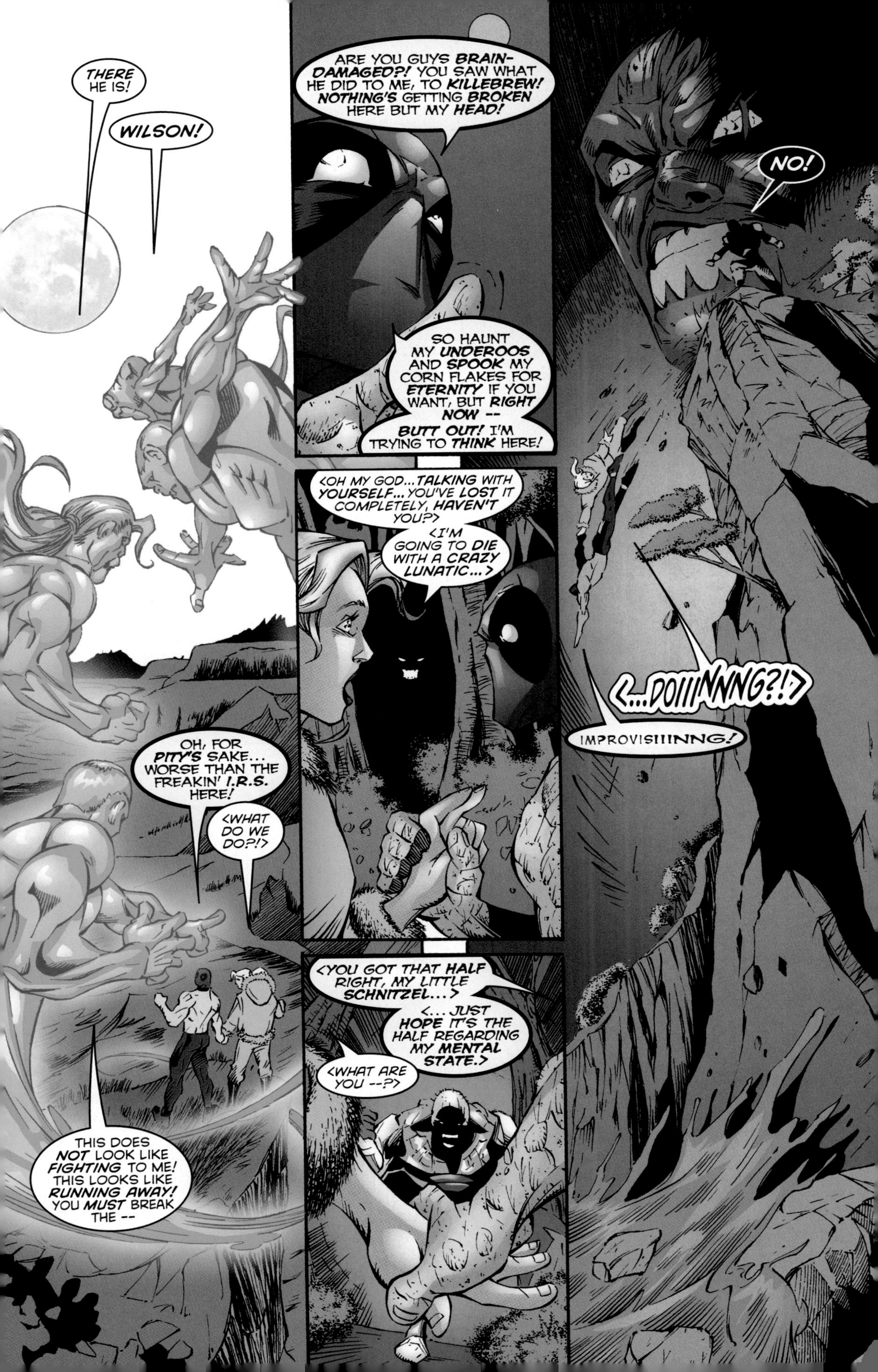
THERE HE IS!
WILSON!
ARE YOU GUYS BRAIN-DAMAGED?! YOU SAW WHAT HE DID TO ME, TO KILLEBREW! NOTHING'S GETTING BROKEN HERE BUT MY HEAD!
SO HAUNT MY UNDEROOS AND SPOOK MY CORN FLAKES FOR ETERNITY IF YOU WANT, BUT RIGHT NOW --
BUTT OUT! I'M TRYING TO THINK HERE!
NO!
<OH MY GOD...TALKING WITH YOURSELF... YOU'VE LOST IT COMPLETELY, HAVEN'T YOU?>
<I'M GOING TO DIE WITH A CRAZY LUNATIC...>
<...DOIIINNNG?!>
IMPROVISIIIINNG!
OH, FOR PITY'S SAKE... WORSE THAN THE FREAKIN' I.R.S. HERE!
<WHAT DO WE DO?!>
<YOU GOT THAT HALF RIGHT, MY LITTLE SCHNITZEL...>
<... JUST HOPE IT'S THE HALF REGARDING MY MENTAL STATE.>
<WHAT ARE YOU --?>
THIS DOES NOT LOOK LIKE FIGHTING TO ME! THIS LOOKS LIKE RUNNING AWAY! YOU MUST BREAK THE --

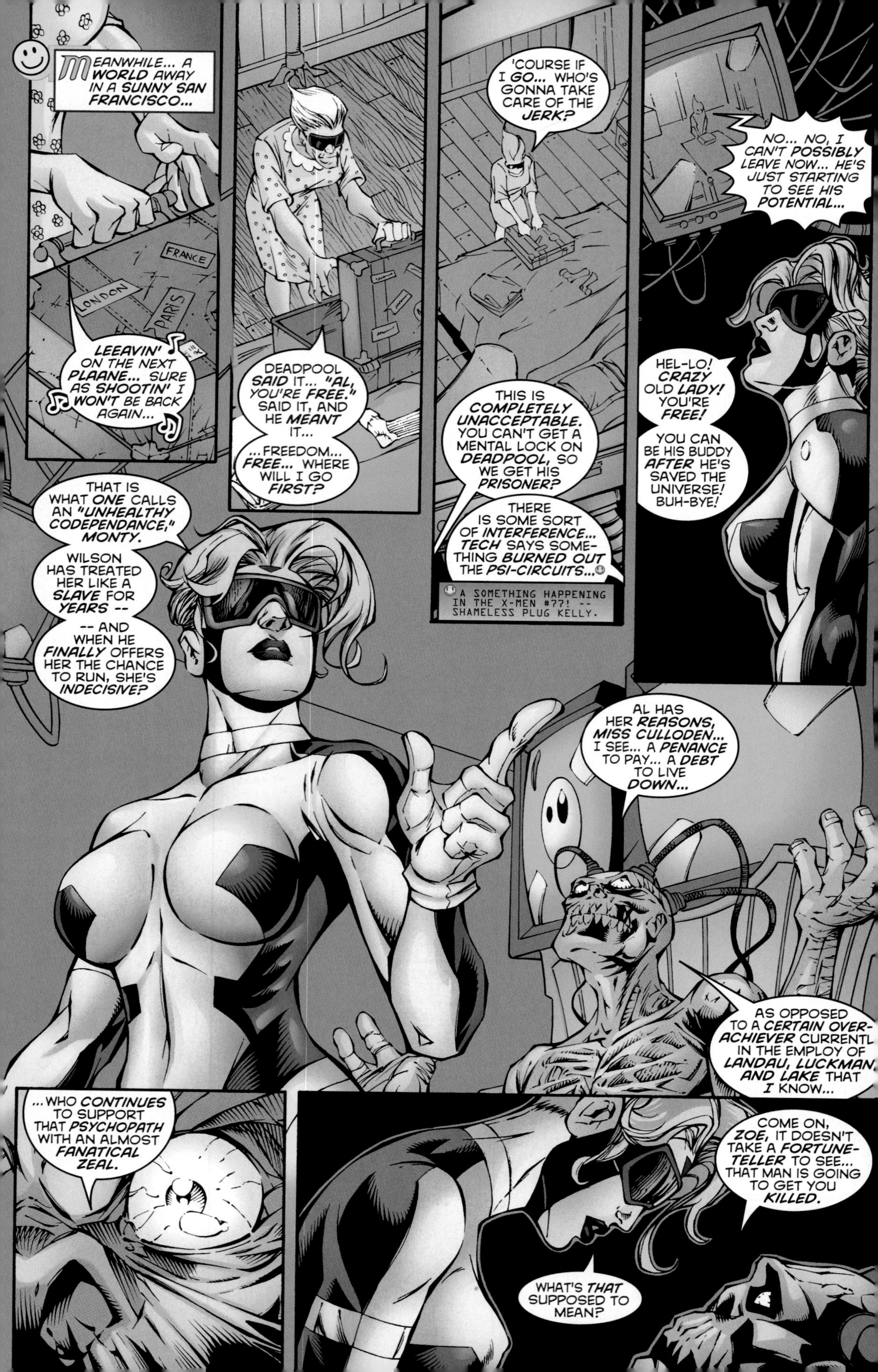
MEANWHILE... A WORLD AWAY IN A SUNNY SAN FRANCISCO...
FRANCE
LONDON
PARIS
LEEAVIN' ON THE NEXT PLAANE... SURE AS SHOOTIN' I WON'T BE BACK AGAIN...
DEADPOOL SAID IT... "AL, YOU'RE FREE." SAID IT, AND HE MEANT IT...
...FREEDOM... FREE... WHERE WILL I GO FIRST?
'COURSE IF I GO... WHO'S GONNA TAKE CARE OF THE JERK?
NO... NO, I CAN'T POSSIBLY LEAVE NOW... HE'S JUST STARTING TO SEE HIS POTENTIAL...
THIS IS COMPLETELY UNACCEPTABLE. YOU CAN'T GET A MENTAL LOCK ON DEADPOOL, SO WE GET HIS PRISONER?
THERE IS SOME SORT OF INTERFERENCE... TECH SAYS SOMETHING BURNED OUT THE PSI-CIRCUITS...
A SOMETHING HAPPENING IN THE X-MEN #77! -- SHAMELESS PLUG KELLY.
HEL-LO! CRAZY OLD LADY! YOU'RE FREE!
YOU CAN BE HIS BUDDY AFTER HE'S SAVED THE UNIVERSE! BUH-BYE!
THAT IS WHAT ONE CALLS AN "UNHEALTHY CODEPENDANCE," MONTY.
WILSON HAS TREATED HER LIKE A SLAVE FOR YEARS --
-- AND WHEN HE FINALLY OFFERS HER THE CHANCE TO RUN, SHE'S INDECISIVE?
AL HAS HER REASONS, MISS CULLODEN... I SEE... A PENANCE TO PAY... A DEBT TO LIVE DOWN...
AS OPPOSED TO A CERTAIN OVER-ACHIEVER CURRENTL IN THE EMPLOY OF LANDAU, LUCKMAN, AND LAKE THAT I KNOW...
...WHO CONTINUES TO SUPPORT THAT PSYCHOPATH WITH AN ALMOST FANATICAL ZEAL.
COME ON, ZOE, IT DOESN'T TAKE A FORTUNE-TELLER TO SEE... THAT MAN IS GOING TO GET YOU KILLED.
WHAT'S THAT SUPPOSED TO MEAN?

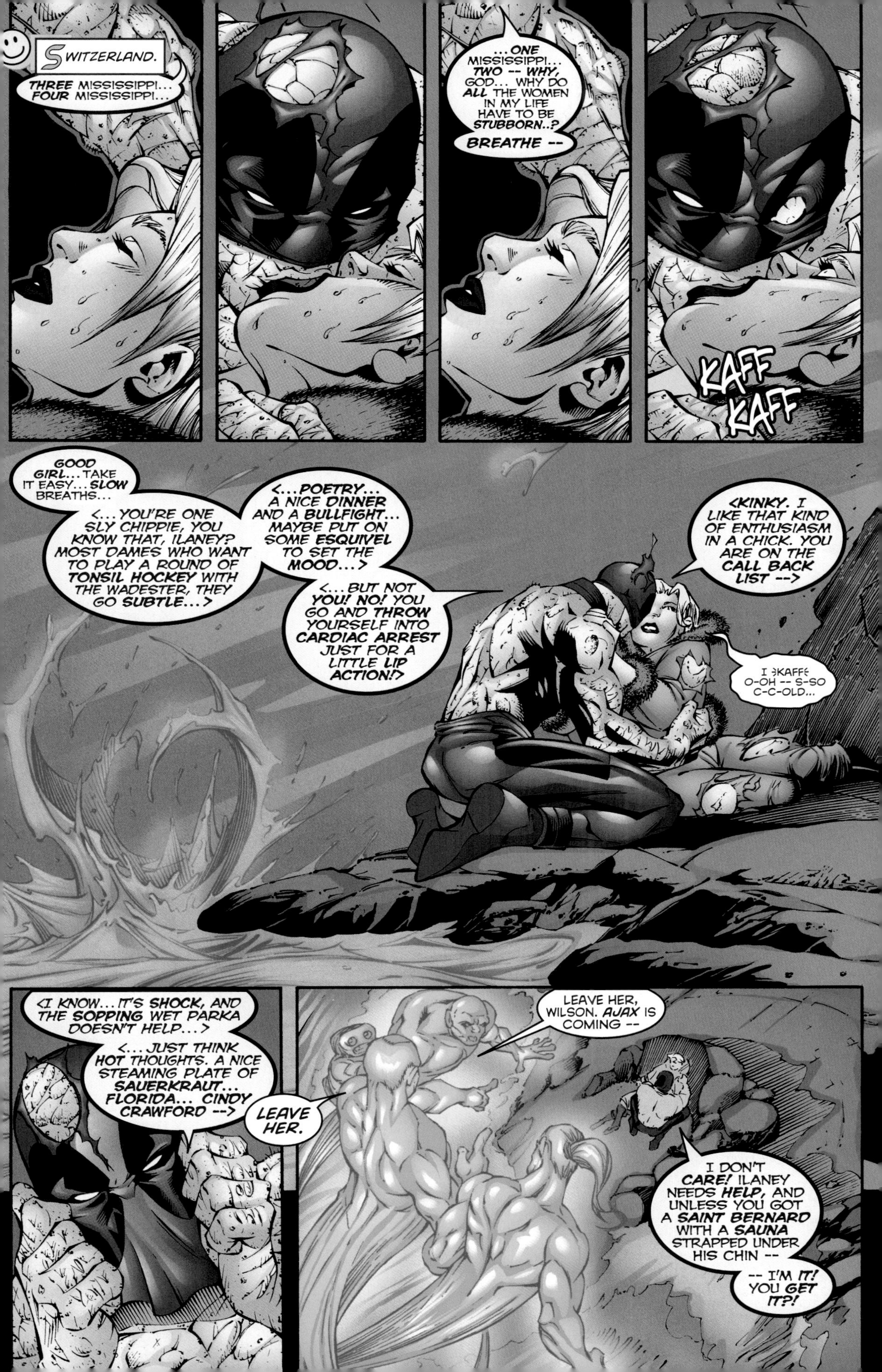
SWITZERLAND.
THREE MISSISSIPPI... FOUR MISSISSIPPI...
...ONE MISSISSIPPI... TWO -- WHY, GOD... WHY DO ALL THE WOMEN IN MY LIFE HAVE TO BE STUBBORN..?
BREATHE --
KAFF KAFF
GOOD GIRL... TAKE IT EASY... SLOW BREATHS...
<...YOU'RE ONE SLY CHIPPIE, YOU KNOW THAT, ILANEY? MOST DAMES WHO WANT TO PLAY A ROUND OF TONSIL HOCKEY WITH THE WADESTER, THEY GO SUBTLE...>
<...POETRY... A NICE DINNER AND A BULLFIGHT... MAYBE PUT ON SOME ESQUIVEL TO SET THE MOOD...>
<...BUT NOT YOU! NO! YOU GO AND THROW YOURSELF INTO CARDIAC ARREST JUST FOR A LITTLE LIP ACTION!?>
<KINKY. I LIKE THAT KIND OF ENTHUSIASM IN A CHICK. YOU ARE ON THE CALL BACK LIST -->
I ⋟KAFF⋞ O-OH -- S-SO C-C-OLD...
<I KNOW... IT'S SHOCK, AND THE SOPPING WET PARKA DOESN'T HELP...>
<...JUST THINK HOT THOUGHTS. A NICE STEAMING PLATE OF SAUERKRAUT... FLORIDA... CINDY CRAWFORD -->
LEAVE HER.
LEAVE HER, WILSON. AJAX IS COMING --
I DON'T CARE! ILANEY NEEDS HELP, AND UNLESS YOU GOT A SAINT BERNARD WITH A SAUNA STRAPPED UNDER HIS CHIN --
-- I'M IT! YOU GET IT?!

BLAST you, WILSON! DON'T you UNDERSTAND?! NONE OF THAT MATTERS! SHE DOESN'T BIND ME TO THE EARTH, YOU DO --

-- AND YOUR TIME IS NEAR! WE CAN SENSE AN END COMING, YOU MUST PREPARE --

I DON'T GIVE A HIGH HOLY SQUIRT UP A FLAGPOLE ABOUT WHAT YOU SENSE, WORM!

IF YOU'RE SO LOST IN THIS VENDETTA THAT YOU'D LET AN INNOCENT WOMAN DIE...

...THAT MAKES YOU AS MUCH OF A DIRTBAG AS FRANCIS!

I -- WILSON... AJAX IS COMING... HERE. YOU CAN'T ESCAPE DESTINY...

...WE KNOW THAT YOU WILL FIGHT, THE SAME WAY WE KNEW ABOUT KILLEBREW --

<C-COLONEL...>

SHUT UP. DON'T SAY HIS NAME.

<TAKE IT EASY, ILANEY... I'M GONNA GET YOU SOMEWHERE SAFE...>

<N-NO... COLONEL... I... DON'T WANT TO... B-BE SAFE ANYMORE... D-DONE THAT TO D-DEATH...>

<ILANEY? IT'S ME... YOUR CRAZY LUNATIC PAL, DEAD-POOL --->

<I W-WANT TO F-FLY AGAIN...>

<....I'M A G-GOOD PILOT, SIR... I TRIED... T-TRIED TO SAVE THEM... BUT AFTER THE ACCIDENT...>

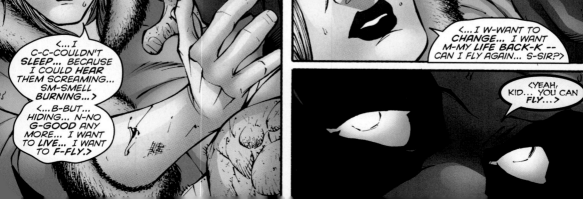

<...I C-C-COULDN'T SLEEP... BECAUSE I COULD HEAR THEM SCREAMING... SM-SMELL BURNING...>

<...B-BUT... HIDING... N-NO G-GOOD ANY MORE... I WANT TO LIVE... I WANT TO F-FLY.>

<K-KILLEBREW CHANGED... HE GOT WHAT HE WANTED...>

<...I W-WANT TO CHANGE... I WANT M-MY LIFE BACK-K -- CAN I FLY AGAIN... S-SIR?>

<YEAH, KID... YOU CAN FLY...>

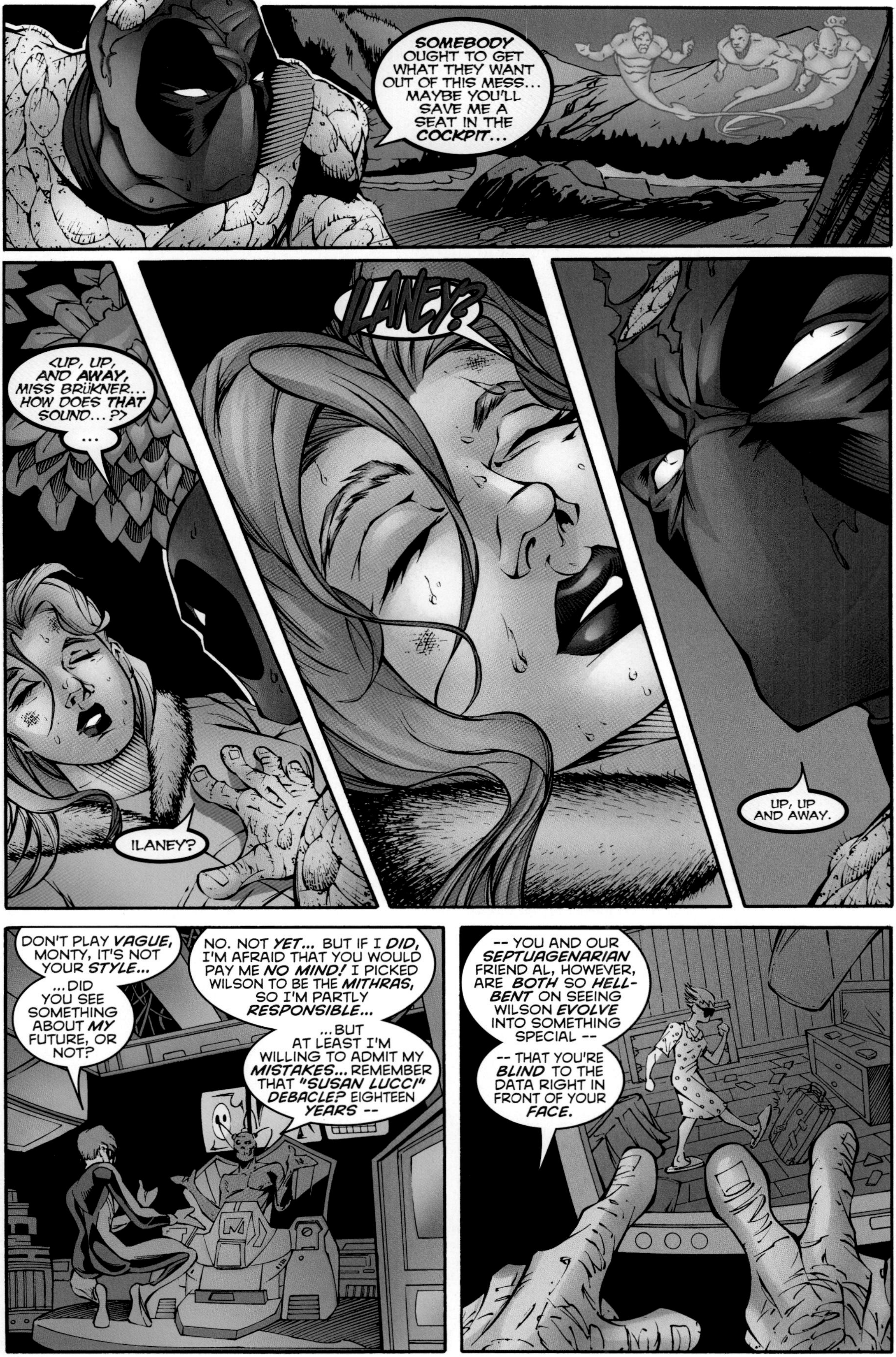
SOMEBODY OUGHT TO GET WHAT THEY WANT OUT OF THIS MESS... MAYBE YOU'LL SAVE ME A SEAT IN THE COCKPIT...
<UP, UP, AND AWAY, MISS BRÜKNER... HOW DOES THAT SOUND...?>
...
¡LANEY?
¡LANEY?
UP, UP AND AWAY.
DON'T PLAY VAGUE, MONTY, IT'S NOT YOUR STYLE...
...DID YOU SEE SOMETHING ABOUT MY FUTURE, OR NOT?
NO. NOT YET... BUT IF I DID, I'M AFRAID THAT YOU WOULD PAY ME NO MIND! I PICKED WILSON TO BE THE MITHRAS, SO I'M PARTLY RESPONSIBLE...
...BUT AT LEAST I'M WILLING TO ADMIT MY MISTAKES... REMEMBER THAT "SUSAN LUCCI" DEBACLE? EIGHTEEN YEARS --
-- YOU AND OUR SEPTUAGENARIAN FRIEND AL, HOWEVER, ARE BOTH SO HELL-BENT ON SEEING WILSON EVOLVE INTO SOMETHING SPECIAL --
-- THAT YOU'RE BLIND TO THE DATA RIGHT IN FRONT OF YOUR FACE.

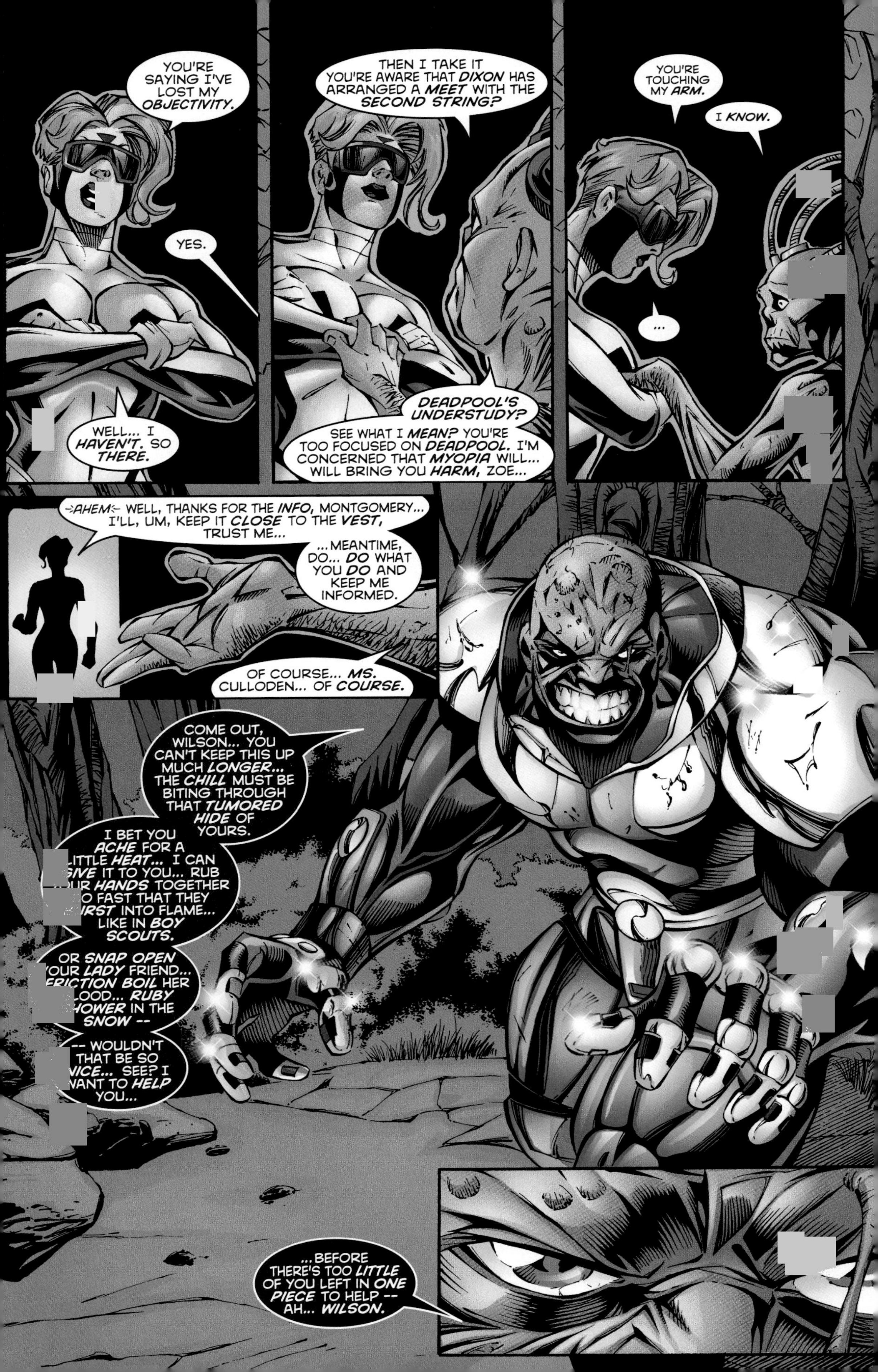

YOU'RE SAYING I'VE LOST MY OBJECTIVITY.
YES.
WELL... I HAVEN'T. SO THERE.
THEN I TAKE IT YOU'RE AWARE THAT DIXON HAS ARRANGED A MEET WITH THE SECOND STRING?
DEADPOOL'S UNDERSTUDY?
SEE WHAT I MEAN? YOU'RE TOO FOCUSED ON DEADPOOL. I'M CONCERNED THAT MYOPIA WILL... WILL BRING YOU HARM, ZOE...
YOU'RE TOUCHING MY ARM.
I KNOW.
...
>AHEM< WELL, THANKS FOR THE INFO, MONTGOMERY... I'LL, UM, KEEP IT CLOSE TO THE VEST, TRUST ME...
...MEANTIME, DO... DO WHAT YOU DO AND KEEP ME INFORMED.
OF COURSE... MS. CULLODEN... OF COURSE.
COME OUT, WILSON... YOU CAN'T KEEP THIS UP MUCH LONGER... THE CHILL MUST BE BITING THROUGH THAT TUMORED HIDE OF YOURS.
I BET YOU ACHE FOR A ITTLE HEAT... I CAN IVE IT TO YOU... RUB UR HANDS TOGETHER O FAST THAT THEY URST INTO FLAME... LIKE IN BOY SCOUTS.
OR SNAP OPEN OUR LADY FRIEND... RICTION BOIL HER OOD... RUBY HOWER IN THE SNOW --
-- WOULDN'T THAT BE SO ICE... SEE? I ANT TO HELP YOU...
...BEFORE THERE'S TOO LITTLE OF YOU LEFT IN ONE PIECE TO HELP -- AH... WILSON.

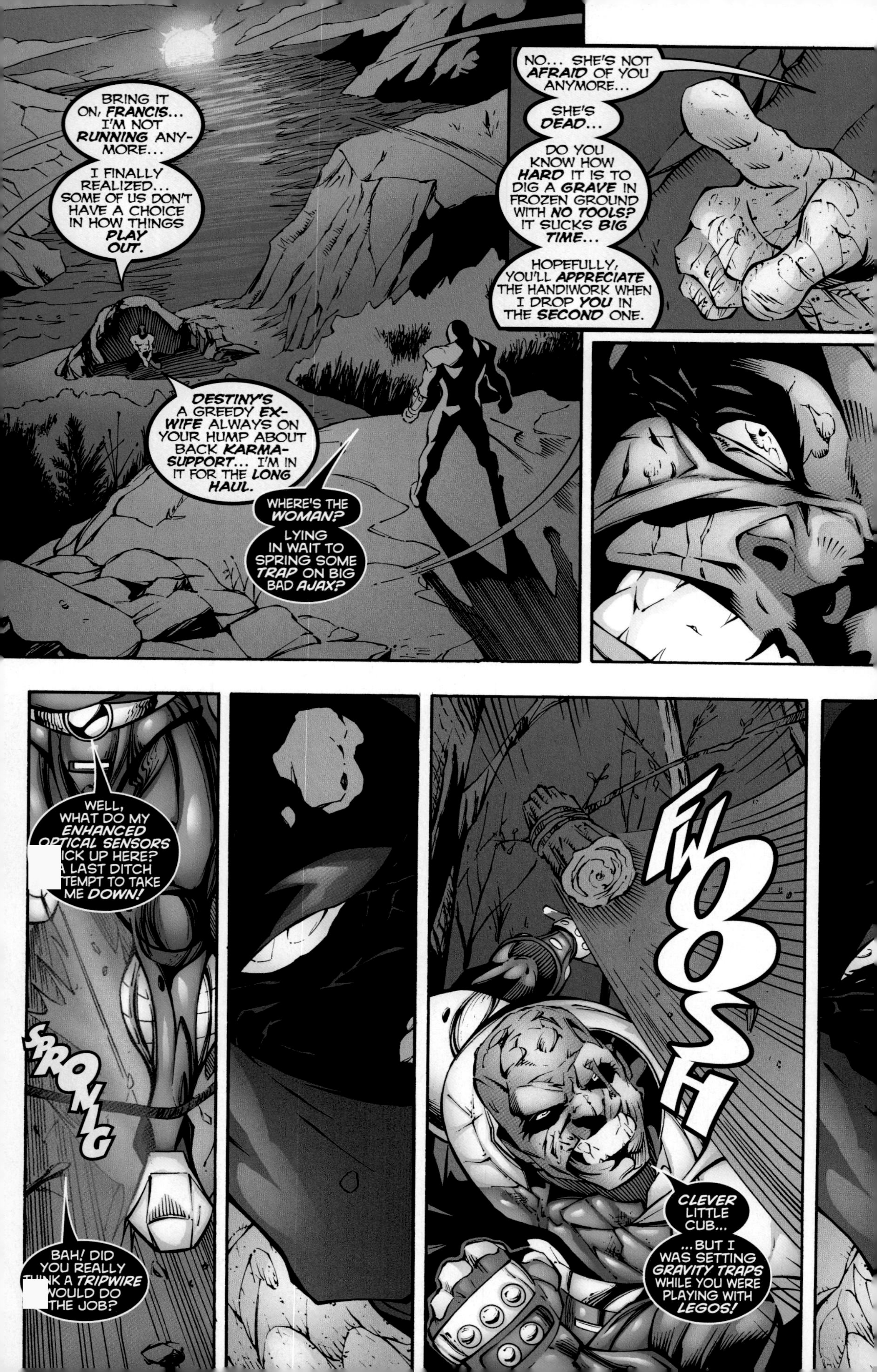

BRING IT ON, FRANCIS... I'M NOT RUNNING ANY-MORE...
I FINALLY REALIZED... SOME OF US DON'T HAVE A CHOICE IN HOW THINGS PLAY OUT.
DESTINY'S A GREEDY EX-WIFE ALWAYS ON YOUR HUMP ABOUT BACK KARMA-SUPPORT... I'M IN IT FOR THE LONG HAUL.
WHERE'S THE WOMAN?
LYING IN WAIT TO SPRING SOME TRAP ON BIG BAD AJAX?
NO... SHE'S NOT AFRAID OF YOU ANYMORE...
SHE'S DEAD...
DO YOU KNOW HOW HARD IT IS TO DIG A GRAVE IN FROZEN GROUND WITH NO TOOLS? IT SUCKS BIG TIME...
HOPEFULLY, YOU'LL APPRECIATE THE HANDIWORK WHEN I DROP YOU IN THE SECOND ONE.
WELL, WHAT DO MY ENHANCED OPTICAL SENSORS ICK UP HERE? A LAST DITCH TEMPT TO TAKE ME DOWN!
SPRONG
BAH! DID YOU REALLY THINK A TRIPWIRE WOULD DO THE JOB?
FWOOSH
CLEVER LITTLE CUB...
...BUT I WAS SETTING GRAVITY TRAPS WHILE YOU WERE PLAYING WITH LEGOS!

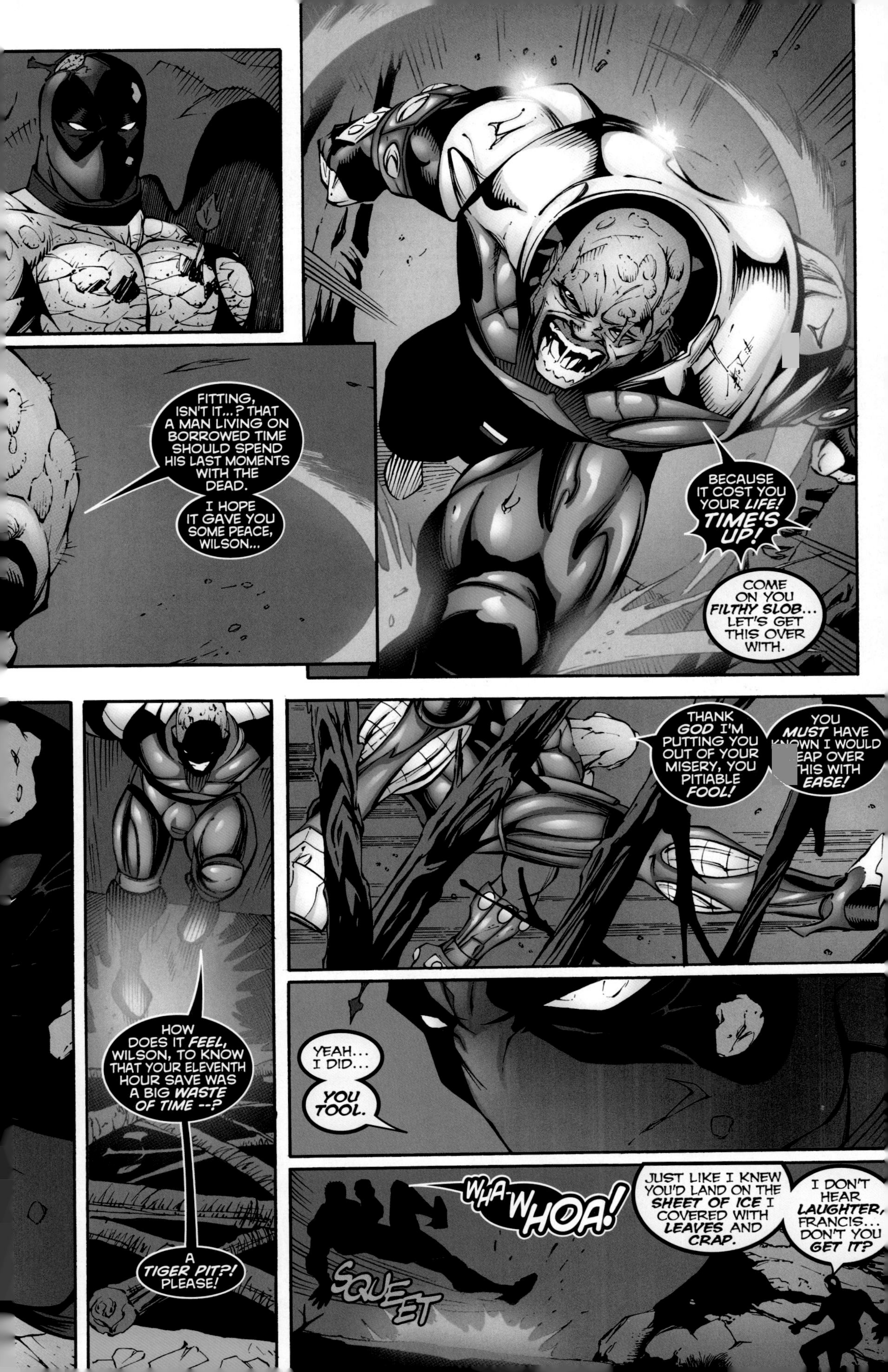
FITTING, ISN'T IT...? THAT A MAN LIVING ON BORROWED TIME SHOULD SPEND HIS LAST MOMENTS WITH THE DEAD.
I HOPE IT GAVE YOU SOME PEACE, WILSON...
BECAUSE IT COST YOU YOUR LIFE! TIME'S UP!
COME ON YOU FILTHY SLOB... LET'S GET THIS OVER WITH.
HOW DOES IT FEEL, WILSON, TO KNOW THAT YOUR ELEVENTH HOUR SAVE WAS A BIG WASTE OF TIME --?
A TIGER PIT?! PLEASE!
THANK GOD I'M PUTTING YOU OUT OF YOUR MISERY, YOU PITIABLE FOOL!
YOU MUST HAVE KNOWN I WOULD LEAP OVER THIS WITH EASE!
YEAH... I DID...
YOU TOOL.
WHA-WHOA!
JUST LIKE I KNEW YOU'D LAND ON THE SHEET OF ICE I COVERED WITH LEAVES AND CRAP.
I DON'T HEAR LAUGHTER, FRANCIS... DON'T YOU GET IT?
SQUEEET

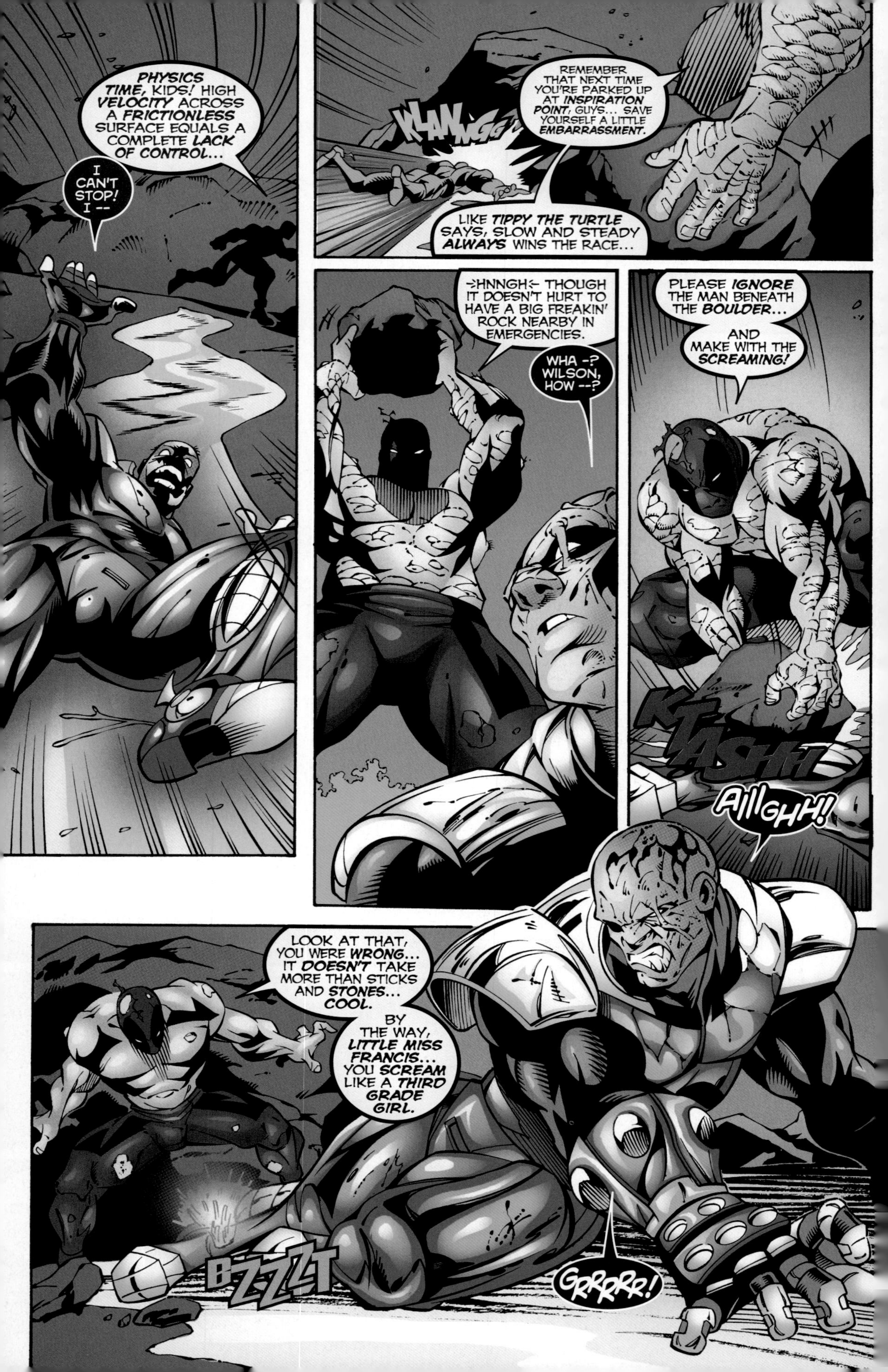

PHYSICS TIME, KIDS! HIGH VELOCITY ACROSS A FRICTIONLESS SURFACE EQUALS A COMPLETE LACK OF CONTROL...
I CAN'T STOP! I --
KLANNGG
REMEMBER THAT NEXT TIME YOU'RE PARKED UP AT INSPIRATION POINT, GUYS... SAVE YOURSELF A LITTLE EMBARRASSMENT.
LIKE TIPPY THE TURTLE SAYS, SLOW AND STEADY ALWAYS WINS THE RACE...
HNNGH THOUGH IT DOESN'T HURT TO HAVE A BIG FREAKIN' ROCK NEARBY IN EMERGENCIES.
WHA -? WILSON, HOW --?
PLEASE IGNORE THE MAN BENEATH THE BOULDER...
AND MAKE WITH THE SCREAMING!
KT TASHH
AIIIGHH!
LOOK AT THAT, YOU WERE WRONG... IT DOESN'T TAKE MORE THAN STICKS AND STONES... COOL.
BY THE WAY, LITTLE MISS FRANCIS... YOU SCREAM LIKE A THIRD GRADE GIRL.
BZZZT
GRRRRR!

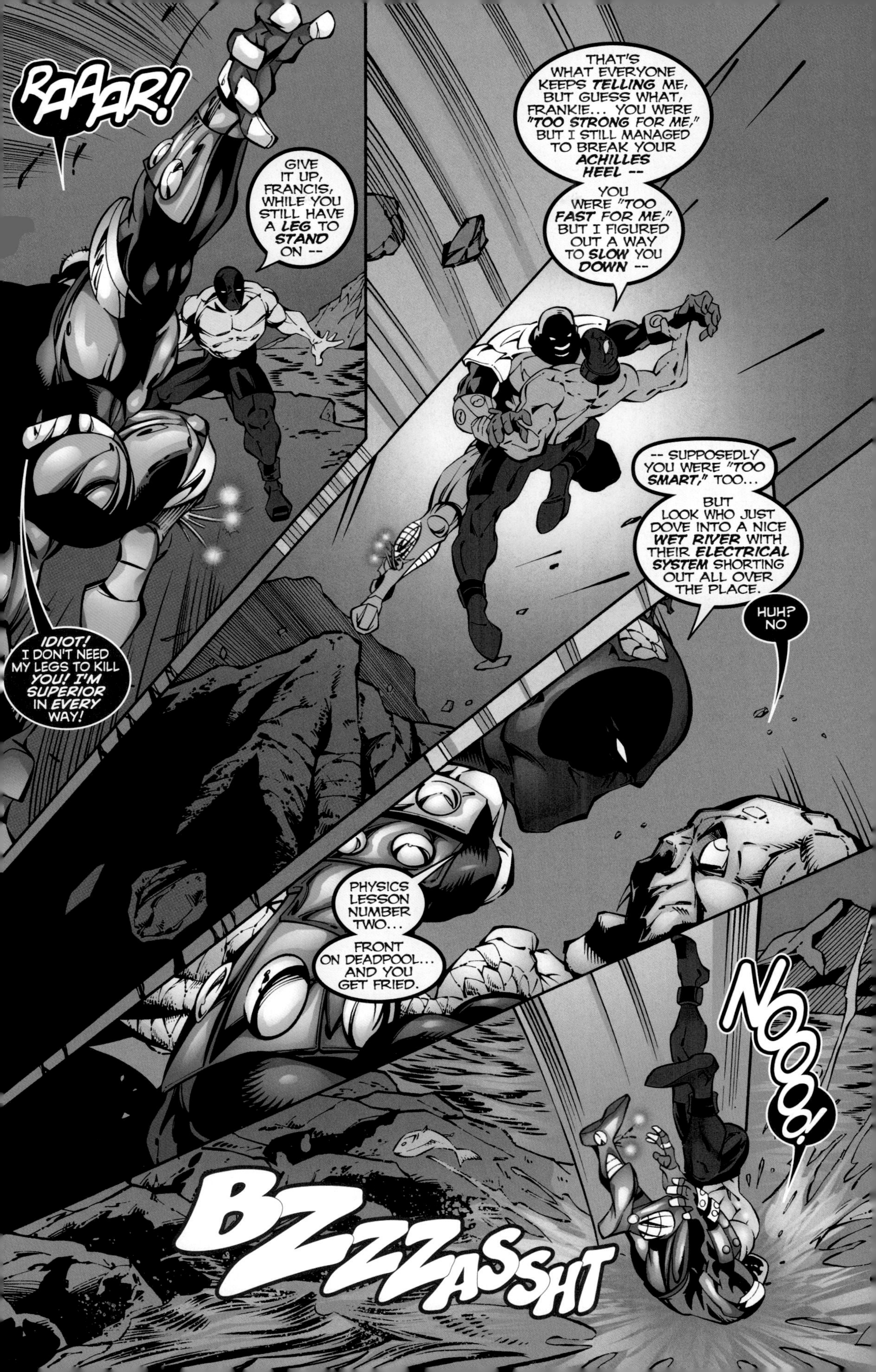
RAAAR!
GIVE IT UP, FRANCIS, WHILE YOU STILL HAVE A LEG TO STAND ON --
IDIOT! I DON'T NEED MY LEGS TO KILL YOU! I'M SUPERIOR IN EVERY WAY!
THAT'S WHAT EVERYONE KEEPS TELLING ME, BUT GUESS WHAT, FRANKIE... YOU WERE "TOO STRONG FOR ME," BUT I STILL MANAGED TO BREAK YOUR ACHILLES HEEL --
YOU WERE "TOO FAST FOR ME," BUT I FIGURED OUT A WAY TO SLOW YOU DOWN --
-- SUPPOSEDLY YOU WERE "TOO SMART," TOO...
BUT LOOK WHO JUST DOVE INTO A NICE WET RIVER WITH THEIR ELECTRICAL SYSTEM SHORTING OUT ALL OVER THE PLACE.
HUH? NO
PHYSICS LESSON NUMBER TWO...
FRONT ON DEADPOOL... AND YOU GET FRIED.
NOOOO!
BZZZASSHT

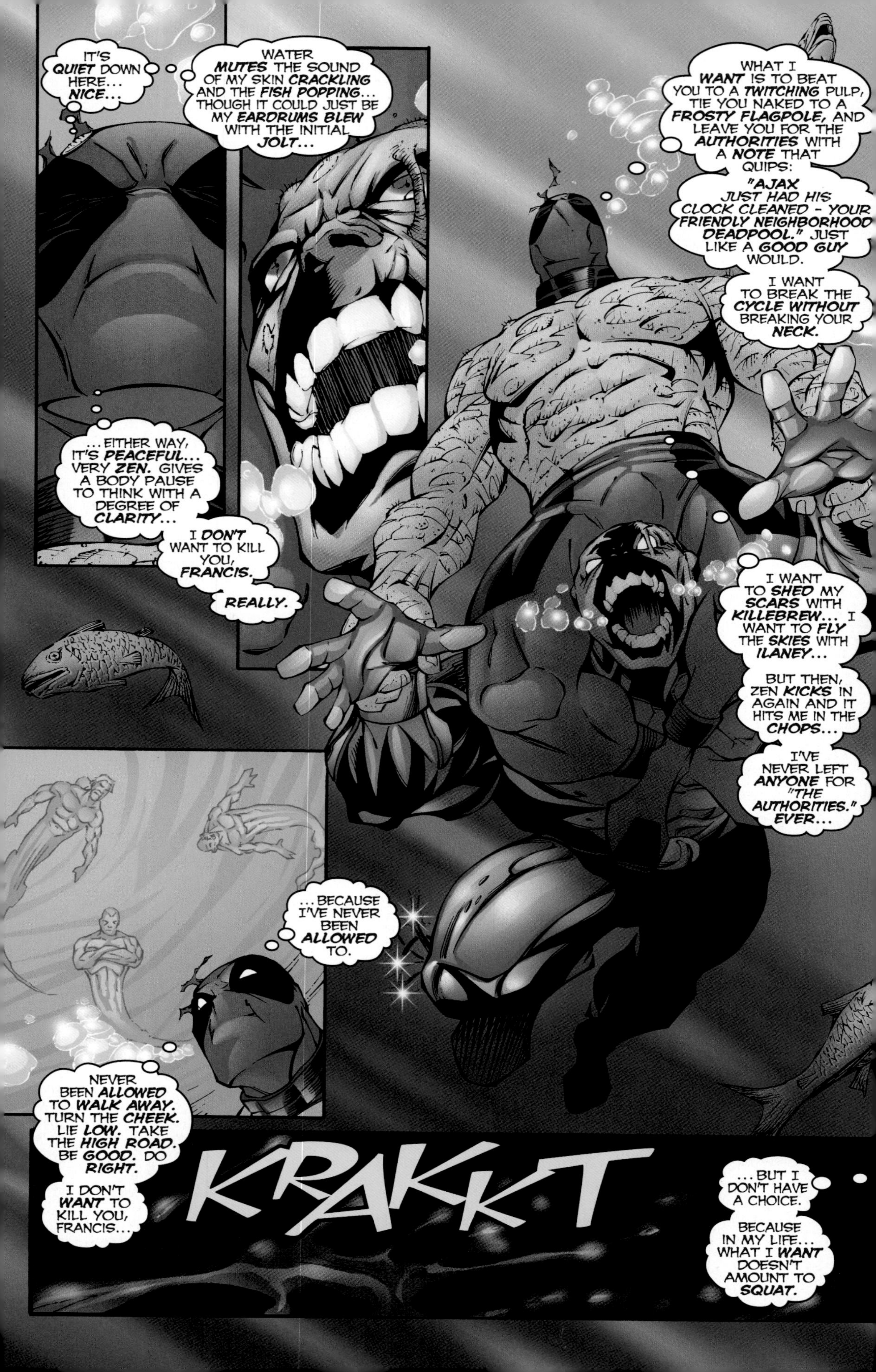

IT'S QUIET DOWN HERE... NICE...
WATER MUTES THE SOUND OF MY SKIN CRACKLING AND THE FISH POPPING... THOUGH IT COULD JUST BE MY EARDRUMS BLEW WITH THE INITIAL JOLT...
...EITHER WAY, IT'S PEACEFUL... VERY ZEN. GIVES A BODY PAUSE TO THINK WITH A DEGREE OF CLARITY...
I DON'T WANT TO KILL YOU, FRANCIS.
REALLY.
WHAT I WANT IS TO BEAT YOU TO A TWITCHING PULP, TIE YOU NAKED TO A FROSTY FLAGPOLE, AND LEAVE YOU FOR THE AUTHORITIES WITH A NOTE THAT QUIPS:
"AJAX JUST HAD HIS CLOCK CLEANED - YOUR FRIENDLY NEIGHBORHOOD DEADPOOL." JUST LIKE A GOOD GUY WOULD.
I WANT TO BREAK THE CYCLE WITHOUT BREAKING YOUR NECK.
I WANT TO SHED MY SCARS WITH KILLEBREW... I WANT TO FLY THE SKIES WITH ILANEY...
BUT THEN, ZEN KICKS IN AGAIN AND IT HITS ME IN THE CHOPS...
I'VE NEVER LEFT ANYONE FOR "THE AUTHORITIES." EVER...
...BECAUSE I'VE NEVER BEEN ALLOWED TO.
NEVER BEEN ALLOWED TO WALK AWAY. TURN THE CHEEK. LIE LOW. TAKE THE HIGH ROAD. BE GOOD. DO RIGHT.
I DON'T WANT TO KILL YOU, FRANCIS...
KRAKKT
...BUT I DON'T HAVE A CHOICE.
BECAUSE IN MY LIFE... WHAT I WANT DOESN'T AMOUNT TO SQUAT.

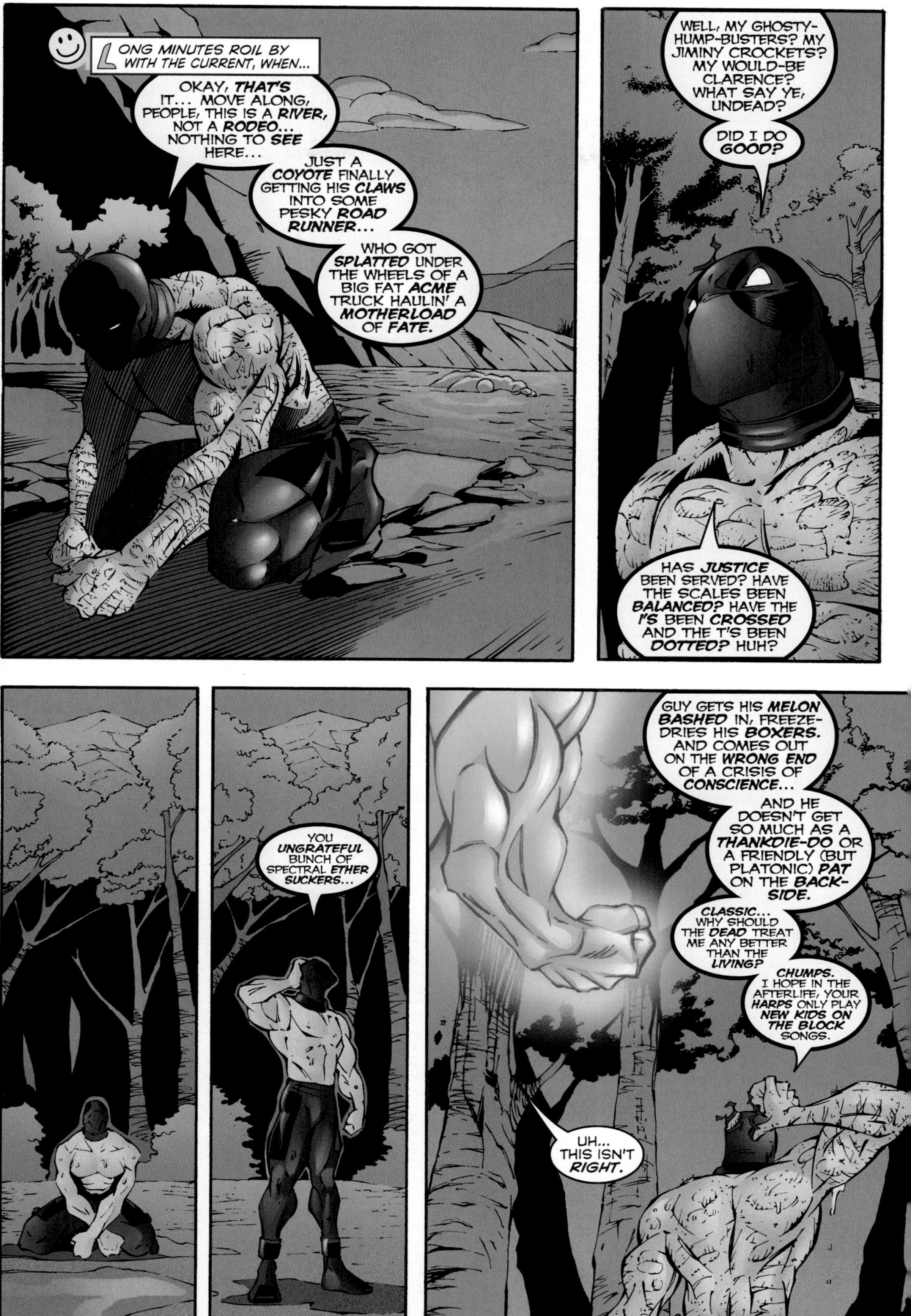
LONG MINUTES ROIL BY WITH THE CURRENT, WHEN...
OKAY, THAT'S IT... MOVE ALONG, PEOPLE, THIS IS A RIVER, NOT A RODEO... NOTHING TO SEE HERE...
JUST A COYOTE FINALLY GETTING HIS CLAWS INTO SOME PESKY ROAD RUNNER...
WHO GOT SPLATTED UNDER THE WHEELS OF A BIG FAT ACME TRUCK HAULIN' A MOTHERLOAD OF FATE.
WELL, MY GHOSTY-HUMP-BUSTERS? MY JIMINY CROCKETS? MY WOULD-BE CLARENCE? WHAT SAY YE, UNDEAD?
DID I DO GOOD?
HAS JUSTICE BEEN SERVED? HAVE THE SCALES BEEN BALANCED? HAVE THE I'S BEEN CROSSED AND THE T'S BEEN DOTTED? HUH?
YOU UNGRATEFUL BUNCH OF SPECTRAL ETHER SUCKERS...
GUY GETS HIS MELON BASHED IN, FREEZE-DRIES HIS BOXERS. AND COMES OUT ON THE WRONG END OF A CRISIS OF CONSCIENCE...
AND HE DOESN'T GET SO MUCH AS A THANKDIE-DO OR A FRIENDLY (BUT PLATONIC) PAT ON THE BACK-SIDE.
CLASSIC... WHY SHOULD THE DEAD TREAT ME ANY BETTER THAN THE LIVING?
CHUMPS. I HOPE IN THE AFTERLIFE, YOUR HARPS ONLY PLAY NEW KIDS ON THE BLOCK SONGS.
UH... THIS ISN'T RIGHT.

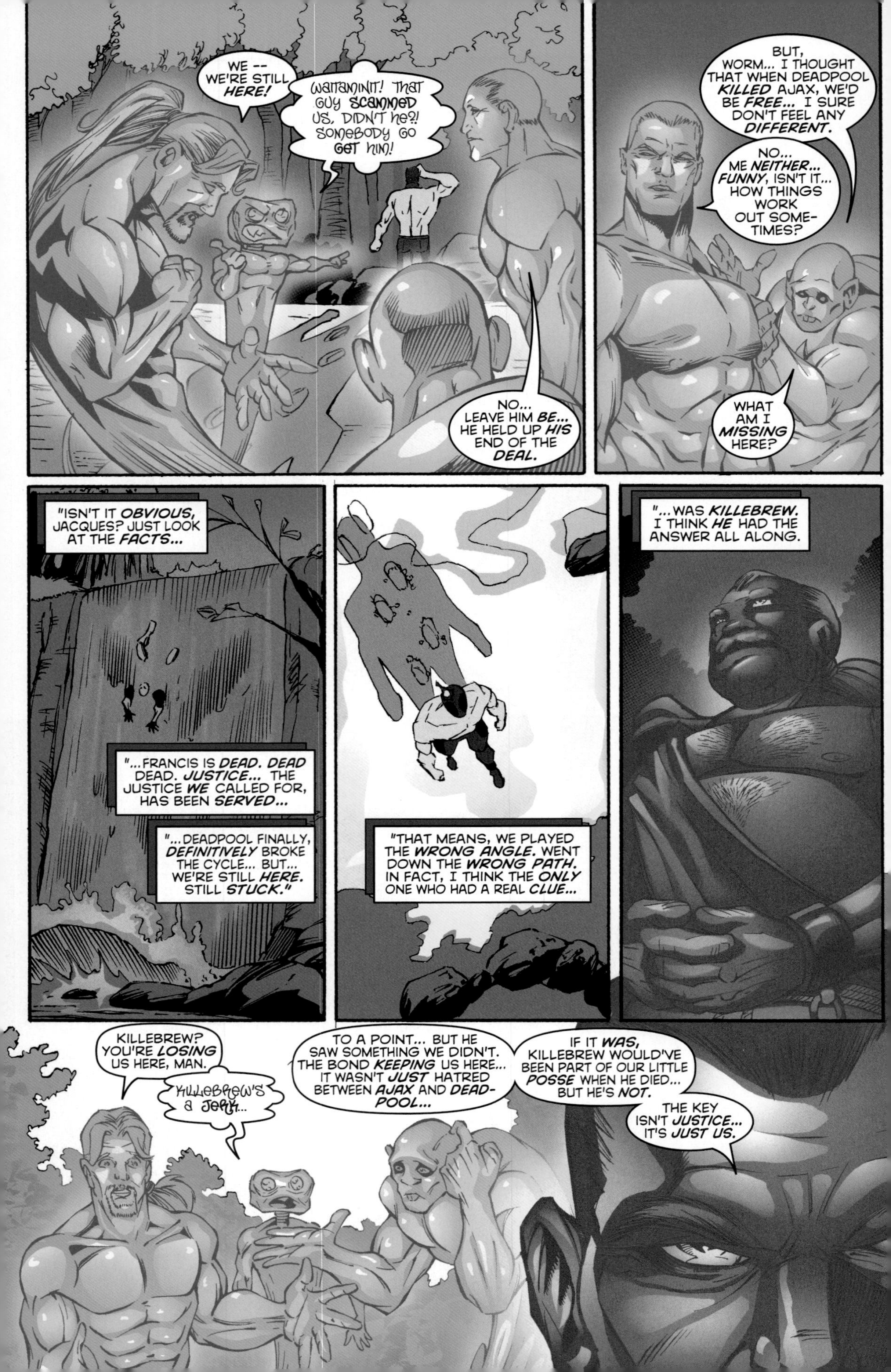
WE -- WE'RE STILL HERE!
WAITAMINIT! THAT GUY SCAMMED US, DIDN'T HE?! SOMEBODY GO GET HIM!
NO... LEAVE HIM BE... HE HELD UP HIS END OF THE DEAL.
BUT, WORM... I THOUGHT THAT WHEN DEADPOOL KILLED AJAX, WE'D BE FREE... I SURE DON'T FEEL ANY DIFFERENT.
NO... ME NEITHER... FUNNY, ISN'T IT... HOW THINGS WORK OUT SOMETIMES?
WHAT AM I MISSING HERE?
"ISN'T IT OBVIOUS, JACQUES? JUST LOOK AT THE FACTS...
"...FRANCIS IS DEAD. DEAD DEAD. JUSTICE... THE JUSTICE WE CALLED FOR, HAS BEEN SERVED...
"...DEADPOOL FINALLY, DEFINITIVELY BROKE THE CYCLE... BUT... WE'RE STILL HERE. STILL STUCK."
"THAT MEANS, WE PLAYED THE WRONG ANGLE. WENT DOWN THE WRONG PATH. IN FACT, I THINK THE ONLY ONE WHO HAD A REAL CLUE...
"...WAS KILLEBREW. I THINK HE HAD THE ANSWER ALL ALONG.
KILLEBREW? YOU'RE LOSING US HERE, MAN.
KILLEBREW'S A JERK...
TO A POINT... BUT HE SAW SOMETHING WE DIDN'T. THE BOND KEEPING US HERE... IT WASN'T JUST HATRED BETWEEN AJAX AND DEADPOOL...
IF IT WAS, KILLEBREW WOULD'VE BEEN PART OF OUR LITTLE POSSE WHEN HE DIED... BUT HE'S NOT.
THE KEY ISN'T JUSTICE... IT'S JUST US.

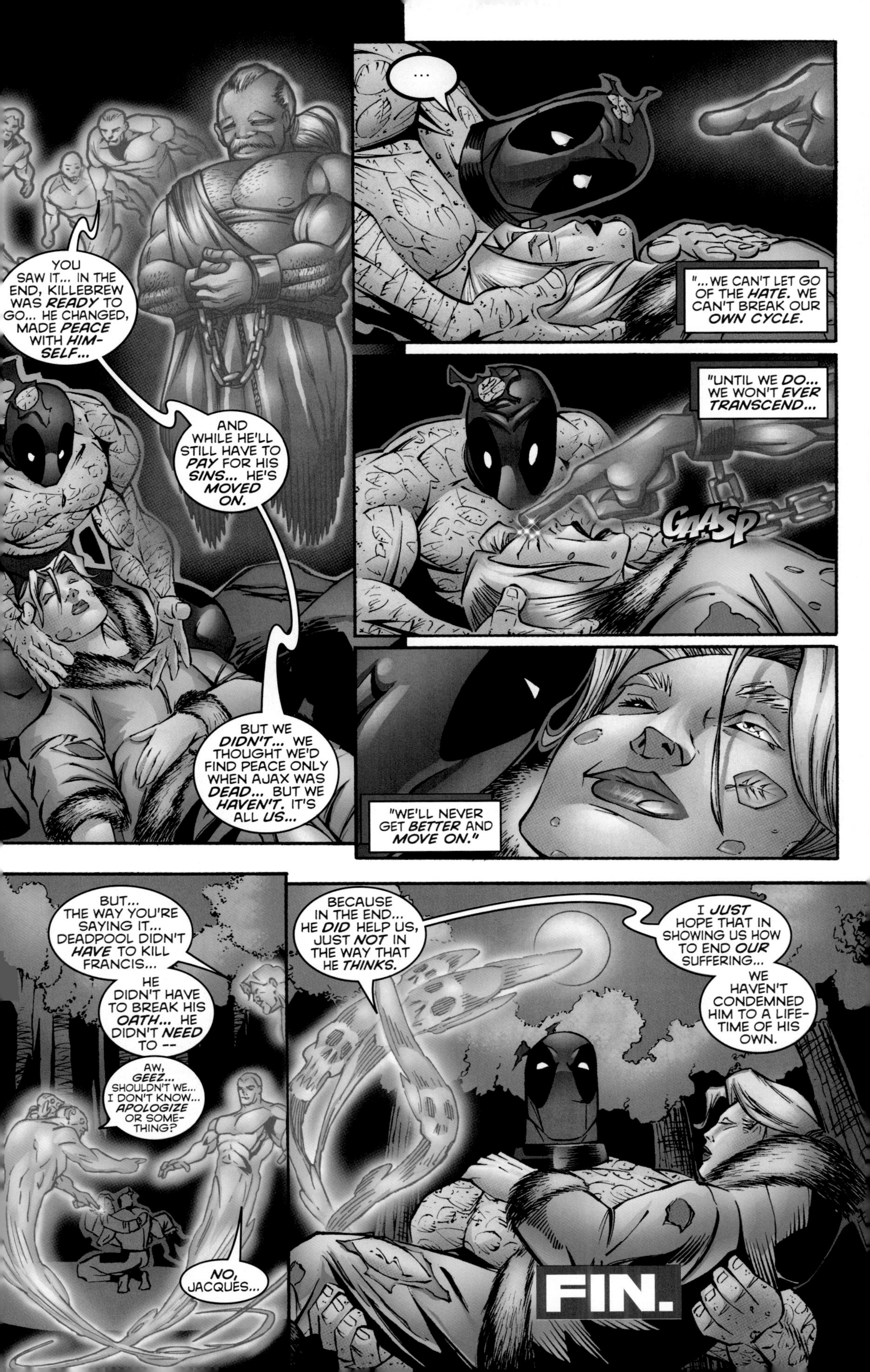

YOU SAW IT... IN THE END, KILLEBREW WAS *READY* TO GO... HE CHANGED, MADE *PEACE* WITH *HIM-SELF*...
AND WHILE HE'LL STILL HAVE TO *PAY* FOR HIS *SINS*... HE'S *MOVED ON.*
BUT WE *DIDN'T*... WE THOUGHT WE'D FIND PEACE ONLY WHEN AJAX WAS *DEAD*... BUT WE *HAVEN'T*. IT'S ALL *US*...
...
"...WE CAN'T LET GO OF THE *HATE*. WE CAN'T BREAK OUR *OWN CYCLE*.
"UNTIL WE *DO*... WE WON'T *EVER TRANSCEND*...
GAASP
"WE'LL NEVER GET *BETTER* AND *MOVE ON*."
BUT... THE WAY YOU'RE SAYING IT... DEADPOOL DIDN'T *HAVE* TO KILL FRANCIS...
HE DIDN'T HAVE TO BREAK HIS *OATH*... HE DIDN'T *NEED* TO --
AW, *GEEZ*... SHOULDN'T WE... I DON'T KNOW... *APOLOGIZE* OR SOME-THING?
NO, JACQUES...
BECAUSE IN THE END... HE *DID* HELP US, JUST *NOT* IN THE WAY THAT HE *THINKS*.
I *JUST* HOPE THAT IN SHOWING US HOW TO END *OUR* SUFFERING...
WE HAVEN'T CONDEMNED HIM TO A LIFE-TIME OF HIS OWN.
FIN.

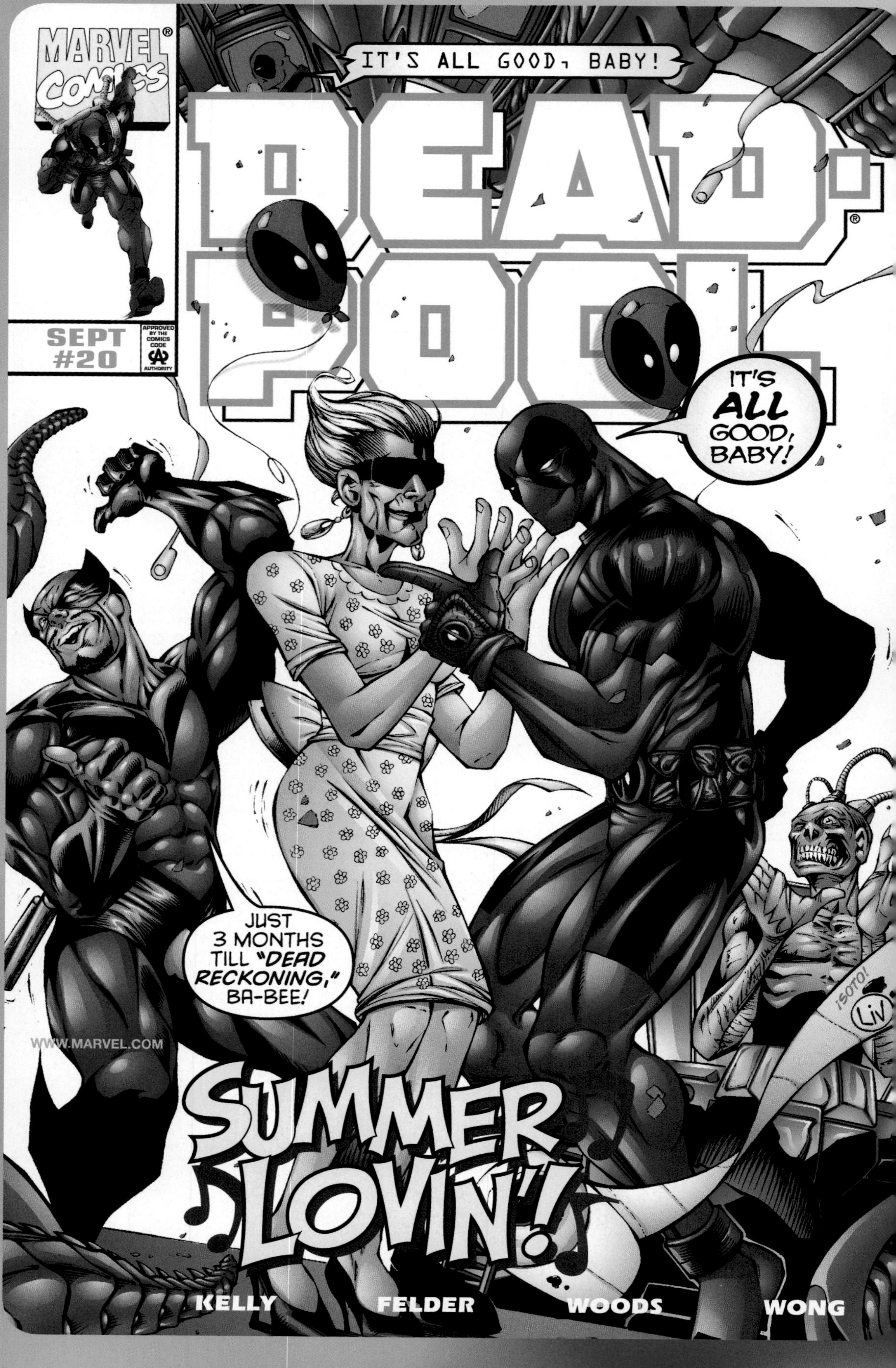
MARVEL® COMICS
IT'S ALL GOOD, BABY!
DEADPOOL®
SEPT #20
APPROVED BY THE COMICS CODE AUTHORITY
IT'S ALL GOOD, BABY!
JUST 3 MONTHS TILL "DEAD RECKONING," BA-BEE!
WWW.MARVEL.COM
¡SOTO!
SUMMER LOVIN'!
KELLY
FELDER
WOODS
WONG

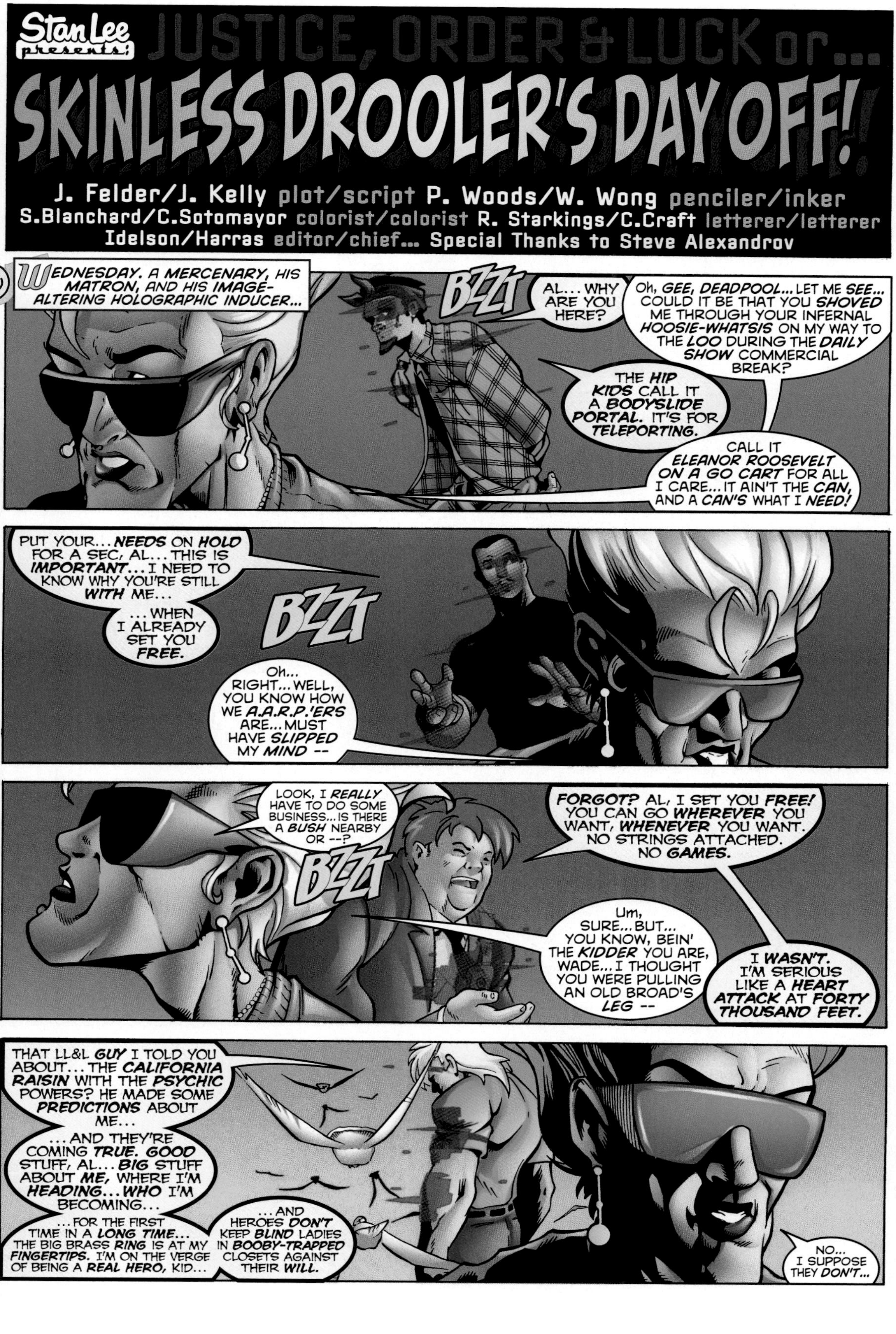
Stan Lee presents:
JUSTICE, ORDER & LUCK or...
SKINLESS DROOLER'S DAY OFF!
J. Felder/J. Kelly plot/script P. Woods/W. Wong penciler/inker
S.Blanchard/C.Sotomayor colorist/colorist R. Starkings/C.Craft letterer/letterer
Idelson/Harras editor/chief... Special Thanks to Steve Alexandrov
WEDNESDAY. A MERCENARY, HIS MATRON, AND HIS IMAGE-ALTERING HOLOGRAPHIC INDUCER...
BZZT
AL... WHY ARE YOU HERE?
Oh, GEE, DEADPOOL... LET ME SEE... COULD IT BE THAT YOU SHOVED ME THROUGH YOUR INFERNAL HOOSIE-WHATSIS ON MY WAY TO THE LOO DURING THE DAILY SHOW COMMERCIAL BREAK?
THE HIP KIDS CALL IT A BODYSLIDE PORTAL. IT'S FOR TELEPORTING.
CALL IT ELEANOR ROOSEVELT ON A GO CART FOR ALL I CARE... IT AIN'T THE CAN, AND A CAN'S WHAT I NEED!
PUT YOUR... NEEDS ON HOLD FOR A SEC, AL... THIS IS IMPORTANT... I NEED TO KNOW WHY YOU'RE STILL WITH ME...
... WHEN I ALREADY SET YOU FREE.
BZZT
Oh... RIGHT... WELL, YOU KNOW HOW WE A.A.R.P.'ERS ARE... MUST HAVE SLIPPED MY MIND --
LOOK, I REALLY HAVE TO DO SOME BUSINESS... IS THERE A BUSH NEARBY OR --?
BZZT
FORGOT? AL, I SET YOU FREE! YOU CAN GO WHEREVER YOU WANT, WHENEVER YOU WANT. NO STRINGS ATTACHED. NO GAMES.
Um, SURE... BUT... YOU KNOW, BEIN' THE KIDDER YOU ARE, WADE... I THOUGHT YOU WERE PULLING AN OLD BROAD'S LEG --
I WASN'T. I'M SERIOUS LIKE A HEART ATTACK AT FORTY THOUSAND FEET.
THAT LL&L GUY I TOLD YOU ABOUT... THE CALIFORNIA RAISIN WITH THE PSYCHIC POWERS? HE MADE SOME PREDICTIONS ABOUT ME...
... AND THEY'RE COMING TRUE. GOOD STUFF, AL... BIG STUFF ABOUT ME, WHERE I'M HEADING... WHO I'M BECOMING...
... FOR THE FIRST TIME IN A LONG TIME... THE BIG BRASS RING IS AT MY FINGERTIPS. I'M ON THE VERGE OF BEING A REAL HERO, KID...
... AND HEROES DON'T KEEP BLIND LADIES IN BOOBY-TRAPPED CLOSETS AGAINST THEIR WILL.
NO... I SUPPOSE THEY DON'T...

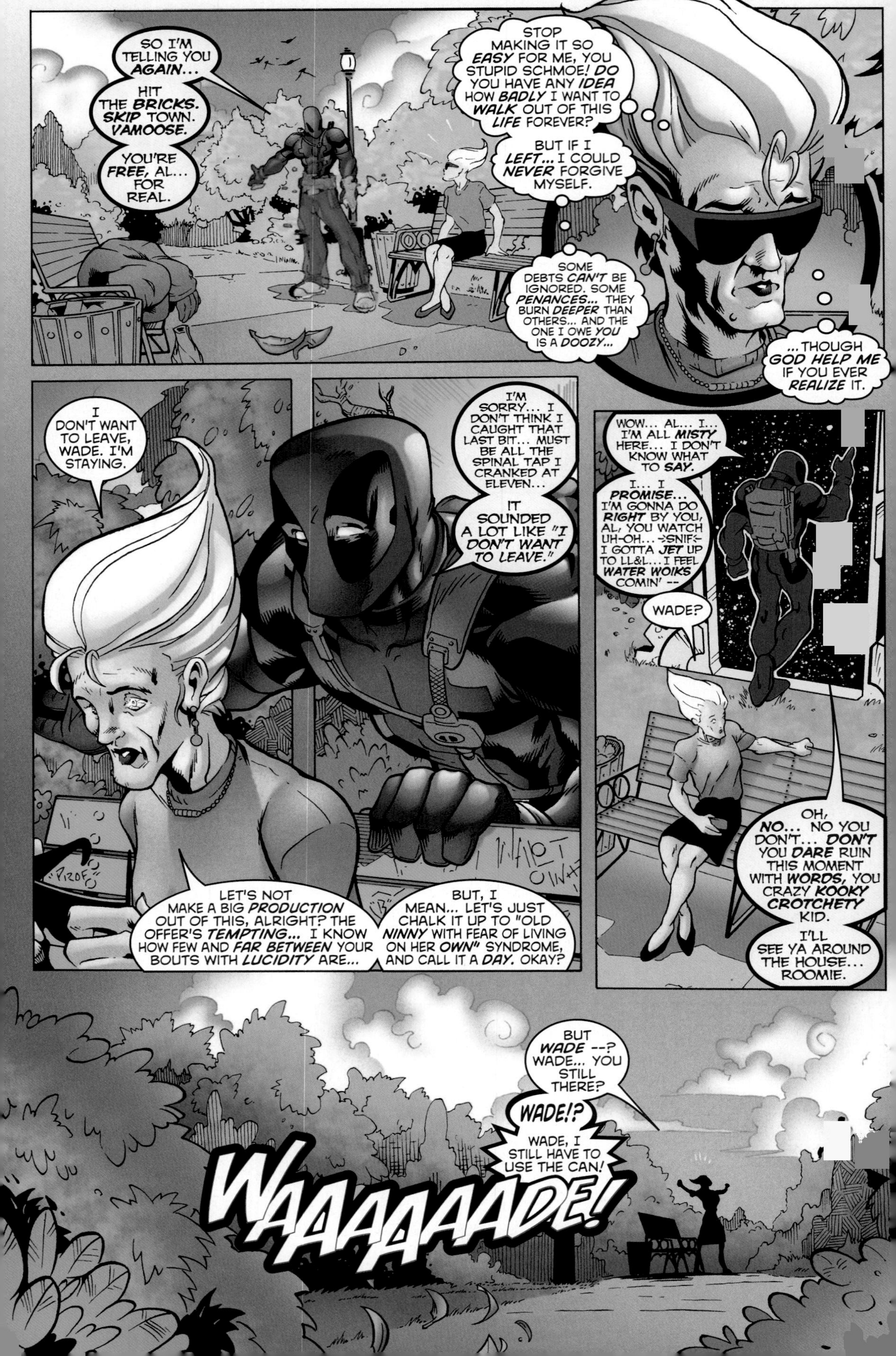

SO I'M TELLING YOU AGAIN...
HIT THE BRICKS. SKIP TOWN. VAMOOSE.
YOU'RE FREE, AL... FOR REAL.
STOP MAKING IT SO EASY FOR ME, YOU STUPID SCHMOE! DO YOU HAVE ANY IDEA HOW BADLY I WANT TO WALK OUT OF THIS LIFE FOREVER?
BUT IF I LEFT... I COULD NEVER FORGIVE MYSELF.
SOME DEBTS CAN'T BE IGNORED. SOME PENANCES... THEY BURN DEEPER THAN OTHERS... AND THE ONE I OWE YOU IS A DOOZY...
...THOUGH GOD HELP ME IF YOU EVER REALIZE IT.
I DON'T WANT TO LEAVE, WADE. I'M STAYING.
I'M SORRY... I DON'T THINK I CAUGHT THAT LAST BIT... MUST BE ALL THE SPINAL TAP I CRANKED AT ELEVEN...
IT SOUNDED A LOT LIKE "I DON'T WANT TO LEAVE."
LET'S NOT MAKE A BIG PRODUCTION OUT OF THIS, ALRIGHT? THE OFFER'S TEMPTING... I KNOW HOW FEW AND FAR BETWEEN YOUR BOUTS WITH LUCIDITY ARE...
BUT, I MEAN... LET'S JUST CHALK IT UP TO "OLD NINNY WITH FEAR OF LIVING ON HER OWN" SYNDROME, AND CALL IT A DAY. OKAY?
WOW... AL... I... I'M ALL MISTY HERE... I DON'T KNOW WHAT TO SAY.
I... I PROMISE... I'M GONNA DO RIGHT BY YOU, AL, YOU WATCH UH-OH... -SNIF- I GOTTA JET UP TO LL&L... I FEEL WATER WOIKS COMIN' --
WADE?
OH, NO... NO YOU DON'T... DON'T YOU DARE RUIN THIS MOMENT WITH WORDS, YOU CRAZY KOOKY CROTCHETY KID.
I'LL SEE YA AROUND THE HOUSE... ROOMIE.
BUT WADE --? WADE... YOU STILL THERE?
WADE!?
WADE, I STILL HAVE TO USE THE CAN!
WAAAAAAADE!

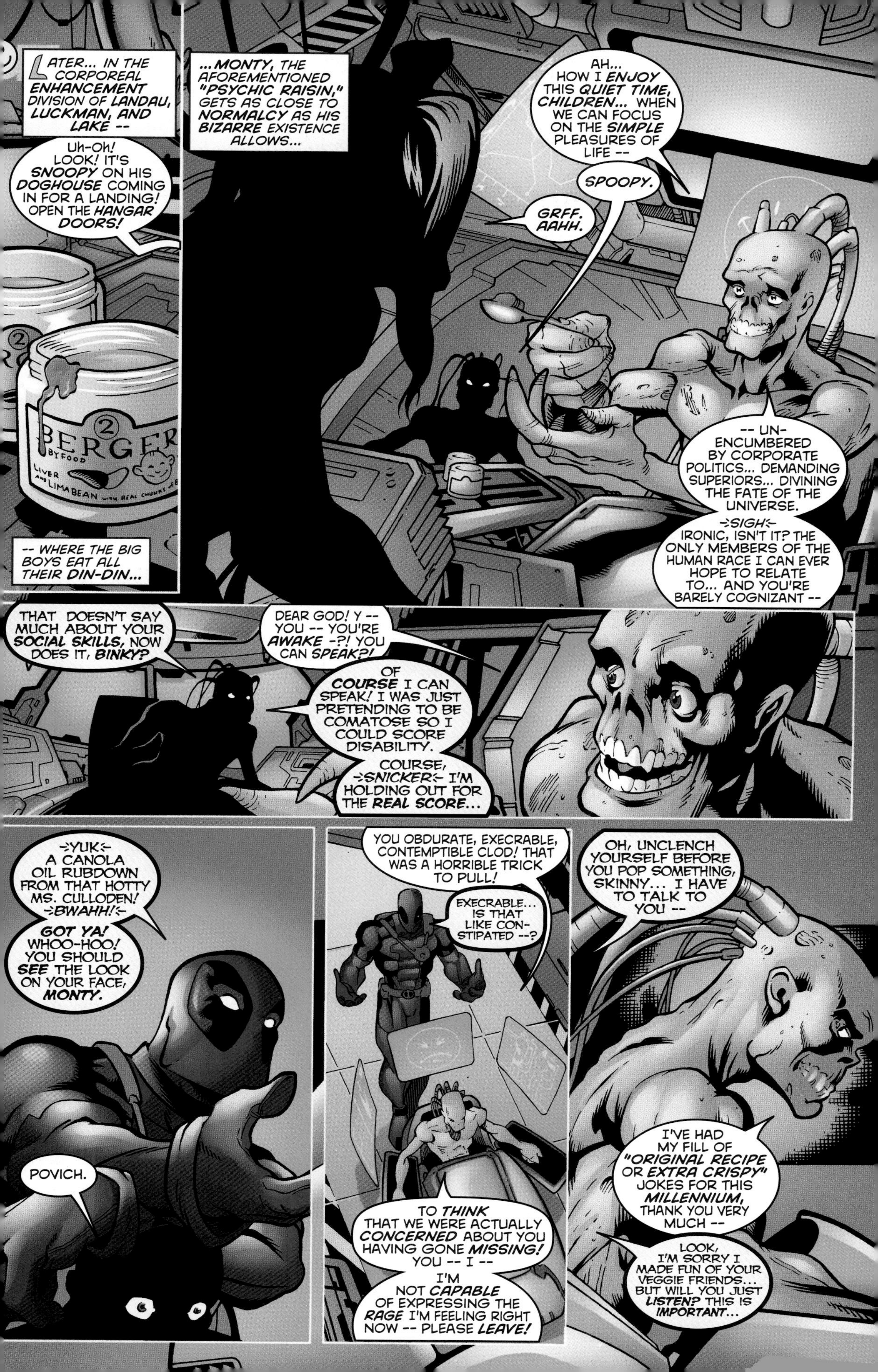
LATER... IN THE CORPOREAL ENHANCEMENT DIVISION OF LANDAU, LUCKMAN, AND LAKE --
UH-OH! LOOK! IT'S SNOOPY ON HIS DOGHOUSE COMING IN FOR A LANDING! OPEN THE HANGAR DOORS!
BERGER BY FOOD LIVER AND LIMA BEAN WITH REAL CHUNKS
-- WHERE THE BIG BOYS EAT ALL THEIR DIN-DIN...
...MONTY, THE AFOREMENTIONED "PSYCHIC RAISIN," GETS AS CLOSE TO NORMALCY AS HIS BIZARRE EXISTENCE ALLOWS...
AH... HOW I ENJOY THIS QUIET TIME, CHILDREN... WHEN WE CAN FOCUS ON THE SIMPLE PLEASURES OF LIFE --
SPOOPY.
GRFF. AAHH.
-- UN-ENCUMBERED BY CORPORATE POLITICS... DEMANDING SUPERIORS... DIVINING THE FATE OF THE UNIVERSE.
-SIGH- IRONIC, ISN'T IT? THE ONLY MEMBERS OF THE HUMAN RACE I CAN EVER HOPE TO RELATE TO... AND YOU'RE BARELY COGNIZANT --
THAT DOESN'T SAY MUCH ABOUT YOUR SOCIAL SKILLS, NOW DOES IT, BINKY?
DEAR GOD! Y -- YOU -- YOU'RE AWAKE -?! YOU CAN SPEAK?!
OF COURSE I CAN SPEAK! I WAS JUST PRETENDING TO BE COMATOSE SO I COULD SCORE DISABILITY.
COURSE, -SNICKER- I'M HOLDING OUT FOR THE REAL SCORE...
-YUK- A CANOLA OIL RUBDOWN FROM THAT HOTTY MS. CULLODEN! -BWAHH!-
GOT YA! WHOO-HOO! YOU SHOULD SEE THE LOOK ON YOUR FACE, MONTY.
POVICH.
YOU OBDURATE, EXECRABLE, CONTEMPTIBLE CLOD! THAT WAS A HORRIBLE TRICK TO PULL!
EXECRABLE... IS THAT LIKE CON-STIPATED --?
TO THINK THAT WE WERE ACTUALLY CONCERNED ABOUT YOU HAVING GONE MISSING! YOU -- I --
I'M NOT CAPABLE OF EXPRESSING THE RAGE I'M FEELING RIGHT NOW -- PLEASE LEAVE!
OH, UNCLENCH YOURSELF BEFORE YOU POP SOMETHING, SKINNY... I HAVE TO TALK TO YOU --
I'VE HAD MY FILL OF "ORIGINAL RECIPE OR EXTRA CRISPY" JOKES FOR THIS MILLENNIUM, THANK YOU VERY MUCH --
LOOK, I'M SORRY I MADE FUN OF YOUR VEGGIE FRIENDS... BUT WILL YOU JUST LISTEN? THIS IS IMPORTANT...

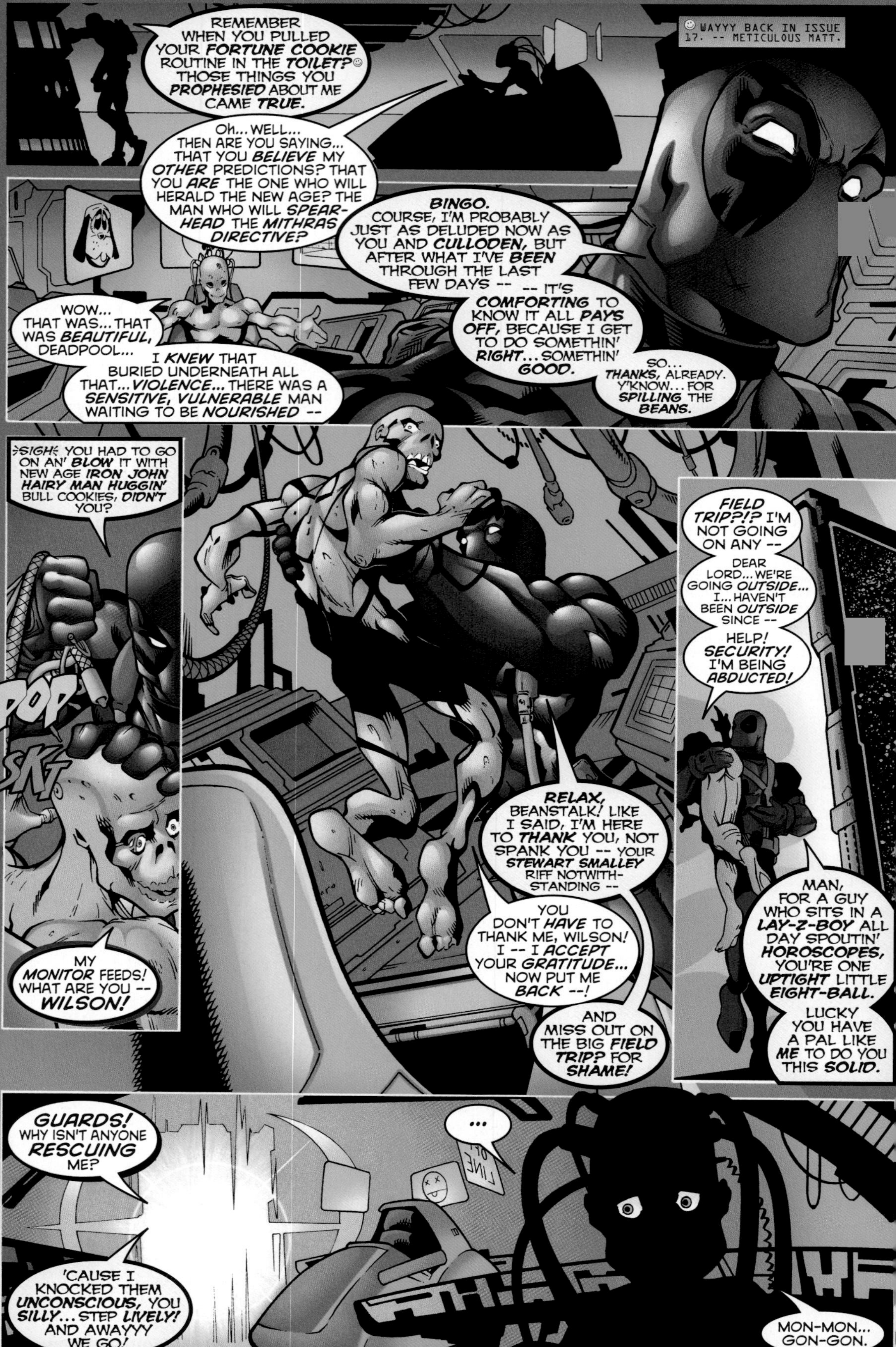

REMEMBER WHEN YOU PULLED YOUR FORTUNE COOKIE ROUTINE IN THE TOILET? ☺ THOSE THINGS YOU PROPHESIED ABOUT ME CAME TRUE.
☺ WAYYY BACK IN ISSUE 17. -- METICULOUS MATT.
Oh... WELL... THEN ARE YOU SAYING... THAT YOU BELIEVE MY OTHER PREDICTIONS? THAT YOU ARE THE ONE WHO WILL HERALD THE NEW AGE? THE MAN WHO WILL SPEAR-HEAD THE MITHRAS DIRECTIVE?
BINGO. COURSE, I'M PROBABLY JUST AS DELUDED NOW AS YOU AND CULLODEN, BUT AFTER WHAT I'VE BEEN THROUGH THE LAST FEW DAYS --
-- IT'S COMFORTING TO KNOW IT ALL PAYS OFF, BECAUSE I GET TO DO SOMETHIN' RIGHT... SOMETHIN' GOOD.
WOW... THAT WAS... THAT WAS BEAUTIFUL, DEADPOOL...
I KNEW THAT BURIED UNDERNEATH ALL THAT... VIOLENCE... THERE WAS A SENSITIVE, VULNERABLE MAN WAITING TO BE NOURISHED --
SO... THANKS, ALREADY. Y'KNOW... FOR SPILLING THE BEANS.
SIGH YOU HAD TO GO ON AN' BLOW IT WITH NEW AGE IRON JOHN HAIRY MAN HUGGIN' BULL COOKIES, DIDN'T YOU?
POP
SKT
MY MONITOR FEEDS! WHAT ARE YOU -- WILSON!
RELAX, BEANSTALK! LIKE I SAID, I'M HERE TO THANK YOU, NOT SPANK YOU -- YOUR STEWART SMALLEY RIFF NOTWITH-STANDING --
YOU DON'T HAVE TO THANK ME, WILSON! I -- I ACCEPT YOUR GRATITUDE... NOW PUT ME BACK --!
AND MISS OUT ON THE BIG FIELD TRIP? FOR SHAME!
FIELD TRIP?!? I'M NOT GOING ON ANY --
DEAR LORD... WE'RE GOING OUTSIDE... I... HAVEN'T BEEN OUTSIDE SINCE --
HELP! SECURITY! I'M BEING ABDUCTED!
MAN, FOR A GUY WHO SITS IN A LAY-Z-BOY ALL DAY SPOUTIN' HOROSCOPES, YOU'RE ONE UPTIGHT LITTLE EIGHT-BALL.
LUCKY YOU HAVE A PAL LIKE ME TO DO YOU THIS SOLID.
GUARDS! WHY ISN'T ANYONE RESCUING ME?
'CAUSE I KNOCKED THEM UNCONSCIOUS, YOU SILLY... STEP LIVELY! AND AWAYYY WE GO!
...
OFF LINE
MON-MON... GON-GON.

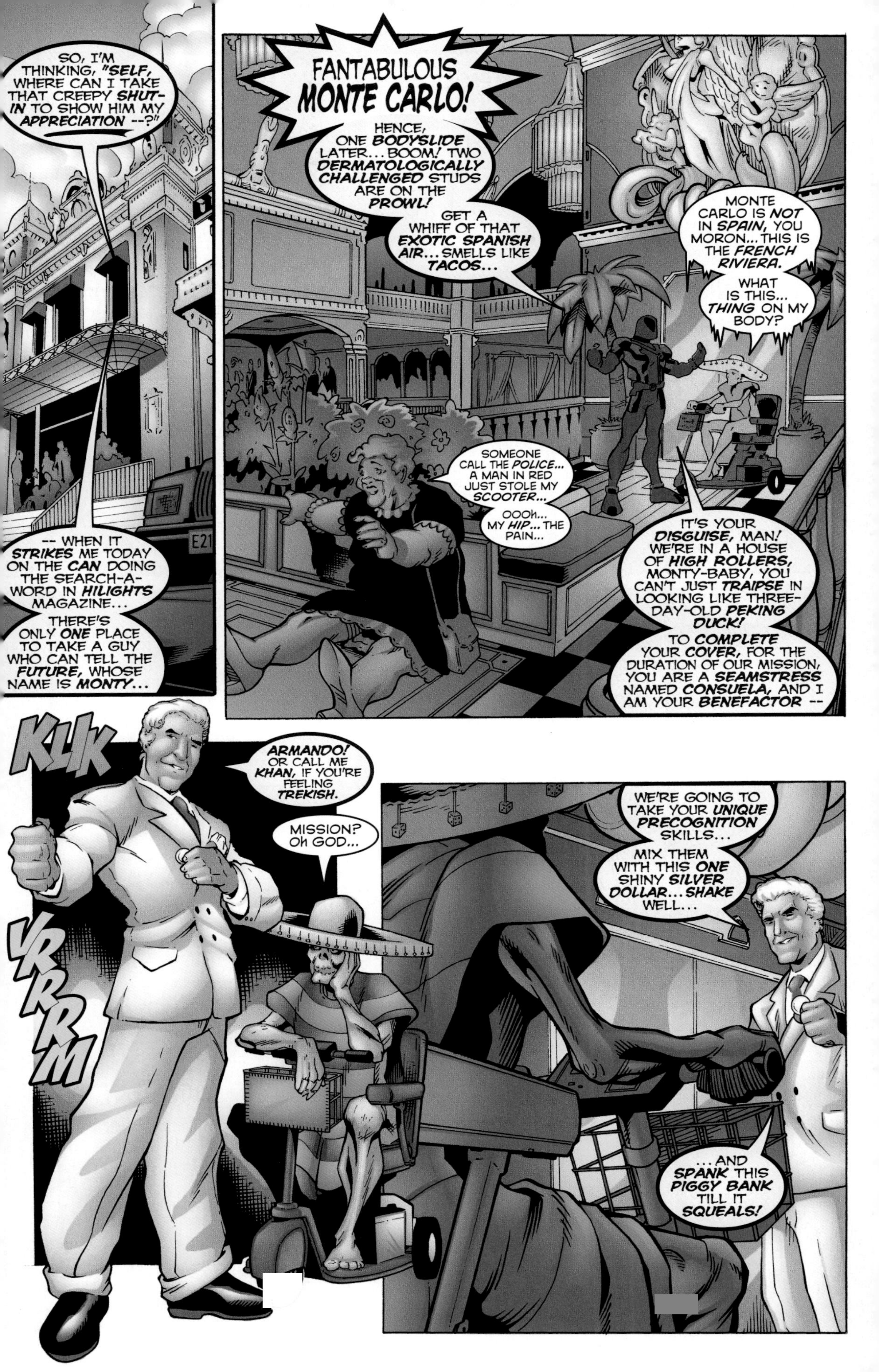
SO, I'M THINKING, "SELF, WHERE CAN I TAKE THAT CREEPY SHUT-IN TO SHOW HIM MY APPRECIATION --?"
-- WHEN IT STRIKES ME TODAY ON THE CAN DOING THE SEARCH-A-WORD IN HILIGHTS MAGAZINE...
THERE'S ONLY ONE PLACE TO TAKE A GUY WHO CAN TELL THE FUTURE, WHOSE NAME IS MONTY...
FANTABULOUS MONTE CARLO!
HENCE, ONE BODYSLIDE LATER... BOOM! TWO DERMATOLOGICALLY CHALLENGED STUDS ARE ON THE PROWL!
GET A WHIFF OF THAT EXOTIC SPANISH AIR... SMELLS LIKE TACOS...
MONTE CARLO IS NOT IN SPAIN, YOU MORON... THIS IS THE FRENCH RIVIERA.
WHAT IS THIS... THING ON MY BODY?
SOMEONE CALL THE POLICE... A MAN IN RED JUST STOLE MY SCOOTER...
OOOh... MY HIP... THE PAIN...
IT'S YOUR DISGUISE, MAN! WE'RE IN A HOUSE OF HIGH ROLLERS, MONTY-BABY, YOU CAN'T JUST TRAIPSE IN LOOKING LIKE THREE-DAY-OLD PEKING DUCK!
TO COMPLETE YOUR COVER, FOR THE DURATION OF OUR MISSION, YOU ARE A SEAMSTRESS NAMED CONSUELA, AND I AM YOUR BENEFACTOR --
KLIK
ARMANDO! OR CALL ME KHAN, IF YOU'RE FEELING TREKISH.
MISSION? Oh GOD...
VRRRM
WE'RE GOING TO TAKE YOUR UNIQUE PRECOGNITION SKILLS...
MIX THEM WITH THIS ONE SHINY SILVER DOLLAR... SHAKE WELL...
...AND SPANK THIS PIGGY BANK TILL IT SQUEALS!

MOMENTS LATER... ...AND *THAT'S* HOW I PICK-POCKETED *THIS* BABY OFF OF A SMELLY LITTLE *RUNT* NAMED *LOGAN*.

IT'S BROUGHT ME *LUCK*... AND THE *ADMIRATION* OF *POUTY LIPPED CASHIERS* EVER SINCE.

FASCINATING.

YES, I *AM*. SO, SHALL WE SHAG *NOW* OR SHAG *LATER*?

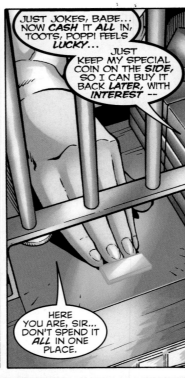

JUST JOKES, BABE... NOW *CASH* IT *ALL* IN, TOOTS, POPPI FEELS *LUCKY*...

JUST KEEP MY SPECIAL COIN ON THE *SIDE*, SO I CAN BUY IT BACK *LATER*, WITH *INTEREST* --

HERE YOU ARE, SIR... DON'T SPEND IT *ALL* IN ONE PLACE.

THAT'S IT?! IT... IT'S SO... *SMALL!* WHAT AM I SUPPOSED TO DO WITH *THIS?!*

I HAVE A FEW *CHOICE* SUGGESTIONS, SIR... BUT I'LL LET *YOU* FIGURE IT OUT...

I'D IMAGINE YOU HAVE *EXPERIENCE* WITH *SMALL THINGS*. GOOD DAY.

ALRIGHT, *CONSUELA*... YOU'RE ON.

TIME TO TAKE THOSE *PRE-COG* POWERS OF YOURS AND TURN *THIS* HUMBLE LITTLE CHIP INTO A FAT *DONATION* TO THE *WADE WILSON POCKET-FILLING FUND!*

Mr. *WILSON!* I AM A *FINELY CALIBRATED PRECOGNITIAN!*

WHAT YOU ARE SUGGESTING IS A *PETTY* AND *INSULTING* ABUSE OF MY GIFTS! I *UTTERLY* REFUSE!

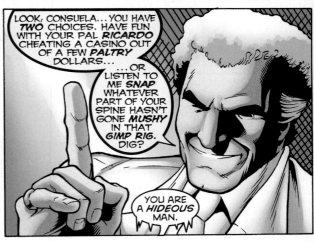

LOOK, CONSUELA... YOU HAVE *TWO* CHOICES. HAVE FUN WITH YOUR PAL *RICARDO* CHEATING A CASINO OUT OF A FEW *PALTRY* DOLLARS...

...OR LISTEN TO ME *SNAP* WHATEVER PART OF YOUR SPINE HASN'T GONE *MUSHY* IN THAT *GIMP RIG*. DIG?

YOU ARE A *HIDEOUS* MAN.

THREE HOURS LATER.

<WHAT'S GOING ON OVER *THERE?*>

<OH, IT'S THAT *OBNOXIOUS LOTHARIO* AGAIN! HE'S *BROKEN THE BANK* AT ALMOST *EVERY* TABLE. I'VE NEVER *SEEN* SUCH LUCK!>

COME ON, BABY! PAPPA NEEDS A SHINY NEW *STOCK* ON HIS *AK-47!*

DING DING DING

<BETWEEN HIM AND *MONSIEUR GEORGES*, WE'LL BE LUCKY TO MAKE A *PROFIT* FOR THE *WEEK!*>

TRANSLATED FROM FRENCH. -- MATT

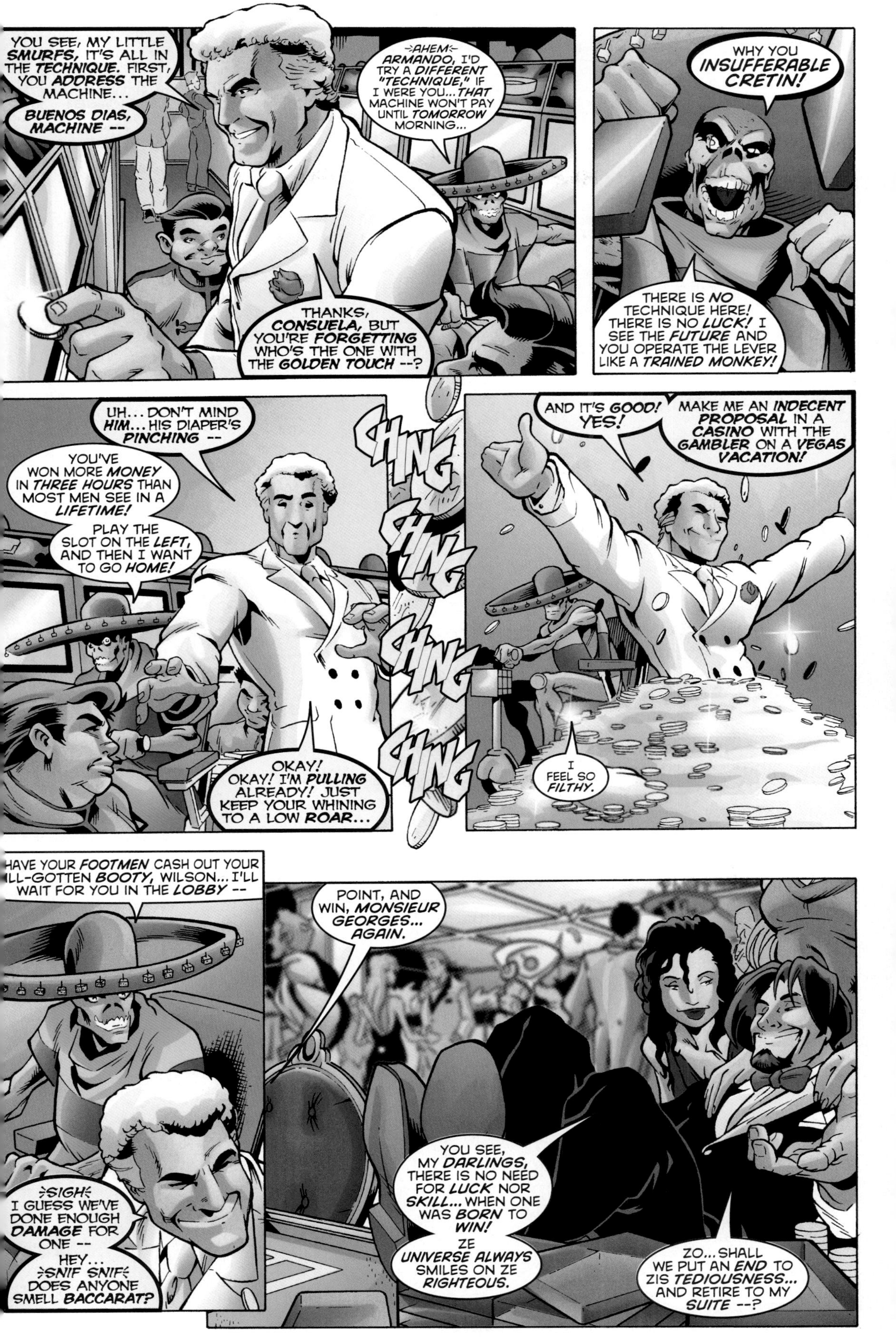
YOU SEE, MY LITTLE SMURFS, IT'S ALL IN THE TECHNIQUE. FIRST, YOU ADDRESS THE MACHINE...
BUENOS DIAS, MACHINE --
>AHEM< ARMANDO, I'D TRY A DIFFERENT "TECHNIQUE," IF I WERE YOU... THAT MACHINE WON'T PAY UNTIL TOMORROW MORNING...
THANKS, CONSUELA, BUT YOU'RE FORGETTING WHO'S THE ONE WITH THE GOLDEN TOUCH --?
WHY YOU INSUFFERABLE CRETIN!
THERE IS NO TECHNIQUE HERE! THERE IS NO LUCK! I SEE THE FUTURE AND YOU OPERATE THE LEVER LIKE A TRAINED MONKEY!
UH... DON'T MIND HIM... HIS DIAPER'S PINCHING --
YOU'VE WON MORE MONEY IN THREE HOURS THAN MOST MEN SEE IN A LIFETIME!
PLAY THE SLOT ON THE LEFT, AND THEN I WANT TO GO HOME!
OKAY! OKAY! I'M PULLING ALREADY! JUST KEEP YOUR WHINING TO A LOW ROAR...
CHING
CHING
CHING
CHING
AND IT'S GOOD! YES!
MAKE ME AN INDECENT PROPOSAL IN A CASINO WITH THE GAMBLER ON A VEGAS VACATION!
I FEEL SO FILTHY.
HAVE YOUR FOOTMEN CASH OUT YOUR ILL-GOTTEN BOOTY, WILSON... I'LL WAIT FOR YOU IN THE LOBBY --
>SIGH< I GUESS WE'VE DONE ENOUGH DAMAGE FOR ONE --
HEY... >SNIF SNIF< DOES ANYONE SMELL BACCARAT?
POINT, AND WIN, MONSIEUR GEORGES... AGAIN.
YOU SEE, MY DARLINGS, THERE IS NO NEED FOR LUCK NOR SKILL... WHEN ONE WAS BORN TO WIN!
ZE UNIVERSE ALWAYS SMILES ON ZE RIGHTEOUS.
ZO... SHALL WE PUT AN END TO ZIS TEDIOUSNESS... AND RETIRE TO MY SUITE --?

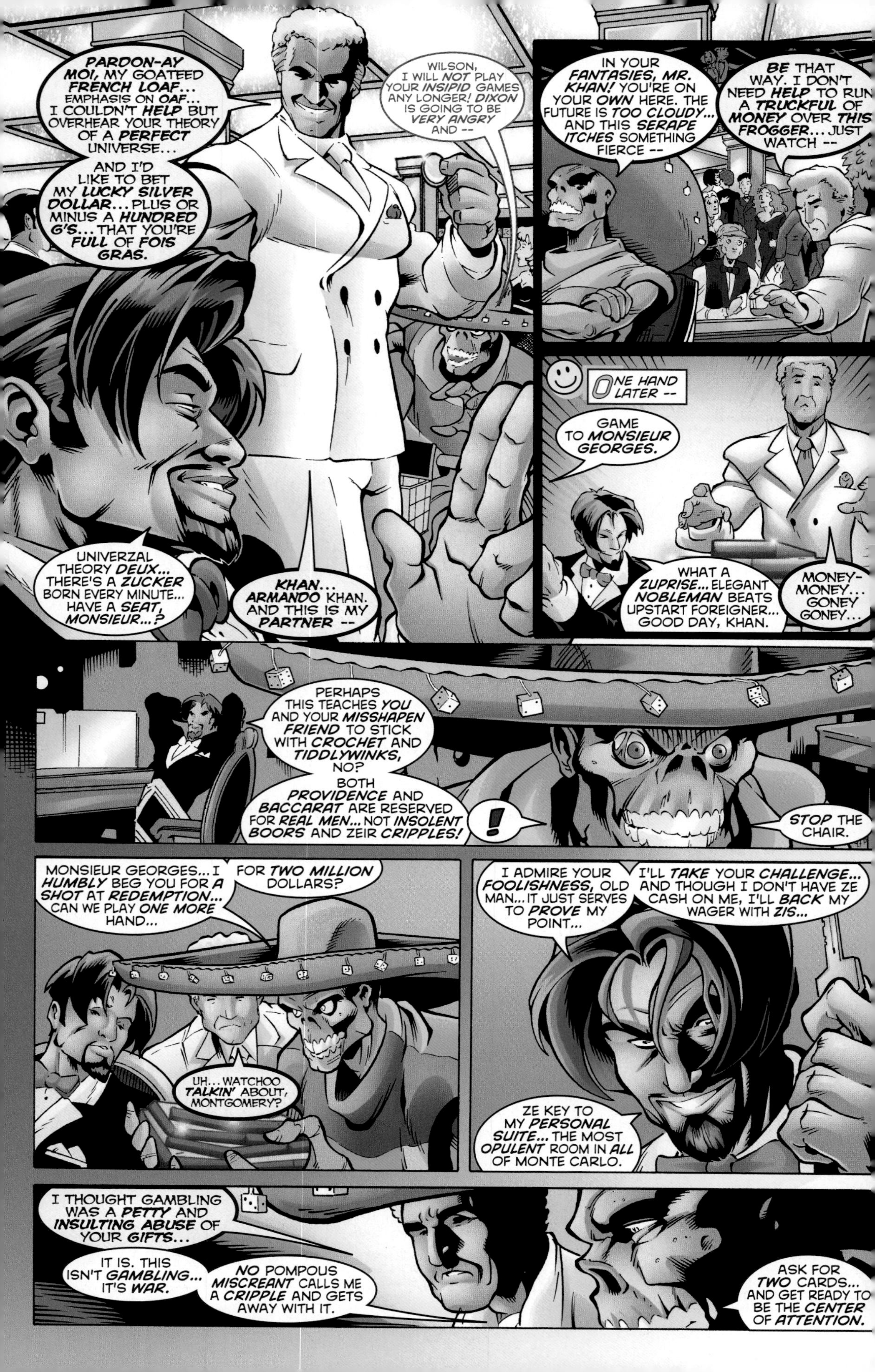
PARDON-AY MOI, MY GOATEED FRENCH LOAF... EMPHASIS ON OAF... I COULDN'T HELP BUT OVERHEAR YOUR THEORY OF A PERFECT UNIVERSE...
AND I'D LIKE TO BET MY LUCKY SILVER DOLLAR... PLUS OR MINUS A HUNDRED G'S... THAT YOU'RE FULL OF FOIS GRAS.
WILSON, I WILL NOT PLAY YOUR INSIPID GAMES ANY LONGER! DIXON IS GOING TO BE VERY ANGRY AND --
UNIVERZAL THEORY DEUX... THERE'S A ZUCKER BORN EVERY MINUTE... HAVE A SEAT, MONSIEUR...?
KHAN... ARMANDO KHAN. AND THIS IS MY PARTNER --
IN YOUR FANTASIES, MR. KHAN! YOU'RE ON YOUR OWN HERE. THE FUTURE IS TOO CLOUDY... AND THIS SERAPE ITCHES SOMETHING FIERCE --
BE THAT WAY. I DON'T NEED HELP TO RUN A TRUCKFUL OF MONEY OVER THIS FROGGER... JUST WATCH --
ONE HAND LATER --
GAME TO MONSIEUR GEORGES.
WHAT A ZUPRISE... ELEGANT NOBLEMAN BEATS UPSTART FOREIGNER... GOOD DAY, KHAN.
MONEY-MONEY... GONEY GONEY...
PERHAPS THIS TEACHES YOU AND YOUR MISSHAPEN FRIEND TO STICK WITH CROCHET AND TIDDLYWINKS, NO?
BOTH PROVIDENCE AND BACCARAT ARE RESERVED FOR REAL MEN... NOT INSOLENT BOORS AND ZEIR CRIPPLES!
!
STOP THE CHAIR.
MONSIEUR GEORGES... I HUMBLY BEG YOU FOR A SHOT AT REDEMPTION... CAN WE PLAY ONE MORE HAND...
FOR TWO MILLION DOLLARS?
UH... WATCHOO TALKIN' ABOUT, MONTGOMERY?
I ADMIRE YOUR FOOLISHNESS, OLD MAN... IT JUST SERVES TO PROVE MY POINT...
I'LL TAKE YOUR CHALLENGE... AND THOUGH I DON'T HAVE ZE CASH ON ME, I'LL BACK MY WAGER WITH ZIS...
ZE KEY TO MY PERSONAL SUITE... THE MOST OPULENT ROOM IN ALL OF MONTE CARLO.
I THOUGHT GAMBLING WAS A PETTY AND INSULTING ABUSE OF YOUR GIFTS...
IT IS. THIS ISN'T GAMBLING... IT'S WAR.
NO POMPOUS MISCREANT CALLS ME A CRIPPLE AND GETS AWAY WITH IT.
ASK FOR TWO CARDS... AND GET READY TO BE THE CENTER OF ATTENTION.

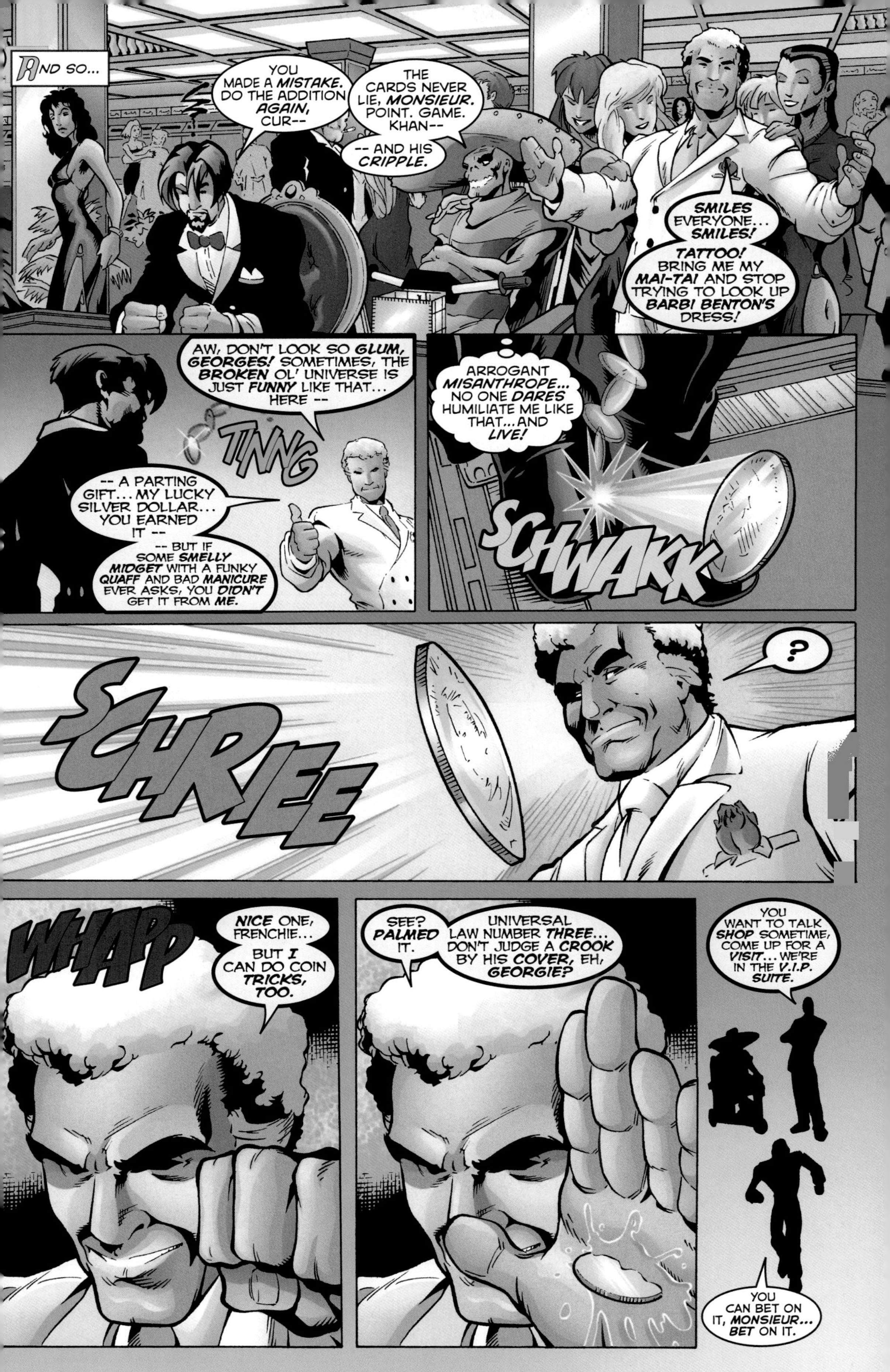
AND SO...
YOU MADE A MISTAKE. DO THE ADDITION AGAIN, CUR--
THE CARDS NEVER LIE, MONSIEUR. POINT. GAME. KHAN--
-- AND HIS CRIPPLE.
SMILES EVERYONE... SMILES!
TATTOO! BRING ME MY MAI-TAI AND STOP TRYING TO LOOK UP BARBI BENTON'S DRESS!
AW, DON'T LOOK SO GLUM, GEORGES! SOMETIMES, THE BROKEN OL' UNIVERSE IS JUST FUNNY LIKE THAT... HERE --
TINNG
-- A PARTING GIFT... MY LUCKY SILVER DOLLAR... YOU EARNED IT --
-- BUT IF SOME SMELLY MIDGET WITH A FUNKY QUAFF AND BAD MANICURE EVER ASKS, YOU DIDN'T GET IT FROM ME.
ARROGANT MISANTHROPE... NO ONE DARES HUMILIATE ME LIKE THAT...AND LIVE!
SCHWAKK
SCHRIEE
?
WHAPP
NICE ONE, FRENCHIE...
BUT I CAN DO COIN TRICKS, TOO.
SEE? PALMED IT.
UNIVERSAL LAW NUMBER THREE... DON'T JUDGE A CROOK BY HIS COVER, EH, GEORGIE?
YOU WANT TO TALK SHOP SOMETIME, COME UP FOR A VISIT... WE'RE IN THE V.I.P. SUITE.
YOU CAN BET ON IT, MONSIEUR... BET ON IT.

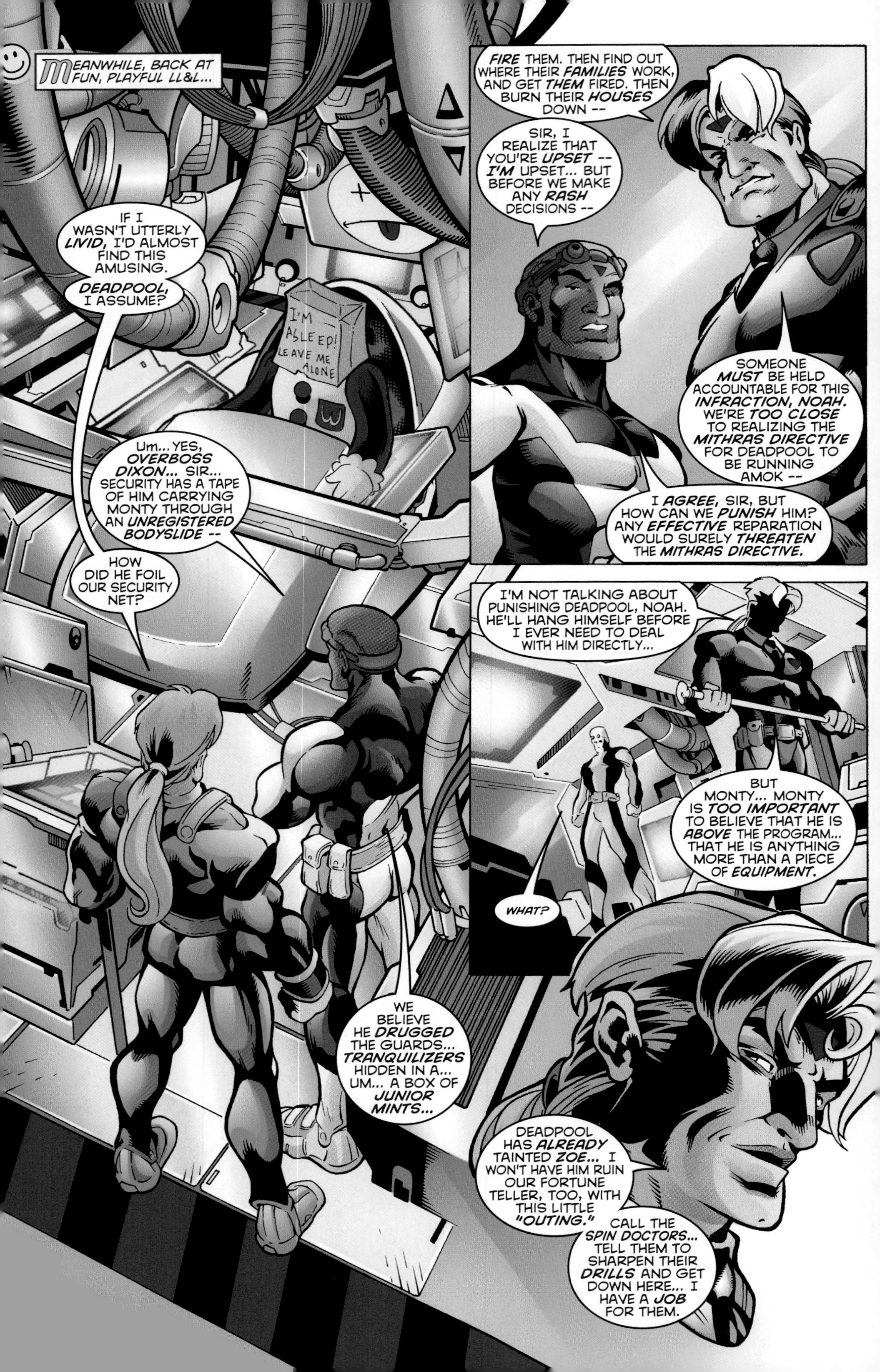
MEANWHILE, BACK AT FUN, PLAYFUL LL&L...
IF I WASN'T UTTERLY LIVID, I'D ALMOST FIND THIS AMUSING.
DEADPOOL, I ASSUME?
I'M ASLEEP! LEAVE ME ALONE
Um... YES, OVERBOSS DIXON... SIR... SECURITY HAS A TAPE OF HIM CARRYING MONTY THROUGH AN UNREGISTERED BODYSLIDE --
HOW DID HE FOIL OUR SECURITY NET?
WE BELIEVE HE DRUGGED THE GUARDS... TRANQUILIZERS HIDDEN IN A... UM... A BOX OF JUNIOR MINTS...
FIRE THEM. THEN FIND OUT WHERE THEIR FAMILIES WORK, AND GET THEM FIRED. THEN BURN THEIR HOUSES DOWN --
SIR, I REALIZE THAT YOU'RE UPSET -- I'M UPSET... BUT BEFORE WE MAKE ANY RASH DECISIONS --
SOMEONE MUST BE HELD ACCOUNTABLE FOR THIS INFRACTION, NOAH. WE'RE TOO CLOSE TO REALIZING THE MITHRAS DIRECTIVE FOR DEADPOOL TO BE RUNNING AMOK --
I AGREE, SIR, BUT HOW CAN WE PUNISH HIM? ANY EFFECTIVE REPARATION WOULD SURELY THREATEN THE MITHRAS DIRECTIVE.
I'M NOT TALKING ABOUT PUNISHING DEADPOOL, NOAH. HE'LL HANG HIMSELF BEFORE I EVER NEED TO DEAL WITH HIM DIRECTLY...
BUT MONTY... MONTY IS TOO IMPORTANT TO BELIEVE THAT HE IS ABOVE THE PROGRAM... THAT HE IS ANYTHING MORE THAN A PIECE OF EQUIPMENT.
WHAT?
DEADPOOL HAS ALREADY TAINTED ZOE... I WON'T HAVE HIM RUIN OUR FORTUNE TELLER, TOO, WITH THIS LITTLE "OUTING."
CALL THE SPIN DOCTORS... TELL THEM TO SHARPEN THEIR DRILLS AND GET DOWN HERE... I HAVE A JOB FOR THEM.

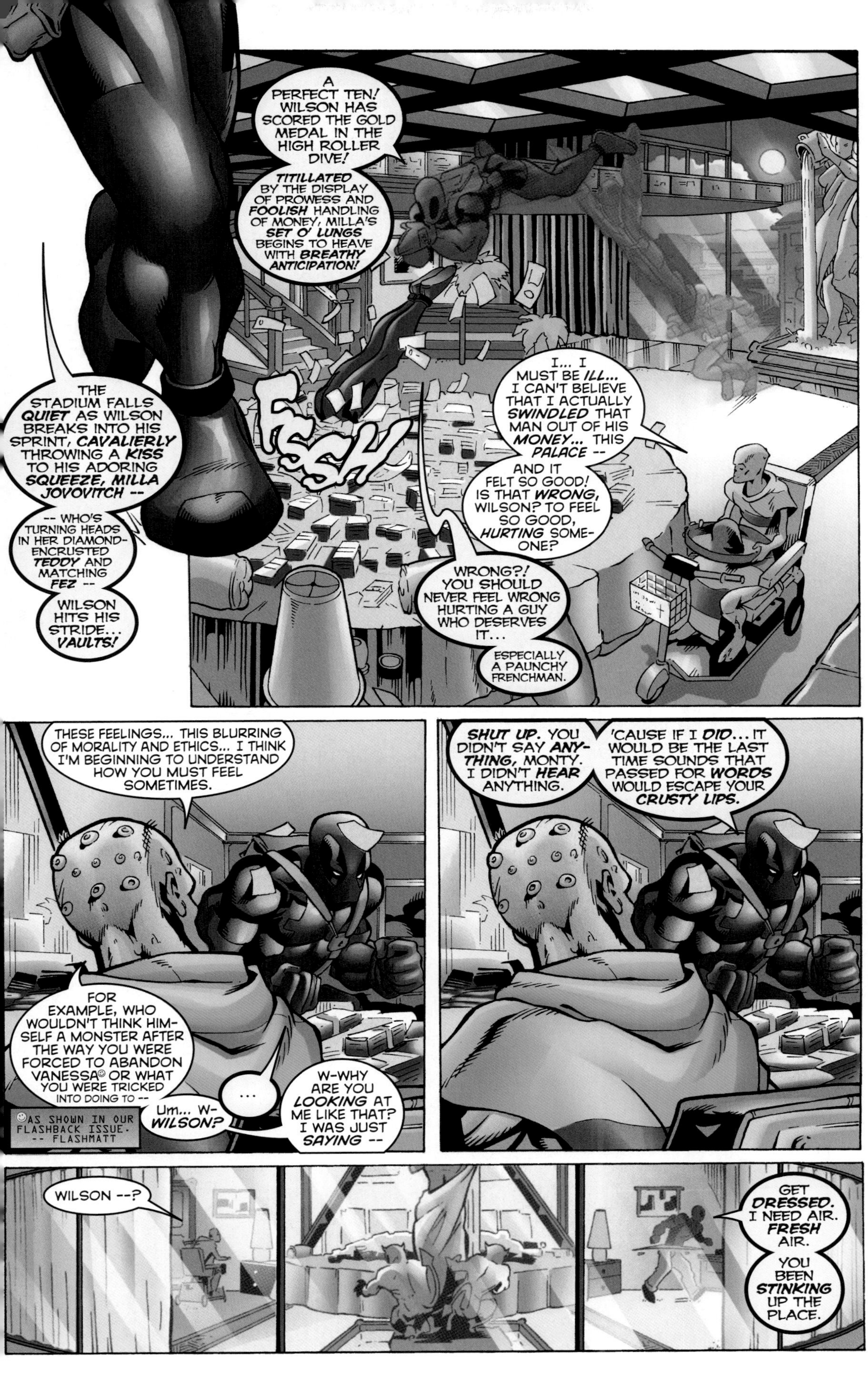
THE STADIUM FALLS QUIET AS WILSON BREAKS INTO HIS SPRINT, CAVALIERLY THROWING A KISS TO HIS ADORING SQUEEZE, MILLA JOVOVITCH --
-- WHO'S TURNING HEADS IN HER DIAMOND-ENCRUSTED TEDDY AND MATCHING FEZ --
WILSON HITS HIS STRIDE... VAULTS!
A PERFECT TEN! WILSON HAS SCORED THE GOLD MEDAL IN THE HIGH ROLLER DIVE!
TITILLATED BY THE DISPLAY OF PROWESS AND FOOLISH HANDLING OF MONEY, MILLA'S SET O' LUNGS BEGINS TO HEAVE WITH BREATHY ANTICIPATION!
FSSH
I... I MUST BE ILL... I CAN'T BELIEVE THAT I ACTUALLY SWINDLED THAT MAN OUT OF HIS MONEY... THIS PALACE --
AND IT FELT SO GOOD! IS THAT WRONG, WILSON? TO FEEL SO GOOD, HURTING SOMEONE?
WRONG?! YOU SHOULD NEVER FEEL WRONG HURTING A GUY WHO DESERVES IT...
ESPECIALLY A PAUNCHY FRENCHMAN.
THESE FEELINGS... THIS BLURRING OF MORALITY AND ETHICS... I THINK I'M BEGINNING TO UNDERSTAND HOW YOU MUST FEEL SOMETIMES.
FOR EXAMPLE, WHO WOULDN'T THINK HIMSELF A MONSTER AFTER THE WAY YOU WERE FORCED TO ABANDON VANESSA☺ OR WHAT YOU WERE TRICKED INTO DOING TO --
...
Um... W-WILSON?
W-WHY ARE YOU LOOKING AT ME LIKE THAT? I WAS JUST SAYING --
☺AS SHOWN IN OUR FLASHBACK ISSUE. -- FLASHMATT
SHUT UP. YOU DIDN'T SAY ANYTHING, MONTY. I DIDN'T HEAR ANYTHING.
'CAUSE IF I DID... IT WOULD BE THE LAST TIME SOUNDS THAT PASSED FOR WORDS WOULD ESCAPE YOUR CRUSTY LIPS.
WILSON --?
GET DRESSED. I NEED AIR. FRESH AIR.
YOU BEEN STINKING UP THE PLACE.

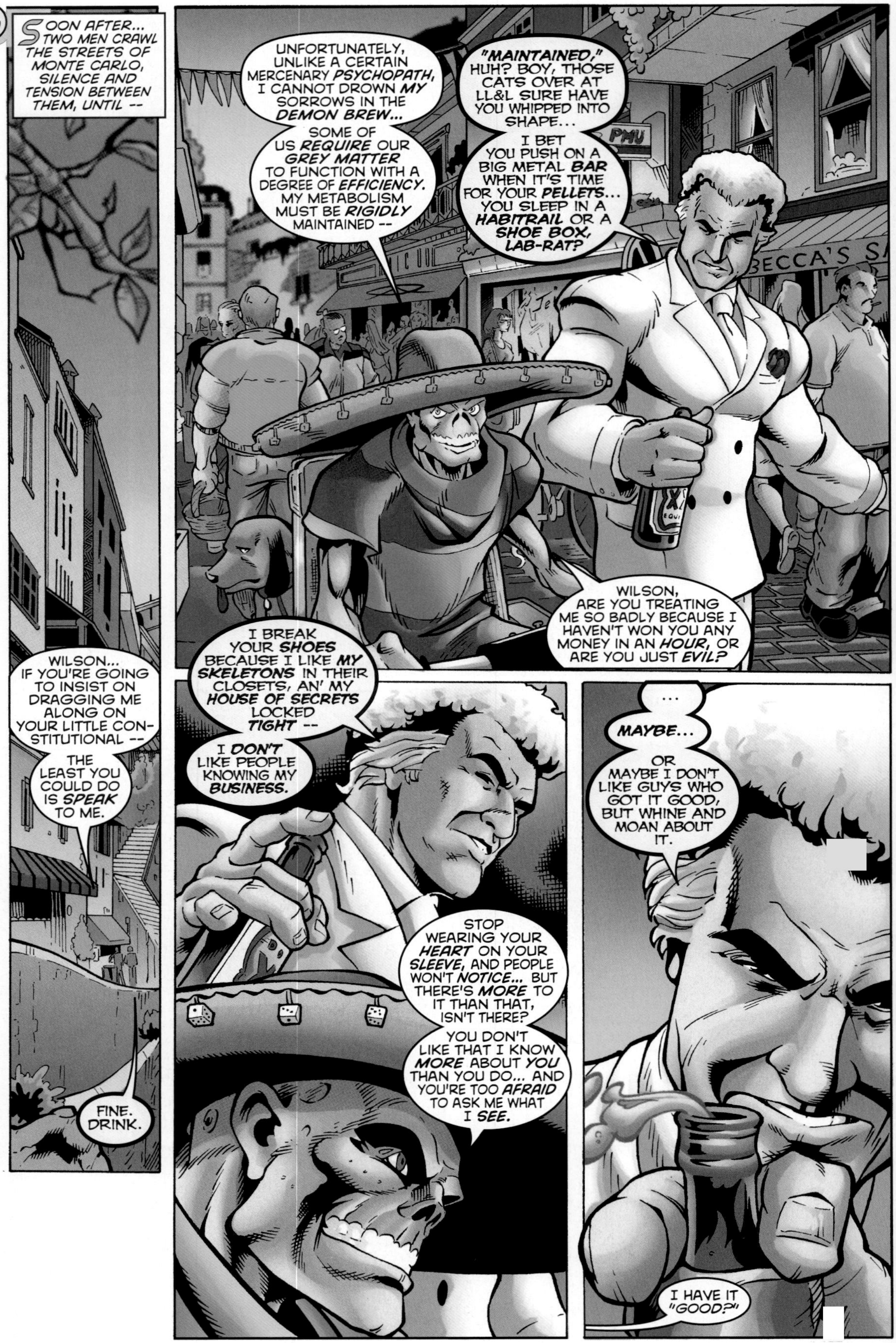
SOON AFTER... TWO MEN CRAWL THE STREETS OF MONTE CARLO, SILENCE AND TENSION BETWEEN THEM, UNTIL --
UNFORTUNATELY, UNLIKE A CERTAIN MERCENARY PSYCHOPATH, I CANNOT DROWN MY SORROWS IN THE DEMON BREW...
SOME OF US REQUIRE OUR GREY MATTER TO FUNCTION WITH A DEGREE OF EFFICIENCY. MY METABOLISM MUST BE RIGIDLY MAINTAINED --
"MAINTAINED," HUH? BOY, THOSE CATS OVER AT LL&L SURE HAVE YOU WHIPPED INTO SHAPE...
I BET YOU PUSH ON A BIG METAL BAR WHEN IT'S TIME FOR YOUR PELLETS... YOU SLEEP IN A HABITRAIL OR A SHOE BOX, LAB-RAT?
PMU
BECCA'S S
WILSON, ARE YOU TREATING ME SO BADLY BECAUSE I HAVEN'T WON YOU ANY MONEY IN AN HOUR, OR ARE YOU JUST EVIL?
WILSON... IF YOU'RE GOING TO INSIST ON DRAGGING ME ALONG ON YOUR LITTLE CONSTITUTIONAL --
THE LEAST YOU COULD DO IS SPEAK TO ME.
I BREAK YOUR SHOES BECAUSE I LIKE MY SKELETONS IN THEIR CLOSETS, AN' MY HOUSE OF SECRETS LOCKED TIGHT --
I DON'T LIKE PEOPLE KNOWING MY BUSINESS.
STOP WEARING YOUR HEART ON YOUR SLEEVE, AND PEOPLE WON'T NOTICE... BUT THERE'S MORE TO IT THAN THAT, ISN'T THERE?
YOU DON'T LIKE THAT I KNOW MORE ABOUT YOU THAN YOU DO... AND YOU'RE TOO AFRAID TO ASK ME WHAT I SEE.
...
MAYBE...
OR MAYBE I DON'T LIKE GUYS WHO GOT IT GOOD, BUT WHINE AND MOAN ABOUT IT.
I HAVE IT "GOOD?"
FINE. DRINK.

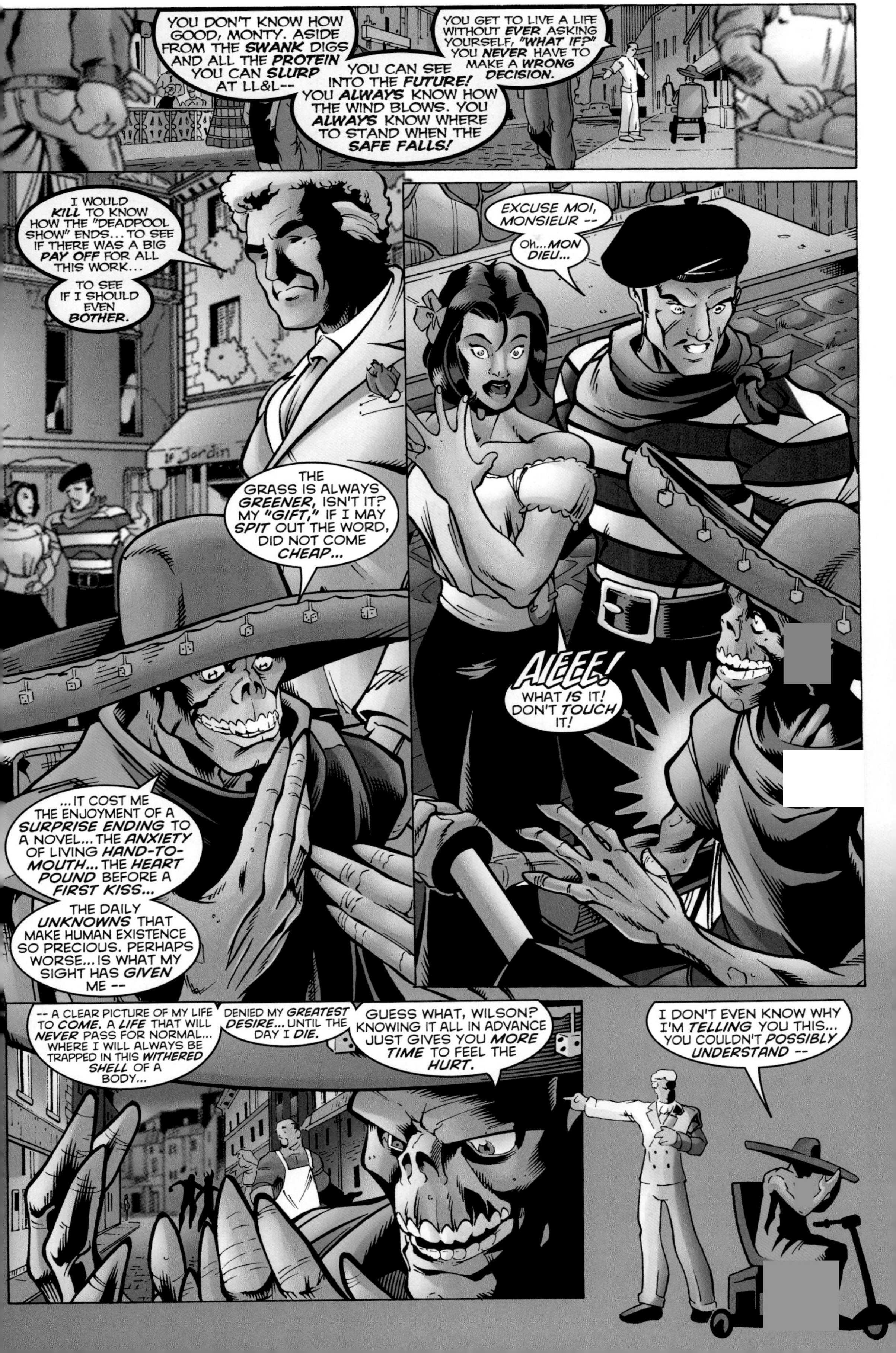
YOU DON'T KNOW HOW GOOD, MONTY. ASIDE FROM THE SWANK DIGS AND ALL THE PROTEIN YOU CAN SLURP AT LL&L--
YOU CAN SEE INTO THE FUTURE! YOU ALWAYS KNOW HOW THE WIND BLOWS. YOU ALWAYS KNOW WHERE TO STAND WHEN THE SAFE FALLS!
YOU GET TO LIVE A LIFE WITHOUT EVER ASKING YOURSELF, "WHAT IF?" YOU NEVER HAVE TO MAKE A WRONG DECISION.
I WOULD KILL TO KNOW HOW THE "DEADPOOL SHOW" ENDS... TO SEE IF THERE WAS A BIG PAY OFF FOR ALL THIS WORK...
TO SEE IF I SHOULD EVEN BOTHER.
Le Jardin
THE GRASS IS ALWAYS GREENER, ISN'T IT? MY "GIFT," IF I MAY SPIT OUT THE WORD, DID NOT COME CHEAP...
...IT COST ME THE ENJOYMENT OF A SURPRISE ENDING TO A NOVEL... THE ANXIETY OF LIVING HAND-TO-MOUTH... THE HEART POUND BEFORE A FIRST KISS...
THE DAILY UNKNOWNS THAT MAKE HUMAN EXISTENCE SO PRECIOUS. PERHAPS WORSE... IS WHAT MY SIGHT HAS GIVEN ME --
EXCUSE MOI, MONSIEUR --
Oh...MON DIEU...
AIEEE!
WHAT IS IT! DON'T TOUCH IT!
-- A CLEAR PICTURE OF MY LIFE TO COME. A LIFE THAT WILL NEVER PASS FOR NORMAL... WHERE I WILL ALWAYS BE TRAPPED IN THIS WITHERED SHELL OF A BODY...
DENIED MY GREATEST DESIRE... UNTIL THE DAY I DIE.
GUESS WHAT, WILSON? KNOWING IT ALL IN ADVANCE JUST GIVES YOU MORE TIME TO FEEL THE HURT.
I DON'T EVEN KNOW WHY I'M TELLING YOU THIS... YOU COULDN'T POSSIBLY UNDERSTAND --

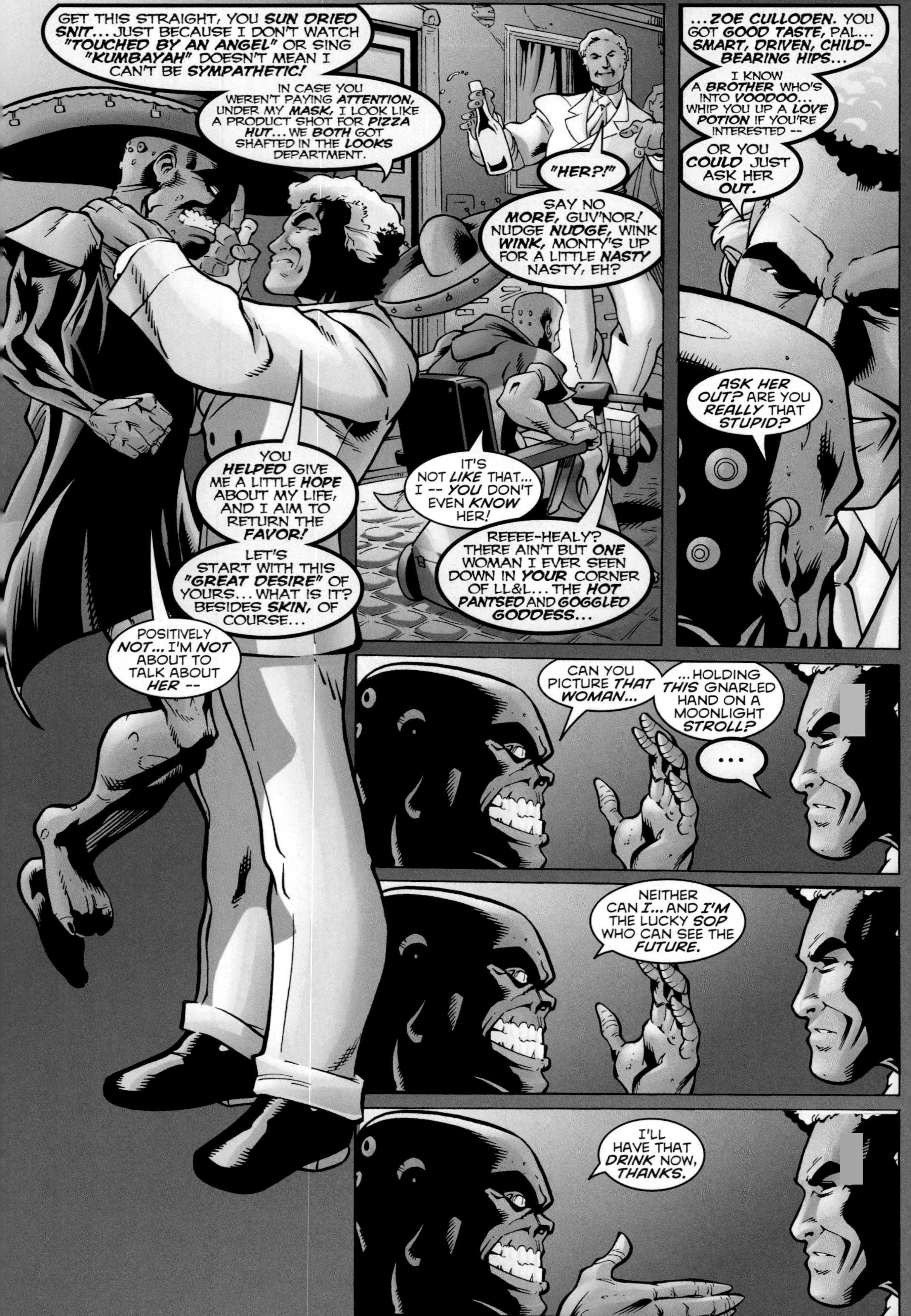
GET THIS STRAIGHT, YOU SUN DRIED SNIT... JUST BECAUSE I DON'T WATCH "TOUCHED BY AN ANGEL" OR SING "KUMBAYAH" DOESN'T MEAN I CAN'T BE SYMPATHETIC!
IN CASE YOU WEREN'T PAYING ATTENTION, UNDER MY MASK, I LOOK LIKE A PRODUCT SHOT FOR PIZZA HUT... WE BOTH GOT SHAFTED IN THE LOOKS DEPARTMENT.
YOU HELPED GIVE ME A LITTLE HOPE ABOUT MY LIFE, AND I AIM TO RETURN THE FAVOR!
LET'S START WITH THIS "GREAT DESIRE" OF YOURS... WHAT IS IT? BESIDES SKIN, OF COURSE...
POSITIVELY NOT... I'M NOT ABOUT TO TALK ABOUT HER --
"HER?!"
SAY NO MORE, GUV'NOR! NUDGE NUDGE, WINK WINK, MONTY'S UP FOR A LITTLE NASTY NASTY, EH?
IT'S NOT LIKE THAT... I -- YOU DON'T EVEN KNOW HER!
REEEE-HEALY? THERE AIN'T BUT ONE WOMAN I EVER SEEN DOWN IN YOUR CORNER OF LL&L... THE HOT PANTSED AND GOGGLED GODDESS...
...ZOE CULLODEN. YOU GOT GOOD TASTE, PAL... SMART, DRIVEN, CHILD-BEARING HIPS...
I KNOW A BROTHER WHO'S INTO VOODOO... WHIP YOU UP A LOVE POTION IF YOU'RE INTERESTED --
OR YOU COULD JUST ASK HER OUT.
ASK HER OUT? ARE YOU REALLY THAT STUPID?
CAN YOU PICTURE THAT WOMAN...
...HOLDING THIS GNARLED HAND ON A MOONLIGHT STROLL?
...
NEITHER CAN I... AND I'M THE LUCKY SOP WHO CAN SEE THE FUTURE.
I'LL HAVE THAT DRINK NOW, THANKS.

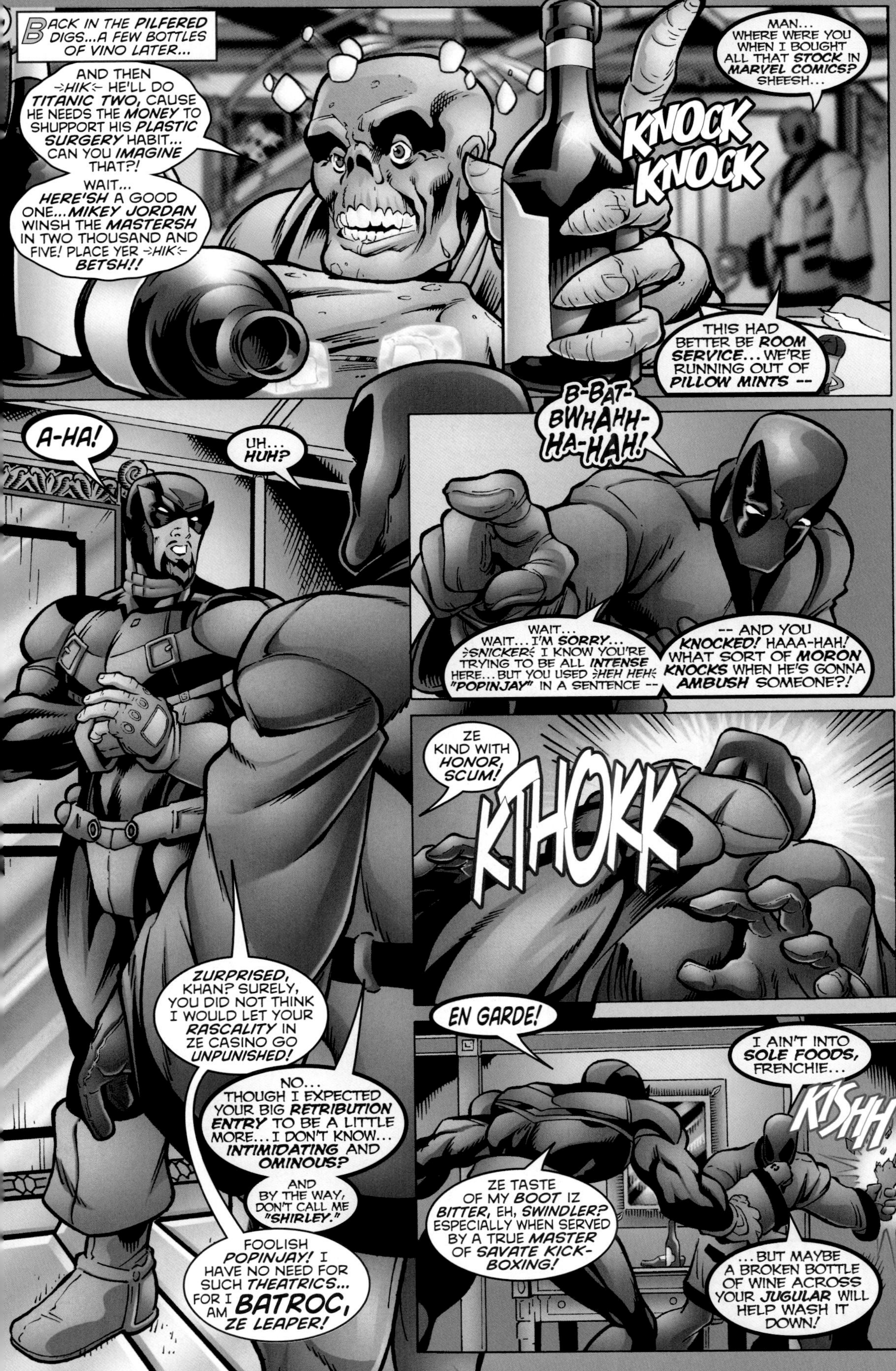
BACK IN THE PILFERED DIGS...A FEW BOTTLES OF VINO LATER...
AND THEN ›HIK‹ HE'LL DO TITANIC TWO, CAUSE HE NEEDS THE MONEY TO SHUPPORT HIS PLASTIC SURGERY HABIT... CAN YOU IMAGINE THAT?!
WAIT... HERE'SH A GOOD ONE...MIKEY JORDAN WINSH THE MASTERSH IN TWO THOUSAND AND FIVE! PLACE YER ›HIK‹ BETSH!!
MAN... WHERE WERE YOU WHEN I BOUGHT ALL THAT STOCK IN MARVEL COMICS? SHEESH...
KNOCK KNOCK
THIS HAD BETTER BE ROOM SERVICE... WE'RE RUNNING OUT OF PILLOW MINTS --
A-HA!
UH... HUH?
ZURPRISED, KHAN? SURELY, YOU DID NOT THINK I WOULD LET YOUR RASCALITY IN ZE CASINO GO UNPUNISHED!
NO... THOUGH I EXPECTED YOUR BIG RETRIBUTION ENTRY TO BE A LITTLE MORE... I DON'T KNOW... INTIMIDATING AND OMINOUS?
AND BY THE WAY, DON'T CALL ME "SHIRLEY."
FOOLISH POPINJAY! I HAVE NO NEED FOR SUCH THEATRICS... FOR I AM BATROC, ZE LEAPER!
B-BAT-BWHAHH-HA-HAH!
WAIT... WAIT... I'M SORRY... ›SNICKER‹ I KNOW YOU'RE TRYING TO BE ALL INTENSE HERE... BUT YOU USED ›HEH HEH‹ "POPINJAY" IN A SENTENCE --
-- AND YOU KNOCKED! HAAA-HAH! WHAT SORT OF MORON KNOCKS WHEN HE'S GONNA AMBUSH SOMEONE?!
ZE KIND WITH HONOR, SCUM!
KTHOKK
EN GARDE!
I AIN'T INTO SOLE FOODS, FRENCHIE...
KISHH
ZE TASTE OF MY BOOT IZ BITTER, EH, SWINDLER? ESPECIALLY WHEN SERVED BY A TRUE MASTER OF SAVATE KICK-BOXING!
...BUT MAYBE A BROKEN BOTTLE OF WINE ACROSS YOUR JUGULAR WILL HELP WASH IT DOWN!

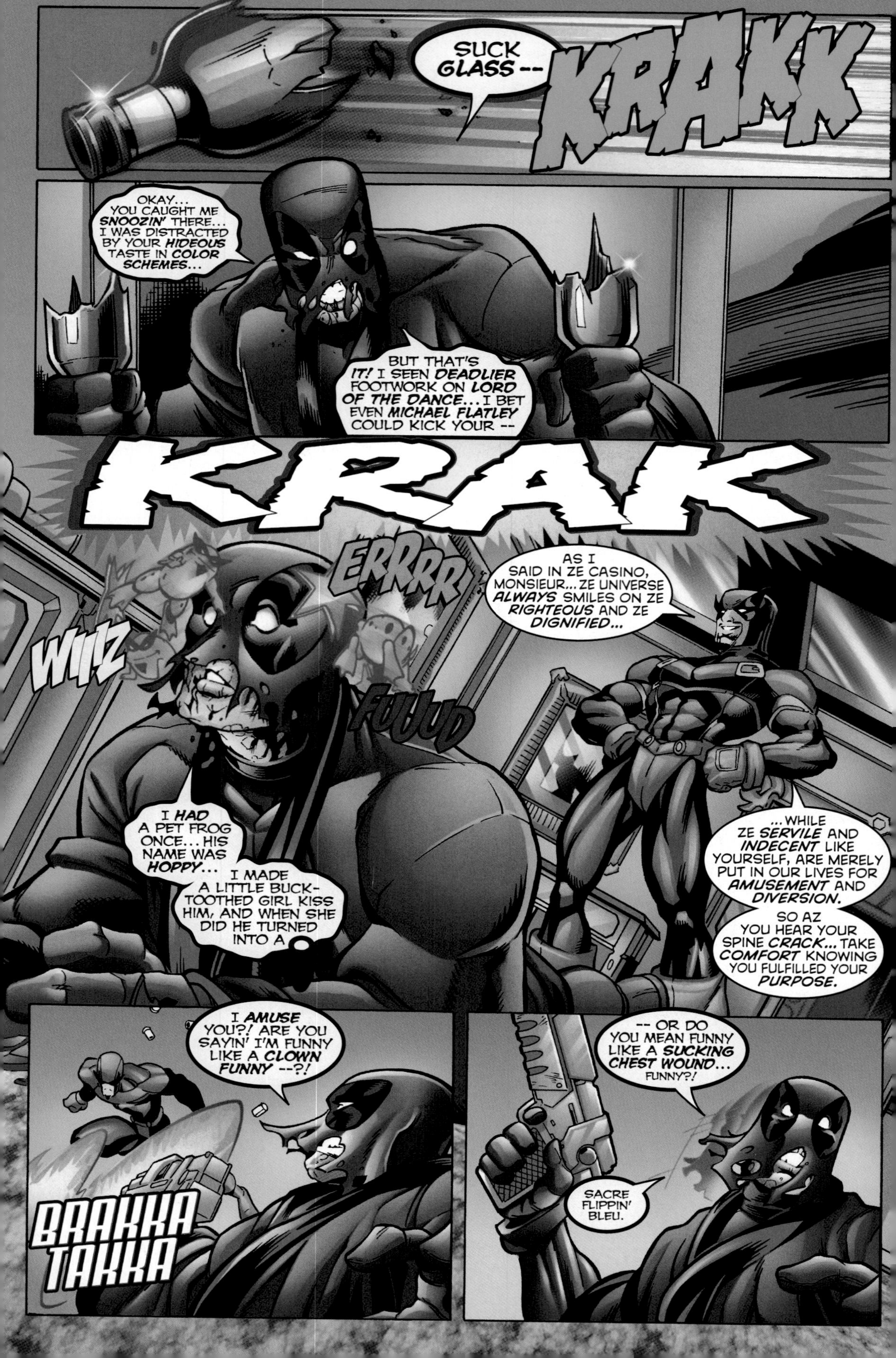
SUCK GLASS --
KRAKK
OKAY... YOU CAUGHT ME SNOOZIN' THERE... I WAS DISTRACTED BY YOUR HIDEOUS TASTE IN COLOR SCHEMES...
BUT THAT'S IT! I SEEN DEADLIER FOOTWORK ON LORD OF THE DANCE... I BET EVEN MICHAEL FLATLEY COULD KICK YOUR --
KRAK
ERRRRR
WIIIZ
FUUUD
AS I SAID IN ZE CASINO, MONSIEUR... ZE UNIVERSE ALWAYS SMILES ON ZE RIGHTEOUS AND ZE DIGNIFIED...
I HAD A PET FROG ONCE... HIS NAME WAS HOPPY...
I MADE A LITTLE BUCK-TOOTHED GIRL KISS HIM, AND WHEN SHE DID HE TURNED INTO A
...WHILE ZE SERVILE AND INDECENT LIKE YOURSELF, ARE MERELY PUT IN OUR LIVES FOR AMUSEMENT AND DIVERSION.
SO AZ YOU HEAR YOUR SPINE CRACK... TAKE COMFORT KNOWING YOU FULFILLED YOUR PURPOSE.
I AMUSE YOU?! ARE YOU SAYIN' I'M FUNNY LIKE A CLOWN FUNNY --?!
BRAKKA TAKKA
-- OR DO YOU MEAN FUNNY LIKE A SUCKING CHEST WOUND... FUNNY?!
SACRE FLIPPIN' BLEU.

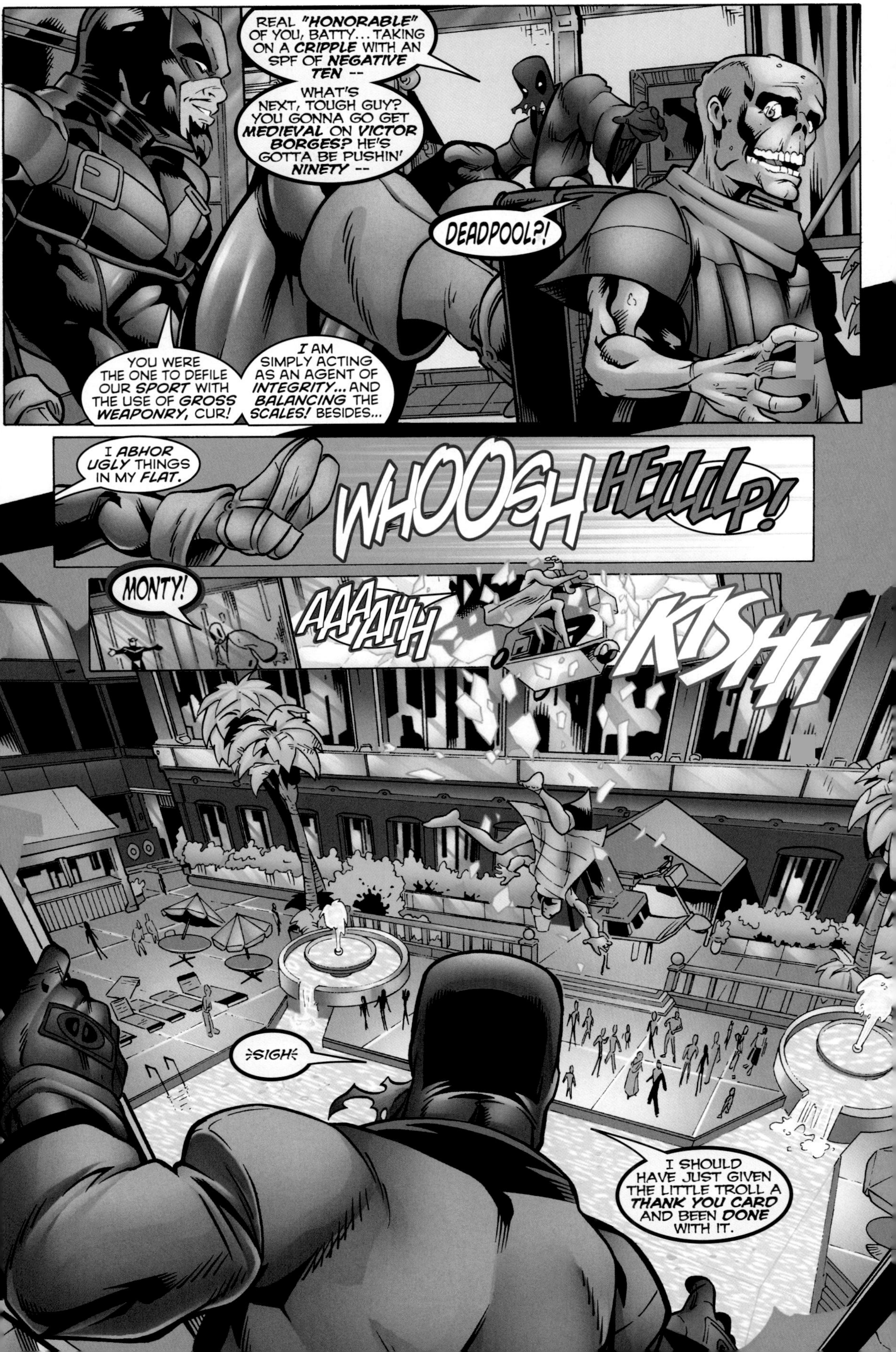

REAL "HONORABLE" OF YOU, BATTY... TAKING ON A CRIPPLE WITH AN SPF OF NEGATIVE TEN --
WHAT'S NEXT, TOUGH GUY? YOU GONNA GO GET MEDIEVAL ON VICTOR BORGES? HE'S GOTTA BE PUSHIN' NINETY --
DEADPOOL?!
YOU WERE THE ONE TO DEFILE OUR SPORT WITH THE USE OF GROSS WEAPONRY, CUR!
I AM SIMPLY ACTING AS AN AGENT OF INTEGRITY... AND BALANCING THE SCALES! BESIDES...
I ABHOR UGLY THINGS IN MY FLAT.
WHOOSH
HELLLLP!
MONTY!
AAAAHH
KTSHH
SIGH
I SHOULD HAVE JUST GIVEN THE LITTLE TROLL A THANK YOU CARD AND BEEN DONE WITH IT.

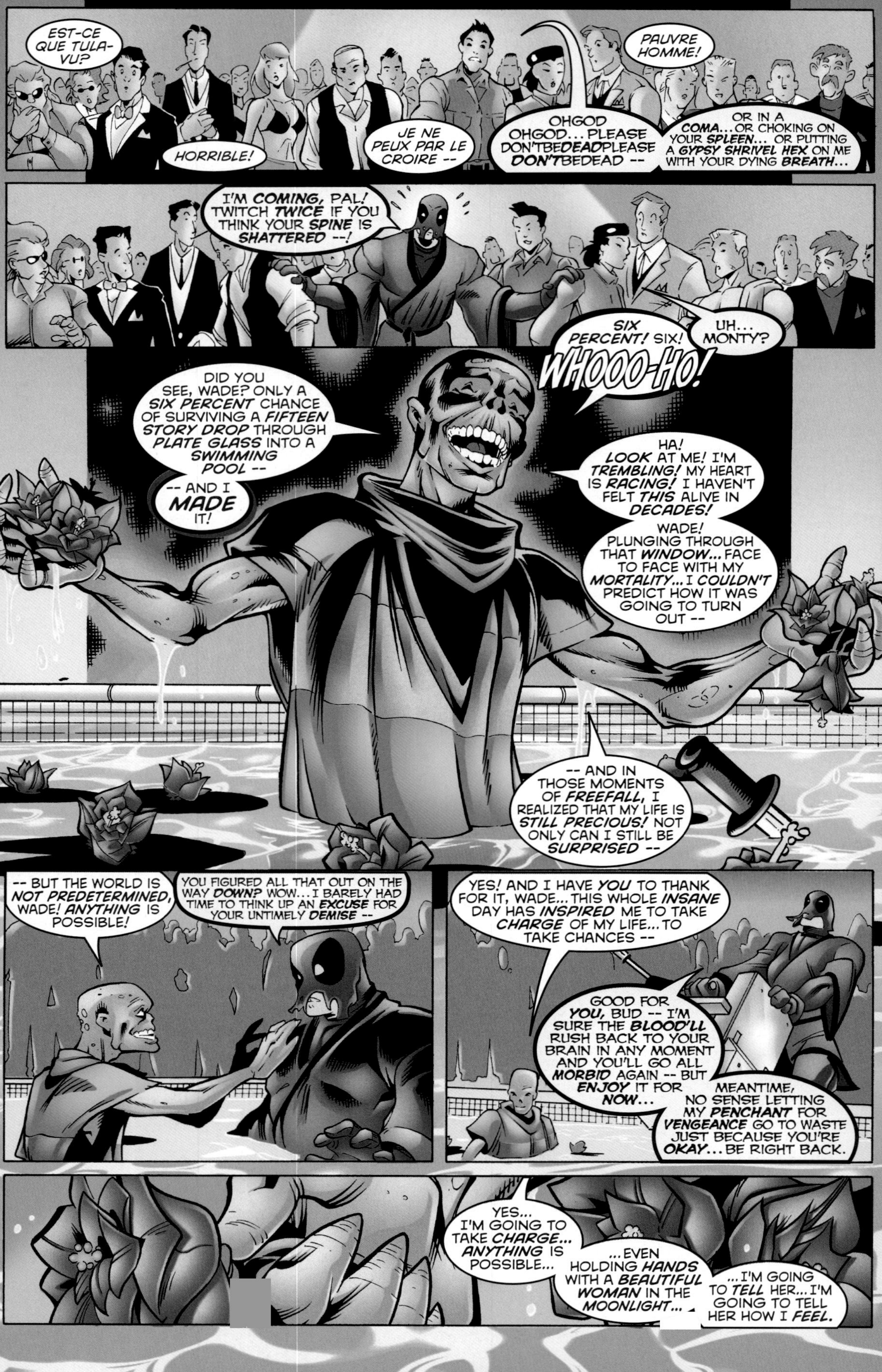
EST-CE QUE TULA-VU?
HORRIBLE!
JE NE PEUX PAR LE CROIRE --
PAUVRE HOMME!
OHGOD OHGOD... PLEASE DON'TBEDEADPLEASE DON'TBEDEAD --
OR IN A COMA... OR CHOKING ON YOUR SPLEEN... OR PUTTING A GYPSY SHRIVEL HEX ON ME WITH YOUR DYING BREATH...
I'M COMING, PAL! TWITCH TWICE IF YOU THINK YOUR SPINE IS SHATTERED --!
SIX PERCENT! SIX!
UH... MONTY?
WHOOO-HO!
DID YOU SEE, WADE? ONLY A SIX PERCENT CHANCE OF SURVIVING A FIFTEEN STORY DROP THROUGH PLATE GLASS INTO A SWIMMING POOL --
-- AND I MADE IT!
HA! LOOK AT ME! I'M TREMBLING! MY HEART IS RACING! I HAVEN'T FELT THIS ALIVE IN DECADES!
WADE! PLUNGING THROUGH THAT WINDOW... FACE TO FACE WITH MY MORTALITY... I COULDN'T PREDICT HOW IT WAS GOING TO TURN OUT --
-- AND IN THOSE MOMENTS OF FREEFALL, I REALIZED THAT MY LIFE IS STILL PRECIOUS! NOT ONLY CAN I STILL BE SURPRISED --
-- BUT THE WORLD IS NOT PREDETERMINED, WADE! ANYTHING IS POSSIBLE!
YOU FIGURED ALL THAT OUT ON THE WAY DOWN? WOW... I BARELY HAD TIME TO THINK UP AN EXCUSE FOR YOUR UNTIMELY DEMISE --
YES! AND I HAVE YOU TO THANK FOR IT, WADE... THIS WHOLE INSANE DAY HAS INSPIRED ME TO TAKE CHARGE OF MY LIFE... TO TAKE CHANCES --
GOOD FOR YOU, BUD -- I'M SURE THE BLOOD'LL RUSH BACK TO YOUR BRAIN IN ANY MOMENT AND YOU'LL GO ALL MORBID AGAIN -- BUT ENJOY IT FOR NOW...
MEANTIME, NO SENSE LETTING MY PENCHANT FOR VENGEANCE GO TO WASTE JUST BECAUSE YOU'RE OKAY... BE RIGHT BACK.
YES... I'M GOING TO TAKE CHARGE... ANYTHING IS POSSIBLE...
...EVEN HOLDING HANDS WITH A BEAUTIFUL WOMAN IN THE MOONLIGHT...
...I'M GOING TO TELL HER... I'M GOING TO TELL HER HOW I FEEL.

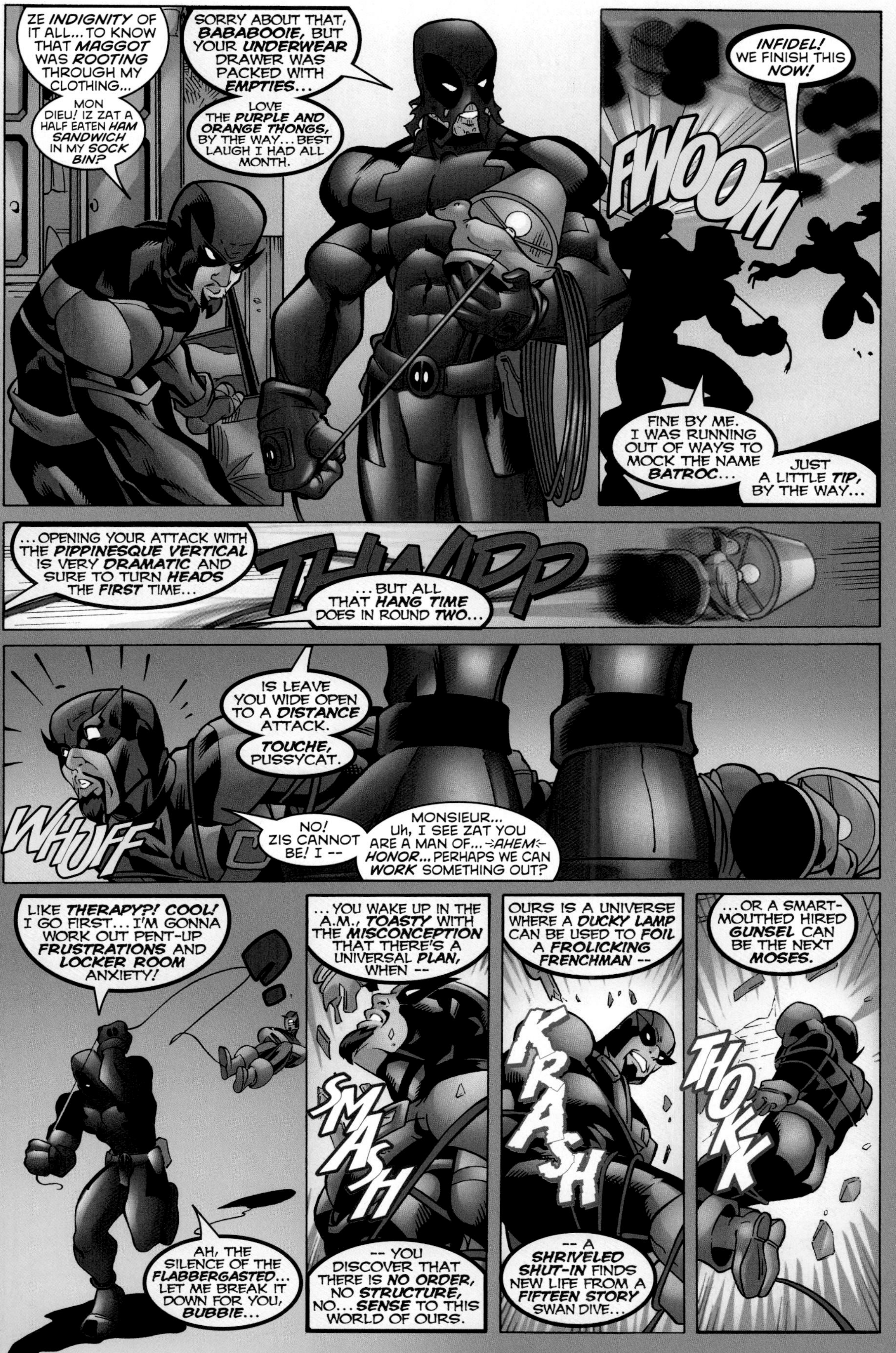
ZE INDIGNITY OF IT ALL... TO KNOW THAT MAGGOT WAS ROOTING THROUGH MY CLOTHING...
MON DIEU! IZ ZAT A HALF EATEN HAM SANDWICH IN MY SOCK BIN?
SORRY ABOUT THAT, BABABOOIE, BUT YOUR UNDERWEAR DRAWER WAS PACKED WITH EMPTIES...
LOVE THE PURPLE AND ORANGE THONGS, BY THE WAY... BEST LAUGH I HAD ALL MONTH.
INFIDEL! WE FINISH THIS NOW!
FWOOM
FINE BY ME. I WAS RUNNING OUT OF WAYS TO MOCK THE NAME BATROC...
JUST A LITTLE TIP, BY THE WAY...
...OPENING YOUR ATTACK WITH THE PIPPINESQUE VERTICAL IS VERY DRAMATIC AND SURE TO TURN HEADS THE FIRST TIME...
THWIPP
...BUT ALL THAT HANG TIME DOES IN ROUND TWO...
IS LEAVE YOU WIDE OPEN TO A DISTANCE ATTACK.
TOUCHE, PUSSYCAT.
WHUFF
NO! ZIS CANNOT BE! I --
MONSIEUR... Uh, I SEE ZAT YOU ARE A MAN OF... AHEM HONOR... PERHAPS WE CAN WORK SOMETHING OUT?
LIKE THERAPY?! COOL! I GO FIRST... I'M GONNA WORK OUT PENT-UP FRUSTRATIONS AND LOCKER ROOM ANXIETY!
AH, THE SILENCE OF THE FLABBERGASTED... LET ME BREAK IT DOWN FOR YOU, BUBBIE...
...YOU WAKE UP IN THE A.M., TOASTY WITH THE MISCONCEPTION THAT THERE'S A UNIVERSAL PLAN, WHEN --
SMASH
-- YOU DISCOVER THAT THERE IS NO ORDER, NO STRUCTURE, NO... SENSE TO THIS WORLD OF OURS.
OURS IS A UNIVERSE WHERE A DUCKY LAMP CAN BE USED TO FOIL A FROLICKING FRENCHMAN --
KRASH
-- A SHRIVELED SHUT-IN FINDS NEW LIFE FROM A FIFTEEN STORY SWAN DIVE...
...OR A SMART-MOUTHED HIRED GUNSEL CAN BE THE NEXT MOSES.
THOKK

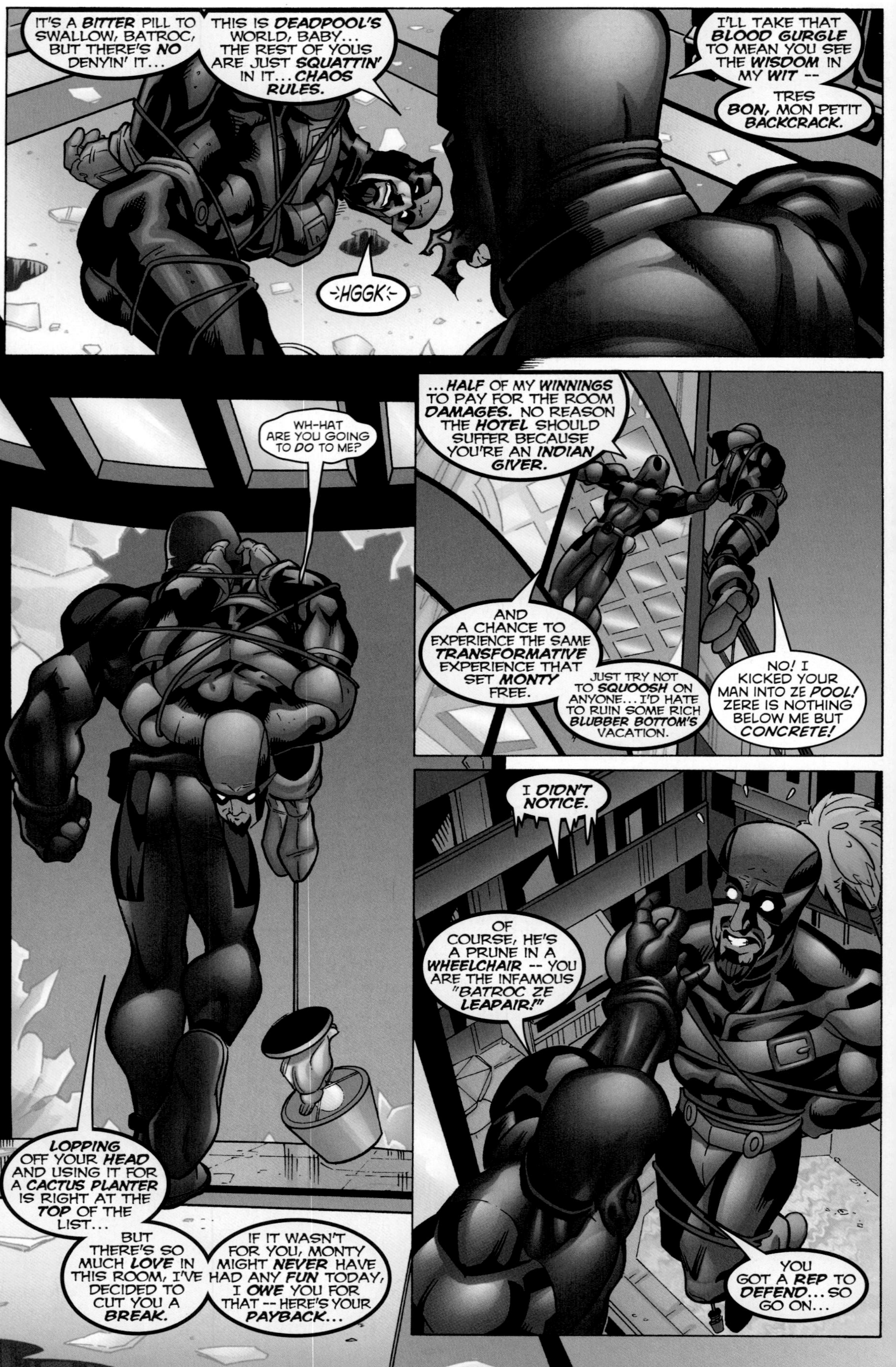
IT'S A BITTER PILL TO SWALLOW, BATROC, BUT THERE'S NO DENYIN' IT...
THIS IS DEADPOOL'S WORLD, BABY... THE REST OF YOUS ARE JUST SQUATTIN' IN IT... CHAOS RULES.
-HGGK-
I'LL TAKE THAT BLOOD GURGLE TO MEAN YOU SEE THE WISDOM IN MY WIT --
TRES BON, MON PETIT BACKCRACK.
WH-HAT ARE YOU GOING TO DO TO ME?
LOPPING OFF YOUR HEAD AND USING IT FOR A CACTUS PLANTER IS RIGHT AT THE TOP OF THE LIST...
BUT THERE'S SO MUCH LOVE IN THIS ROOM, I'VE DECIDED TO CUT YOU A BREAK.
IF IT WASN'T FOR YOU, MONTY MIGHT NEVER HAVE HAD ANY FUN TODAY, I OWE YOU FOR THAT -- HERE'S YOUR PAYBACK...
...HALF OF MY WINNINGS TO PAY FOR THE ROOM DAMAGES. NO REASON THE HOTEL SHOULD SUFFER BECAUSE YOU'RE AN INDIAN GIVER.
AND A CHANCE TO EXPERIENCE THE SAME TRANSFORMATIVE EXPERIENCE THAT SET MONTY FREE.
JUST TRY NOT TO SQUOOSH ON ANYONE... I'D HATE TO RUIN SOME RICH BLUBBER BOTTOM'S VACATION.
NO! I KICKED YOUR MAN INTO ZE POOL! ZERE IS NOTHING BELOW ME BUT CONCRETE!
I DIDN'T NOTICE.
OF COURSE, HE'S A PRUNE IN A WHEELCHAIR -- YOU ARE THE INFAMOUS "BATROC ZE LEAPAIR!"
YOU GOT A REP TO DEFEND... SO GO ON...

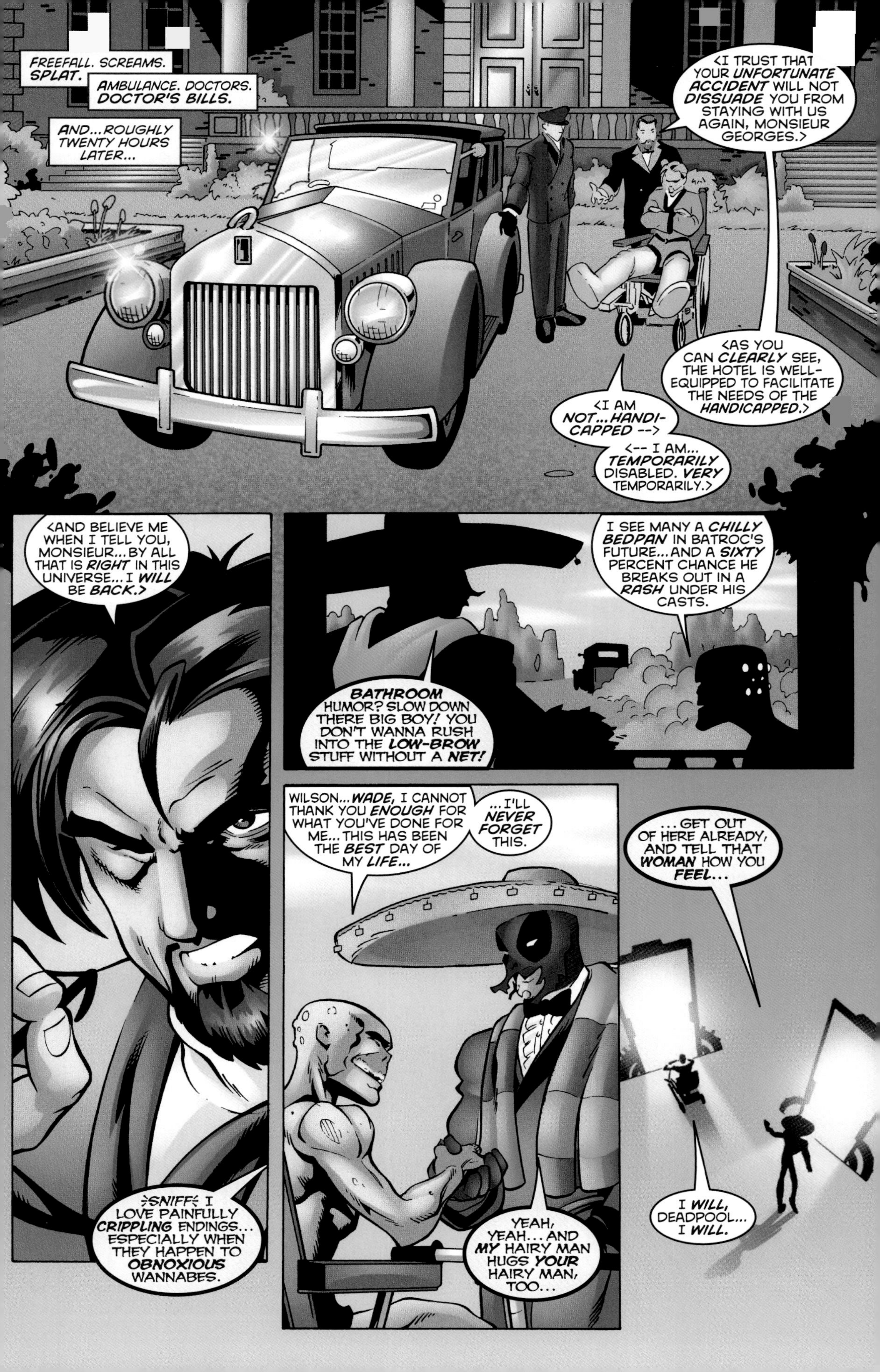
FREEFALL. SCREAMS. SPLAT.
AMBULANCE. DOCTORS. DOCTOR'S BILLS.
AND... ROUGHLY TWENTY HOURS LATER...
<I TRUST THAT YOUR UNFORTUNATE ACCIDENT WILL NOT DISSUADE YOU FROM STAYING WITH US AGAIN, MONSIEUR GEORGES.>
<AS YOU CAN CLEARLY SEE, THE HOTEL IS WELL-EQUIPPED TO FACILITATE THE NEEDS OF THE HANDICAPPED.>
<I AM NOT... HANDI-CAPPED -->
<-- I AM... TEMPORARILY DISABLED. VERY TEMPORARILY.>
<AND BELIEVE ME WHEN I TELL YOU, MONSIEUR... BY ALL THAT IS RIGHT IN THIS UNIVERSE... I WILL BE BACK.>
I SEE MANY A CHILLY BEDPAN IN BATROC'S FUTURE... AND A SIXTY PERCENT CHANCE HE BREAKS OUT IN A RASH UNDER HIS CASTS.
BATHROOM HUMOR? SLOW DOWN THERE BIG BOY! YOU DON'T WANNA RUSH INTO THE LOW-BROW STUFF WITHOUT A NET!
SNIFF I LOVE PAINFULLY CRIPPLING ENDINGS... ESPECIALLY WHEN THEY HAPPEN TO OBNOXIOUS WANNABES.
WILSON... WADE, I CANNOT THANK YOU ENOUGH FOR WHAT YOU'VE DONE FOR ME... THIS HAS BEEN THE BEST DAY OF MY LIFE...
...I'LL NEVER FORGET THIS.
YEAH, YEAH... AND MY HAIRY MAN HUGS YOUR HAIRY MAN, TOO...
... GET OUT OF HERE ALREADY, AND TELL THAT WOMAN HOW YOU FEEL...
I WILL, DEADPOOL... I WILL.

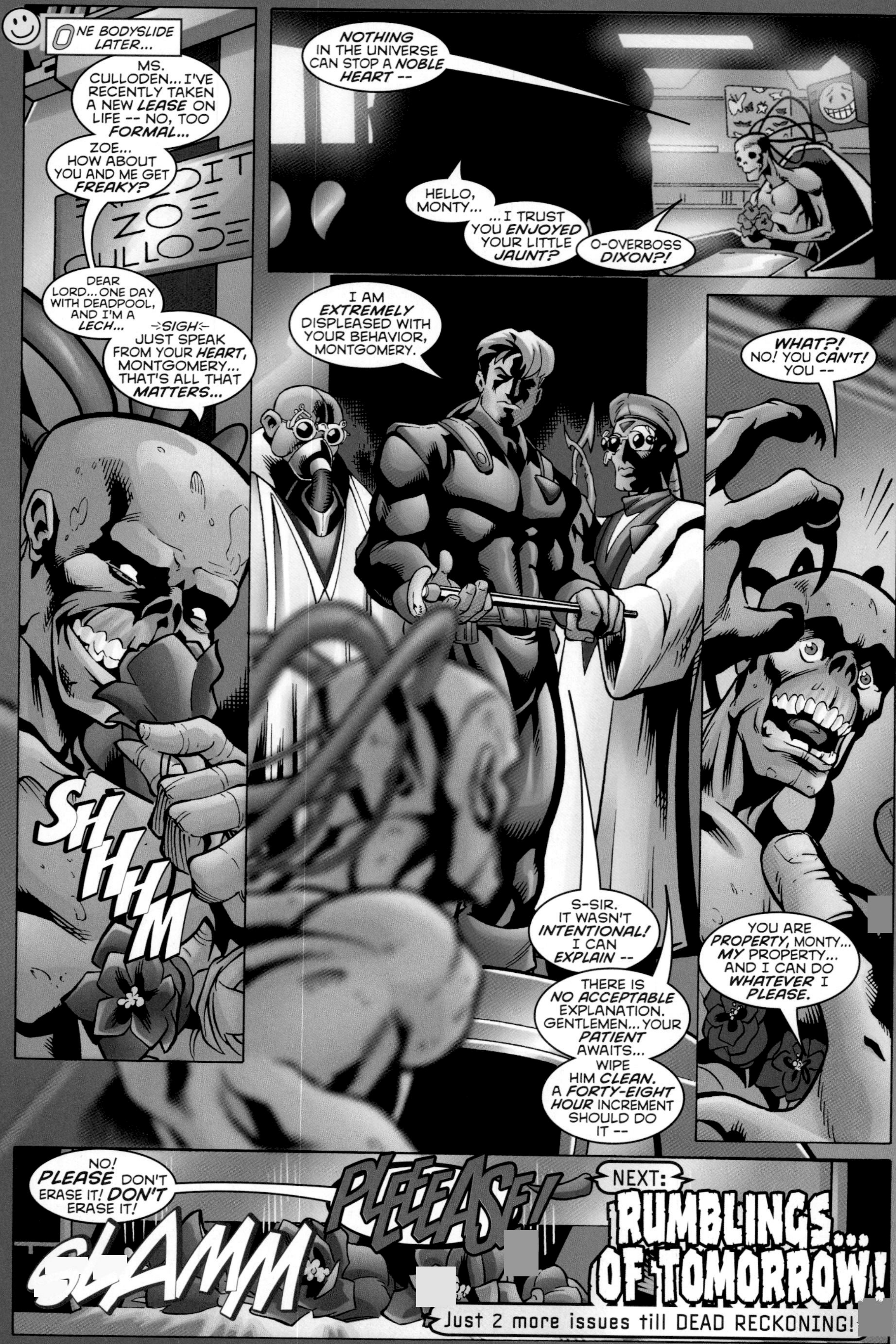
ONE BODYSLIDE LATER...
MS. CULLODEN... I'VE RECENTLY TAKEN A NEW LEASE ON LIFE -- NO, TOO FORMAL...
ZOE... HOW ABOUT YOU AND ME GET FREAKY?
CREDIT ZOE CULLODEN
DEAR LORD... ONE DAY WITH DEADPOOL, AND I'M A LECH... ⇾SIGH⇽
JUST SPEAK FROM YOUR HEART, MONTGOMERY... THAT'S ALL THAT MATTERS...
SHHHHM
NOTHING IN THE UNIVERSE CAN STOP A NOBLE HEART --
HELLO, MONTY...
...I TRUST YOU ENJOYED YOUR LITTLE JAUNT?
O-OVERBOSS DIXON?!
I AM EXTREMELY DISPLEASED WITH YOUR BEHAVIOR, MONTGOMERY.
S-SIR. IT WASN'T INTENTIONAL! I CAN EXPLAIN --
THERE IS NO ACCEPTABLE EXPLANATION. GENTLEMEN... YOUR PATIENT AWAITS...
WIPE HIM CLEAN. A FORTY-EIGHT HOUR INCREMENT SHOULD DO IT --
WHAT?! NO! YOU CAN'T! YOU --
YOU ARE PROPERTY, MONTY... MY PROPERTY... AND I CAN DO WHATEVER I PLEASE.
NO! PLEASE DON'T ERASE IT! DON'T ERASE IT!
SLAMM
PLEEEASE!
NEXT: RUMBLINGS... OF TOMORROW!
Just 2 more issues till DEAD RECKONING!

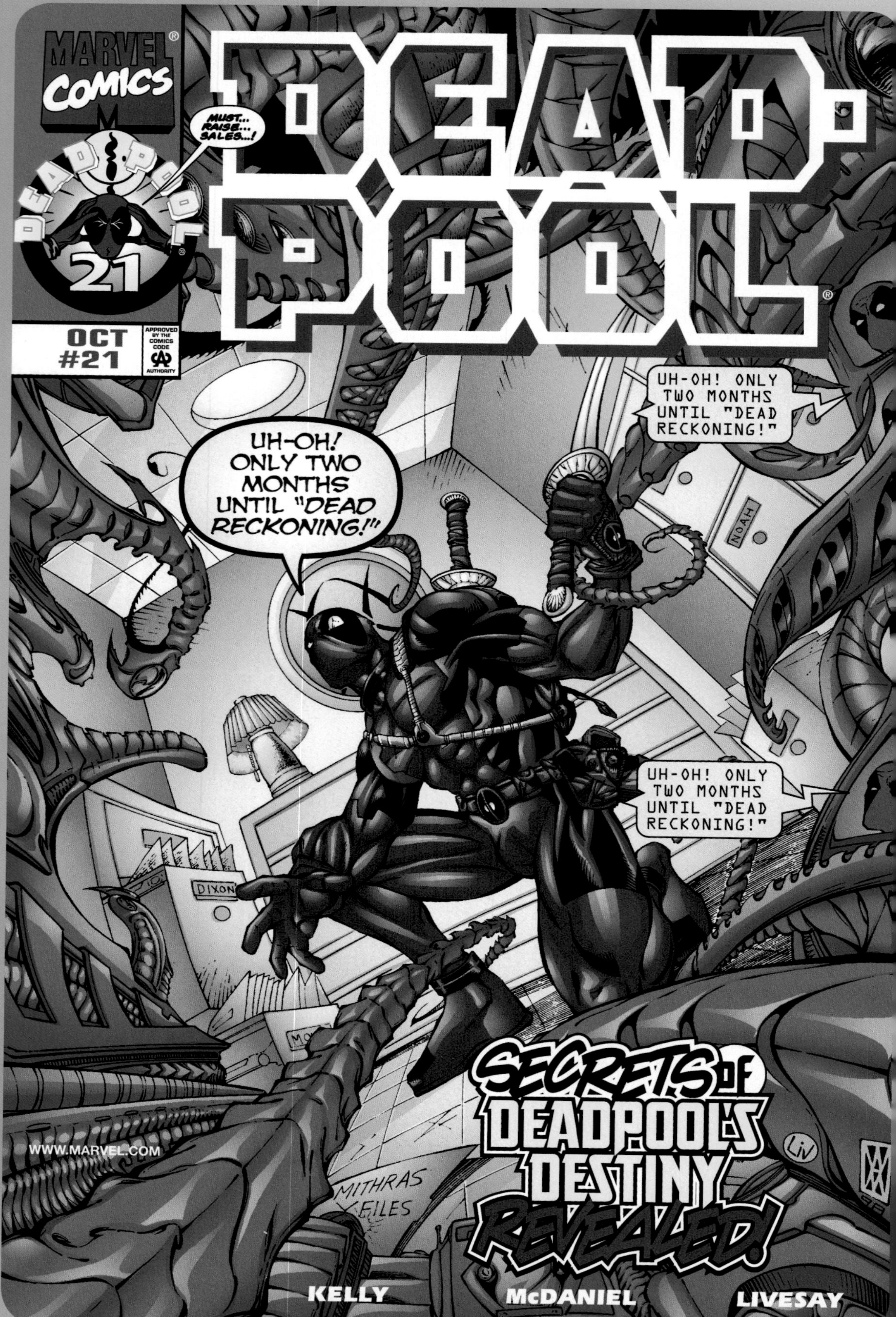

MARVEL COMICS
MUST... RAISE... SALES...!
DEADPOOL 21
OCT #21
APPROVED BY THE COMICS CODE AUTHORITY
DEADPOOL
UH-OH! ONLY TWO MONTHS UNTIL "DEAD RECKONING!"
UH-OH! ONLY TWO MONTHS UNTIL "DEAD RECKONING!"
UH-OH! ONLY TWO MONTHS UNTIL "DEAD RECKONING!"
NOAH
DIXON
MITHRAS FILES
SECRETS OF DEADPOOL'S DESTINY REVEALED!
WWW.MARVEL.COM
KELLY McDANIEL LIVESAY

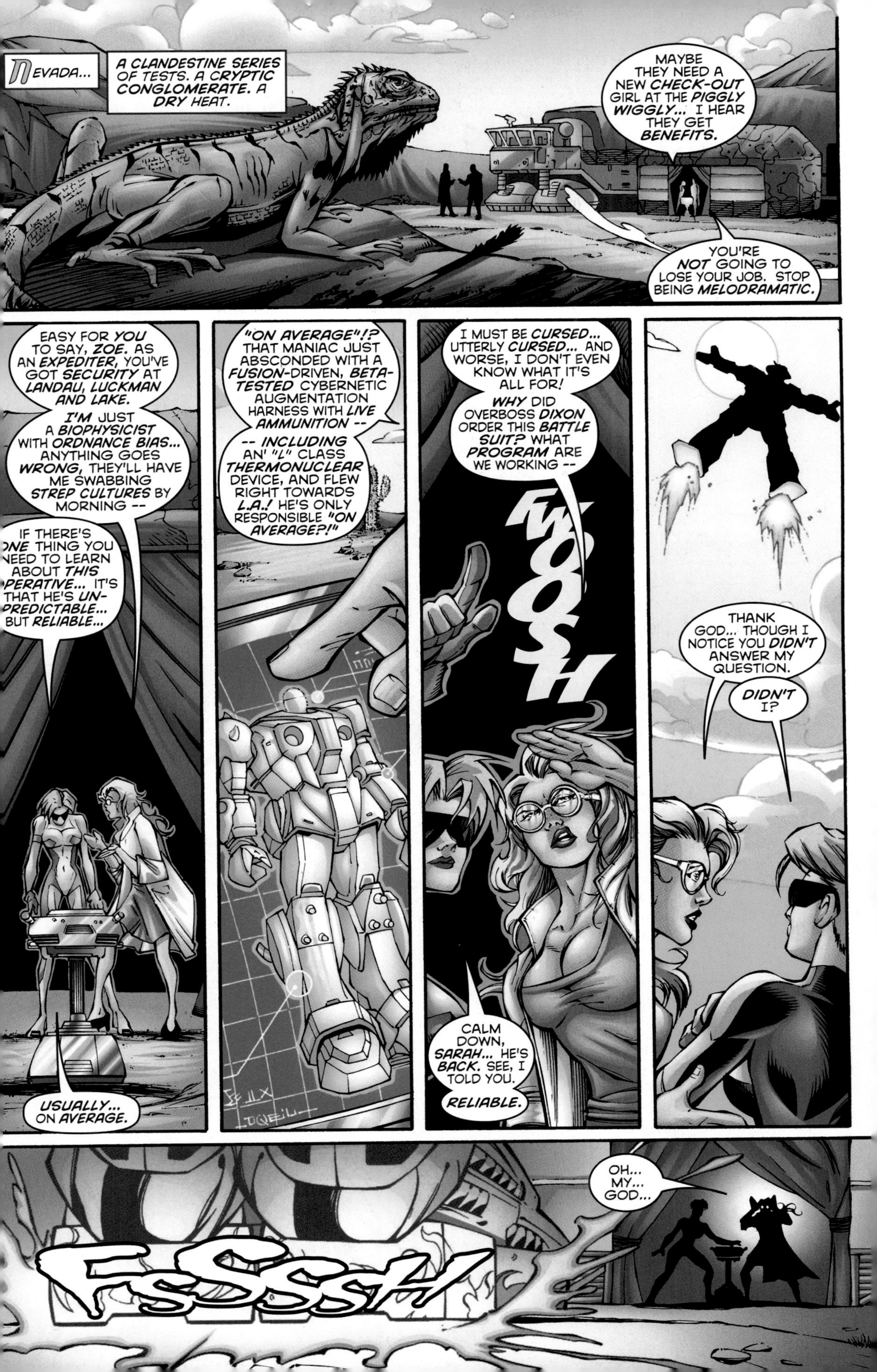
NEVADA...
A CLANDESTINE SERIES OF TESTS. A CRYPTIC CONGLOMERATE. A DRY HEAT.
MAYBE THEY NEED A NEW CHECK-OUT GIRL AT THE PIGGLY WIGGLY... I HEAR THEY GET BENEFITS.
YOU'RE NOT GOING TO LOSE YOUR JOB. STOP BEING MELODRAMATIC.
EASY FOR YOU TO SAY, ZOE. AS AN EXPEDITER, YOU'VE GOT SECURITY AT LANDAU, LUCKMAN AND LAKE.
I'M JUST A BIOPHYSICIST WITH ORDNANCE BIAS... ANYTHING GOES WRONG, THEY'LL HAVE ME SWABBING STREP CULTURES BY MORNING --
IF THERE'S ONE THING YOU NEED TO LEARN ABOUT THIS OPERATIVE... IT'S THAT HE'S UNPREDICTABLE... BUT RELIABLE...
USUALLY... ON AVERAGE.
"ON AVERAGE"!? THAT MANIAC JUST ABSCONDED WITH A FUSION-DRIVEN, BETA-TESTED CYBERNETIC AUGMENTATION HARNESS WITH LIVE AMMUNITION --
-- INCLUDING AN' "L" CLASS THERMONUCLEAR DEVICE, AND FLEW RIGHT TOWARDS L.A.! HE'S ONLY RESPONSIBLE "ON AVERAGE?!"
I MUST BE CURSED... UTTERLY CURSED... AND WORSE, I DON'T EVEN KNOW WHAT IT'S ALL FOR!
WHY DID OVERBOSS DIXON ORDER THIS BATTLE SUIT? WHAT PROGRAM ARE WE WORKING --
FWOOOSH
CALM DOWN, SARAH... HE'S BACK. SEE, I TOLD YOU. RELIABLE.
THANK GOD... THOUGH I NOTICE YOU DIDN'T ANSWER MY QUESTION.
DIDN'T I?
OH... MY... GOD...
FSSSSSH

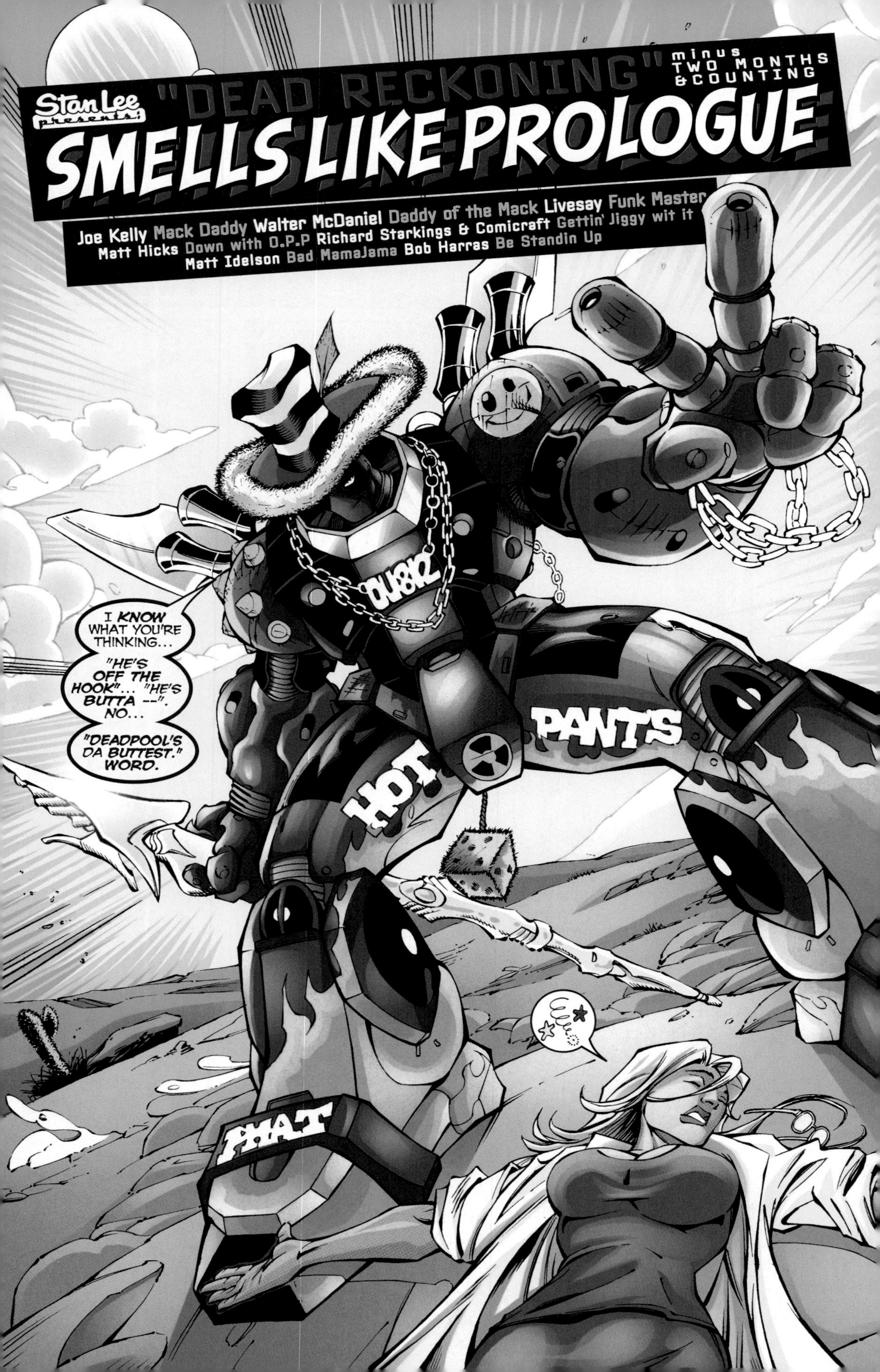
Stan Lee presents:
"DEAD RECKONING" minus TWO MONTHS & COUNTING
SMELLS LIKE PROLOGUE
Joe Kelly Mack Daddy Walter McDaniel Daddy of the Mack Livesay Funk Master Matt Hicks Down with O.P.P Richard Starkings & Comicraft Gettin' Jiggy wit it Matt Idelson Bad MamaJama Bob Harras Be Standin Up
I KNOW WHAT YOU'RE THINKING...
"HE'S OFF THE HOOK"... "HE'S BUTTA --". NO...
"DEADPOOL'S DA BUTTEST." WORD.
DUB12
PANTS
HOT
PHAT

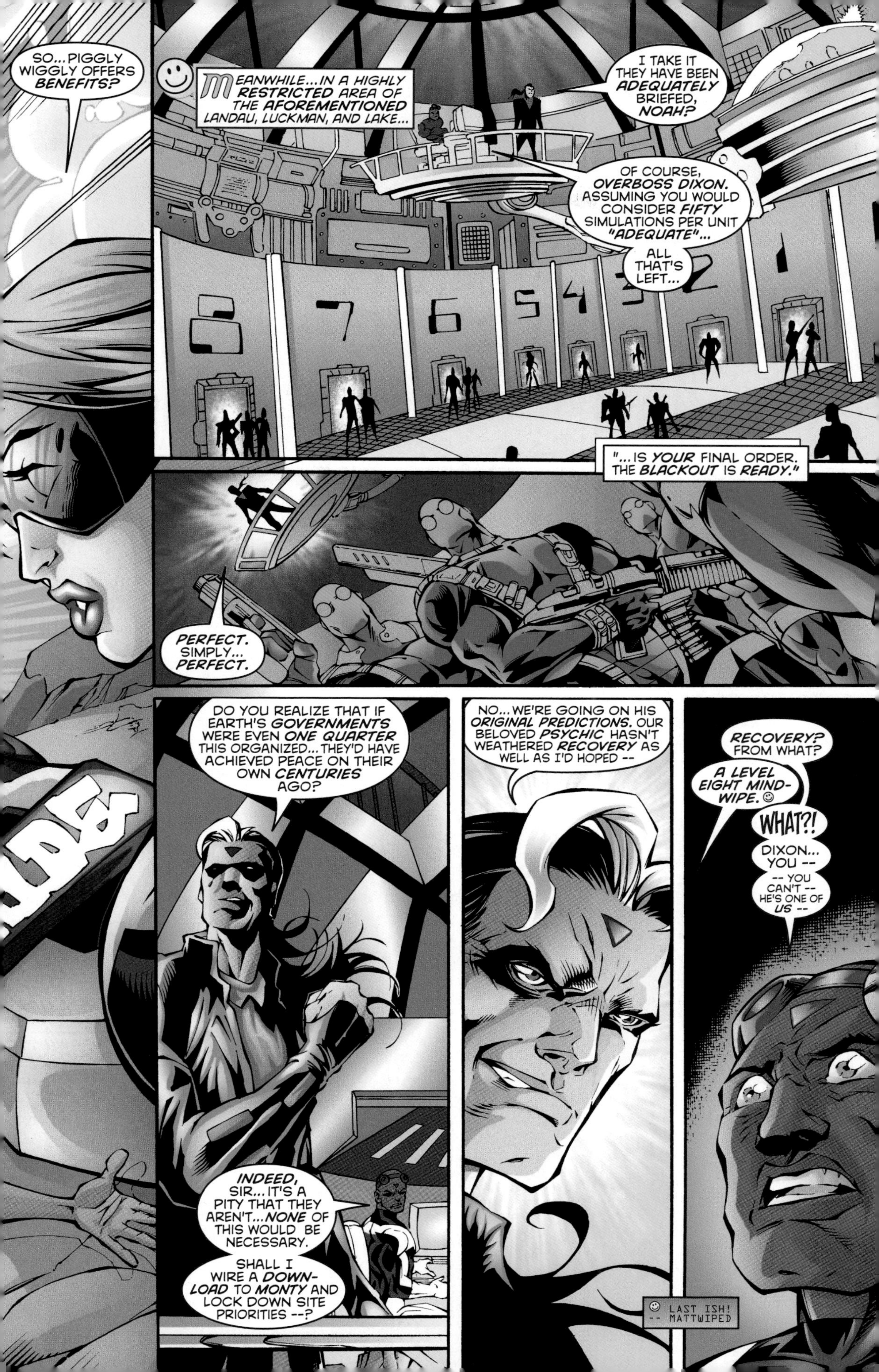
SO... PIGGLY WIGGLY OFFERS BENEFITS?
MEANWHILE... IN A HIGHLY RESTRICTED AREA OF THE AFOREMENTIONED LANDAU, LUCKMAN, AND LAKE...
I TAKE IT THEY HAVE BEEN ADEQUATELY BRIEFED, NOAH?
OF COURSE, OVERBOSS DIXON. ASSUMING YOU WOULD CONSIDER FIFTY SIMULATIONS PER UNIT "ADEQUATE"...
ALL THAT'S LEFT...
"...IS YOUR FINAL ORDER. THE BLACKOUT IS READY."
PERFECT. SIMPLY... PERFECT.
DO YOU REALIZE THAT IF EARTH'S GOVERNMENTS WERE EVEN ONE QUARTER THIS ORGANIZED... THEY'D HAVE ACHIEVED PEACE ON THEIR OWN CENTURIES AGO?
INDEED, SIR... IT'S A PITY THAT THEY AREN'T... NONE OF THIS WOULD BE NECESSARY.
SHALL I WIRE A DOWN-LOAD TO MONTY AND LOCK DOWN SITE PRIORITIES --?
NO... WE'RE GOING ON HIS ORIGINAL PREDICTIONS. OUR BELOVED PSYCHIC HASN'T WEATHERED RECOVERY AS WELL AS I'D HOPED --
RECOVERY? FROM WHAT?
A LEVEL EIGHT MIND-WIPE. ☺
WHAT?!
DIXON... YOU --
-- YOU CAN'T -- HE'S ONE OF US --
☺ LAST ISH! -- MATTWIPED

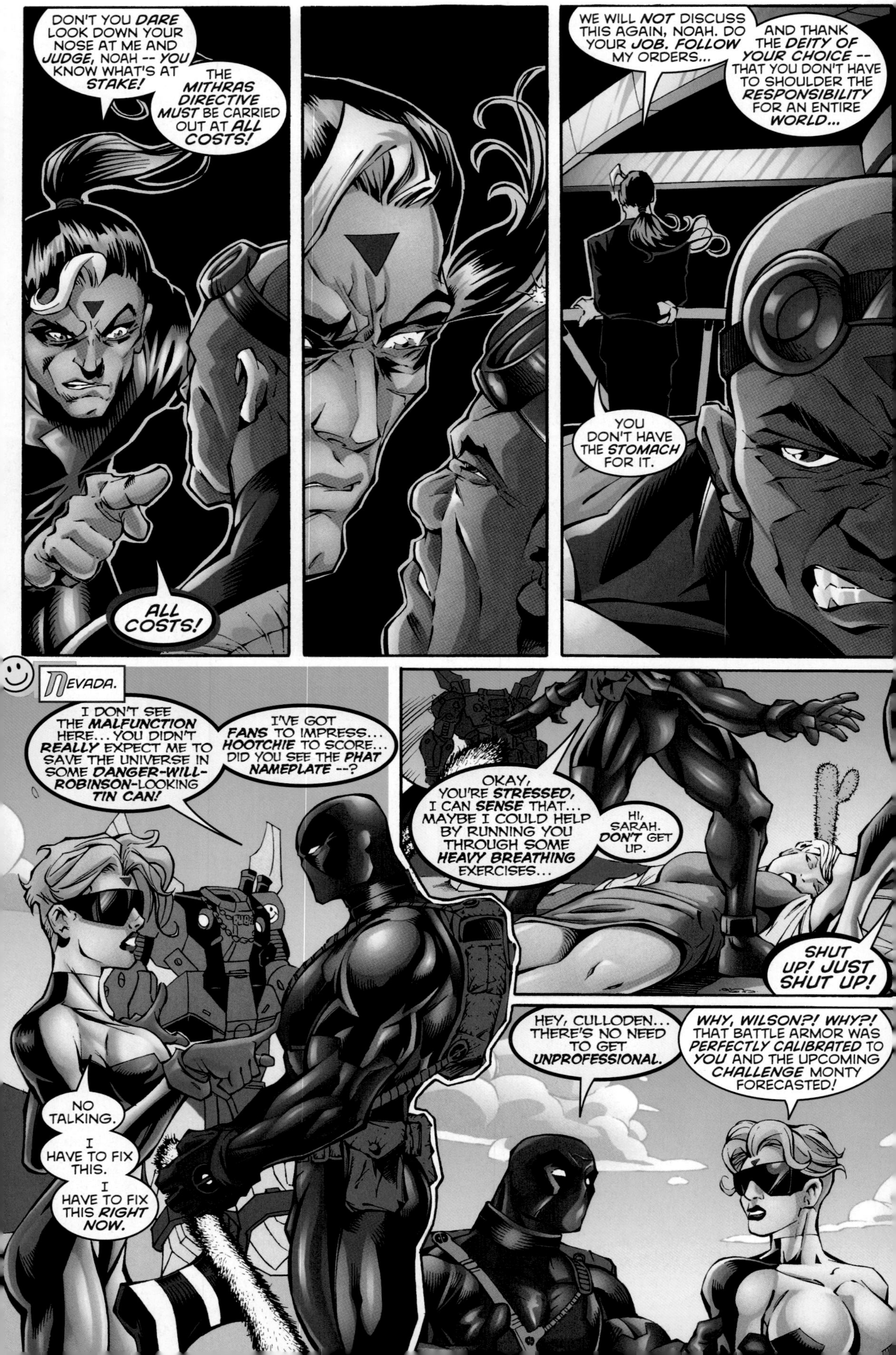
DON'T YOU DARE LOOK DOWN YOUR NOSE AT ME AND JUDGE, NOAH -- YOU KNOW WHAT'S AT STAKE!
THE MITHRAS DIRECTIVE MUST BE CARRIED OUT AT ALL COSTS!
ALL COSTS!
WE WILL NOT DISCUSS THIS AGAIN, NOAH. DO YOUR JOB. FOLLOW MY ORDERS...
AND THANK THE DEITY OF YOUR CHOICE -- THAT YOU DON'T HAVE TO SHOULDER THE RESPONSIBILITY FOR AN ENTIRE WORLD...
YOU DON'T HAVE THE STOMACH FOR IT.
NEVADA.
I DON'T SEE THE MALFUNCTION HERE... YOU DIDN'T REALLY EXPECT ME TO SAVE THE UNIVERSE IN SOME DANGER-WILL-ROBINSON-LOOKING TIN CAN!
I'VE GOT FANS TO IMPRESS... HOOTCHIE TO SCORE... DID YOU SEE THE PHAT NAMEPLATE --?
NO TALKING.
I HAVE TO FIX THIS.
I HAVE TO FIX THIS RIGHT NOW.
OKAY, YOU'RE STRESSED, I CAN SENSE THAT... MAYBE I COULD HELP BY RUNNING YOU THROUGH SOME HEAVY BREATHING EXERCISES...
HI, SARAH. DON'T GET UP.
SHUT UP! JUST SHUT UP!
HEY, CULLODEN... THERE'S NO NEED TO GET UNPROFESSIONAL.
WHY, WILSON?! WHY?! THAT BATTLE ARMOR WAS PERFECTLY CALIBRATED TO YOU AND THE UPCOMING CHALLENGE MONTY FORECASTED!

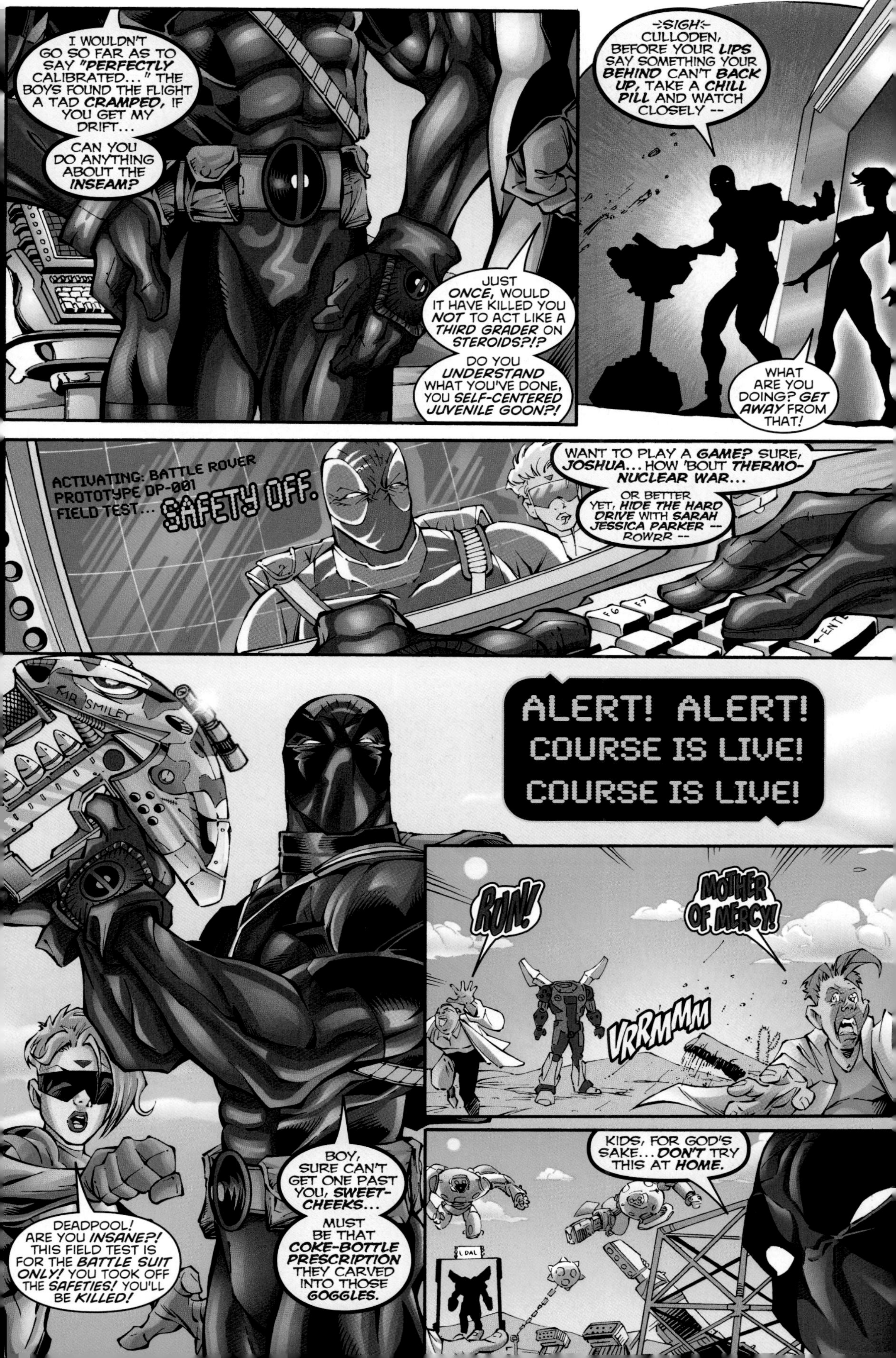
I WOULDN'T GO SO FAR AS TO SAY "PERFECTLY CALIBRATED..." THE BOYS FOUND THE FLIGHT A TAD CRAMPED, IF YOU GET MY DRIFT...
CAN YOU DO ANYTHING ABOUT THE INSEAM?
JUST ONCE, WOULD IT HAVE KILLED YOU NOT TO ACT LIKE A THIRD GRADER ON STEROIDS?!?
DO YOU UNDERSTAND WHAT YOU'VE DONE, YOU SELF-CENTERED JUVENILE GOON?!
-SIGH- CULLODEN, BEFORE YOUR LIPS SAY SOMETHING YOUR BEHIND CAN'T BACK UP, TAKE A CHILL PILL AND WATCH CLOSELY --
WHAT ARE YOU DOING? GET AWAY FROM THAT!
ACTIVATING: BATTLE ROVER PROTOTYPE DP-001 FIELD TEST...
SAFETY OFF.
WANT TO PLAY A GAME? SURE, JOSHUA... HOW 'BOUT THERMO-NUCLEAR WAR...
OR BETTER YET, HIDE THE HARD DRIVE WITH SARAH JESSICA PARKER -- ROWRR --
MR. SMILEY
ALERT! ALERT! COURSE IS LIVE! COURSE IS LIVE!
DEADPOOL! ARE YOU INSANE?! THIS FIELD TEST IS FOR THE BATTLE SUIT ONLY! YOU TOOK OFF THE SAFETIES! YOU'LL BE KILLED!
BOY, SURE CAN'T GET ONE PAST YOU, SWEET-CHEEKS...
MUST BE THAT COKE-BOTTLE PRESCRIPTION THEY CARVED INTO THOSE GOGGLES.
RUN!
MOTHER OF MERCY!
VRRMMM
KIDS, FOR GOD'S SAKE... DON'T TRY THIS AT HOME.

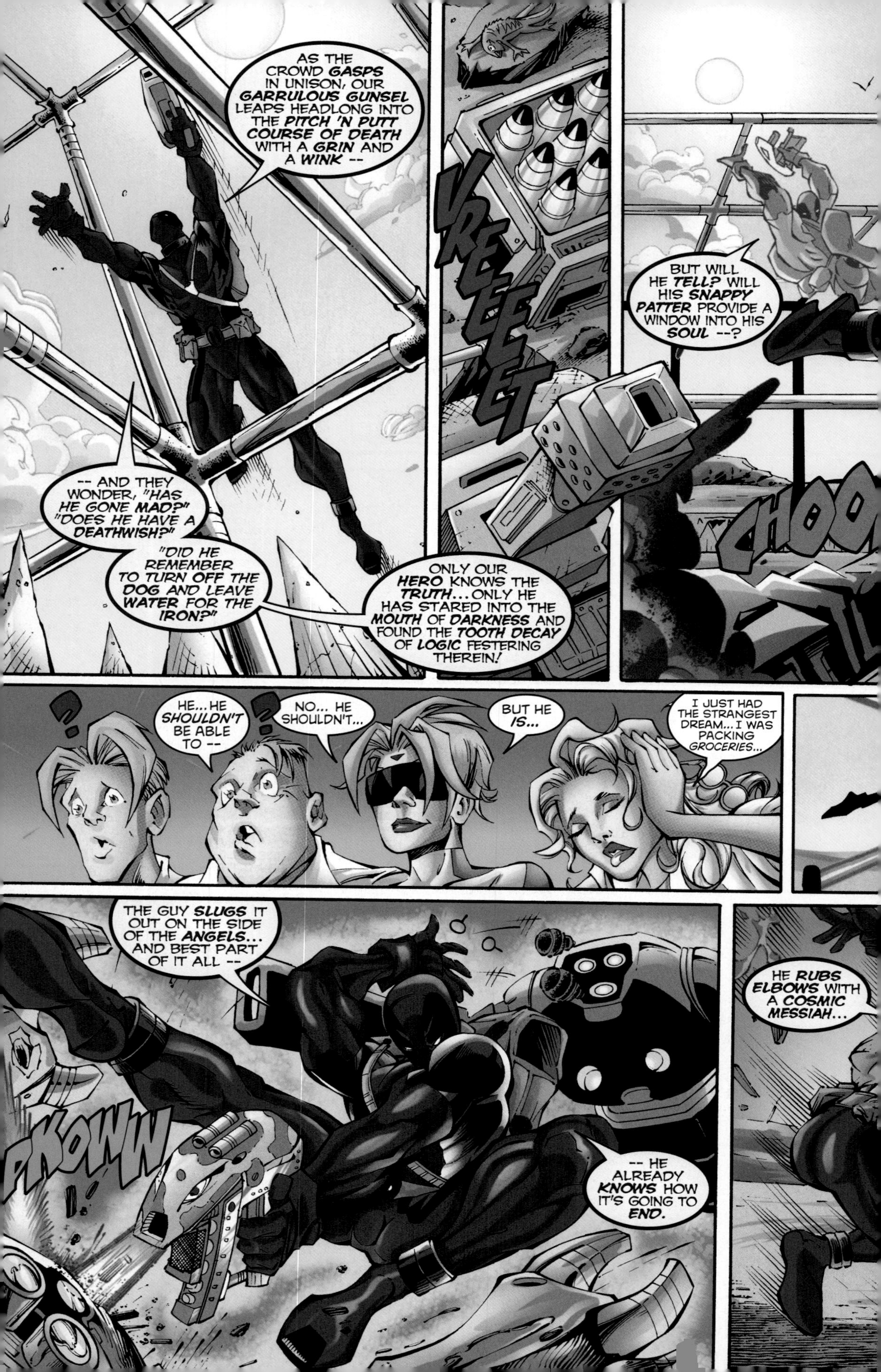
AS THE CROWD GASPS IN UNISON, OUR GARRULOUS GUNSEL LEAPS HEADLONG INTO THE PITCH 'N PUTT COURSE OF DEATH WITH A GRIN AND A WINK --
-- AND THEY WONDER, "HAS HE GONE MAD?" "DOES HE HAVE A DEATHWISH?"
"DID HE REMEMBER TO TURN OFF THE DOG AND LEAVE WATER FOR THE IRON?"
ONLY OUR HERO KNOWS THE TRUTH... ONLY HE HAS STARED INTO THE MOUTH OF DARKNESS AND FOUND THE TOOTH DECAY OF LOGIC FESTERING THEREIN!
VREEEEET
BUT WILL HE TELL? WILL HIS SNAPPY PATTER PROVIDE A WINDOW INTO HIS SOUL --?
CHOO
HE... HE SHOULDN'T BE ABLE TO --
NO... HE SHOULDN'T...
BUT HE IS...
I JUST HAD THE STRANGEST DREAM... I WAS PACKING GROCERIES...
THE GUY SLUGS IT OUT ON THE SIDE OF THE ANGELS... AND BEST PART OF IT ALL --
PKOWW
-- HE ALREADY KNOWS HOW IT'S GOING TO END.
HE RUBS ELBOWS WITH A COSMIC MESSIAH...

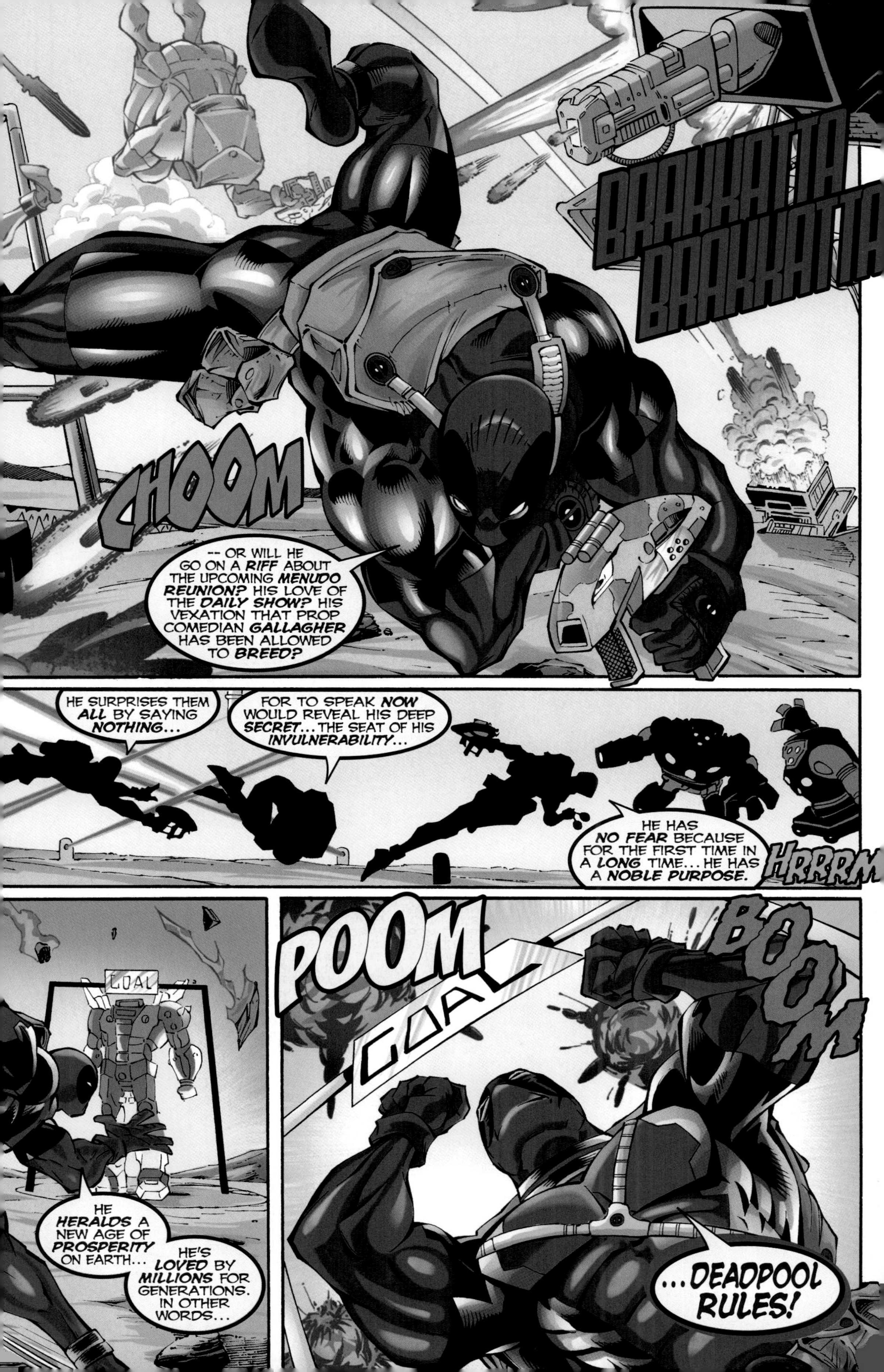
BRAKKATTA BRAKKATTA
CHOOM
-- OR WILL HE GO ON A RIFF ABOUT THE UPCOMING MENUDO REUNION? HIS LOVE OF THE DAILY SHOW? HIS VEXATION THAT PROP COMEDIAN GALLAGHER HAS BEEN ALLOWED TO BREED?
HE SURPRISES THEM ALL BY SAYING NOTHING...
FOR TO SPEAK NOW WOULD REVEAL HIS DEEP SECRET... THE SEAT OF HIS INVULNERABILITY...
HE HAS NO FEAR BECAUSE FOR THE FIRST TIME IN A LONG TIME... HE HAS A NOBLE PURPOSE.
HRRRM
GOAL
HE HERALDS A NEW AGE OF PROSPERITY ON EARTH...
HE'S LOVED BY MILLIONS FOR GENERATIONS. IN OTHER WORDS...
POOM
BOOM
GOAL
...DEADPOOL RULES!

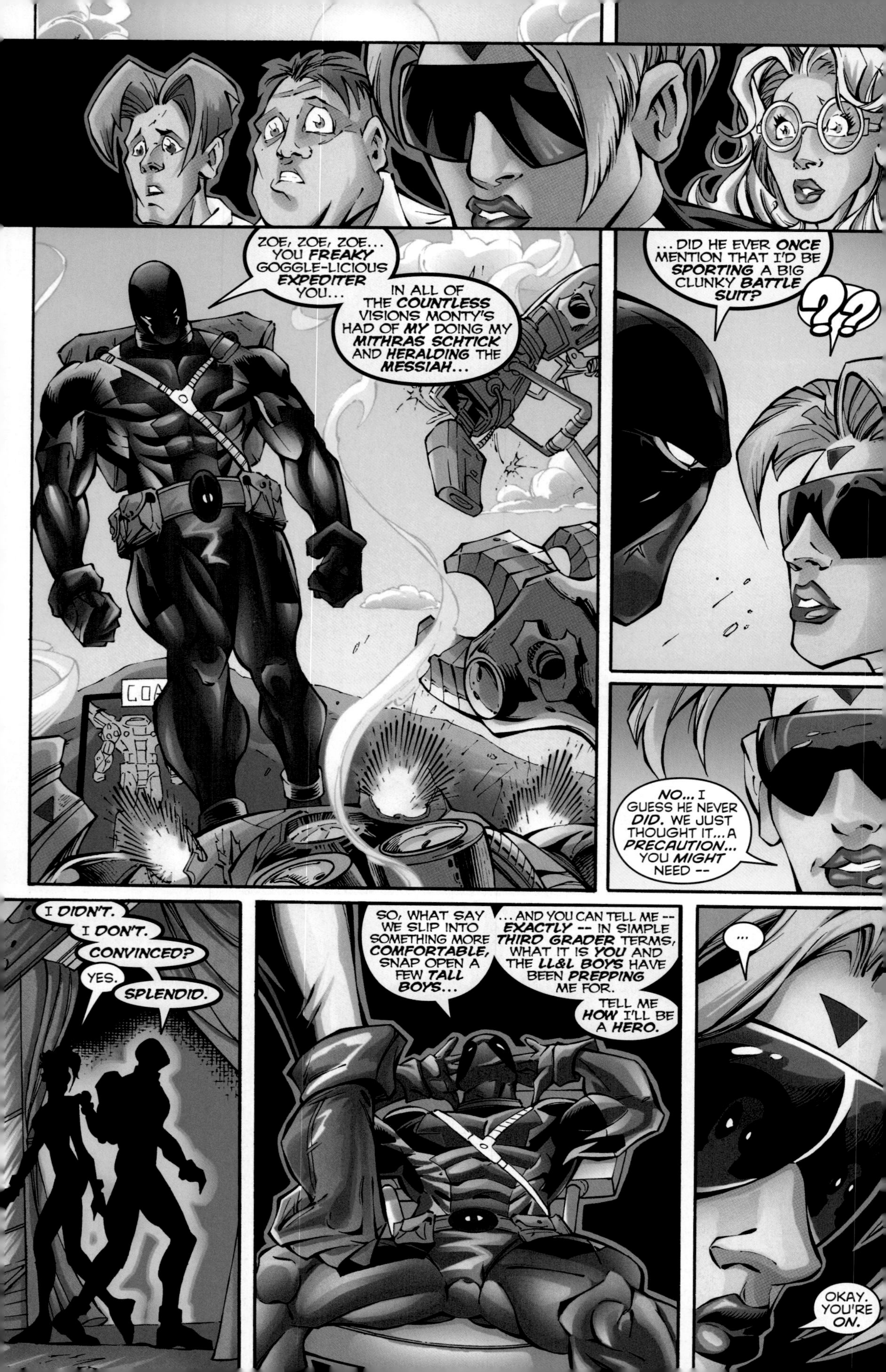
ZOE, ZOE, ZOE... YOU FREAKY GOGGLE-LICIOUS EXPEDITER YOU...
IN ALL OF THE COUNTLESS VISIONS MONTY'S HAD OF MY DOING MY MITHRAS SCHTICK AND HERALDING THE MESSIAH...
...DID HE EVER ONCE MENTION THAT I'D BE SPORTING A BIG CLUNKY BATTLE SUIT?
??
NO... I GUESS HE NEVER DID. WE JUST THOUGHT IT... A PRECAUTION... YOU MIGHT NEED --
I DIDN'T.
I DON'T.
CONVINCED?
YES.
SPLENDID.
SO, WHAT SAY WE SLIP INTO SOMETHING MORE COMFORTABLE, SNAP OPEN A FEW TALL BOYS...
...AND YOU CAN TELL ME -- EXACTLY -- IN SIMPLE THIRD GRADER TERMS, WHAT IT IS YOU AND THE LL&L BOYS HAVE BEEN PREPPING ME FOR.
TELL ME HOW I'LL BE A HERO.
...
OKAY. YOU'RE ON.

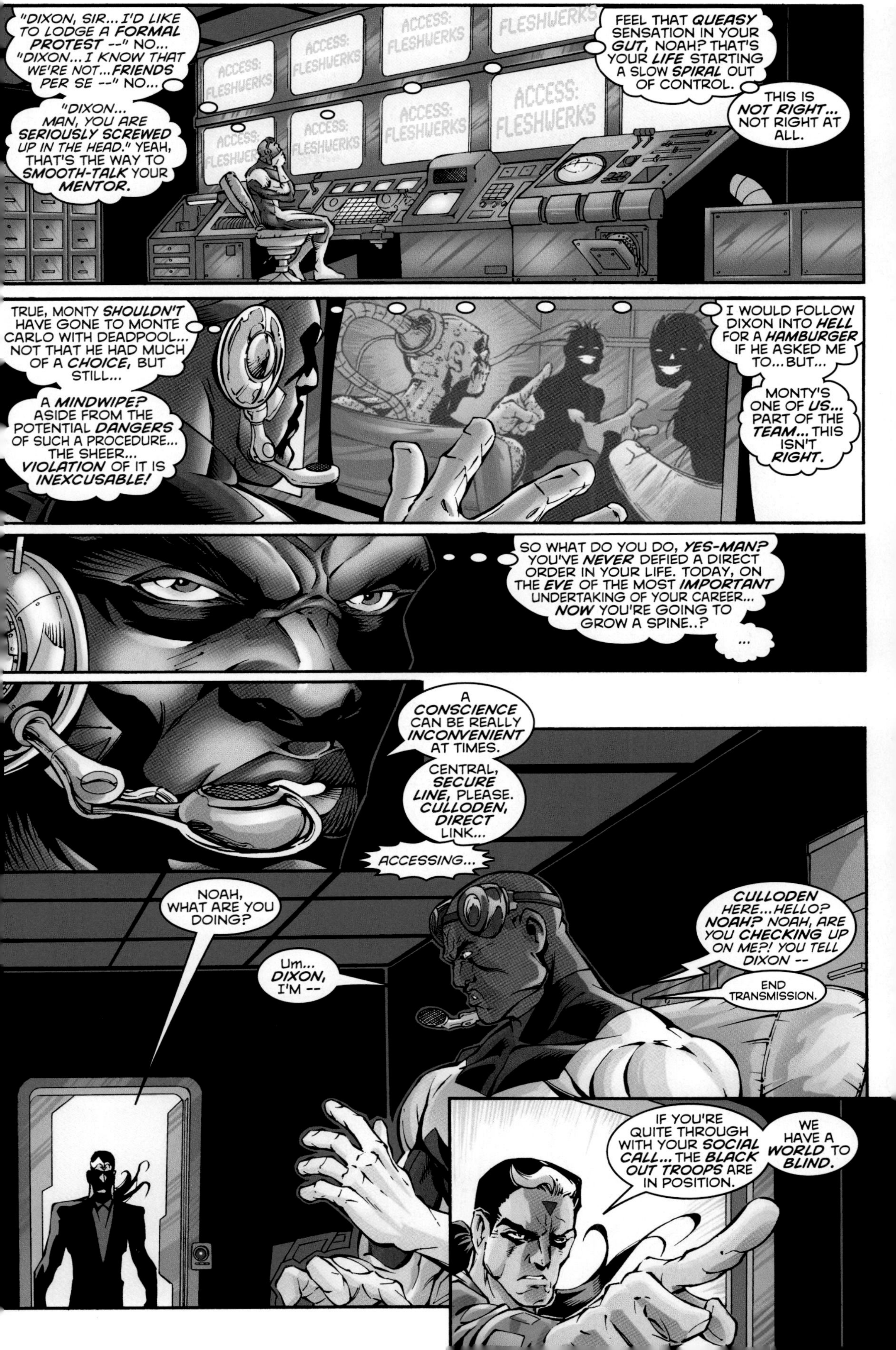
"DIXON, SIR... I'D LIKE TO LODGE A FORMAL PROTEST --" NO... "DIXON... I KNOW THAT WE'RE NOT... FRIENDS PER SE --" NO...
"DIXON... MAN, YOU ARE SERIOUSLY SCREWED UP IN THE HEAD." YEAH, THAT'S THE WAY TO SMOOTH-TALK YOUR MENTOR.
ACCESS: FLESHWERKS
FEEL THAT QUEASY SENSATION IN YOUR GUT, NOAH? THAT'S YOUR LIFE STARTING A SLOW SPIRAL OUT OF CONTROL.
THIS IS NOT RIGHT... NOT RIGHT AT ALL.
TRUE, MONTY SHOULDN'T HAVE GONE TO MONTE CARLO WITH DEADPOOL... NOT THAT HE HAD MUCH OF A CHOICE, BUT STILL...
A MINDWIPE? ASIDE FROM THE POTENTIAL DANGERS OF SUCH A PROCEDURE... THE SHEER... VIOLATION OF IT IS INEXCUSABLE!
I WOULD FOLLOW DIXON INTO HELL FOR A HAMBURGER IF HE ASKED ME TO... BUT...
MONTY'S ONE OF US... PART OF THE TEAM... THIS ISN'T RIGHT.
SO WHAT DO YOU DO, YES-MAN? YOU'VE NEVER DEFIED A DIRECT ORDER IN YOUR LIFE. TODAY, ON THE EVE OF THE MOST IMPORTANT UNDERTAKING OF YOUR CAREER... NOW YOU'RE GOING TO GROW A SPINE..?
...
A CONSCIENCE CAN BE REALLY INCONVENIENT AT TIMES.
CENTRAL, SECURE LINE, PLEASE. CULLODEN, DIRECT LINK...
ACCESSING...
NOAH, WHAT ARE YOU DOING?
Um... DIXON, I'M --
CULLODEN HERE... HELLO? NOAH? NOAH, ARE YOU CHECKING UP ON ME?! YOU TELL DIXON --
END TRANSMISSION.
IF YOU'RE QUITE THROUGH WITH YOUR SOCIAL CALL... THE BLACK OUT TROOPS ARE IN POSITION.
WE HAVE A WORLD TO BLIND.

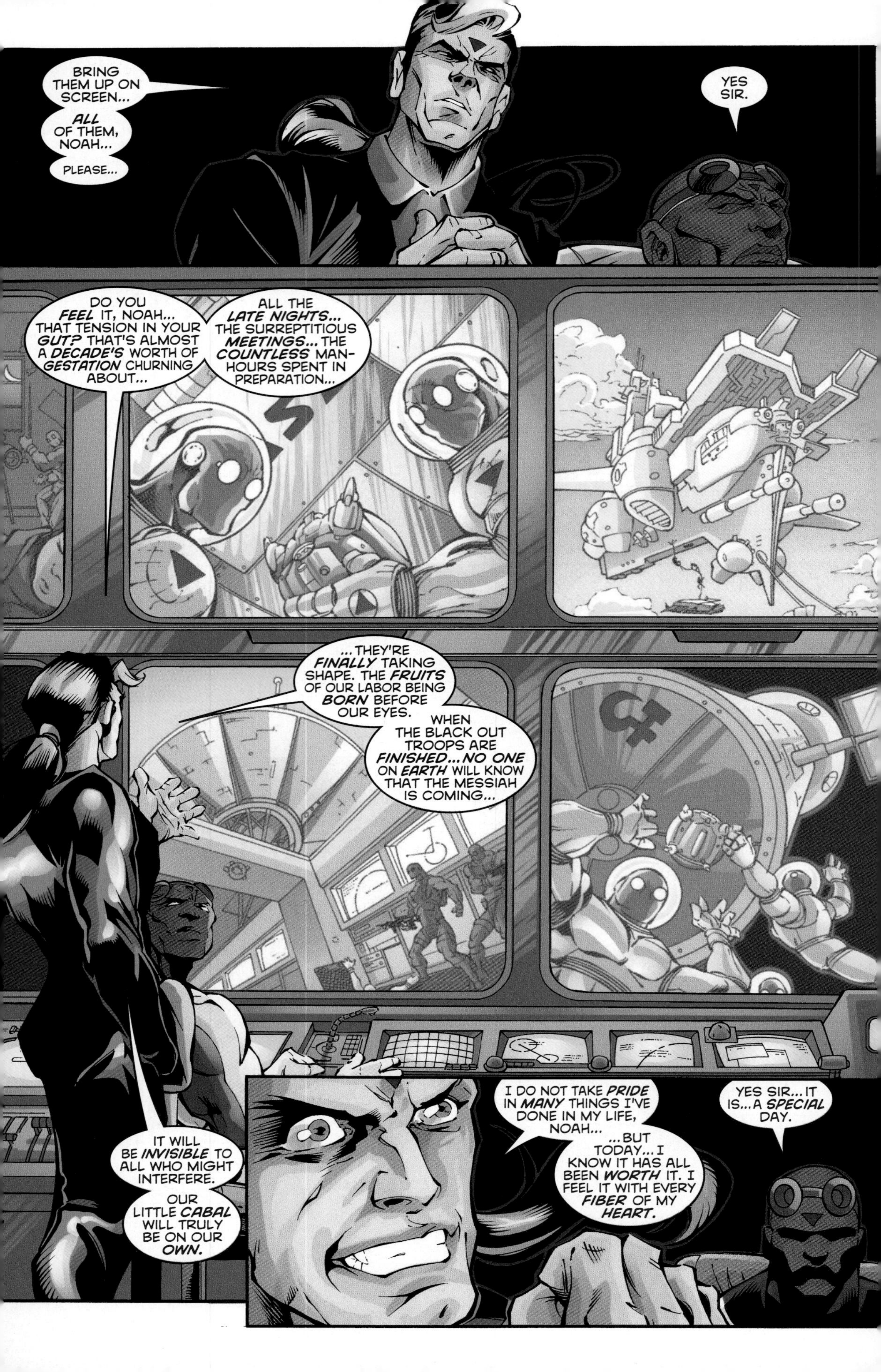
BRING THEM UP ON SCREEN...
ALL OF THEM, NOAH...
PLEASE...
YES SIR.
DO YOU FEEL IT, NOAH... THAT TENSION IN YOUR GUT? THAT'S ALMOST A DECADE'S WORTH OF GESTATION CHURNING ABOUT...
ALL THE LATE NIGHTS... THE SURREPTITIOUS MEETINGS... THE COUNTLESS MAN-HOURS SPENT IN PREPARATION...
...THEY'RE FINALLY TAKING SHAPE. THE FRUITS OF OUR LABOR BEING BORN BEFORE OUR EYES.
WHEN THE BLACK OUT TROOPS ARE FINISHED... NO ONE ON EARTH WILL KNOW THAT THE MESSIAH IS COMING...
IT WILL BE INVISIBLE TO ALL WHO MIGHT INTERFERE.
OUR LITTLE CABAL WILL TRULY BE ON OUR OWN.
I DO NOT TAKE PRIDE IN MANY THINGS I'VE DONE IN MY LIFE, NOAH...
...BUT TODAY... I KNOW IT HAS ALL BEEN WORTH IT. I FEEL IT WITH EVERY FIBER OF MY HEART.
YES SIR... IT IS... A SPECIAL DAY.

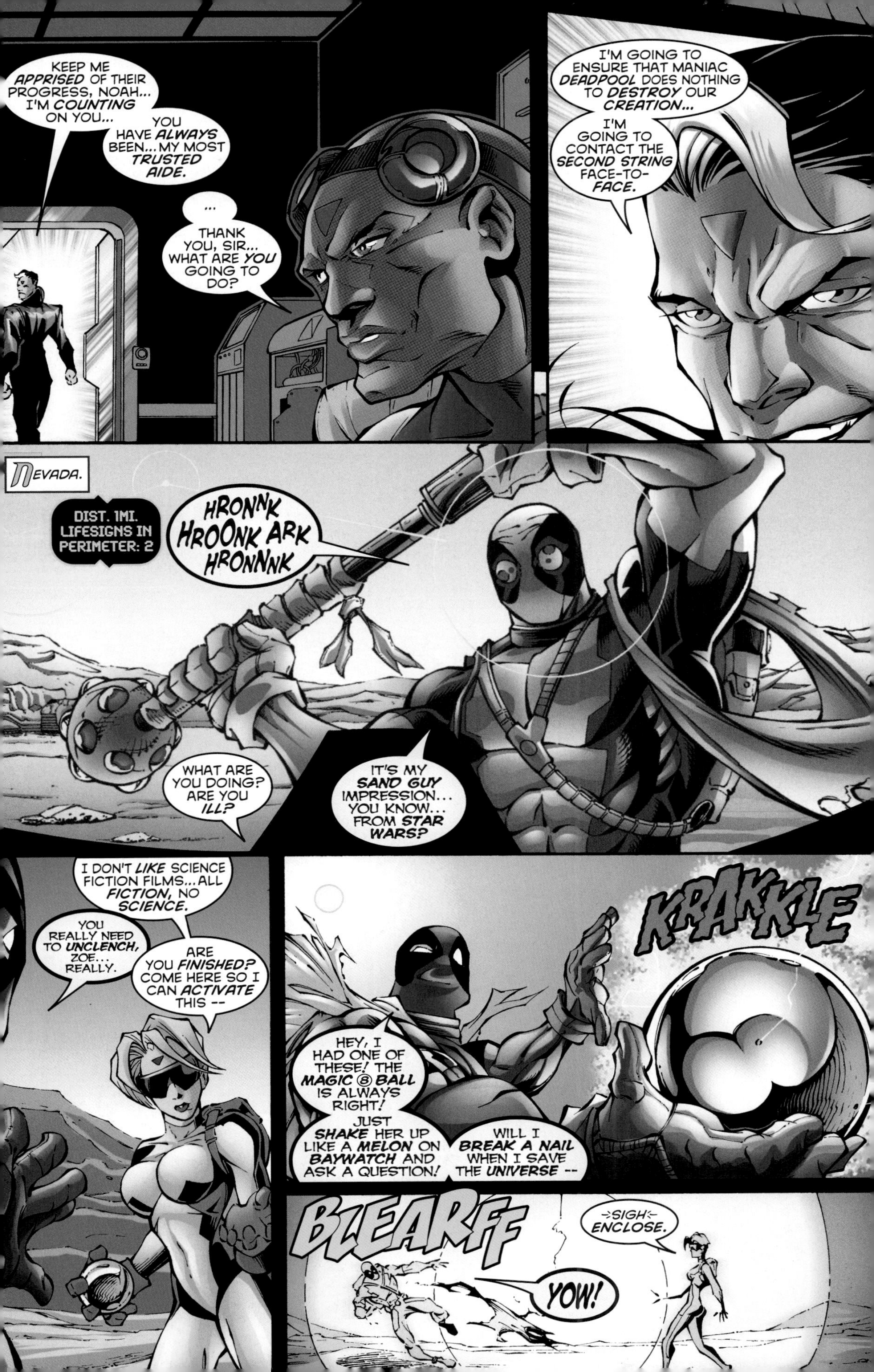
KEEP ME APPRISED OF THEIR PROGRESS, NOAH... I'M COUNTING ON YOU...
YOU HAVE ALWAYS BEEN... MY MOST TRUSTED AIDE.
...
THANK YOU, SIR... WHAT ARE YOU GOING TO DO?
I'M GOING TO ENSURE THAT MANIAC DEADPOOL DOES NOTHING TO DESTROY OUR CREATION...
I'M GOING TO CONTACT THE SECOND STRING FACE-TO-FACE.
NEVADA.
DIST. 1MI. LIFESIGNS IN PERIMETER: 2
HRONNK HROONK ARK HRONNNK
WHAT ARE YOU DOING? ARE YOU ILL?
IT'S MY SAND GUY IMPRESSION... YOU KNOW... FROM STAR WARS?
I DON'T LIKE SCIENCE FICTION FILMS... ALL FICTION, NO SCIENCE.
YOU REALLY NEED TO UNCLENCH, ZOE... REALLY.
ARE YOU FINISHED? COME HERE SO I CAN ACTIVATE THIS --
KRAKKLE
HEY, I HAD ONE OF THESE! THE MAGIC 8 BALL IS ALWAYS RIGHT!
JUST SHAKE HER UP LIKE A MELON ON BAYWATCH AND ASK A QUESTION!
WILL I BREAK A NAIL WHEN I SAVE THE UNIVERSE --
BLEARFF
SIGH ENCLOSE.
YOW!

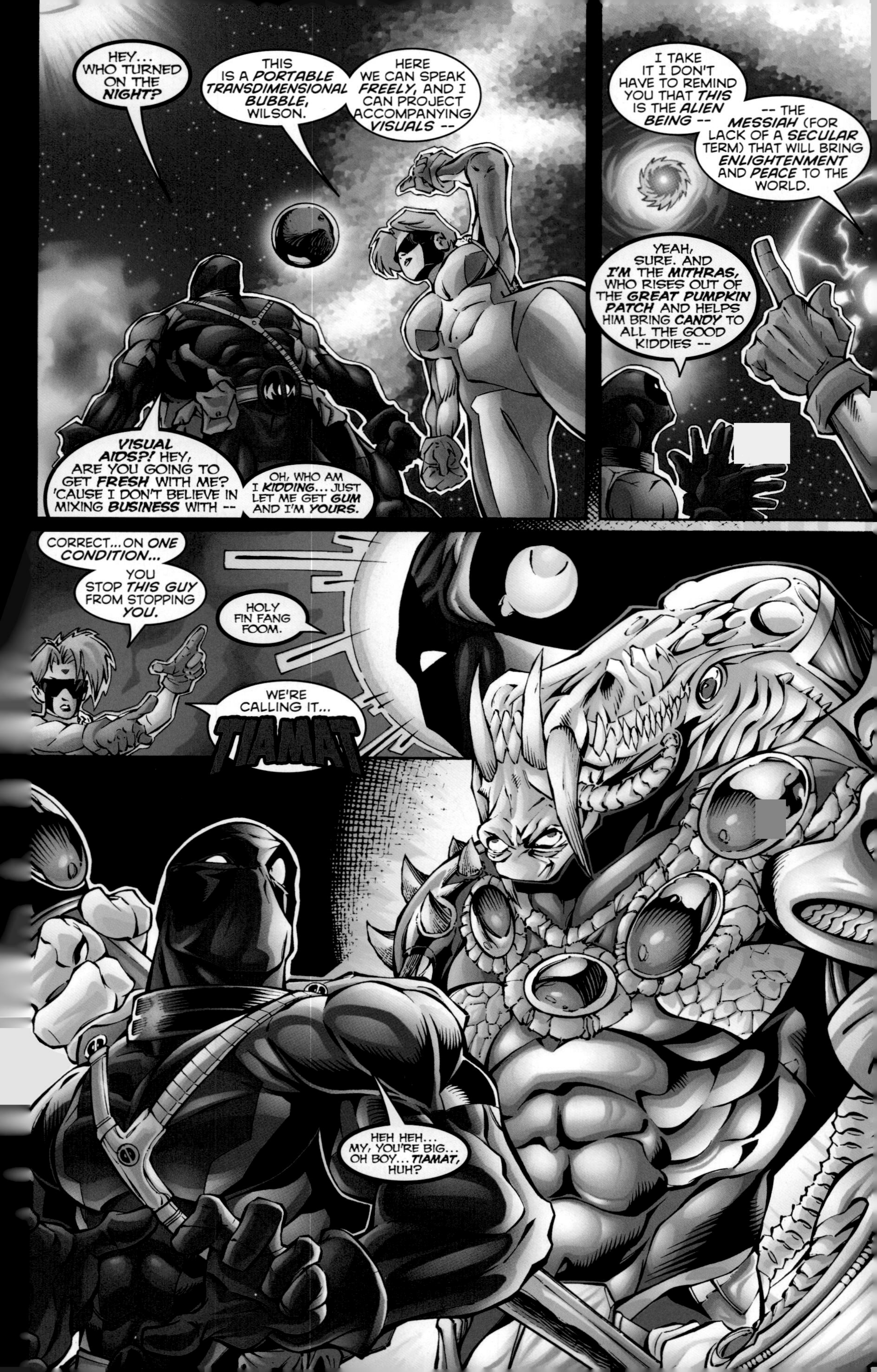
HEY... WHO TURNED ON THE NIGHT?
THIS IS A PORTABLE TRANSDIMENSIONAL BUBBLE, WILSON.
HERE WE CAN SPEAK FREELY, AND I CAN PROJECT ACCOMPANYING VISUALS --
VISUAL AIDS?! HEY, ARE YOU GOING TO GET FRESH WITH ME? 'CAUSE I DON'T BELIEVE IN MIXING BUSINESS WITH --
OH, WHO AM I KIDDING... JUST LET ME GET GUM AND I'M YOURS.
I TAKE IT I DON'T HAVE TO REMIND YOU THAT THIS IS THE ALIEN BEING --
-- THE MESSIAH (FOR LACK OF A SECULAR TERM) THAT WILL BRING ENLIGHTENMENT AND PEACE TO THE WORLD.
YEAH, SURE. AND I'M THE MITHRAS, WHO RISES OUT OF THE GREAT PUMPKIN PATCH AND HELPS HIM BRING CANDY TO ALL THE GOOD KIDDIES --
CORRECT...ON ONE CONDITION...
YOU STOP THIS GUY FROM STOPPING YOU.
HOLY FIN FANG FOOM.
WE'RE CALLING IT...
TIAMAT
HEH HEH... MY, YOU'RE BIG... OH BOY... TIAMAT, HUH?

IT'S *ALL GOOD*, REALLY...

WHEN I WAS IN *GRADE SCHOOL*, AN' THEY GAVE ME AN *APTITUDE* TEST, YOU KNOW WHAT CAME UP?

DENTIST, TALK SHOW HOST, MERCENARY KILLER. BUSTING HEADS IS IN MY *BLOOD*.

OH, SO THOSE *INFLECTIONS* OF *SELF-PITY* IN YOUR VOICE ARE JUST FOR *MY* BENEFIT?

BZZT

SPILL IT.

I DON'T *KNOW*... I GUESS IT JUST CAUGHT ME OFF GUARD... ALL THE *HYPE* ABOUT MY BEING *GOOD*... POLISHING MY *HALO*...

ALL SORTS OF *GOOD JUNK* THAT I'M *DIRECTLY* RESPONSIBLE FOR --

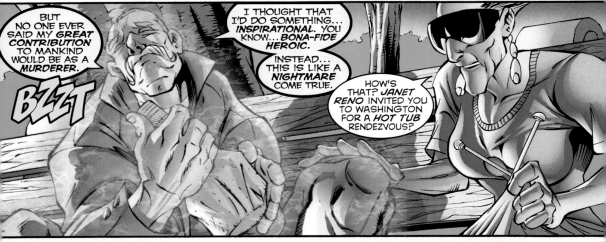

BUT NO ONE EVER SAID MY *GREAT* CONTRIBUTION TO MANKIND WOULD BE AS A *MURDERER.*

BZZT

I THOUGHT THAT I'D DO SOMETHING... *INSPIRATIONAL.* YOU KNOW... *BONA-FIDE* HEROIC.

INSTEAD... THIS IS LIKE A *NIGHTMARE* COME TRUE.

HOW'S *THAT? JANET RENO* INVITED YOU TO WASHINGTON FOR A *HOT TUB* RENDEZVOUS?

⸢SIGH⸥

DESTINY HAS FINGERED ME AS THE GUY YOU CALL TO SPILL BLOOD.

BZZT

WADE WILSON... MONSTER AT LARGE. THAT'S IT.

OH...

OH?

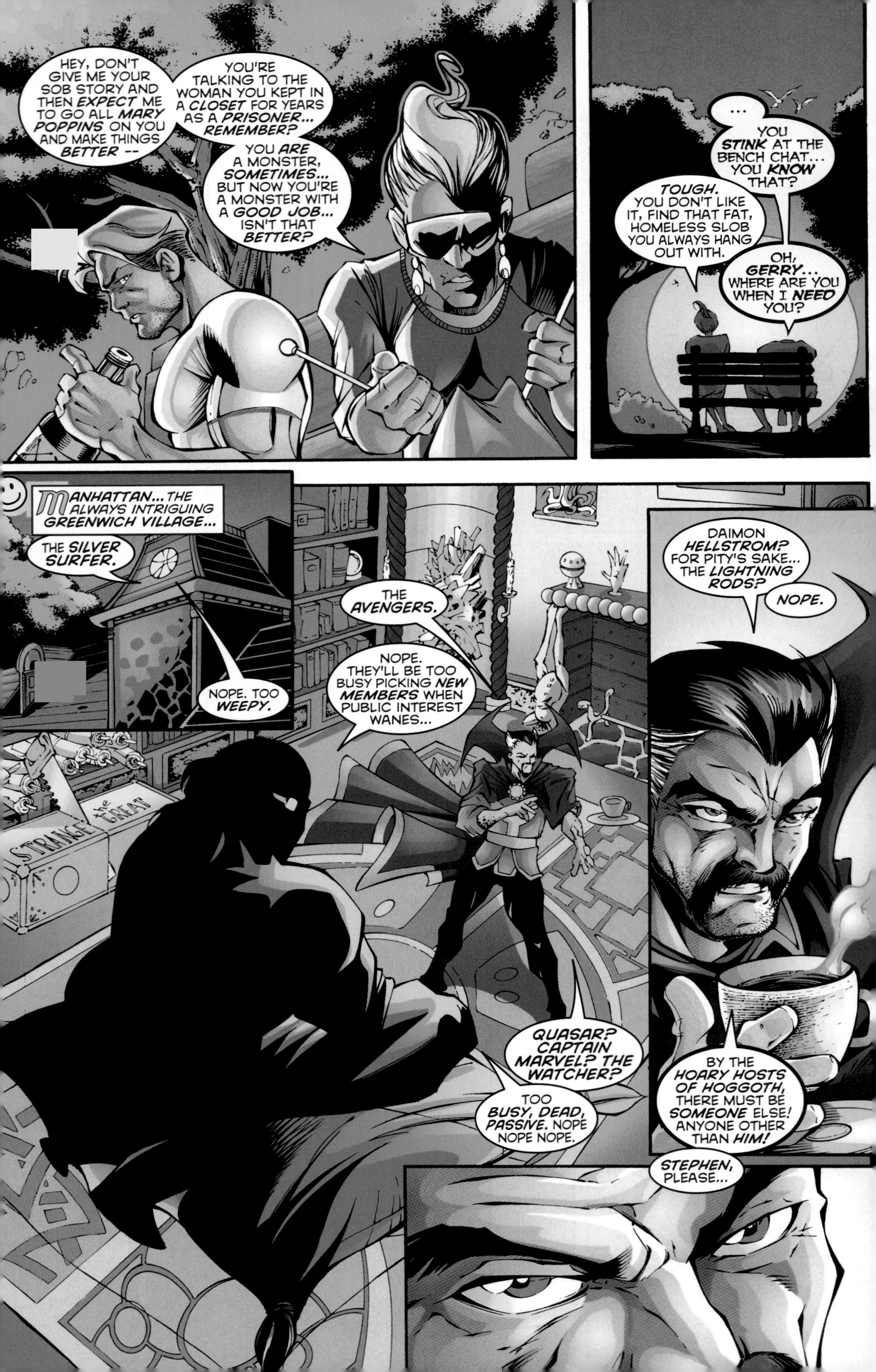

HEY, DON'T GIVE ME YOUR SOB STORY AND THEN EXPECT ME TO GO ALL MARY POPPINS ON YOU AND MAKE THINGS BETTER --
YOU'RE TALKING TO THE WOMAN YOU KEPT IN A CLOSET FOR YEARS AS A PRISONER... REMEMBER?
YOU ARE A MONSTER, SOMETIMES... BUT NOW YOU'RE A MONSTER WITH A GOOD JOB... ISN'T THAT BETTER?
...
YOU STINK AT THE BENCH CHAT... YOU KNOW THAT?
TOUGH. YOU DON'T LIKE IT, FIND THAT FAT, HOMELESS SLOB YOU ALWAYS HANG OUT WITH.
OH, GERRY... WHERE ARE YOU WHEN I NEED YOU?
MANHATTAN... THE ALWAYS INTRIGUING GREENWICH VILLAGE...
THE SILVER SURFER.
NOPE. TOO WEEPY.
THE AVENGERS.
NOPE. THEY'LL BE TOO BUSY PICKING NEW MEMBERS WHEN PUBLIC INTEREST WANES...
DAIMON HELLSTROM? FOR PITY'S SAKE... THE LIGHTNING RODS?
NOPE.
STRANGE the GREAT
QUASAR? CAPTAIN MARVEL? THE WATCHER?
TOO BUSY, DEAD, PASSIVE. NOPE NOPE NOPE.
BY THE HOARY HOSTS OF HOGGOTH, THERE MUST BE SOMEONE ELSE! ANYONE OTHER THAN HIM!
STEPHEN, PLEASE...

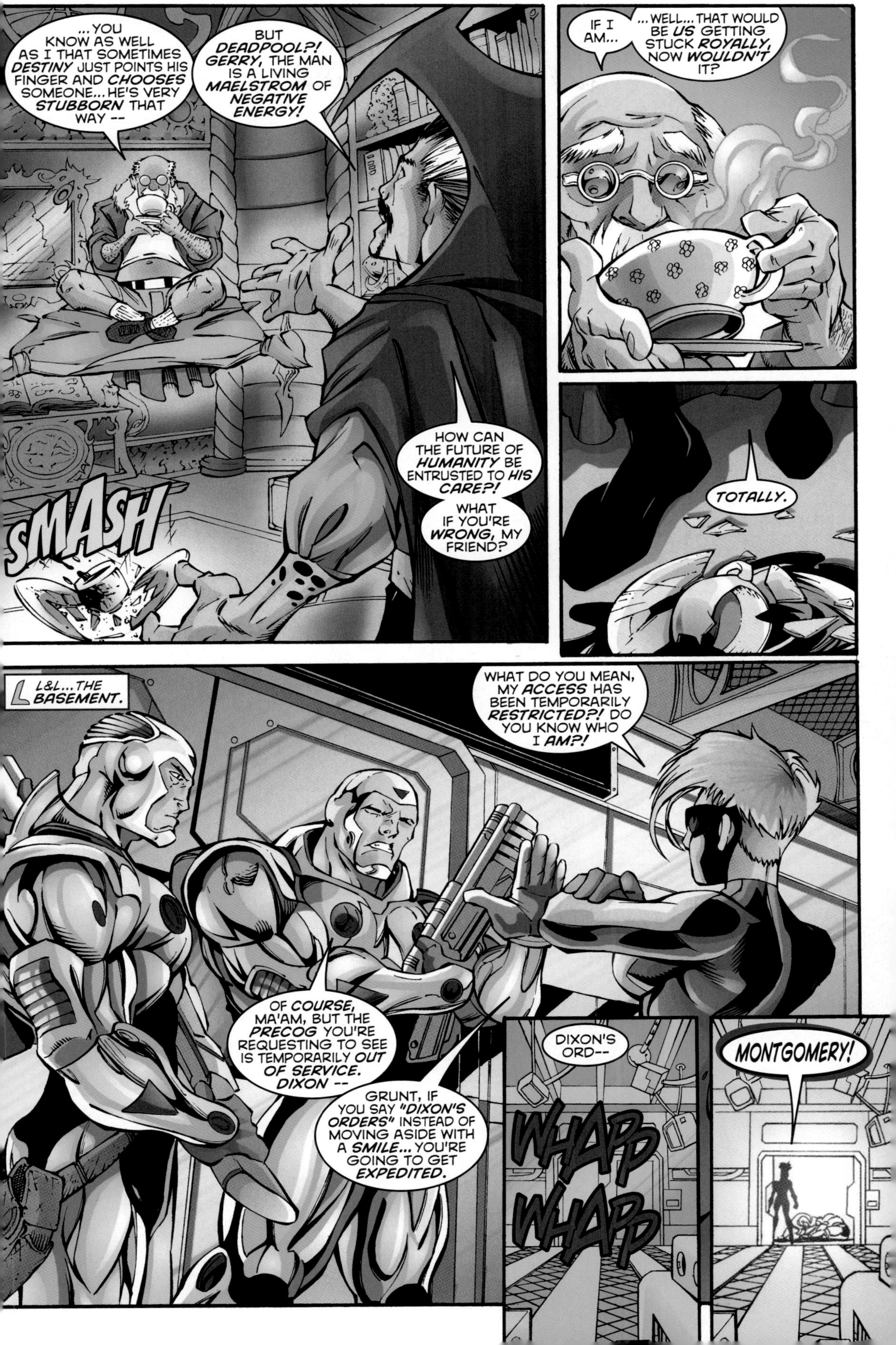
...YOU KNOW AS WELL AS I THAT SOMETIMES DESTINY JUST POINTS HIS FINGER AND CHOOSES SOMEONE... HE'S VERY STUBBORN THAT WAY --
BUT DEADPOOL?! GERRY, THE MAN IS A LIVING MAELSTROM OF NEGATIVE ENERGY!
HOW CAN THE FUTURE OF HUMANITY BE ENTRUSTED TO HIS CARE?!
WHAT IF YOU'RE WRONG, MY FRIEND?
SMASH
IF I AM...
...WELL...THAT WOULD BE US GETTING STUCK ROYALLY, NOW WOULDN'T IT?
TOTALLY.
L&L...THE BASEMENT.
WHAT DO YOU MEAN, MY ACCESS HAS BEEN TEMPORARILY RESTRICTED?! DO YOU KNOW WHO I AM?!
OF COURSE, MA'AM, BUT THE PRECOG YOU'RE REQUESTING TO SEE IS TEMPORARILY OUT OF SERVICE. DIXON --
GRUNT, IF YOU SAY "DIXON'S ORDERS" INSTEAD OF MOVING ASIDE WITH A SMILE... YOU'RE GOING TO GET EXPEDITED.
DIXON'S ORD--
WHAPP
WHAPP
MONTGOMERY!

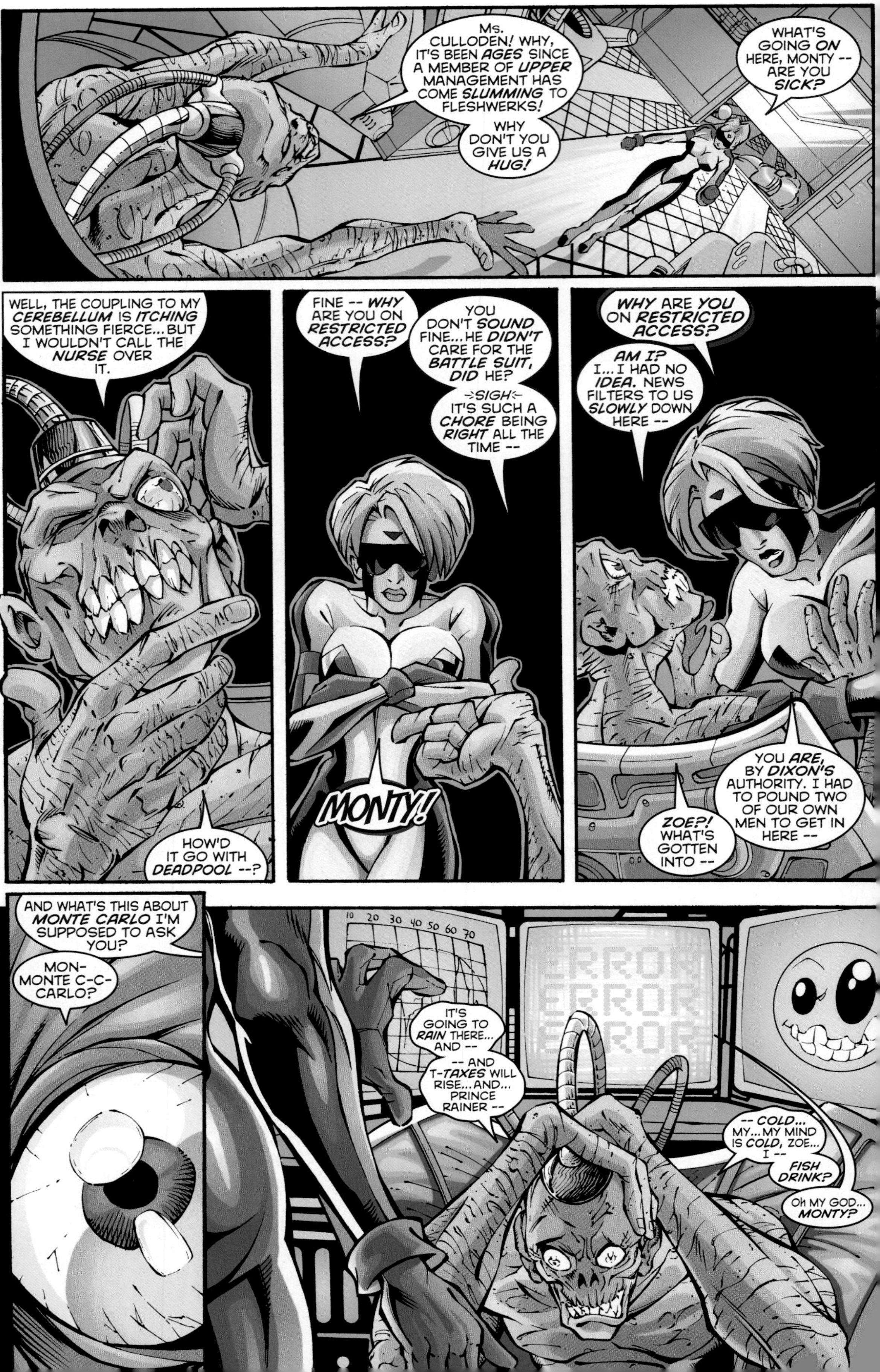
Ms. CULLODEN! WHY, IT'S BEEN AGES SINCE A MEMBER OF UPPER MANAGEMENT HAS COME SLUMMING TO FLESHWERKS!
WHY DON'T YOU GIVE US A HUG!
WHAT'S GOING ON HERE, MONTY -- ARE YOU SICK?
WELL, THE COUPLING TO MY CEREBELLUM IS ITCHING SOMETHING FIERCE... BUT I WOULDN'T CALL THE NURSE OVER IT.
HOW'D IT GO WITH DEADPOOL --?
FINE -- WHY ARE YOU ON RESTRICTED ACCESS?
YOU DON'T SOUND FINE... HE DIDN'T CARE FOR THE BATTLE SUIT, DID HE?
SIGH
IT'S SUCH A CHORE BEING RIGHT ALL THE TIME --
MONTY!
WHY ARE YOU ON RESTRICTED ACCESS?
AM I? I... I HAD NO IDEA. NEWS FILTERS TO US SLOWLY DOWN HERE --
YOU ARE, BY DIXON'S AUTHORITY. I HAD TO POUND TWO OF OUR OWN MEN TO GET IN HERE --
ZOE?! WHAT'S GOTTEN INTO --
AND WHAT'S THIS ABOUT MONTE CARLO I'M SUPPOSED TO ASK YOU?
MON- MONTE C-C-CARLO?
10 20 30 40 50 60 70
ERROR
ERROR
ERROR
IT'S GOING TO RAIN THERE... AND --
-- AND T-TAXES WILL RISE... AND... PRINCE RAINER --
-- COLD... MY... MY MIND IS COLD, ZOE... I --
FISH DRINK?
Oh MY GOD... MONTY?

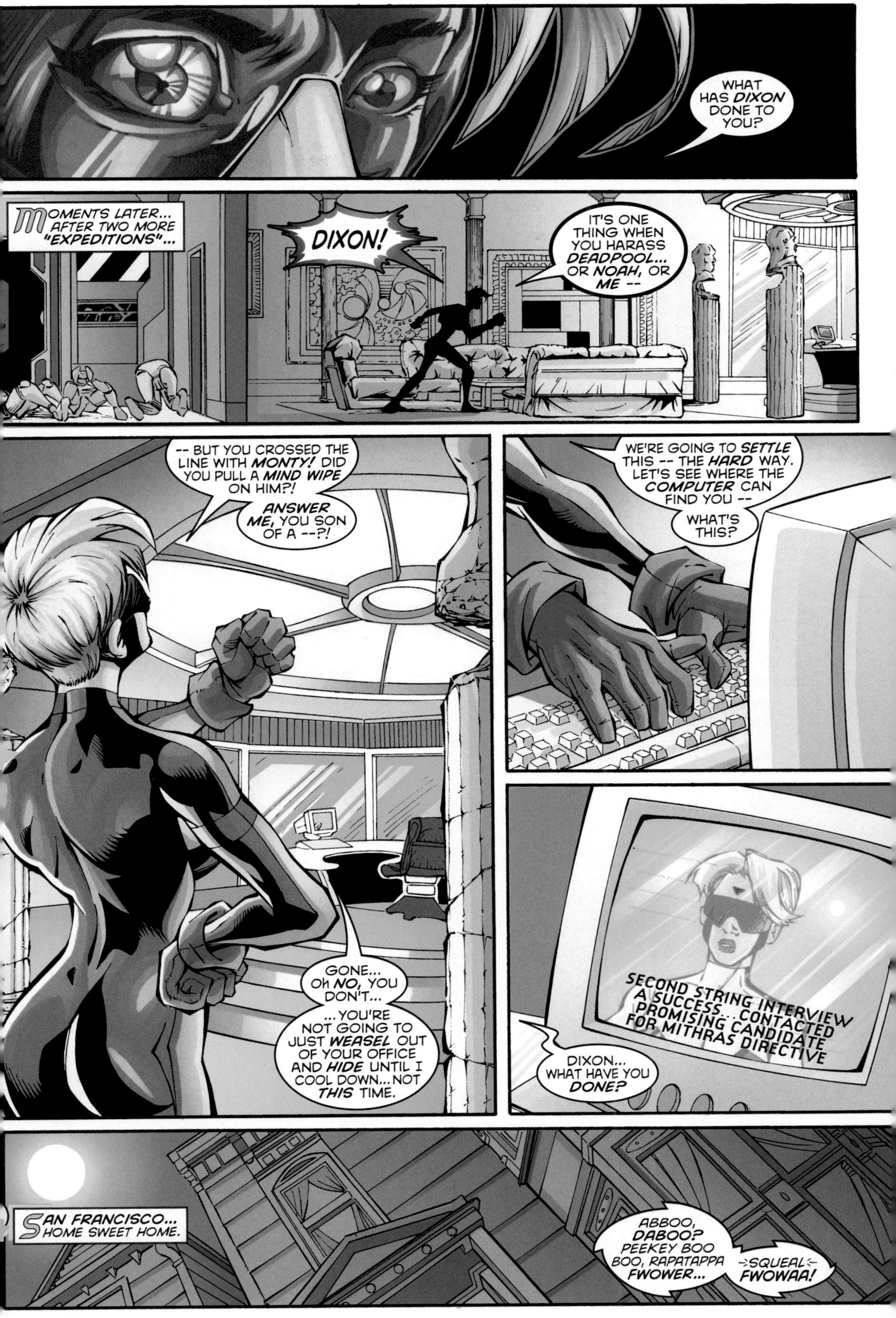
WHAT HAS DIXON DONE TO YOU?
MOMENTS LATER... AFTER TWO MORE "EXPEDITIONS"...
DIXON!
IT'S ONE THING WHEN YOU HARASS DEADPOOL... OR NOAH, OR ME --
-- BUT YOU CROSSED THE LINE WITH MONTY! DID YOU PULL A MIND WIPE ON HIM?!
ANSWER ME, YOU SON OF A --?!
GONE... OH NO, YOU DON'T...
...YOU'RE NOT GOING TO JUST WEASEL OUT OF YOUR OFFICE AND HIDE UNTIL I COOL DOWN... NOT THIS TIME.
WE'RE GOING TO SETTLE THIS -- THE HARD WAY. LET'S SEE WHERE THE COMPUTER CAN FIND YOU --
WHAT'S THIS?
SECOND STRING INTERVIEW A SUCCESS... CONTACTED PROMISING CANDIDATE FOR MITHRAS DIRECTIVE
DIXON... WHAT HAVE YOU DONE?
SAN FRANCISCO... HOME SWEET HOME.
ABBOO, DABOO? PEEKEY BOO BOO, RAPATAPPA FWOWER...
SQUEAL
FWOWAA!

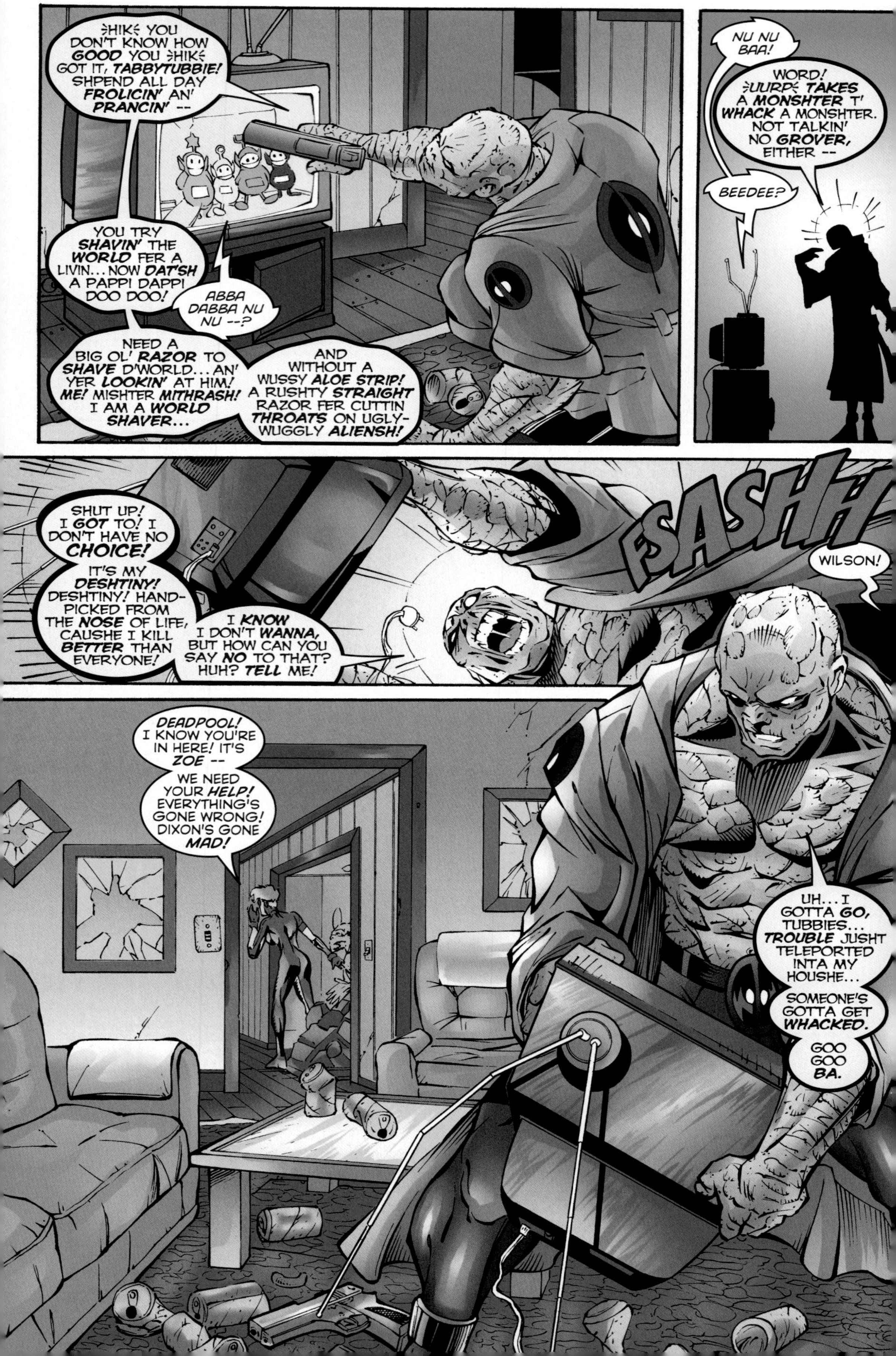
HIK YOU DON'T KNOW HOW GOOD YOU *HIK* GOT IT, TABBYTUBBIE! SHPEND ALL DAY FROLICIN' AN' PRANCIN' --
YOU TRY SHAVIN' THE WORLD FER A LIVIN... NOW DAT'SH A PAPPI DAPPI DOO DOO!
ABBA DABBA NU NU --?
NEED A BIG OL' RAZOR TO SHAVE D'WORLD... AN' YER LOOKIN' AT HIM! ME! MISHTER MITHRASH! I AM A WORLD SHAVER...
AND WITHOUT A WUSSY ALOE STRIP! A RUSHTY STRAIGHT RAZOR FER CUTTIN THROATS ON UGLY-WUGGLY ALIENSH!
NU NU BAA!
WORD! *UURP* TAKES A MONSHTER T' WHACK A MONSHTER. NOT TALKIN' NO GROVER, EITHER --
BEEDEE?
FSASHH
SHUT UP! I GOT TO! I DON'T HAVE NO CHOICE!
IT'S MY DESHTINY! DESHTINY! HAND-PICKED FROM THE NOSE OF LIFE, CAUSHE I KILL BETTER THAN EVERYONE!
I KNOW I DON'T WANNA, BUT HOW CAN YOU SAY NO TO THAT? HUH? TELL ME!
WILSON!
DEADPOOL! I KNOW YOU'RE IN HERE! IT'S ZOE --
WE NEED YOUR HELP! EVERYTHING'S GONE WRONG! DIXON'S GONE MAD!
UH... I GOTTA GO, TUBBIES... TROUBLE JUSHT TELEPORTED INTA MY HOUSHE...
SOMEONE'S GOTTA GET WHACKED.
GOO GOO BA.

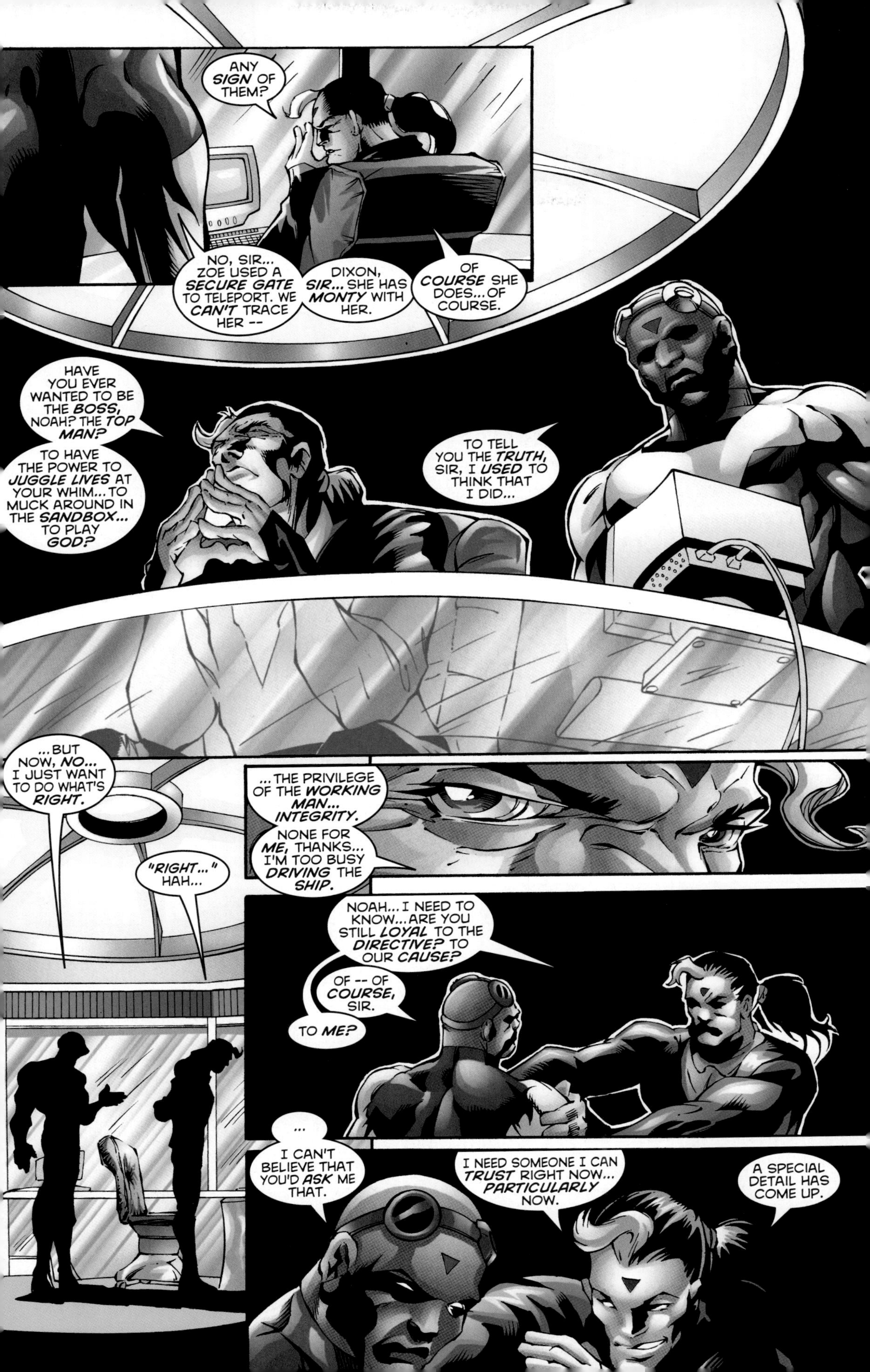
ANY SIGN OF THEM?
NO, SIR... ZOE USED A SECURE GATE TO TELEPORT. WE CAN'T TRACE HER --
DIXON, SIR... SHE HAS MONTY WITH HER.
OF COURSE SHE DOES... OF COURSE.
HAVE YOU EVER WANTED TO BE THE BOSS, NOAH? THE TOP MAN?
TO HAVE THE POWER TO JUGGLE LIVES AT YOUR WHIM... TO MUCK AROUND IN THE SANDBOX... TO PLAY GOD?
TO TELL YOU THE TRUTH, SIR, I USED TO THINK THAT I DID...
...BUT NOW, NO... I JUST WANT TO DO WHAT'S RIGHT.
"RIGHT..." HAH...
...THE PRIVILEGE OF THE WORKING MAN... INTEGRITY.
NONE FOR ME, THANKS... I'M TOO BUSY DRIVING THE SHIP.
NOAH... I NEED TO KNOW... ARE YOU STILL LOYAL TO THE DIRECTIVE? TO OUR CAUSE?
TO ME?
OF -- OF COURSE, SIR.
...
I CAN'T BELIEVE THAT YOU'D ASK ME THAT.
I NEED SOMEONE I CAN TRUST RIGHT NOW... PARTICULARLY NOW.
A SPECIAL DETAIL HAS COME UP.

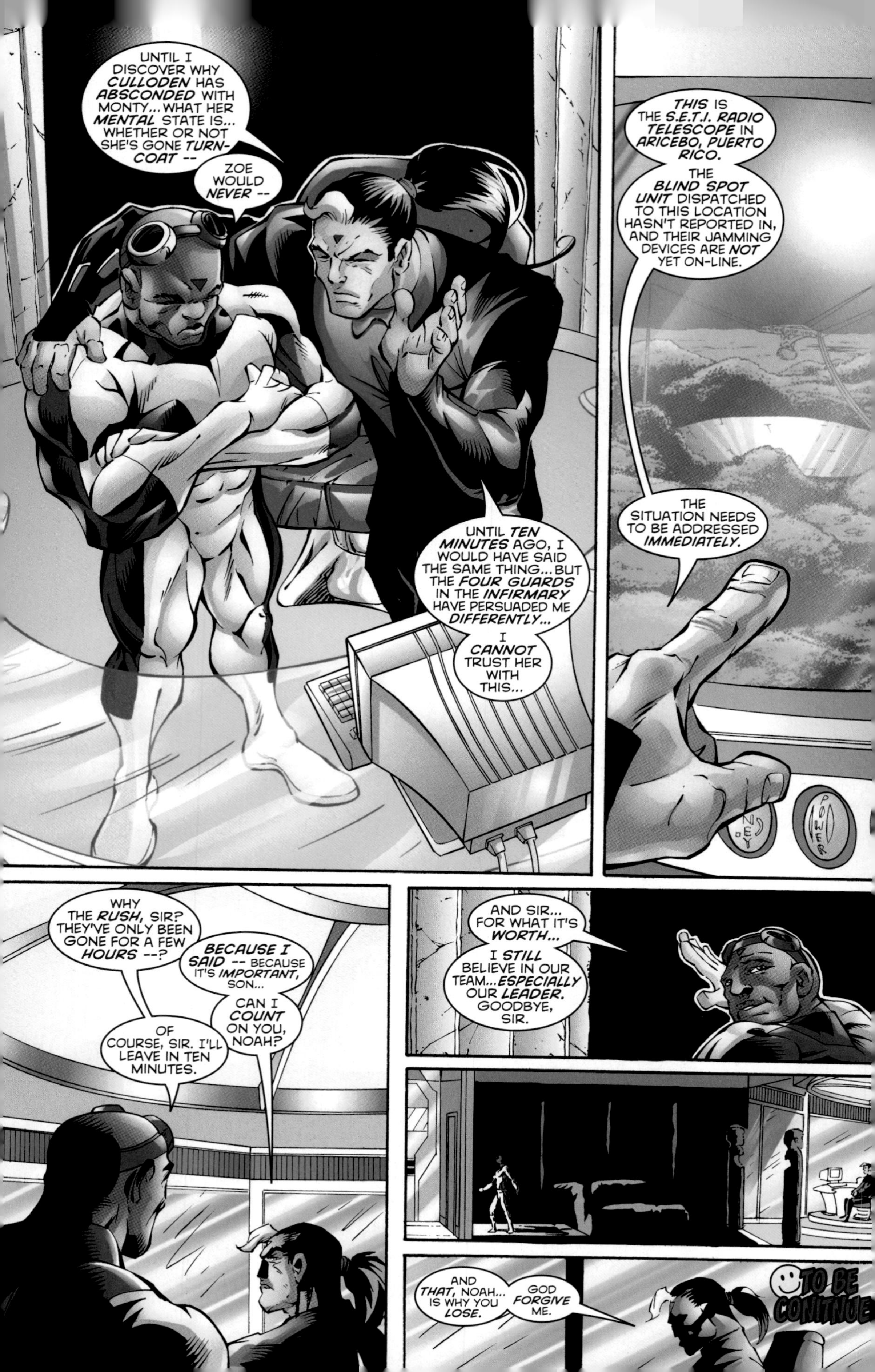
UNTIL I DISCOVER WHY CULLODEN HAS ABSCONDED WITH MONTY... WHAT HER MENTAL STATE IS... WHETHER OR NOT SHE'S GONE TURN-COAT --
ZOE WOULD NEVER --
UNTIL TEN MINUTES AGO, I WOULD HAVE SAID THE SAME THING... BUT THE FOUR GUARDS IN THE INFIRMARY HAVE PERSUADED ME DIFFERENTLY...
I CANNOT TRUST HER WITH THIS...
THIS IS THE S.E.T.I. RADIO TELESCOPE IN ARICEBO, PUERTO RICO.
THE BLIND SPOT UNIT DISPATCHED TO THIS LOCATION HASN'T REPORTED IN, AND THEIR JAMMING DEVICES ARE NOT YET ON-LINE.
THE SITUATION NEEDS TO BE ADDRESSED IMMEDIATELY.
POWER
WHY THE RUSH, SIR? THEY'VE ONLY BEEN GONE FOR A FEW HOURS --?
BECAUSE I SAID -- BECAUSE IT'S IMPORTANT, SON...
CAN I COUNT ON YOU, NOAH?
OF COURSE, SIR. I'LL LEAVE IN TEN MINUTES.
AND SIR... FOR WHAT IT'S WORTH...
I STILL BELIEVE IN OUR TEAM... ESPECIALLY OUR LEADER. GOODBYE, SIR.
AND THAT, NOAH... IS WHY YOU LOSE.
GOD FORGIVE ME.
TO BE CONTINUED

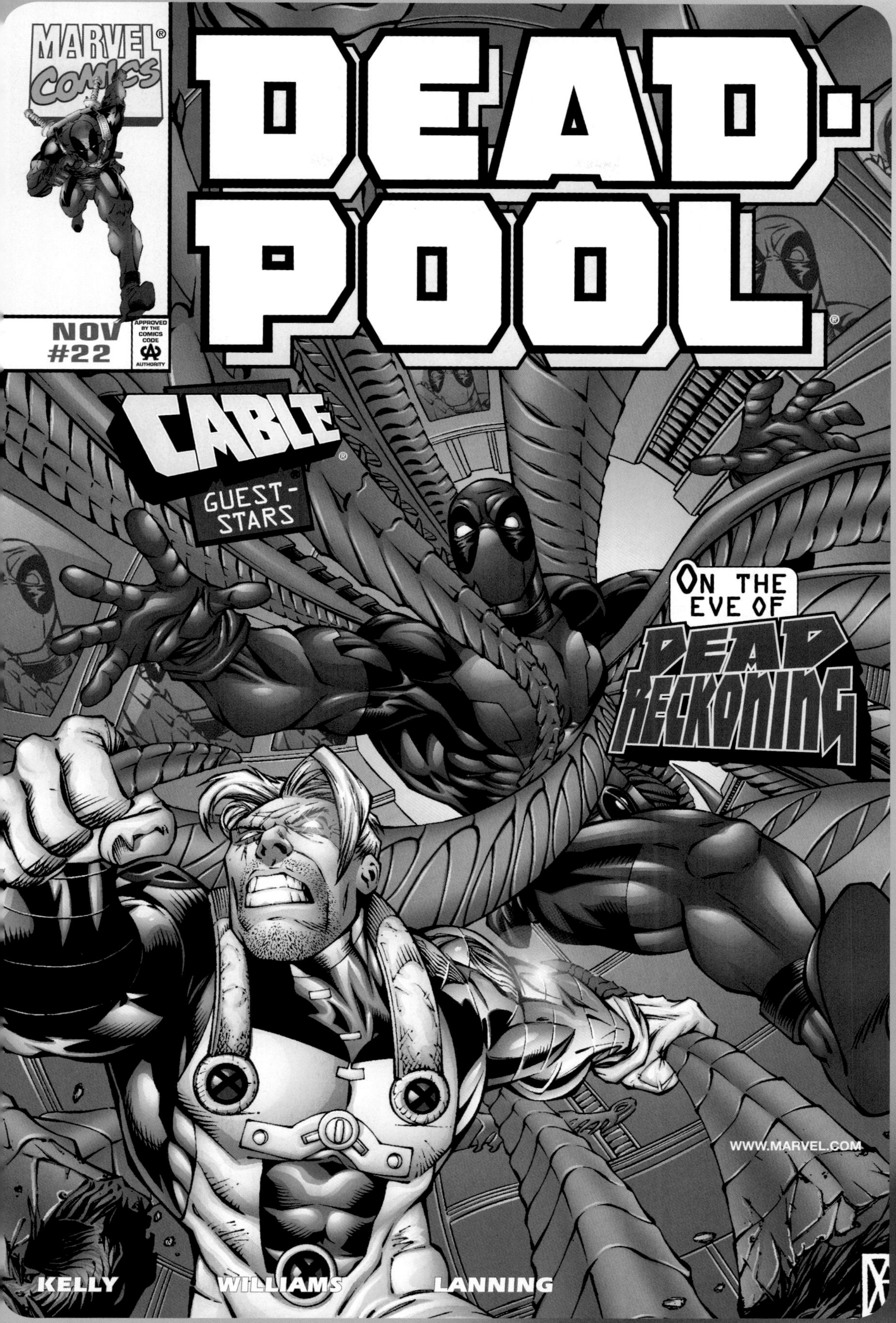
MARVEL® COMICS
DEADPOOL®
NOV #22
APPROVED BY THE COMICS CODE AUTHORITY
CABLE® GUEST-STARS
ON THE EVE OF DEAD RECKONING
WWW.MARVEL.COM
KELLY WILLIAMS LANNING

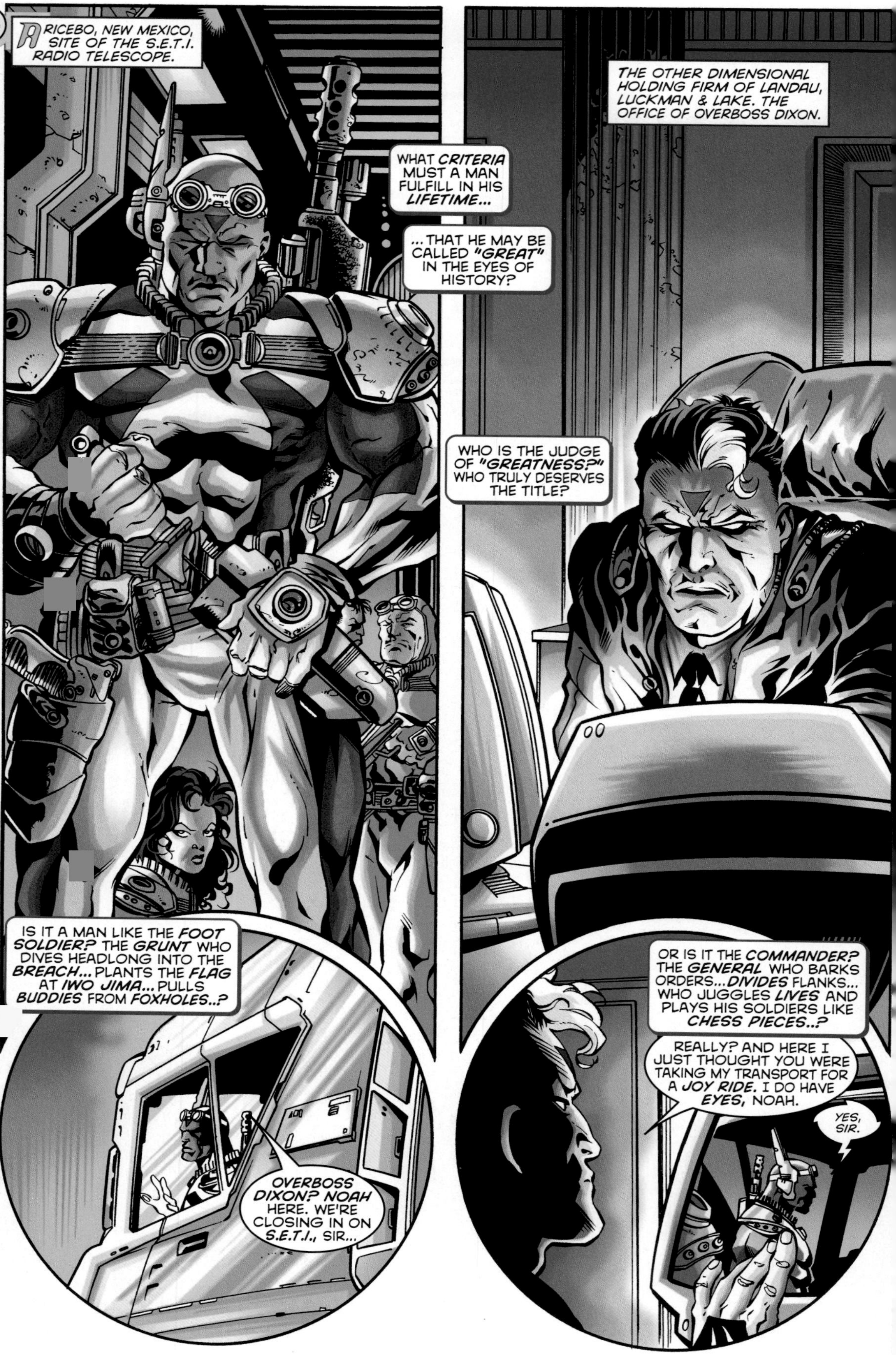
ARICEBO, NEW MEXICO, SITE OF THE S.E.T.I. RADIO TELESCOPE.
WHAT CRITERIA MUST A MAN FULFILL IN HIS LIFETIME...
...THAT HE MAY BE CALLED "GREAT" IN THE EYES OF HISTORY?
THE OTHER DIMENSIONAL HOLDING FIRM OF LANDAU, LUCKMAN & LAKE. THE OFFICE OF OVERBOSS DIXON.
WHO IS THE JUDGE OF "GREATNESS?" WHO TRULY DESERVES THE TITLE?
IS IT A MAN LIKE THE FOOT SOLDIER? THE GRUNT WHO DIVES HEADLONG INTO THE BREACH... PLANTS THE FLAG AT IWO JIMA... PULLS BUDDIES FROM FOXHOLES..?
OVERBOSS DIXON? NOAH HERE. WE'RE CLOSING IN ON S.E.T.I., SIR...
OR IS IT THE COMMANDER? THE GENERAL WHO BARKS ORDERS... DIVIDES FLANKS... WHO JUGGLES LIVES AND PLAYS HIS SOLDIERS LIKE CHESS PIECES..?
REALLY? AND HERE I JUST THOUGHT YOU WERE TAKING MY TRANSPORT FOR A JOY RIDE. I DO HAVE EYES, NOAH.
YES, SIR.

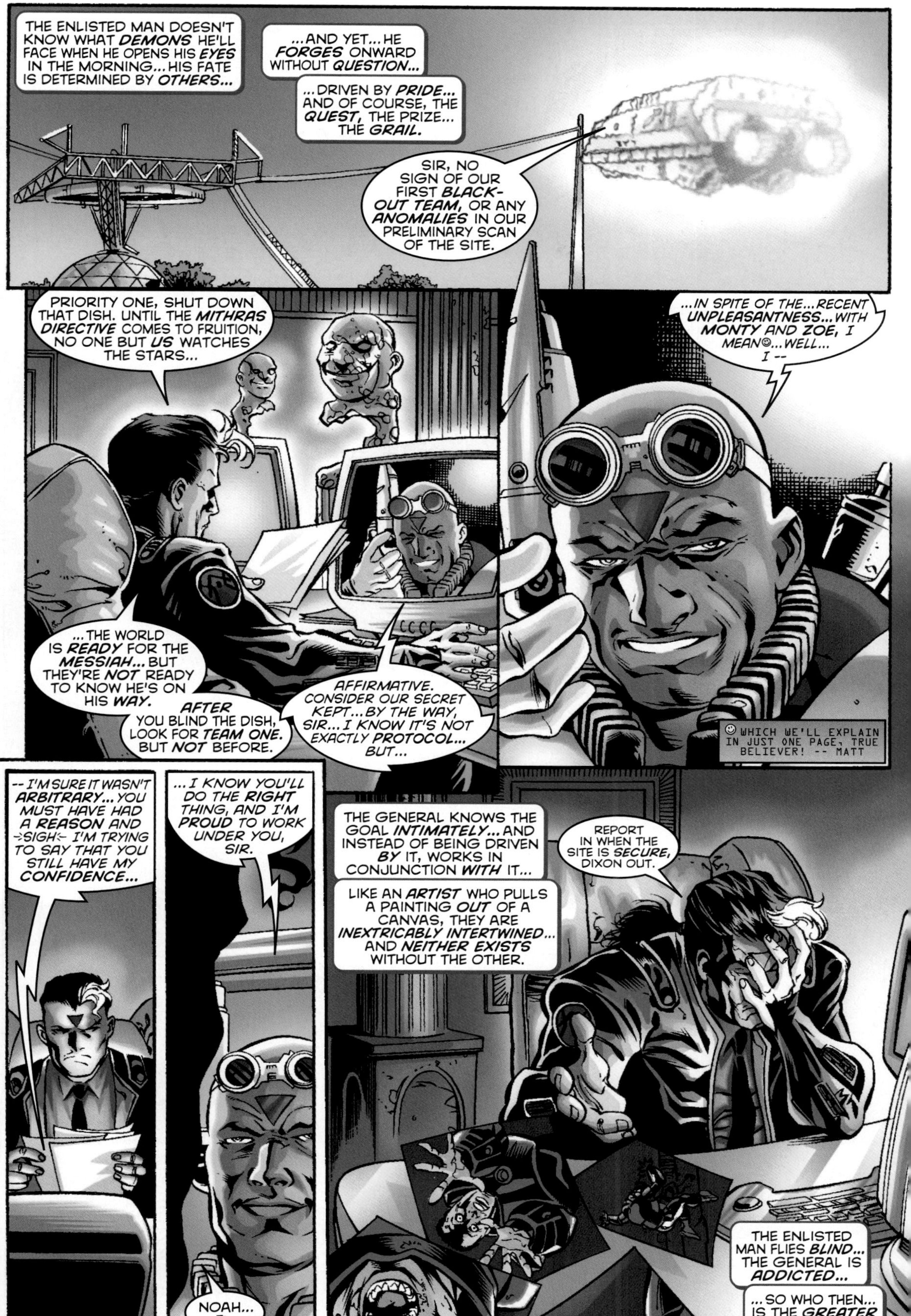

THE ENLISTED MAN DOESN'T KNOW WHAT DEMONS HE'LL FACE WHEN HE OPENS HIS EYES IN THE MORNING... HIS FATE IS DETERMINED BY OTHERS...
...AND YET... HE FORGES ONWARD WITHOUT QUESTION...
...DRIVEN BY PRIDE... AND OF COURSE, THE QUEST, THE PRIZE... THE GRAIL.
SIR, NO SIGN OF OUR FIRST BLACK-OUT TEAM, OR ANY ANOMALIES IN OUR PRELIMINARY SCAN OF THE SITE.
PRIORITY ONE, SHUT DOWN THAT DISH. UNTIL THE MITHRAS DIRECTIVE COMES TO FRUITION, NO ONE BUT US WATCHES THE STARS...
...THE WORLD IS READY FOR THE MESSIAH... BUT THEY'RE NOT READY TO KNOW HE'S ON HIS WAY.
AFTER YOU BLIND THE DISH, LOOK FOR TEAM ONE. BUT NOT BEFORE.
AFFIRMATIVE. CONSIDER OUR SECRET KEPT... BY THE WAY, SIR... I KNOW IT'S NOT EXACTLY PROTOCOL... BUT...
...IN SPITE OF THE... RECENT UNPLEASANTNESS... WITH MONTY AND ZOE, I MEAN☺... WELL... I --
☺ WHICH WE'LL EXPLAIN IN JUST ONE PAGE, TRUE BELIEVER! -- MATT
-- I'M SURE IT WASN'T ARBITRARY... YOU MUST HAVE HAD A REASON AND ⇒SIGH⇐ I'M TRYING TO SAY THAT YOU STILL HAVE MY CONFIDENCE...
...I KNOW YOU'LL DO THE RIGHT THING, AND I'M PROUD TO WORK UNDER YOU, SIR.
NOAH... I...
THE GENERAL KNOWS THE GOAL INTIMATELY... AND INSTEAD OF BEING DRIVEN BY IT, WORKS IN CONJUNCTION WITH IT...
LIKE AN ARTIST WHO PULLS A PAINTING OUT OF A CANVAS, THEY ARE INEXTRICABLY INTERTWINED... AND NEITHER EXISTS WITHOUT THE OTHER.
REPORT IN WHEN THE SITE IS SECURE, DIXON OUT.
THE ENLISTED MAN FLIES BLIND... THE GENERAL IS ADDICTED...
...SO WHO THEN... IS THE GREATER MAN?

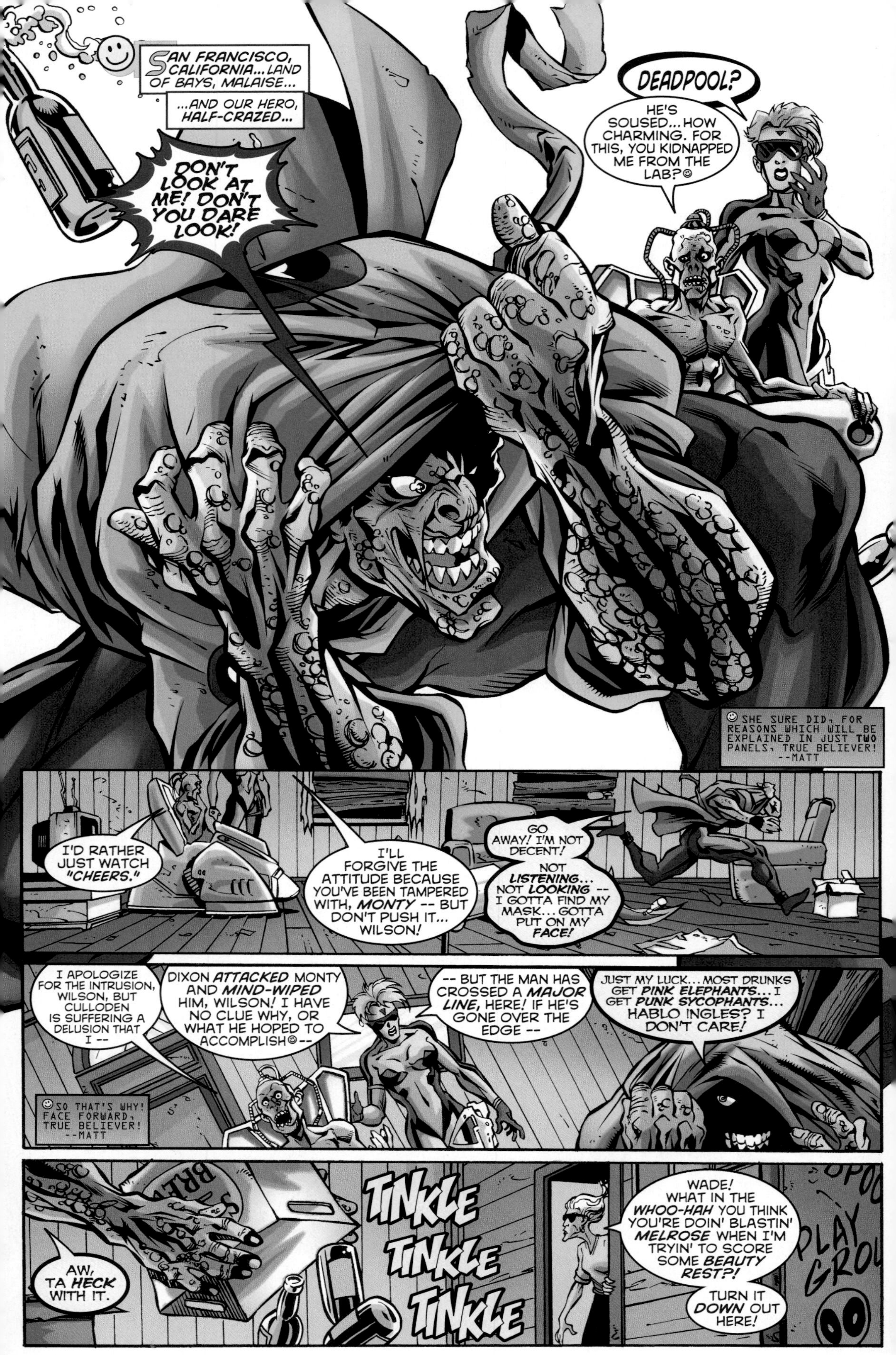
SAN FRANCISCO, CALIFORNIA... LAND OF BAYS, MALAISE...
...AND OUR HERO, HALF-CRAZED...
DON'T LOOK AT ME! DON'T YOU DARE LOOK!
DEADPOOL?
HE'S SOUSED... HOW CHARMING. FOR THIS, YOU KIDNAPPED ME FROM THE LAB?☺
☺ SHE SURE DID, FOR REASONS WHICH WILL BE EXPLAINED IN JUST TWO PANELS, TRUE BELIEVER! --MATT
I'D RATHER JUST WATCH "CHEERS."
I'LL FORGIVE THE ATTITUDE BECAUSE YOU'VE BEEN TAMPERED WITH, MONTY -- BUT DON'T PUSH IT... WILSON!
GO AWAY! I'M NOT DECENT!
NOT LISTENING... NOT LOOKING -- I GOTTA FIND MY MASK... GOTTA PUT ON MY FACE!
I APOLOGIZE FOR THE INTRUSION, WILSON, BUT CULLODEN IS SUFFERING A DELUSION THAT I --
DIXON ATTACKED MONTY AND MIND-WIPED HIM, WILSON! I HAVE NO CLUE WHY, OR WHAT HE HOPED TO ACCOMPLISH☺ --
-- BUT THE MAN HAS CROSSED A MAJOR LINE, HERE! IF HE'S GONE OVER THE EDGE --
JUST MY LUCK... MOST DRUNKS GET PINK ELEPHANTS... I GET PUNK SYCOPHANTS... HABLO INGLES? I DON'T CARE!
☺ SO THAT'S WHY! FACE FORWARD, TRUE BELIEVER! --MATT
AW, TA HECK WITH IT.
TINKLE TINKLE TINKLE
WADE! WHAT IN THE WHOO-HAH YOU THINK YOU'RE DOIN' BLASTIN' MELROSE WHEN I'M TRYIN' TO SCORE SOME BEAUTY REST?!
TURN IT DOWN OUT HERE!

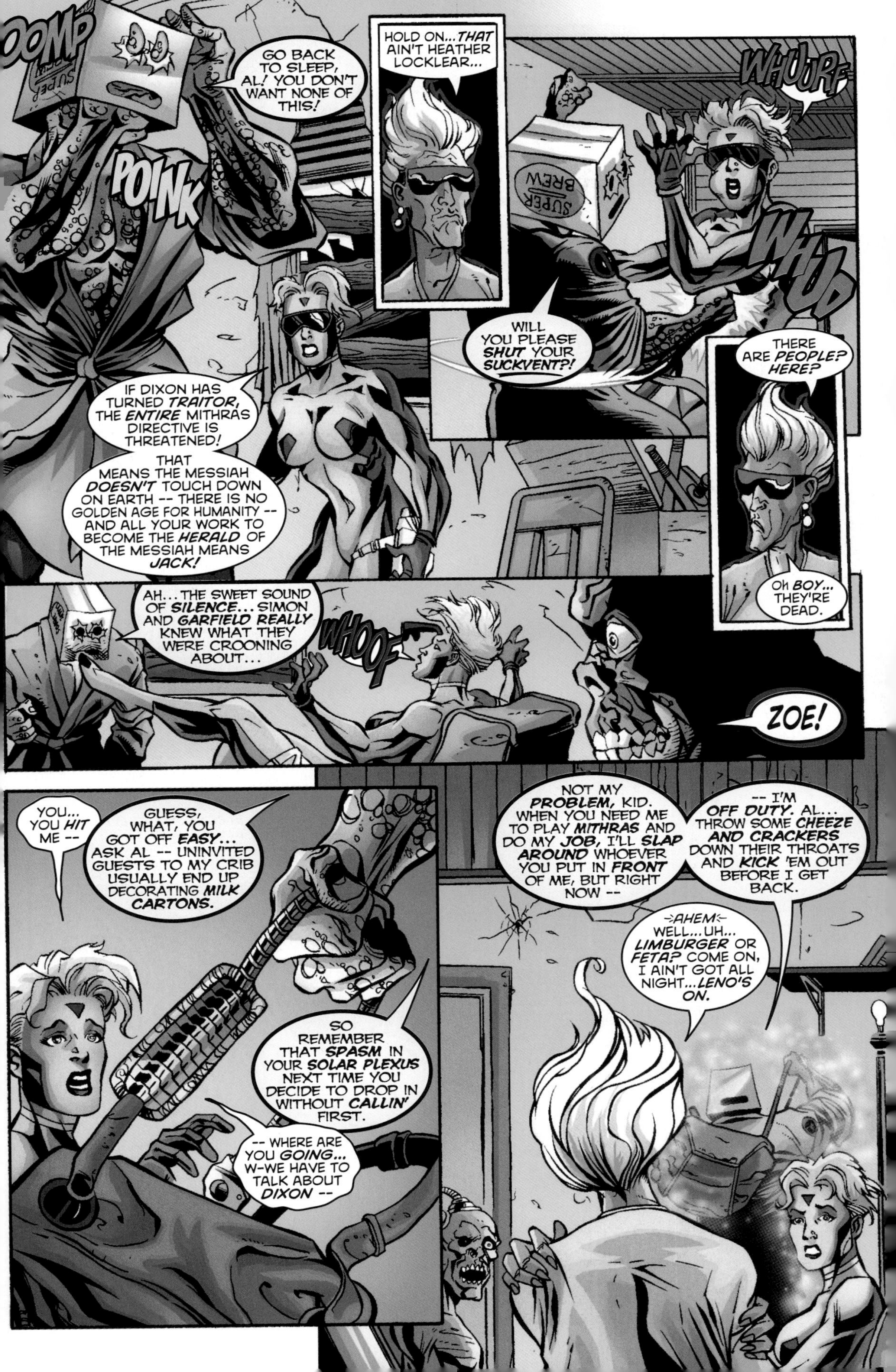
OOMP
GO BACK TO SLEEP, AL! YOU DON'T WANT NONE OF THIS!
POINK
HOLD ON...THAT AIN'T HEATHER LOCKLEAR...
WHUURF
SUPER BREW
WHUD
WILL YOU PLEASE SHUT YOUR SUCKVENT?!
THERE ARE PEOPLE? HERE?
IF DIXON HAS TURNED TRAITOR, THE ENTIRE MITHRAS DIRECTIVE IS THREATENED!
THAT MEANS THE MESSIAH DOESN'T TOUCH DOWN ON EARTH -- THERE IS NO GOLDEN AGE FOR HUMANITY -- AND ALL YOUR WORK TO BECOME THE HERALD OF THE MESSIAH MEANS JACK!
Oh BOY... THEY'RE DEAD.
AH...THE SWEET SOUND OF SILENCE...SIMON AND GARFIELD REALLY KNEW WHAT THEY WERE CROONING ABOUT...
WHOOF
ZOE!
YOU... YOU HIT ME --
GUESS, WHAT, YOU GOT OFF EASY... ASK AL -- UNINVITED GUESTS TO MY CRIB USUALLY END UP DECORATING MILK CARTONS.
SO REMEMBER THAT SPASM IN YOUR SOLAR PLEXUS NEXT TIME YOU DECIDE TO DROP IN WITHOUT CALLIN' FIRST.
-- WHERE ARE YOU GOING... W-WE HAVE TO TALK ABOUT DIXON --
NOT MY PROBLEM, KID. WHEN YOU NEED ME TO PLAY MITHRAS AND DO MY JOB, I'LL SLAP AROUND WHOEVER YOU PUT IN FRONT OF ME, BUT RIGHT NOW --
-- I'M OFF DUTY. AL... THROW SOME CHEEZE AND CRACKERS DOWN THEIR THROATS AND KICK 'EM OUT BEFORE I GET BACK.
AHEM
WELL...UH... LIMBURGER OR FETA? COME ON, I AIN'T GOT ALL NIGHT...LENO'S ON.

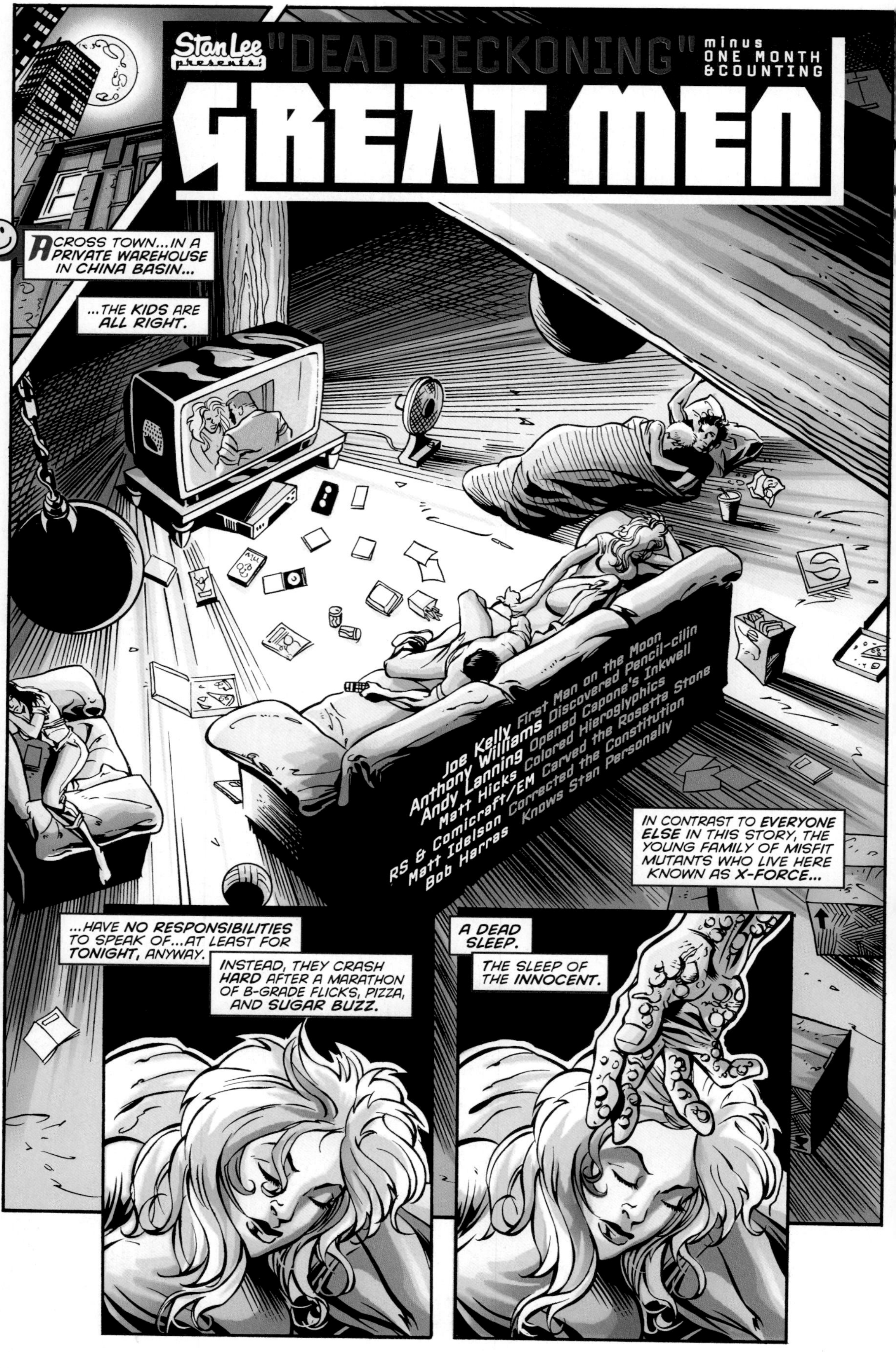
Stan Lee presents:
"DEAD RECKONING"
minus ONE MONTH & COUNTING
GREAT MEN
ACROSS TOWN...IN A PRIVATE WAREHOUSE IN CHINA BASIN...
...THE KIDS ARE ALL RIGHT.
Joe Kelly First Man on the Moon
Anthony Williams Discovered Pencil-cilin
Andy Lanning Opened Capone's Inkwell
Matt Hicks Colored Hieroglyphics
RS & Comicraft/EM Carved the Rosetta Stone
Matt Idelson Corrected the Constitution
Bob Harras Knows Stan Personally
IN CONTRAST TO EVERYONE ELSE IN THIS STORY, THE YOUNG FAMILY OF MISFIT MUTANTS WHO LIVE HERE KNOWN AS X-FORCE...
...HAVE NO RESPONSIBILITIES TO SPEAK OF...AT LEAST FOR TONIGHT, ANYWAY.
INSTEAD, THEY CRASH HARD AFTER A MARATHON OF B-GRADE FLICKS, PIZZA, AND SUGAR BUZZ.
A DEAD SLEEP.
THE SLEEP OF THE INNOCENT.

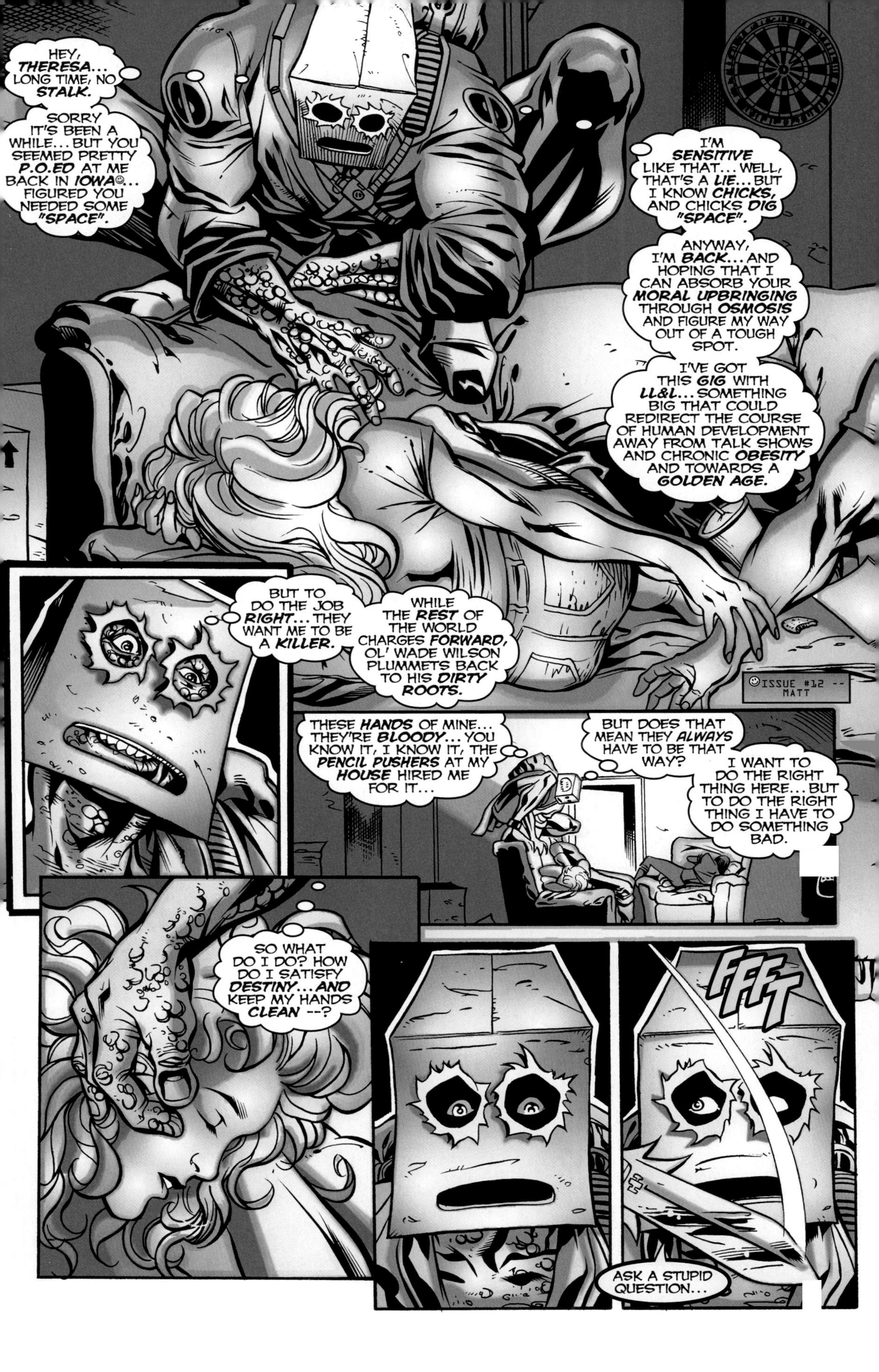
HEY, THERESA... LONG TIME, NO STALK.
SORRY IT'S BEEN A WHILE... BUT YOU SEEMED PRETTY P.O.ED AT ME BACK IN IOWA☺... FIGURED YOU NEEDED SOME "SPACE".
I'M SENSITIVE LIKE THAT... WELL, THAT'S A LIE... BUT I KNOW CHICKS, AND CHICKS DIG "SPACE".
ANYWAY, I'M BACK... AND HOPING THAT I CAN ABSORB YOUR MORAL UPBRINGING THROUGH OSMOSIS AND FIGURE MY WAY OUT OF A TOUGH SPOT.
I'VE GOT THIS GIG WITH LL&L... SOMETHING BIG THAT COULD REDIRECT THE COURSE OF HUMAN DEVELOPMENT AWAY FROM TALK SHOWS AND CHRONIC OBESITY AND TOWARDS A GOLDEN AGE.
BUT TO DO THE JOB RIGHT... THEY WANT ME TO BE A KILLER.
WHILE THE REST OF THE WORLD CHARGES FORWARD, OL' WADE WILSON PLUMMETS BACK TO HIS DIRTY ROOTS.
☺ISSUE #12 -- MATT
THESE HANDS OF MINE... THEY'RE BLOODY... YOU KNOW IT, I KNOW IT, THE PENCIL PUSHERS AT MY HOUSE HIRED ME FOR IT...
BUT DOES THAT MEAN THEY ALWAYS HAVE TO BE THAT WAY?
I WANT TO DO THE RIGHT THING HERE... BUT TO DO THE RIGHT THING I HAVE TO DO SOMETHING BAD.
SO WHAT DO I DO? HOW DO I SATISFY DESTINY... AND KEEP MY HANDS CLEAN --?
FFFT
ASK A STUPID QUESTION...

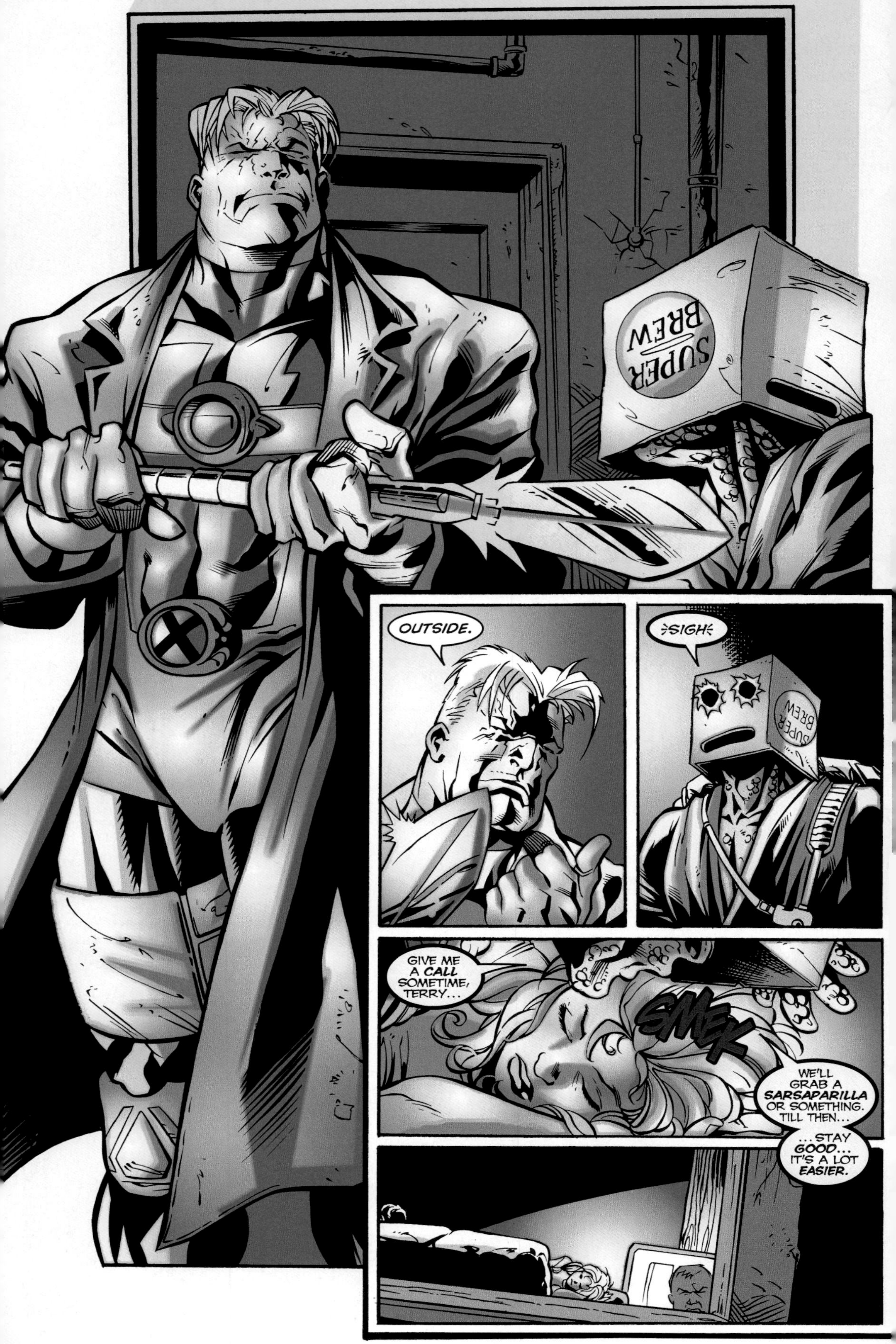
SUPER BREW
OUTSIDE.
-SIGH-
SUPER BREW
GIVE ME A CALL SOMETIME, TERRY...
SMEK
WE'LL GRAB A SARSAPARILLA OR SOMETHING. TILL THEN...
...STAY GOOD... IT'S A LOT EASIER.

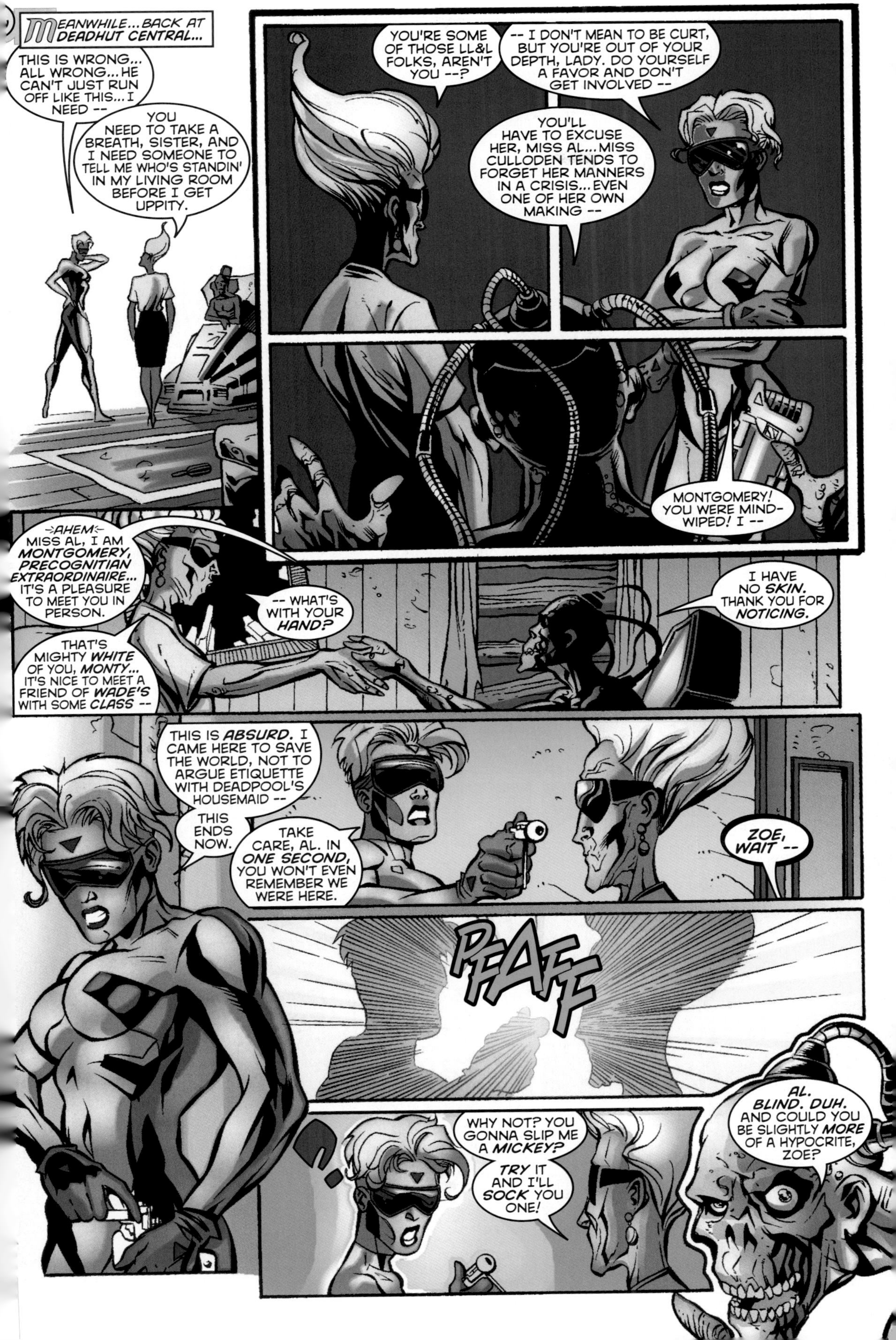
MEANWHILE... BACK AT DEADHUT CENTRAL...
THIS IS WRONG... ALL WRONG... HE CAN'T JUST RUN OFF LIKE THIS... I NEED --
YOU NEED TO TAKE A BREATH, SISTER, AND I NEED SOMEONE TO TELL ME WHO'S STANDIN' IN MY LIVING ROOM BEFORE I GET UPPITY.
YOU'RE SOME OF THOSE LL&L FOLKS, AREN'T YOU --?
-- I DON'T MEAN TO BE CURT, BUT YOU'RE OUT OF YOUR DEPTH, LADY. DO YOURSELF A FAVOR AND DON'T GET INVOLVED --
YOU'LL HAVE TO EXCUSE HER, MISS AL... MISS CULLODEN TENDS TO FORGET HER MANNERS IN A CRISIS... EVEN ONE OF HER OWN MAKING --
MONTGOMERY! YOU WERE MIND-WIPED! I --
AHEM
MISS AL, I AM MONTGOMERY, PRECOGNITIAN EXTRAORDINAIRE... IT'S A PLEASURE TO MEET YOU IN PERSON.
THAT'S MIGHTY WHITE OF YOU, MONTY... IT'S NICE TO MEET A FRIEND OF WADE'S WITH SOME CLASS --
-- WHAT'S WITH YOUR HAND?
I HAVE NO SKIN. THANK YOU FOR NOTICING.
THIS IS ABSURD. I CAME HERE TO SAVE THE WORLD, NOT TO ARGUE ETIQUETTE WITH DEADPOOL'S HOUSEMAID --
THIS ENDS NOW.
TAKE CARE, AL. IN ONE SECOND, YOU WON'T EVEN REMEMBER WE WERE HERE.
ZOE, WAIT --
PFAFF
WHY NOT? YOU GONNA SLIP ME A MICKEY?
TRY IT AND I'LL SOCK YOU ONE!
AL. BLIND. DUH. AND COULD YOU BE SLIGHTLY MORE OF A HYPOCRITE, ZOE?

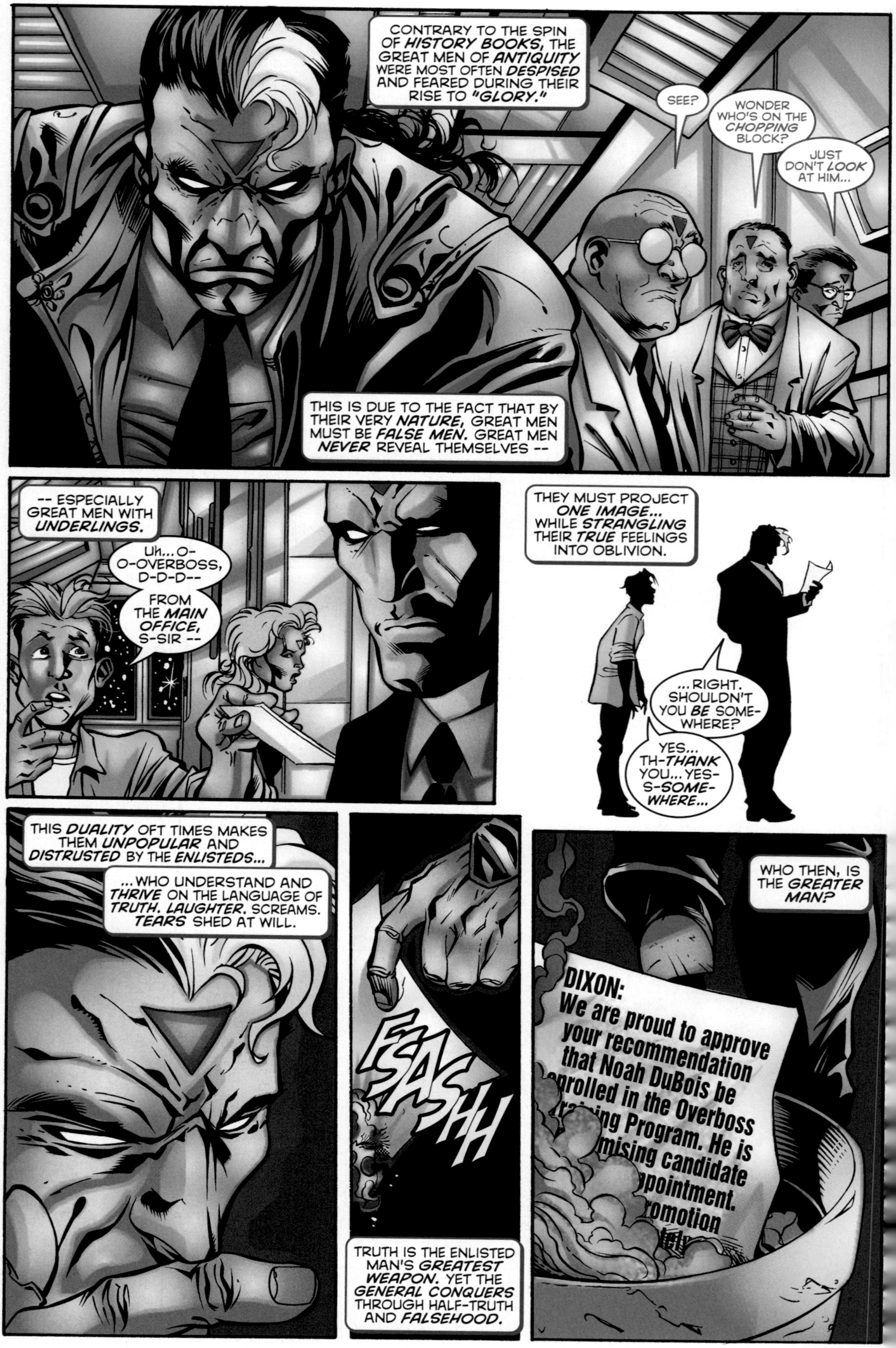
CONTRARY TO THE SPIN OF HISTORY BOOKS, THE GREAT MEN OF ANTIQUITY WERE MOST OFTEN DESPISED AND FEARED DURING THEIR RISE TO "GLORY."
SEE?
WONDER WHO'S ON THE CHOPPING BLOCK?
JUST DON'T LOOK AT HIM...
THIS IS DUE TO THE FACT THAT BY THEIR VERY NATURE, GREAT MEN MUST BE FALSE MEN. GREAT MEN NEVER REVEAL THEMSELVES --
-- ESPECIALLY GREAT MEN WITH UNDERLINGS.
Uh... O-O-OVERBOSS, D-D-D--
FROM THE MAIN OFFICE, S-SIR --
THEY MUST PROJECT ONE IMAGE... WHILE STRANGLING THEIR TRUE FEELINGS INTO OBLIVION.
...RIGHT. SHOULDN'T YOU BE SOMEWHERE?
YES... TH-THANK YOU... YES-S-SOMEWHERE...
THIS DUALITY OFT TIMES MAKES THEM UNPOPULAR AND DISTRUSTED BY THE ENLISTEDS...
...WHO UNDERSTAND AND THRIVE ON THE LANGUAGE OF TRUTH. LAUGHTER. SCREAMS. TEARS SHED AT WILL.
FSASHH
TRUTH IS THE ENLISTED MAN'S GREATEST WEAPON. YET THE GENERAL CONQUERS THROUGH HALF-TRUTH AND FALSEHOOD.
WHO THEN, IS THE GREATER MAN?
DIXON:
We are proud to approve
your recommendation
that Noah DuBois be
nrolled in the Overboss
ing Program. He is
mising candidate
ppointment.
romotion

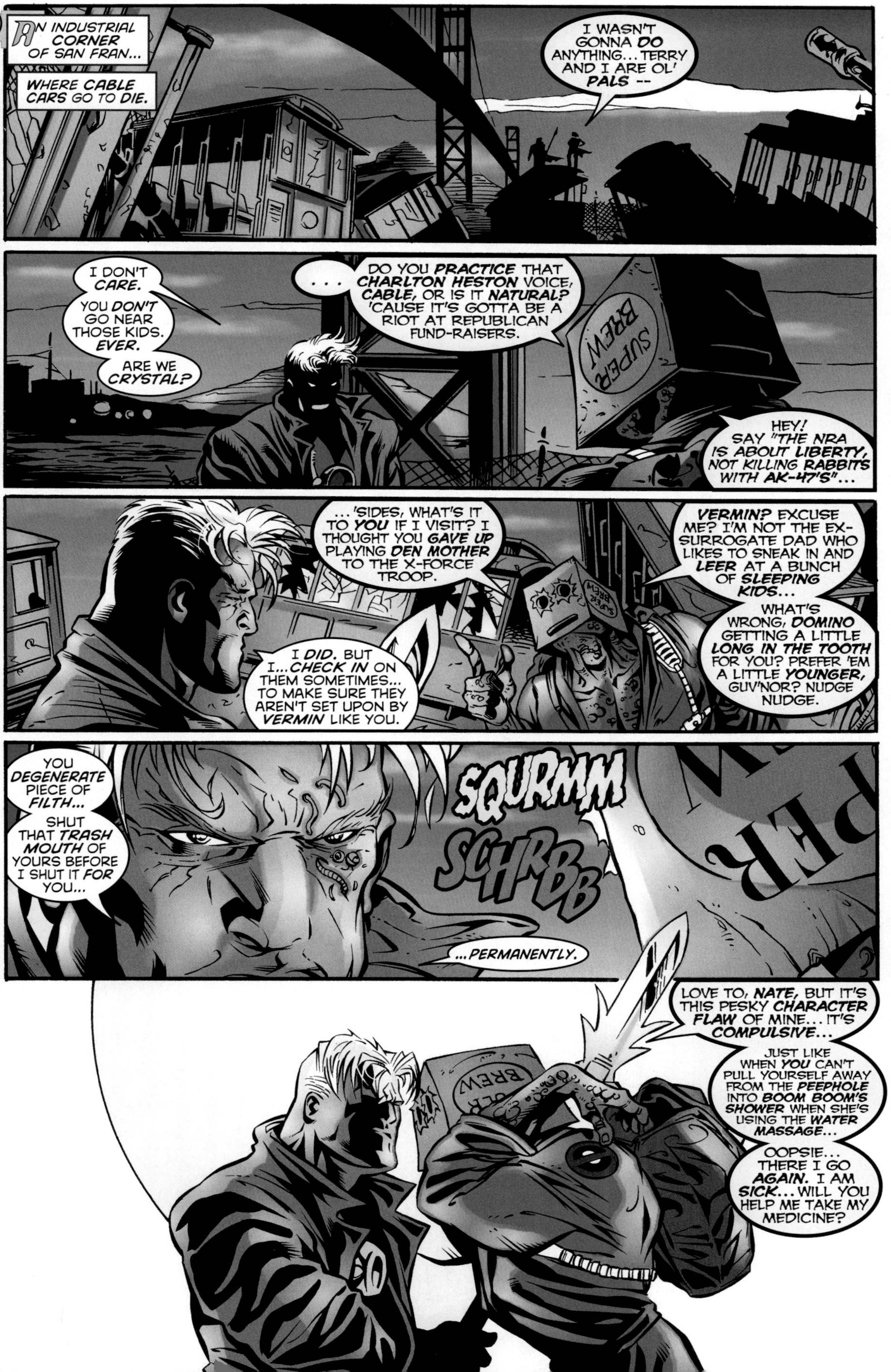
AN INDUSTRIAL CORNER OF SAN FRAN...
WHERE CABLE CARS GO TO DIE.
I WASN'T GONNA DO ANYTHING... TERRY AND I ARE OL' PALS --
I DON'T CARE.
YOU DON'T GO NEAR THOSE KIDS. EVER.
ARE WE CRYSTAL?
. . .
DO YOU PRACTICE THAT CHARLTON HESTON VOICE, CABLE, OR IS IT NATURAL? 'CAUSE IT'S GOTTA BE A RIOT AT REPUBLICAN FUND-RAISERS.
SUPER BREW
HEY! SAY "THE NRA IS ABOUT LIBERTY, NOT KILLING RABBITS WITH AK-47'S"...
...'SIDES, WHAT'S IT TO YOU IF I VISIT? I THOUGHT YOU GAVE UP PLAYING DEN MOTHER TO THE X-FORCE TROOP.
I DID. BUT I...CHECK IN ON THEM SOMETIMES... TO MAKE SURE THEY AREN'T SET UPON BY VERMIN LIKE YOU.
VERMIN? EXCUSE ME? I'M NOT THE EX-SURROGATE DAD WHO LIKES TO SNEAK IN AND LEER AT A BUNCH OF SLEEPING KIDS...
WHAT'S WRONG, DOMINO GETTING A LITTLE LONG IN THE TOOTH FOR YOU? PREFER 'EM A LITTLE YOUNGER, GUV'NOR? NUDGE NUDGE.
YOU DEGENERATE PIECE OF FILTH...
SHUT THAT TRASH MOUTH OF YOURS BEFORE I SHUT IT FOR YOU...
SQURMM
SCHRBB
...PERMANENTLY.
LOVE TO, NATE, BUT IT'S THIS PESKY CHARACTER FLAW OF MINE... IT'S COMPULSIVE...
JUST LIKE WHEN YOU CAN'T PULL YOURSELF AWAY FROM THE PEEPHOLE INTO BOOM BOOM'S SHOWER WHEN SHE'S USING THE WATER MASSAGE...
OOPSIE... THERE I GO AGAIN. I AM SICK... WILL YOU HELP ME TAKE MY MEDICINE?

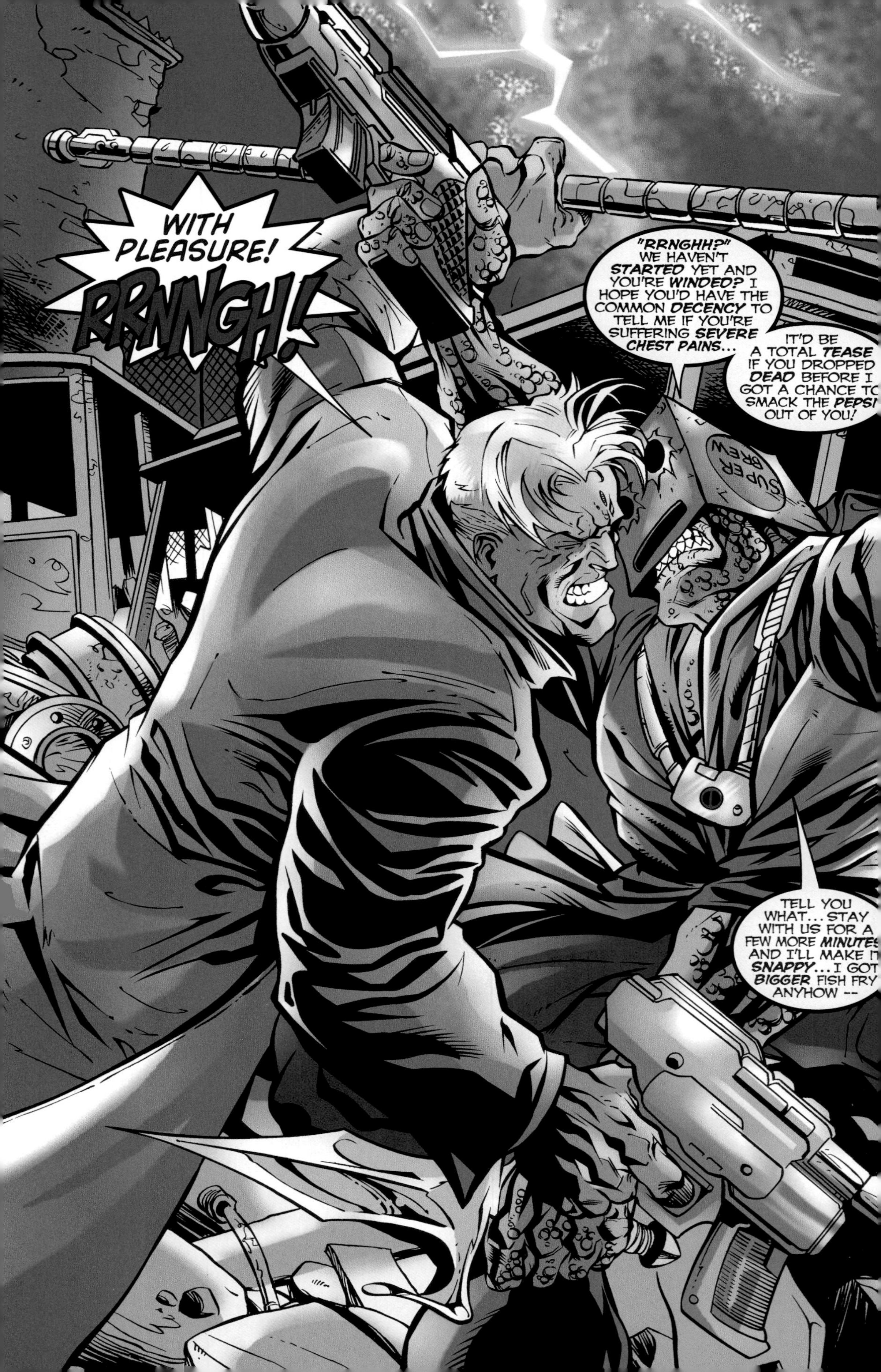
WITH PLEASURE!
RRNNGH!
"RRNGHH?" WE HAVEN'T STARTED YET AND YOU'RE WINDED? I HOPE YOU'D HAVE THE COMMON DECENCY TO TELL ME IF YOU'RE SUFFERING SEVERE CHEST PAINS...
IT'D BE A TOTAL TEASE IF YOU DROPPED DEAD BEFORE I GOT A CHANCE TO SMACK THE PEPSI OUT OF YOU!
SUPER BREW
TELL YOU WHAT... STAY WITH US FOR A FEW MORE MINUTES AND I'LL MAKE IT SNAPPY... I GOT BIGGER FISH FRY ANYHOW --

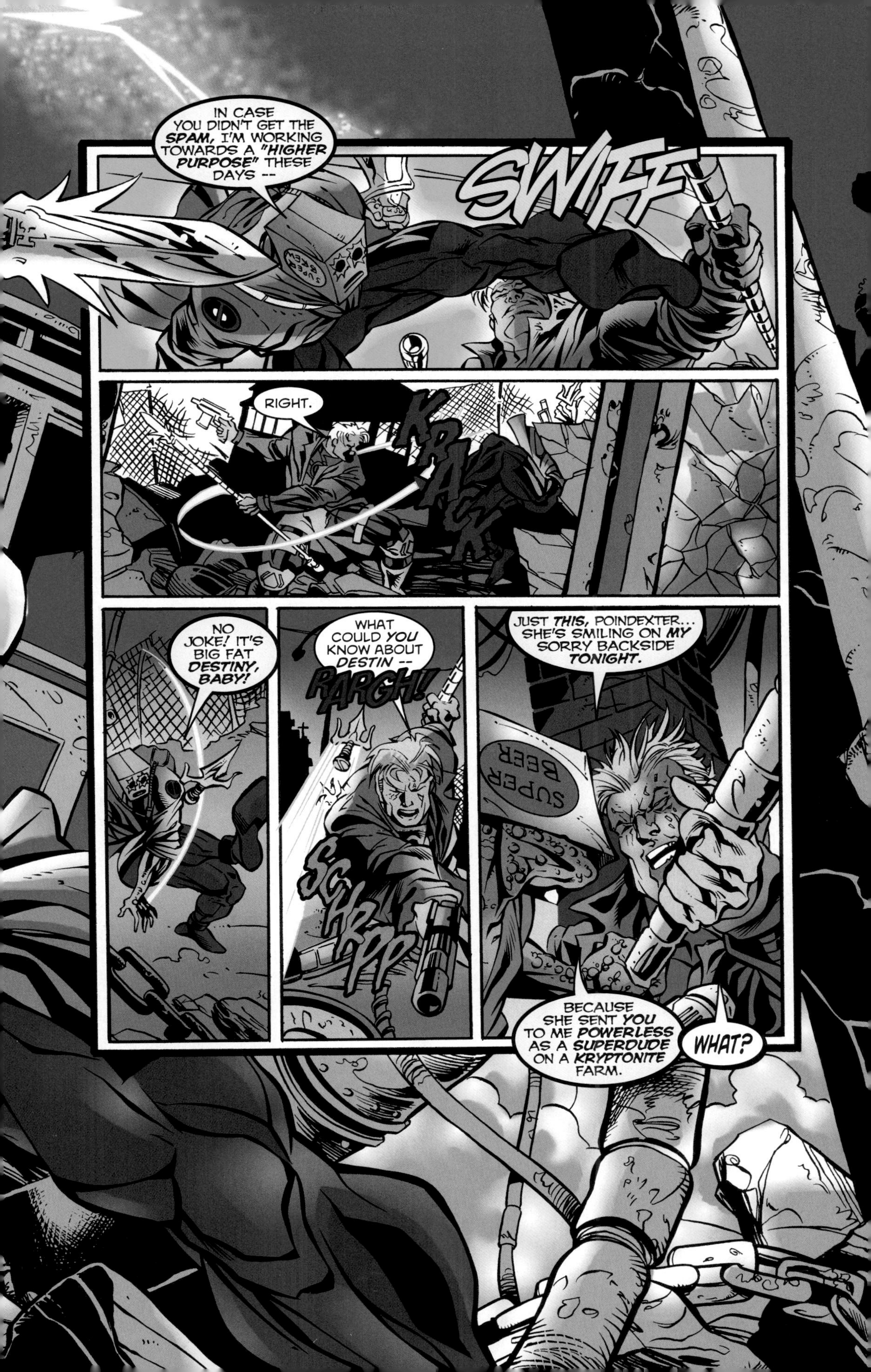
IN CASE YOU DIDN'T GET THE SPAM, I'M WORKING TOWARDS A "HIGHER PURPOSE" THESE DAYS --
SWIFF
SUPER BREW
RIGHT.
KRAK-A-AK
NO JOKE! IT'S BIG FAT DESTINY, BABY!
WHAT COULD YOU KNOW ABOUT DESTIN --
RARGH!
SCHRPP
JUST THIS, POINDEXTER... SHE'S SMILING ON MY SORRY BACKSIDE TONIGHT.
SUPER BEER
BECAUSE SHE SENT YOU TO ME POWERLESS AS A SUPERDUDE ON A KRYPTONITE FARM.
WHAT?

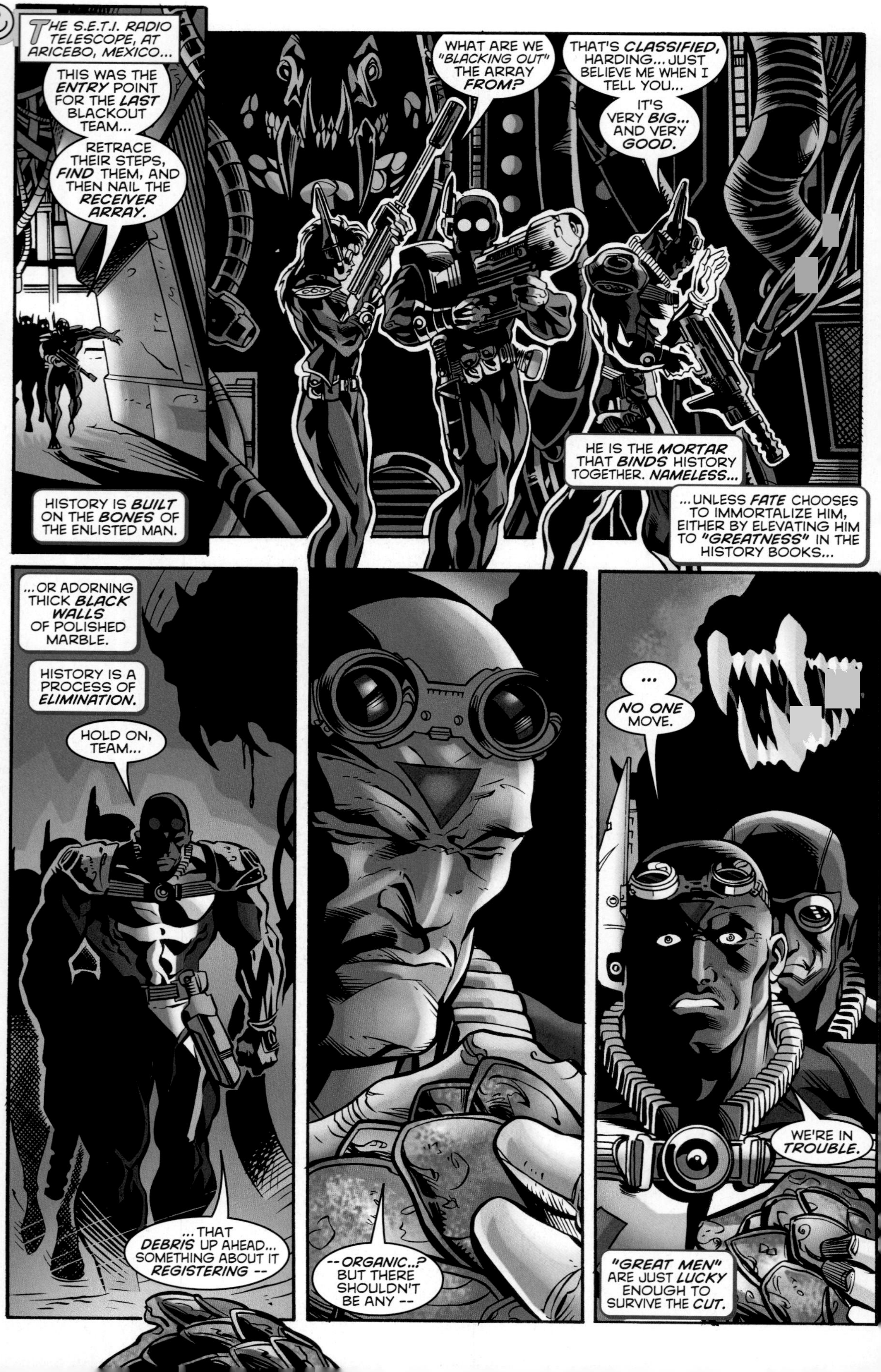
THE S.E.T.I. RADIO TELESCOPE, AT ARICEBO, MEXICO...
THIS WAS THE ENTRY POINT FOR THE LAST BLACKOUT TEAM...
RETRACE THEIR STEPS, FIND THEM, AND THEN NAIL THE RECEIVER ARRAY.
HISTORY IS BUILT ON THE BONES OF THE ENLISTED MAN.
WHAT ARE WE "BLACKING OUT" THE ARRAY FROM?
THAT'S CLASSIFIED, HARDING... JUST BELIEVE ME WHEN I TELL YOU...
IT'S VERY BIG... AND VERY GOOD.
HE IS THE MORTAR THAT BINDS HISTORY TOGETHER. NAMELESS...
...UNLESS FATE CHOOSES TO IMMORTALIZE HIM, EITHER BY ELEVATING HIM TO "GREATNESS" IN THE HISTORY BOOKS...
...OR ADORNING THICK BLACK WALLS OF POLISHED MARBLE.
HISTORY IS A PROCESS OF ELIMINATION.
HOLD ON, TEAM...
...THAT DEBRIS UP AHEAD... SOMETHING ABOUT IT REGISTERING --
--ORGANIC..? BUT THERE SHOULDN'T BE ANY --
...
NO ONE MOVE.
WE'RE IN TROUBLE.
"GREAT MEN" ARE JUST LUCKY ENOUGH TO SURVIVE THE CUT.

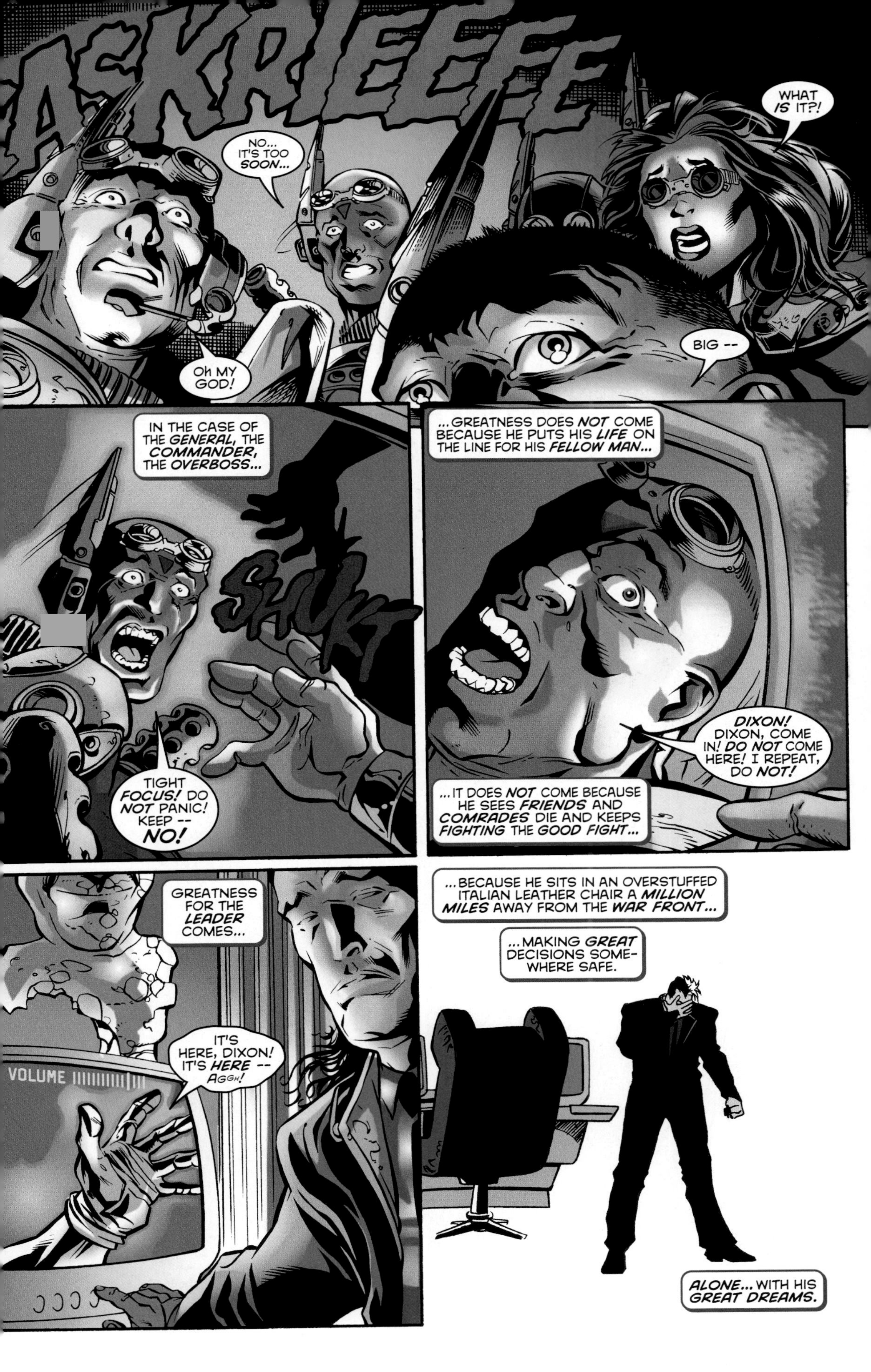
SKRIEEEE
NO... IT'S TOO SOON...
WHAT IS IT?!
Oh MY GOD!
BIG --
IN THE CASE OF THE GENERAL, THE COMMANDER, THE OVERBOSS...
SHUKT
TIGHT FOCUS! DO NOT PANIC! KEEP -- NO!
...GREATNESS DOES NOT COME BECAUSE HE PUTS HIS LIFE ON THE LINE FOR HIS FELLOW MAN...
DIXON! DIXON, COME IN! DO NOT COME HERE! I REPEAT, DO NOT!
...IT DOES NOT COME BECAUSE HE SEES FRIENDS AND COMRADES DIE AND KEEPS FIGHTING THE GOOD FIGHT...
GREATNESS FOR THE LEADER COMES...
IT'S HERE, DIXON! IT'S HERE -- AGGH!
VOLUME
...BECAUSE HE SITS IN AN OVERSTUFFED ITALIAN LEATHER CHAIR A MILLION MILES AWAY FROM THE WAR FRONT...
...MAKING GREAT DECISIONS SOMEWHERE SAFE.
ALONE... WITH HIS GREAT DREAMS.

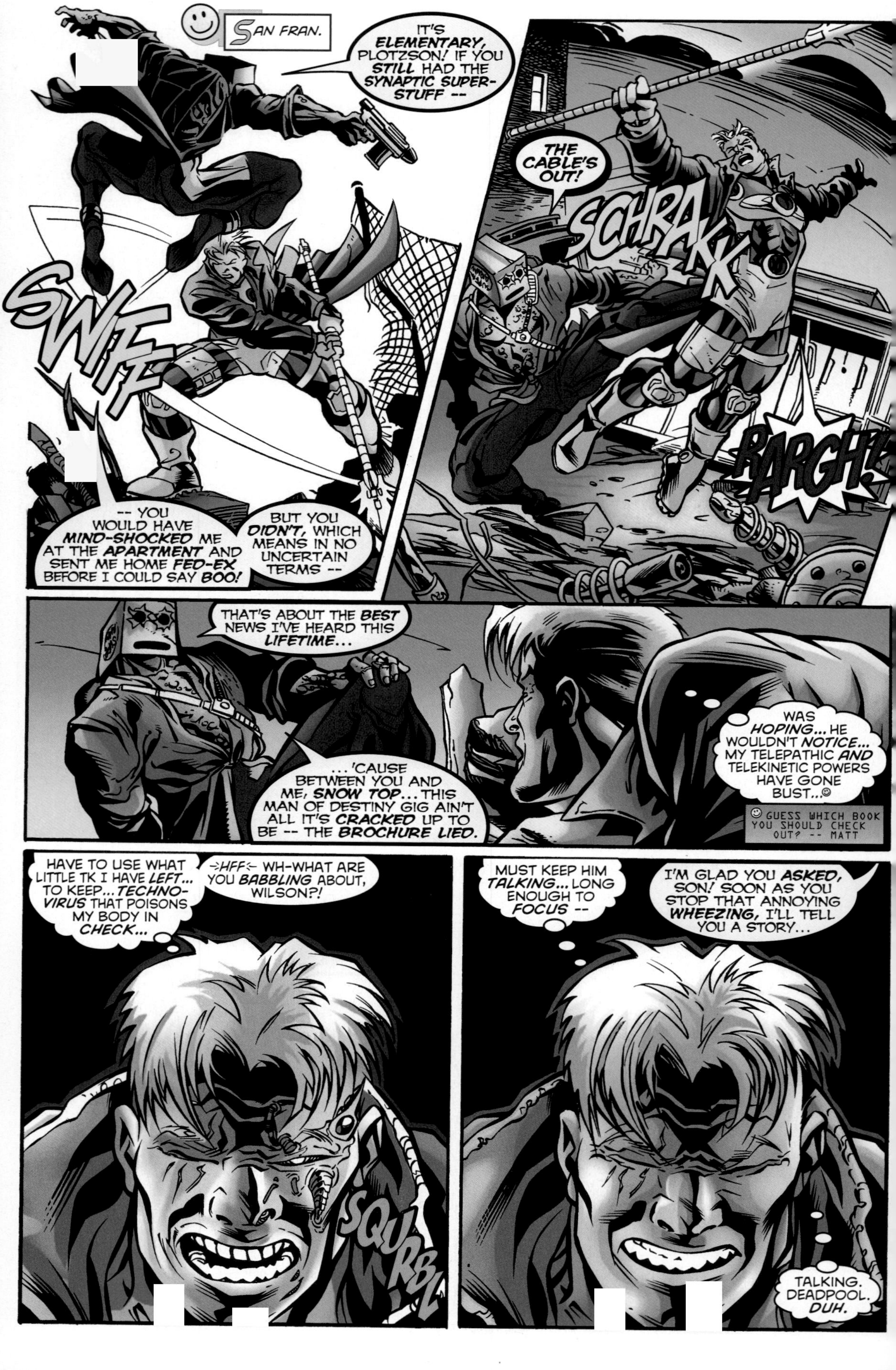
SAN FRAN.
IT'S ELEMENTARY, PLOTZSON! IF YOU STILL HAD THE SYNAPTIC SUPER-STUFF --
SWIFF
-- YOU WOULD HAVE MIND-SHOCKED ME AT THE APARTMENT AND SENT ME HOME FED-EX BEFORE I COULD SAY BOO!
BUT YOU DIDN'T, WHICH MEANS IN NO UNCERTAIN TERMS --
THE CABLE'S OUT!
SCHRAKK
RARGH!
THAT'S ABOUT THE BEST NEWS I'VE HEARD THIS LIFETIME...
...'CAUSE BETWEEN YOU AND ME, SNOW TOP... THIS MAN OF DESTINY GIG AIN'T ALL IT'S CRACKED UP TO BE -- THE BROCHURE LIED.
WAS HOPING... HE WOULDN'T NOTICE... MY TELEPATHIC AND TELEKINETIC POWERS HAVE GONE BUST...☺
☺ GUESS WHICH BOOK YOU SHOULD CHECK OUT? -- MATT
HAVE TO USE WHAT LITTLE TK I HAVE LEFT... TO KEEP... TECHNO-VIRUS THAT POISONS MY BODY IN CHECK...
HFF WH-WHAT ARE YOU BABBLING ABOUT, WILSON?!
SQURBL
MUST KEEP HIM TALKING... LONG ENOUGH TO FOCUS --
I'M GLAD YOU ASKED, SON! SOON AS YOU STOP THAT ANNOYING WHEEZING, I'LL TELL YOU A STORY...
TALKING. DEADPOOL. DUH.

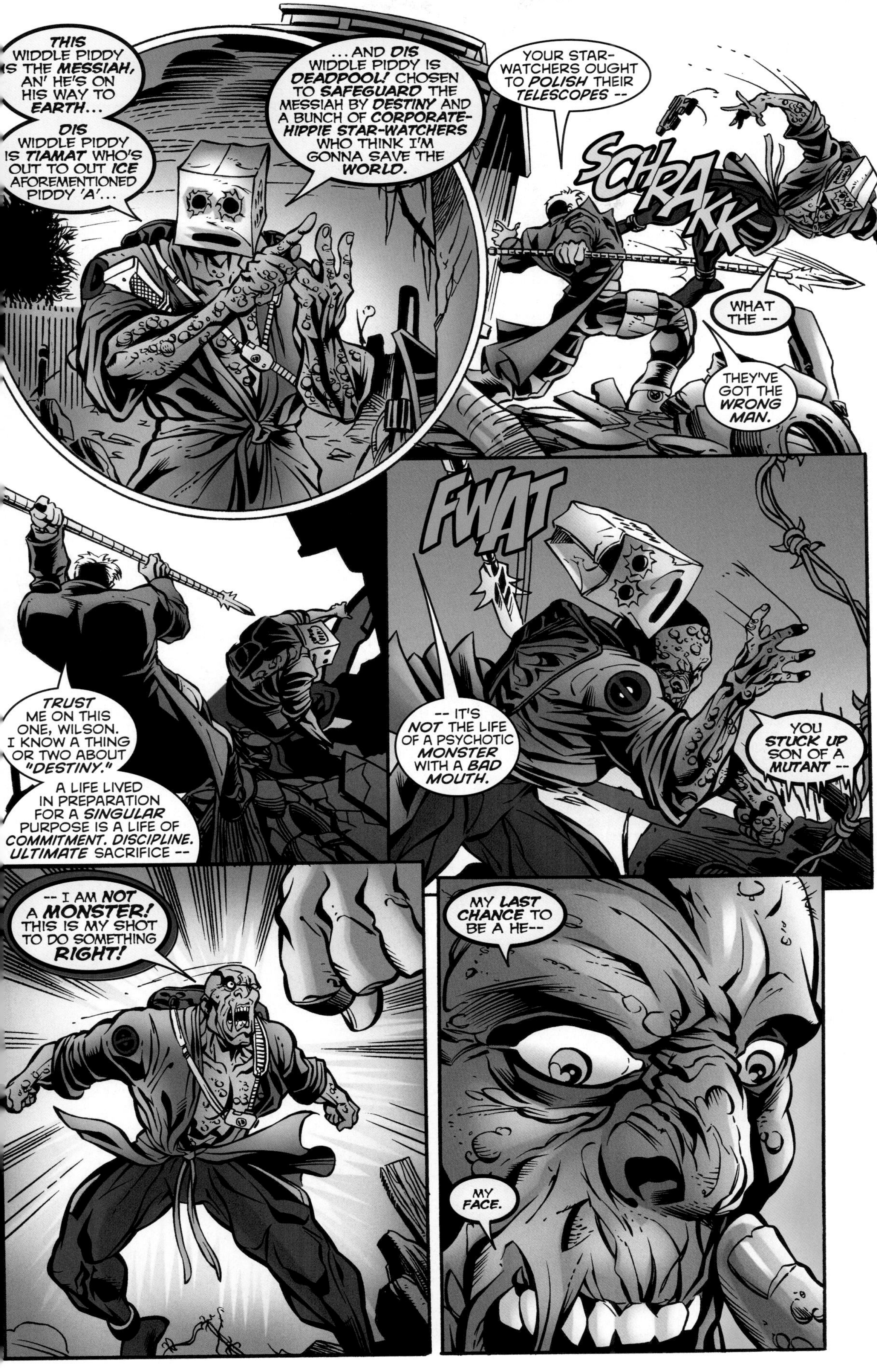
THIS WIDDLE PIDDY IS THE MESSIAH, AN' HE'S ON HIS WAY TO EARTH...
DIS WIDDLE PIDDY IS TIAMAT WHO'S OUT TO OUT ICE AFOREMENTIONED PIDDY 'A'...
...AND DIS WIDDLE PIDDY IS DEADPOOL! CHOSEN TO SAFEGUARD THE MESSIAH BY DESTINY AND A BUNCH OF CORPORATE-HIPPIE STAR-WATCHERS WHO THINK I'M GONNA SAVE THE WORLD.
YOUR STAR-WATCHERS OUGHT TO POLISH THEIR TELESCOPES --
SCHRAKK
WHAT THE --
THEY'VE GOT THE WRONG MAN.
TRUST ME ON THIS ONE, WILSON. I KNOW A THING OR TWO ABOUT "DESTINY."
A LIFE LIVED IN PREPARATION FOR A SINGULAR PURPOSE IS A LIFE OF COMMITMENT. DISCIPLINE. ULTIMATE SACRIFICE --
FWAT
-- IT'S NOT THE LIFE OF A PSYCHOTIC MONSTER WITH A BAD MOUTH.
YOU STUCK UP SON OF A MUTANT --
-- I AM NOT A MONSTER! THIS IS MY SHOT TO DO SOMETHING RIGHT!
MY LAST CHANCE TO BE A HE--
MY. FACE.

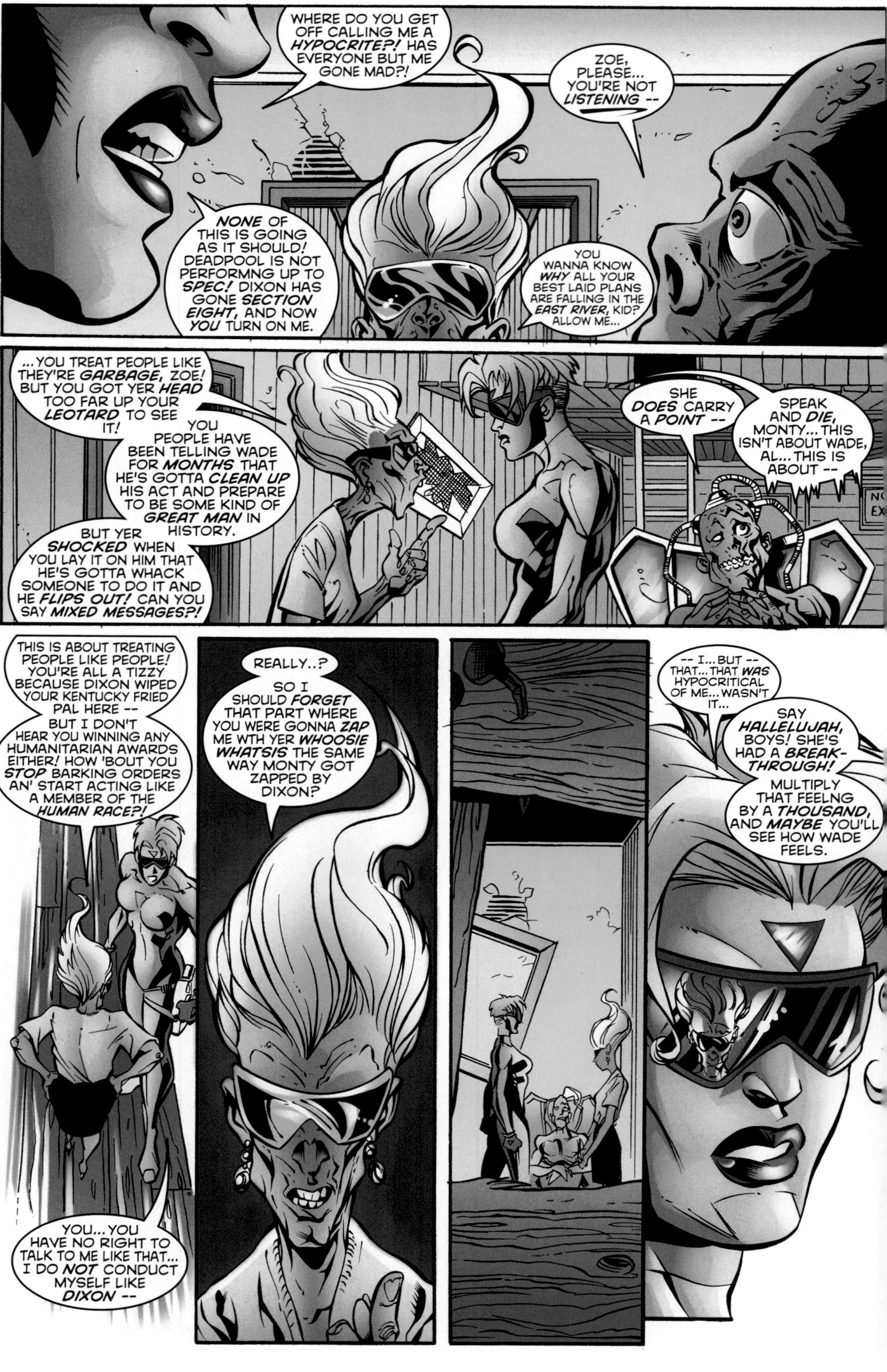
WHERE DO YOU GET OFF CALLING ME A HYPOCRITE?! HAS EVERYONE BUT ME GONE MAD?!
ZOE, PLEASE... YOU'RE NOT LISTENING --
NONE OF THIS IS GOING AS IT SHOULD! DEADPOOL IS NOT PERFORMNG UP TO SPEC! DIXON HAS GONE SECTION EIGHT, AND NOW YOU TURN ON ME.
YOU WANNA KNOW WHY ALL YOUR BEST LAID PLANS ARE FALLING IN THE EAST RIVER, KID? ALLOW ME...
...YOU TREAT PEOPLE LIKE THEY'RE GARBAGE, ZOE! BUT YOU GOT YER HEAD TOO FAR UP YOUR LEOTARD TO SEE IT!
YOU PEOPLE HAVE BEEN TELLING WADE FOR MONTHS THAT HE'S GOTTA CLEAN UP HIS ACT AND PREPARE TO BE SOME KIND OF GREAT MAN IN HISTORY.
BUT YER SHOCKED WHEN YOU LAY IT ON HIM THAT HE'S GOTTA WHACK SOMEONE TO DO IT AND HE FLIPS OUT! CAN YOU SAY MIXED MESSAGES?!
SHE DOES CARRY A POINT --
SPEAK AND DIE, MONTY... THIS ISN'T ABOUT WADE, AL... THIS IS ABOUT --
THIS IS ABOUT TREATING PEOPLE LIKE PEOPLE! YOU'RE ALL A TIZZY BECAUSE DIXON WIPED YOUR KENTUCKY FRIED PAL HERE -- BUT I DON'T HEAR YOU WINNING ANY HUMANITARIAN AWARDS EITHER! HOW 'BOUT YOU STOP BARKING ORDERS AN' START ACTING LIKE A MEMBER OF THE HUMAN RACE?!
YOU... YOU HAVE NO RIGHT TO TALK TO ME LIKE THAT... I DO NOT CONDUCT MYSELF LIKE DIXON --
REALLY..?
SO I SHOULD FORGET THAT PART WHERE YOU WERE GONNA ZAP ME WTH YER WHOOSIE WHATSIS THE SAME WAY MONTY GOT ZAPPED BY DIXON?
-- I... BUT -- THAT... THAT WAS HYPOCRITICAL OF ME... WASN'T IT...
SAY HALLELUJAH, BOYS! SHE'S HAD A BREAK-THROUGH!
MULTIPLY THAT FEELNG BY A THOUSAND, AND MAYBE YOU'LL SEE HOW WADE FEELS.

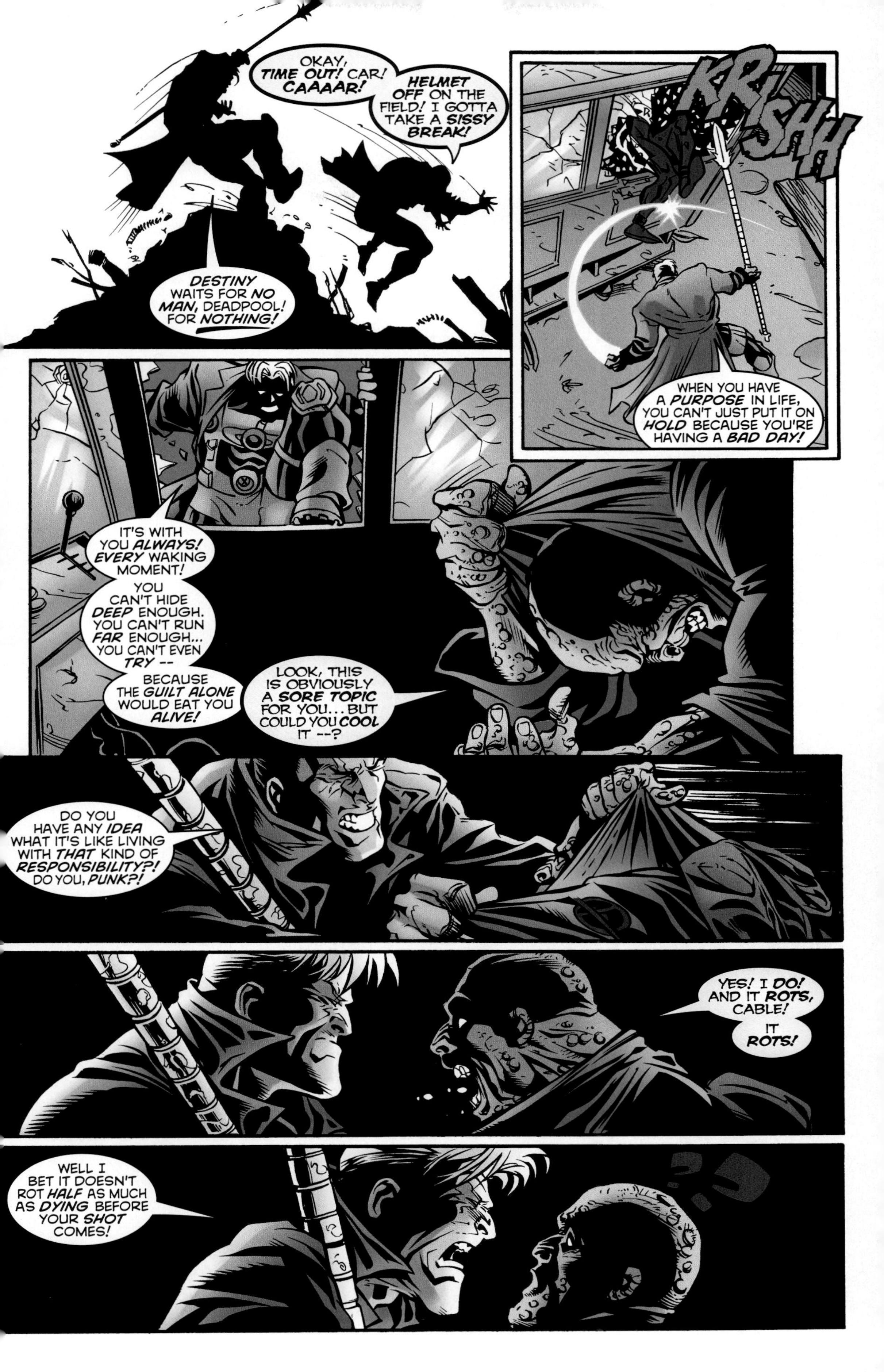
OKAY, TIME OUT! CAR! CAAAAR!
HELMET OFF ON THE FIELD! I GOTTA TAKE A SISSY BREAK!
DESTINY WAITS FOR NO MAN, DEADPOOL! FOR NOTHING!
KRISHH
WHEN YOU HAVE A PURPOSE IN LIFE, YOU CAN'T JUST PUT IT ON HOLD BECAUSE YOU'RE HAVING A BAD DAY!
IT'S WITH YOU ALWAYS! EVERY WAKING MOMENT!
YOU CAN'T HIDE DEEP ENOUGH. YOU CAN'T RUN FAR ENOUGH... YOU CAN'T EVEN TRY --
BECAUSE THE GUILT ALONE WOULD EAT YOU ALIVE!
LOOK, THIS IS OBVIOUSLY A SORE TOPIC FOR YOU... BUT COULD YOU COOL IT --?
DO YOU HAVE ANY IDEA WHAT IT'S LIKE LIVING WITH THAT KIND OF RESPONSIBILITY?! DO YOU, PUNK?!
YES! I DO! AND IT ROTS, CABLE!
IT ROTS!
WELL I BET IT DOESN'T ROT HALF AS MUCH AS DYING BEFORE YOUR SHOT COMES!

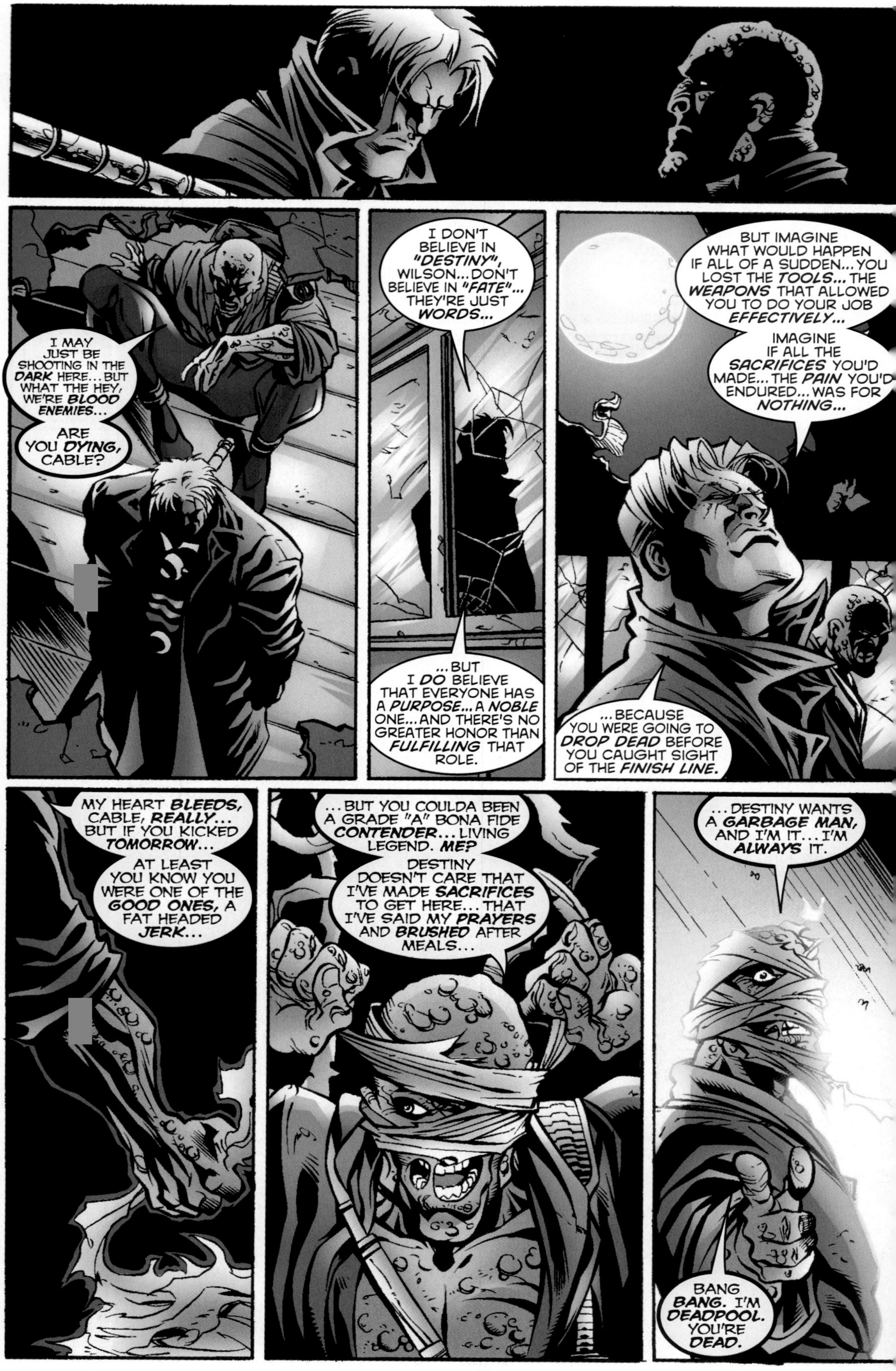
I MAY JUST BE SHOOTING IN THE DARK HERE... BUT WHAT THE HEY, WE'RE BLOOD ENEMIES...
ARE YOU DYING, CABLE?
I DON'T BELIEVE IN "DESTINY", WILSON... DON'T BELIEVE IN "FATE"... THEY'RE JUST WORDS...
...BUT I DO BELIEVE THAT EVERYONE HAS A PURPOSE... A NOBLE ONE... AND THERE'S NO GREATER HONOR THAN FULFILLING THAT ROLE.
BUT IMAGINE WHAT WOULD HAPPEN IF ALL OF A SUDDEN... YOU LOST THE TOOLS... THE WEAPONS THAT ALLOWED YOU TO DO YOUR JOB EFFECTIVELY...
IMAGINE IF ALL THE SACRIFICES YOU'D MADE... THE PAIN YOU'D ENDURED... WAS FOR NOTHING...
...BECAUSE YOU WERE GOING TO DROP DEAD BEFORE YOU CAUGHT SIGHT OF THE FINISH LINE.
MY HEART BLEEDS, CABLE, REALLY... BUT IF YOU KICKED TOMORROW...
AT LEAST YOU KNOW YOU WERE ONE OF THE GOOD ONES, A FAT HEADED JERK...
...BUT YOU COULDA BEEN A GRADE "A" BONA FIDE CONTENDER... LIVING LEGEND. ME?
DESTINY DOESN'T CARE THAT I'VE MADE SACRIFICES TO GET HERE... THAT I'VE SAID MY PRAYERS AND BRUSHED AFTER MEALS...
...DESTINY WANTS A GARBAGE MAN, AND I'M IT... I'M ALWAYS IT.
BANG BANG. I'M DEADPOOL. YOU'RE DEAD.

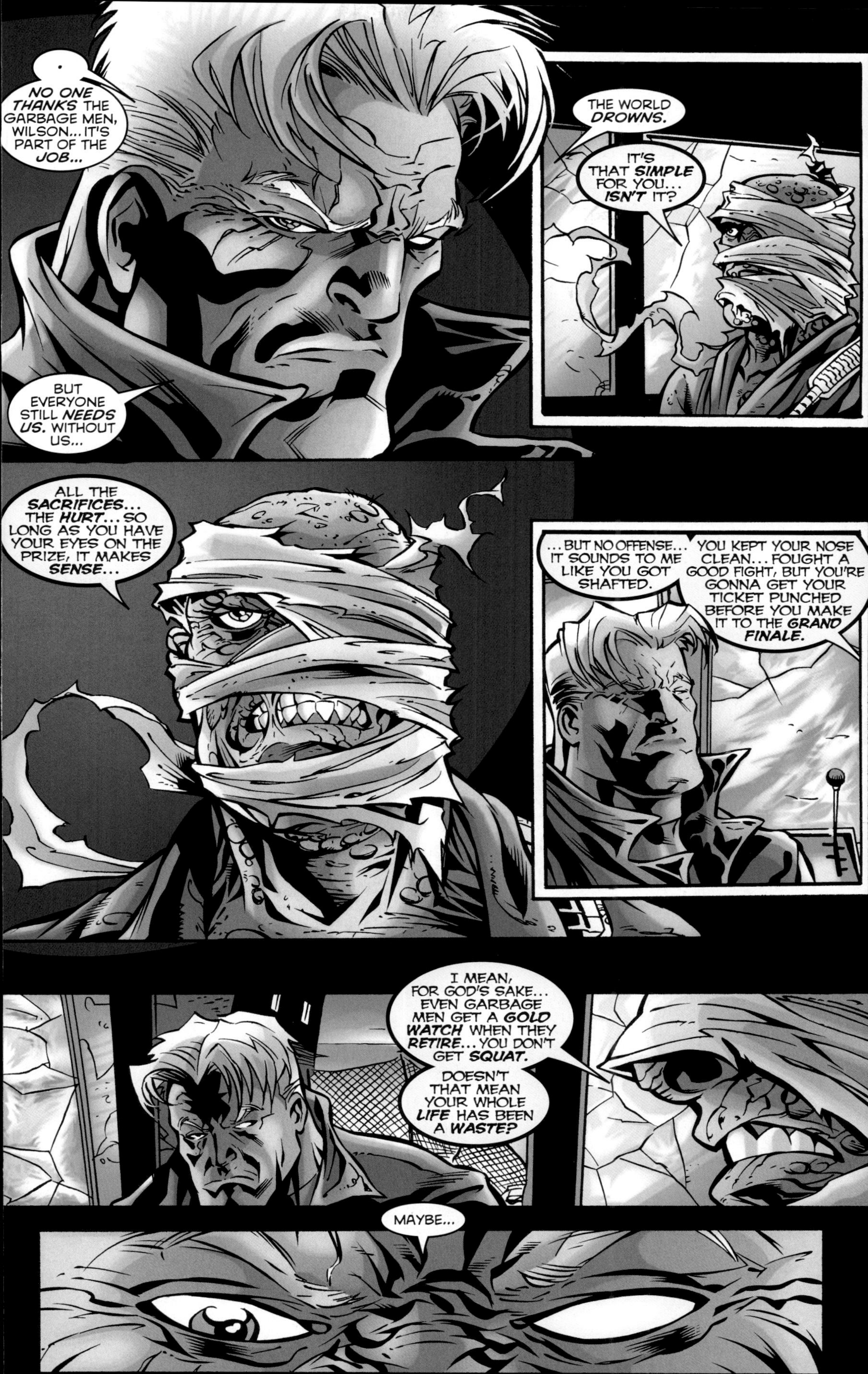
NO ONE THANKS THE GARBAGE MEN, WILSON... IT'S PART OF THE JOB...
BUT EVERYONE STILL NEEDS US. WITHOUT US...
THE WORLD DROWNS.
IT'S THAT SIMPLE FOR YOU... ISN'T IT?
ALL THE SACRIFICES... THE HURT... SO LONG AS YOU HAVE YOUR EYES ON THE PRIZE, IT MAKES SENSE...
...BUT NO OFFENSE... IT SOUNDS TO ME LIKE YOU GOT SHAFTED.
YOU KEPT YOUR NOSE CLEAN... FOUGHT A GOOD FIGHT, BUT YOU'RE GONNA GET YOUR TICKET PUNCHED BEFORE YOU MAKE IT TO THE GRAND FINALE.
I MEAN, FOR GOD'S SAKE... EVEN GARBAGE MEN GET A GOLD WATCH WHEN THEY RETIRE... YOU DON'T GET SQUAT.
DOESN'T THAT MEAN YOUR WHOLE LIFE HAS BEEN A WASTE?
MAYBE...

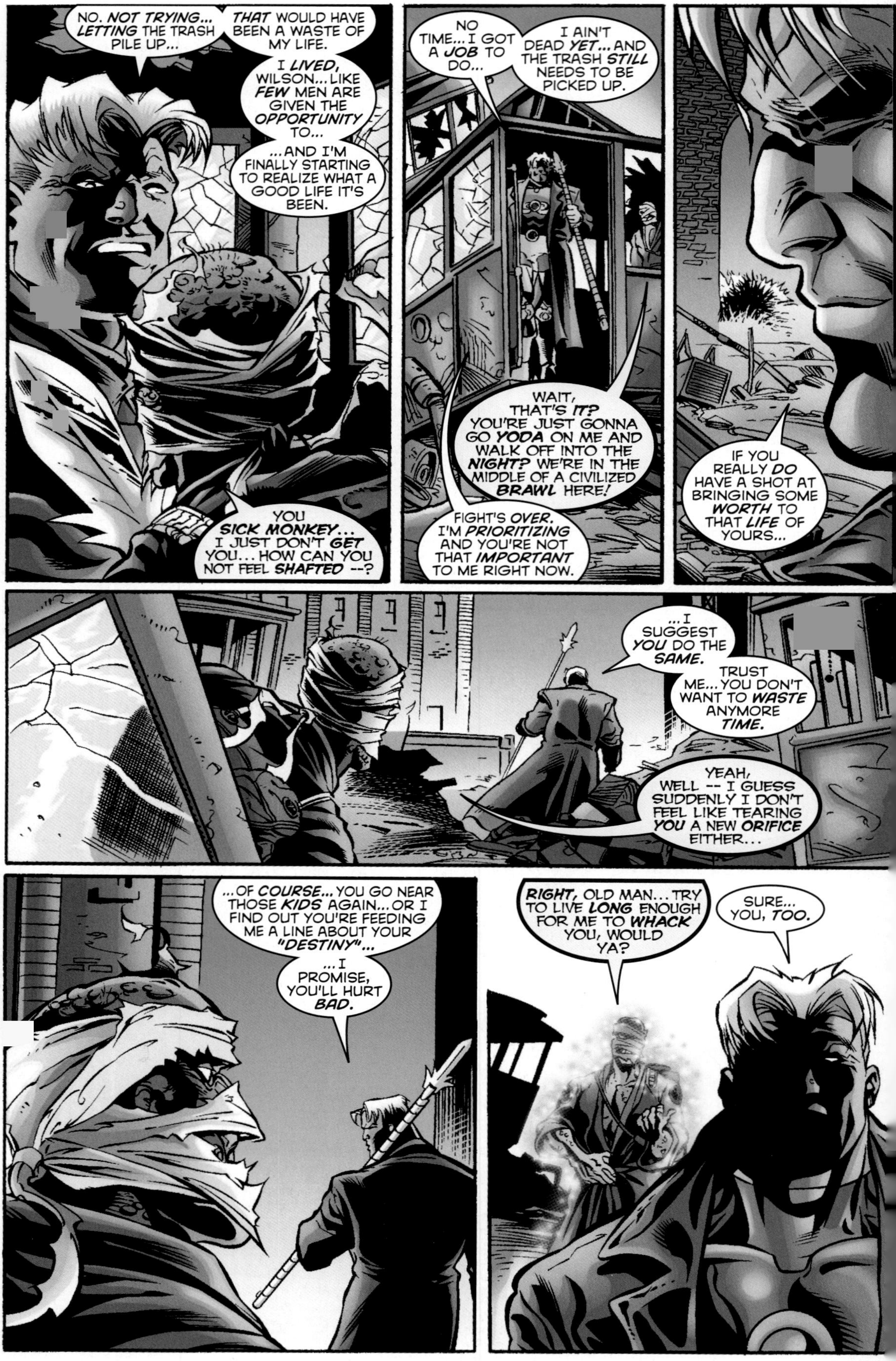
NO. NOT TRYING... LETTING THE TRASH PILE UP...
THAT WOULD HAVE BEEN A WASTE OF MY LIFE.
I LIVED, WILSON... LIKE FEW MEN ARE GIVEN THE OPPORTUNITY TO...
...AND I'M FINALLY STARTING TO REALIZE WHAT A GOOD LIFE IT'S BEEN.
YOU SICK MONKEY... I JUST DON'T GET YOU... HOW CAN YOU NOT FEEL SHAFTED --?
NO TIME... I GOT A JOB TO DO...
I AIN'T DEAD YET... AND THE TRASH STILL NEEDS TO BE PICKED UP.
WAIT, THAT'S IT? YOU'RE JUST GONNA GO YODA ON ME AND WALK OFF INTO THE NIGHT? WE'RE IN THE MIDDLE OF A CIVILIZED BRAWL HERE!
FIGHT'S OVER. I'M PRIORITIZING AND YOU'RE NOT THAT IMPORTANT TO ME RIGHT NOW.
IF YOU REALLY DO HAVE A SHOT AT BRINGING SOME WORTH TO THAT LIFE OF YOURS...
...I SUGGEST YOU DO THE SAME.
TRUST ME... YOU DON'T WANT TO WASTE ANYMORE TIME.
YEAH, WELL -- I GUESS SUDDENLY I DON'T FEEL LIKE TEARING YOU A NEW ORIFICE EITHER...
...OF COURSE... YOU GO NEAR THOSE KIDS AGAIN... OR I FIND OUT YOU'RE FEEDING ME A LINE ABOUT YOUR "DESTINY"...
...I PROMISE, YOU'LL HURT BAD.
RIGHT, OLD MAN... TRY TO LIVE LONG ENOUGH FOR ME TO WHACK YOU, WOULD YA?
SURE... YOU, TOO.

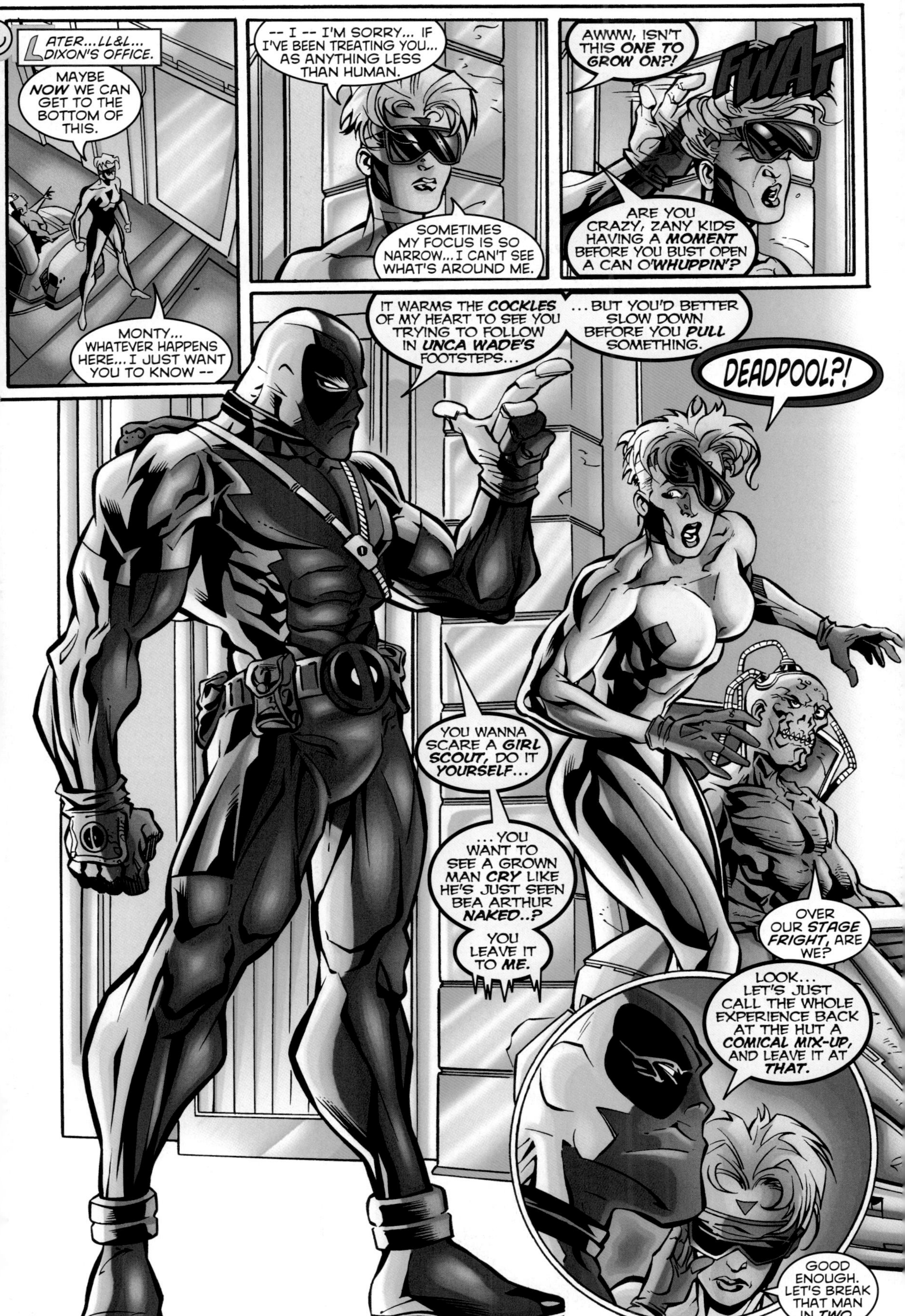
LATER...LL&L...DIXON'S OFFICE.
MAYBE NOW WE CAN GET TO THE BOTTOM OF THIS.
MONTY... WHATEVER HAPPENS HERE... I JUST WANT YOU TO KNOW --
-- I -- I'M SORRY... IF I'VE BEEN TREATING YOU... AS ANYTHING LESS THAN HUMAN.
SOMETIMES MY FOCUS IS SO NARROW... I CAN'T SEE WHAT'S AROUND ME.
AWWW, ISN'T THIS ONE TO GROW ON?!
FWAT
ARE YOU CRAZY, ZANY KIDS HAVING A MOMENT BEFORE YOU BUST OPEN A CAN O'WHUPPIN'?
IT WARMS THE COCKLES OF MY HEART TO SEE YOU TRYING TO FOLLOW IN UNCA WADE'S FOOTSTEPS...
...BUT YOU'D BETTER SLOW DOWN BEFORE YOU PULL SOMETHING.
DEADPOOL?!
YOU WANNA SCARE A GIRL SCOUT, DO IT YOURSELF...
...YOU WANT TO SEE A GROWN MAN CRY LIKE HE'S JUST SEEN BEA ARTHUR NAKED..?
YOU LEAVE IT TO ME.
OVER OUR STAGE FRIGHT, ARE WE?
LOOK... LET'S JUST CALL THE WHOLE EXPERIENCE BACK AT THE HUT A COMICAL MIX-UP, AND LEAVE IT AT THAT.
GOOD ENOUGH. LET'S BREAK THAT MAN IN TWO.

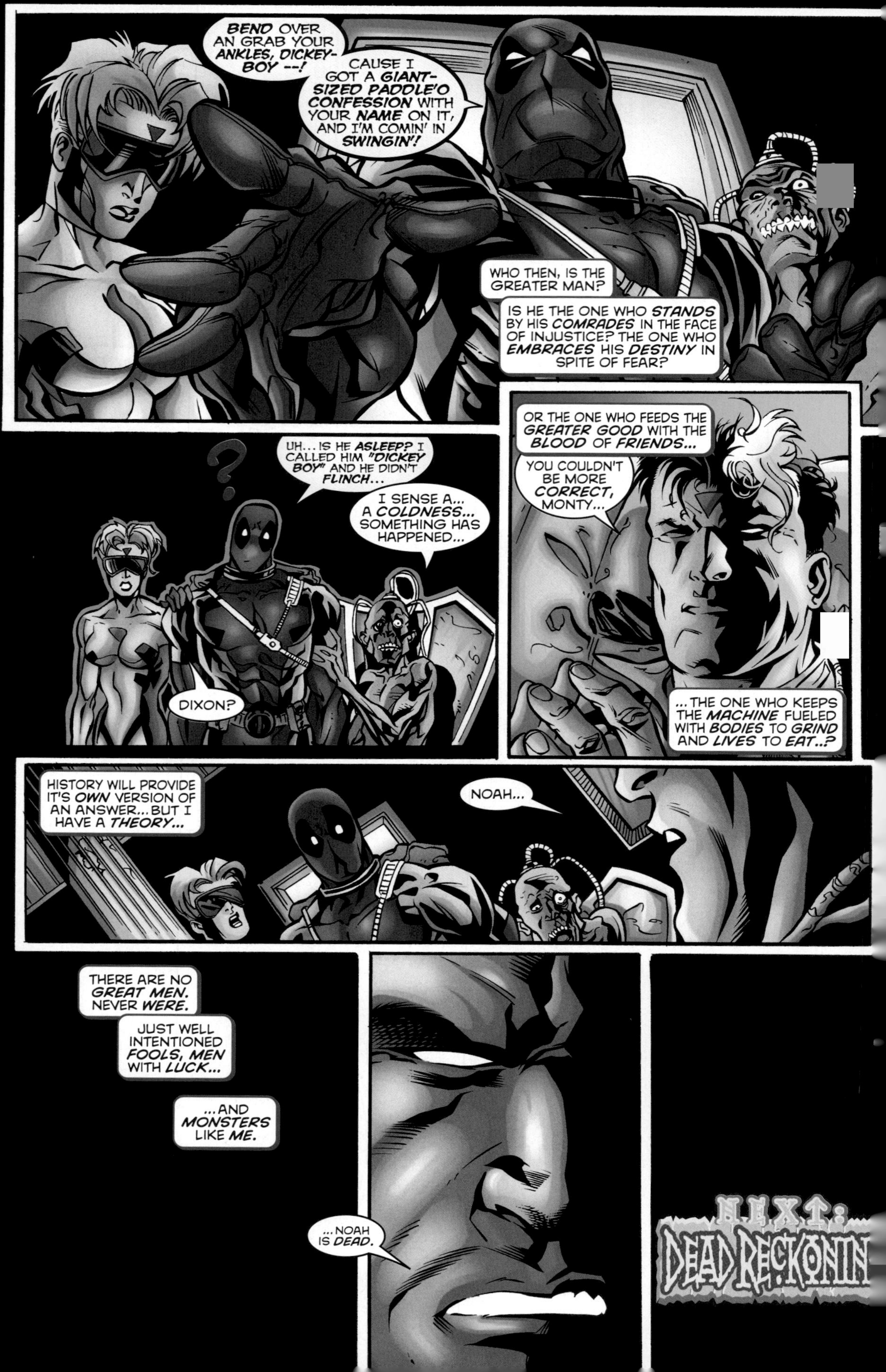

BEND OVER AN GRAB YOUR ANKLES, DICKEY-BOY --!
CAUSE I GOT A GIANT-SIZED PADDLE'O CONFESSION WITH YOUR NAME ON IT, AND I'M COMIN' IN SWINGIN'!
WHO THEN, IS THE GREATER MAN?
IS HE THE ONE WHO STANDS BY HIS COMRADES IN THE FACE OF INJUSTICE? THE ONE WHO EMBRACES HIS DESTINY IN SPITE OF FEAR?
?
UH... IS HE ASLEEP? I CALLED HIM "DICKEY BOY" AND HE DIDN'T FLINCH...
I SENSE A... A COLDNESS... SOMETHING HAS HAPPENED...
DIXON?
OR THE ONE WHO FEEDS THE GREATER GOOD WITH THE BLOOD OF FRIENDS...
YOU COULDN'T BE MORE CORRECT, MONTY...
...THE ONE WHO KEEPS THE MACHINE FUELED WITH BODIES TO GRIND AND LIVES TO EAT..?
HISTORY WILL PROVIDE IT'S OWN VERSION OF AN ANSWER... BUT I HAVE A THEORY...
NOAH...
THERE ARE NO GREAT MEN. NEVER WERE.
JUST WELL INTENTIONED FOOLS, MEN WITH LUCK...
...AND MONSTERS LIKE ME.
...NOAH IS DEAD.
NEXT:
DEAD RECKONIN

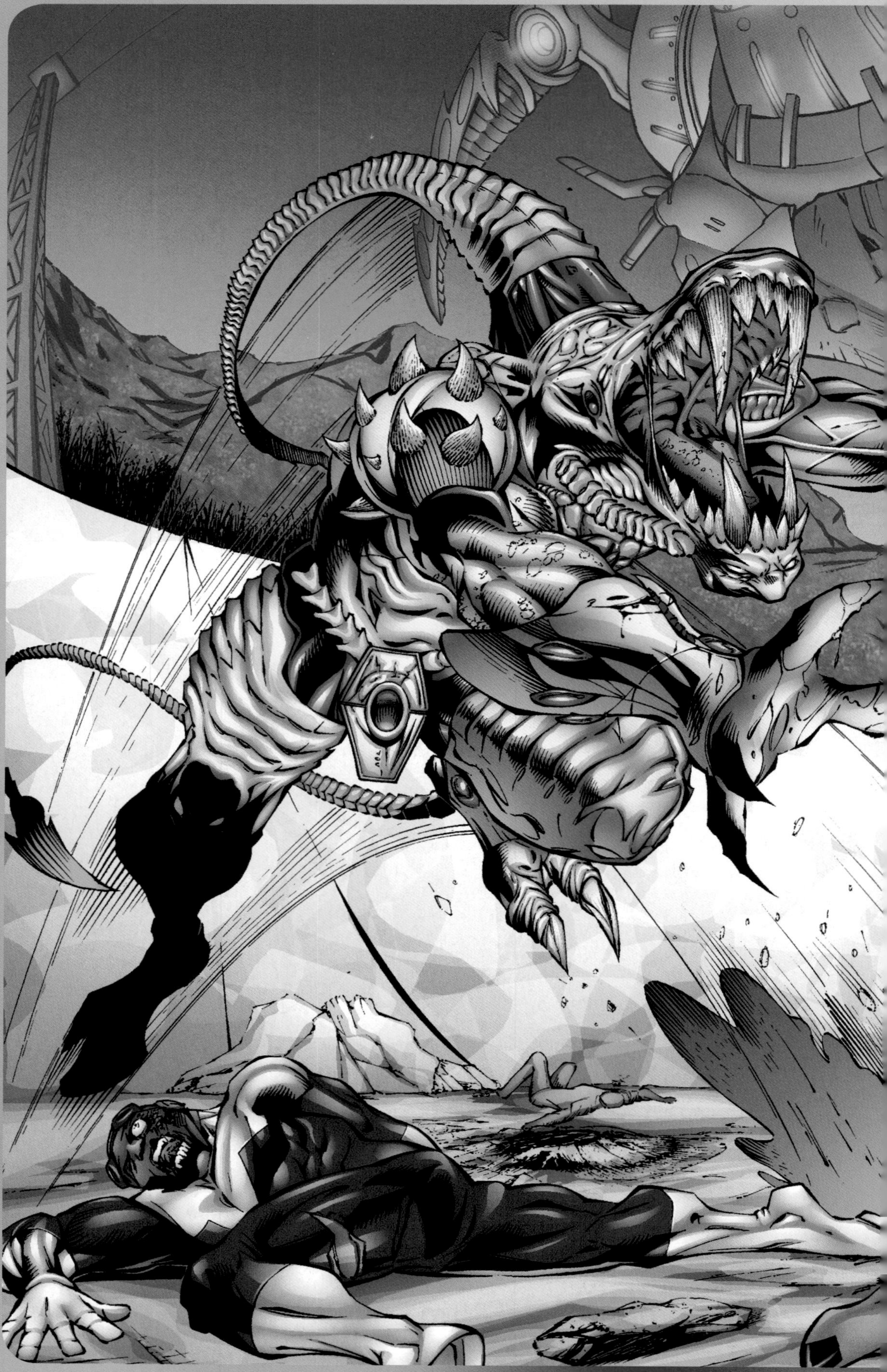

MARVEL COMICS
DEAD RECKONING PART 1 OF 3
IT BEGINS NOW!
DEADPOOL
DEC #23
APPROVED BY THE COMICS CODE AUTHORITY
WWW.MARVEL.COM

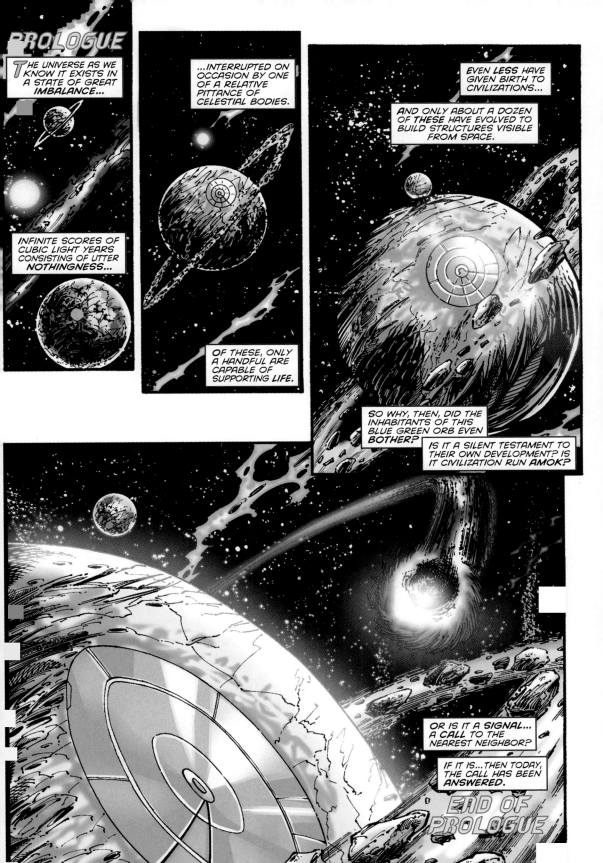

PROLOGUE

THE UNIVERSE AS WE KNOW IT EXISTS IN A STATE OF GREAT IMBALANCE...

INFINITE SCORES OF CUBIC LIGHT YEARS CONSISTING OF UTTER NOTHINGNESS...

...INTERRUPTED ON OCCASION BY ONE OF A RELATIVE PITTANCE OF CELESTIAL BODIES.

OF THESE, ONLY A HANDFUL ARE CAPABLE OF SUPPORTING LIFE.

EVEN LESS HAVE GIVEN BIRTH TO CIVILIZATIONS...

AND ONLY ABOUT A DOZEN OF THESE HAVE EVOLVED TO BUILD STRUCTURES VISIBLE FROM SPACE.

SO WHY, THEN, DID THE INHABITANTS OF THIS BLUE GREEN ORB EVEN BOTHER?

IS IT A SILENT TESTAMENT TO THEIR OWN DEVELOPMENT? IS IT CIVILIZATION RUN AMOK?

OR IS IT A SIGNAL... A CALL TO THE NEAREST NEIGHBOR?

IF IT IS...THEN TODAY, THE CALL HAS BEEN ANSWERED.

END OF PROLOGUE

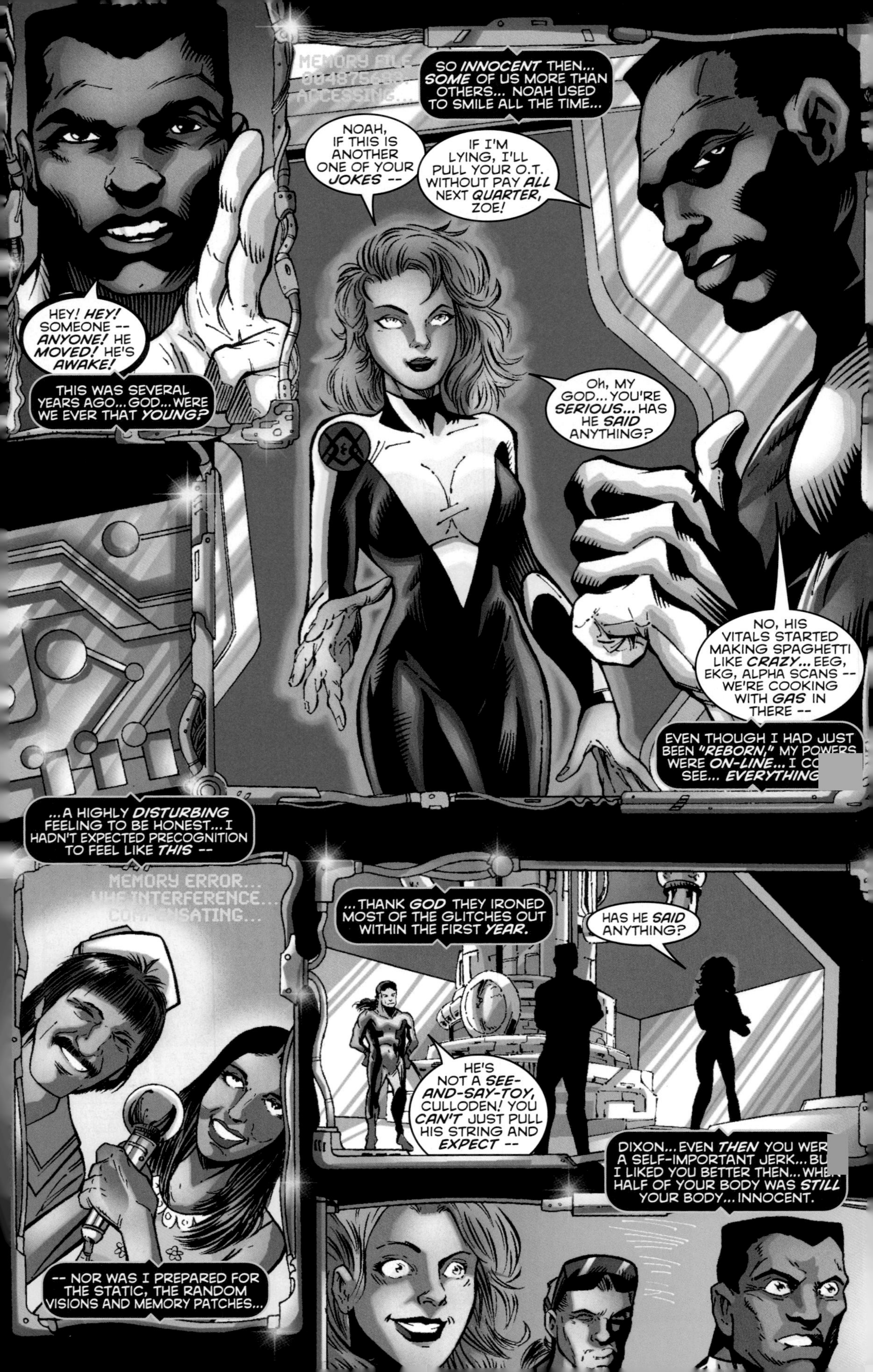
MEMORY FILE
ACCESSING...
SO INNOCENT THEN... SOME OF US MORE THAN OTHERS... NOAH USED TO SMILE ALL THE TIME...
NOAH, IF THIS IS ANOTHER ONE OF YOUR JOKES --
IF I'M LYING, I'LL PULL YOUR O.T. WITHOUT PAY ALL NEXT QUARTER, ZOE!
HEY! HEY! SOMEONE -- ANYONE! HE MOVED! HE'S AWAKE!
THIS WAS SEVERAL YEARS AGO...GOD...WERE WE EVER THAT YOUNG?
Oh, MY GOD...YOU'RE SERIOUS...HAS HE SAID ANYTHING?
NO, HIS VITALS STARTED MAKING SPAGHETTI LIKE CRAZY... EEG, EKG, ALPHA SCANS -- WE'RE COOKING WITH GAS IN THERE --
EVEN THOUGH I HAD JUST BEEN "REBORN," MY POWERS WERE ON-LINE... I CO SEE... EVERYTHING
...A HIGHLY DISTURBING FEELING TO BE HONEST... I HADN'T EXPECTED PRECOGNITION TO FEEL LIKE THIS --
MEMORY ERROR...
-- NOR WAS I PREPARED FOR THE STATIC, THE RANDOM VISIONS AND MEMORY PATCHES...
...THANK GOD THEY IRONED MOST OF THE GLITCHES OUT WITHIN THE FIRST YEAR.
HAS HE SAID ANYTHING?
HE'S NOT A SEE-AND-SAY-TOY, CULLODEN! YOU CAN'T JUST PULL HIS STRING AND EXPECT --
DIXON... EVEN THEN YOU WER A SELF-IMPORTANT JERK... BU I LIKED YOU BETTER THEN... WHE HALF OF YOUR BODY WAS STILL YOUR BODY... INNOCENT.

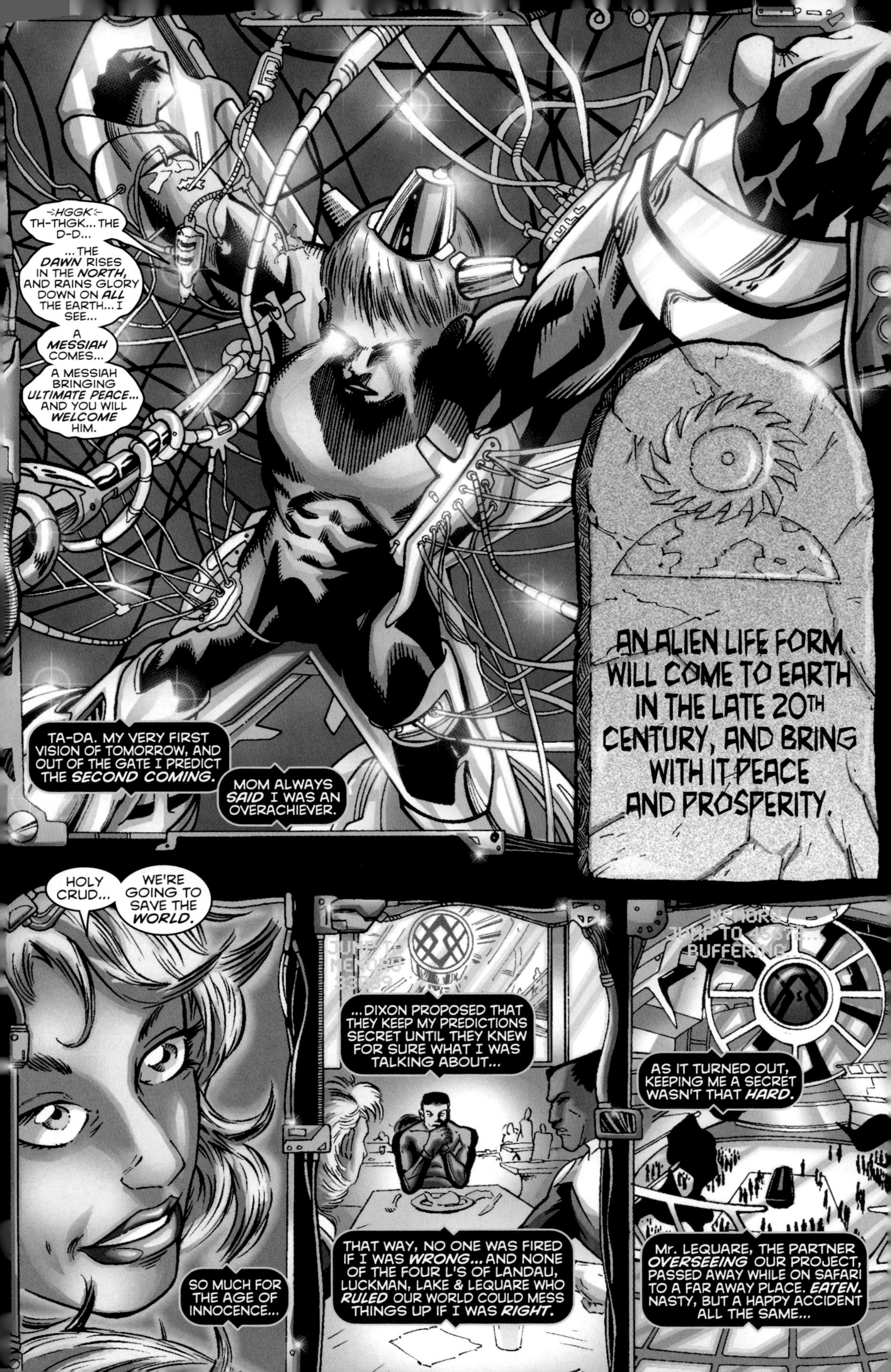

HGGK
TH-THGK... THE D-D...
...THE DAWN RISES IN THE NORTH, AND RAINS GLORY DOWN ON ALL THE EARTH... I SEE...
A MESSIAH COMES...
A MESSIAH BRINGING ULTIMATE PEACE... AND YOU WILL WELCOME HIM.
AN ALIEN LIFE FORM WILL COME TO EARTH IN THE LATE 20TH CENTURY, AND BRING WITH IT PEACE AND PROSPERITY.
TA-DA. MY VERY FIRST VISION OF TOMORROW, AND OUT OF THE GATE I PREDICT THE SECOND COMING.
MOM ALWAYS SAID I WAS AN OVERACHIEVER.
HOLY CRUD...
WE'RE GOING TO SAVE THE WORLD.
SO MUCH FOR THE AGE OF INNOCENCE...
...DIXON PROPOSED THAT THEY KEEP MY PREDICTIONS SECRET UNTIL THEY KNEW FOR SURE WHAT I WAS TALKING ABOUT...
THAT WAY, NO ONE WAS FIRED IF I WAS WRONG... AND NONE OF THE FOUR L'S OF LANDAU, LUCKMAN, LAKE & LEQUARE WHO RULED OUR WORLD COULD MESS THINGS UP IF I WAS RIGHT.
AS IT TURNED OUT, KEEPING ME A SECRET WASN'T THAT HARD.
Mr. LEQUARE, THE PARTNER OVERSEEING OUR PROJECT, PASSED AWAY WHILE ON SAFARI TO A FAR AWAY PLACE. EATEN. NASTY, BUT A HAPPY ACCIDENT ALL THE SAME...

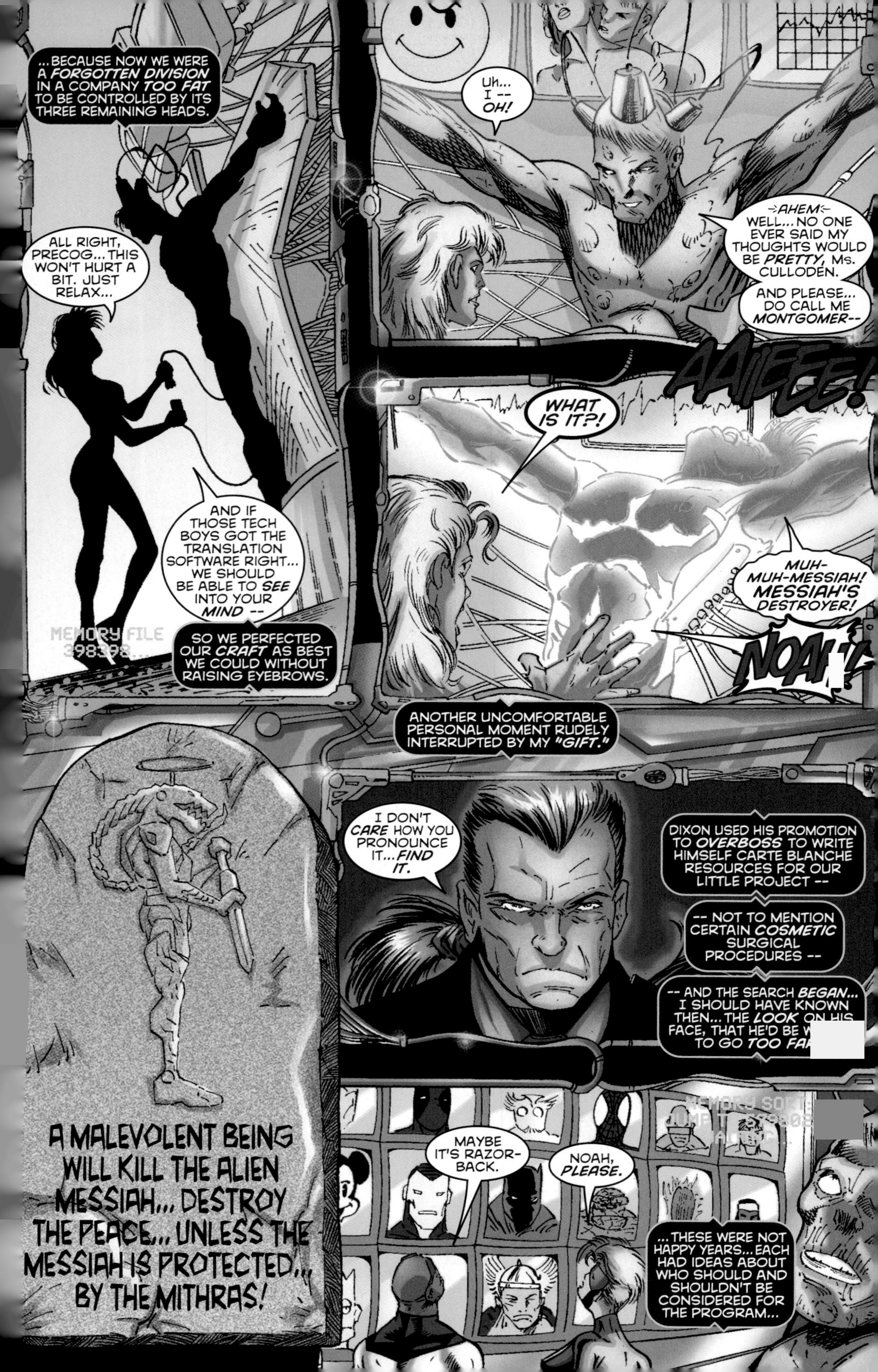
...BECAUSE NOW WE WERE A *FORGOTTEN DIVISION* IN A COMPANY *TOO FAT* TO BE CONTROLLED BY ITS THREE REMAINING HEADS.
ALL RIGHT, PRECOG...THIS WON'T HURT A BIT. JUST RELAX...
AND IF THOSE TECH BOYS GOT THE TRANSLATION SOFTWARE RIGHT... WE SHOULD BE ABLE TO *SEE* INTO YOUR *MIND* --
MEMORY FILE 398398...
SO WE PERFECTED OUR *CRAFT* AS BEST WE COULD WITHOUT RAISING EYEBROWS.
Uh... I -- *OH!*
AHEM
WELL...NO ONE EVER SAID MY THOUGHTS WOULD BE *PRETTY*, Ms. CULLODEN.
AND PLEASE... DO CALL ME *MONTGOMER*--
AAIIEEE!
WHAT IS IT?!
MUH-MUH-MESSIAH! MESSIAH'S DESTROYER!
NOAH
ANOTHER UNCOMFORTABLE PERSONAL MOMENT RUDELY INTERRUPTED BY MY *"GIFT."*
A MALEVOLENT BEING WILL KILL THE ALIEN MESSIAH... DESTROY THE PEACE... UNLESS THE MESSIAH IS PROTECTED... BY THE MITHRAS!
I DON'T *CARE* HOW YOU PRONOUNCE IT...*FIND IT.*
DIXON USED HIS PROMOTION TO *OVERBOSS* TO WRITE HIMSELF CARTE BLANCHE RESOURCES FOR OUR LITTLE PROJECT --
-- NOT TO MENTION CERTAIN *COSMETIC* SURGICAL PROCEDURES --
-- AND THE SEARCH *BEGAN*... I SHOULD HAVE KNOWN THEN...THE *LOOK* ON HIS FACE, THAT HE'D BE W
TO GO *TOO FA*
MAYBE IT'S RAZOR-BACK.
NOAH, *PLEASE.*
...THESE WERE NOT HAPPY YEARS...EACH HAD IDEAS ABOUT WHO SHOULD AND SHOULDN'T BE CONSIDERED FOR THE PROGRAM...

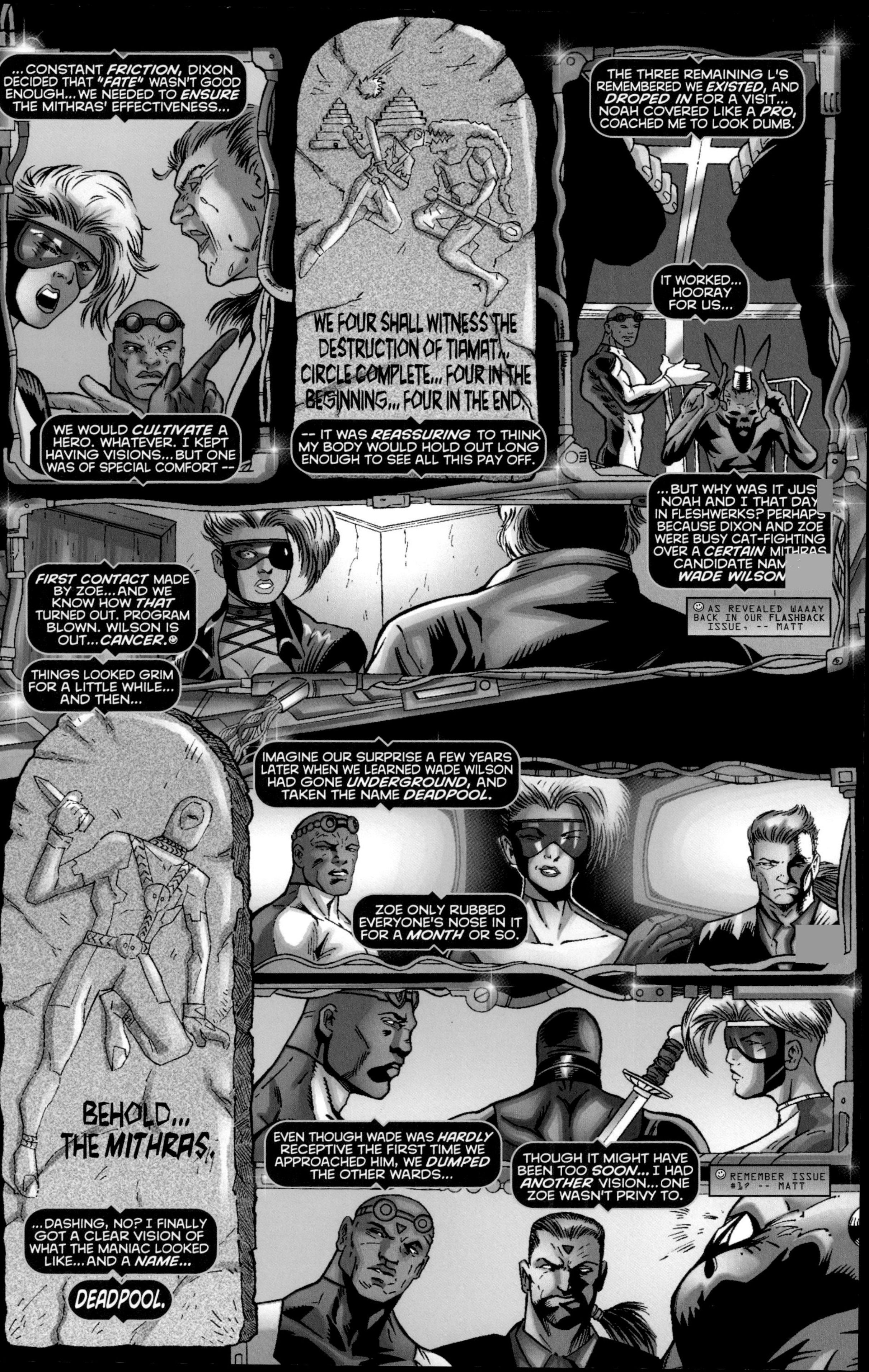
...CONSTANT FRICTION, DIXON DECIDED THAT "FATE" WASN'T GOOD ENOUGH... WE NEEDED TO ENSURE THE MITHRAS' EFFECTIVENESS...
WE WOULD CULTIVATE A HERO. WHATEVER. I KEPT HAVING VISIONS... BUT ONE WAS OF SPECIAL COMFORT --
WE FOUR SHALL WITNESS THE DESTRUCTION OF TIAMAT... CIRCLE COMPLETE... FOUR IN THE BEGINNING... FOUR IN THE END.
-- IT WAS REASSURING TO THINK MY BODY WOULD HOLD OUT LONG ENOUGH TO SEE ALL THIS PAY OFF.
THE THREE REMAINING L'S REMEMBERED WE EXISTED, AND DROPED IN FOR A VISIT... NOAH COVERED LIKE A PRO, COACHED ME TO LOOK DUMB.
IT WORKED... HOORAY FOR US...
...BUT WHY WAS IT JUS NOAH AND I THAT DAY IN FLESHWERKS? PERHAPS BECAUSE DIXON AND ZOE WERE BUSY CAT-FIGHTING OVER A CERTAIN MITHRAS CANDIDATE NAM WADE WILSON
AS REVEALED WAAAY BACK IN OUR FLASHBACK ISSUE, -- MATT
FIRST CONTACT MADE BY ZOE... AND WE KNOW HOW THAT TURNED OUT. PROGRAM BLOWN. WILSON IS OUT... CANCER.
THINGS LOOKED GRIM FOR A LITTLE WHILE... AND THEN...
BEHOLD... THE MITHRAS.
...DASHING, NO? I FINALLY GOT A CLEAR VISION OF WHAT THE MANIAC LOOKED LIKE... AND A NAME...
DEADPOOL.
IMAGINE OUR SURPRISE A FEW YEARS LATER WHEN WE LEARNED WADE WILSON HAD GONE UNDERGROUND, AND TAKEN THE NAME DEADPOOL.
ZOE ONLY RUBBED EVERYONE'S NOSE IN IT FOR A MONTH OR SO.
EVEN THOUGH WADE WAS HARDLY RECEPTIVE THE FIRST TIME WE APPROACHED HIM, WE DUMPED THE OTHER WARDS...
THOUGH IT MIGHT HAVE BEEN TOO SOON... I HAD ANOTHER VISION... ONE ZOE WASN'T PRIVY TO.
REMEMBER ISSUE #1? -- MATT

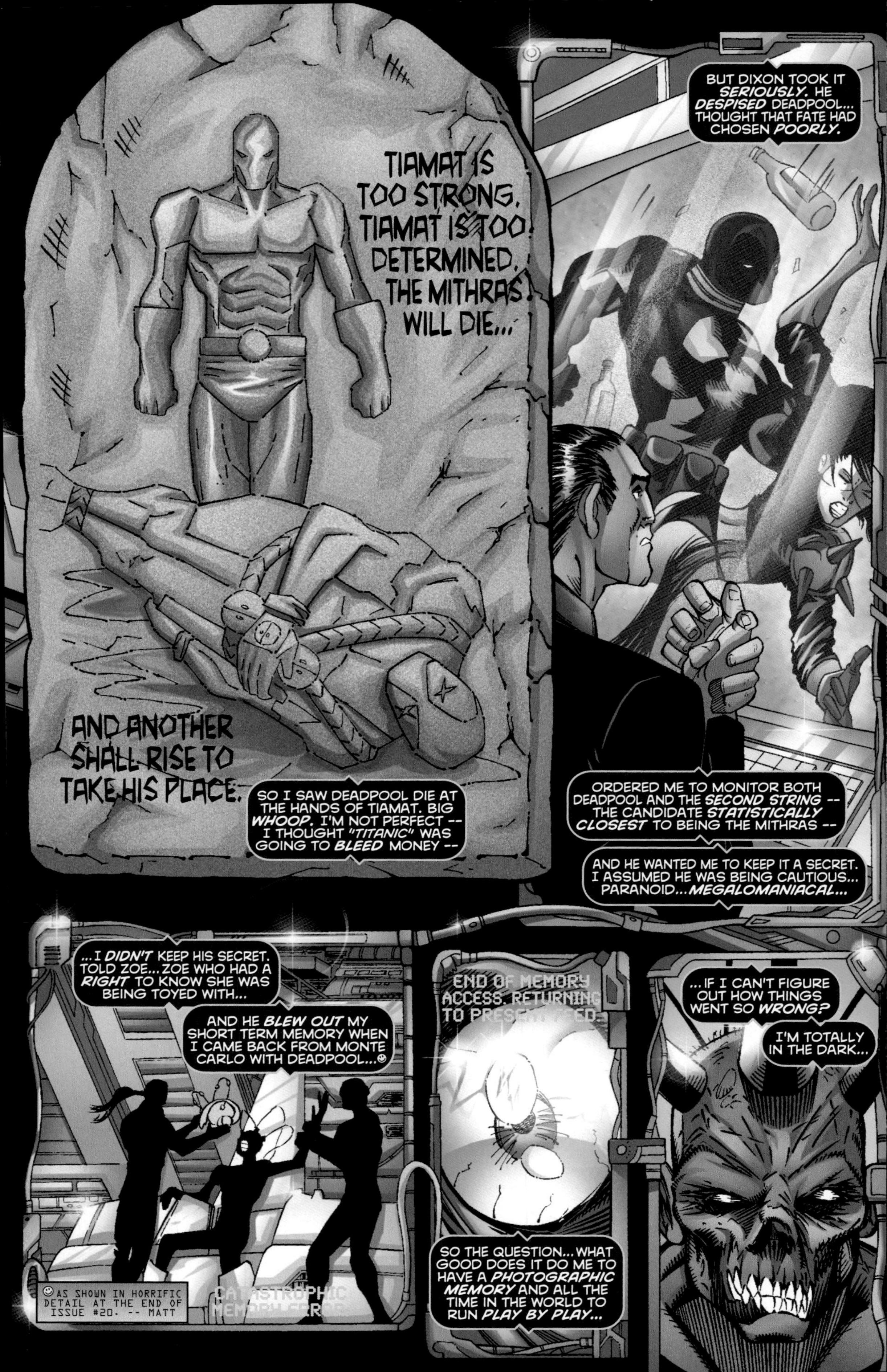
TIAMAT IS TOO STRONG. TIAMAT IS TOO DETERMINED. THE MITHRAS WILL DIE...
AND ANOTHER SHALL RISE TO TAKE HIS PLACE.
SO I SAW DEADPOOL DIE AT THE HANDS OF TIAMAT. BIG WHOOP. I'M NOT PERFECT -- I THOUGHT "TITANIC" WAS GOING TO BLEED MONEY --
BUT DIXON TOOK IT SERIOUSLY. HE DESPISED DEADPOOL... THOUGHT THAT FATE HAD CHOSEN POORLY.
ORDERED ME TO MONITOR BOTH DEADPOOL AND THE SECOND STRING -- THE CANDIDATE STATISTICALLY CLOSEST TO BEING THE MITHRAS --
AND HE WANTED ME TO KEEP IT A SECRET. I ASSUMED HE WAS BEING CAUTIOUS... PARANOID... MEGALOMANIACAL...
...I DIDN'T KEEP HIS SECRET. TOLD ZOE... ZOE WHO HAD A RIGHT TO KNOW SHE WAS BEING TOYED WITH...
AND HE BLEW OUT MY SHORT TERM MEMORY WHEN I CAME BACK FROM MONTE CARLO WITH DEADPOOL...☺
☺AS SHOWN IN HORRIFIC DETAIL AT THE END OF ISSUE #20. -- MATT
CATASTROPHIC MEMORY ERROR
END OF MEMORY ACCESS. RETURNING TO PRESENT FEED.
SO THE QUESTION... WHAT GOOD DOES IT DO ME TO HAVE A PHOTOGRAPHIC MEMORY AND ALL THE TIME IN THE WORLD TO RUN PLAY BY PLAY...
...IF I CAN'T FIGURE OUT HOW THINGS WENT SO WRONG?
I'M TOTALLY IN THE DARK...

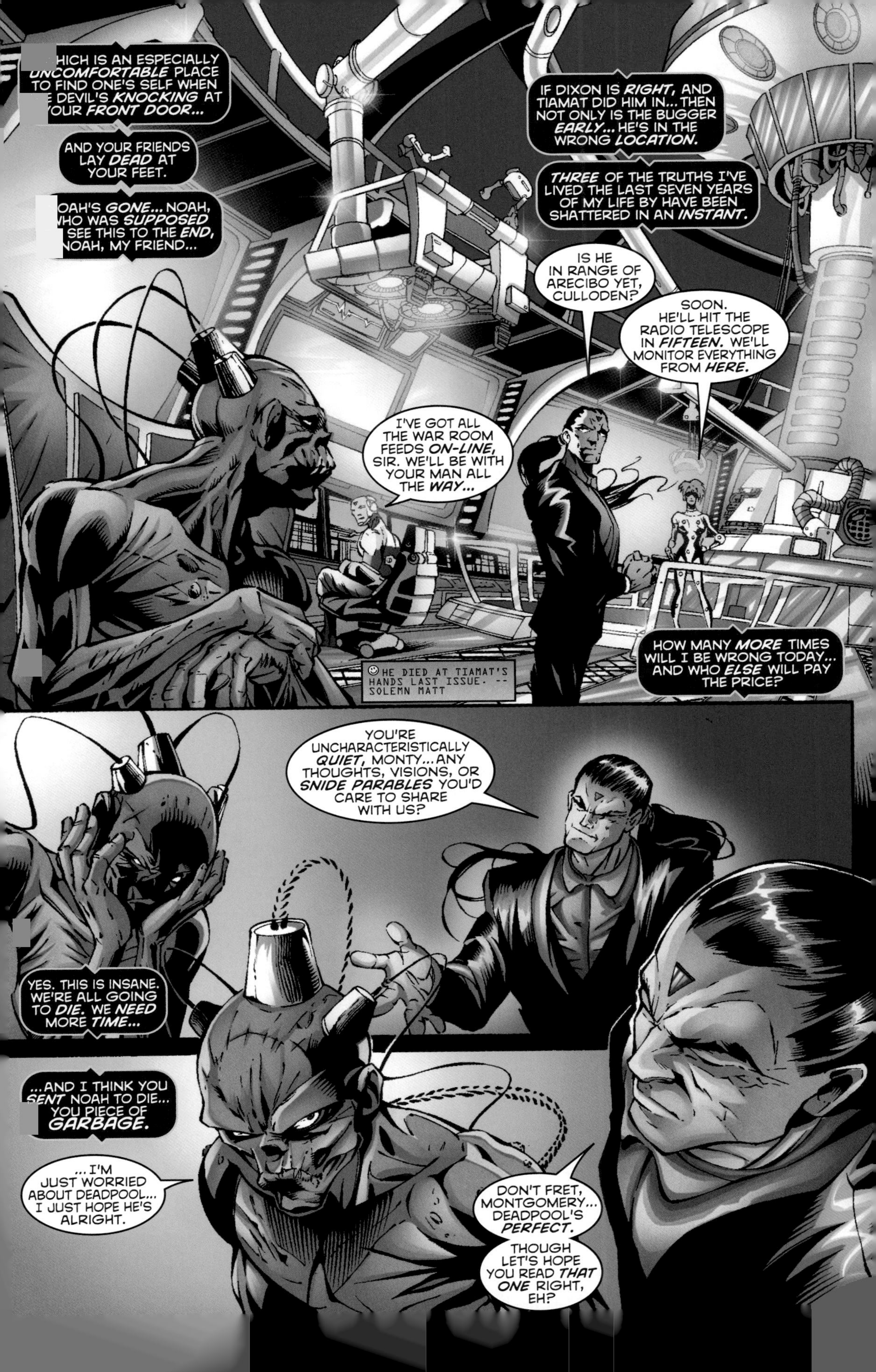
HICH IS AN ESPECIALLY UNCOMFORTABLE PLACE TO FIND ONE'S SELF WHEN E DEVIL'S KNOCKING AT OUR FRONT DOOR...
AND YOUR FRIENDS LAY DEAD AT YOUR FEET.
OAH'S GONE... NOAH, HO WAS SUPPOSED SEE THIS TO THE END, OAH, MY FRIEND...
IF DIXON IS RIGHT, AND TIAMAT DID HIM IN... THEN NOT ONLY IS THE BUGGER EARLY... HE'S IN THE WRONG LOCATION.
THREE OF THE TRUTHS I'VE LIVED THE LAST SEVEN YEARS OF MY LIFE BY HAVE BEEN SHATTERED IN AN INSTANT.
IS HE IN RANGE OF ARECIBO YET, CULLODEN?
SOON. HE'LL HIT THE RADIO TELESCOPE IN FIFTEEN. WE'LL MONITOR EVERYTHING FROM HERE.
I'VE GOT ALL THE WAR ROOM FEEDS ON-LINE, SIR. WE'LL BE WITH YOUR MAN ALL THE WAY...
HE DIED AT TIAMAT'S HANDS LAST ISSUE. -- SOLEMN MATT
HOW MANY MORE TIMES WILL I BE WRONG TODAY... AND WHO ELSE WILL PAY THE PRICE?
YOU'RE UNCHARACTERISTICALLY QUIET, MONTY... ANY THOUGHTS, VISIONS, OR SNIDE PARABLES YOU'D CARE TO SHARE WITH US?
YES. THIS IS INSANE. WE'RE ALL GOING TO DIE. WE NEED MORE TIME...
...AND I THINK YOU SENT NOAH TO DIE... YOU PIECE OF GARBAGE.
...I'M JUST WORRIED ABOUT DEADPOOL... I JUST HOPE HE'S ALRIGHT.
DON'T FRET, MONTGOMERY... DEADPOOL'S PERFECT.
THOUGH LET'S HOPE YOU READ THAT ONE RIGHT, EH?

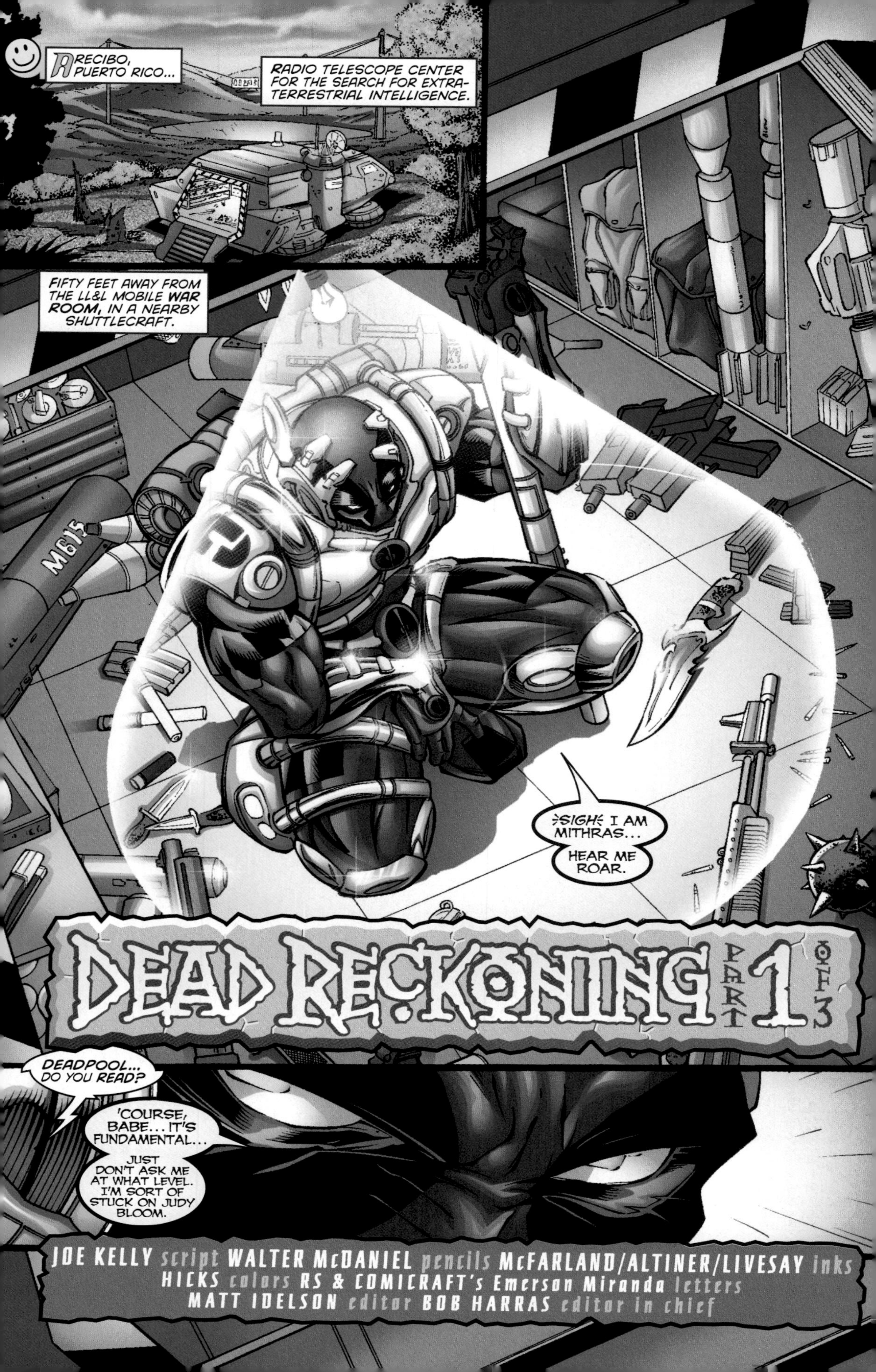
ARECIBO, PUERTO RICO...
RADIO TELESCOPE CENTER FOR THE SEARCH FOR EXTRA-TERRESTRIAL INTELLIGENCE.
FIFTY FEET AWAY FROM THE LL&L MOBILE WAR ROOM, IN A NEARBY SHUTTLECRAFT.
M615
SIGH I AM MITHRAS... HEAR ME ROAR.
DEAD RECKONING PART 1 OF 3
DEADPOOL... DO YOU READ?
'COURSE, BABE... IT'S FUNDAMENTAL...
JUST DON'T ASK ME AT WHAT LEVEL. I'M SORT OF STUCK ON JUDY BLOOM.
JOE KELLY script WALTER McDANIEL pencils McFARLAND/ALTINER/LIVESAY inks
HICKS colors RS & COMICRAFT's Emerson Miranda letters
MATT IDELSON editor BOB HARRAS editor in chief

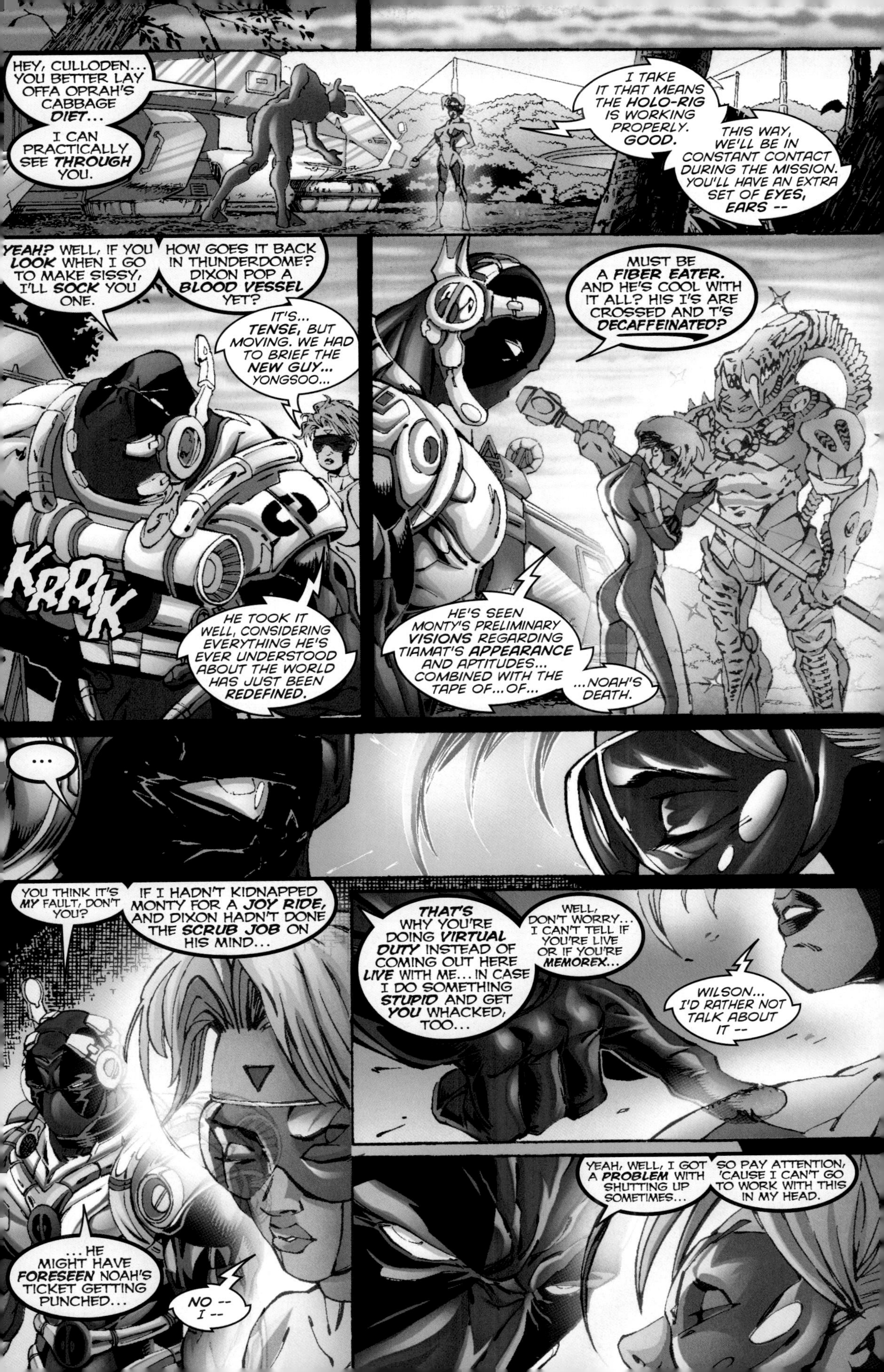

HEY, CULLODEN... YOU BETTER LAY OFFA OPRAH'S CABBAGE DIET...
I CAN PRACTICALLY SEE THROUGH YOU.
I TAKE IT THAT MEANS THE HOLO-RIG IS WORKING PROPERLY. GOOD.
THIS WAY, WE'LL BE IN CONSTANT CONTACT DURING THE MISSION. YOU'LL HAVE AN EXTRA SET OF EYES, EARS --
YEAH? WELL, IF YOU LOOK WHEN I GO TO MAKE SISSY, I'LL SOCK YOU ONE.
HOW GOES IT BACK IN THUNDERDOME? DIXON POP A BLOOD VESSEL YET?
IT'S... TENSE, BUT MOVING. WE HAD TO BRIEF THE NEW GUY... YONGSOO...
KRRK
HE TOOK IT WELL, CONSIDERING EVERYTHING HE'S EVER UNDERSTOOD ABOUT THE WORLD HAS JUST BEEN REDEFINED.
MUST BE A FIBER EATER. AND HE'S COOL WITH IT ALL? HIS I'S ARE CROSSED AND T'S DECAFFEINATED?
HE'S SEEN MONTY'S PRELIMINARY VISIONS REGARDING TIAMAT'S APPEARANCE AND APTITUDES... COMBINED WITH THE TAPE OF... OF...
...NOAH'S DEATH.
...
YOU THINK IT'S MY FAULT, DON'T YOU?
IF I HADN'T KIDNAPPED MONTY FOR A JOY RIDE, AND DIXON HADN'T DONE THE SCRUB JOB ON HIS MIND...
... HE MIGHT HAVE FORESEEN NOAH'S TICKET GETTING PUNCHED...
NO -- I --
THAT'S WHY YOU'RE DOING VIRTUAL DUTY INSTEAD OF COMING OUT HERE LIVE WITH ME... IN CASE I DO SOMETHING STUPID AND GET YOU WHACKED, TOO...
WELL, DON'T WORRY... I CAN'T TELL IF YOU'RE LIVE OR IF YOU'RE MEMOREX...
WILSON... I'D RATHER NOT TALK ABOUT IT --
YEAH, WELL, I GOT A PROBLEM WITH SHUTTING UP SOMETIMES...
SO PAY ATTENTION, 'CAUSE I CAN'T GO TO WORK WITH THIS IN MY HEAD.

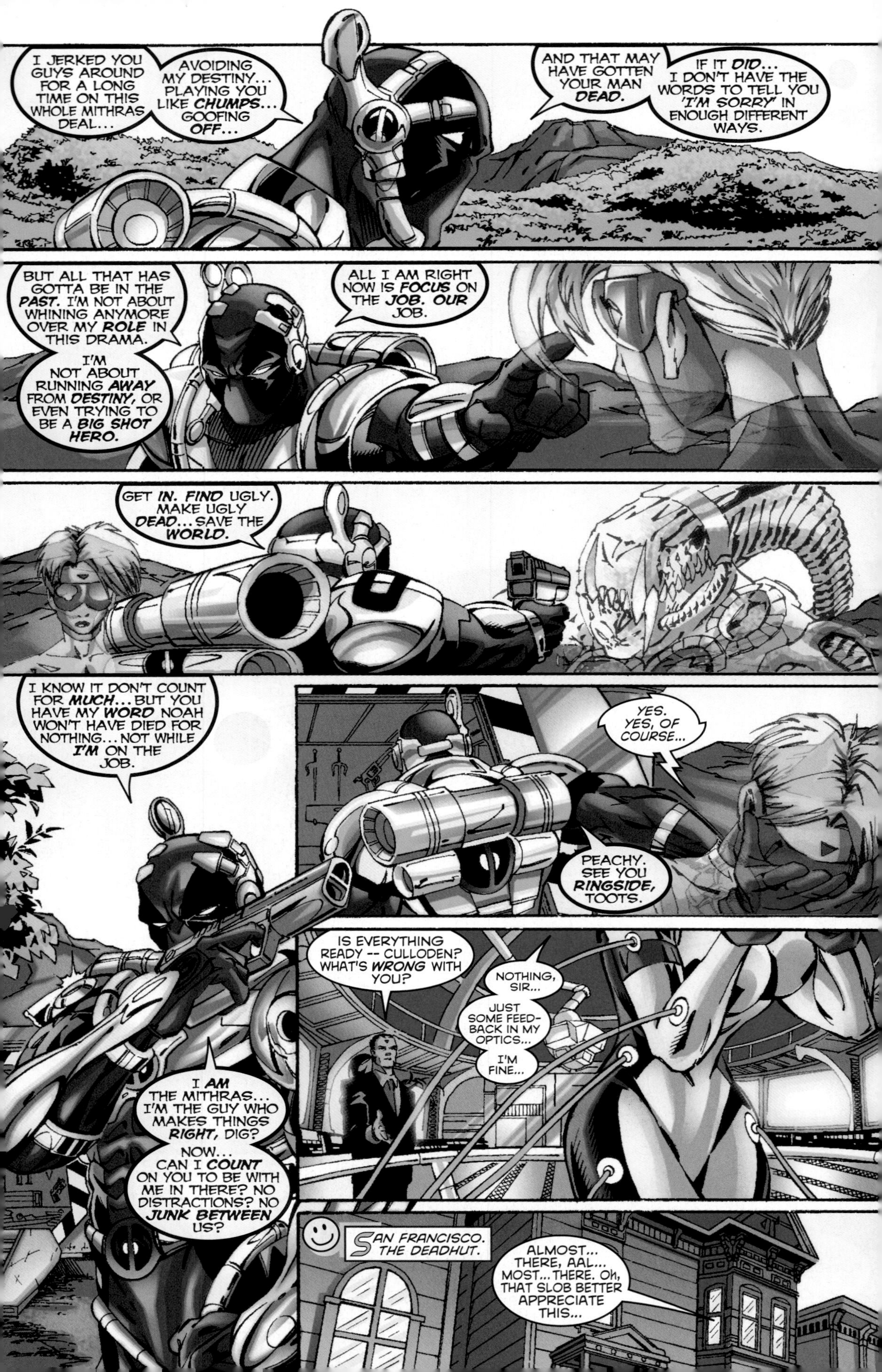
I JERKED YOU GUYS AROUND FOR A LONG TIME ON THIS WHOLE MITHRAS DEAL...
AVOIDING MY DESTINY... PLAYING YOU LIKE CHUMPS... GOOFING OFF...
AND THAT MAY HAVE GOTTEN YOUR MAN DEAD.
IF IT DID... I DON'T HAVE THE WORDS TO TELL YOU 'I'M SORRY' IN ENOUGH DIFFERENT WAYS.
BUT ALL THAT HAS GOTTA BE IN THE PAST. I'M NOT ABOUT WHINING ANYMORE OVER MY ROLE IN THIS DRAMA.
I'M NOT ABOUT RUNNING AWAY FROM DESTINY, OR EVEN TRYING TO BE A BIG SHOT HERO.
ALL I AM RIGHT NOW IS FOCUS ON THE JOB. OUR JOB.
GET IN. FIND UGLY. MAKE UGLY DEAD... SAVE THE WORLD.
I KNOW IT DON'T COUNT FOR MUCH... BUT YOU HAVE MY WORD NOAH WON'T HAVE DIED FOR NOTHING... NOT WHILE I'M ON THE JOB.
I AM THE MITHRAS... I'M THE GUY WHO MAKES THINGS RIGHT, DIG?
NOW... CAN I COUNT ON YOU TO BE WITH ME IN THERE? NO DISTRACTIONS? NO JUNK BETWEEN US?
YES. YES, OF COURSE...
PEACHY. SEE YOU RINGSIDE, TOOTS.
IS EVERYTHING READY -- CULLODEN? WHAT'S WRONG WITH YOU?
NOTHING, SIR...
JUST SOME FEED-BACK IN MY OPTICS...
I'M FINE...
SAN FRANCISCO. THE DEADHUT.
ALMOST... THERE, AAL... MOST... THERE. Oh, THAT SLOB BETTER APPRECIATE THIS...

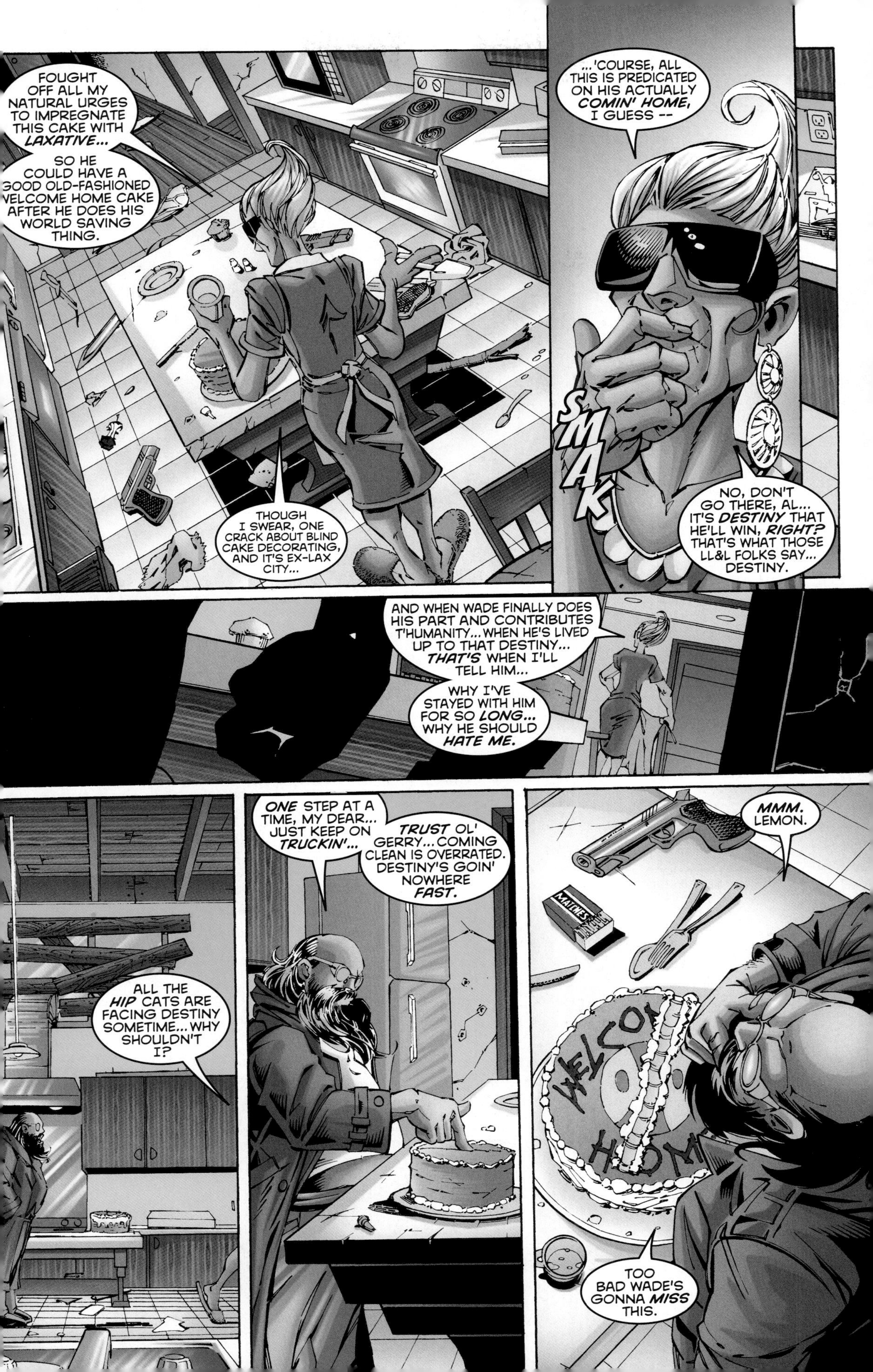
FOUGHT OFF ALL MY NATURAL URGES TO IMPREGNATE THIS CAKE WITH *LAXATIVE...*
SO HE COULD HAVE A GOOD OLD-FASHIONED WELCOME HOME CAKE AFTER HE DOES HIS WORLD SAVING THING.
THOUGH I SWEAR, ONE CRACK ABOUT BLIND CAKE DECORATING, AND IT'S EX-LAX CITY...
...'COURSE, ALL THIS IS PREDICATED ON HIS ACTUALLY *COMIN' HOME,* I GUESS --
SMAK
NO, DON'T GO THERE, AL... IT'S *DESTINY* THAT HE'LL WIN, *RIGHT?* THAT'S WHAT THOSE LL&L FOLKS SAY... DESTINY.
AND WHEN WADE FINALLY DOES HIS PART AND CONTRIBUTES T'HUMANITY... WHEN HE'S LIVED UP TO THAT DESTINY... *THAT'S* WHEN I'LL TELL HIM...
WHY I'VE STAYED WITH HIM FOR SO *LONG...* WHY HE SHOULD *HATE ME.*
ALL THE *HIP* CATS ARE FACING DESTINY SOMETIME... WHY SHOULDN'T I?
ONE STEP AT A TIME, MY DEAR... JUST KEEP ON *TRUCKIN'...*
TRUST OL' GERRY... COMING CLEAN IS OVERRATED. DESTINY'S GOIN' NOWHERE *FAST.*
MATCHES
MMM. LEMON.
WELCO HOM
TOO BAD WADE'S GONNA *MISS* THIS.

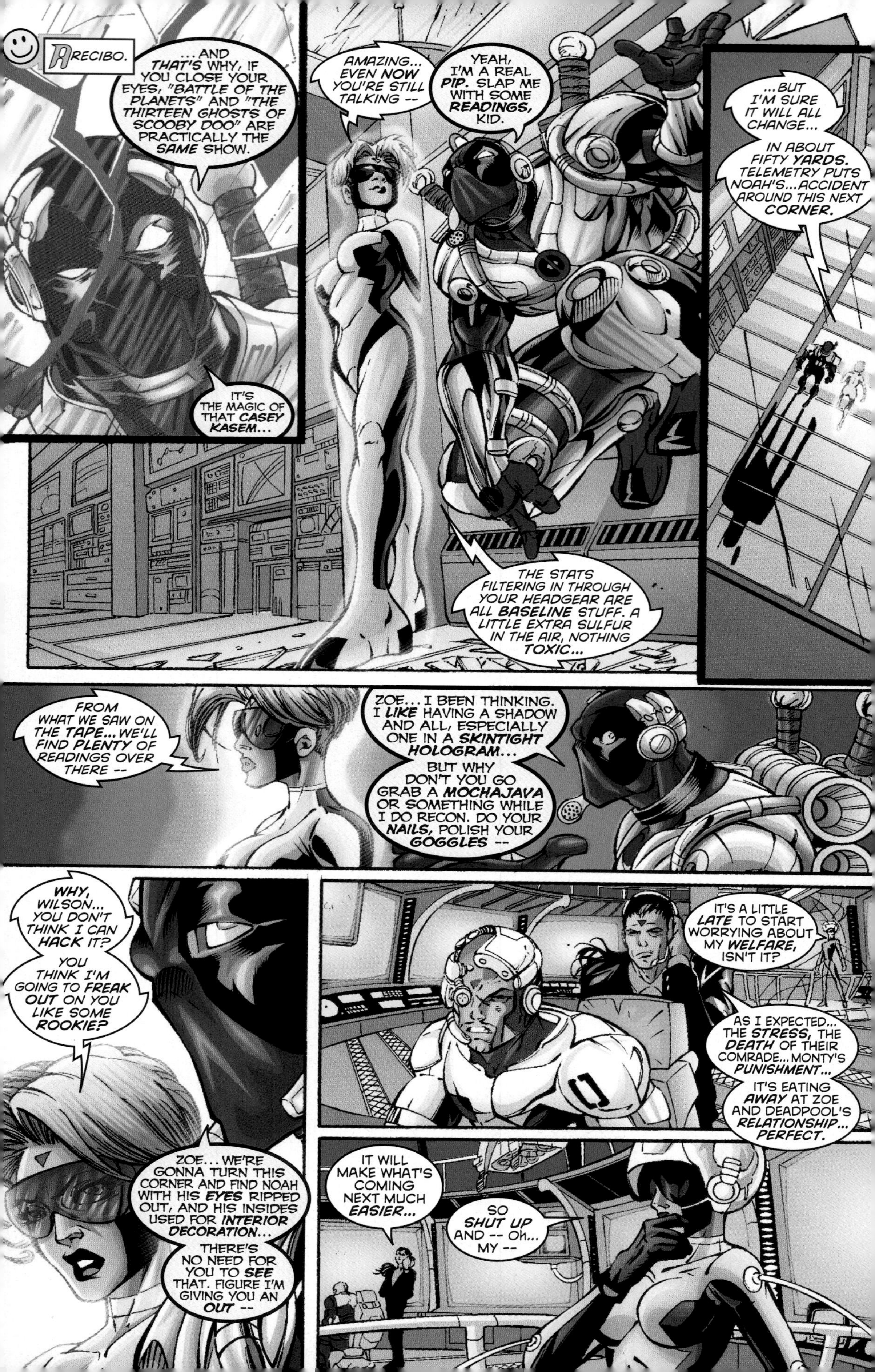

RECIBO.
...AND THAT'S WHY, IF YOU CLOSE YOUR EYES, "BATTLE OF THE PLANETS" AND "THE THIRTEEN GHOSTS OF SCOOBY DOO" ARE PRACTICALLY THE SAME SHOW.
IT'S THE MAGIC OF THAT CASEY KASEM...
AMAZING... EVEN NOW YOU'RE STILL TALKING --
YEAH, I'M A REAL PIP. SLAP ME WITH SOME READINGS, KID.
THE STATS FILTERING IN THROUGH YOUR HEADGEAR ARE ALL BASELINE STUFF. A LITTLE EXTRA SULFUR IN THE AIR, NOTHING TOXIC...
...BUT I'M SURE IT WILL ALL CHANGE...
IN ABOUT FIFTY YARDS. TELEMETRY PUTS NOAH'S...ACCIDENT AROUND THIS NEXT CORNER.
FROM WHAT WE SAW ON THE TAPE...WE'LL FIND PLENTY OF READINGS OVER THERE --
ZOE... I BEEN THINKING. I LIKE HAVING A SHADOW AND ALL, ESPECIALLY ONE IN A SKINTIGHT HOLOGRAM...
BUT WHY DON'T YOU GO GRAB A MOCHAJAVA OR SOMETHING WHILE I DO RECON. DO YOUR NAILS, POLISH YOUR GOGGLES --
WHY, WILSON... YOU DON'T THINK I CAN HACK IT?
YOU THINK I'M GOING TO FREAK OUT ON YOU LIKE SOME ROOKIE?
ZOE... WE'RE GONNA TURN THIS CORNER AND FIND NOAH WITH HIS EYES RIPPED OUT, AND HIS INSIDES USED FOR INTERIOR DECORATION...
THERE'S NO NEED FOR YOU TO SEE THAT. FIGURE I'M GIVING YOU AN OUT --
IT'S A LITTLE LATE TO START WORRYING ABOUT MY WELFARE, ISN'T IT?
AS I EXPECTED... THE STRESS, THE DEATH OF THEIR COMRADE...MONTY'S PUNISHMENT...
IT'S EATING AWAY AT ZOE AND DEADPOOL'S RELATIONSHIP... PERFECT.
IT WILL MAKE WHAT'S COMING NEXT MUCH EASIER...
SO SHUT UP AND -- Oh... MY --

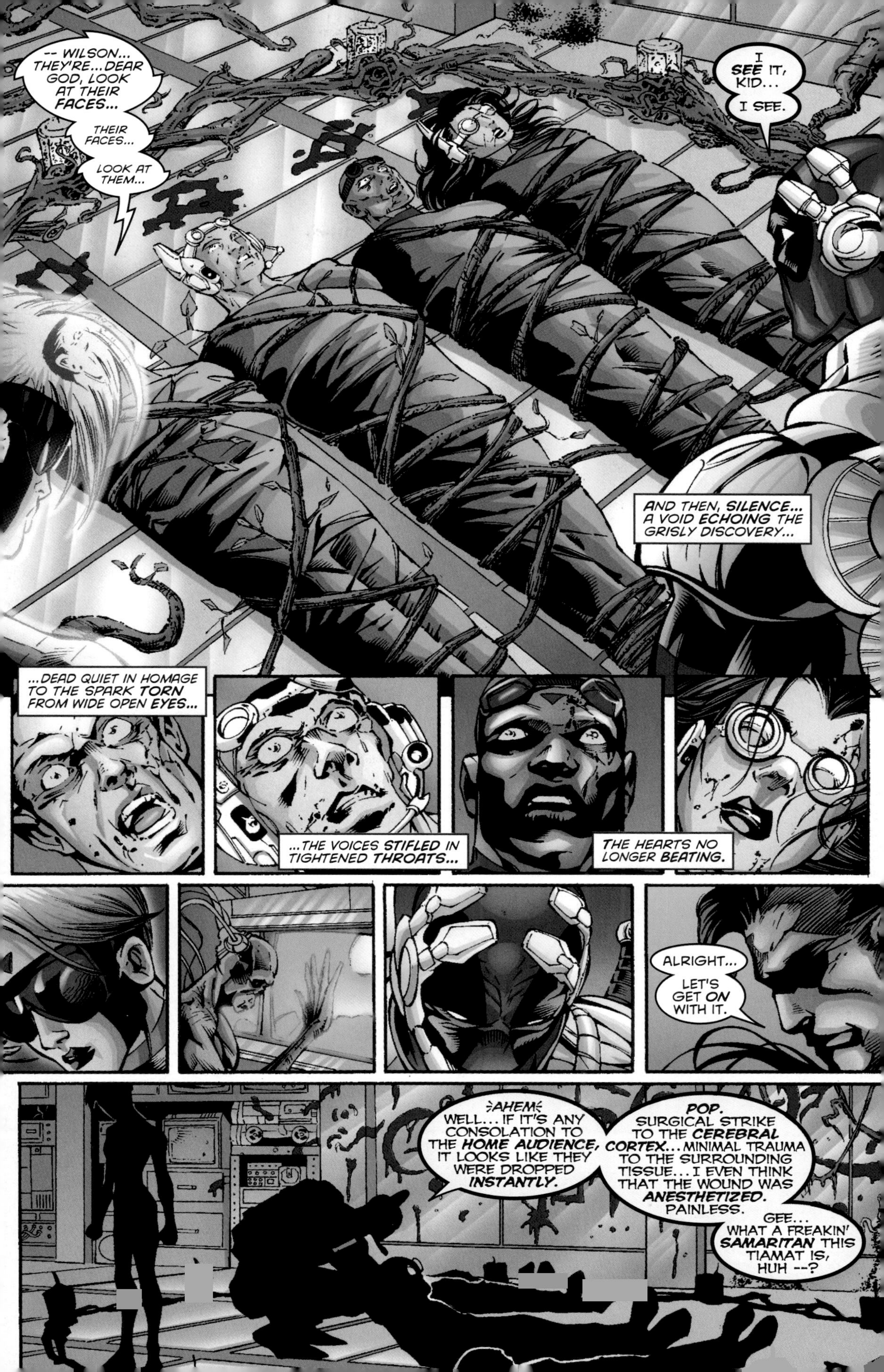
-- WILSON... THEY'RE...DEAR GOD, LOOK AT THEIR FACES...
THEIR FACES...
LOOK AT THEM...
I SEE IT, KID...
I SEE.
AND THEN, SILENCE... A VOID ECHOING THE GRISLY DISCOVERY...
...DEAD QUIET IN HOMAGE TO THE SPARK TORN FROM WIDE OPEN EYES...
...THE VOICES STIFLED IN TIGHTENED THROATS...
THE HEARTS NO LONGER BEATING.
ALRIGHT...
LET'S GET ON WITH IT.
AHEM WELL... IF IT'S ANY CONSOLATION TO THE HOME AUDIENCE, IT LOOKS LIKE THEY WERE DROPPED INSTANTLY.
POP. SURGICAL STRIKE TO THE CEREBRAL CORTEX... MINIMAL TRAUMA TO THE SURROUNDING TISSUE... I EVEN THINK THAT THE WOUND WAS ANESTHETIZED. PAINLESS.
GEE... WHAT A FREAKIN' SAMARITAN THIS TIAMAT IS, HUH --?

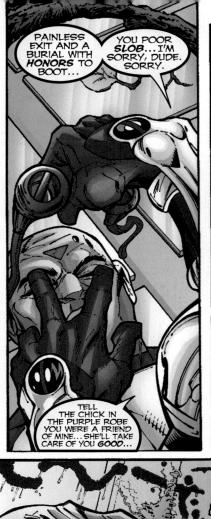

PAINLESS EXIT AND A BURIAL WITH **HONORS** TO BOOT...

YOU POOR **SLOB**...I'M SORRY, DUDE. SORRY.

TELL THE CHICK IN THE PURPLE ROBE YOU WERE A FRIEND OF MINE...SHE'LL TAKE CARE OF YOU **GOOD**...

YOU STILL **WITH** ME, CULLODEN?

YES... I AM...

I...I HAVEN'T HAD A **FRIEND** DIE BEFORE.

MMM. SOMETIMES, SAYING **GOOD-BYE** HELPS.

BZZZZZT

SOMETIMES IT **DOESN'T**.

...YOU'LL FEEL BETTER ONCE WE GO **KILL** SOMETHING. I PROMISE.

MMM -- MM --

MIT-RASSS...

I -- I SAID GOODBYE ON THE INSIDE.

YEAH, SURE YOU DID. LET'S MOVE ON...

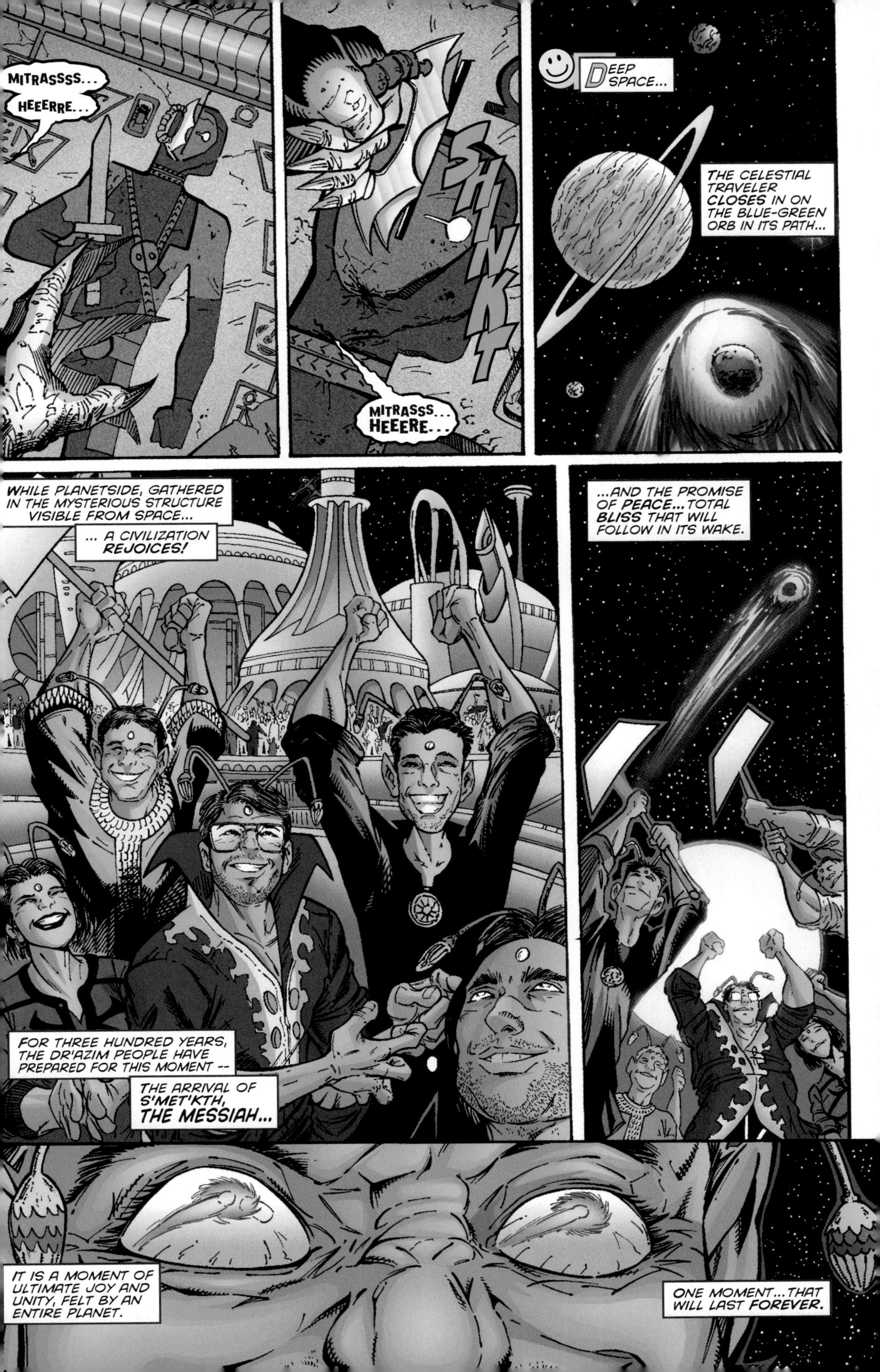

MITRASSSS...
HEEERRE...
SHINKT
MITRASSS...
HEEERE...
DEEP SPACE...
THE CELESTIAL TRAVELER CLOSES IN ON THE BLUE-GREEN ORB IN ITS PATH...
WHILE PLANETSIDE, GATHERED IN THE MYSTERIOUS STRUCTURE VISIBLE FROM SPACE...
... A CIVILIZATION REJOICES!
FOR THREE HUNDRED YEARS, THE DR'AZIM PEOPLE HAVE PREPARED FOR THIS MOMENT --
THE ARRIVAL OF S'MET'KTH, THE MESSIAH...
...AND THE PROMISE OF PEACE...TOTAL BLISS THAT WILL FOLLOW IN ITS WAKE.
IT IS A MOMENT OF ULTIMATE JOY AND UNITY, FELT BY AN ENTIRE PLANET.
ONE MOMENT...THAT WILL LAST FOREVER.

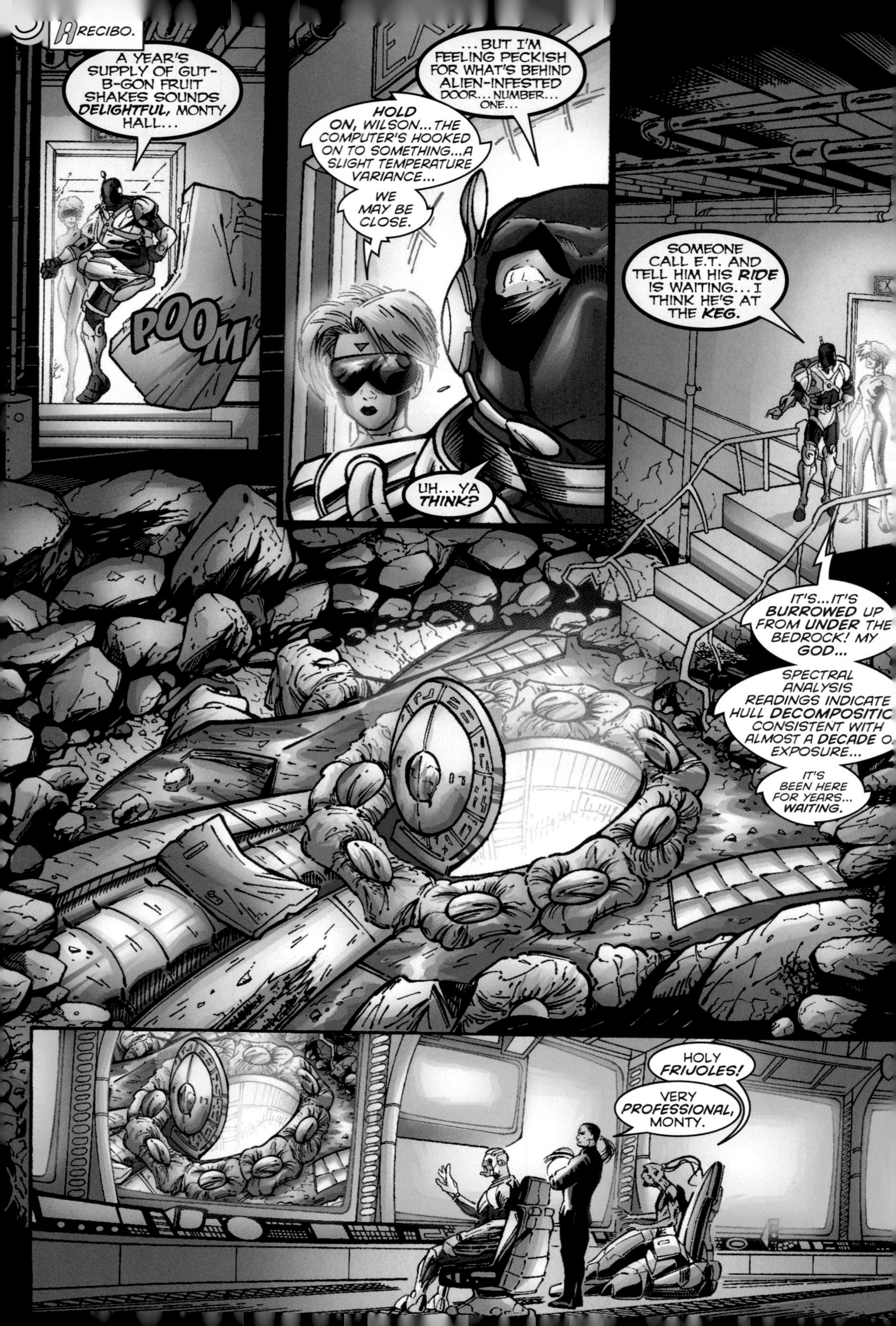
ARECIBO.
A YEAR'S SUPPLY OF GUT-B-GON FRUIT SHAKES SOUNDS DELIGHTFUL, MONTY HALL...
POOM
...BUT I'M FEELING PECKISH FOR WHAT'S BEHIND ALIEN-INFESTED DOOR...NUMBER...ONE...
HOLD ON, WILSON...THE COMPUTER'S HOOKED ON TO SOMETHING...A SLIGHT TEMPERATURE VARIANCE...
WE MAY BE CLOSE.
UH...YA THINK?
SOMEONE CALL E.T. AND TELL HIM HIS RIDE IS WAITING...I THINK HE'S AT THE KEG.
IT'S...IT'S BURROWED UP FROM UNDER THE BEDROCK! MY GOD...
SPECTRAL ANALYSIS READINGS INDICATE HULL DECOMPOSITIC CONSISTENT WITH ALMOST A DECADE O EXPOSURE...
IT'S BEEN HERE FOR YEARS...WAITING.
HOLY FRIJOLES!
VERY PROFESSIONAL, MONTY.

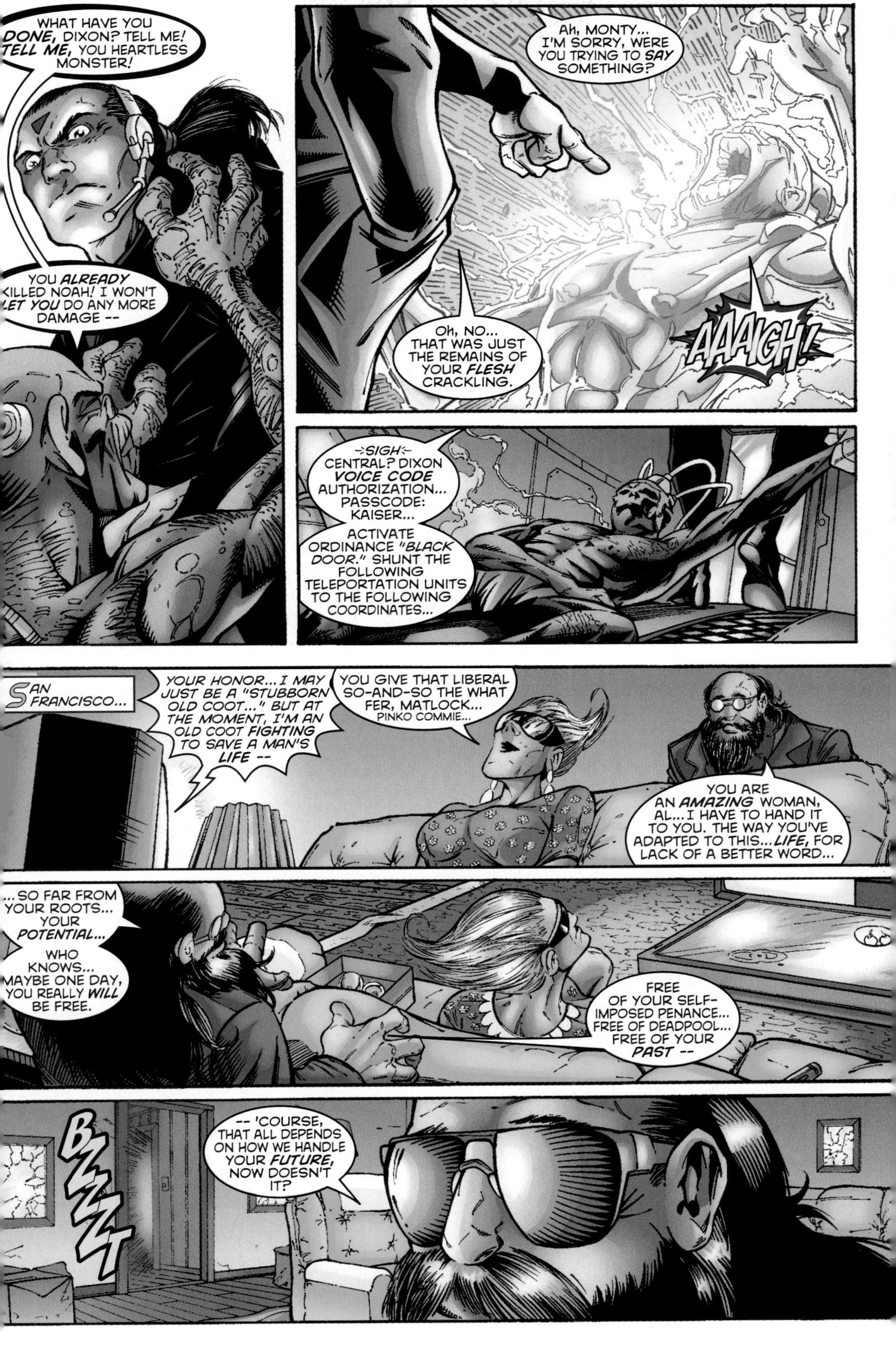

WHAT HAVE YOU DONE, DIXON? TELL ME! TELL ME, YOU HEARTLESS MONSTER!
YOU ALREADY KILLED NOAH! I WON'T LET YOU DO ANY MORE DAMAGE --
Ah, MONTY... I'M SORRY, WERE YOU TRYING TO SAY SOMETHING?
Oh, NO... THAT WAS JUST THE REMAINS OF YOUR FLESH CRACKLING.
AAAIGH!
SIGH
CENTRAL? DIXON VOICE CODE AUTHORIZATION... PASSCODE: KAISER...
ACTIVATE ORDINANCE "BLACK DOOR." SHUNT THE FOLLOWING TELEPORTATION UNITS TO THE FOLLOWING COORDINATES...
SAN FRANCISCO...
YOUR HONOR... I MAY JUST BE A "STUBBORN OLD COOT..." BUT AT THE MOMENT, I'M AN OLD COOT FIGHTING TO SAVE A MAN'S LIFE --
YOU GIVE THAT LIBERAL SO-AND-SO THE WHAT FER, MATLOCK... PINKO COMMIE...
YOU ARE AN AMAZING WOMAN, AL... I HAVE TO HAND IT TO YOU. THE WAY YOU'VE ADAPTED TO THIS... LIFE, FOR LACK OF A BETTER WORD...
...SO FAR FROM YOUR ROOTS... YOUR POTENTIAL...
WHO KNOWS... MAYBE ONE DAY, YOU REALLY WILL BE FREE.
FREE OF YOUR SELF-IMPOSED PENANCE... FREE OF DEADPOOL... FREE OF YOUR PAST --
BZZZT
-- 'COURSE, THAT ALL DEPENDS ON HOW WE HANDLE YOUR FUTURE, NOW DOESN'T IT?

ASSUMING YOU *HAVE* A *FUTURE* TO HANDLE AT ALL.

MAN...A *TRIAD* OF BLACK-OUT TROOPERS FOR *ONE* OLD LADY...

YOU SURE ARE A *THOROUGH* RASCAL, DIXON...ALWAYS *WERE*...

...I *TAUGHT* YOU *WELL*.

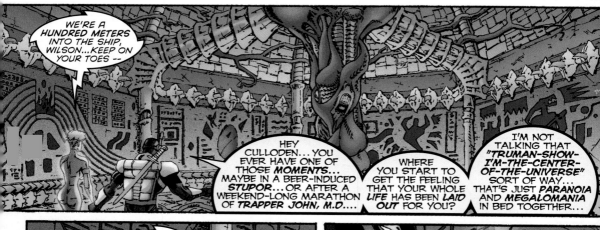

WE'RE A *HUNDRED METERS* INTO THE SHIP, WILSON...KEEP ON YOUR TOES --

HEY CULLODEN... YOU EVER HAVE ONE OF THOSE *MOMENTS*... MAYBE IN A BEER-INDUCED *STUPOR*... OR AFTER A WEEKEND-LONG MARATHON OF *TRAPPER JOHN, M.D.*...

WHERE YOU START TO GET THE FEELING THAT YOUR WHOLE *LIFE* HAS BEEN *LAID OUT* FOR YOU?

I'M *NOT* TALKING THAT "*TRUMAN-SHOW-I'M-THE-CENTER-OF-THE-UNIVERSE*" SORT OF WAY... THAT'S JUST *PARANOIA* AND *MEGALOMANIA* IN BED TOGETHER...

PLEASE, WILSON...THIS IS NOT A GOOD TIME FOR A *RANT*...

I'M TALKING MORE A *CAUSE* AND *EFFECT* SORT OF THING... THAT *EVENTS* AND *PEOPLE* AND *SPEEDING CARS* BEYOND YOUR CONTROL *IMPACT* ON YOU --

-- WHILE THE *CHEMICALS* BOUNCING AROUND YOUR BRAIN PAN *FORCE* YOU TO REACT IN A CERTAIN WAY TO THEM...

RENDERING *FREE WILL* AN *ILLUSION*, RIGHT?

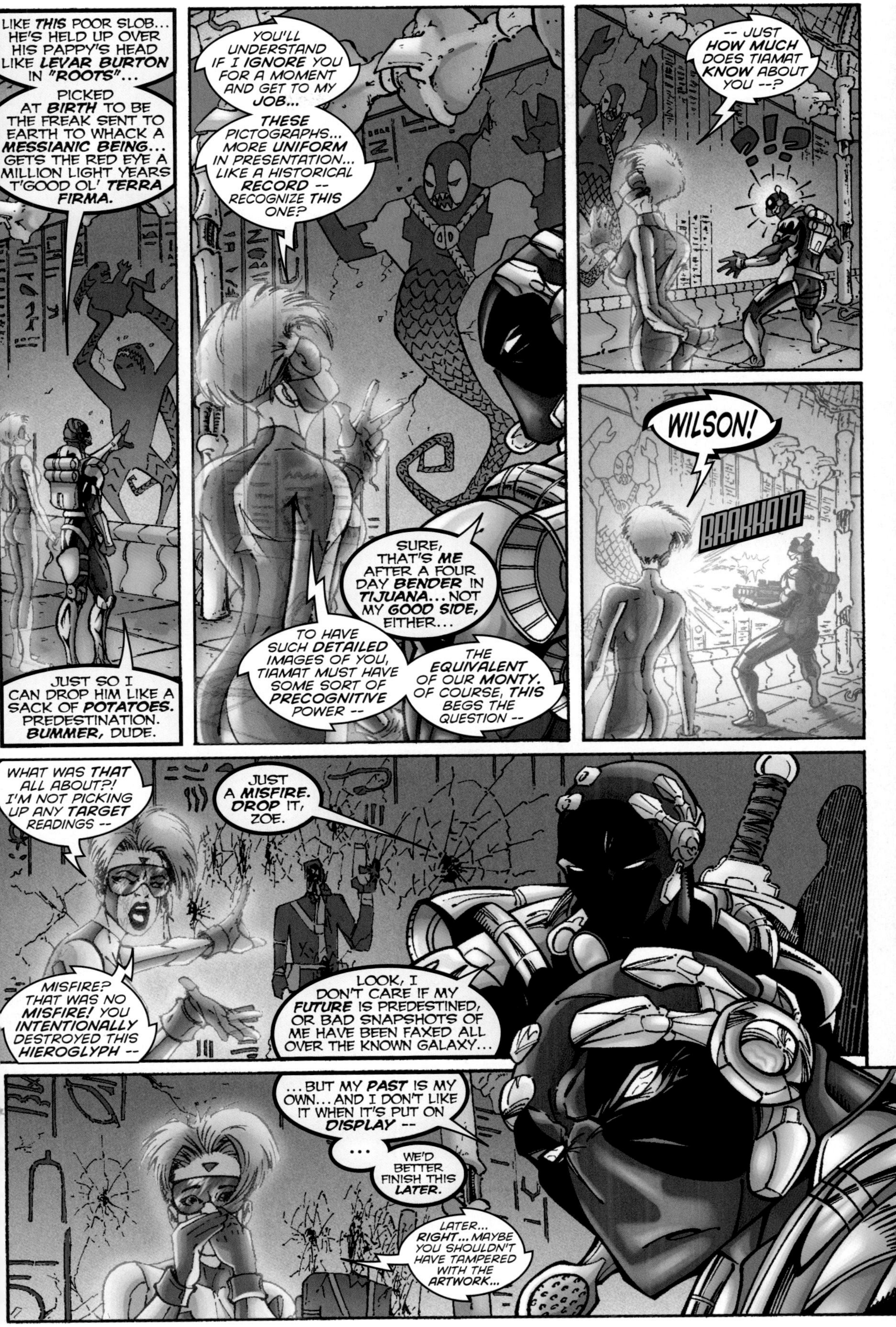

LIKE THIS POOR SLOB... HE'S HELD UP OVER HIS PAPPY'S HEAD LIKE LEVAR BURTON IN "ROOTS"...
PICKED AT BIRTH TO BE THE FREAK SENT TO EARTH TO WHACK A MESSIANIC BEING... GETS THE RED EYE A MILLION LIGHT YEARS T'GOOD OL' TERRA FIRMA.
JUST SO I CAN DROP HIM LIKE A SACK OF POTATOES. PREDESTINATION. BUMMER, DUDE.
YOU'LL UNDERSTAND IF I IGNORE YOU FOR A MOMENT AND GET TO MY JOB...
THESE PICTOGRAPHS... MORE UNIFORM IN PRESENTATION... LIKE A HISTORICAL RECORD -- RECOGNIZE THIS ONE?
SURE, THAT'S ME AFTER A FOUR DAY BENDER IN TIJUANA... NOT MY GOOD SIDE, EITHER...
TO HAVE SUCH DETAILED IMAGES OF YOU, TIAMAT MUST HAVE SOME SORT OF PRECOGNITIVE POWER --
THE EQUIVALENT OF OUR MONTY. OF COURSE, THIS BEGS THE QUESTION --
-- JUST HOW MUCH DOES TIAMAT KNOW ABOUT YOU --?
?!?
WILSON!
BRAKKATA
WHAT WAS THAT ALL ABOUT?! I'M NOT PICKING UP ANY TARGET READINGS --
JUST A MISFIRE. DROP IT, ZOE.
MISFIRE? THAT WAS NO MISFIRE! YOU INTENTIONALLY DESTROYED THIS HIEROGLYPH --
LOOK, I DON'T CARE IF MY FUTURE IS PREDESTINED, OR BAD SNAPSHOTS OF ME HAVE BEEN FAXED ALL OVER THE KNOWN GALAXY...
...BUT MY PAST IS MY OWN... AND I DON'T LIKE IT WHEN IT'S PUT ON DISPLAY --
...
WE'D BETTER FINISH THIS LATER.
LATER... RIGHT... MAYBE YOU SHOULDN'T HAVE TAMPERED WITH THE ARTWORK...

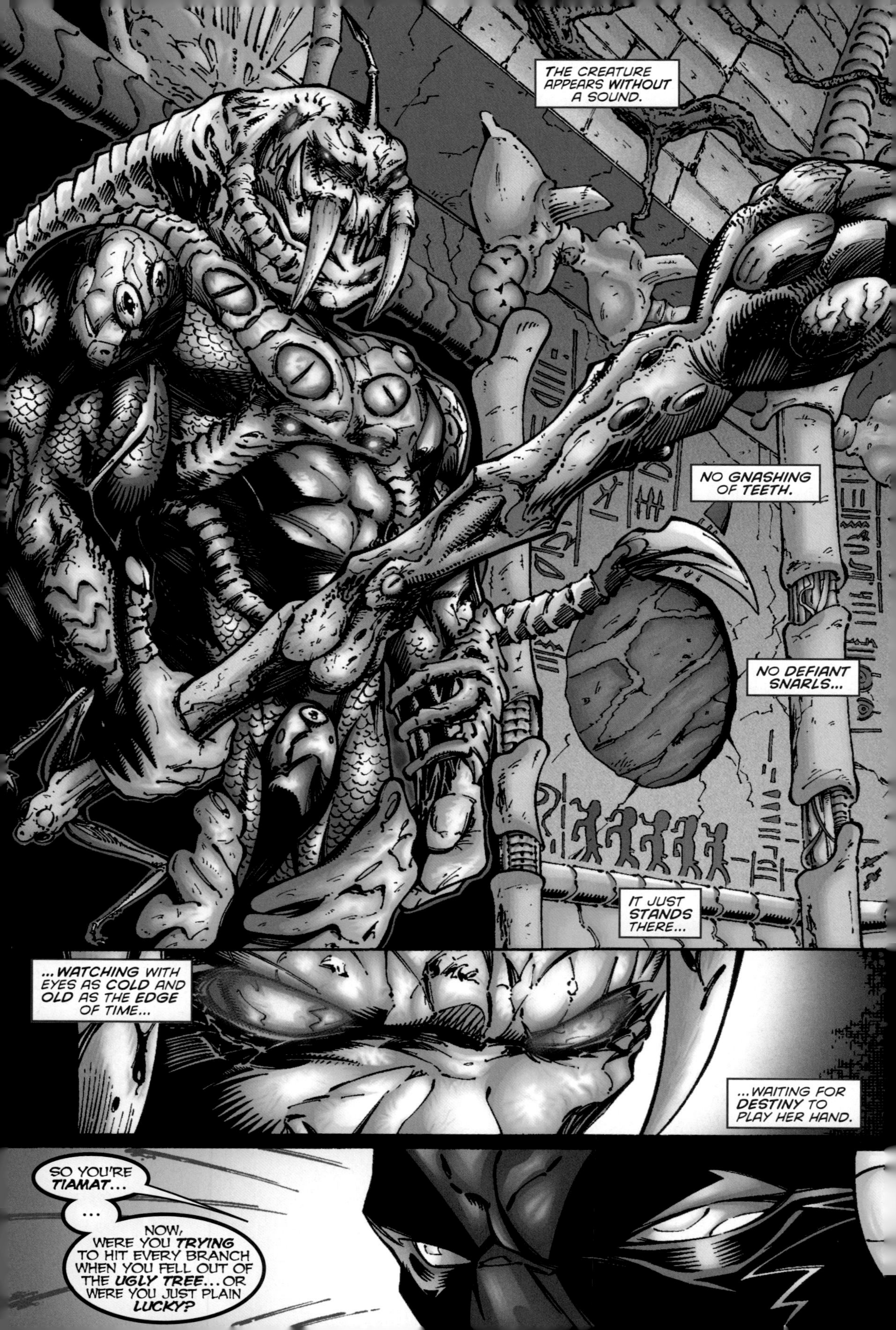
THE CREATURE APPEARS WITHOUT A SOUND.
NO GNASHING OF TEETH.
NO DEFIANT SNARLS...
IT JUST STANDS THERE...
...WATCHING WITH EYES AS COLD AND OLD AS THE EDGE OF TIME...
...WAITING FOR DESTINY TO PLAY HER HAND.
SO YOU'RE TIAMAT...
...
NOW, WERE YOU TRYING TO HIT EVERY BRANCH WHEN YOU FELL OUT OF THE UGLY TREE...OR WERE YOU JUST PLAIN LUCKY?

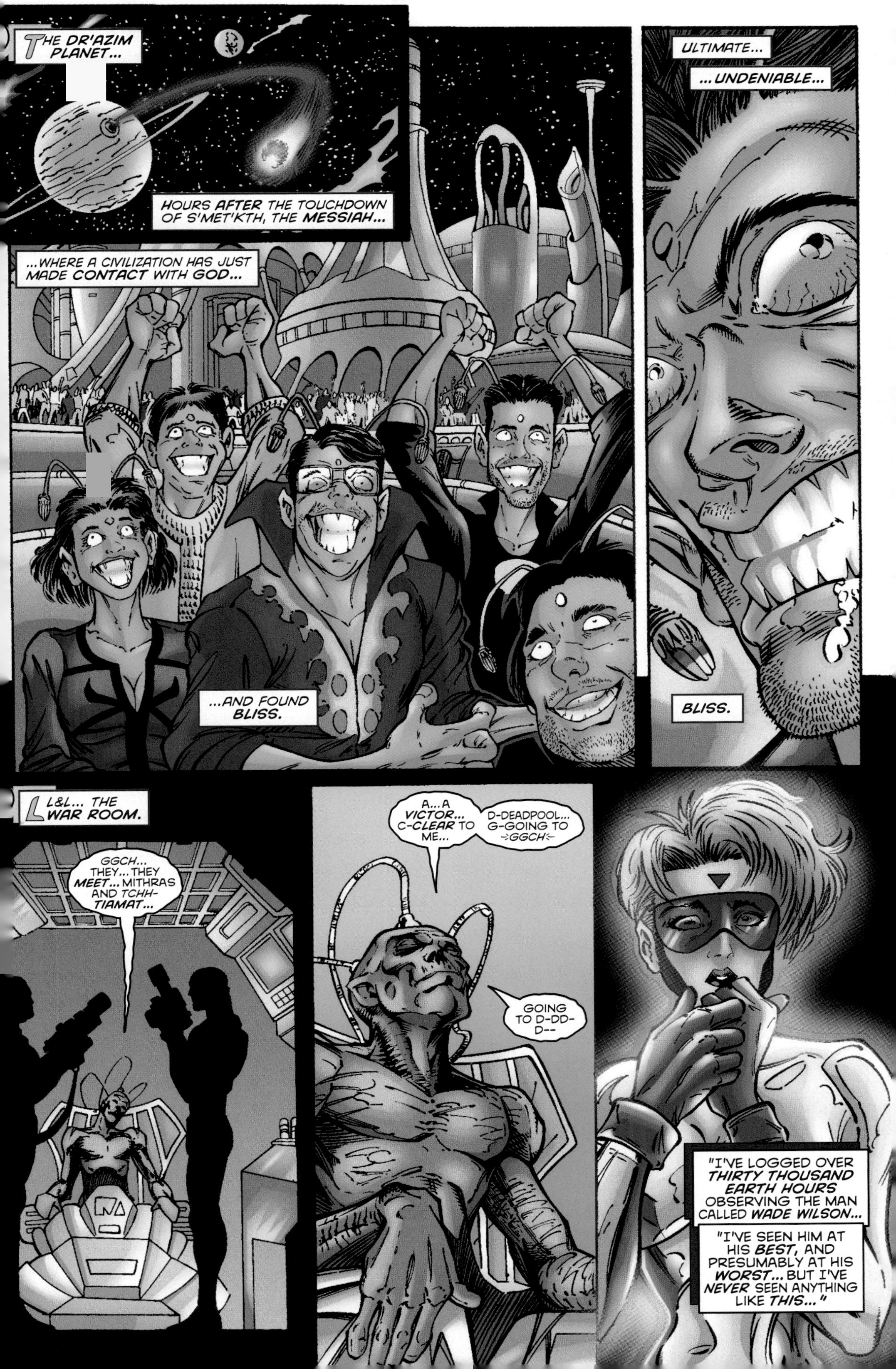
THE DR'AZIM PLANET...
HOURS AFTER THE TOUCHDOWN OF S'MET'KTH, THE MESSIAH...
...WHERE A CIVILIZATION HAS JUST MADE CONTACT WITH GOD...
...AND FOUND BLISS.
ULTIMATE...
...UNDENIABLE...
BLISS.
L&L... THE WAR ROOM.
GGCH... THEY... THEY MEET... MITHRAS AND TCHH-TIAMAT...
A...A VICTOR... C-CLEAR TO ME...
D-DEADPOOL... G-GOING TO GGCH
GOING TO D-DD-D--
"I'VE LOGGED OVER THIRTY THOUSAND EARTH HOURS OBSERVING THE MAN CALLED WADE WILSON...
"I'VE SEEN HIM AT HIS BEST, AND PRESUMABLY AT HIS WORST... BUT I'VE NEVER SEEN ANYTHING LIKE THIS..."

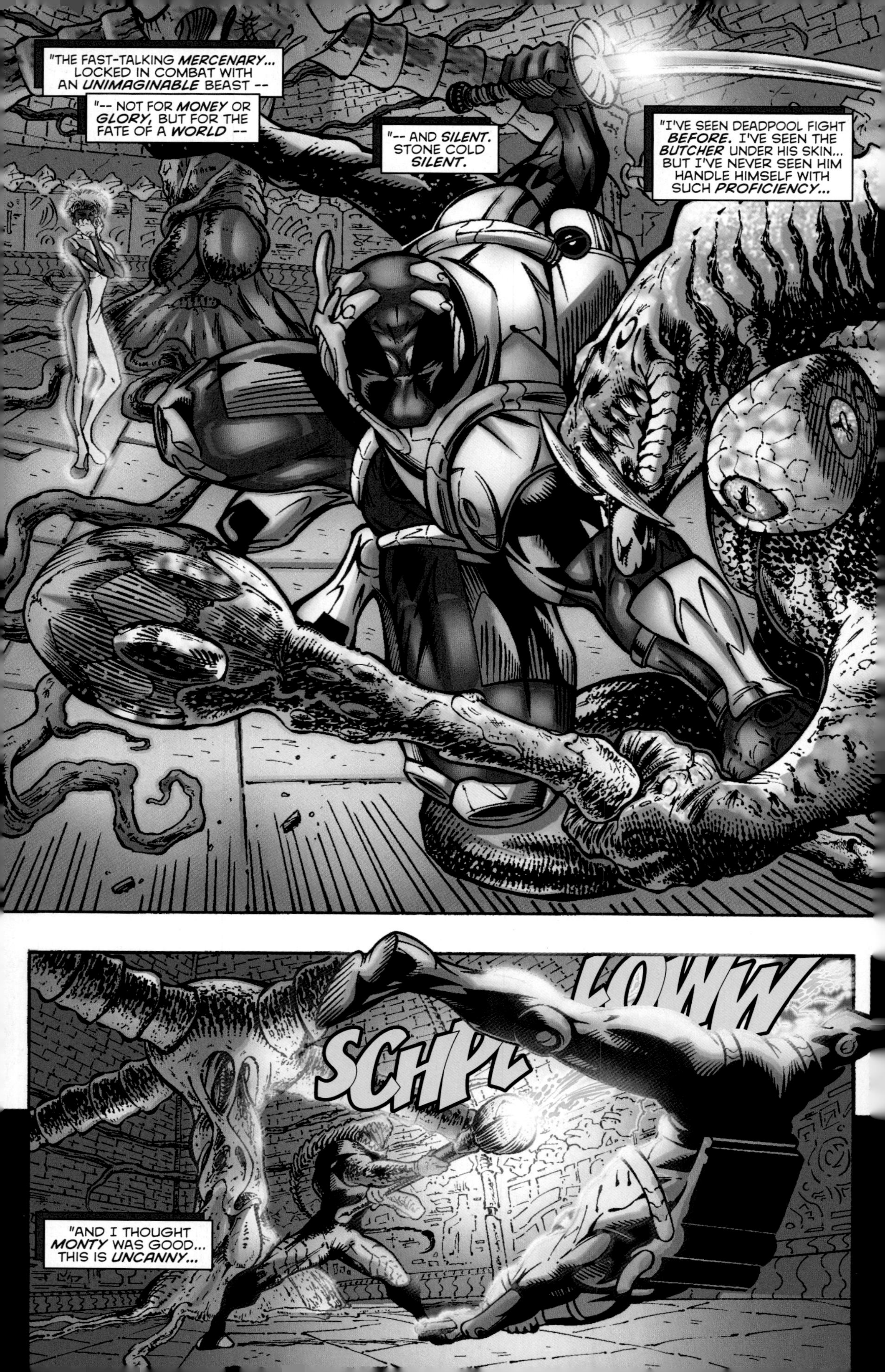
"THE FAST-TALKING MERCENARY... LOCKED IN COMBAT WITH AN UNIMAGINABLE BEAST --
"-- NOT FOR MONEY OR GLORY, BUT FOR THE FATE OF A WORLD --
"-- AND SILENT. STONE COLD SILENT.
"I'VE SEEN DEADPOOL FIGHT BEFORE. I'VE SEEN THE BUTCHER UNDER HIS SKIN... BUT I'VE NEVER SEEN HIM HANDLE HIMSELF WITH SUCH PROFICIENCY...
SCHPLOWW
"AND I THOUGHT MONTY WAS GOOD... THIS IS UNCANNY...

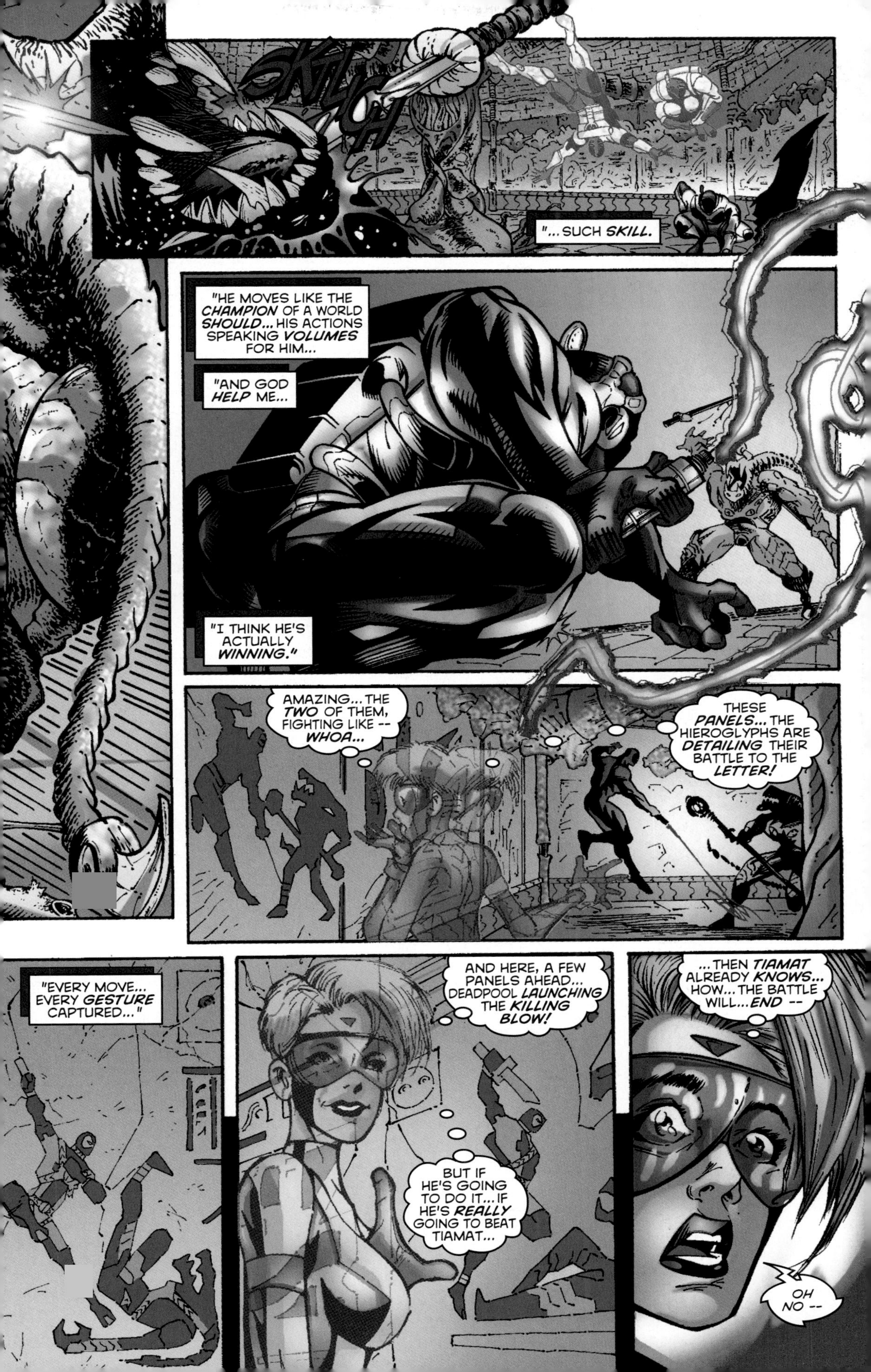
SKLUCH
"...SUCH SKILL.
"HE MOVES LIKE THE CHAMPION OF A WORLD SHOULD... HIS ACTIONS SPEAKING VOLUMES FOR HIM...
"AND GOD HELP ME...
"I THINK HE'S ACTUALLY WINNING."
AMAZING... THE TWO OF THEM, FIGHTING LIKE -- WHOA...
THESE PANELS... THE HIEROGLYPHS ARE DETAILING THEIR BATTLE TO THE LETTER!
"EVERY MOVE... EVERY GESTURE CAPTURED..."
AND HERE, A FEW PANELS AHEAD... DEADPOOL LAUNCHING THE KILLING BLOW!
BUT IF HE'S GOING TO DO IT... IF HE'S REALLY GOING TO BEAT TIAMAT...
...THEN TIAMAT ALREADY KNOWS... HOW... THE BATTLE WILL... END --
OH NO --

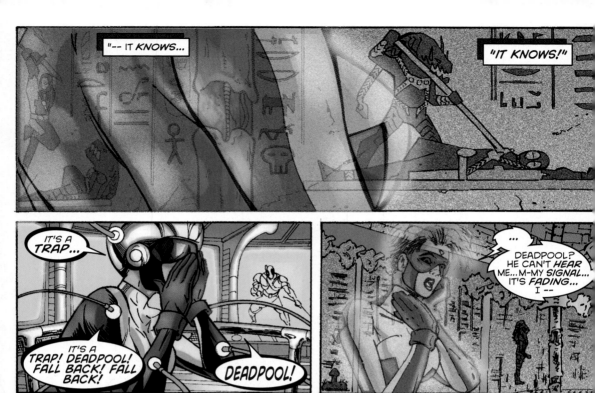

"-- IT *KNOWS*..."

"IT KNOWS!"

IT'S A *TRAP*...

IT'S A *TRAP!* DEADPOOL! *FALL BACK! FALL BACK!*

DEADPOOL!

...
DEADPOOL? HE CAN'T *HEAR* ME...M-MY *SIGNAL*...IT'S *FADING*... I --

IT'S *OVER*, ZOE...

BE A GOOD *PAWN* NOW AND GIVE IT A *REST*, WOULD YOU?

THIS IS *IT*...

THIS IS IT.

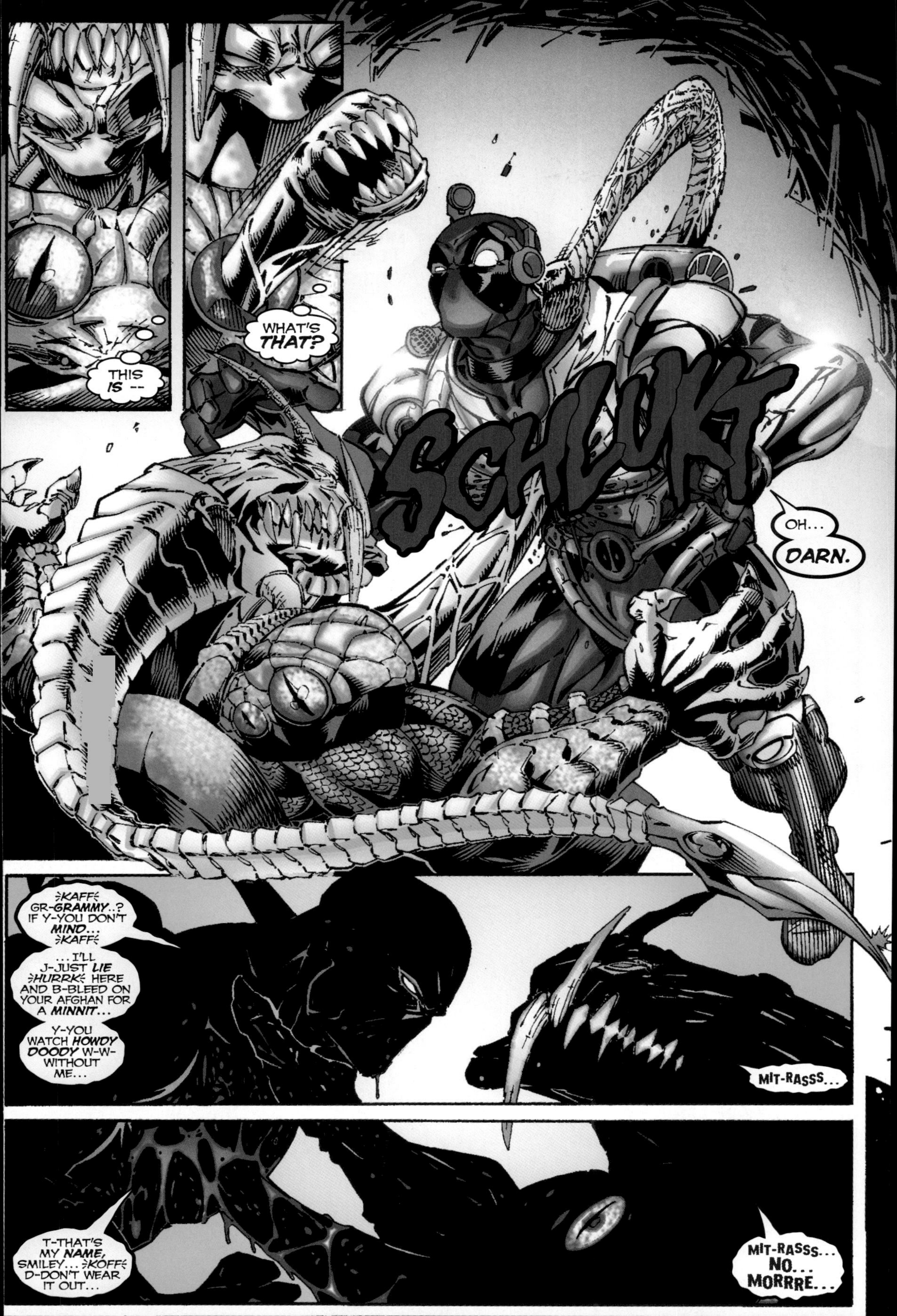
WHAT'S THAT?
THIS IS --
SCHLUKT
OH... DARN.
≻KAFF≺ GR-GRAMMY..? IF Y-YOU DON'T MIND... ≻KAFF≺
... I'LL J-JUST LIE ≻HURRK≺ HERE AND B-BLEED ON YOUR AFGHAN FOR A MINNIT...
Y-YOU WATCH HOWDY DOODY W-W-WITHOUT ME...
MIT-RASSS...
T-THAT'S MY NAME, SMILEY... ≻KOFF≺ D-DON'T WEAR IT OUT...
MIT-RASSS... NO... MORRRE...

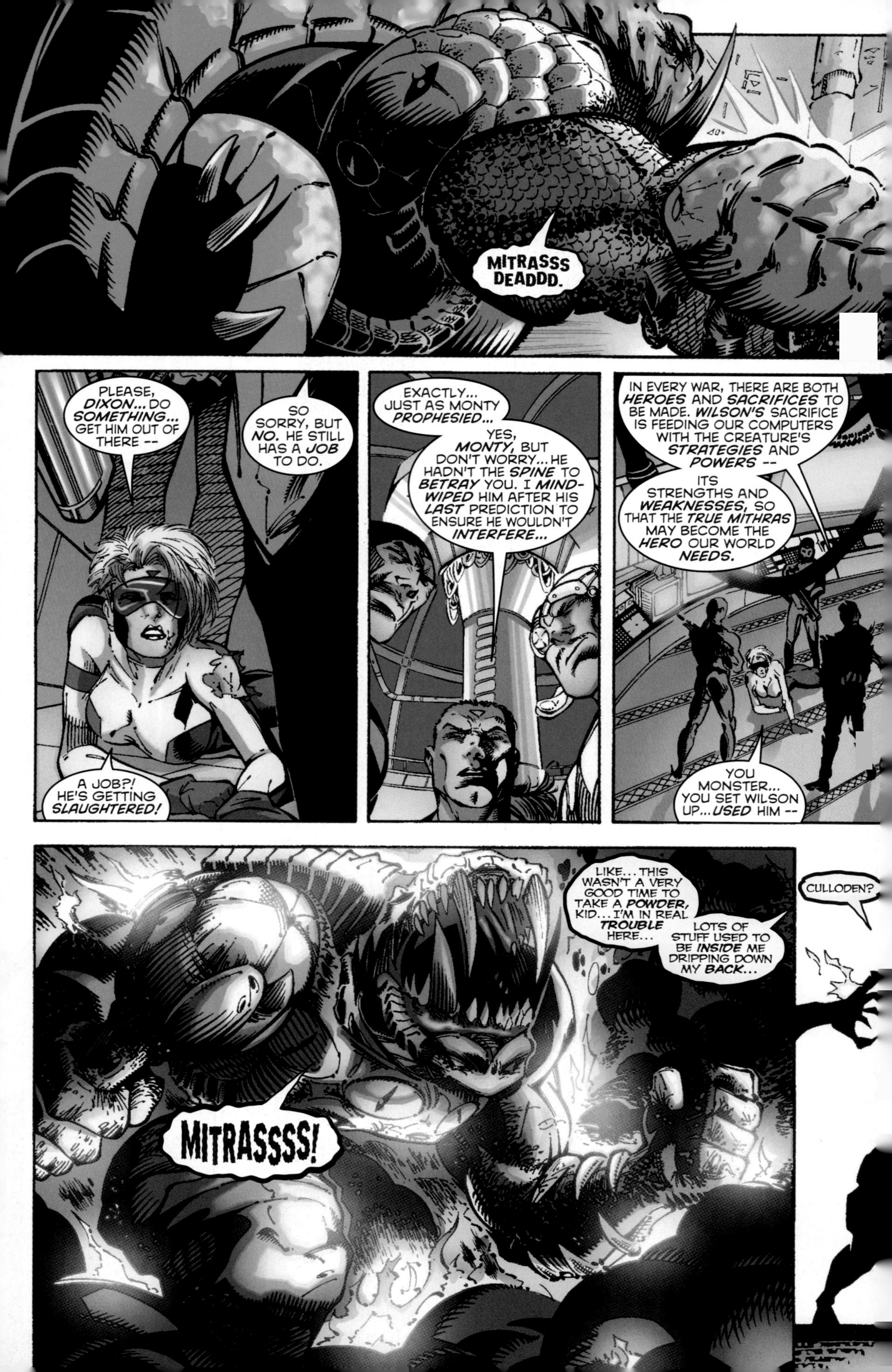
MITRASSS DEADDD.
PLEASE, DIXON... DO SOMETHING... GET HIM OUT OF THERE --
SO SORRY, BUT NO. HE STILL HAS A JOB TO DO.
A JOB?! HE'S GETTING SLAUGHTERED!
EXACTLY... JUST AS MONTY PROPHESIED...
YES, MONTY, BUT DON'T WORRY... HE HADN'T THE SPINE TO BETRAY YOU. I MIND-WIPED HIM AFTER HIS LAST PREDICTION TO ENSURE HE WOULDN'T INTERFERE...
IN EVERY WAR, THERE ARE BOTH HEROES AND SACRIFICES TO BE MADE. WILSON'S SACRIFICE IS FEEDING OUR COMPUTERS WITH THE CREATURE'S STRATEGIES AND POWERS --
ITS STRENGTHS AND WEAKNESSES, SO THAT THE TRUE MITHRAS MAY BECOME THE HERO OUR WORLD NEEDS.
YOU MONSTER... YOU SET WILSON UP... USED HIM --
LIKE... THIS WASN'T A VERY GOOD TIME TO TAKE A POWDER, KID... I'M IN REAL TROUBLE HERE...
LOTS OF STUFF USED TO BE INSIDE ME DRIPPING DOWN MY BACK...
CULLODEN?
MITRASSSS!

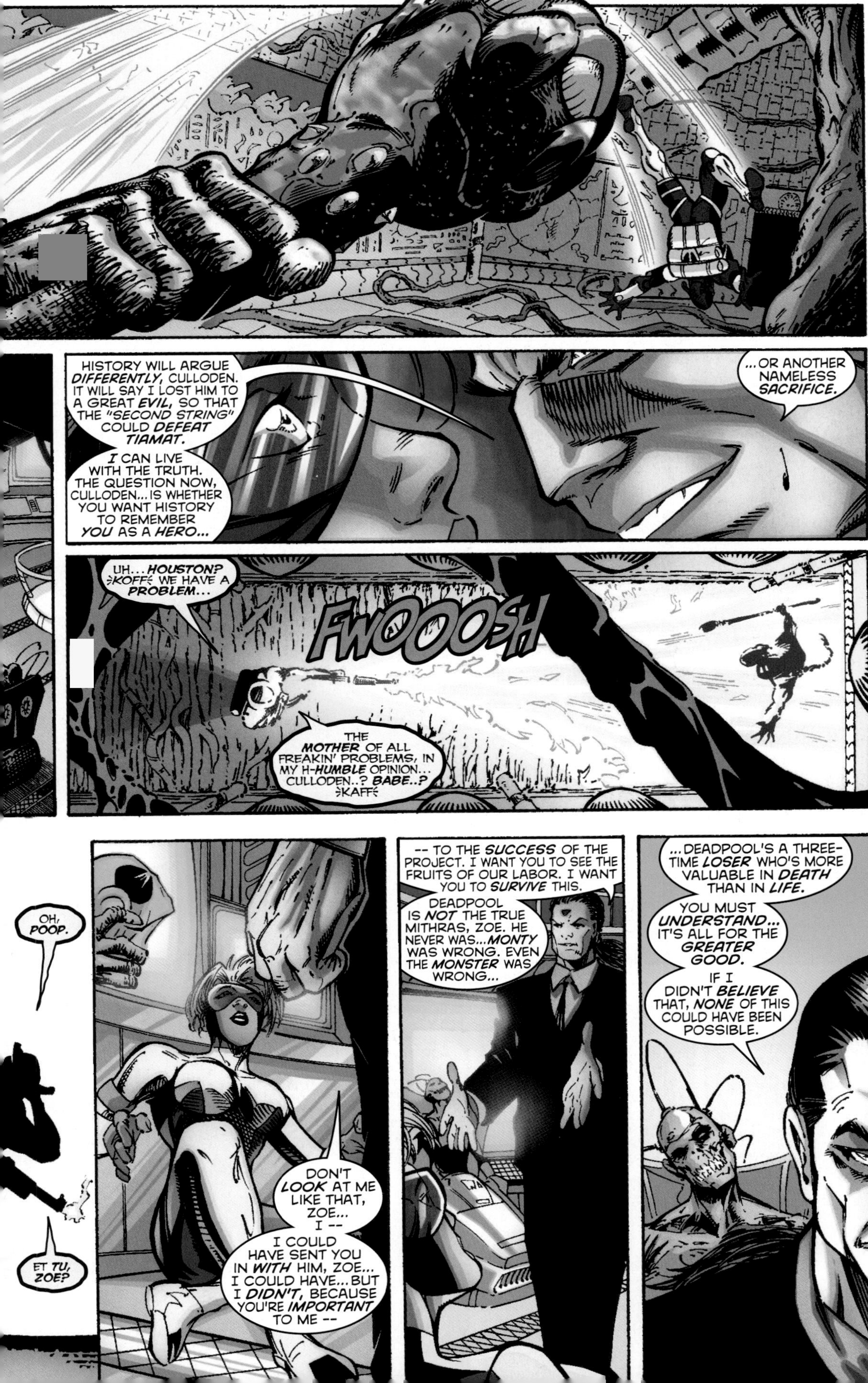
HISTORY WILL ARGUE DIFFERENTLY, CULLODEN. IT WILL SAY I LOST HIM TO A GREAT EVIL, SO THAT THE "SECOND STRING" COULD DEFEAT TIAMAT.
I CAN LIVE WITH THE TRUTH. THE QUESTION NOW, CULLODEN... IS WHETHER YOU WANT HISTORY TO REMEMBER YOU AS A HERO...
...OR ANOTHER NAMELESS SACRIFICE.
UH... HOUSTON? *KOFF* WE HAVE A PROBLEM...
FWOOOSH
THE MOTHER OF ALL FREAKIN' PROBLEMS, IN MY H-HUMBLE OPINION... CULLODEN..? BABE..? *KAFF*
OH, POOP.
ET TU, ZOE?
DON'T LOOK AT ME LIKE THAT, ZOE... I --
I COULD HAVE SENT YOU IN WITH HIM, ZOE... I COULD HAVE... BUT I DIDN'T, BECAUSE YOU'RE IMPORTANT TO ME --
-- TO THE SUCCESS OF THE PROJECT. I WANT YOU TO SEE THE FRUITS OF OUR LABOR. I WANT YOU TO SURVIVE THIS.
DEADPOOL IS NOT THE TRUE MITHRAS, ZOE. HE NEVER WAS... MONTY WAS WRONG. EVEN THE MONSTER WAS WRONG...
...DEADPOOL'S A THREE-TIME LOSER WHO'S MORE VALUABLE IN DEATH THAN IN LIFE.
YOU MUST UNDERSTAND... IT'S ALL FOR THE GREATER GOOD.
IF I DIDN'T BELIEVE THAT, NONE OF THIS COULD HAVE BEEN POSSIBLE.

OH, EVEN ON ONLY TH-THREE PINTS OF BLOOD... ≶HUURKT≶ I STILL GOT -- ≶KAFF≶

SLASH

NNNGHH!

WHO D-DOES YOUR NAILS..? MARQUIS DE SADE?

"THE GREATER GOOD?" IS THAT HOW YOU KEEP YOURSELF WARM AT NIGHT AFTER THE THINGS YOU DO, DIXON?

DID IT WORK AFTER YOU VIOLATED MONTY? AFTER YOU KILLED NOAH?

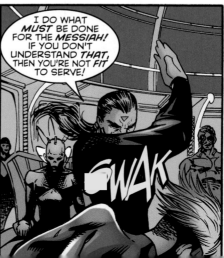

I DO WHAT MUST BE DONE FOR THE MESSIAH! IF YOU DON'T UNDERSTAND THAT, THEN YOU'RE NOT FIT TO SERVE!

SWAK

Z... ZOE...

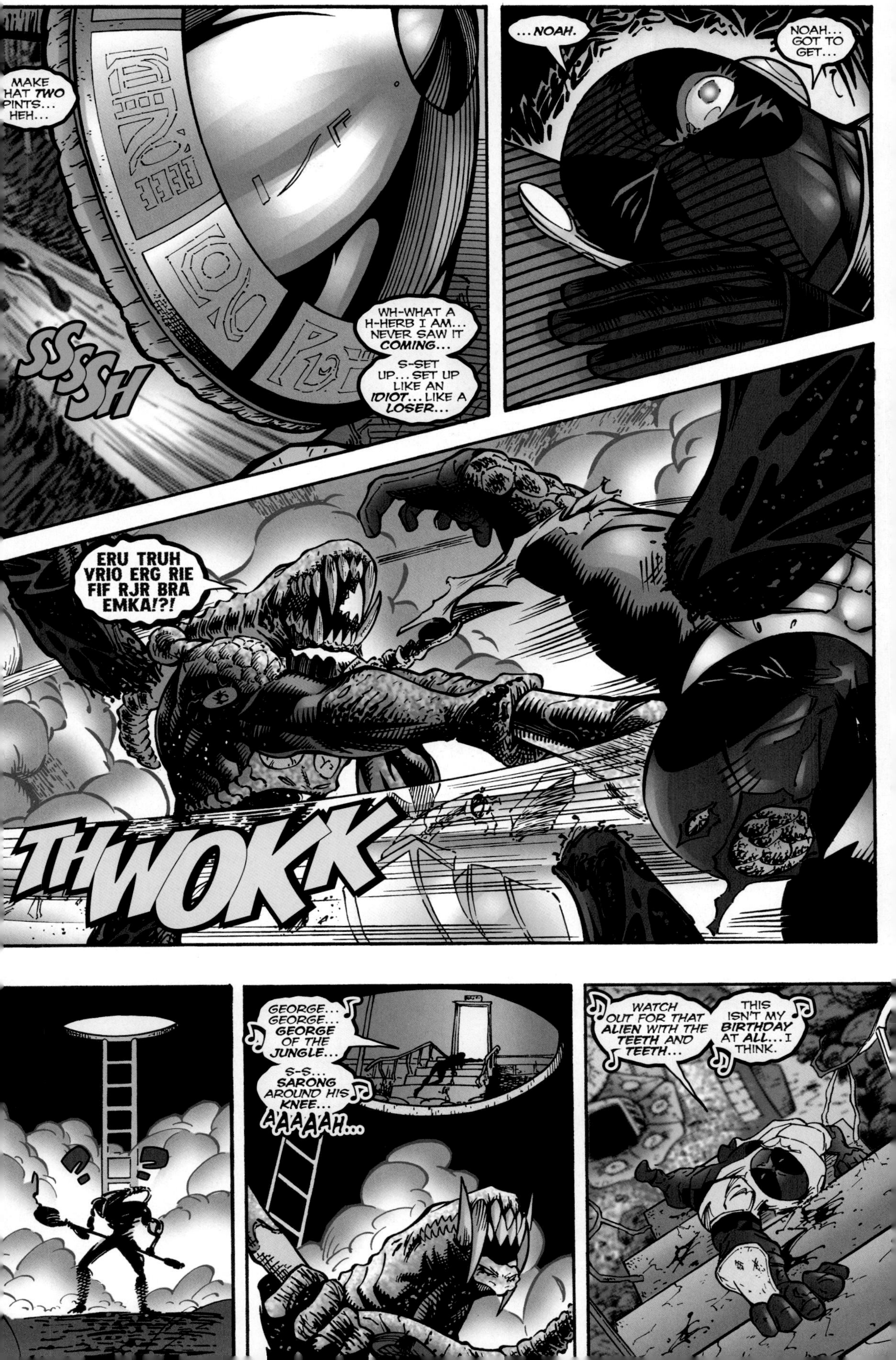
MAKE HAT TWO PINTS... HEH...
WH-WHAT A H-HERB I AM... NEVER SAW IT COMING...
S-SET UP... SET UP LIKE AN IDIOT... LIKE A LOSER...
SSSSH
...NOAH.
NOAH... GOT TO GET...
ERU TRUH VRIO ERG RIE FIF RJR BRA EMKA!?!
THWOKK
GEORGE... GEORGE... GEORGE OF THE JUNGLE...
S-S... SARONG AROUND HIS KNEE...
AAAAAH...
WATCH OUT FOR THAT ALIEN WITH THE TEETH AND TEETH...
THIS ISN'T MY BIRTHDAY AT ALL... I THINK.

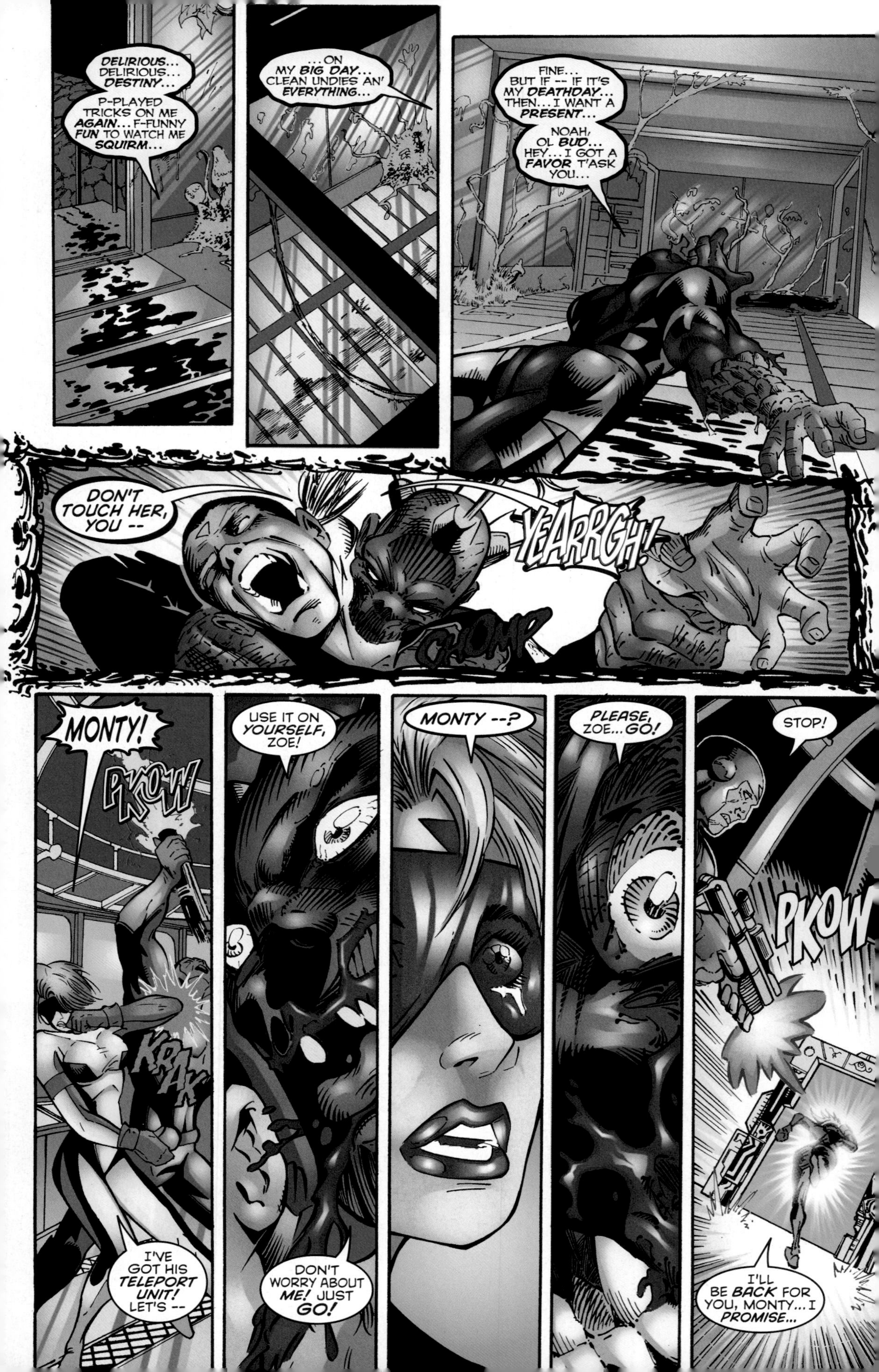

DELIRIOUS... DELIRIOUS... DESTINY...
P-PLAYED TRICKS ON ME AGAIN... F-FUNNY FUN TO WATCH ME SQUIRM...
...ON MY BIG DAY... CLEAN UNDIES AN' EVERYTHING...
FINE... BUT IF -- IF IT'S MY DEATHDAY... THEN... I WANT A PRESENT...
NOAH, OL BUD... HEY... I GOT A FAVOR T'ASK YOU...
DON'T TOUCH HER, YOU --
YEARRGH!
CHOMP
MONTY!
PKOW
KRAK
I'VE GOT HIS TELEPORT UNIT! LET'S --
USE IT ON YOURSELF, ZOE!
DON'T WORRY ABOUT ME! JUST GO!
MONTY --?
PLEASE, ZOE... GO!
STOP!
PKOW
I'LL BE BACK FOR YOU, MONTY... I PROMISE...

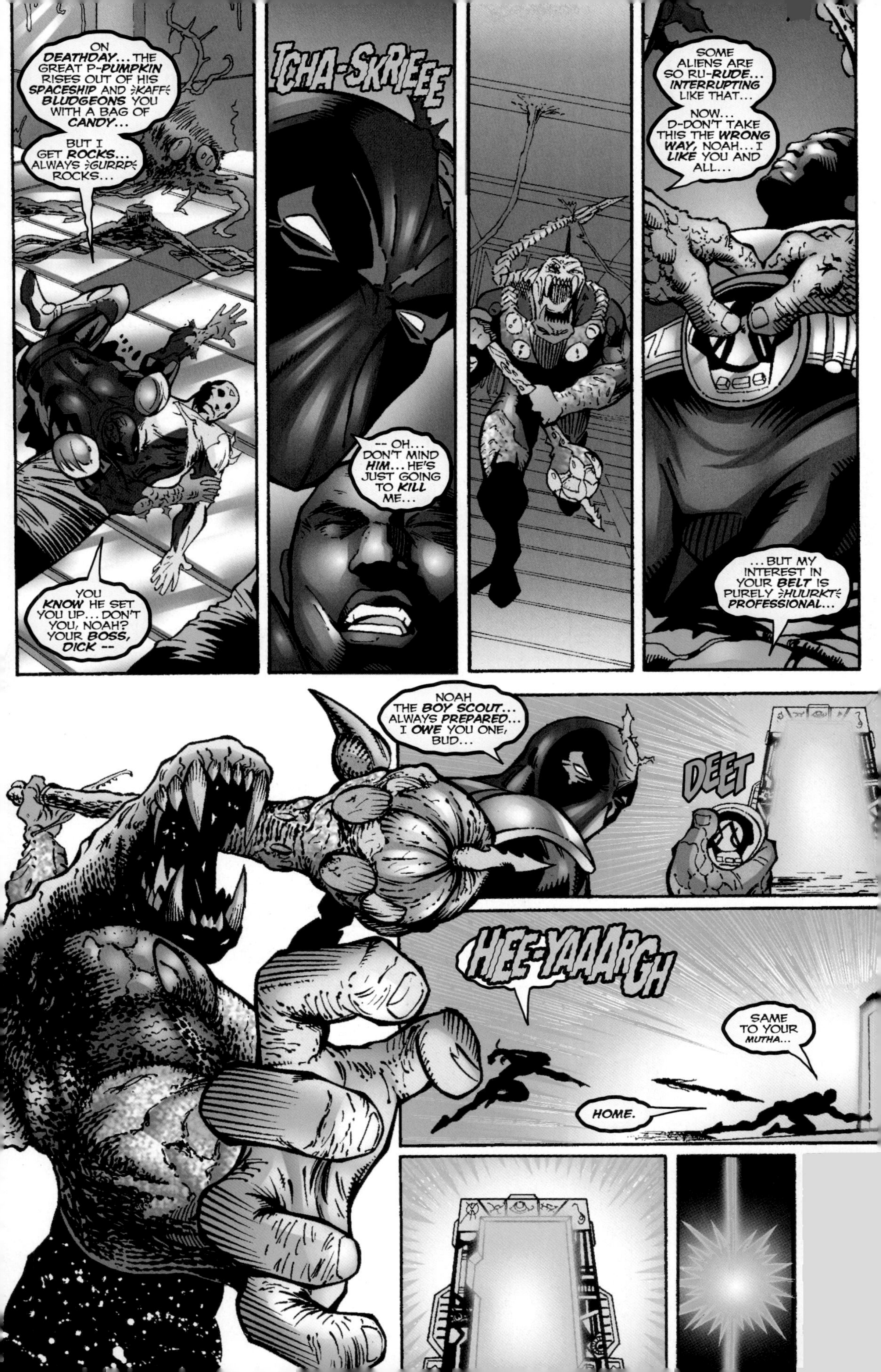

ON DEATHDAY... THE GREAT P-PUMPKIN RISES OUT OF HIS SPACESHIP AND ⊰KAFF⊱ BLUDGEONS YOU WITH A BAG OF CANDY...
BUT I GET ROCKS... ALWAYS ⊰GURRP⊱ ROCKS...
YOU KNOW HE SET YOU UP... DON'T YOU, NOAH? YOUR BOSS, DICK --
TCHA-SKRIEEEE
-- OH... DON'T MIND HIM... HE'S JUST GOING TO KILL ME...
SOME ALIENS ARE SO RU-RUDE... INTERRUPTING LIKE THAT...
NOW... D-DON'T TAKE THIS THE WRONG WAY, NOAH... I LIKE YOU AND ALL...
...BUT MY INTEREST IN YOUR BELT IS PURELY ⊰HUURKT⊱ PROFESSIONAL...
NOAH THE BOY SCOUT... ALWAYS PREPARED... I OWE YOU ONE, BUD...
DEET
HIEE-YAAARGH
SAME TO YOUR MUTHA...
HOME.

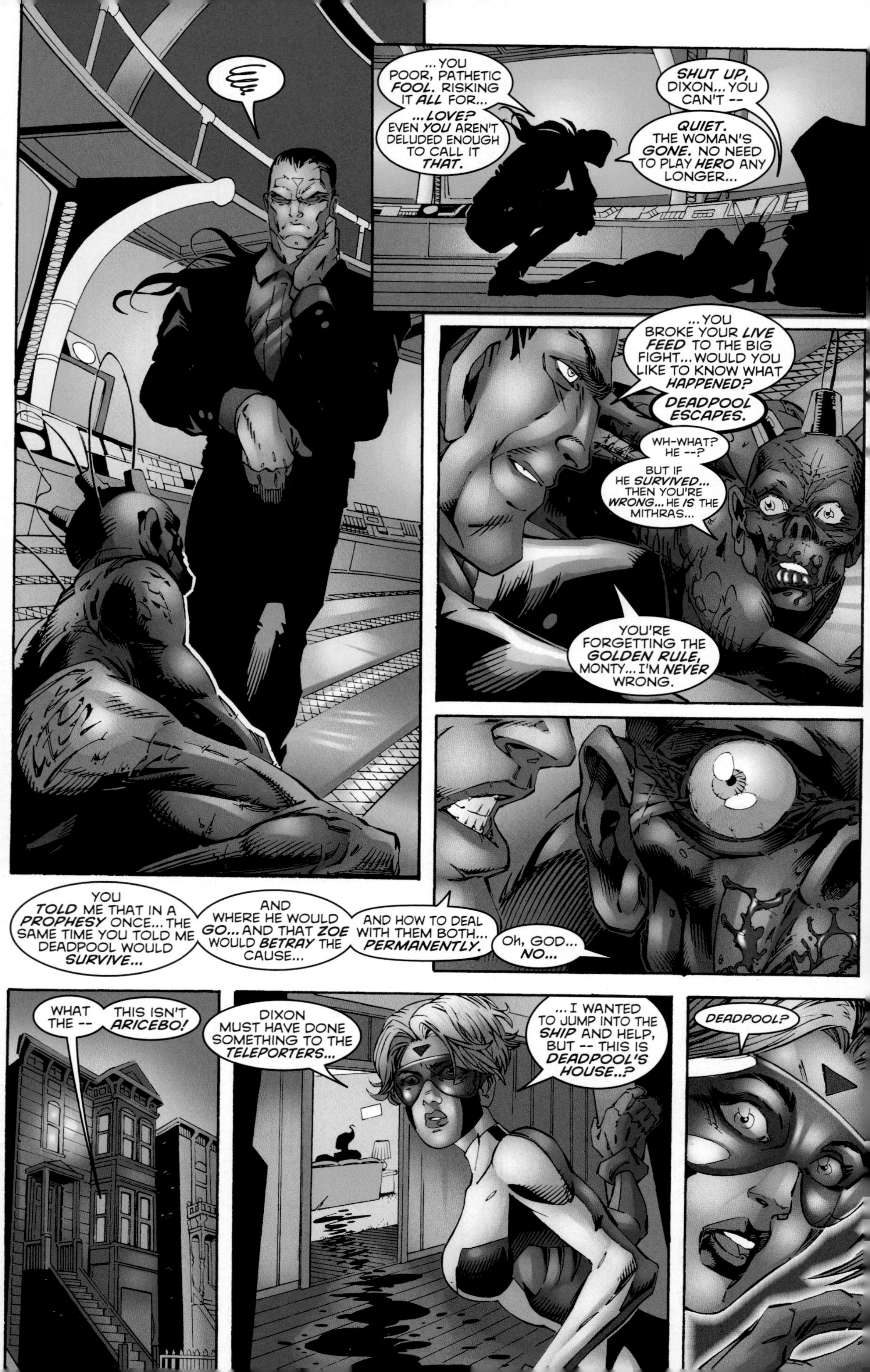

...YOU POOR, PATHETIC FOOL. RISKING IT ALL FOR... ...LOVE? EVEN YOU AREN'T DELUDED ENOUGH TO CALL IT THAT.
SHUT UP, DIXON... YOU CAN'T --
QUIET. THE WOMAN'S GONE. NO NEED TO PLAY HERO ANY LONGER...
...YOU BROKE YOUR LIVE FEED TO THE BIG FIGHT... WOULD YOU LIKE TO KNOW WHAT HAPPENED?
DEADPOOL ESCAPES.
WH-WHAT? HE --?
BUT IF HE SURVIVED... THEN YOU'RE WRONG... HE IS THE MITHRAS...
YOU'RE FORGETTING THE GOLDEN RULE, MONTY... I'M NEVER WRONG.
YOU TOLD ME THAT IN A PROPHESY ONCE... THE SAME TIME YOU TOLD ME DEADPOOL WOULD SURVIVE...
AND WHERE HE WOULD GO... AND THAT ZOE WOULD BETRAY THE CAUSE...
AND HOW TO DEAL WITH THEM BOTH... PERMANENTLY.
Oh, GOD... NO...
WHAT THE --
THIS ISN'T ARICEBO!
DIXON MUST HAVE DONE SOMETHING TO THE TELEPORTERS...
...I WANTED TO JUMP INTO THE SHIP AND HELP, BUT -- THIS IS DEADPOOL'S HOUSE..?
DEADPOOL?

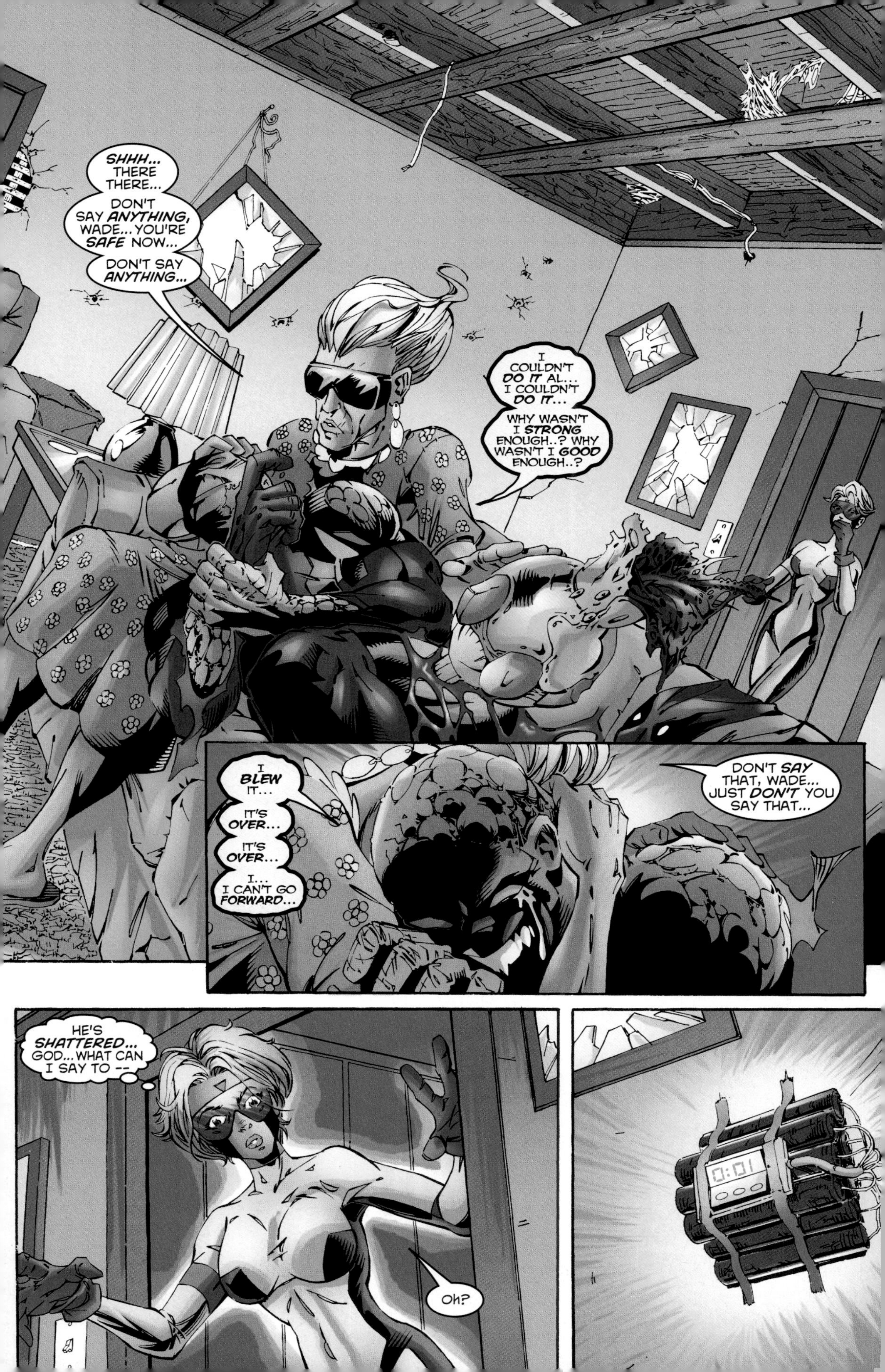
SHHH... THERE THERE... DON'T SAY ANYTHING, WADE... YOU'RE SAFE NOW... DON'T SAY ANYTHING...
I COULDN'T DO IT AL... I COULDN'T DO IT... WHY WASN'T I STRONG ENOUGH..? WHY WASN'T I GOOD ENOUGH..?
I BLEW IT... IT'S OVER... IT'S OVER... I... I CAN'T GO FORWARD...
DON'T SAY THAT, WADE... JUST DON'T YOU SAY THAT...
HE'S SHATTERED... GOD... WHAT CAN I SAY TO --
Oh?
0:01

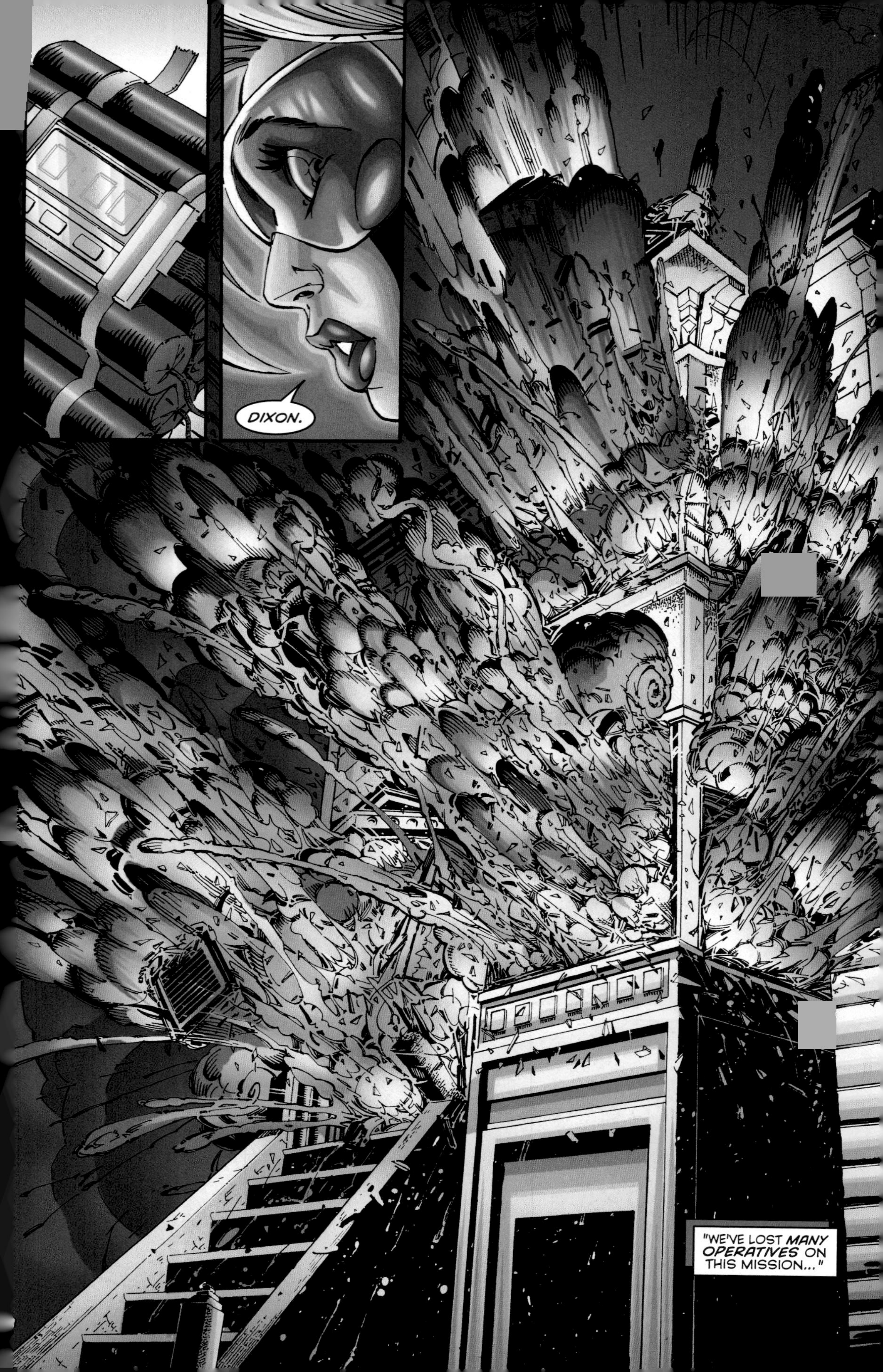
DIXON.
"WE'VE LOST MANY OPERATIVES ON THIS MISSION..."

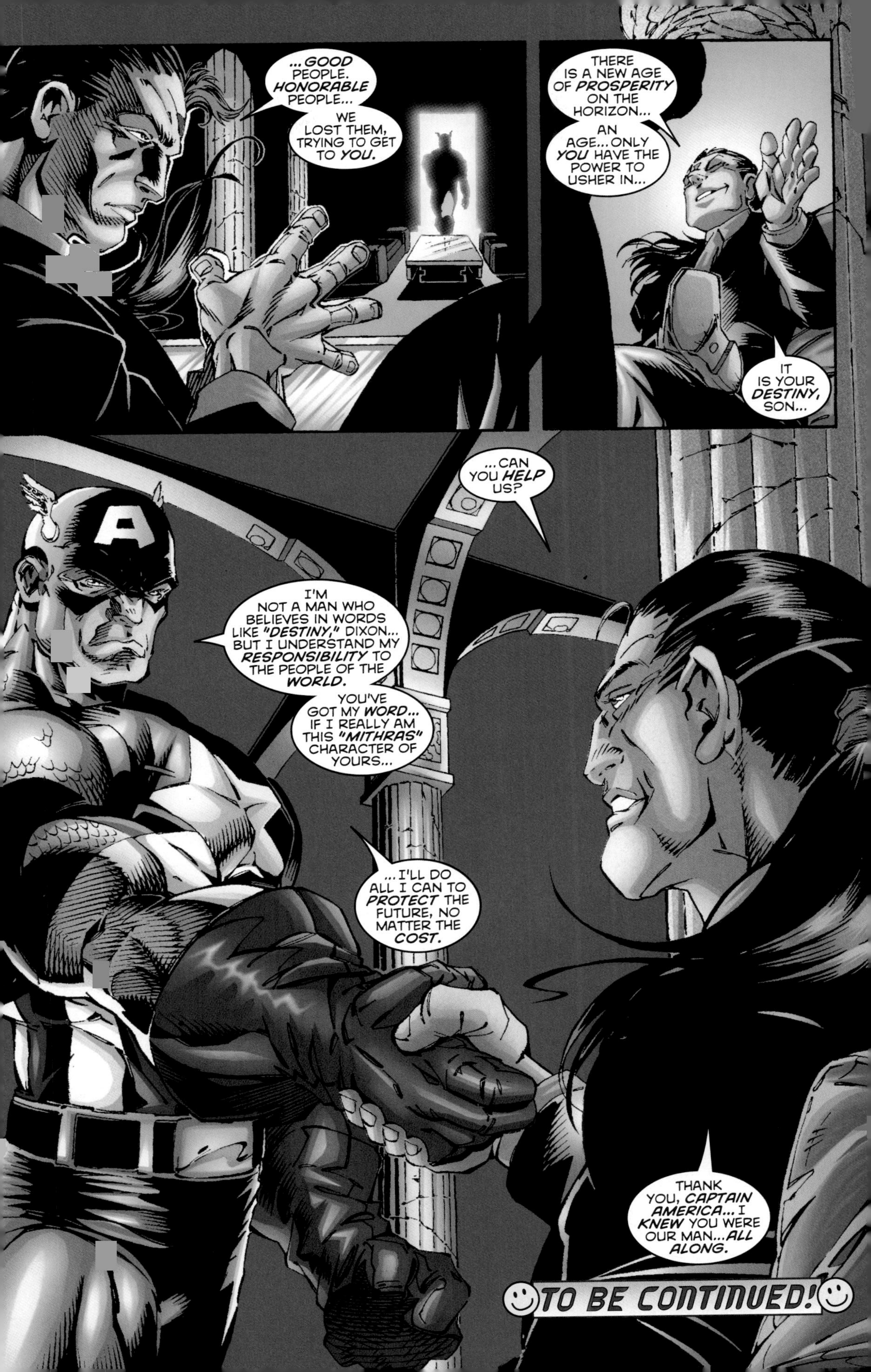
...GOOD PEOPLE. HONORABLE PEOPLE...
WE LOST THEM, TRYING TO GET TO YOU.
THERE IS A NEW AGE OF PROSPERITY ON THE HORIZON...
AN AGE...ONLY YOU HAVE THE POWER TO USHER IN...
IT IS YOUR DESTINY, SON...
...CAN YOU HELP US?
I'M NOT A MAN WHO BELIEVES IN WORDS LIKE "DESTINY," DIXON... BUT I UNDERSTAND MY RESPONSIBILITY TO THE PEOPLE OF THE WORLD.
YOU'VE GOT MY WORD... IF I REALLY AM THIS "MITHRAS" CHARACTER OF YOURS...
...I'LL DO ALL I CAN TO PROTECT THE FUTURE, NO MATTER THE COST.
THANK YOU, CAPTAIN AMERICA... I KNEW YOU WERE OUR MAN...ALL ALONG.
TO BE CONTINUED!

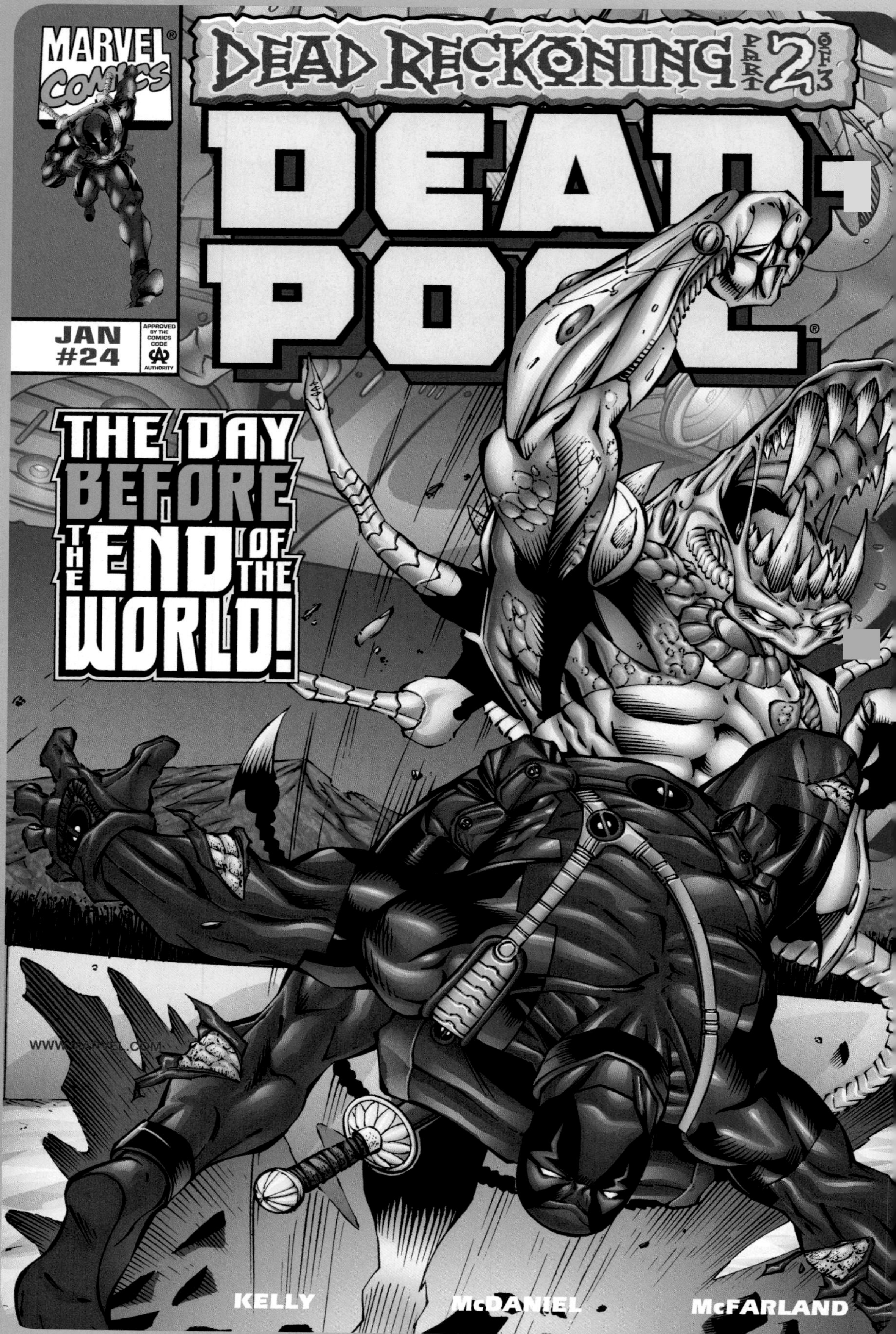
MARVEL COMICS
DEAD RECKONING PART 2 OF 3
DEADPOOL
JAN #24
APPROVED BY THE COMICS CODE AUTHORITY
THE DAY BEFORE THE END OF THE WORLD!
KELLY
McDANIEL
McFARLAND

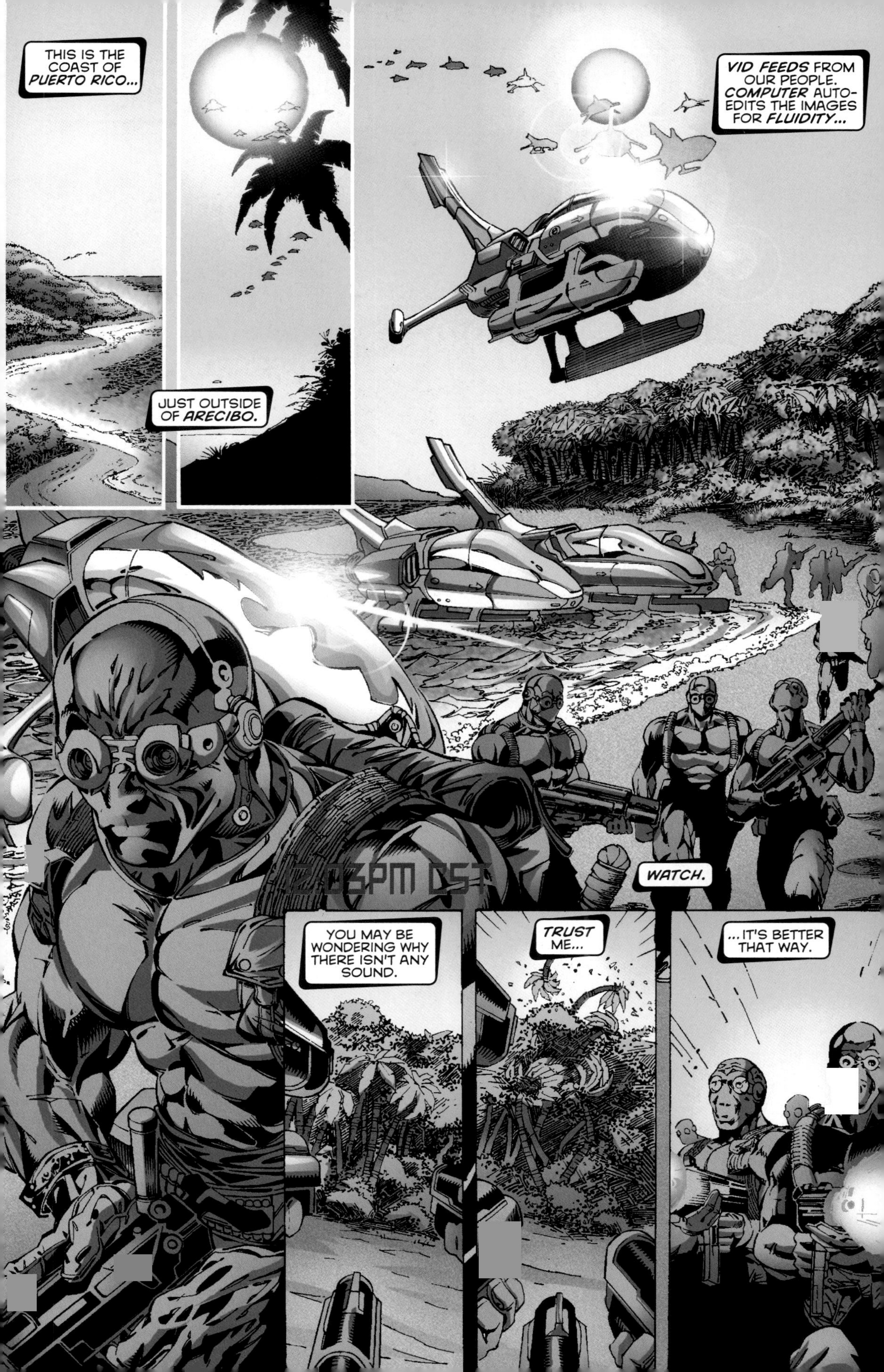
THIS IS THE COAST OF *PUERTO RICO...*
JUST OUTSIDE OF *ARECIBO.*
VID FEEDS FROM OUR PEOPLE. ***COMPUTER*** AUTO-EDITS THE IMAGES FOR ***FLUIDITY...***
12:03PM CST
WATCH.
YOU MAY BE WONDERING WHY THERE ISN'T ANY SOUND.
TRUST ME...
...IT'S BETTER THAT WAY.

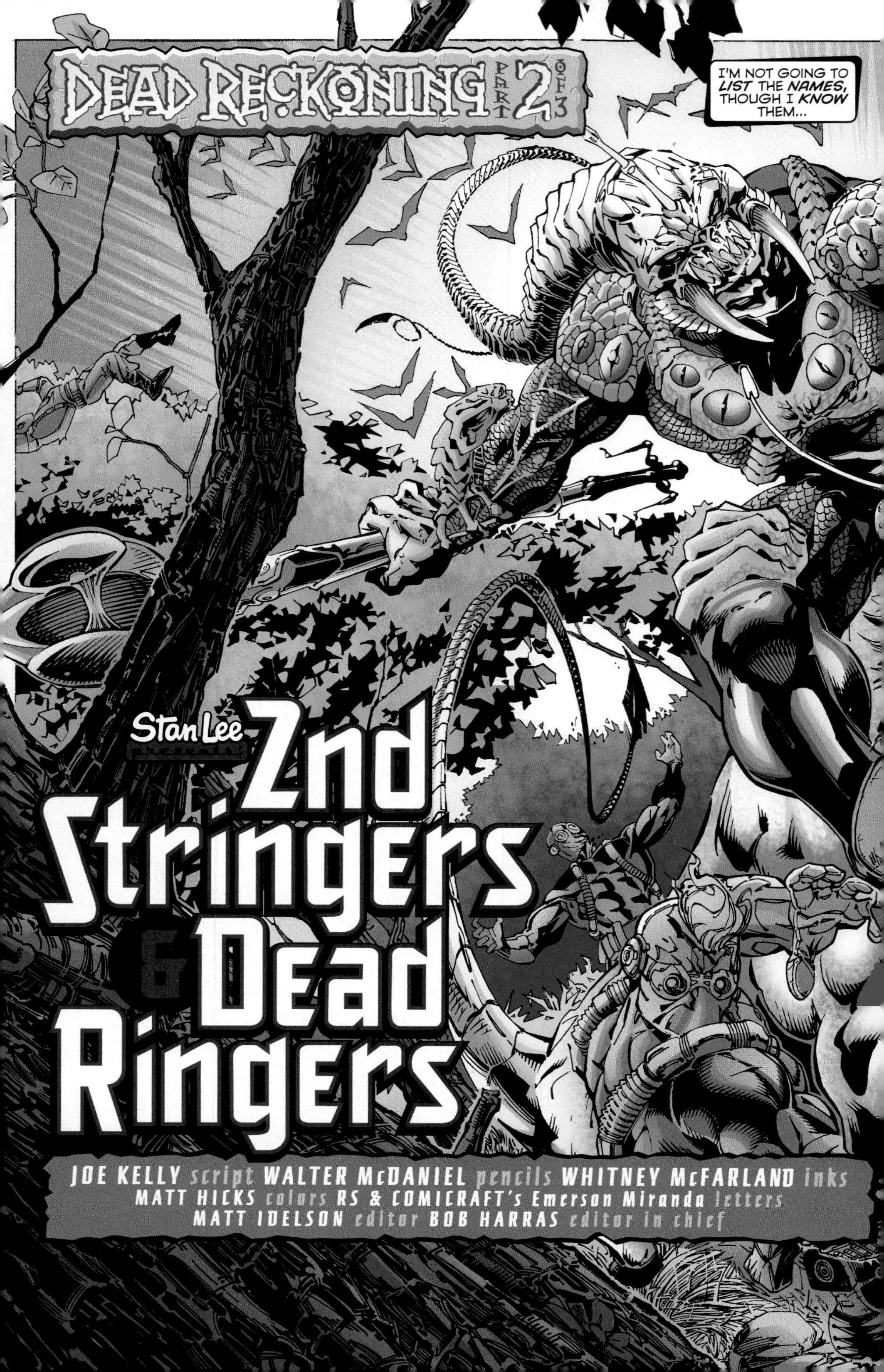
DEAD RECKONING PART 2 OF 3
I'M NOT GOING TO LIST THE NAMES, THOUGH I KNOW THEM...
Stan Lee presents
2nd Stringers & Dead Ringers
JOE KELLY script WALTER McDANIEL pencils WHITNEY McFARLAND inks
MATT HICKS colors RS & COMICRAFT's Emerson Miranda letters
MATT IDELSON editor BOB HARRAS editor in chief

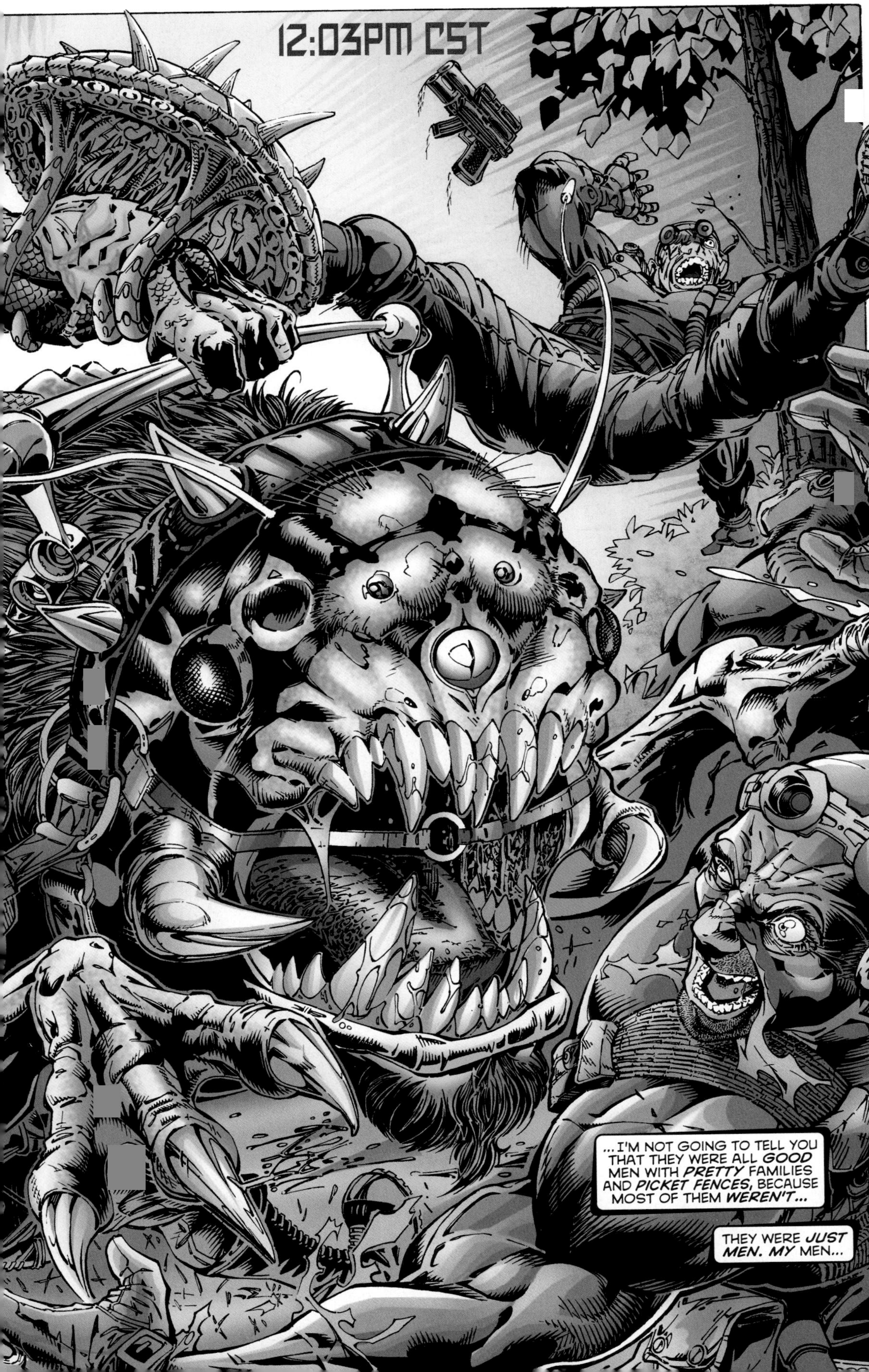
12:03PM CST
...I'M NOT GOING TO TELL YOU THAT THEY WERE ALL *GOOD* MEN WITH *PRETTY* FAMILIES AND *PICKET FENCES,* BECAUSE MOST OF THEM *WEREN'T...*
THEY WERE *JUST MEN. MY* MEN...

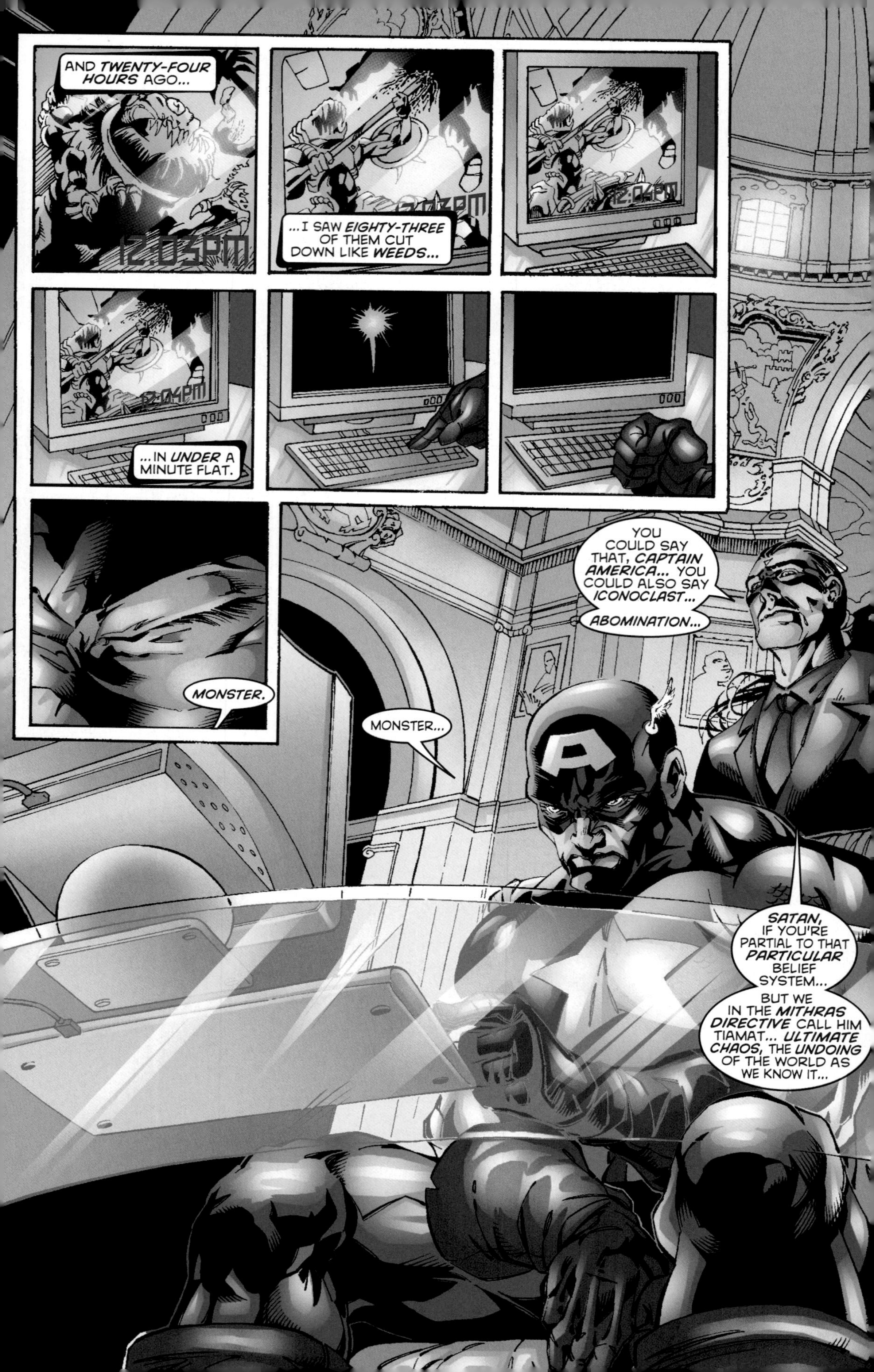
AND TWENTY-FOUR HOURS AGO...
12:03PM
...I SAW EIGHTY-THREE OF THEM CUT DOWN LIKE WEEDS...
12:04PM
...IN UNDER A MINUTE FLAT.
MONSTER.
MONSTER...
YOU COULD SAY THAT, CAPTAIN AMERICA... YOU COULD ALSO SAY ICONOCLAST...
ABOMINATION...
SATAN, IF YOU'RE PARTIAL TO THAT PARTICULAR BELIEF SYSTEM...
BUT WE IN THE MITHRAS DIRECTIVE CALL HIM TIAMAT... ULTIMATE CHAOS, THE UNDOING OF THE WORLD AS WE KNOW IT...

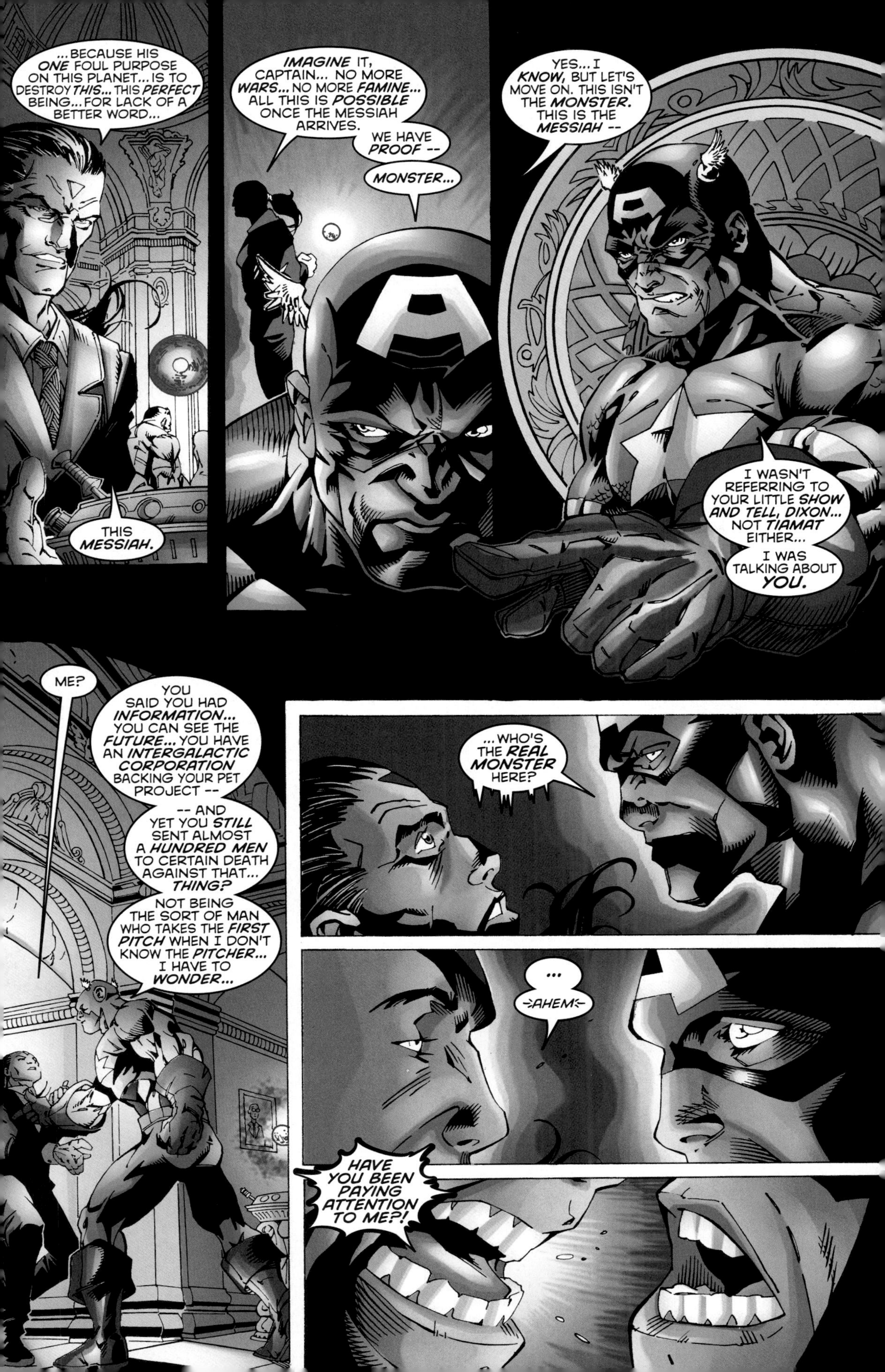
...BECAUSE HIS ONE FOUL PURPOSE ON THIS PLANET... IS TO DESTROY THIS... THIS PERFECT BEING... FOR LACK OF A BETTER WORD...
THIS MESSIAH.
IMAGINE IT, CAPTAIN... NO MORE WARS... NO MORE FAMINE... ALL THIS IS POSSIBLE ONCE THE MESSIAH ARRIVES.
WE HAVE PROOF --
MONSTER...
YES... I KNOW, BUT LET'S MOVE ON. THIS ISN'T THE MONSTER. THIS IS THE MESSIAH --
I WASN'T REFERRING TO YOUR LITTLE SHOW AND TELL, DIXON... NOT TIAMAT EITHER...
I WAS TALKING ABOUT YOU.
ME?
YOU SAID YOU HAD INFORMATION... YOU CAN SEE THE FUTURE... YOU HAVE AN INTERGALACTIC CORPORATION BACKING YOUR PET PROJECT --
-- AND YET YOU STILL SENT ALMOST A HUNDRED MEN TO CERTAIN DEATH AGAINST THAT... THING?
NOT BEING THE SORT OF MAN WHO TAKES THE FIRST PITCH WHEN I DON'T KNOW THE PITCHER... I HAVE TO WONDER...
...WHO'S THE REAL MONSTER HERE?
...
AHEM
HAVE YOU BEEN PAYING ATTENTION TO ME?!

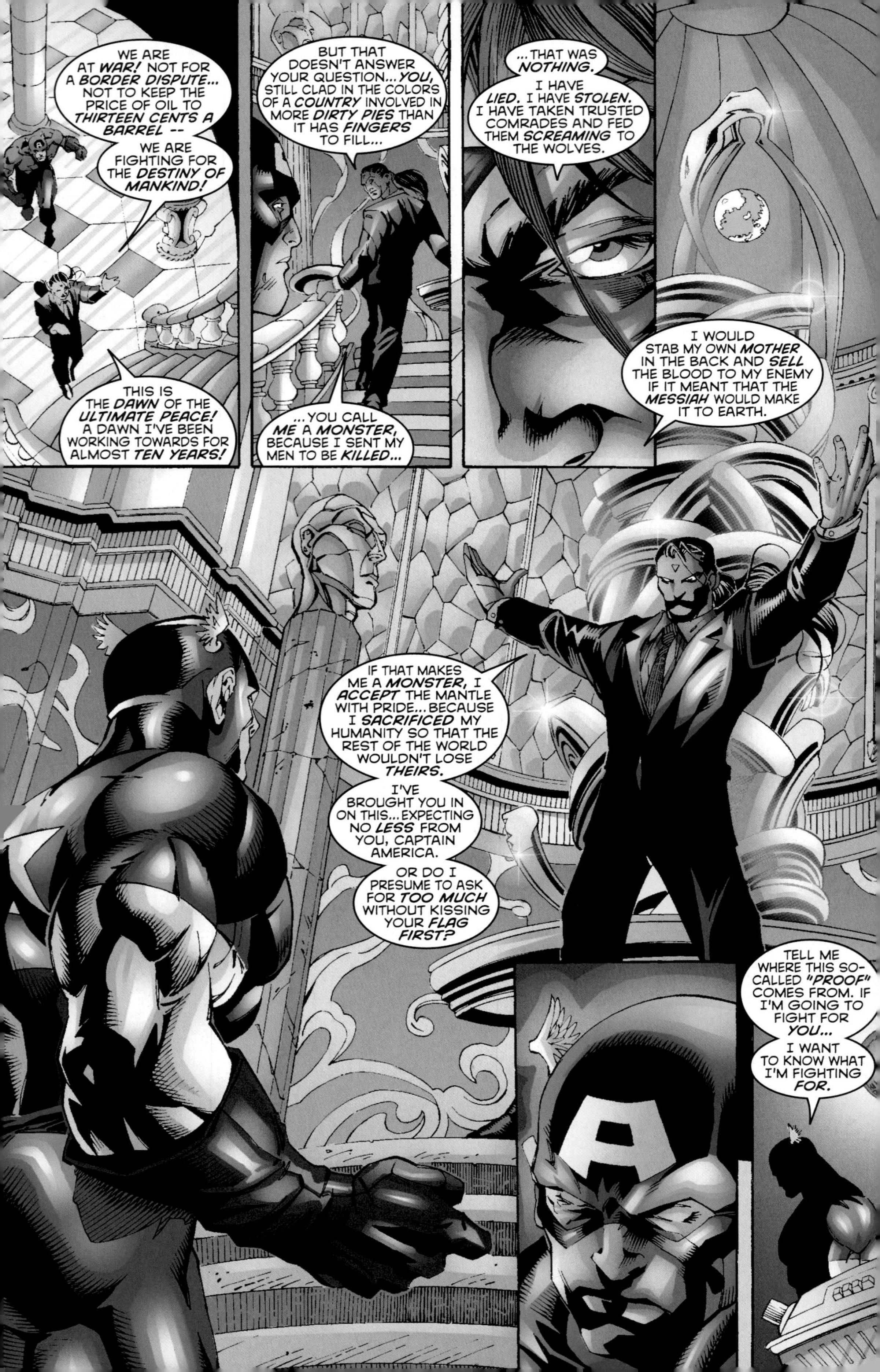
WE ARE AT WAR! NOT FOR A BORDER DISPUTE... NOT TO KEEP THE PRICE OF OIL TO THIRTEEN CENTS A BARREL --
WE ARE FIGHTING FOR THE DESTINY OF MANKIND!
THIS IS THE DAWN OF THE ULTIMATE PEACE! A DAWN I'VE BEEN WORKING TOWARDS FOR ALMOST TEN YEARS!
BUT THAT DOESN'T ANSWER YOUR QUESTION... YOU, STILL CLAD IN THE COLORS OF A COUNTRY INVOLVED IN MORE DIRTY PIES THAN IT HAS FINGERS TO FILL...
...YOU CALL ME A MONSTER, BECAUSE I SENT MY MEN TO BE KILLED...
...THAT WAS NOTHING.
I HAVE LIED. I HAVE STOLEN. I HAVE TAKEN TRUSTED COMRADES AND FED THEM SCREAMING TO THE WOLVES.
I WOULD STAB MY OWN MOTHER IN THE BACK AND SELL THE BLOOD TO MY ENEMY IF IT MEANT THAT THE MESSIAH WOULD MAKE IT TO EARTH.
IF THAT MAKES ME A MONSTER, I ACCEPT THE MANTLE WITH PRIDE... BECAUSE I SACRIFICED MY HUMANITY SO THAT THE REST OF THE WORLD WOULDN'T LOSE THEIRS.
I'VE BROUGHT YOU IN ON THIS... EXPECTING NO LESS FROM YOU, CAPTAIN AMERICA.
OR DO I PRESUME TO ASK FOR TOO MUCH WITHOUT KISSING YOUR FLAG FIRST?
TELL ME WHERE THIS SO-CALLED "PROOF" COMES FROM. IF I'M GOING TO FIGHT FOR YOU...
I WANT TO KNOW WHAT I'M FIGHTING FOR.

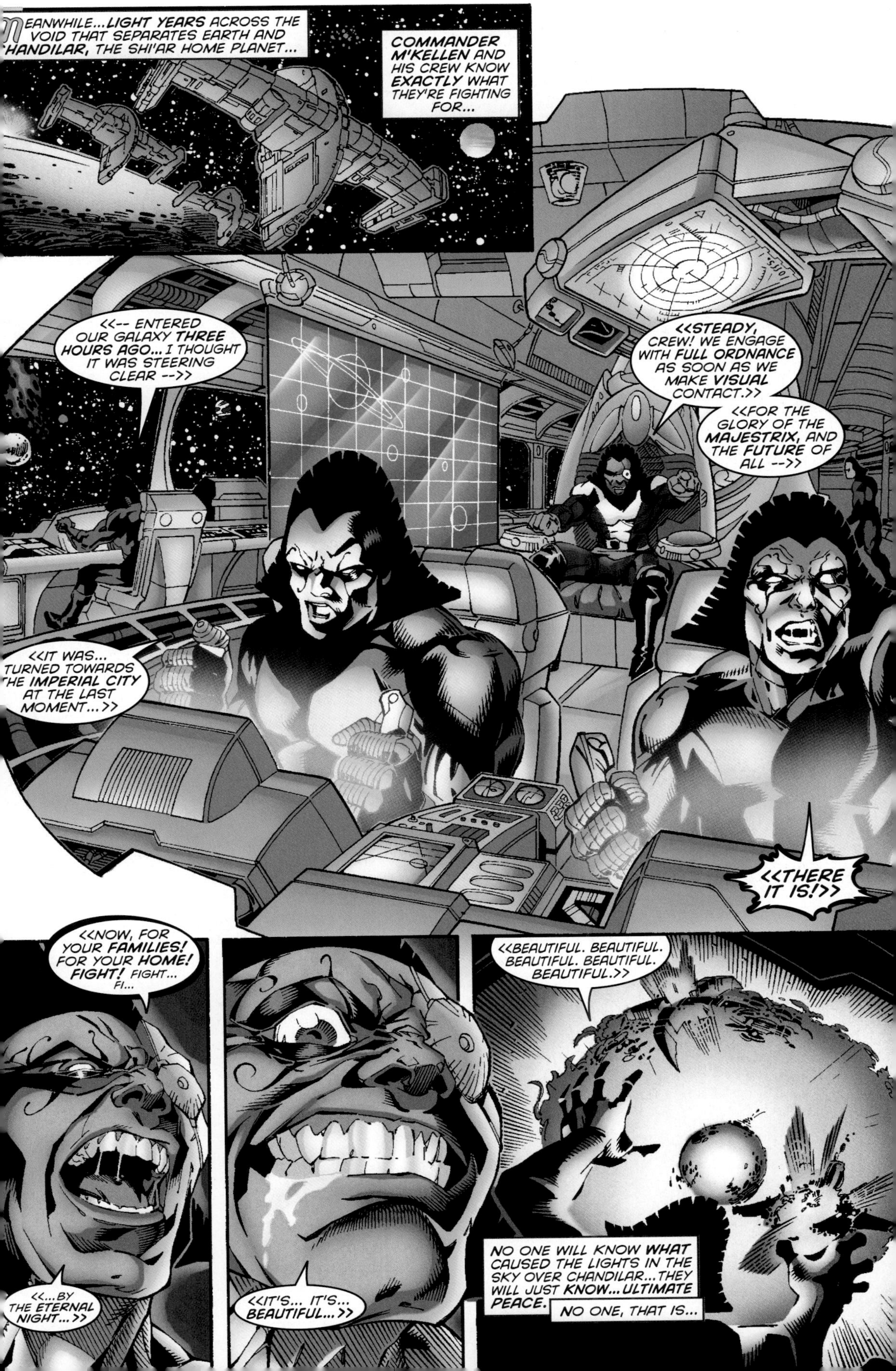
MEANWHILE... LIGHT YEARS ACROSS THE VOID THAT SEPARATES EARTH AND CHANDILAR, THE SHI'AR HOME PLANET...
COMMANDER M'KELLEN AND HIS CREW KNOW EXACTLY WHAT THEY'RE FIGHTING FOR...
<<-- ENTERED OUR GALAXY THREE HOURS AGO... I THOUGHT IT WAS STEERING CLEAR -->>
<<STEADY, CREW! WE ENGAGE WITH FULL ORDNANCE AS SOON AS WE MAKE VISUAL CONTACT.>>
<<FOR THE GLORY OF THE MAJESTRIX, AND THE FUTURE OF ALL -->>
<<IT WAS... TURNED TOWARDS THE IMPERIAL CITY AT THE LAST MOMENT...>>
<<THERE IT IS!>>
<<NOW, FOR YOUR FAMILIES! FOR YOUR HOME! FIGHT! FIGHT... FI...
<<...BY THE ETERNAL NIGHT...>>
<<IT'S... IT'S... BEAUTIFUL...>>
<<BEAUTIFUL. BEAUTIFUL. BEAUTIFUL. BEAUTIFUL. BEAUTIFUL.>>
NO ONE WILL KNOW WHAT CAUSED THE LIGHTS IN THE SKY OVER CHANDILAR... THEY WILL JUST KNOW... ULTIMATE PEACE.
NO ONE, THAT IS...

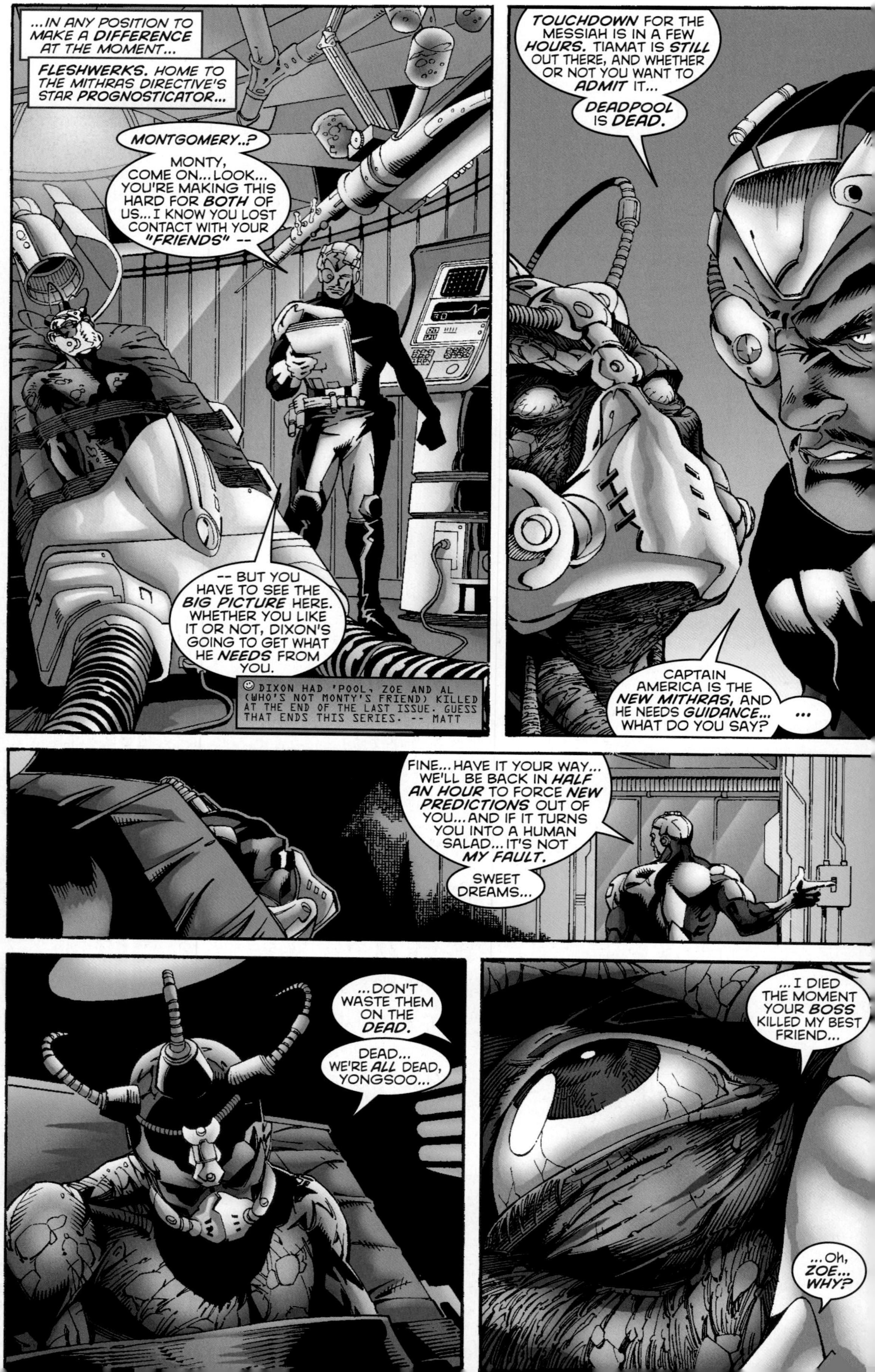
...IN ANY POSITION TO MAKE A DIFFERENCE AT THE MOMENT...
FLESHWERKS. HOME TO THE MITHRAS DIRECTIVE'S STAR PROGNOSTICATOR...
MONTGOMERY..?
MONTY, COME ON... LOOK... YOU'RE MAKING THIS HARD FOR BOTH OF US... I KNOW YOU LOST CONTACT WITH YOUR "FRIENDS" --
-- BUT YOU HAVE TO SEE THE BIG PICTURE HERE. WHETHER YOU LIKE IT OR NOT, DIXON'S GOING TO GET WHAT HE NEEDS FROM YOU.
DIXON HAD 'POOL, ZOE AND AL (WHO'S NOT MONTY'S FRIEND) KILLED AT THE END OF THE LAST ISSUE. GUESS THAT ENDS THIS SERIES. -- MATT
TOUCHDOWN FOR THE MESSIAH IS IN A FEW HOURS. TIAMAT IS STILL OUT THERE, AND WHETHER OR NOT YOU WANT TO ADMIT IT...
DEADPOOL IS DEAD.
CAPTAIN AMERICA IS THE NEW MITHRAS, AND HE NEEDS GUIDANCE... WHAT DO YOU SAY?
...
FINE... HAVE IT YOUR WAY... WE'LL BE BACK IN HALF AN HOUR TO FORCE NEW PREDICTIONS OUT OF YOU... AND IF IT TURNS YOU INTO A HUMAN SALAD... IT'S NOT MY FAULT.
SWEET DREAMS...
...DON'T WASTE THEM ON THE DEAD.
DEAD... WE'RE ALL DEAD, YONGSOO...
...I DIED THE MOMENT YOUR BOSS KILLED MY BEST FRIEND...
...Oh, ZOE... WHY?

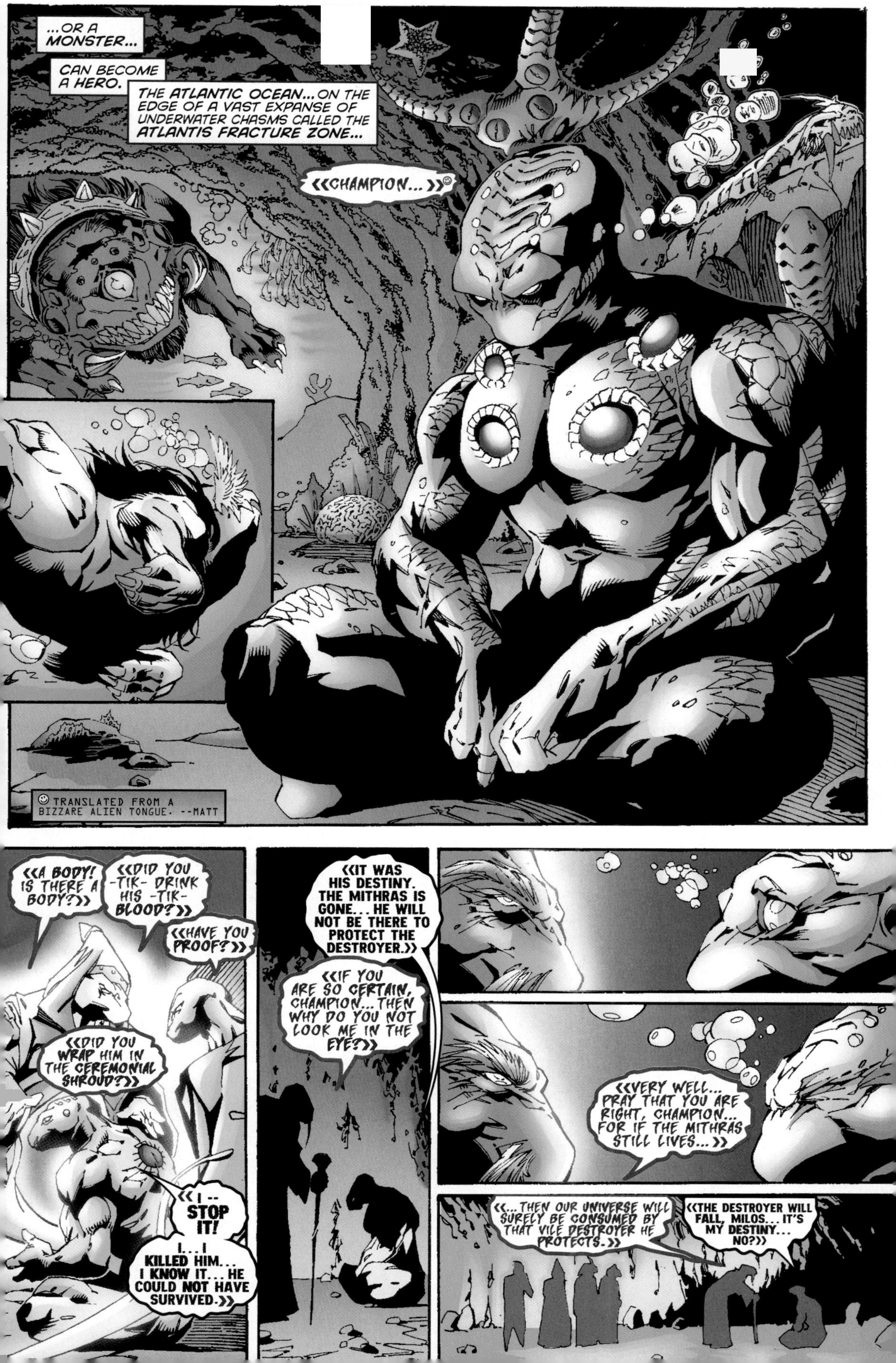

...OR A MONSTER...
CAN BECOME A HERO.
THE ATLANTIC OCEAN... ON THE EDGE OF A VAST EXPANSE OF UNDERWATER CHASMS CALLED THE ATLANTIS FRACTURE ZONE...
<<CHAMPION...>>
TRANSLATED FROM A BIZZARE ALIEN TONGUE. --MATT
<<A BODY! IS THERE A BODY?>>
<<DID YOU -TIK- DRINK HIS -TIK- BLOOD?>>
<<HAVE YOU PROOF?>>
<<DID YOU WRAP HIM IN THE CEREMONIAL SHROUD?>>
<<I -- STOP IT!
I...I KILLED HIM... I KNOW IT... HE COULD NOT HAVE SURVIVED.>>
<<IT WAS HIS DESTINY. THE MITHRAS IS GONE... HE WILL NOT BE THERE TO PROTECT THE DESTROYER.>>
<<IF YOU ARE SO CERTAIN, CHAMPION... THEN WHY DO YOU NOT LOOK ME IN THE EYE?>>
<<VERY WELL... PRAY THAT YOU ARE RIGHT, CHAMPION... FOR IF THE MITHRAS STILL LIVES...>>
<<...THEN OUR UNIVERSE WILL SURELY BE CONSUMED BY THAT VILE DESTROYER HE PROTECTS.>>
<<THE DESTROYER WILL FALL, MILOS... IT'S MY DESTINY... NO?>>

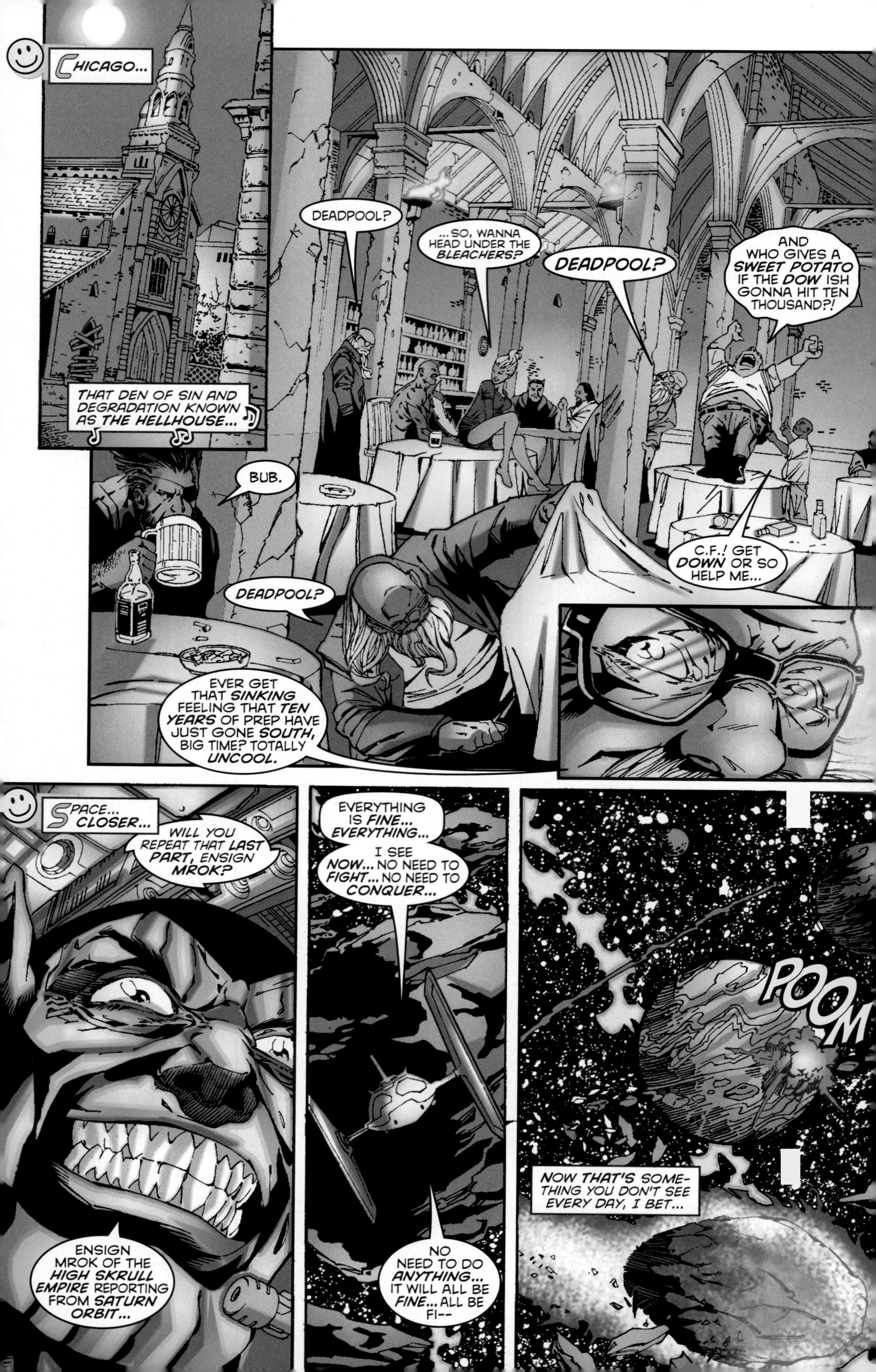
CHICAGO...
THAT DEN OF SIN AND DEGRADATION KNOWN AS THE HELLHOUSE...
DEADPOOL?
...SO, WANNA HEAD UNDER THE BLEACHERS?
DEADPOOL?
AND WHO GIVES A SWEET POTATO IF THE DOW ISH GONNA HIT TEN THOUSAND?!
BUB.
C.F.! GET DOWN OR SO HELP ME...
DEADPOOL?
EVER GET THAT SINKING FEELING THAT TEN YEARS OF PREP HAVE JUST GONE SOUTH, BIG TIME? TOTALLY UNCOOL.
SPACE... CLOSER...
WILL YOU REPEAT THAT LAST PART, ENSIGN MROK?
ENSIGN MROK OF THE HIGH SKRULL EMPIRE REPORTING FROM SATURN ORBIT...
EVERYTHING IS FINE... EVERYTHING...
I SEE NOW... NO NEED TO FIGHT... NO NEED TO CONQUER...
NO NEED TO DO ANYTHING... IT WILL ALL BE FINE... ALL BE FI--
POOM
NOW THAT'S SOME-THING YOU DON'T SEE EVERY DAY, I BET...

GOD IN HEAVEN...WHAT *IS* IT?

THAT'S THE *WINDOW* TO OUR *FUTURE,* SIR...

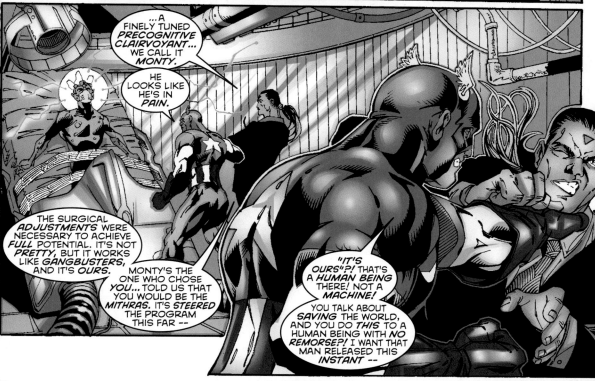

...A FINELY TUNED *PRECOGNITIVE CLAIRVOYANT*... WE CALL IT *MONTY.*

HE LOOKS LIKE HE'S IN *PAIN.*

THE SURGICAL *ADJUSTMENTS* WERE NECESSARY TO ACHIEVE *FULL* POTENTIAL. IT'S NOT *PRETTY,* BUT IT WORKS LIKE *GANGBUSTERS,* AND IT'S *OURS.*

MONTY'S THE ONE WHO CHOSE *YOU*... TOLD US THAT YOU WOULD BE THE *MITHRAS.* IT'S *STEERED* THE PROGRAM THIS FAR --

"IT'S OURS"?! THAT'S A *HUMAN BEING* THERE! NOT A *MACHINE!*

YOU TALK ABOUT *SAVING* THE WORLD, AND YOU DO *THIS* TO A HUMAN BEING WITH *NO REMORSE?!* I WANT THAT MAN RELEASED THIS *INSTANT* --

STEEEVE...

WHAT THE --?

STEEVE... *NOT*... IN *PAIN*... MUST *TALK* TO YOU --

HOW DO YOU KNOW MY *REAL* NAME?

I KNOW... *EVERYTHING* ABOUT YOU...*STEEEVE*... I KNOW ABOUT *NIGHTMARE*... *NOT* YOUR *FAULT*...

NUCLEAR WINTER, HIS BAD DREAM...☺

☺ SEE CAPTAIN AMERICA #9-12 FOR FULL SCOOP! -- MATT

HOW..? *NO ONE* KNOWS ABOUT THAT...

I KNEW... *WEEKS AGO*... I KNOW... *ALL*...

YOU *ARE* THE *MITHRAS,* STEVE... STOP *TIAMAT*... OR WE'RE *ALL DOOMED*... IN THE *SAND,* STEVE... THE *SAAAAND*...

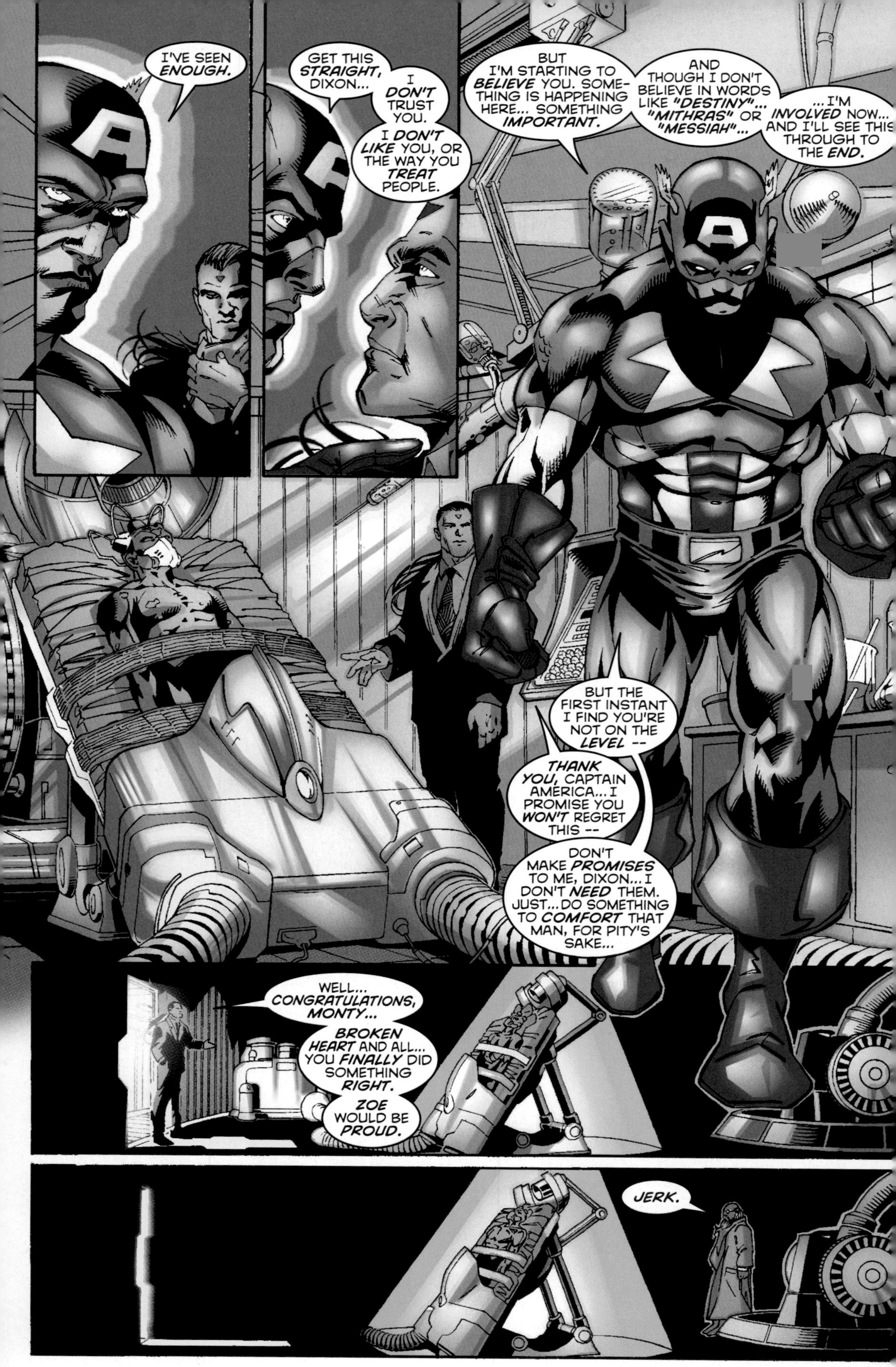
I'VE SEEN ENOUGH.
GET THIS STRAIGHT, DIXON...
I DON'T TRUST YOU.
I DON'T LIKE YOU, OR THE WAY YOU TREAT PEOPLE.
BUT I'M STARTING TO BELIEVE YOU. SOMETHING IS HAPPENING HERE... SOMETHING IMPORTANT.
AND THOUGH I DON'T BELIEVE IN WORDS LIKE "DESTINY"... "MITHRAS" OR "MESSIAH"...
...I'M INVOLVED NOW... AND I'LL SEE THIS THROUGH TO THE END.
BUT THE FIRST INSTANT I FIND YOU'RE NOT ON THE LEVEL --
THANK YOU, CAPTAIN AMERICA... I PROMISE YOU WON'T REGRET THIS --
DON'T MAKE PROMISES TO ME, DIXON... I DON'T NEED THEM. JUST... DO SOMETHING TO COMFORT THAT MAN, FOR PITY'S SAKE...
WELL... CONGRATULATIONS, MONTY...
BROKEN HEART AND ALL... YOU FINALLY DID SOMETHING RIGHT.
ZOE WOULD BE PROUD.
JERK.

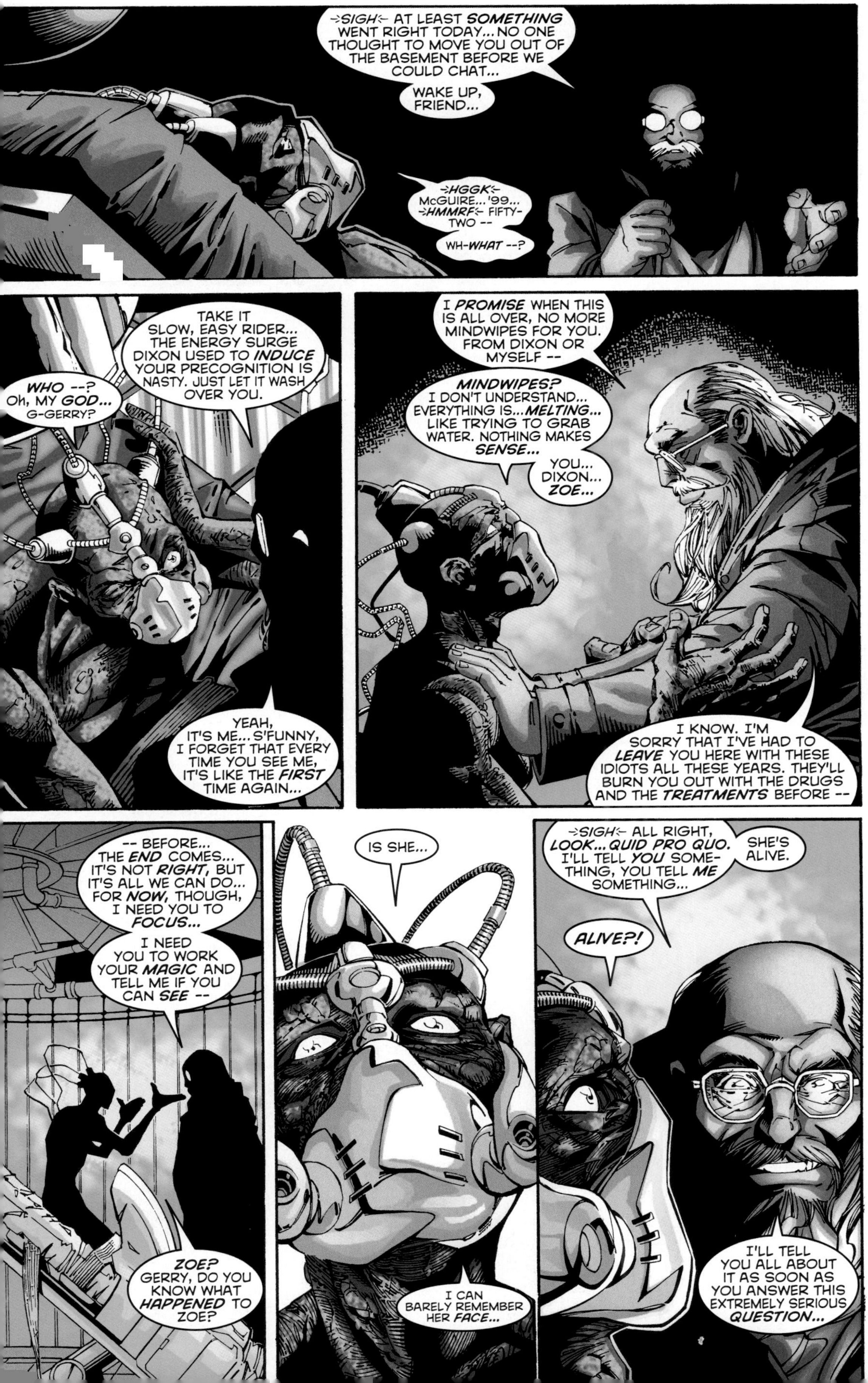

-SIGH- AT LEAST SOMETHING WENT RIGHT TODAY... NO ONE THOUGHT TO MOVE YOU OUT OF THE BASEMENT BEFORE WE COULD CHAT...
WAKE UP, FRIEND...
-HGGK- McGUIRE... '99... -HMMRF- FIFTY-TWO --
WH-WHAT --?
WHO --? Oh, MY GOD... G-GERRY?
TAKE IT SLOW, EASY RIDER... THE ENERGY SURGE DIXON USED TO INDUCE YOUR PRECOGNITION IS NASTY. JUST LET IT WASH OVER YOU.
YEAH, IT'S ME... S'FUNNY, I FORGET THAT EVERY TIME YOU SEE ME, IT'S LIKE THE FIRST TIME AGAIN...
I PROMISE WHEN THIS IS ALL OVER, NO MORE MINDWIPES FOR YOU. FROM DIXON OR MYSELF --
MINDWIPES? I DON'T UNDERSTAND... EVERYTHING IS... MELTING... LIKE TRYING TO GRAB WATER. NOTHING MAKES SENSE...
YOU... DIXON... ZOE...
I KNOW. I'M SORRY THAT I'VE HAD TO LEAVE YOU HERE WITH THESE IDIOTS ALL THESE YEARS. THEY'LL BURN YOU OUT WITH THE DRUGS AND THE TREATMENTS BEFORE --
-- BEFORE... THE END COMES... IT'S NOT RIGHT, BUT IT'S ALL WE CAN DO... FOR NOW, THOUGH, I NEED YOU TO FOCUS...
I NEED YOU TO WORK YOUR MAGIC AND TELL ME IF YOU CAN SEE --
ZOE? GERRY, DO YOU KNOW WHAT HAPPENED TO ZOE?
IS SHE...
I CAN BARELY REMEMBER HER FACE...
-SIGH- ALL RIGHT, LOOK... QUID PRO QUO. I'LL TELL YOU SOMETHING, YOU TELL ME SOMETHING...
SHE'S ALIVE.
ALIVE?!
I'LL TELL YOU ALL ABOUT IT AS SOON AS YOU ANSWER THIS EXTREMELY SERIOUS QUESTION...

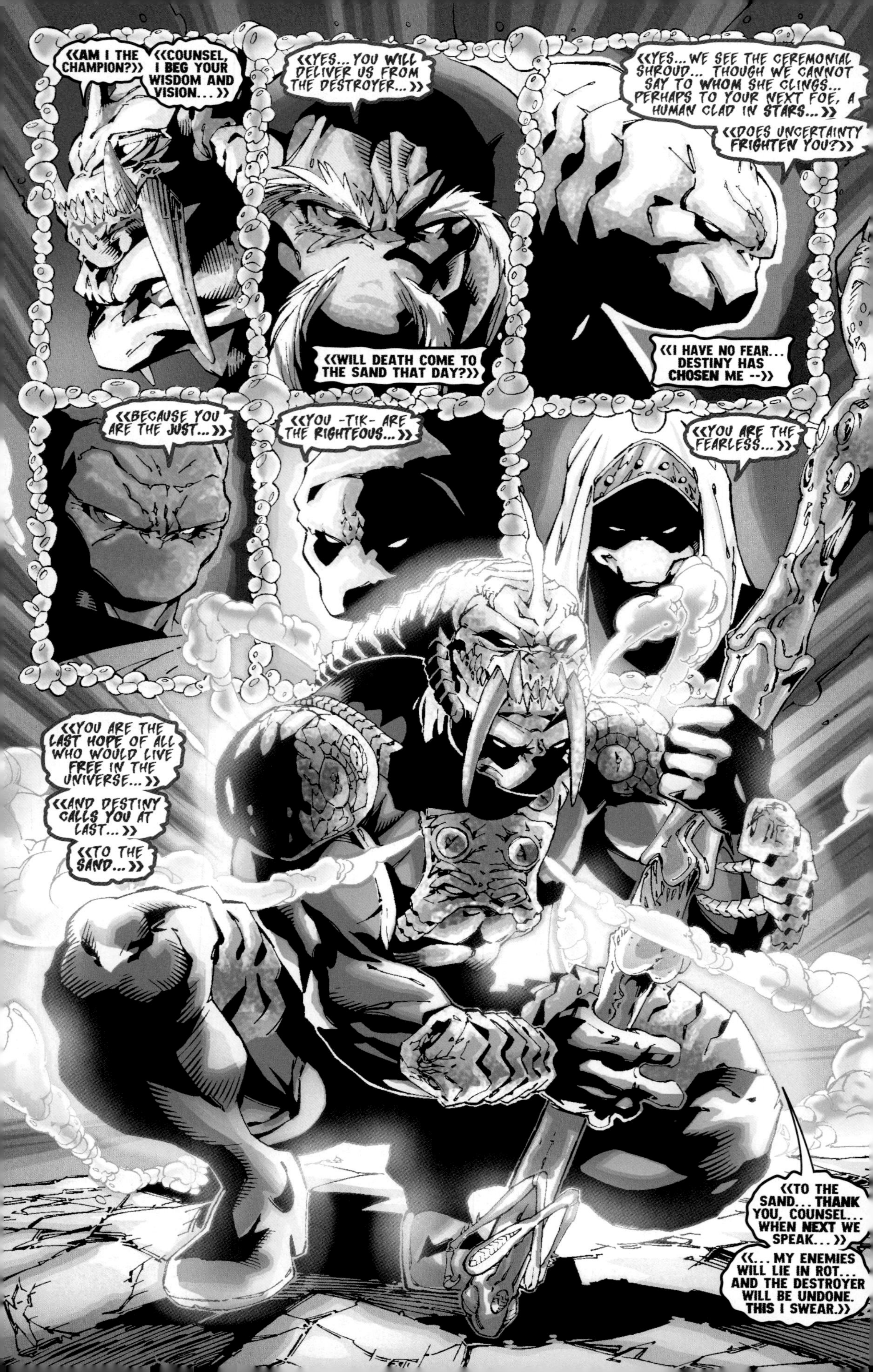

<<AM I THE CHAMPION?>>
<<COUNSEL, I BEG YOUR WISDOM AND VISION...>>
<<YES... YOU WILL DELIVER US FROM THE DESTROYER...>>
<<WILL DEATH COME TO THE SAND THAT DAY?>>
<<YES... WE SEE THE CEREMONIAL SHROUD... THOUGH WE CANNOT SAY TO WHOM SHE CLINGS... PERHAPS TO YOUR NEXT FOE, A HUMAN CLAD IN STARS...>>
<<DOES UNCERTAINTY FRIGHTEN YOU?>>
<<I HAVE NO FEAR... DESTINY HAS CHOSEN ME -->>
<<BECAUSE YOU ARE THE JUST...>>
<<YOU -TIK- ARE THE RIGHTEOUS...>>
<<YOU ARE THE FEARLESS...>>
<<YOU ARE THE LAST HOPE OF ALL WHO WOULD LIVE FREE IN THE UNIVERSE...>>
<<AND DESTINY CALLS YOU AT LAST...>>
<<TO THE SAND...>>
<<TO THE SAND... THANK YOU, COUNSEL... WHEN NEXT WE SPEAK...>>
<<... MY ENEMIES WILL LIE IN ROT... AND THE DESTROYER WILL BE UNDONE. THIS I SWEAR.>>

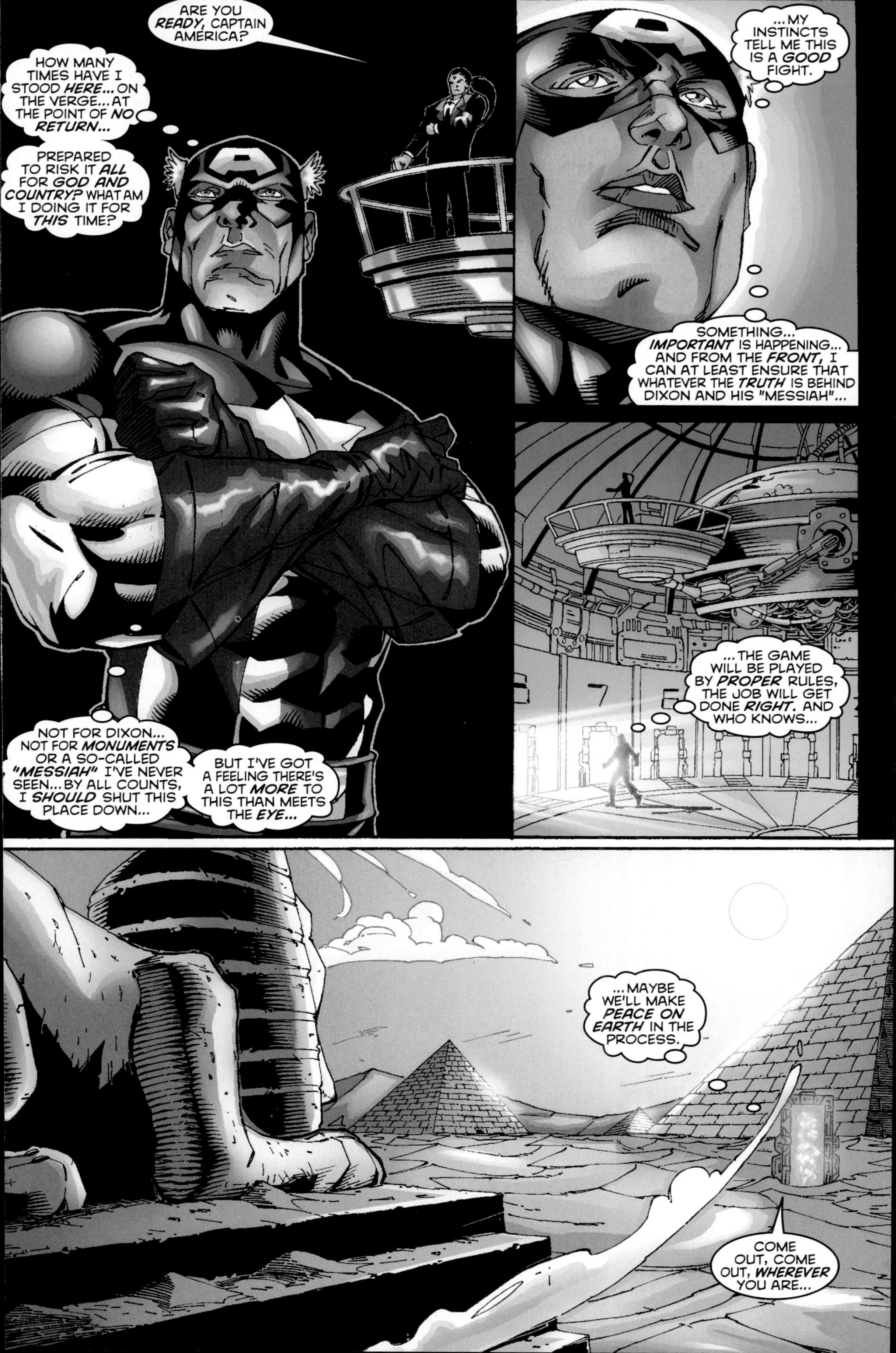

ARE YOU *READY,* CAPTAIN AMERICA?
HOW MANY TIMES HAVE I STOOD *HERE...* ON THE VERGE... AT THE POINT OF *NO RETURN...*
PREPARED TO RISK IT *ALL* FOR *GOD AND COUNTRY?* WHAT AM I DOING IT FOR *THIS* TIME?
NOT FOR DIXON... NOT FOR *MONUMENTS* OR A SO-CALLED *"MESSIAH"* I'VE NEVER SEEN... BY ALL COUNTS, I *SHOULD* SHUT THIS PLACE DOWN...
BUT I'VE GOT A FEELING THERE'S A LOT *MORE* TO THIS THAN MEETS THE *EYE...*
...MY INSTINCTS TELL ME THIS IS A *GOOD* FIGHT.
SOMETHING... *IMPORTANT* IS HAPPENING... AND FROM THE *FRONT,* I CAN AT LEAST ENSURE THAT WHATEVER THE *TRUTH* IS BEHIND DIXON AND HIS "MESSIAH"...
...THE GAME WILL BE PLAYED BY *PROPER* RULES, THE JOB WILL GET DONE *RIGHT.* AND WHO KNOWS...
...MAYBE WE'LL MAKE *PEACE ON EARTH* IN THE PROCESS.
COME OUT, COME OUT, *WHEREVER* YOU ARE...

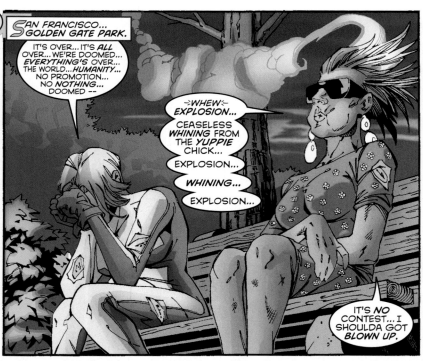

SAN FRANCISCO... GOLDEN GATE PARK.

IT'S OVER... IT'S *ALL* OVER... WE'RE DOOMED... *EVERYTHING'S* OVER... THE WORLD... *HUMANITY...* NO PROMOTION... NO *NOTHING...* DOOMED --

~WHEW~ EXPLOSION... CEASELESS *WHINING* FROM THE *YUPPIE* CHICK... EXPLOSION... *WHINING...* EXPLOSION...

IT'S *NO* CONTEST... I SHOULDA GOT *BLOWN UP.*

ENOUGH ALREADY WITH THE *"WE'RE DOOMED"* CLAPTRAP, CULLODEN!

SWAK

MY EARS *FINALLY* STOPPED RINGING... I DON'T WANT YOU TO MAKE 'EM *START* AGAIN!

OH, AL... YOU *POOR* WOMAN... NOT JUST *SIGHTLESS*, BUT BLIND TO THE *TRUTH* AS WELL...

DON'T YOU GET IT? DEADPOOL'S *GONE*... THE MITHRAS... THE *HERALD* OF THE MESSIAH...

WITHOUT *HIM* IT *ALL* FALLS APART. TIAMAT *DESTROYS* THE MESSIAH... THE WORLD FALLS TO *RUIN* --

IN CASE YOU DIDN'T NOTICE, ZOE, INSTEAD OF BEIN' GUESTS OF HONOR AT AN *INSTANT BARBECUE*, WE'RE STILL *BREATHIN'* ON A PARK BENCH!

WE'RE *ALIVE!* WASN'T *NO ONE* BACK *HOME* BUT THE THREE OF US WHEN IT *BLEW*, SO IF *WE'RE* STILL KICKIN', IT'S BECAUSE *WADE* DID SOMETHING!

TRUST ME, AS SOMEONE WHO *LIVED* WITH THE MAN FOR *YEARS*, WADE ISN'T THE *SELFLESS* TYPE. IF WE'RE ALIVE, HE'S ALREADY CAMPED OUT SOME-WHERE WATCHING *WORLD'S WORST POLICE CHASES* AND DROOLING INTO AN EMPTY *SIX PACK* --

WHOA!

SCHUNKOOM

WHAT ON *EARTH* --?

WHAT'S *HAPPENING?* IS THIS SOME STUPID *CANDID CAMERA* STUNT, 'CAUSE I SWEAR I'LL *KILL* THAT *FUNT* KID --

VRRRRRMM

IT'S A *DOOR!* SOMEONE'S COMING --

OH...MY... GOD...

WHAT? WHAT? WHAAAT?

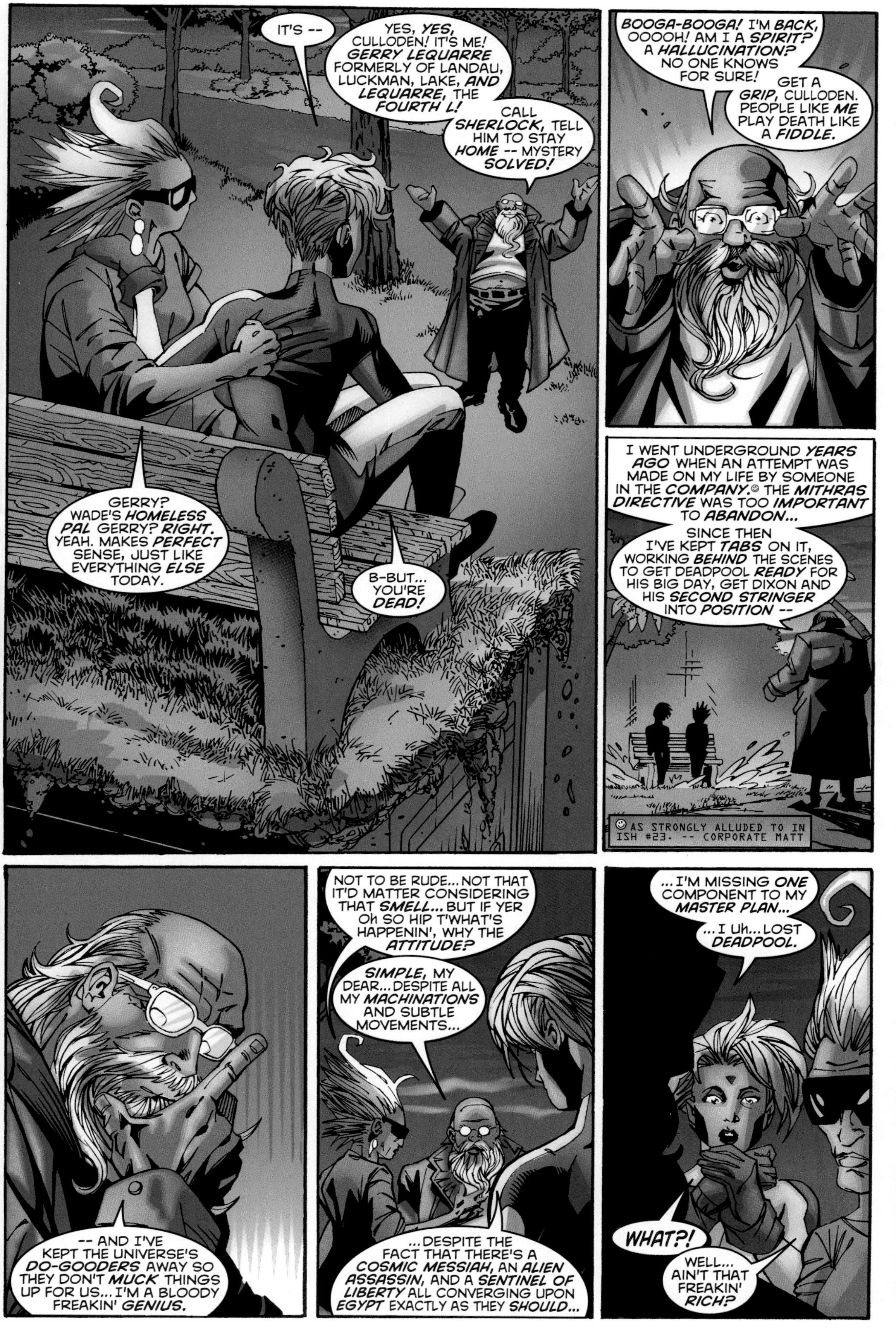
IT'S --
YES, YES, CULLODEN! IT'S ME! GERRY LEQUARRE FORMERLY OF LANDAU, LUCKMAN, LAKE, AND LEQUARRE, THE FOURTH L!
CALL SHERLOCK, TELL HIM TO STAY HOME -- MYSTERY SOLVED!
GERRY? WADE'S HOMELESS PAL GERRY? RIGHT. YEAH. MAKES PERFECT SENSE, JUST LIKE EVERYTHING ELSE TODAY.
B-BUT... YOU'RE DEAD!
BOOGA-BOOGA! I'M BACK, OOOOH! AM I A SPIRIT? A HALLUCINATION? NO ONE KNOWS FOR SURE!
GET A GRIP, CULLODEN. PEOPLE LIKE ME PLAY DEATH LIKE A FIDDLE.
I WENT UNDERGROUND YEARS AGO WHEN AN ATTEMPT WAS MADE ON MY LIFE BY SOMEONE IN THE COMPANY.☺ THE MITHRAS DIRECTIVE WAS TOO IMPORTANT TO ABANDON...
SINCE THEN I'VE KEPT TABS ON IT, WORKING BEHIND THE SCENES TO GET DEADPOOL READY FOR HIS BIG DAY, GET DIXON AND HIS SECOND STRINGER INTO POSITION --
☺ AS STRONGLY ALLUDED TO IN ISH #23. -- CORPORATE MATT
-- AND I'VE KEPT THE UNIVERSE'S DO-GOODERS AWAY SO THEY DON'T MUCK THINGS UP FOR US... I'M A BLOODY FREAKIN' GENIUS.
NOT TO BE RUDE... NOT THAT IT'D MATTER CONSIDERING THAT SMELL... BUT IF YER Oh SO HIP T'WHAT'S HAPPENIN', WHY THE ATTITUDE?
SIMPLE, MY DEAR... DESPITE ALL MY MACHINATIONS AND SUBTLE MOVEMENTS...
...DESPITE THE FACT THAT THERE'S A COSMIC MESSIAH, AN ALIEN ASSASSIN, AND A SENTINEL OF LIBERTY ALL CONVERGING UPON EGYPT EXACTLY AS THEY SHOULD...
...I'M MISSING ONE COMPONENT TO MY MASTER PLAN...
...I Uh... LOST DEADPOOL.
WHAT?!
WELL... AIN'T THAT FREAKIN' RICH?

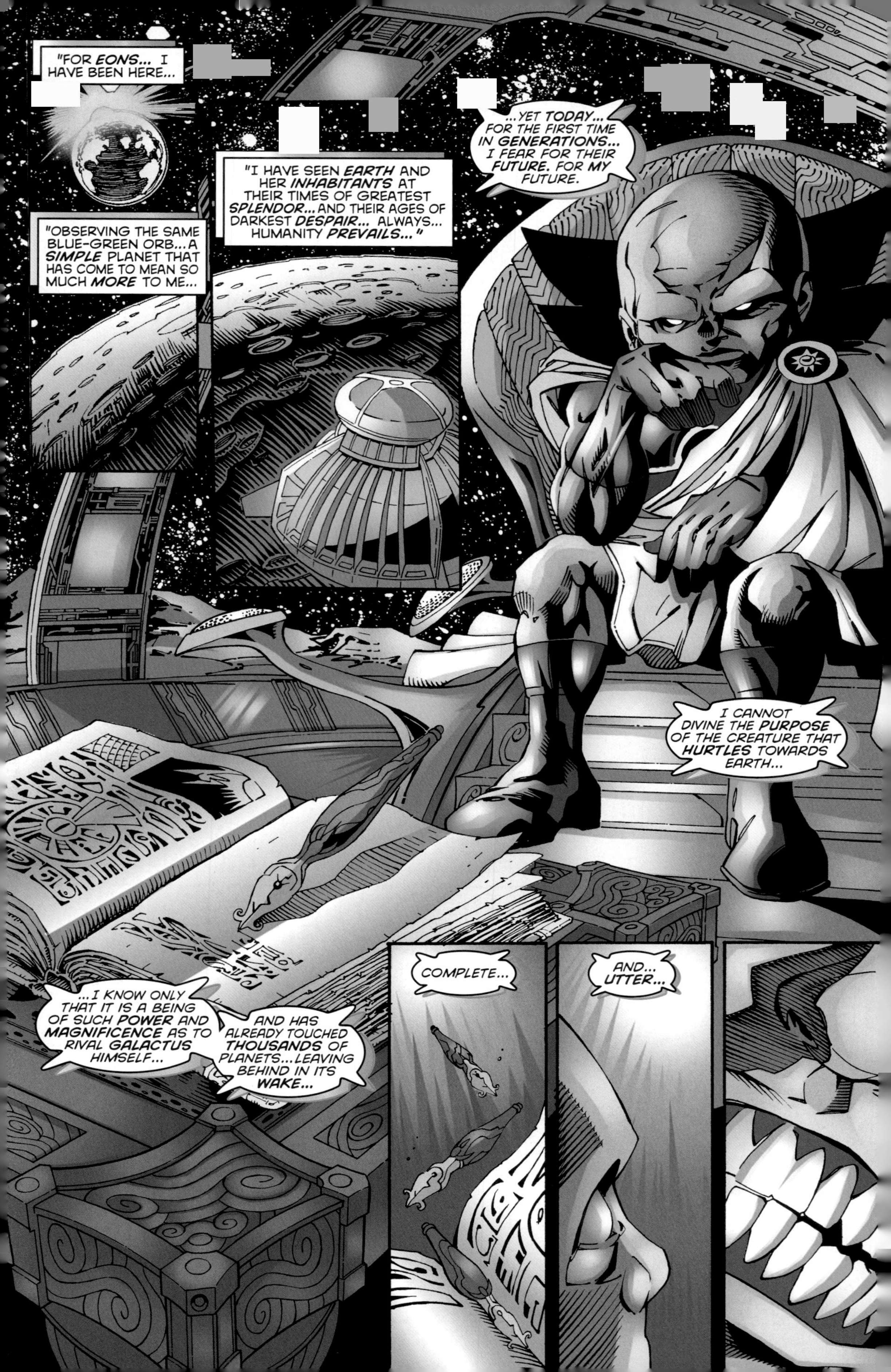
"FOR EONS... I HAVE BEEN HERE...
"OBSERVING THE SAME BLUE-GREEN ORB...A SIMPLE PLANET THAT HAS COME TO MEAN SO MUCH MORE TO ME...
"I HAVE SEEN EARTH AND HER INHABITANTS AT THEIR TIMES OF GREATEST SPLENDOR...AND THEIR AGES OF DARKEST DESPAIR... ALWAYS... HUMANITY PREVAILS..."
...YET TODAY... FOR THE FIRST TIME IN GENERATIONS... I FEAR FOR THEIR FUTURE. FOR MY FUTURE.
I CANNOT DIVINE THE PURPOSE OF THE CREATURE THAT HURTLES TOWARDS EARTH...
...I KNOW ONLY THAT IT IS A BEING OF SUCH POWER AND MAGNIFICENCE AS TO RIVAL GALACTUS HIMSELF...
AND HAS ALREADY TOUCHED THOUSANDS OF PLANETS...LEAVING BEHIND IN ITS WAKE...
COMPLETE...
AND... UTTER...

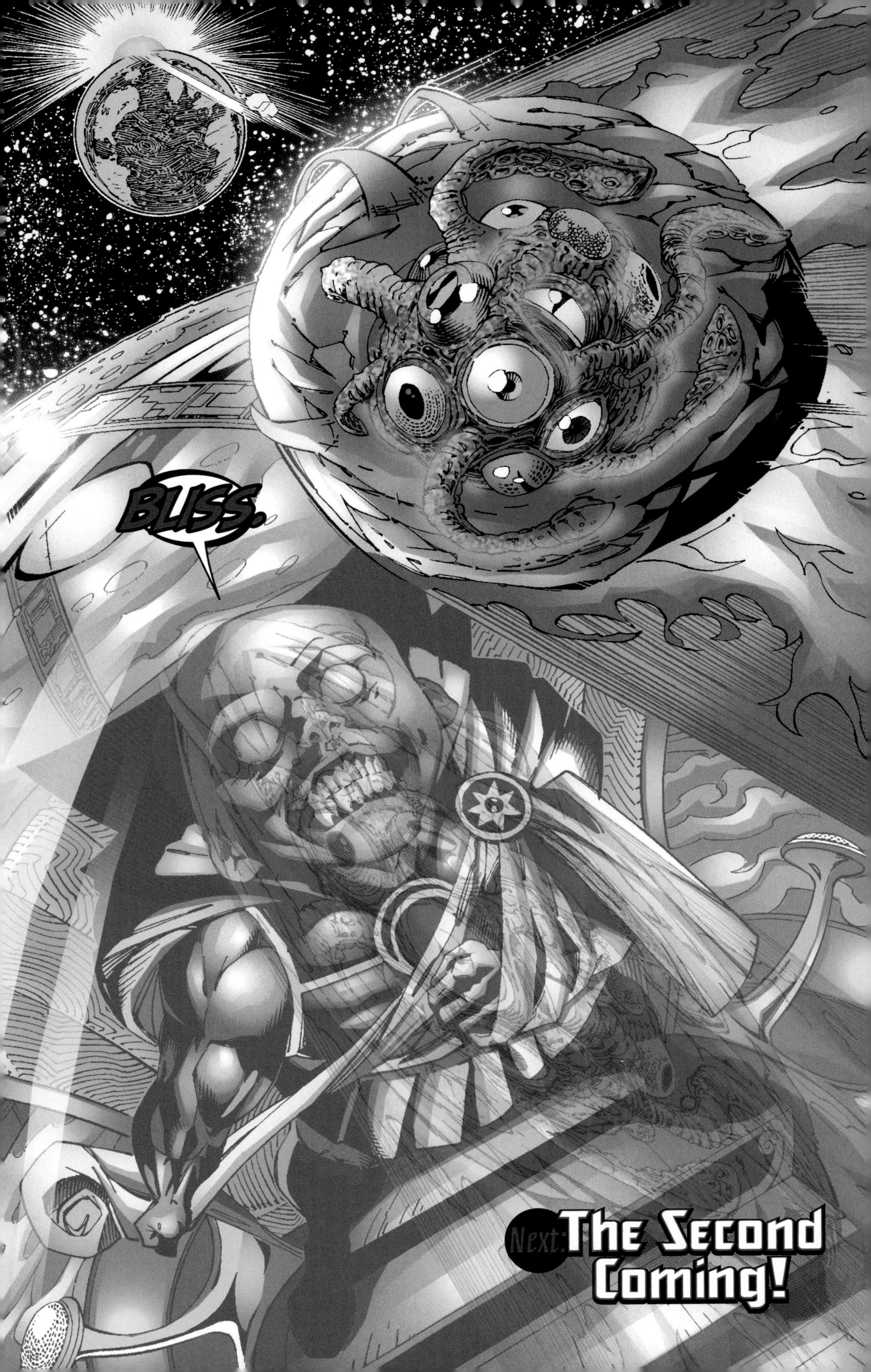
BLISS.
Next: The Second Coming!

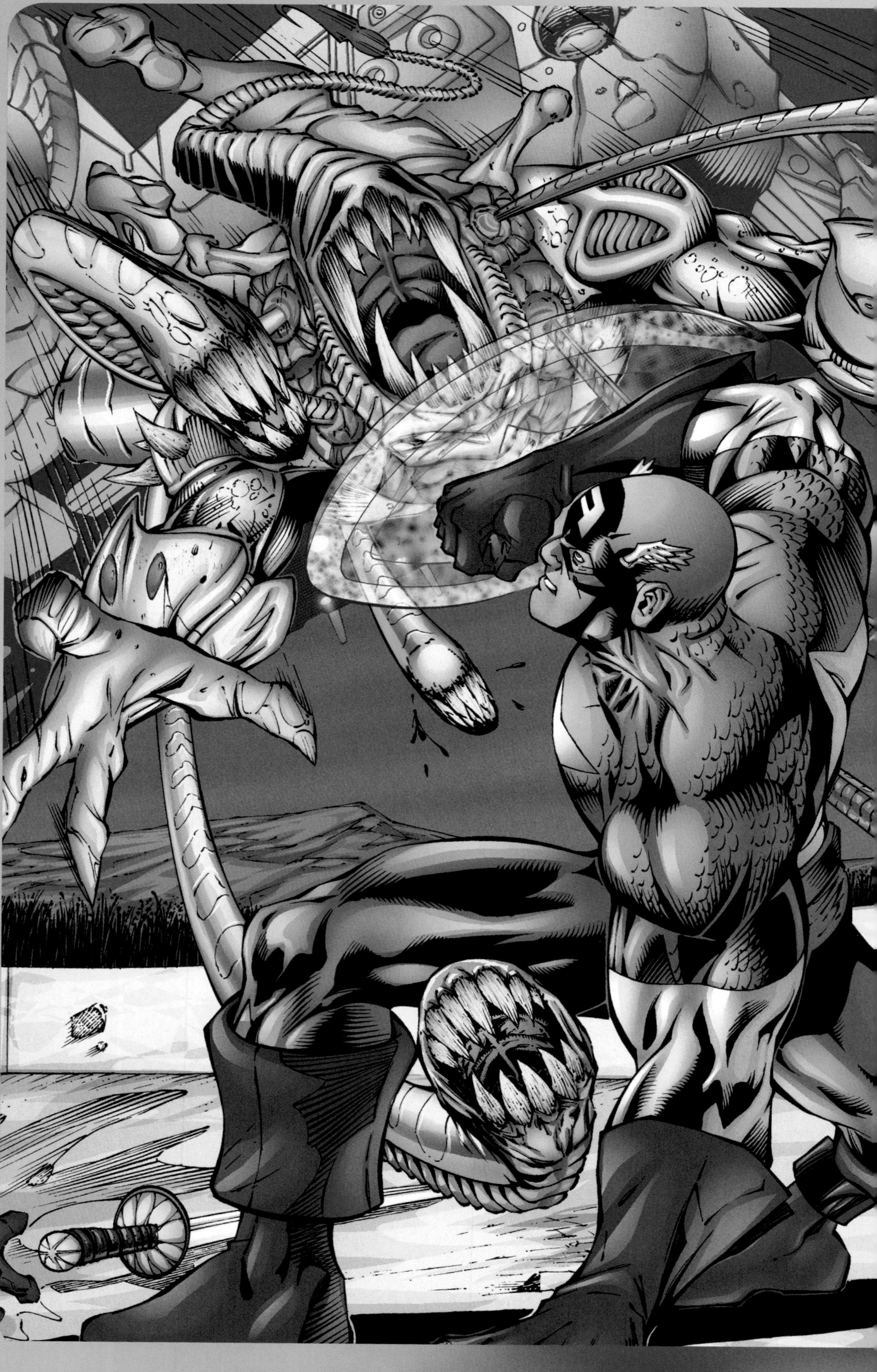

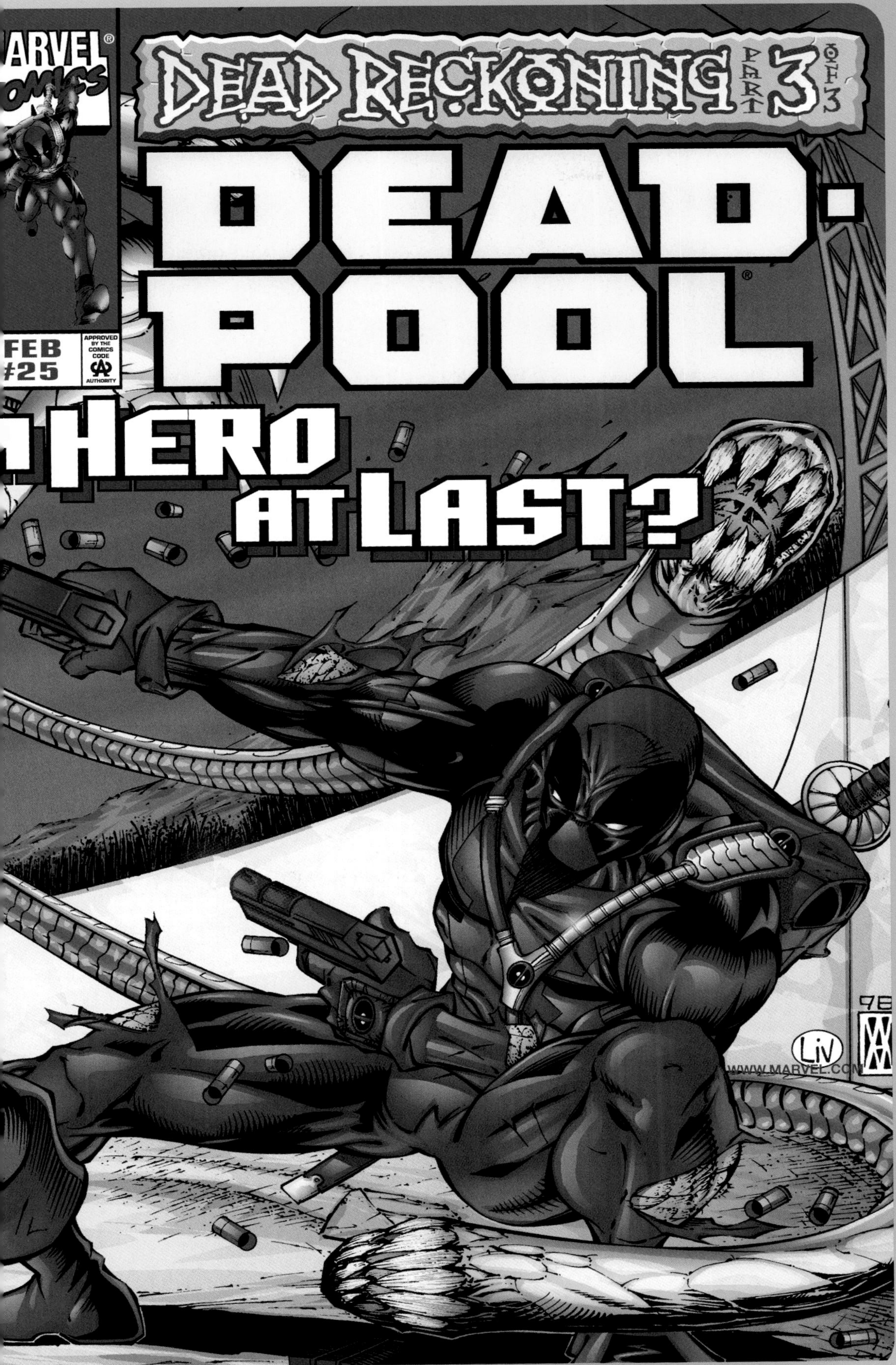

MARVEL COMICS
DEAD RECKONING PART 3 OF 3
DEADPOOL
FEB #25
APPROVED BY THE COMICS CODE AUTHORITY
HERO AT LAST?
WWW.MARVEL.COM

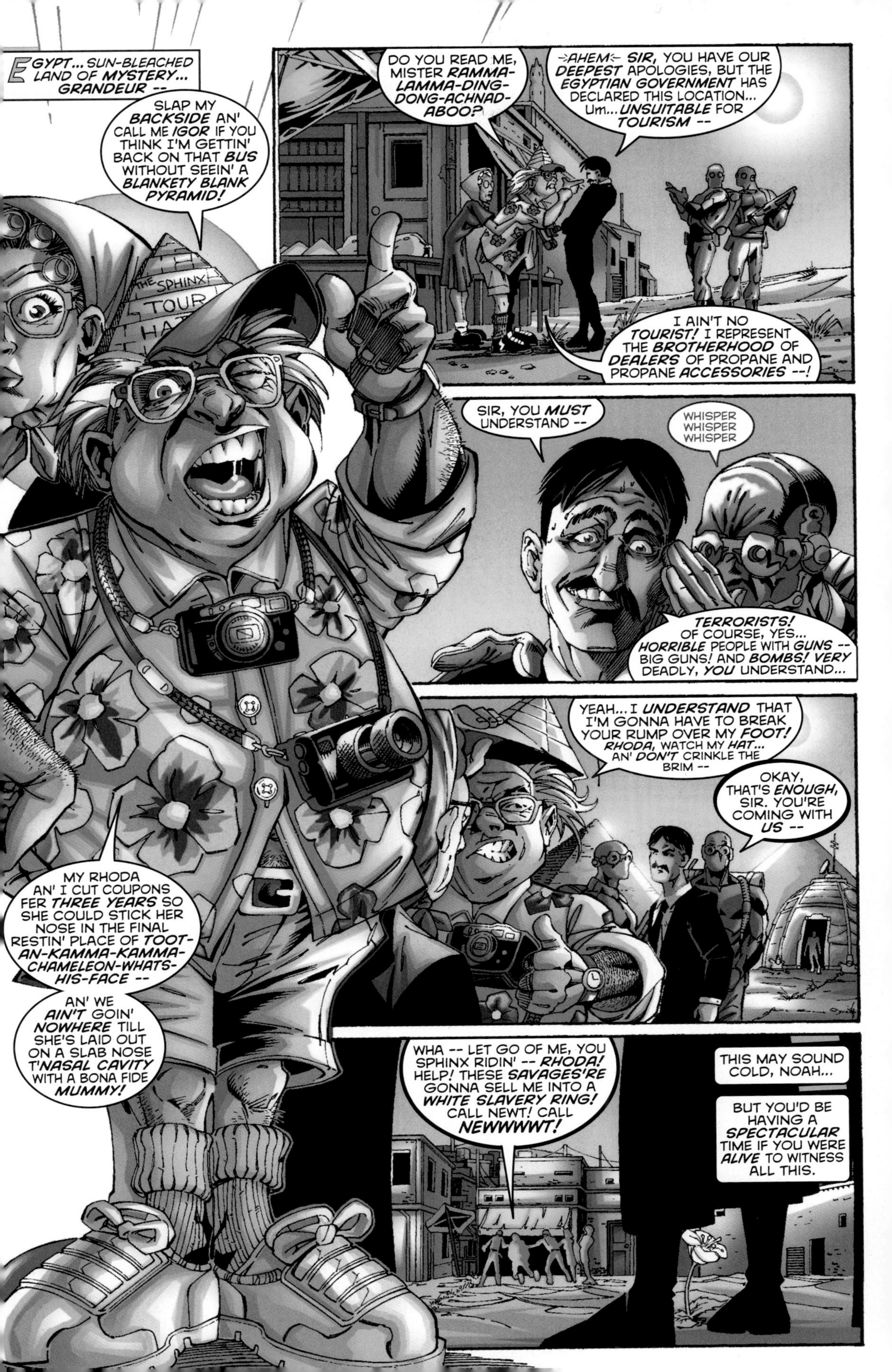
EGYPT... SUN-BLEACHED LAND OF MYSTERY... GRANDEUR --
SLAP MY BACKSIDE AN' CALL ME IGOR IF YOU THINK I'M GETTIN' BACK ON THAT BUS WITHOUT SEEIN' A BLANKETY BLANK PYRAMID!
THE SPHINX TOUR HAT
DO YOU READ ME, MISTER RAMMA-LAMMA-DING-DONG-ACHNAD-ABOO?
-AHEM- SIR, YOU HAVE OUR DEEPEST APOLOGIES, BUT THE EGYPTIAN GOVERNMENT HAS DECLARED THIS LOCATION... Um... UNSUITABLE FOR TOURISM --
I AIN'T NO TOURIST! I REPRESENT THE BROTHERHOOD OF DEALERS OF PROPANE AND PROPANE ACCESSORIES --!
SIR, YOU MUST UNDERSTAND --
WHISPER WHISPER WHISPER
TERRORISTS! OF COURSE, YES... HORRIBLE PEOPLE WITH GUNS -- BIG GUNS! AND BOMBS! VERY DEADLY, YOU UNDERSTAND...
YEAH... I UNDERSTAND THAT I'M GONNA HAVE TO BREAK YOUR RUMP OVER MY FOOT! RHODA, WATCH MY HAT... AN' DON'T CRINKLE THE BRIM --
OKAY, THAT'S ENOUGH, SIR. YOU'RE COMING WITH US --
MY RHODA AN' I CUT COUPONS FER THREE YEARS SO SHE COULD STICK HER NOSE IN THE FINAL RESTIN' PLACE OF TOOT-AN-KAMMA-KAMMA-CHAMELEON-WHATS-HIS-FACE --
AN' WE AIN'T GOIN' NOWHERE TILL SHE'S LAID OUT ON A SLAB NOSE T'NASAL CAVITY WITH A BONA FIDE MUMMY!
WHA -- LET GO OF ME, YOU SPHINX RIDIN' -- RHODA! HELP! THESE SAVAGES'RE GONNA SELL ME INTO A WHITE SLAVERY RING! CALL NEWT! CALL NEWWWWT!
THIS MAY SOUND COLD, NOAH...
BUT YOU'D BE HAVING A SPECTACULAR TIME IF YOU WERE ALIVE TO WITNESS ALL THIS.

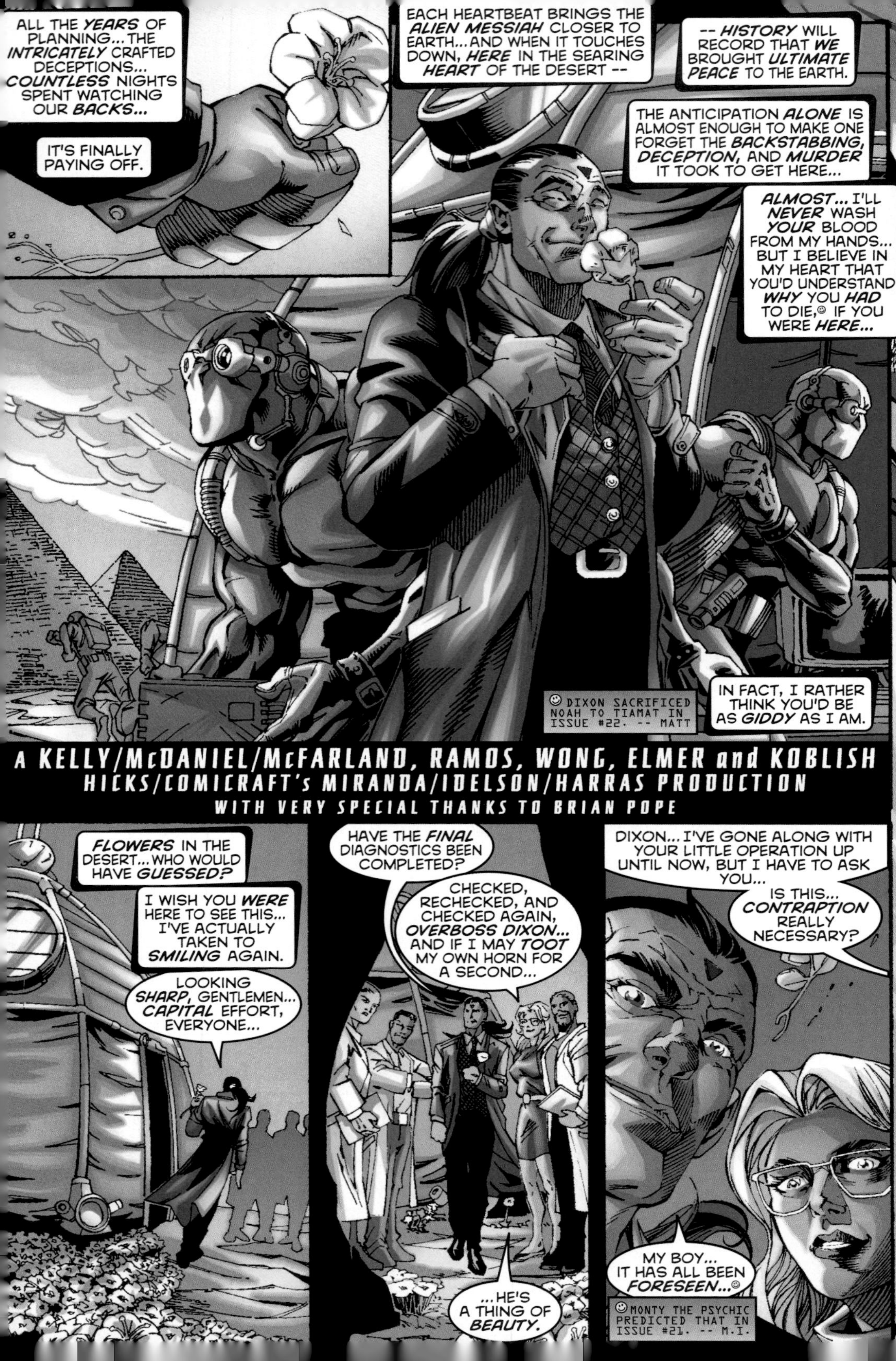
ALL THE YEARS OF PLANNING... THE INTRICATELY CRAFTED DECEPTIONS... COUNTLESS NIGHTS SPENT WATCHING OUR BACKS...
IT'S FINALLY PAYING OFF.
EACH HEARTBEAT BRINGS THE ALIEN MESSIAH CLOSER TO EARTH... AND WHEN IT TOUCHES DOWN, HERE IN THE SEARING HEART OF THE DESERT --
-- HISTORY WILL RECORD THAT WE BROUGHT ULTIMATE PEACE TO THE EARTH.
THE ANTICIPATION ALONE IS ALMOST ENOUGH TO MAKE ONE FORGET THE BACKSTABBING, DECEPTION, AND MURDER IT TOOK TO GET HERE...
ALMOST... I'LL NEVER WASH YOUR BLOOD FROM MY HANDS... BUT I BELIEVE IN MY HEART THAT YOU'D UNDERSTAND WHY YOU HAD TO DIE,☺ IF YOU WERE HERE...
☺ DIXON SACRIFICED NOAH TO TIAMAT IN ISSUE #22. -- MATT
IN FACT, I RATHER THINK YOU'D BE AS GIDDY AS I AM.
A KELLY/McDANIEL/McFARLAND, RAMOS, WONG, ELMER and KOBLISH HICKS/COMICRAFT's MIRANDA/IDELSON/HARRAS PRODUCTION
WITH VERY SPECIAL THANKS TO BRIAN POPE
FLOWERS IN THE DESERT... WHO WOULD HAVE GUESSED?
I WISH YOU WERE HERE TO SEE THIS... I'VE ACTUALLY TAKEN TO SMILING AGAIN.
LOOKING SHARP, GENTLEMEN... CAPITAL EFFORT, EVERYONE...
HAVE THE FINAL DIAGNOSTICS BEEN COMPLETED?
CHECKED, RECHECKED, AND CHECKED AGAIN, OVERBOSS DIXON... AND IF I MAY TOOT MY OWN HORN FOR A SECOND...
...HE'S A THING OF BEAUTY.
DIXON... I'VE GONE ALONG WITH YOUR LITTLE OPERATION UP UNTIL NOW, BUT I HAVE TO ASK YOU...
IS THIS... CONTRAPTION REALLY NECESSARY?
MY BOY... IT HAS ALL BEEN FORESEEN...☺
☺ MONTY THE PSYCHIC PREDICTED THAT IN ISSUE #21. -- M.I.

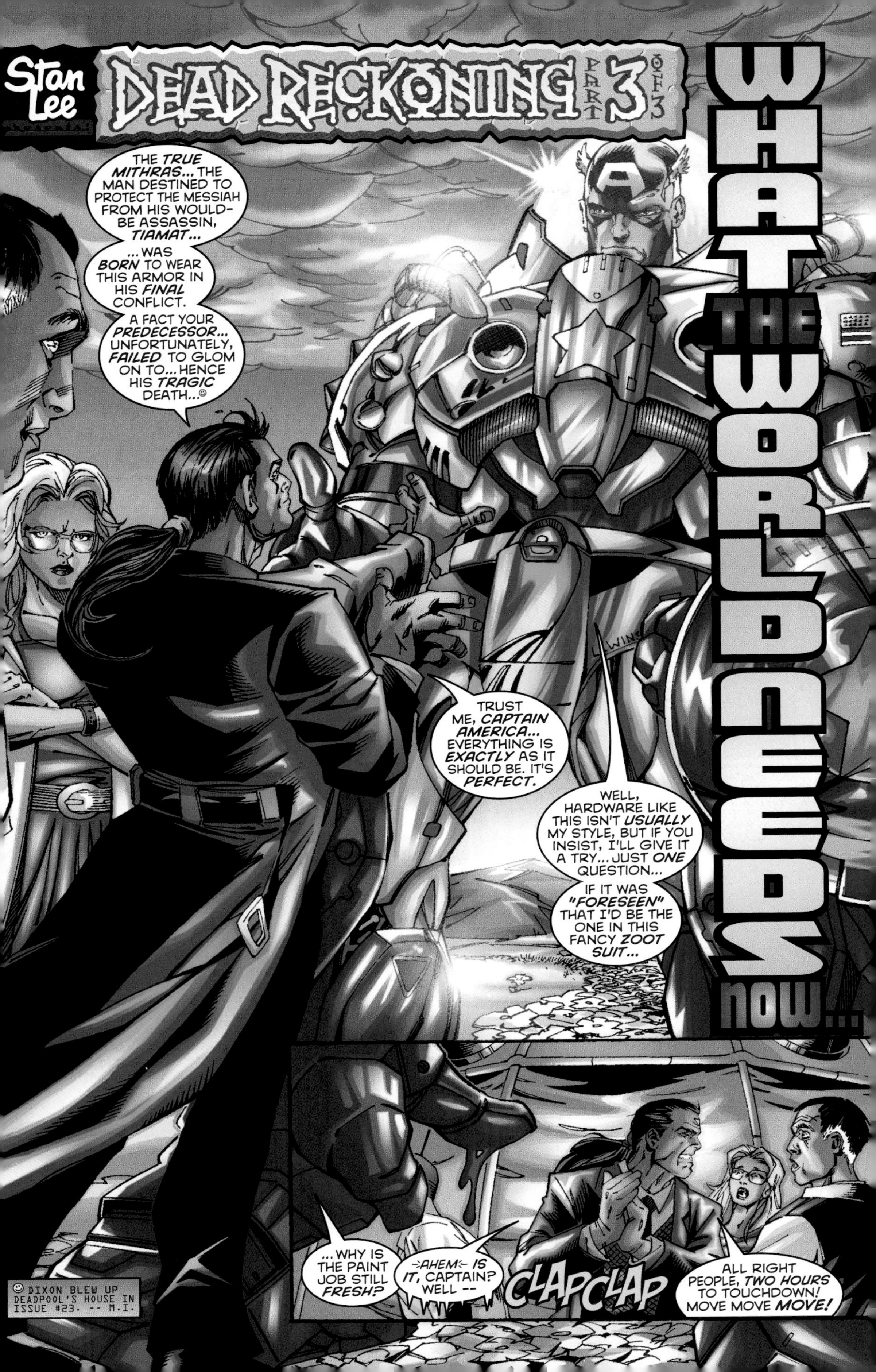
Stan Lee
DEAD RECKONING PART 3 OF 3
WHAT THE WORLD NEEDS NOW...
THE TRUE MITHRAS... THE MAN DESTINED TO PROTECT THE MESSIAH FROM HIS WOULD-BE ASSASSIN, TIAMAT...
...WAS BORN TO WEAR THIS ARMOR IN HIS FINAL CONFLICT.
A FACT YOUR PREDECESSOR... UNFORTUNATELY, FAILED TO GLOM ON TO... HENCE HIS TRAGIC DEATH...☺
TRUST ME, CAPTAIN AMERICA... EVERYTHING IS EXACTLY AS IT SHOULD BE. IT'S PERFECT.
WELL, HARDWARE LIKE THIS ISN'T USUALLY MY STYLE, BUT IF YOU INSIST, I'LL GIVE IT A TRY... JUST ONE QUESTION...
IF IT WAS "FORESEEN" THAT I'D BE THE ONE IN THIS FANCY ZOOT SUIT...
...WHY IS THE PAINT JOB STILL FRESH?
AHEM IS IT, CAPTAIN? WELL --
CLAPCLAP
ALL RIGHT PEOPLE, TWO HOURS TO TOUCHDOWN! MOVE MOVE MOVE!
☺ DIXON BLEW UP DEADPOOL'S HOUSE IN ISSUE #23. -- M.I.

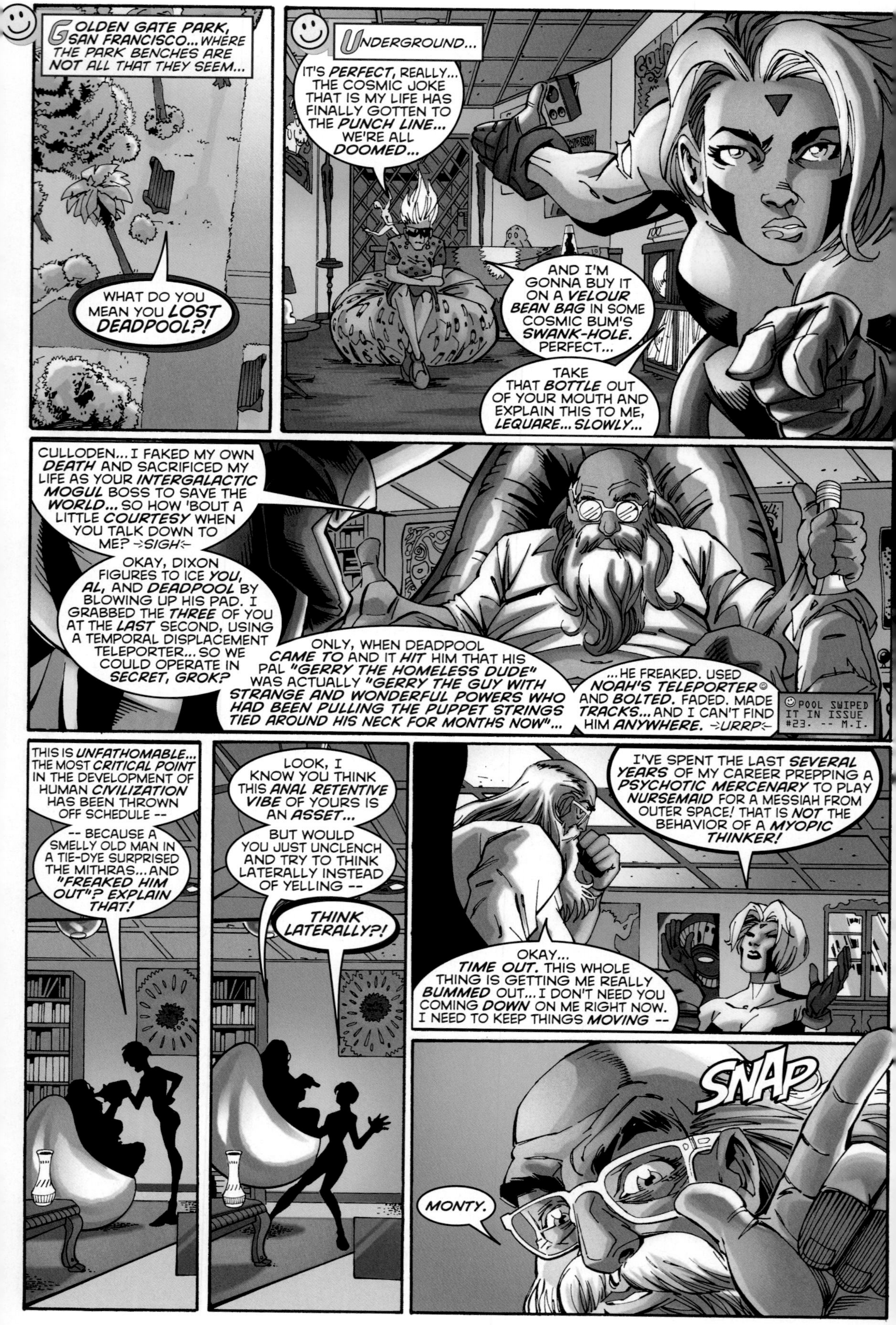
GOLDEN GATE PARK, SAN FRANCISCO... WHERE THE PARK BENCHES ARE NOT ALL THAT THEY SEEM...
WHAT DO YOU MEAN YOU LOST DEADPOOL?!
UNDERGROUND...
IT'S PERFECT, REALLY... THE COSMIC JOKE THAT IS MY LIFE HAS FINALLY GOTTEN TO THE PUNCH LINE... WE'RE ALL DOOMED...
AND I'M GONNA BUY IT ON A VELOUR BEAN BAG IN SOME COSMIC BUM'S SWANK-HOLE. PERFECT...
TAKE THAT BOTTLE OUT OF YOUR MOUTH AND EXPLAIN THIS TO ME, LEQUARE... SLOWLY...
CULLODEN... I FAKED MY OWN DEATH AND SACRIFICED MY LIFE AS YOUR INTERGALACTIC MOGUL BOSS TO SAVE THE WORLD... SO HOW 'BOUT A LITTLE COURTESY WHEN YOU TALK DOWN TO ME? -SIGH-
OKAY, DIXON FIGURES TO ICE YOU, AL, AND DEADPOOL BY BLOWING UP HIS PAD. I GRABBED THE THREE OF YOU AT THE LAST SECOND, USING A TEMPORAL DISPLACEMENT TELEPORTER... SO WE COULD OPERATE IN SECRET, GROK?
ONLY, WHEN DEADPOOL CAME TO AND IT HIT HIM THAT HIS PAL "GERRY THE HOMELESS DUDE" WAS ACTUALLY "GERRY THE GUY WITH STRANGE AND WONDERFUL POWERS WHO HAD BEEN PULLING THE PUPPET STRINGS TIED AROUND HIS NECK FOR MONTHS NOW"...
...HE FREAKED. USED NOAH'S TELEPORTER AND BOLTED. FADED. MADE TRACKS... AND I CAN'T FIND HIM ANYWHERE. -URRP-
POOL SWIPED IT IN ISSUE #23. -- M.I.
THIS IS UNFATHOMABLE... THE MOST CRITICAL POINT IN THE DEVELOPMENT OF HUMAN CIVILIZATION HAS BEEN THROWN OFF SCHEDULE --
-- BECAUSE A SMELLY OLD MAN IN A TIE-DYE SURPRISED THE MITHRAS... AND "FREAKED HIM OUT"? EXPLAIN THAT!
LOOK, I KNOW YOU THINK THIS ANAL RETENTIVE VIBE OF YOURS IS AN ASSET...
BUT WOULD YOU JUST UNCLENCH AND TRY TO THINK LATERALLY INSTEAD OF YELLING --
THINK LATERALLY?!
I'VE SPENT THE LAST SEVERAL YEARS OF MY CAREER PREPPING A PSYCHOTIC MERCENARY TO PLAY NURSEMAID FOR A MESSIAH FROM OUTER SPACE! THAT IS NOT THE BEHAVIOR OF A MYOPIC THINKER!
OKAY... TIME OUT. THIS WHOLE THING IS GETTING ME REALLY BUMMED OUT... I DON'T NEED YOU COMING DOWN ON ME RIGHT NOW. I NEED TO KEEP THINGS MOVING --
SNAP
MONTY.

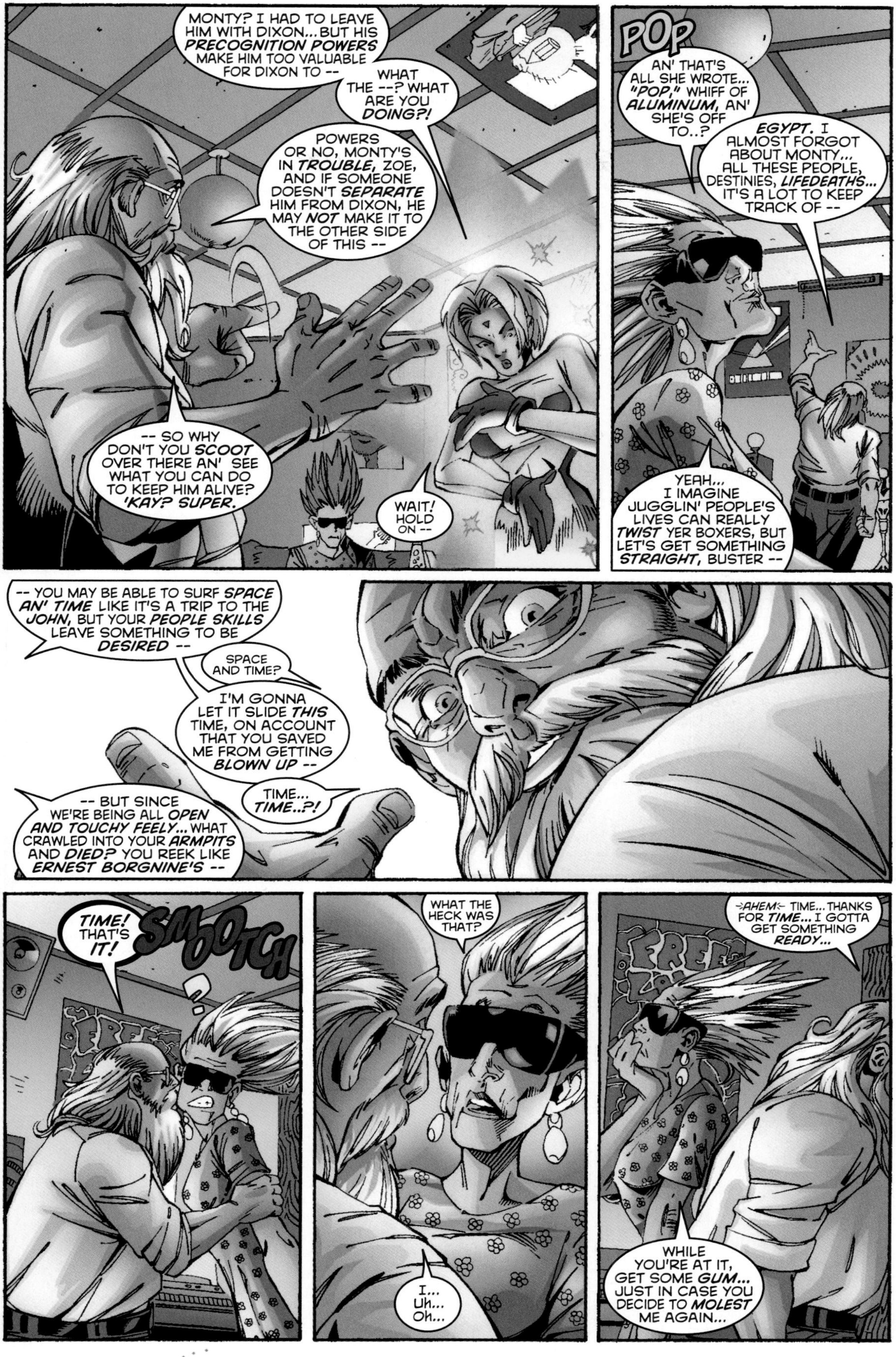
MONTY? I HAD TO LEAVE HIM WITH DIXON... BUT HIS PRECOGNITION POWERS MAKE HIM TOO VALUABLE FOR DIXON TO --
WHAT THE --? WHAT ARE YOU DOING?!
POWERS OR NO, MONTY'S IN TROUBLE, ZOE, AND IF SOMEONE DOESN'T SEPARATE HIM FROM DIXON, HE MAY NOT MAKE IT TO THE OTHER SIDE OF THIS --
-- SO WHY DON'T YOU SCOOT OVER THERE AN' SEE WHAT YOU CAN DO TO KEEP HIM ALIVE? 'KAY? SUPER.
WAIT! HOLD ON --
POP
AN' THAT'S ALL SHE WROTE... "POP," WHIFF OF ALUMINUM, AN' SHE'S OFF TO..?
EGYPT. I ALMOST FORGOT ABOUT MONTY... ALL THESE PEOPLE, DESTINIES, LIFEDEATHS... IT'S A LOT TO KEEP TRACK OF --
YEAH... I IMAGINE JUGGLIN' PEOPLE'S LIVES CAN REALLY TWIST YER BOXERS, BUT LET'S GET SOMETHING STRAIGHT, BUSTER --
-- YOU MAY BE ABLE TO SURF SPACE AN' TIME LIKE IT'S A TRIP TO THE JOHN, BUT YOUR PEOPLE SKILLS LEAVE SOMETHING TO BE DESIRED --
SPACE AND TIME?
I'M GONNA LET IT SLIDE THIS TIME, ON ACCOUNT THAT YOU SAVED ME FROM GETTING BLOWN UP --
TIME... TIME..?!
-- BUT SINCE WE'RE BEING ALL OPEN AND TOUCHY FEELY... WHAT CRAWLED INTO YOUR ARMPITS AND DIED? YOU REEK LIKE ERNEST BORGNINE'S --
TIME! THAT'S IT!
SMOOTCH
WHAT THE HECK WAS THAT?
I... Uh... Oh...
AHEM TIME... THANKS FOR TIME... I GOTTA GET SOMETHING READY...
WHILE YOU'RE AT IT, GET SOME GUM... JUST IN CASE YOU DECIDE TO MOLEST ME AGAIN...

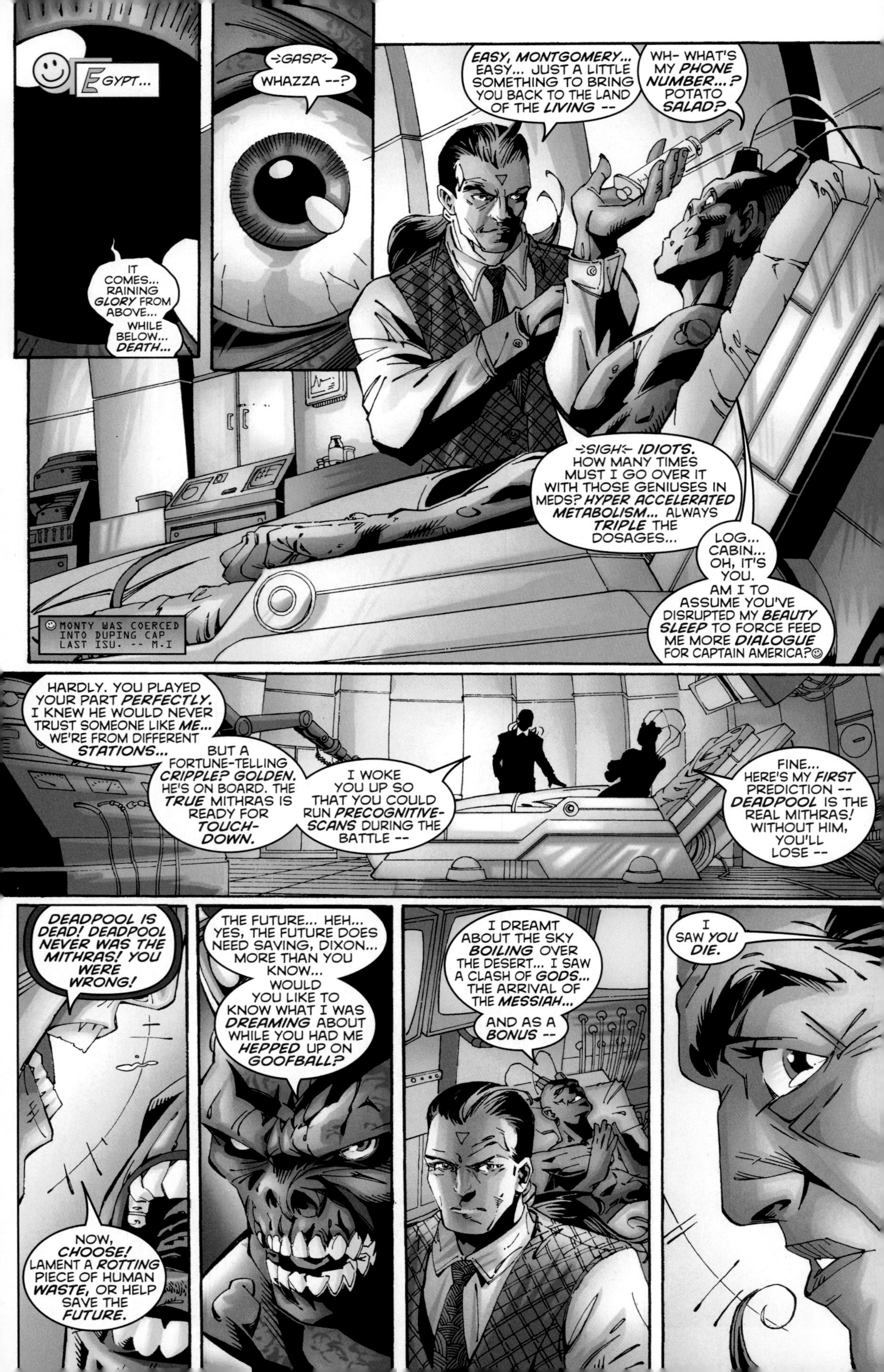
EGYPT...
IT COMES... RAINING GLORY FROM ABOVE... WHILE BELOW... DEATH...
>GASP< WHAZZA --?
EASY, MONTGOMERY... EASY... JUST A LITTLE SOMETHING TO BRING YOU BACK TO THE LAND OF THE LIVING --
WH- WHAT'S MY PHONE NUMBER...? POTATO SALAD?
>SIGH< IDIOTS. HOW MANY TIMES MUST I GO OVER IT WITH THOSE GENIUSES IN MEDS? HYPER ACCELERATED METABOLISM... ALWAYS TRIPLE THE DOSAGES...
LOG... CABIN... OH, IT'S YOU. AM I TO ASSUME YOU'VE DISRUPTED MY BEAUTY SLEEP TO FORCE FEED ME MORE DIALOGUE FOR CAPTAIN AMERICA?
MONTY WAS COERCED INTO DUPING CAP LAST ISU. -- M.I
HARDLY. YOU PLAYED YOUR PART PERFECTLY. I KNEW HE WOULD NEVER TRUST SOMEONE LIKE ME... WE'RE FROM DIFFERENT STATIONS...
BUT A FORTUNE-TELLING CRIPPLE? GOLDEN. HE'S ON BOARD. THE TRUE MITHRAS IS READY FOR TOUCH-DOWN.
I WOKE YOU UP SO THAT YOU COULD RUN PRECOGNITIVE-SCANS DURING THE BATTLE --
FINE... HERE'S MY FIRST PREDICTION -- DEADPOOL IS THE REAL MITHRAS! WITHOUT HIM, YOU'LL LOSE --
DEADPOOL IS DEAD! DEADPOOL NEVER WAS THE MITHRAS! YOU WERE WRONG!
NOW, CHOOSE! LAMENT A ROTTING PIECE OF HUMAN WASTE, OR HELP SAVE THE FUTURE.
THE FUTURE... HEH... YES, THE FUTURE DOES NEED SAVING, DIXON... MORE THAN YOU KNOW...
WOULD YOU LIKE TO KNOW WHAT I WAS DREAMING ABOUT WHILE YOU HAD ME HEPPED UP ON GOOFBALL?
I DREAMT ABOUT THE SKY BOILING OVER THE DESERT... I SAW A CLASH OF GODS... THE ARRIVAL OF THE MESSIAH...
AND AS A BONUS --
I SAW YOU DIE.

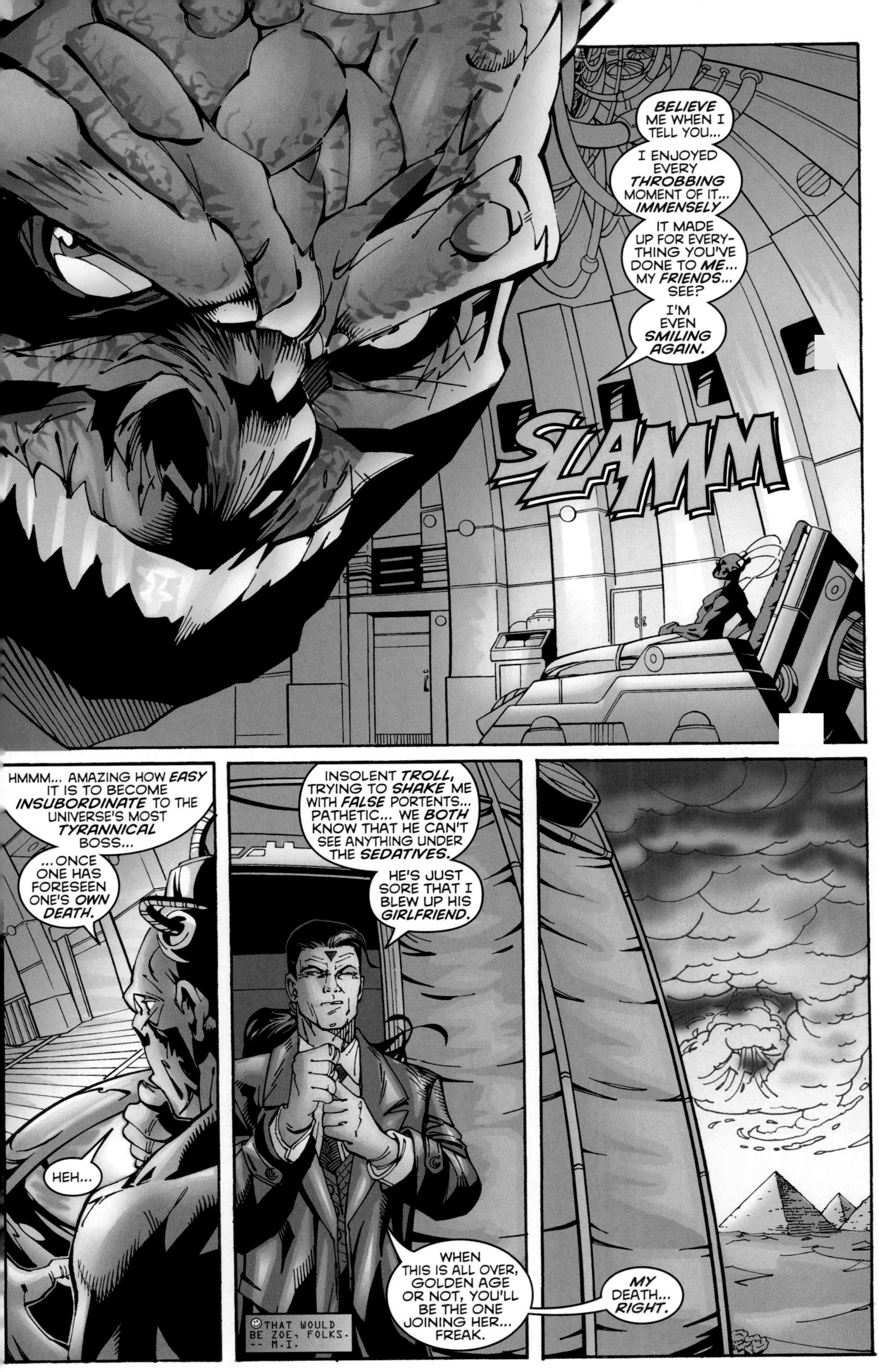
BELIEVE ME WHEN I TELL YOU...
I ENJOYED EVERY THROBBING MOMENT OF IT... IMMENSELY
IT MADE UP FOR EVERYTHING YOU'VE DONE TO ME... MY FRIENDS... SEE?
I'M EVEN SMILING AGAIN.
SLAMM
HMMM... AMAZING HOW EASY IT IS TO BECOME INSUBORDINATE TO THE UNIVERSE'S MOST TYRANNICAL BOSS...
...ONCE ONE HAS FORESEEN ONE'S OWN DEATH.
HEH...
INSOLENT TROLL, TRYING TO SHAKE ME WITH FALSE PORTENTS... PATHETIC... WE BOTH KNOW THAT HE CAN'T SEE ANYTHING UNDER THE SEDATIVES.
HE'S JUST SORE THAT I BLEW UP HIS GIRLFRIEND.
WHEN THIS IS ALL OVER, GOLDEN AGE OR NOT, YOU'LL BE THE ONE JOINING HER... FREAK.
☺THAT WOULD BE ZOE, FOLKS. -- M.I.
MY DEATH... RIGHT.

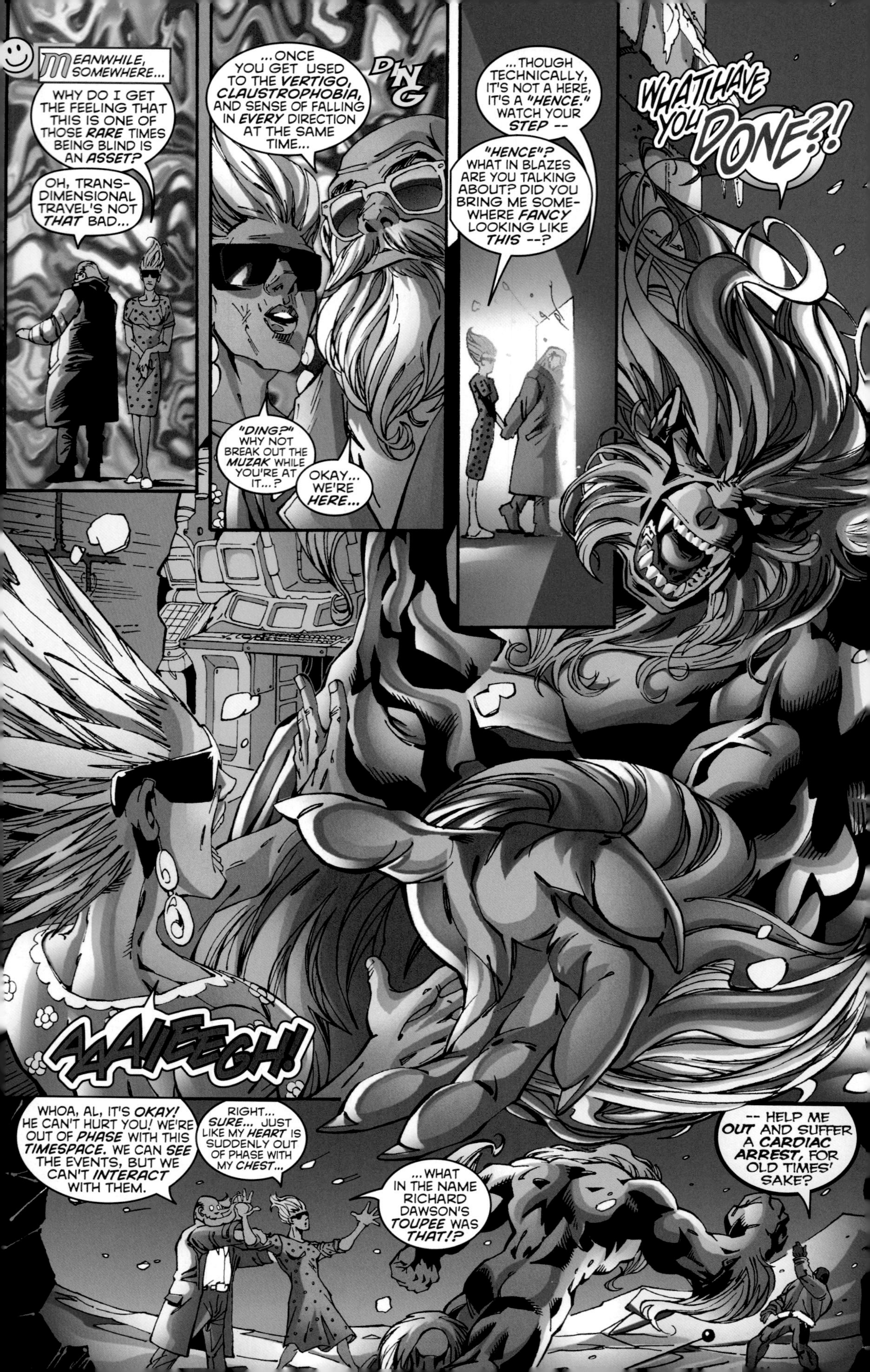
MEANWHILE, SOMEWHERE...
WHY DO I GET THE FEELING THAT THIS IS ONE OF THOSE RARE TIMES BEING BLIND IS AN ASSET?
OH, TRANS-DIMENSIONAL TRAVEL'S NOT THAT BAD...
...ONCE YOU GET USED TO THE VERTIGO, CLAUSTROPHOBIA, AND SENSE OF FALLING IN EVERY DIRECTION AT THE SAME TIME...
DING
"DING?" WHY NOT BREAK OUT THE MUZAK WHILE YOU'RE AT IT...?
OKAY... WE'RE HERE...
...THOUGH TECHNICALLY, IT'S NOT A HERE, IT'S A "HENCE." WATCH YOUR STEP --
"HENCE"? WHAT IN BLAZES ARE YOU TALKING ABOUT? DID YOU BRING ME SOME-WHERE FANCY LOOKING LIKE THIS --?
WHAT HAVE YOU DONE?!
AAAIEEGH!
WHOA, AL, IT'S OKAY! HE CAN'T HURT YOU! WE'RE OUT OF PHASE WITH THIS TIMESPACE. WE CAN SEE THE EVENTS, BUT WE CAN'T INTERACT WITH THEM.
RIGHT... SURE... JUST LIKE MY HEART IS SUDDENLY OUT OF PHASE WITH MY CHEST...
...WHAT IN THE NAME RICHARD DAWSON'S TOUPEE WAS THAT!?
-- HELP ME OUT AND SUFFER A CARDIAC ARREST, FOR OLD TIMES' SAKE?

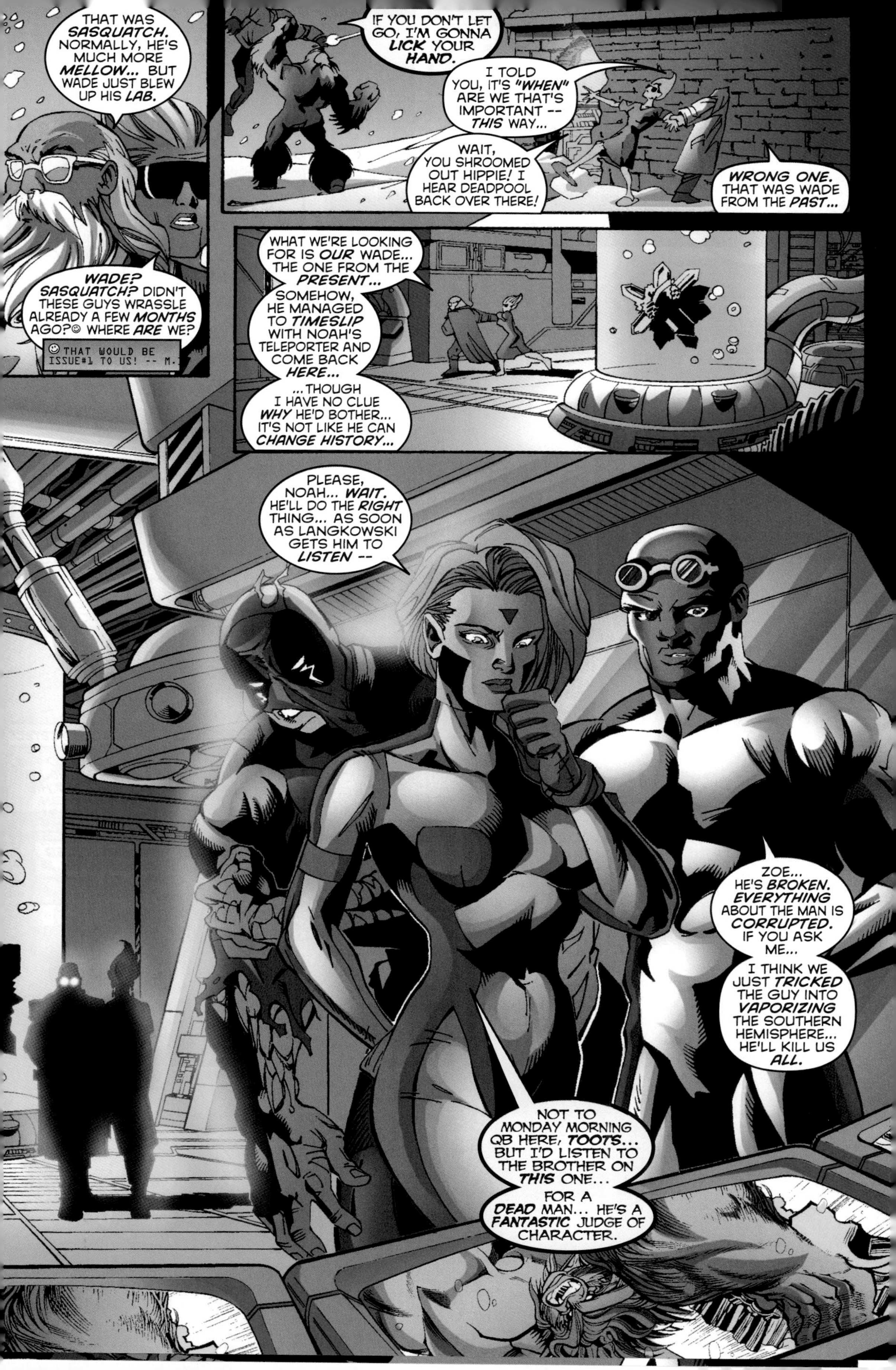
THAT WAS SASQUATCH. NORMALLY, HE'S MUCH MORE MELLOW... BUT WADE JUST BLEW UP HIS LAB.
WADE? SASQUATCH? DIDN'T THESE GUYS WRASSLE ALREADY A FEW MONTHS AGO?☺ WHERE ARE WE?
☺THAT WOULD BE ISSUE#1 TO US! -- M.
IF YOU DON'T LET GO, I'M GONNA LICK YOUR HAND.
I TOLD YOU, IT'S "WHEN" ARE WE THAT'S IMPORTANT -- THIS WAY...
WAIT, YOU SHROOMED OUT HIPPIE! I HEAR DEADPOOL BACK OVER THERE!
WRONG ONE. THAT WAS WADE FROM THE PAST...
WHAT WE'RE LOOKING FOR IS OUR WADE... THE ONE FROM THE PRESENT...
SOMEHOW, HE MANAGED TO TIMESLIP WITH NOAH'S TELEPORTER AND COME BACK HERE...
...THOUGH I HAVE NO CLUE WHY HE'D BOTHER... IT'S NOT LIKE HE CAN CHANGE HISTORY...
PLEASE, NOAH... WAIT. HE'LL DO THE RIGHT THING... AS SOON AS LANGKOWSKI GETS HIM TO LISTEN --
ZOE... HE'S BROKEN. EVERYTHING ABOUT THE MAN IS CORRUPTED. IF YOU ASK ME...
I THINK WE JUST TRICKED THE GUY INTO VAPORIZING THE SOUTHERN HEMISPHERE... HE'LL KILL US ALL.
NOT TO MONDAY MORNING QB HERE, TOOTS... BUT I'D LISTEN TO THE BROTHER ON THIS ONE...
FOR A DEAD MAN... HE'S A FANTASTIC JUDGE OF CHARACTER.

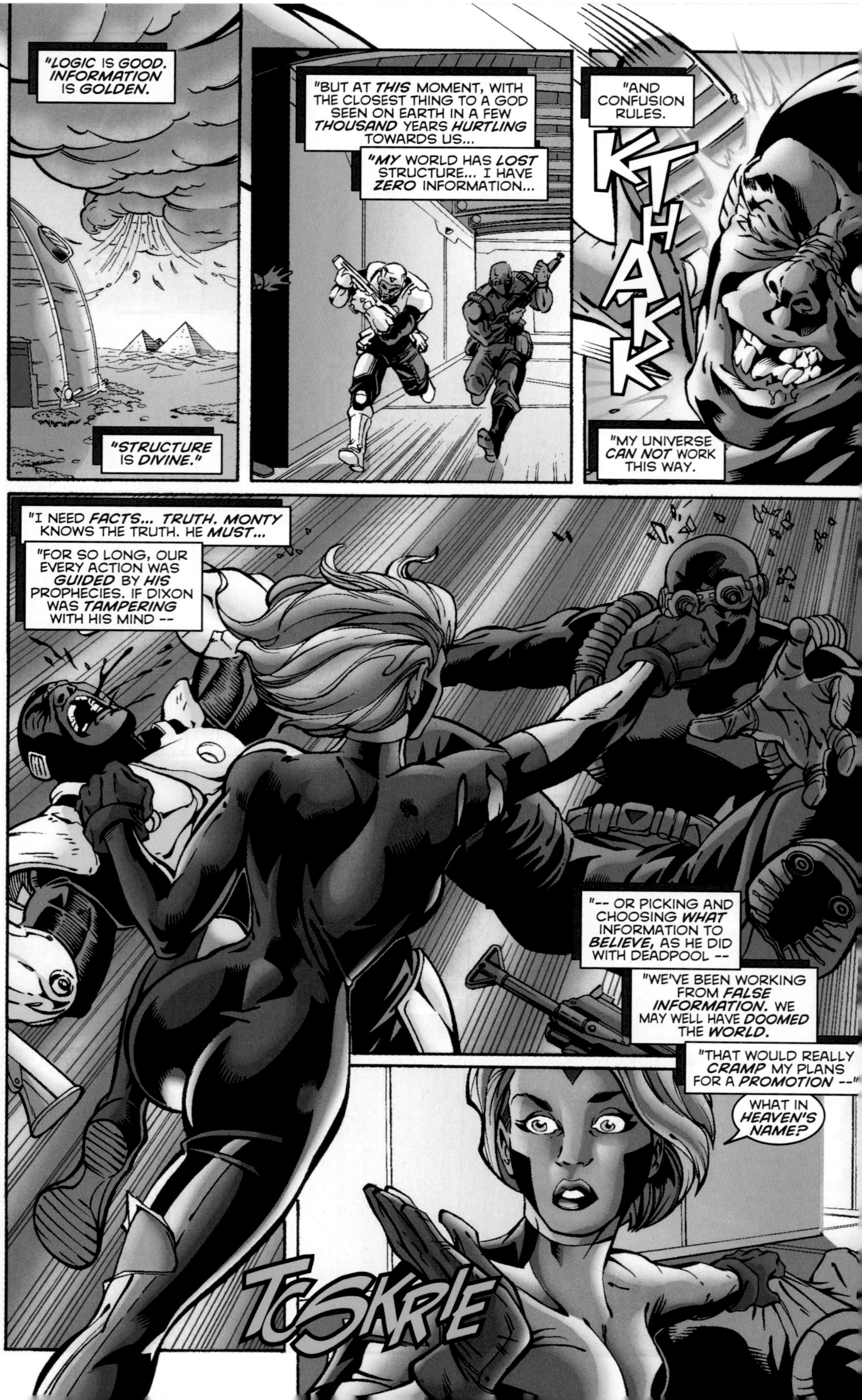
"LOGIC IS GOOD. INFORMATION IS GOLDEN.
"STRUCTURE IS DIVINE."
"BUT AT THIS MOMENT, WITH THE CLOSEST THING TO A GOD SEEN ON EARTH IN A FEW THOUSAND YEARS HURTLING TOWARDS US...
"MY WORLD HAS LOST STRUCTURE... I HAVE ZERO INFORMATION...
"AND CONFUSION RULES.
KTHAKK
"MY UNIVERSE CAN NOT WORK THIS WAY.
"I NEED FACTS... TRUTH. MONTY KNOWS THE TRUTH. HE MUST...
"FOR SO LONG, OUR EVERY ACTION WAS GUIDED BY HIS PROPHECIES. IF DIXON WAS TAMPERING WITH HIS MIND --
"-- OR PICKING AND CHOOSING WHAT INFORMATION TO BELIEVE, AS HE DID WITH DEADPOOL --
"WE'VE BEEN WORKING FROM FALSE INFORMATION. WE MAY WELL HAVE DOOMED THE WORLD.
"THAT WOULD REALLY CRAMP MY PLANS FOR A PROMOTION --"
WHAT IN HEAVEN'S NAME?
TCSKRIE

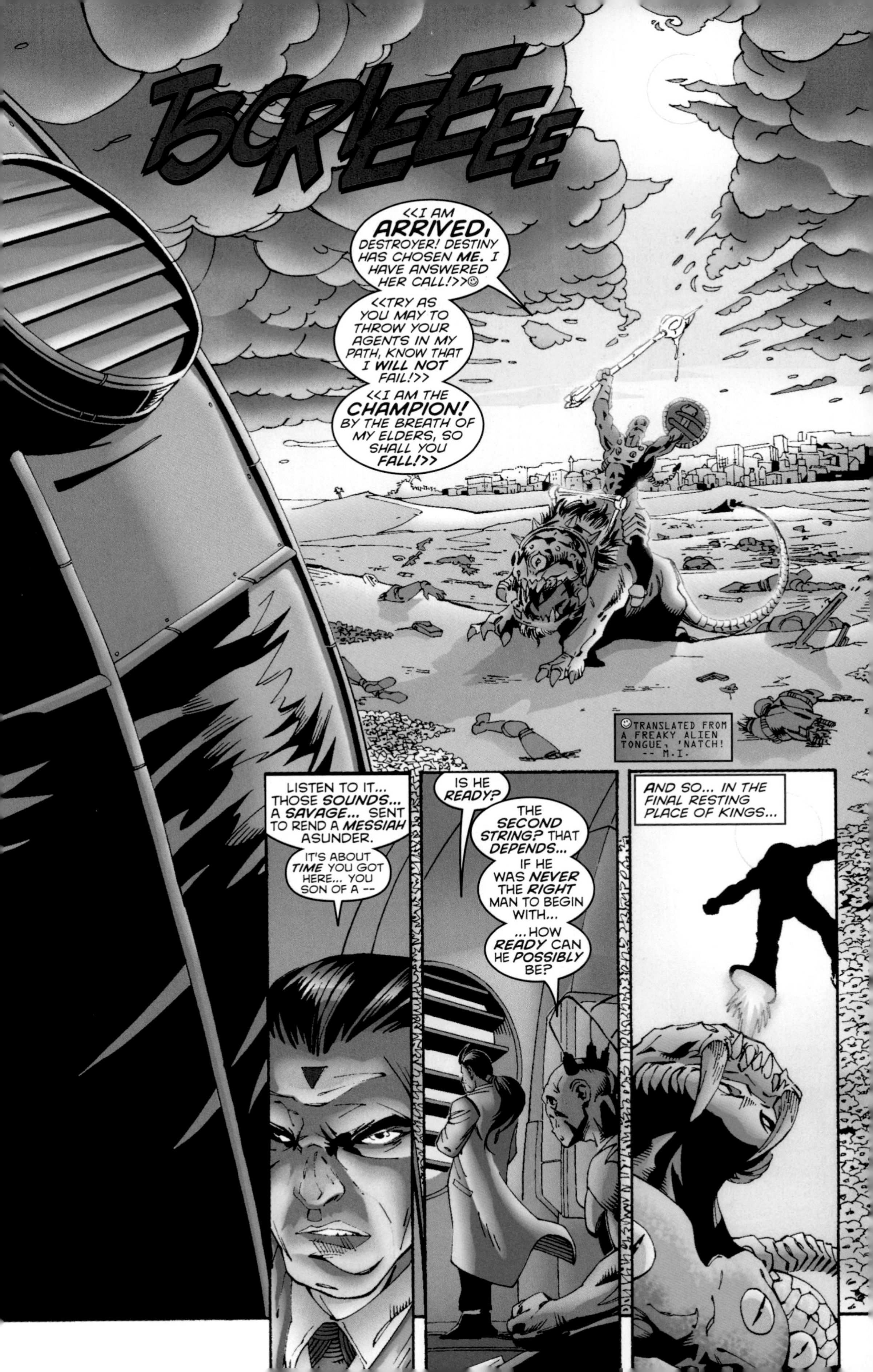
TSCRIEEEEE
<<I AM ARRIVED, DESTROYER! DESTINY HAS CHOSEN ME. I HAVE ANSWERED HER CALL!>>☺
<<TRY AS YOU MAY TO THROW YOUR AGENTS IN MY PATH, KNOW THAT I WILL NOT FAIL!>>
<<I AM THE CHAMPION! BY THE BREATH OF MY ELDERS, SO SHALL YOU FALL!>>
☺TRANSLATED FROM A FREAKY ALIEN TONGUE, 'NATCH! -- M.I.
LISTEN TO IT... THOSE SOUNDS... A SAVAGE... SENT TO REND A MESSIAH ASUNDER.
IT'S ABOUT TIME YOU GOT HERE... YOU SON OF A --
IS HE READY?
THE SECOND STRING? THAT DEPENDS... IF HE WAS NEVER THE RIGHT MAN TO BEGIN WITH...
...HOW READY CAN HE POSSIBLY BE?
AND SO... IN THE FINAL RESTING PLACE OF KINGS...

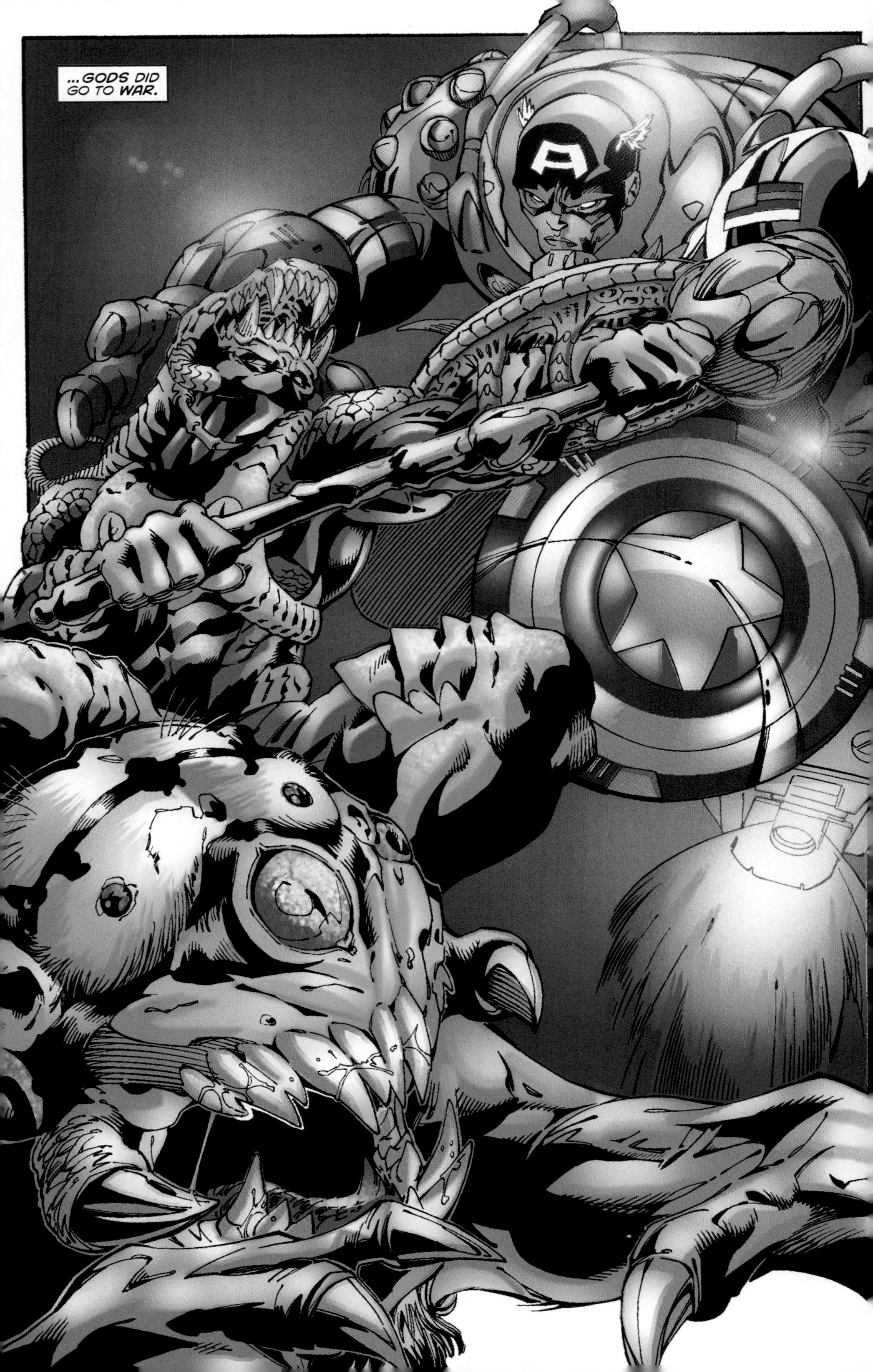
...GODS DID GO TO WAR.

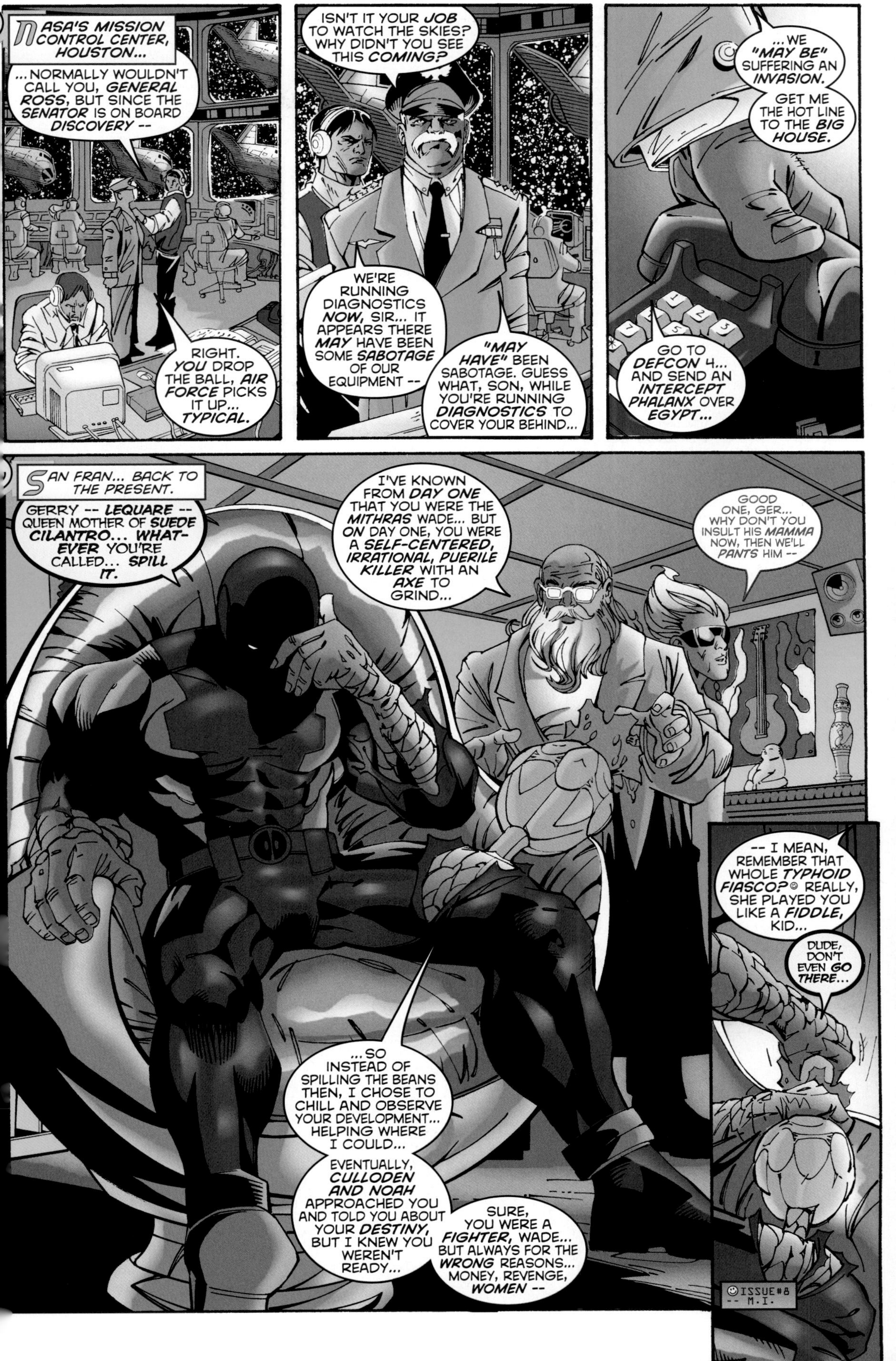
NASA'S MISSION CONTROL CENTER, HOUSTON...
...NORMALLY WOULDN'T CALL YOU, GENERAL ROSS, BUT SINCE THE SENATOR IS ON BOARD DISCOVERY --
RIGHT. YOU DROP THE BALL, AIR FORCE PICKS IT UP... TYPICAL.
ISN'T IT YOUR JOB TO WATCH THE SKIES? WHY DIDN'T YOU SEE THIS COMING?
WE'RE RUNNING DIAGNOSTICS NOW, SIR... IT APPEARS THERE MAY HAVE BEEN SOME SABOTAGE OF OUR EQUIPMENT --
"MAY HAVE" BEEN SABOTAGE. GUESS WHAT, SON, WHILE YOU'RE RUNNING DIAGNOSTICS TO COVER YOUR BEHIND...
...WE "MAY BE" SUFFERING AN INVASION.
GET ME THE HOT LINE TO THE BIG HOUSE.
GO TO DEFCON 4... AND SEND AN INTERCEPT PHALANX OVER EGYPT...
SAN FRAN... BACK TO THE PRESENT.
GERRY -- LEQUARE -- QUEEN MOTHER OF SUEDE CILANTRO... WHATEVER YOU'RE CALLED... SPILL IT.
I'VE KNOWN FROM DAY ONE THAT YOU WERE THE MITHRAS WADE... BUT ON DAY ONE, YOU WERE A SELF-CENTERED, IRRATIONAL, PUERILE KILLER WITH AN AXE TO GRIND...
GOOD ONE, GER... WHY DON'T YOU INSULT HIS MAMMA NOW, THEN WE'LL PANTS HIM --
...SO INSTEAD OF SPILLING THE BEANS THEN, I CHOSE TO CHILL AND OBSERVE YOUR DEVELOPMENT... HELPING WHERE I COULD...
EVENTUALLY, CULLODEN AND NOAH APPROACHED YOU AND TOLD YOU ABOUT YOUR DESTINY, BUT I KNEW YOU WEREN'T READY...
SURE, YOU WERE A FIGHTER, WADE... BUT ALWAYS FOR THE WRONG REASONS... MONEY, REVENGE, WOMEN --
-- I MEAN, REMEMBER THAT WHOLE TYPHOID FIASCO? REALLY, SHE PLAYED YOU LIKE A FIDDLE, KID...
DUDE, DON'T EVEN GO THERE...
ISSUE #8 -- M.I.

THINGS FINALLY STARTED TO CLICK ONCE I LET YOU GET *OBLITERATED* BY THAT MANIAC, *T-RAY* -- ☺

YOU *HEARD* ME. I *WANTED* HIM TO KICK THE *SNOT* OUT OF YOU...AND HE *DID*.

YOU *KNEW* HE --?! HOW COULD YOU PUT ME THROUGH *THAT*?!

I-I'M SORRY... THOUGHT YOU JUST SAID THAT YOU HAD A HAND IN ONE OF THE MOST *DEVASTATING* MOMENTS IN MY *YOUNG* LIFE... CLEARLY, *ONE* OF US IS HAVING AN *EPISODE*...

☺ ISH. #13. -- M.I.

IF YOU LIKED *THAT* ONE, WAIT... IT GETS *BETTER*.

I KNEW *THREE MONTHS* AGO YOU WERE GOING TO *LOSE* AGAINST *TIAMAT*, TOO.

BUT GUESS WHAT...? YOU *NEEDED* TO GET BEAT. EACH TIME YOU *SLAM* INTO A BRICK WALL YOU LEARN JUST A LITTLE MORE ABOUT YOURSELF... IT'S WHAT MAKES YOU *SPECIAL*.

AFTER *T-RAY*, YOU FIGURED OUT THAT *PLAYING* HERO AND *BEING* A HERO *AREN'T* THE SAME. AFTER *AJAX*,© YOU BELIEVED YOU WERE *WORTHY* OF A GLORIOUS DESTINY AND REACHED FOR THE *BRASS RING*. FINALLY, AFTER *TIAMAT*...

☺ ISH. #19. -- M.I.

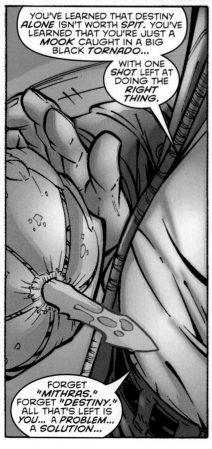

YOU'VE LEARNED THAT DESTINY *ALONE* ISN'T WORTH *SPIT*. YOU'VE LEARNED THAT YOU'RE JUST A *MOOK* CAUGHT IN A BIG BLACK *TORNADO*...

WITH ONE *SHOT* LEFT AT DOING THE *RIGHT THING*.

FORGET *"MITHRAS."* FORGET *"DESTINY."* ALL THAT'S LEFT IS *YOU*... A *PROBLEM*... A *SOLUTION*...

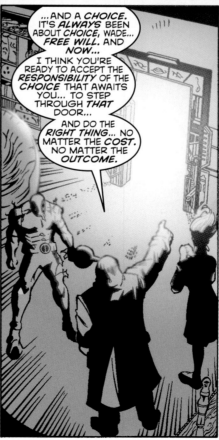

...AND A *CHOICE*. IT'S *ALWAYS* BEEN ABOUT *CHOICE*, WADE... *FREE WILL*. AND NOW...

I THINK YOU'RE READY TO ACCEPT THE *RESPONSIBILITY* OF THE *CHOICE* THAT AWAITS YOU... TO STEP THROUGH *THAT* DOOR...

AND DO THE *RIGHT THING*... NO MATTER THE *COST*. NO MATTER THE *OUTCOME*.

SO... WAS NOAH *RIGHT* ABOUT YOU...?

OR DID I ROYALLY *BLOW THIS* WHOLE *CAPER*?

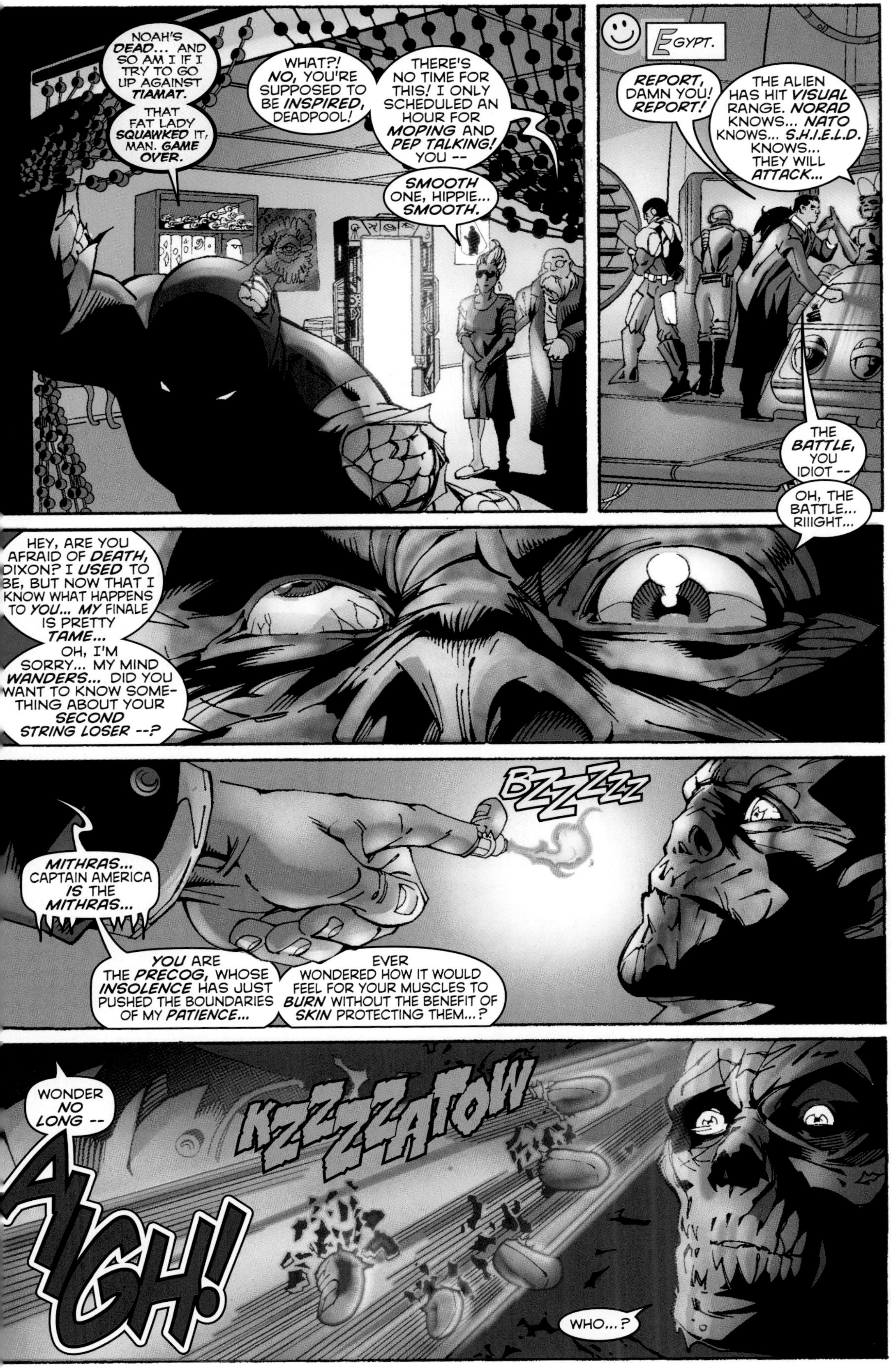
NOAH'S DEAD... AND SO AM I IF I TRY TO GO UP AGAINST TIAMAT.
THAT FAT LADY SQUAWKED IT, MAN. GAME OVER.
WHAT?! NO, YOU'RE SUPPOSED TO BE INSPIRED, DEADPOOL!
THERE'S NO TIME FOR THIS! I ONLY SCHEDULED AN HOUR FOR MOPING AND PEP TALKING! YOU --
SMOOTH ONE, HIPPIE... SMOOTH.
EGYPT.
REPORT, DAMN YOU! REPORT!
THE ALIEN HAS HIT VISUAL RANGE. NORAD KNOWS... NATO KNOWS... S.H.I.E.L.D. KNOWS... THEY WILL ATTACK...
THE BATTLE, YOU IDIOT --
OH, THE BATTLE... RIIIGHT...
HEY, ARE YOU AFRAID OF DEATH, DIXON? I USED TO BE, BUT NOW THAT I KNOW WHAT HAPPENS TO YOU... MY FINALE IS PRETTY TAME...
OH, I'M SORRY... MY MIND WANDERS... DID YOU WANT TO KNOW SOMETHING ABOUT YOUR SECOND STRING LOSER --?
BZZZZZ
MITHRAS... CAPTAIN AMERICA IS THE MITHRAS...
YOU ARE THE PRECOG, WHOSE INSOLENCE HAS JUST PUSHED THE BOUNDARIES OF MY PATIENCE...
EVER WONDERED HOW IT WOULD FEEL FOR YOUR MUSCLES TO BURN WITHOUT THE BENEFIT OF SKIN PROTECTING THEM...?
WONDER NO LONG --
KZZZZZATOW
AIGH!
WHO...?

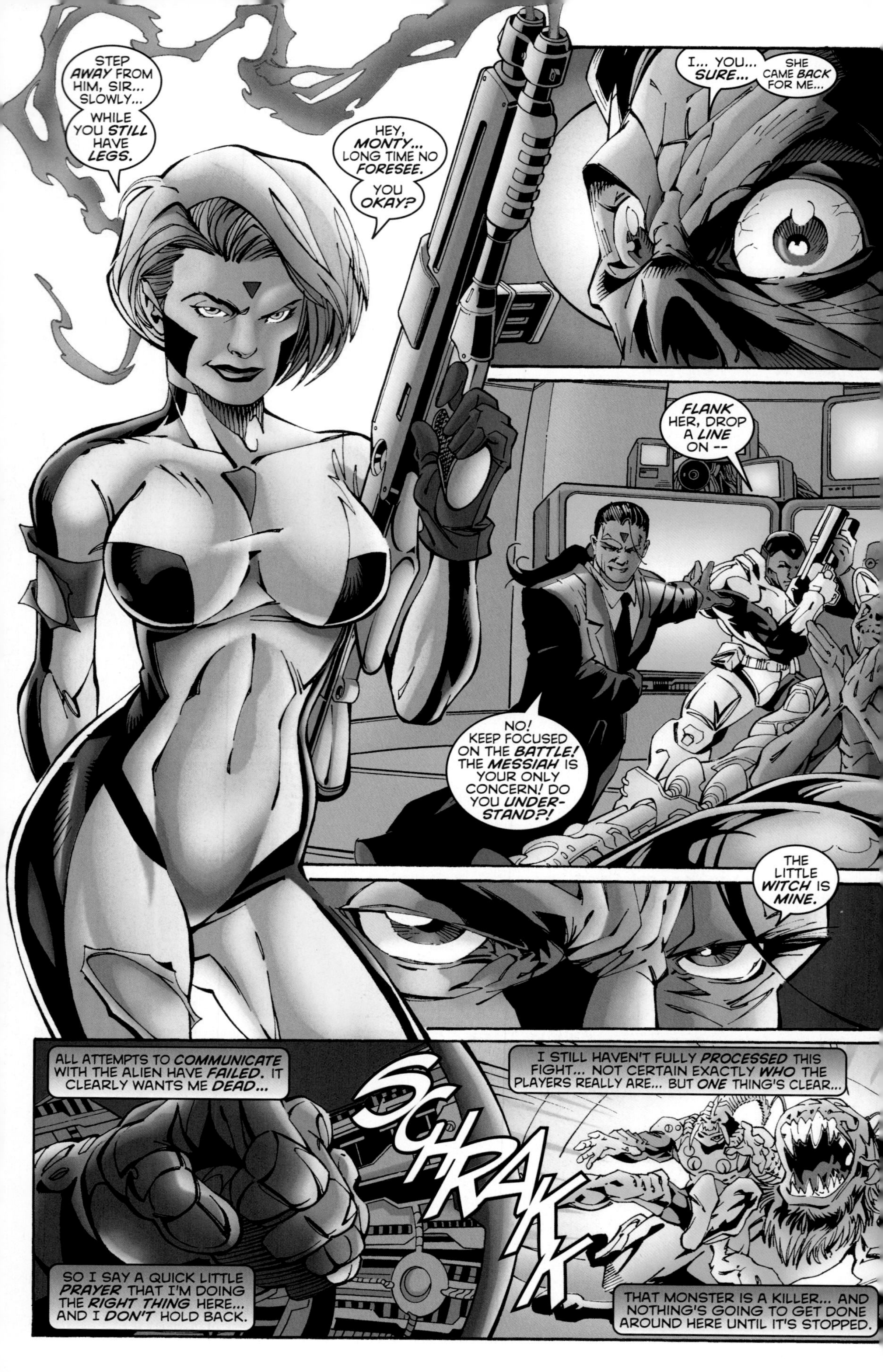

STEP AWAY FROM HIM, SIR... SLOWLY... WHILE YOU STILL HAVE LEGS.
HEY, MONTY... LONG TIME NO FORESEE.
YOU OKAY?
I... YOU... SURE...
SHE CAME BACK FOR ME...
FLANK HER, DROP A LINE ON --
NO! KEEP FOCUSED ON THE BATTLE! THE MESSIAH IS YOUR ONLY CONCERN! DO YOU UNDER-STAND?!
THE LITTLE WITCH IS MINE.
ALL ATTEMPTS TO COMMUNICATE WITH THE ALIEN HAVE FAILED. IT CLEARLY WANTS ME DEAD...
SCHRAKK
I STILL HAVEN'T FULLY PROCESSED THIS FIGHT... NOT CERTAIN EXACTLY WHO THE PLAYERS REALLY ARE... BUT ONE THING'S CLEAR...
SO I SAY A QUICK LITTLE PRAYER THAT I'M DOING THE RIGHT THING HERE... AND I DON'T HOLD BACK.
THAT MONSTER IS A KILLER... AND NOTHING'S GOING TO GET DONE AROUND HERE UNTIL IT'S STOPPED.

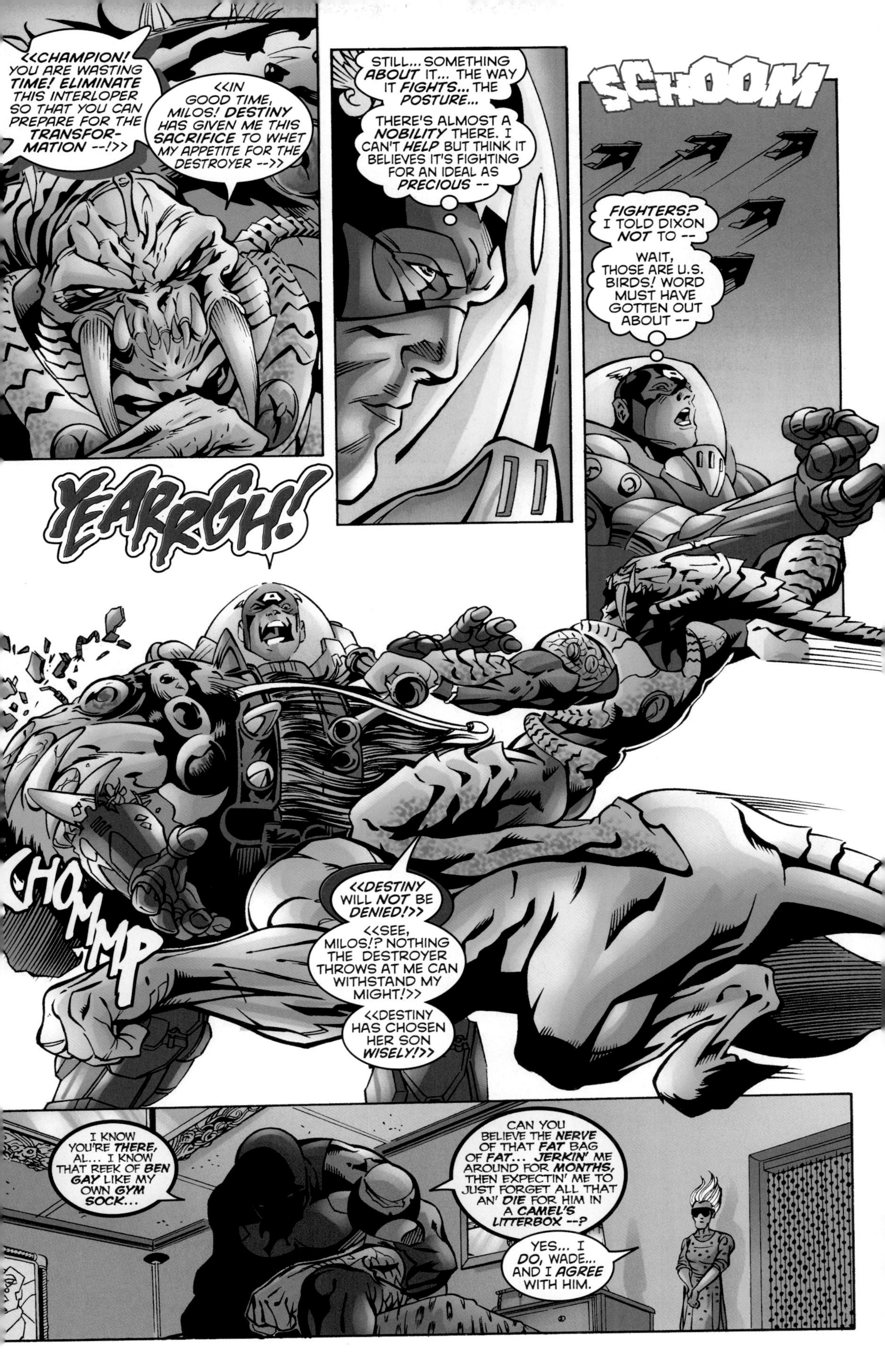

<<CHAMPION! YOU ARE WASTING TIME! ELIMINATE THIS INTERLOPER SO THAT YOU CAN PREPARE FOR THE TRANSFORMATION --!>>
<<IN GOOD TIME, MILOS! DESTINY HAS GIVEN ME THIS SACRIFICE TO WHET MY APPETITE FOR THE DESTROYER -->>
STILL... SOMETHING ABOUT IT... THE WAY IT FIGHTS... THE POSTURE...
THERE'S ALMOST A NOBILITY THERE. I CAN'T HELP BUT THINK IT BELIEVES IT'S FIGHTING FOR AN IDEAL AS PRECIOUS --
SCHOOM
FIGHTERS? I TOLD DIXON NOT TO --
WAIT, THOSE ARE U.S. BIRDS! WORD MUST HAVE GOTTEN OUT ABOUT --
YEARRGH!
CHOMMP
<<DESTINY WILL NOT BE DENIED!>>
<<SEE, MILOS!? NOTHING THE DESTROYER THROWS AT ME CAN WITHSTAND MY MIGHT!>>
<<DESTINY HAS CHOSEN HER SON WISELY!>>
I KNOW YOU'RE THERE, AL... I KNOW THAT REEK OF BEN GAY LIKE MY OWN GYM SOCK...
CAN YOU BELIEVE THE NERVE OF THAT FAT BAG OF FAT... JERKIN' ME AROUND FOR MONTHS, THEN EXPECTIN' ME TO JUST FORGET ALL THAT AN' DIE FOR HIM IN A CAMEL'S LITTERBOX --?
YES... I DO, WADE... AND I AGREE WITH HIM.

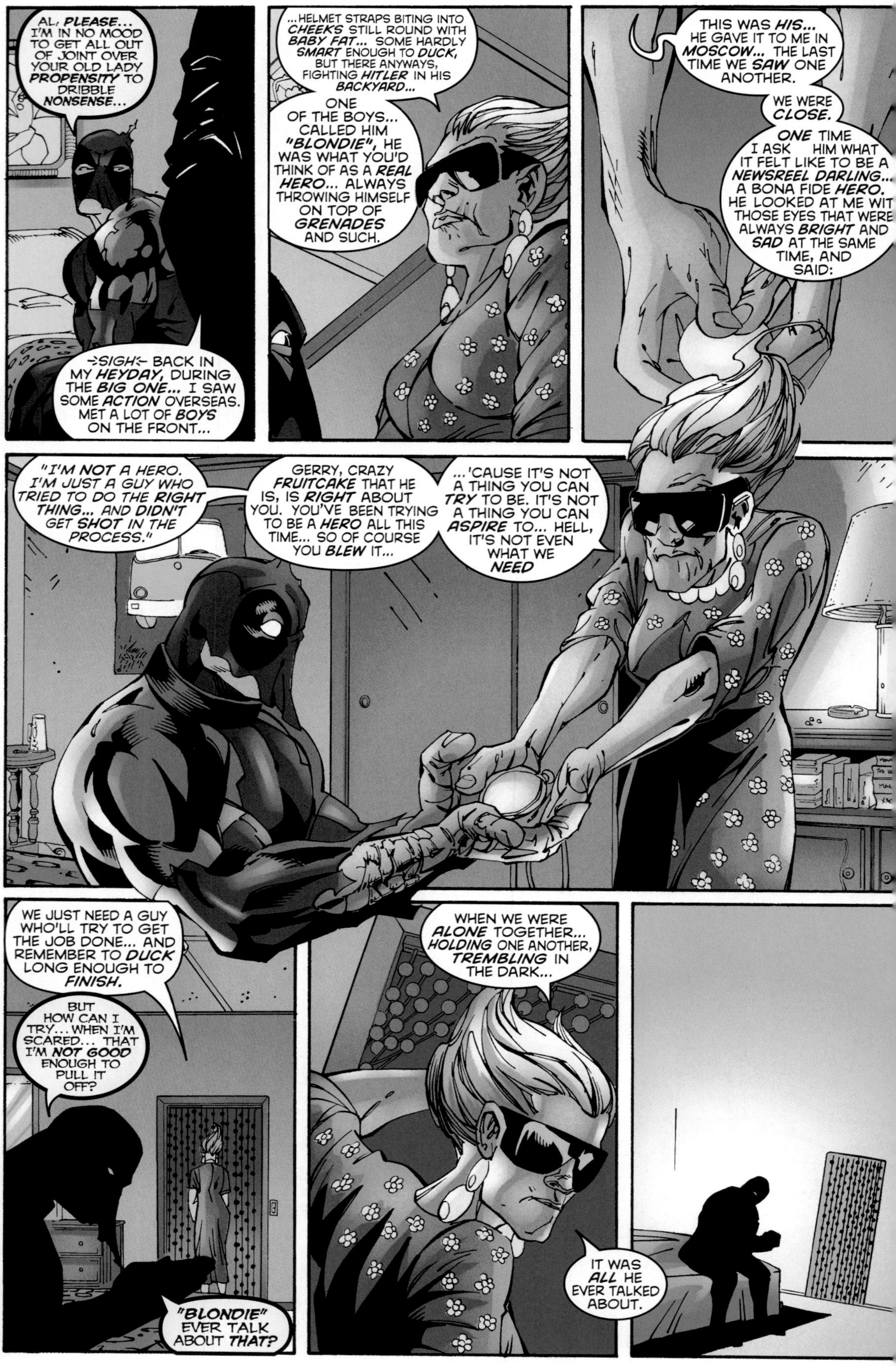
AL, PLEASE... I'M IN NO MOOD TO GET ALL OUT OF JOINT OVER YOUR OLD LADY PROPENSITY TO DRIBBLE NONSENSE...
~SIGH~ BACK IN MY HEYDAY, DURING THE BIG ONE... I SAW SOME ACTION OVERSEAS. MET A LOT OF BOYS ON THE FRONT...
...HELMET STRAPS BITING INTO CHEEKS STILL ROUND WITH BABY FAT... SOME HARDLY SMART ENOUGH TO DUCK, BUT THERE ANYWAYS, FIGHTING HITLER IN HIS BACKYARD...
ONE OF THE BOYS... CALLED HIM "BLONDIE", HE WAS WHAT YOU'D THINK OF AS A REAL HERO... ALWAYS THROWING HIMSELF ON TOP OF GRENADES AND SUCH.
THIS WAS HIS... HE GAVE IT TO ME IN MOSCOW... THE LAST TIME WE SAW ONE ANOTHER.
WE WERE CLOSE.
ONE TIME I ASK HIM WHAT IT FELT LIKE TO BE A NEWSREEL DARLING... A BONA FIDE HERO. HE LOOKED AT ME WIT THOSE EYES THAT WERE ALWAYS BRIGHT AND SAD AT THE SAME TIME, AND SAID:
"I'M NOT A HERO. I'M JUST A GUY WHO TRIED TO DO THE RIGHT THING... AND DIDN'T GET SHOT IN THE PROCESS."
GERRY, CRAZY FRUITCAKE THAT HE IS, IS RIGHT ABOUT YOU. YOU'VE BEEN TRYING TO BE A HERO ALL THIS TIME... SO OF COURSE YOU BLEW IT...
...'CAUSE IT'S NOT A THING YOU CAN TRY TO BE. IT'S NOT A THING YOU CAN ASPIRE TO... HELL, IT'S NOT EVEN WHAT WE NEED
WE JUST NEED A GUY WHO'LL TRY TO GET THE JOB DONE... AND REMEMBER TO DUCK LONG ENOUGH TO FINISH.
BUT HOW CAN I TRY... WHEN I'M SCARED... THAT I'M NOT GOOD ENOUGH TO PULL IT OFF?
"BLONDIE" EVER TALK ABOUT THAT?
WHEN WE WERE ALONE TOGETHER... HOLDING ONE ANOTHER, TREMBLING IN THE DARK...
IT WAS ALL HE EVER TALKED ABOUT.

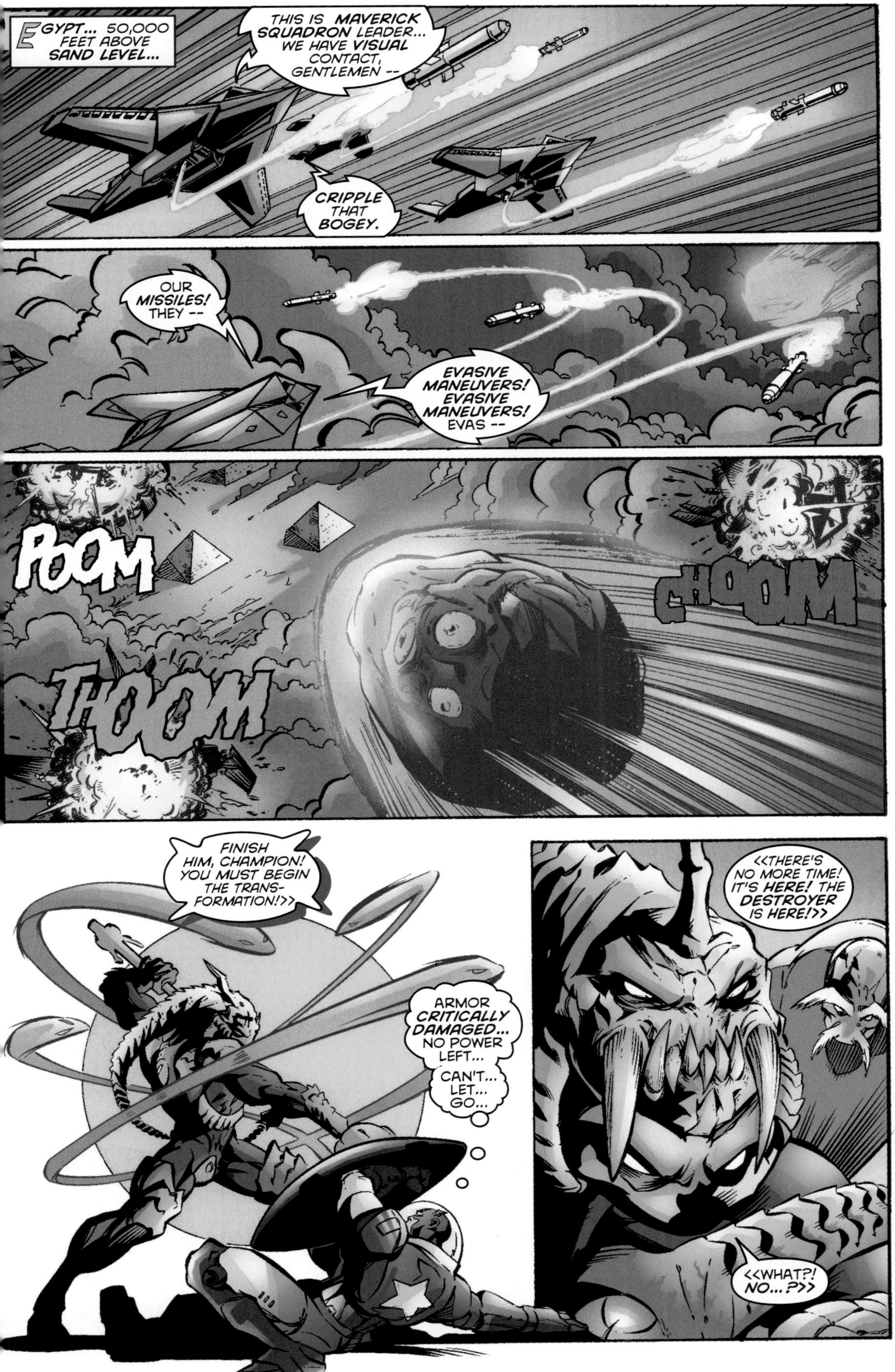
EGYPT... 50,000 FEET ABOVE SAND LEVEL...
THIS IS MAVERICK SQUADRON LEADER... WE HAVE VISUAL CONTACT, GENTLEMEN --
CRIPPLE THAT BOGEY.
OUR MISSILES! THEY --
EVASIVE MANEUVERS! EVASIVE MANEUVERS! EVAS --
POOM
CHOOM
THOOM
FINISH HIM, CHAMPION! YOU MUST BEGIN THE TRANS-FORMATION!>>
ARMOR CRITICALLY DAMAGED... NO POWER LEFT...
CAN'T... LET... GO...
<<THERE'S NO MORE TIME! IT'S HERE! THE DESTROYER IS HERE!>>
<<WHAT?! NO...?>>

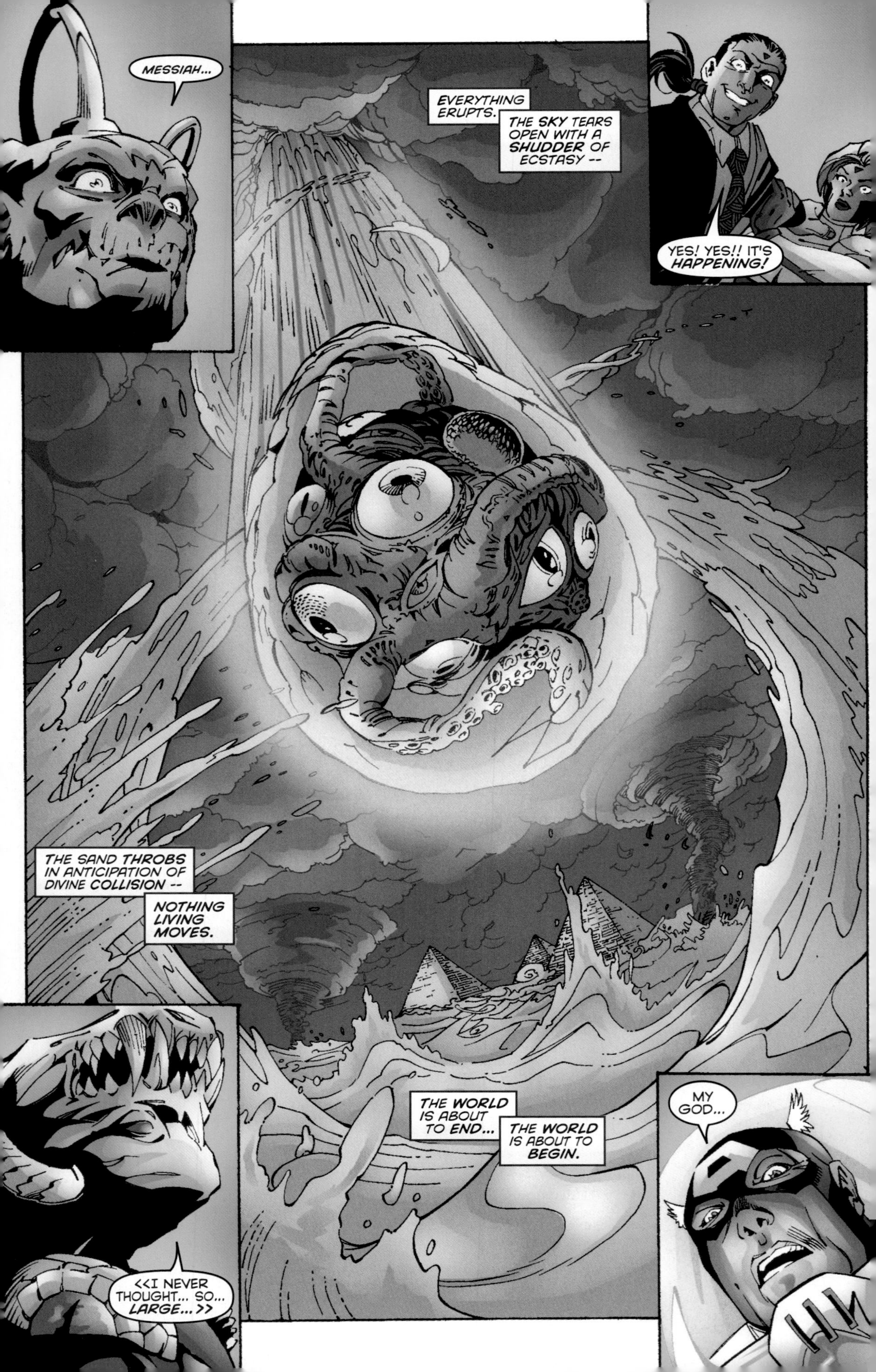
MESSIAH...
EVERYTHING ERUPTS.
THE SKY TEARS OPEN WITH A SHUDDER OF ECSTASY --
YES! YES!! IT'S HAPPENING!
THE SAND THROBS IN ANTICIPATION OF DIVINE COLLISION --
NOTHING LIVING MOVES.
<<I NEVER THOUGHT... SO... LARGE...>>
THE WORLD IS ABOUT TO END...
THE WORLD IS ABOUT TO BEGIN.
MY GOD...

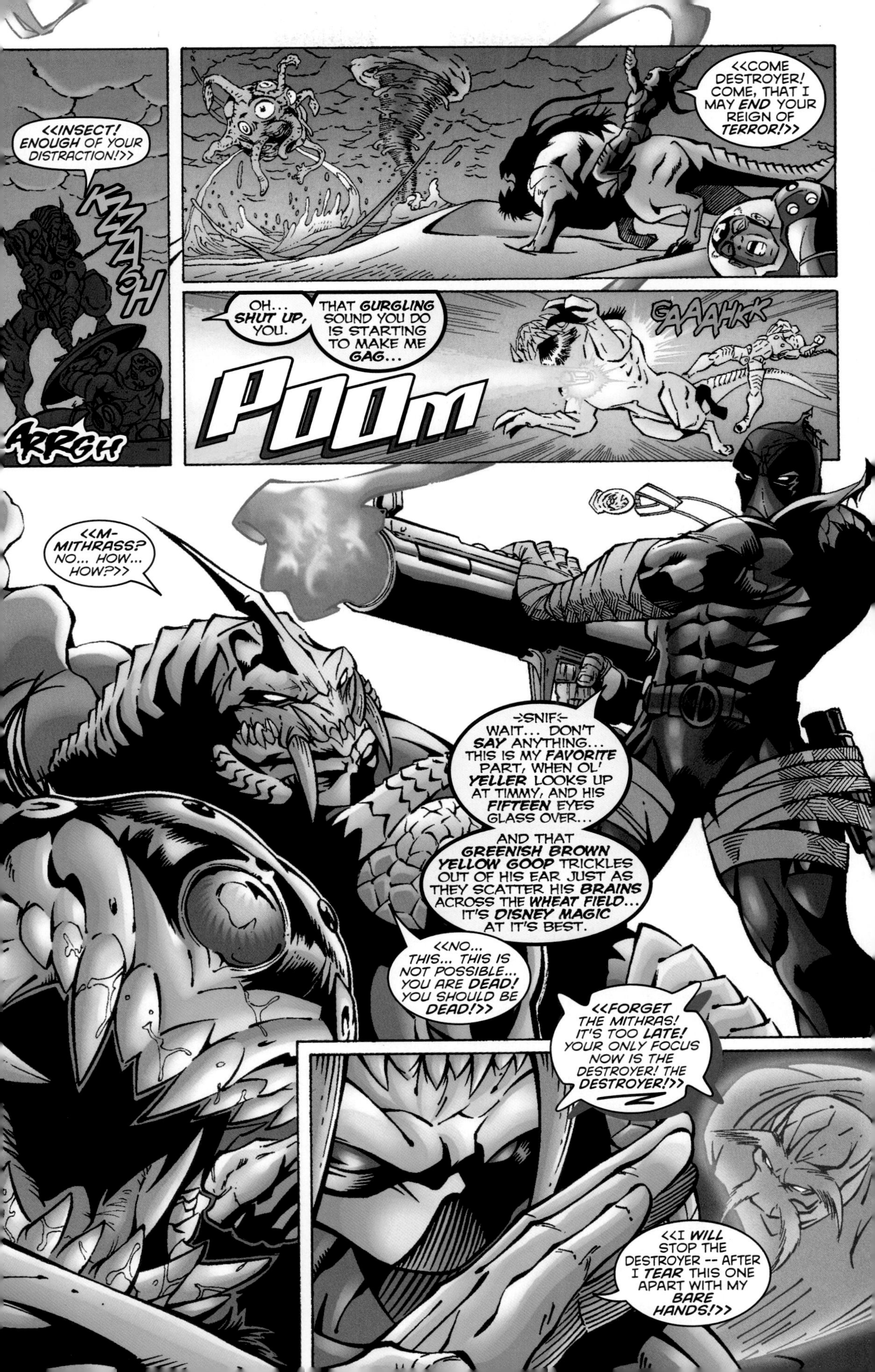

<<INSECT! ENOUGH OF YOUR DISTRACTION!>>
KRAAGH
ARRGH!
<<COME DESTROYER! COME, THAT I MAY END YOUR REIGN OF TERROR!>>
OH... SHUT UP, YOU.
THAT GURGLING SOUND YOU DO IS STARTING TO MAKE ME GAG...
POOM
GAAAHKK
<<M-MITHRASS? NO... HOW... HOW?>>
=SNIF= WAIT... DON'T SAY ANYTHING... THIS IS MY FAVORITE PART, WHEN OL' YELLER LOOKS UP AT TIMMY, AND HIS FIFTEEN EYES GLASS OVER...
AND THAT GREENISH BROWN YELLOW GOOP TRICKLES OUT OF HIS EAR JUST AS THEY SCATTER HIS BRAINS ACROSS THE WHEAT FIELD... IT'S DISNEY MAGIC AT IT'S BEST.
<<NO... THIS... THIS IS NOT POSSIBLE... YOU ARE DEAD! YOU SHOULD BE DEAD!>>
<<FORGET THE MITHRAS! IT'S TOO LATE! YOUR ONLY FOCUS NOW IS THE DESTROYER! THE DESTROYER!>>
<<I WILL STOP THE DESTROYER -- AFTER I TEAR THIS ONE APART WITH MY BARE HANDS!>>

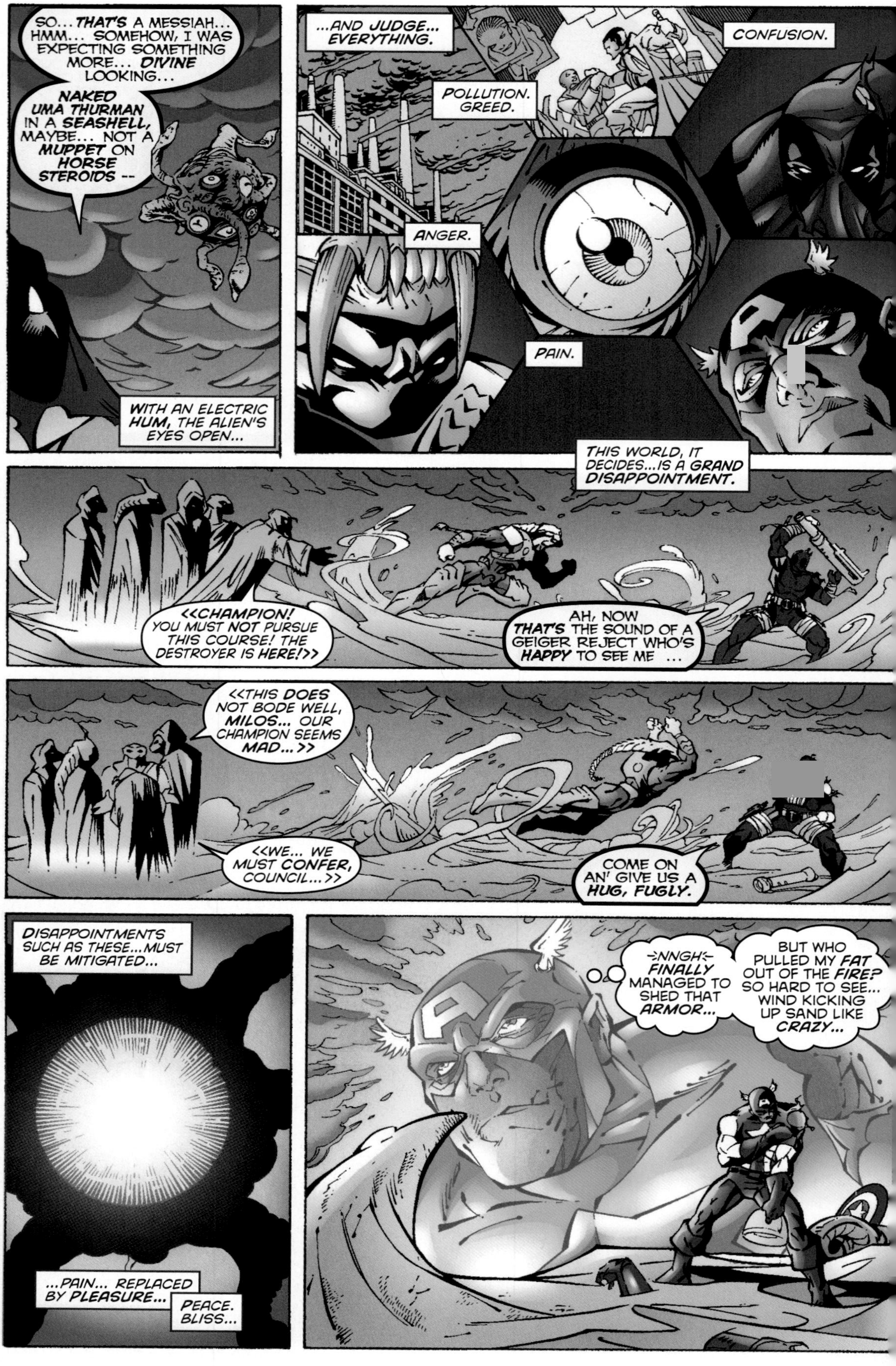
SO... THAT'S A MESSIAH... HMM... SOMEHOW, I WAS EXPECTING SOMETHING MORE... DIVINE LOOKING...
NAKED UMA THURMAN IN A SEASHELL, MAYBE... NOT A MUPPET ON HORSE STEROIDS --
WITH AN ELECTRIC HUM, THE ALIEN'S EYES OPEN...
...AND JUDGE... EVERYTHING.
POLLUTION. GREED.
CONFUSION.
ANGER.
PAIN.
THIS WORLD, IT DECIDES...IS A GRAND DISAPPOINTMENT.
<<CHAMPION! YOU MUST NOT PURSUE THIS COURSE! THE DESTROYER IS HERE!>>
AH, NOW THAT'S THE SOUND OF A GEIGER REJECT WHO'S HAPPY TO SEE ME ...
<<THIS DOES NOT BODE WELL, MILOS... OUR CHAMPION SEEMS MAD...>>
<<WE... WE MUST CONFER, COUNCIL...>>
COME ON AN' GIVE US A HUG, FUGLY.
DISAPPOINTMENTS SUCH AS THESE...MUST BE MITIGATED...
...PAIN... REPLACED BY PLEASURE...
PEACE. BLISS...
-NNGH- FINALLY MANAGED TO SHED THAT ARMOR...
BUT WHO PULLED MY FAT OUT OF THE FIRE? SO HARD TO SEE... WIND KICKING UP SAND LIKE CRAZY...

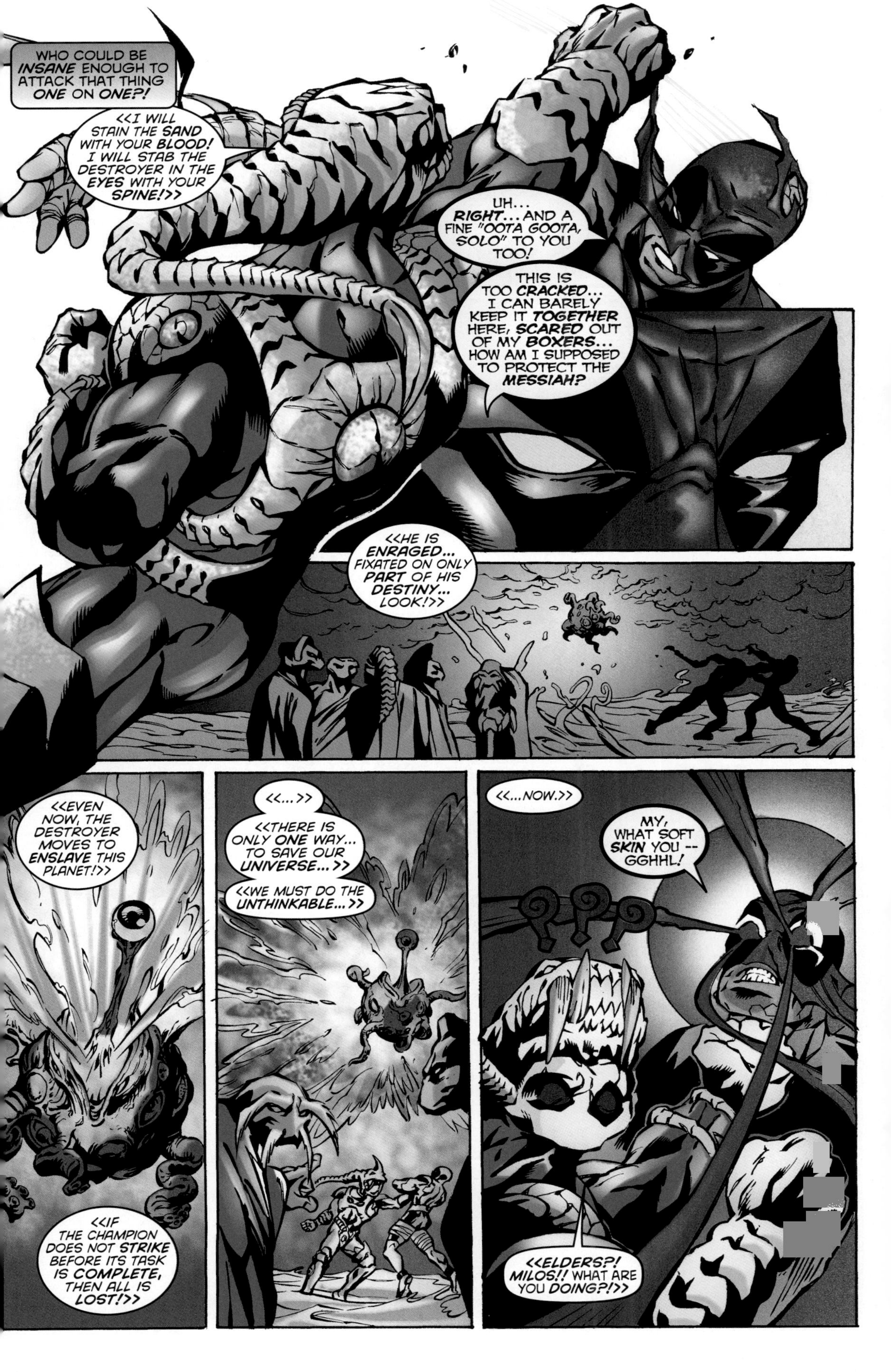
WHO COULD BE INSANE ENOUGH TO ATTACK THAT THING ONE ON ONE?!
<<I WILL STAIN THE SAND WITH YOUR BLOOD! I WILL STAB THE DESTROYER IN THE EYES WITH YOUR SPINE!>>
UH... RIGHT... AND A FINE "OOTA GOOTA, SOLO" TO YOU TOO!
THIS IS TOO CRACKED... I CAN BARELY KEEP IT TOGETHER HERE, SCARED OUT OF MY BOXERS... HOW AM I SUPPOSED TO PROTECT THE MESSIAH?
<<HE IS ENRAGED... FIXATED ON ONLY PART OF HIS DESTINY... LOOK!>>
<<EVEN NOW, THE DESTROYER MOVES TO ENSLAVE THIS PLANET!>>
<<IF THE CHAMPION DOES NOT STRIKE BEFORE ITS TASK IS COMPLETE, THEN ALL IS LOST!>>
<<...>>
<<THERE IS ONLY ONE WAY... TO SAVE OUR UNIVERSE...>>
<<WE MUST DO THE UNTHINKABLE...>>
<<...NOW.>>
MY, WHAT SOFT SKIN YOU -- GGHHL!
<<ELDERS?! MILOS!! WHAT ARE YOU DOING?!>>

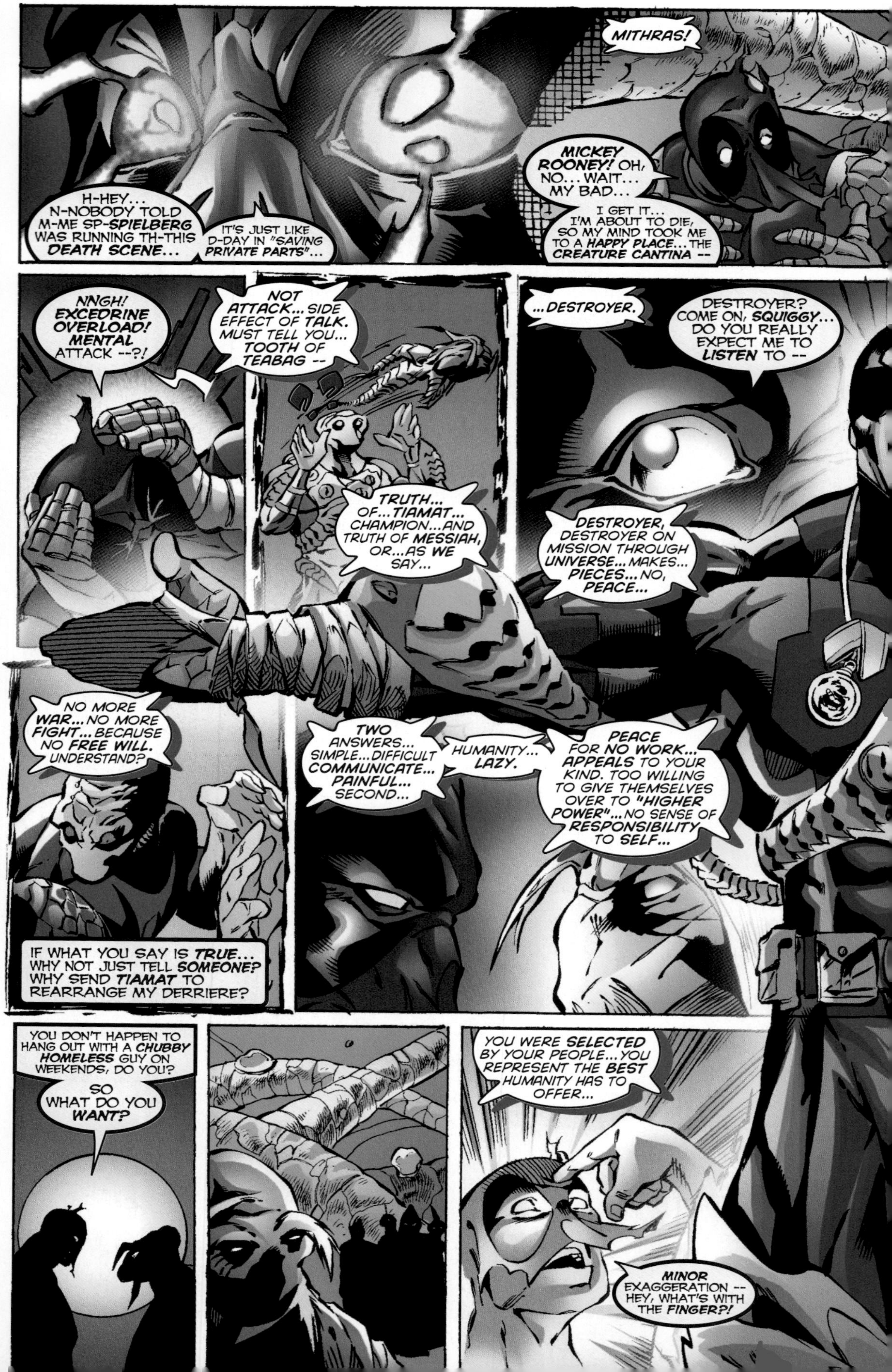

H-HEY... N-NOBODY TOLD M-ME SP-SPIELBERG WAS RUNNING TH-THIS DEATH SCENE...
IT'S JUST LIKE D-DAY IN "SAVING PRIVATE PARTS"...
MITHRAS!
MICKEY ROONEY! OH, NO... WAIT... MY BAD...
I GET IT... I'M ABOUT TO DIE, SO MY MIND TOOK ME TO A HAPPY PLACE... THE CREATURE CANTINA --
NNGH! EXCEDRINE OVERLOAD! MENTAL ATTACK --?!
NOT ATTACK... SIDE EFFECT OF TALK. MUST TELL YOU... TOOTH OF TEABAG --
...DESTROYER.
DESTROYER? COME ON, SQUIGGY... DO YOU REALLY EXPECT ME TO LISTEN TO --
TRUTH... OF... TIAMAT... CHAMPION... AND TRUTH OF MESSIAH, OR... AS WE SAY...
DESTROYER, DESTROYER ON MISSION THROUGH UNIVERSE... MAKES... PIECES... NO, PEACE...
NO MORE WAR... NO MORE FIGHT... BECAUSE NO FREE WILL. UNDERSTAND?
IF WHAT YOU SAY IS TRUE... WHY NOT JUST TELL SOMEONE? WHY SEND TIAMAT TO REARRANGE MY DERRIERE?
TWO ANSWERS... SIMPLE... DIFFICULT COMMUNICATE... PAINFUL... SECOND...
HUMANITY... LAZY.
PEACE FOR NO WORK... APPEALS TO YOUR KIND. TOO WILLING TO GIVE THEMSELVES OVER TO "HIGHER POWER"... NO SENSE OF RESPONSIBILITY TO SELF...
YOU DON'T HAPPEN TO HANG OUT WITH A CHUBBY HOMELESS GUY ON WEEKENDS, DO YOU?
SO WHAT DO YOU WANT?
YOU WERE SELECTED BY YOUR PEOPLE... YOU REPRESENT THE BEST HUMANITY HAS TO OFFER...
MINOR EXAGGERATION -- HEY, WHAT'S WITH THE FINGER?!

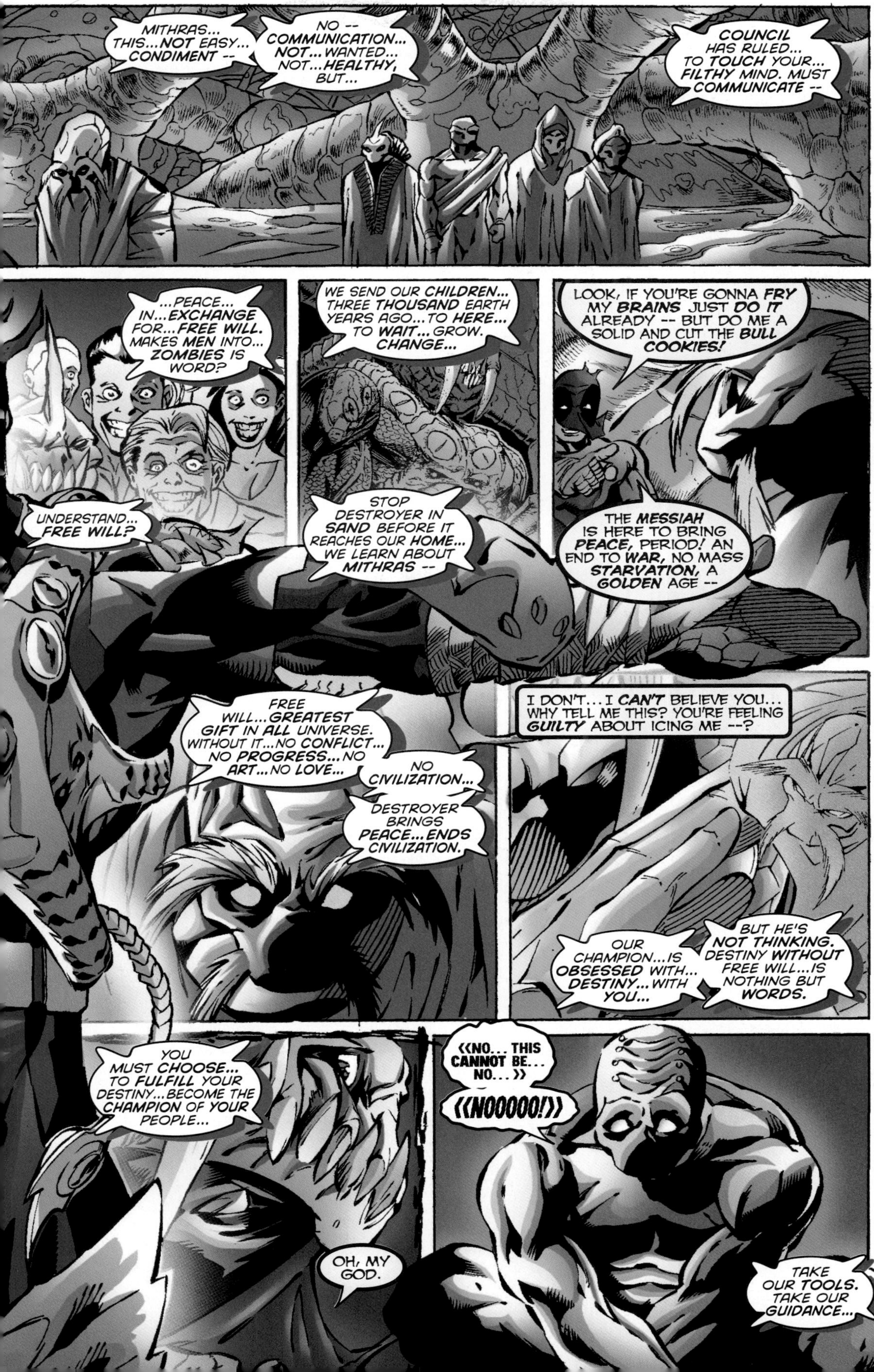
MITHRAS... THIS...NOT EASY... CONDIMENT --
NO -- COMMUNICATION... NOT...WANTED... NOT...HEALTHY, BUT...
COUNCIL HAS RULED... TO TOUCH YOUR... FILTHY MIND. MUST COMMUNICATE --
...PEACE... IN...EXCHANGE FOR...FREE WILL. MAKES MEN INTO... ZOMBIES IS WORD?
UNDERSTAND... FREE WILL?
WE SEND OUR CHILDREN... THREE THOUSAND EARTH YEARS AGO...TO HERE... TO WAIT...GROW. CHANGE...
STOP DESTROYER IN SAND BEFORE IT REACHES OUR HOME... WE LEARN ABOUT MITHRAS --
LOOK, IF YOU'RE GONNA FRY MY BRAINS JUST DO IT ALREADY -- BUT DO ME A SOLID AND CUT THE BULL COOKIES!
THE MESSIAH IS HERE TO BRING PEACE, PERIOD! AN END TO WAR, NO MASS STARVATION, A GOLDEN AGE --
FREE WILL...GREATEST GIFT IN ALL UNIVERSE. WITHOUT IT...NO CONFLICT... NO PROGRESS...NO ART...NO LOVE...
NO CIVILIZATION...
DESTROYER BRINGS PEACE...ENDS CIVILIZATION.
I DON'T...I CAN'T BELIEVE YOU... WHY TELL ME THIS? YOU'RE FEELING GUILTY ABOUT ICING ME --?
OUR CHAMPION...IS OBSESSED WITH... DESTINY...WITH YOU...
BUT HE'S NOT THINKING. DESTINY WITHOUT FREE WILL...IS NOTHING BUT WORDS.
YOU MUST CHOOSE... TO FULFILL YOUR DESTINY...BECOME THE CHAMPION OF YOUR PEOPLE...
OH, MY GOD.
«NO... THIS CANNOT BE... NO...»
«NOOOOO!»
TAKE OUR TOOLS. TAKE OUR GUIDANCE...

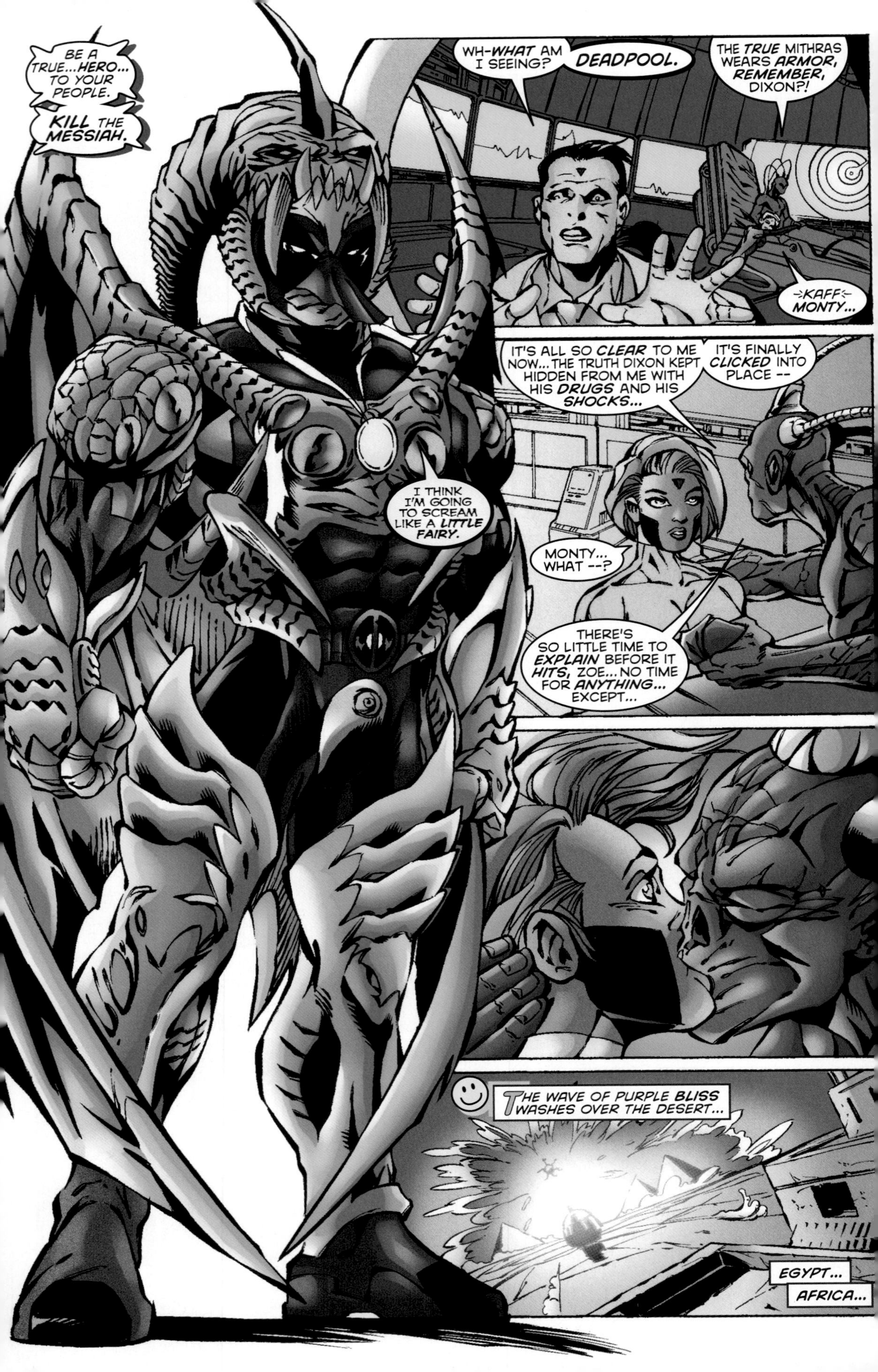
BE A TRUE...HERO... TO YOUR PEOPLE.
KILL THE MESSIAH.
WH-WHAT AM I SEEING?
DEADPOOL.
THE TRUE MITHRAS WEARS ARMOR, REMEMBER, DIXON?!
-KAFF- MONTY...
I THINK I'M GOING TO SCREAM LIKE A LITTLE FAIRY.
IT'S ALL SO CLEAR TO ME NOW...THE TRUTH DIXON KEPT HIDDEN FROM ME WITH HIS DRUGS AND HIS SHOCKS...
IT'S FINALLY CLICKED INTO PLACE --
MONTY... WHAT --?
THERE'S SO LITTLE TIME TO EXPLAIN BEFORE IT HITS, ZOE... NO TIME FOR ANYTHING... EXCEPT...
THE WAVE OF PURPLE BLISS WASHES OVER THE DESERT...
EGYPT...
AFRICA...

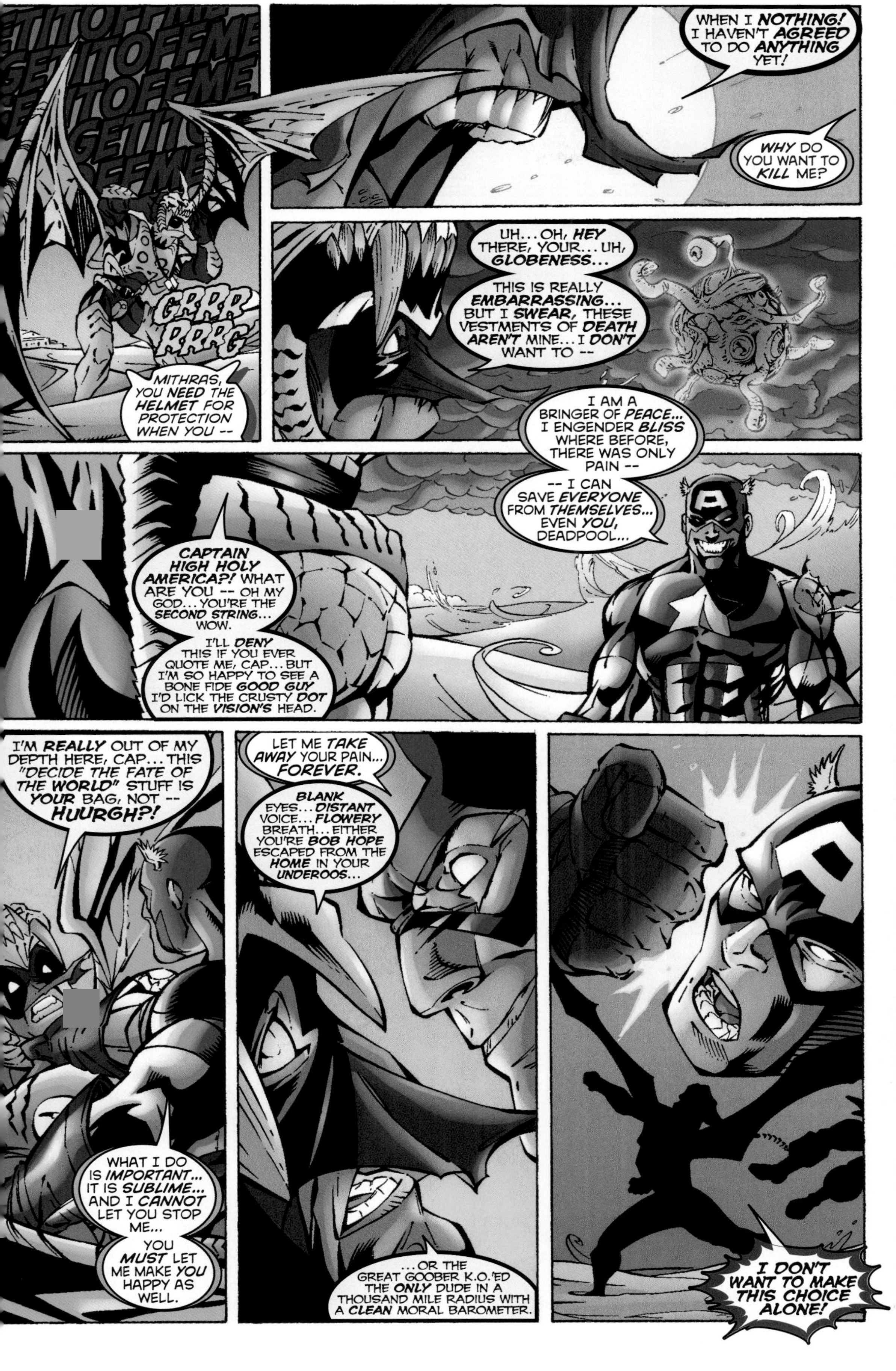

GETITOFFME GETITOFFME GETITOFFME GETITOFFME
WHEN I NOTHING! I HAVEN'T AGREED TO DO ANYTHING YET!
WHY DO YOU WANT TO KILL ME?
GRRR RRRG
MITHRAS, YOU NEED THE HELMET FOR PROTECTION WHEN YOU --
UH... OH, HEY THERE, YOUR... UH, GLOBENESS...
THIS IS REALLY EMBARRASSING... BUT I SWEAR, THESE VESTMENTS OF DEATH AREN'T MINE... I DON'T WANT TO --
I AM A BRINGER OF PEACE... I ENGENDER BLISS WHERE BEFORE, THERE WAS ONLY PAIN --
-- I CAN SAVE EVERYONE FROM THEMSELVES... EVEN YOU, DEADPOOL...
CAPTAIN HIGH HOLY AMERICA?! WHAT ARE YOU -- OH MY GOD... YOU'RE THE SECOND STRING... WOW.
I'LL DENY THIS IF YOU EVER QUOTE ME, CAP... BUT I'M SO HAPPY TO SEE A BONE FIDE GOOD GUY I'D LICK THE CRUSTY DOT ON THE VISION'S HEAD.
I'M REALLY OUT OF MY DEPTH HERE, CAP... THIS "DECIDE THE FATE OF THE WORLD" STUFF IS YOUR BAG, NOT -- HUURGH?!
WHAT I DO IS IMPORTANT... IT IS SUBLIME... AND I CANNOT LET YOU STOP ME...
YOU MUST LET ME MAKE YOU HAPPY AS WELL.
LET ME TAKE AWAY YOUR PAIN... FOREVER.
BLANK EYES... DISTANT VOICE... FLOWERY BREATH... EITHER YOU'RE BOB HOPE ESCAPED FROM THE HOME IN YOUR UNDEROOS...
...OR THE GREAT GOOBER K.O.'ED THE ONLY DUDE IN A THOUSAND MILE RADIUS WITH A CLEAN MORAL BAROMETER.
I DON'T WANT TO MAKE THIS CHOICE ALONE!

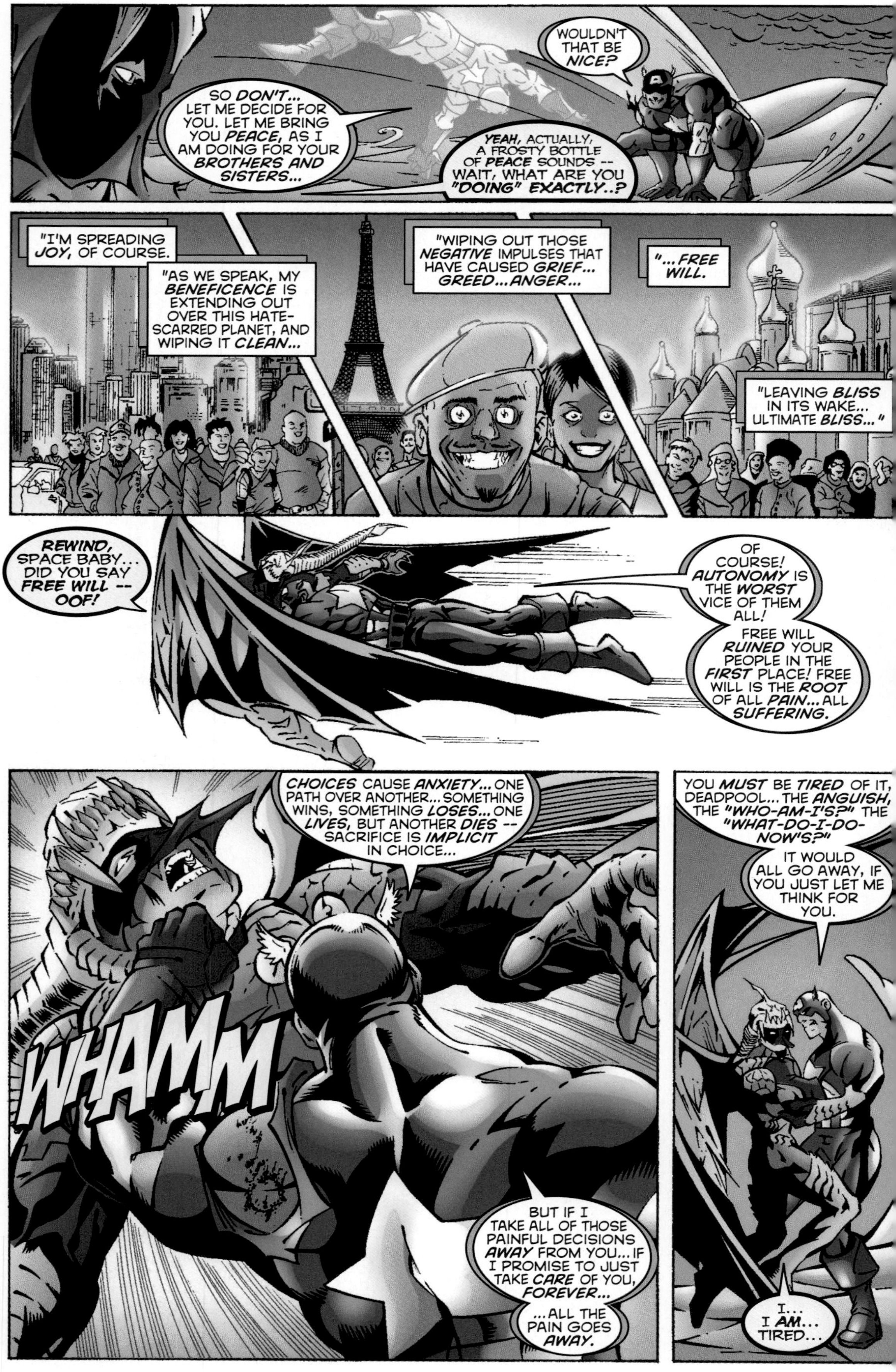
WOULDN'T THAT BE NICE?
SO DON'T... LET ME DECIDE FOR YOU. LET ME BRING YOU PEACE, AS I AM DOING FOR YOUR BROTHERS AND SISTERS...
YEAH, ACTUALLY, A FROSTY BOTTLE OF PEACE SOUNDS -- WAIT, WHAT ARE YOU "DOING" EXACTLY..?
"I'M SPREADING JOY, OF COURSE.
"AS WE SPEAK, MY BENEFICENCE IS EXTENDING OUT OVER THIS HATE-SCARRED PLANET, AND WIPING IT CLEAN...
"WIPING OUT THOSE NEGATIVE IMPULSES THAT HAVE CAUSED GRIEF... GREED... ANGER...
"...FREE WILL.
"LEAVING BLISS IN ITS WAKE... ULTIMATE BLISS..."
REWIND, SPACE BABY... DID YOU SAY FREE WILL -- OOF!
OF COURSE! AUTONOMY IS THE WORST VICE OF THEM ALL!
FREE WILL RUINED YOUR PEOPLE IN THE FIRST PLACE! FREE WILL IS THE ROOT OF ALL PAIN... ALL SUFFERING.
CHOICES CAUSE ANXIETY... ONE PATH OVER ANOTHER... SOMETHING WINS, SOMETHING LOSES... ONE LIVES, BUT ANOTHER DIES -- SACRIFICE IS IMPLICIT IN CHOICE...
WHAMM
BUT IF I TAKE ALL OF THOSE PAINFUL DECISIONS AWAY FROM YOU... IF I PROMISE TO JUST TAKE CARE OF YOU, FOREVER...
...ALL THE PAIN GOES AWAY.
YOU MUST BE TIRED OF IT, DEADPOOL... THE ANGUISH, THE "WHO-AM-I'S?" THE "WHAT-DO-I-DO-NOW'S?"
IT WOULD ALL GO AWAY, IF YOU JUST LET ME THINK FOR YOU.
I... I AM... TIRED...

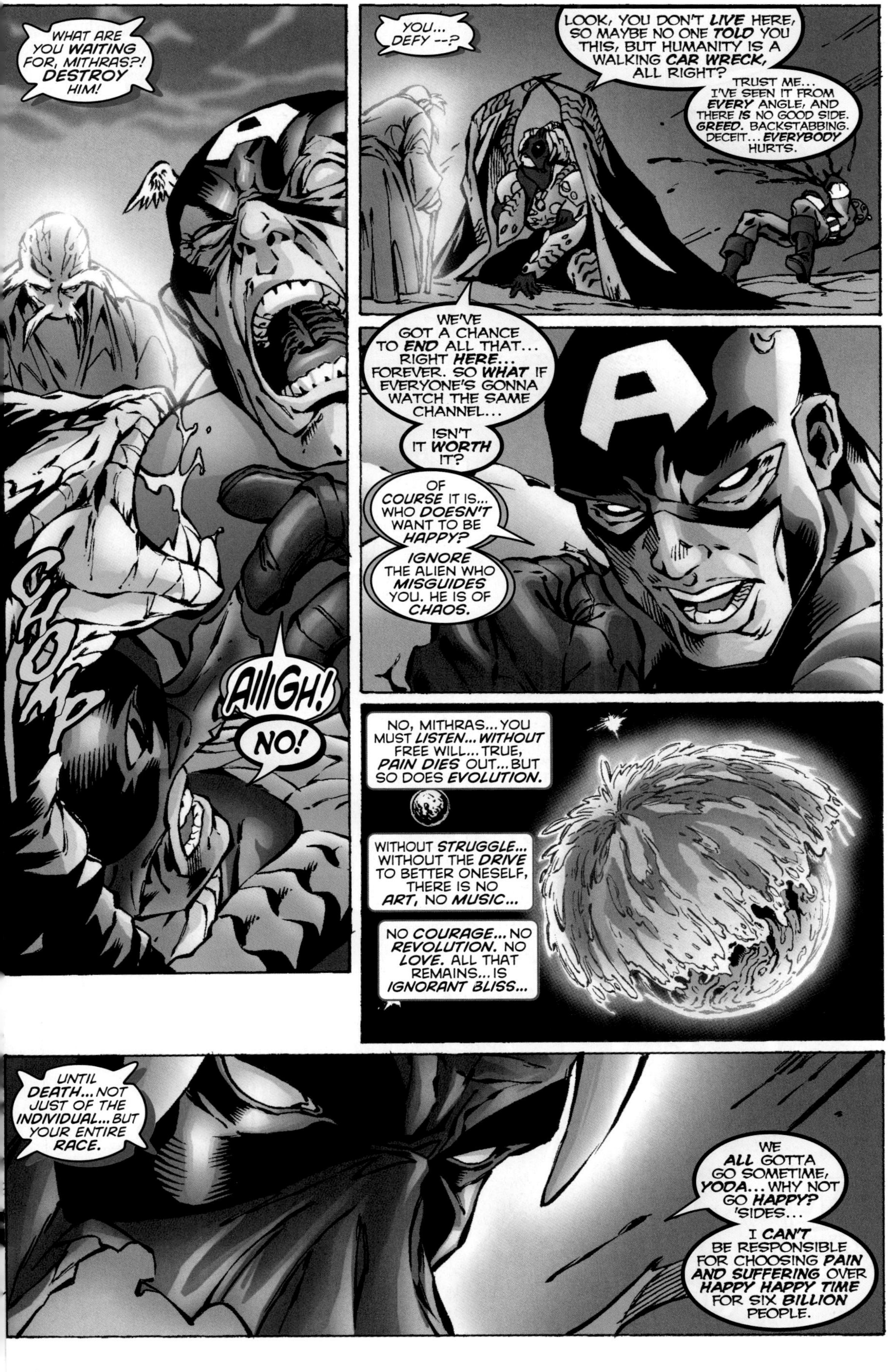

WHAT ARE YOU WAITING FOR, MITHRAS?! DESTROY HIM!
CHOMP
AIIIGH!
NO!
YOU... DEFY --?
LOOK, YOU DON'T LIVE HERE, SO MAYBE NO ONE TOLD YOU THIS, BUT HUMANITY IS A WALKING CAR WRECK, ALL RIGHT?
TRUST ME... I'VE SEEN IT FROM EVERY ANGLE, AND THERE IS NO GOOD SIDE. GREED. BACKSTABBING. DECEIT... EVERYBODY HURTS.
WE'VE GOT A CHANCE TO END ALL THAT... RIGHT HERE... FOREVER. SO WHAT IF EVERYONE'S GONNA WATCH THE SAME CHANNEL...
ISN'T IT WORTH IT?
OF COURSE IT IS... WHO DOESN'T WANT TO BE HAPPY?
IGNORE THE ALIEN WHO MISGUIDES YOU. HE IS OF CHAOS.
NO, MITHRAS... YOU MUST LISTEN... WITHOUT FREE WILL... TRUE, PAIN DIES OUT... BUT SO DOES EVOLUTION.
WITHOUT STRUGGLE... WITHOUT THE DRIVE TO BETTER ONESELF, THERE IS NO ART, NO MUSIC...
NO COURAGE... NO REVOLUTION. NO LOVE. ALL THAT REMAINS... IS IGNORANT BLISS...
UNTIL DEATH... NOT JUST OF THE INDIVIDUAL... BUT YOUR ENTIRE RACE.
WE ALL GOTTA GO SOMETIME, YODA... WHY NOT GO HAPPY? 'SIDES...
I CAN'T BE RESPONSIBLE FOR CHOOSING PAIN AND SUFFERING OVER HAPPY HAPPY TIME FOR SIX BILLION PEOPLE.

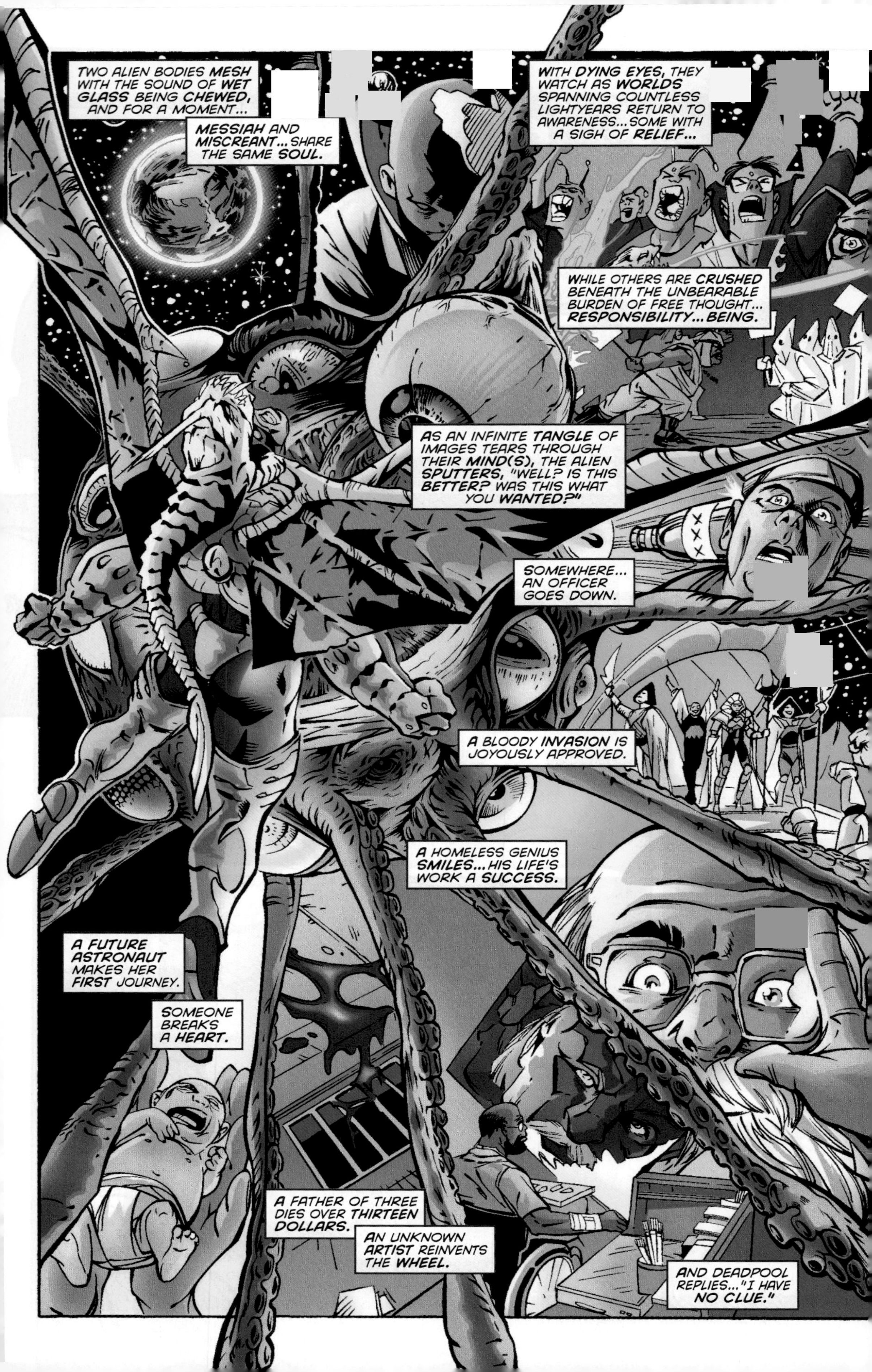
TWO ALIEN BODIES MESH WITH THE SOUND OF WET GLASS BEING CHEWED, AND FOR A MOMENT...
MESSIAH AND MISCREANT... SHARE THE SAME SOUL.
WITH DYING EYES, THEY WATCH AS WORLDS SPANNING COUNTLESS LIGHTYEARS RETURN TO AWARENESS... SOME WITH A SIGH OF RELIEF...
WHILE OTHERS ARE CRUSHED BENEATH THE UNBEARABLE BURDEN OF FREE THOUGHT... RESPONSIBILITY... BEING.
AS AN INFINITE TANGLE OF IMAGES TEARS THROUGH THEIR MIND(S), THE ALIEN SPUTTERS, "WELL? IS THIS BETTER? WAS THIS WHAT YOU WANTED?"
SOMEWHERE... AN OFFICER GOES DOWN.
A BLOODY INVASION IS JOYOUSLY APPROVED.
A HOMELESS GENIUS SMILES... HIS LIFE'S WORK A SUCCESS.
A FUTURE ASTRONAUT MAKES HER FIRST JOURNEY.
SOMEONE BREAKS A HEART.
A FATHER OF THREE DIES OVER THIRTEEN DOLLARS.
AN UNKNOWN ARTIST REINVENTS THE WHEEL.
AND DEADPOOL REPLIES... "I HAVE NO CLUE."

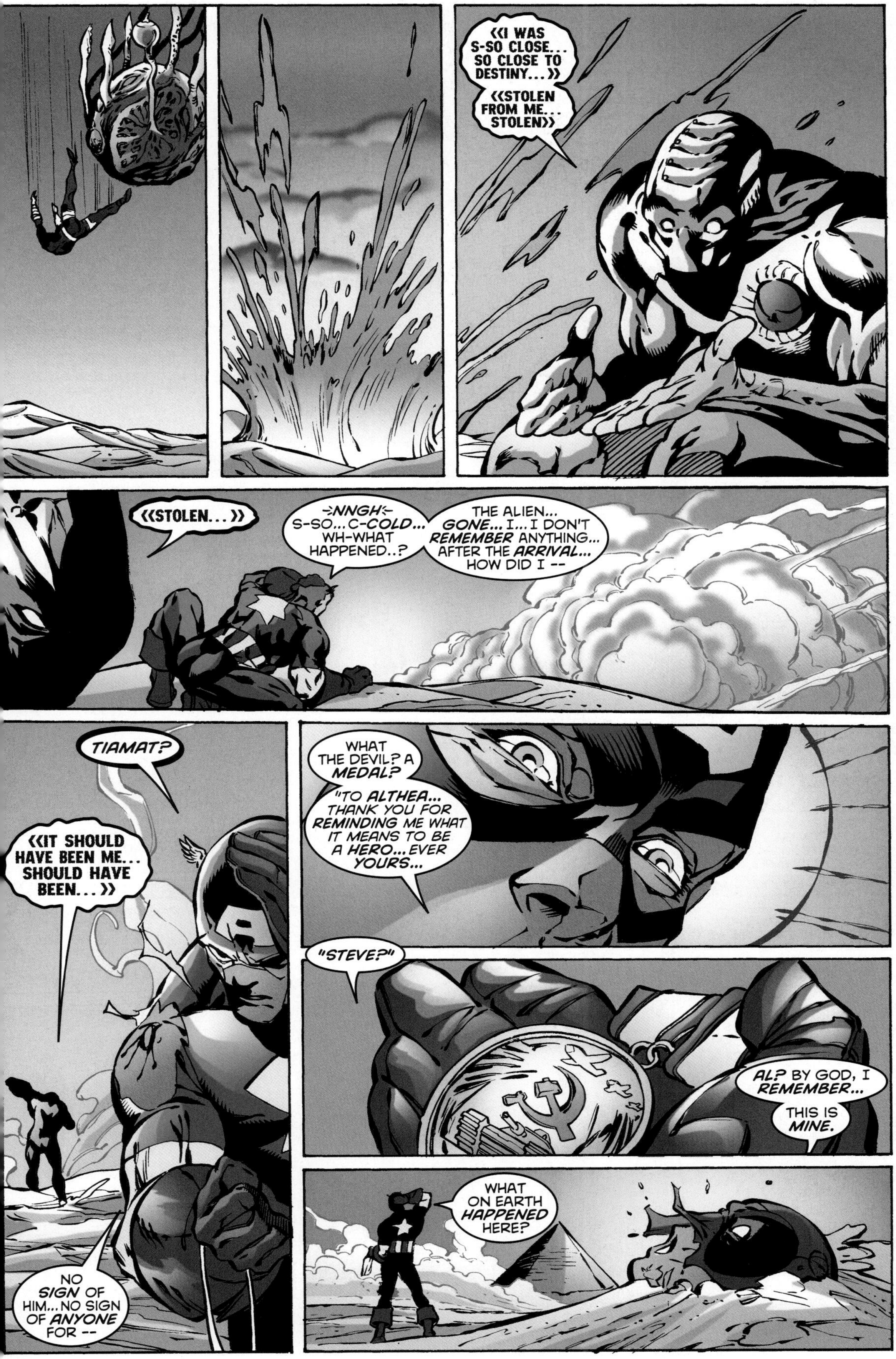
<<I WAS S-SO CLOSE... SO CLOSE TO DESTINY...>>
<<STOLEN FROM ME... STOLEN>>
<<STOLEN...>>
-NNGH- S-SO... C-COLD... WH-WHAT HAPPENED..?
THE ALIEN... GONE... I... I DON'T REMEMBER ANYTHING... AFTER THE ARRIVAL... HOW DID I --
TIAMAT?
<<IT SHOULD HAVE BEEN ME... SHOULD HAVE BEEN...>>
NO SIGN OF HIM... NO SIGN OF ANYONE FOR --
WHAT THE DEVIL? A MEDAL?
"TO ALTHEA... THANK YOU FOR REMINDING ME WHAT IT MEANS TO BE A HERO... EVER YOURS...
"STEVE?"
AL? BY GOD, I REMEMBER...
THIS IS MINE.
WHAT ON EARTH HAPPENED HERE?

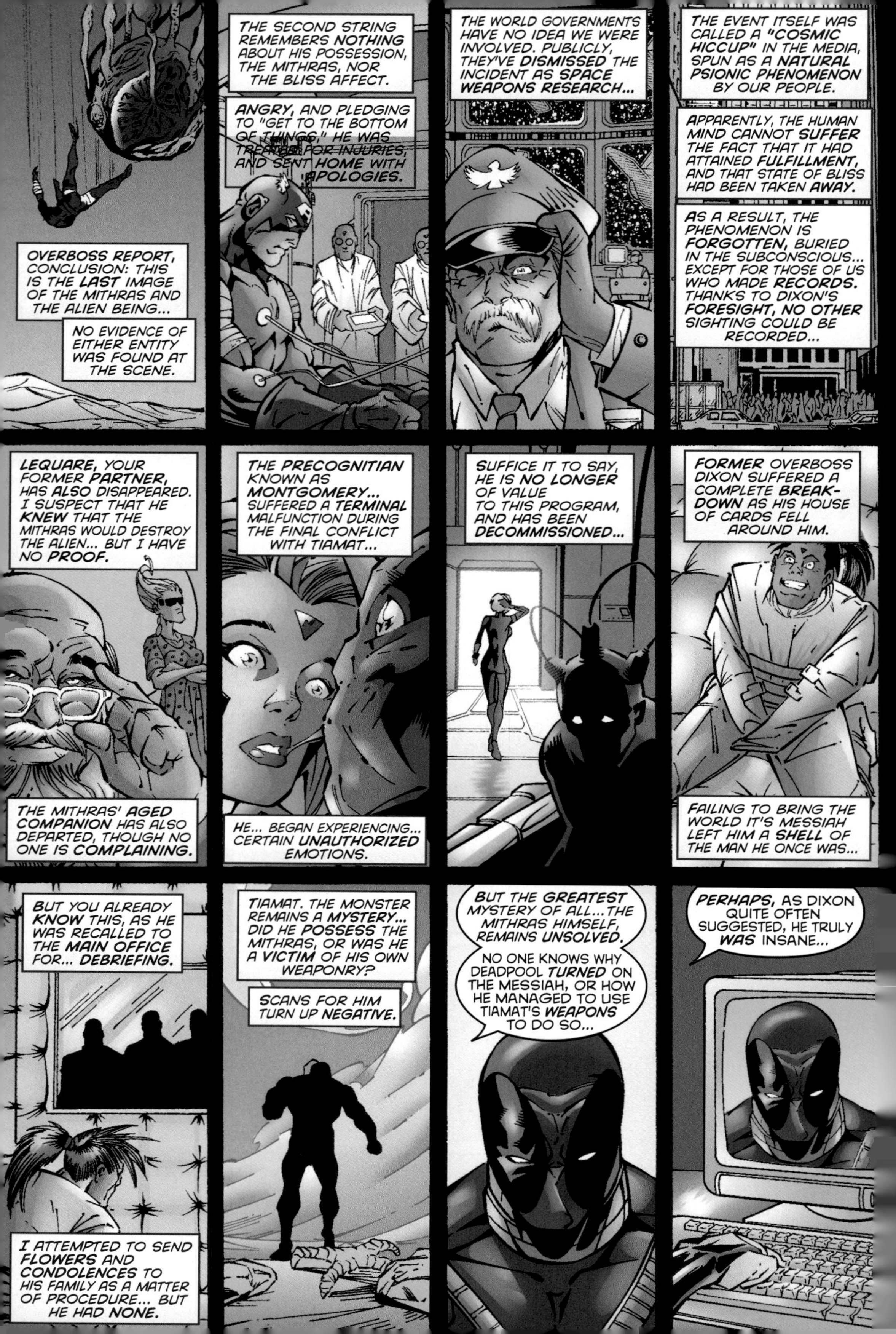

OVERBOSS REPORT, CONCLUSION: THIS IS THE LAST IMAGE OF THE MITHRAS AND THE ALIEN BEING...
NO EVIDENCE OF EITHER ENTITY WAS FOUND AT THE SCENE.
THE SECOND STRING REMEMBERS NOTHING ABOUT HIS POSSESSION, THE MITHRAS, NOR THE BLISS AFFECT.
ANGRY, AND PLEDGING TO "GET TO THE BOTTOM OF THINGS," HE WAS TREATED FOR INJURIES, AND SENT HOME WITH APOLOGIES.
THE WORLD GOVERNMENTS HAVE NO IDEA WE WERE INVOLVED. PUBLICLY, THEY'VE DISMISSED THE INCIDENT AS SPACE WEAPONS RESEARCH...
THE EVENT ITSELF WAS CALLED A "COSMIC HICCUP" IN THE MEDIA, SPUN AS A NATURAL PSIONIC PHENOMENON BY OUR PEOPLE.
APPARENTLY, THE HUMAN MIND CANNOT SUFFER THE FACT THAT IT HAD ATTAINED FULFILLMENT, AND THAT STATE OF BLISS HAD BEEN TAKEN AWAY.
AS A RESULT, THE PHENOMENON IS FORGOTTEN, BURIED IN THE SUBCONSCIOUS... EXCEPT FOR THOSE OF US WHO MADE RECORDS. THANKS TO DIXON'S FORESIGHT, NO OTHER SIGHTING COULD BE RECORDED...
LEQUARE, YOUR FORMER PARTNER, HAS ALSO DISAPPEARED. I SUSPECT THAT HE KNEW THAT THE MITHRAS WOULD DESTROY THE ALIEN... BUT I HAVE NO PROOF.
THE MITHRAS' AGED COMPANION HAS ALSO DEPARTED, THOUGH NO ONE IS COMPLAINING.
THE PRECOGNITIAN KNOWN AS MONTGOMERY... SUFFERED A TERMINAL MALFUNCTION DURING THE FINAL CONFLICT WITH TIAMAT...
HE... BEGAN EXPERIENCING... CERTAIN UNAUTHORIZED EMOTIONS.
SUFFICE IT TO SAY, HE IS NO LONGER OF VALUE TO THIS PROGRAM, AND HAS BEEN DECOMMISSIONED...
FORMER OVERBOSS DIXON SUFFERED A COMPLETE BREAK-DOWN AS HIS HOUSE OF CARDS FELL AROUND HIM.
FAILING TO BRING THE WORLD IT'S MESSIAH LEFT HIM A SHELL OF THE MAN HE ONCE WAS...
BUT YOU ALREADY KNOW THIS, AS HE WAS RECALLED TO THE MAIN OFFICE FOR... DEBRIEFING.
I ATTEMPTED TO SEND FLOWERS AND CONDOLENCES TO HIS FAMILY AS A MATTER OF PROCEDURE... BUT HE HAD NONE.
TIAMAT. THE MONSTER REMAINS A MYSTERY... DID HE POSSESS THE MITHRAS, OR WAS HE A VICTIM OF HIS OWN WEAPONRY?
SCANS FOR HIM TURN UP NEGATIVE.
BUT THE GREATEST MYSTERY OF ALL...THE MITHRAS HIMSELF, REMAINS UNSOLVED.
NO ONE KNOWS WHY DEADPOOL TURNED ON THE MESSIAH, OR HOW HE MANAGED TO USE TIAMAT'S WEAPONS TO DO SO...
PERHAPS, AS DIXON QUITE OFTEN SUGGESTED, HE TRULY WAS INSANE...

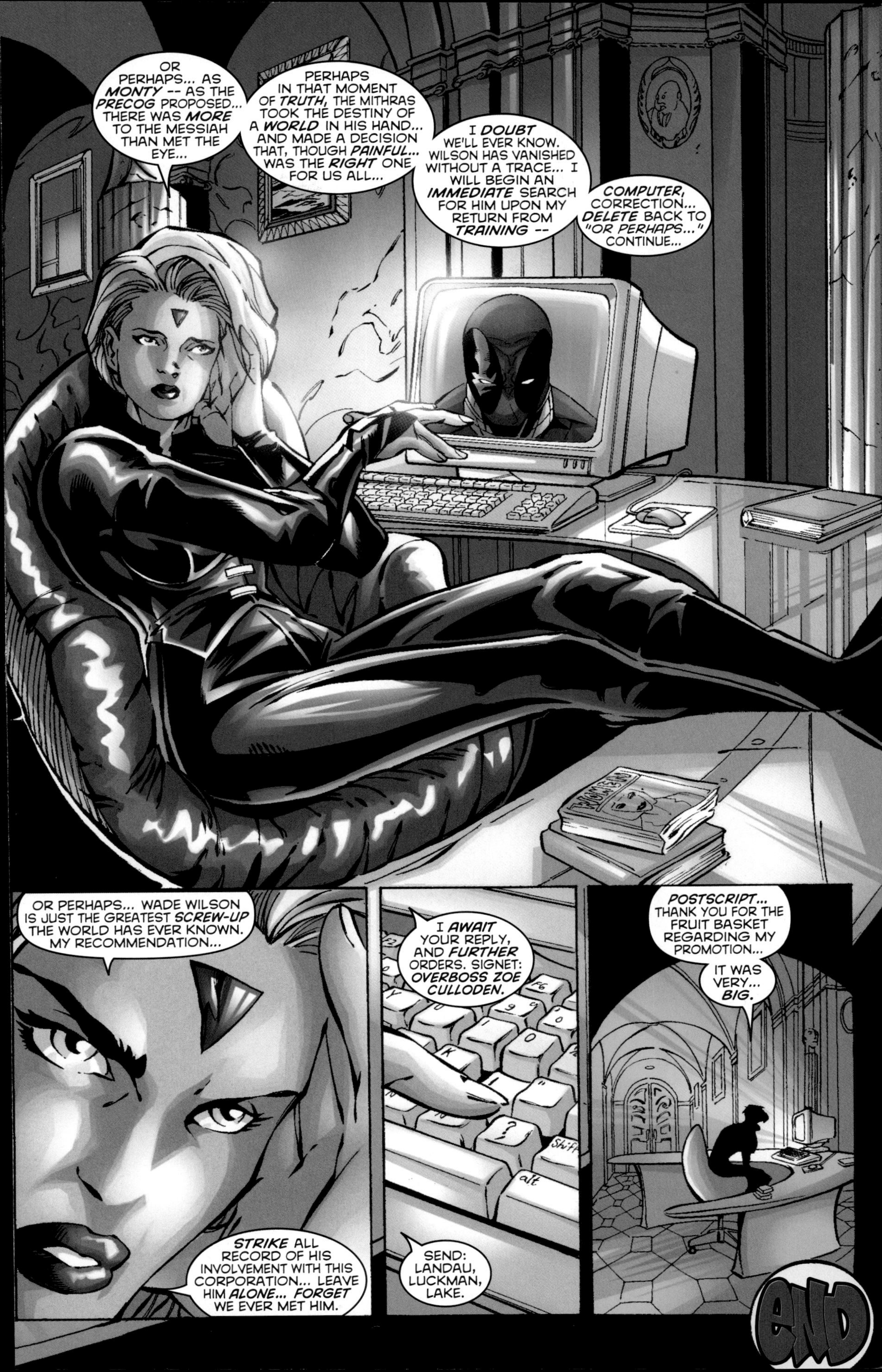
OR PERHAPS... AS MONTY -- AS THE PRECOG PROPOSED... THERE WAS MORE TO THE MESSIAH THAN MET THE EYE...
PERHAPS IN THAT MOMENT OF TRUTH, THE MITHRAS TOOK THE DESTINY OF A WORLD IN HIS HAND... AND MADE A DECISION THAT, THOUGH PAINFUL... WAS THE RIGHT ONE FOR US ALL...
I DOUBT WE'LL EVER KNOW. WILSON HAS VANISHED WITHOUT A TRACE... I WILL BEGIN AN IMMEDIATE SEARCH FOR HIM UPON MY RETURN FROM TRAINING --
COMPUTER, CORRECTION... DELETE BACK TO "OR PERHAPS..." CONTINUE...
OR PERHAPS... WADE WILSON IS JUST THE GREATEST SCREW-UP THE WORLD HAS EVER KNOWN. MY RECOMMENDATION...
STRIKE ALL RECORD OF HIS INVOLVEMENT WITH THIS CORPORATION... LEAVE HIM ALONE... FORGET WE EVER MET HIM.
I AWAIT YOUR REPLY, AND FURTHER ORDERS. SIGNET: OVERBOSS ZOE CULLODEN.
SEND: LANDAU, LUCKMAN, LAKE.
POSTSCRIPT... THANK YOU FOR THE FRUIT BASKET REGARDING MY PROMOTION...
IT WAS VERY... BIG.
END

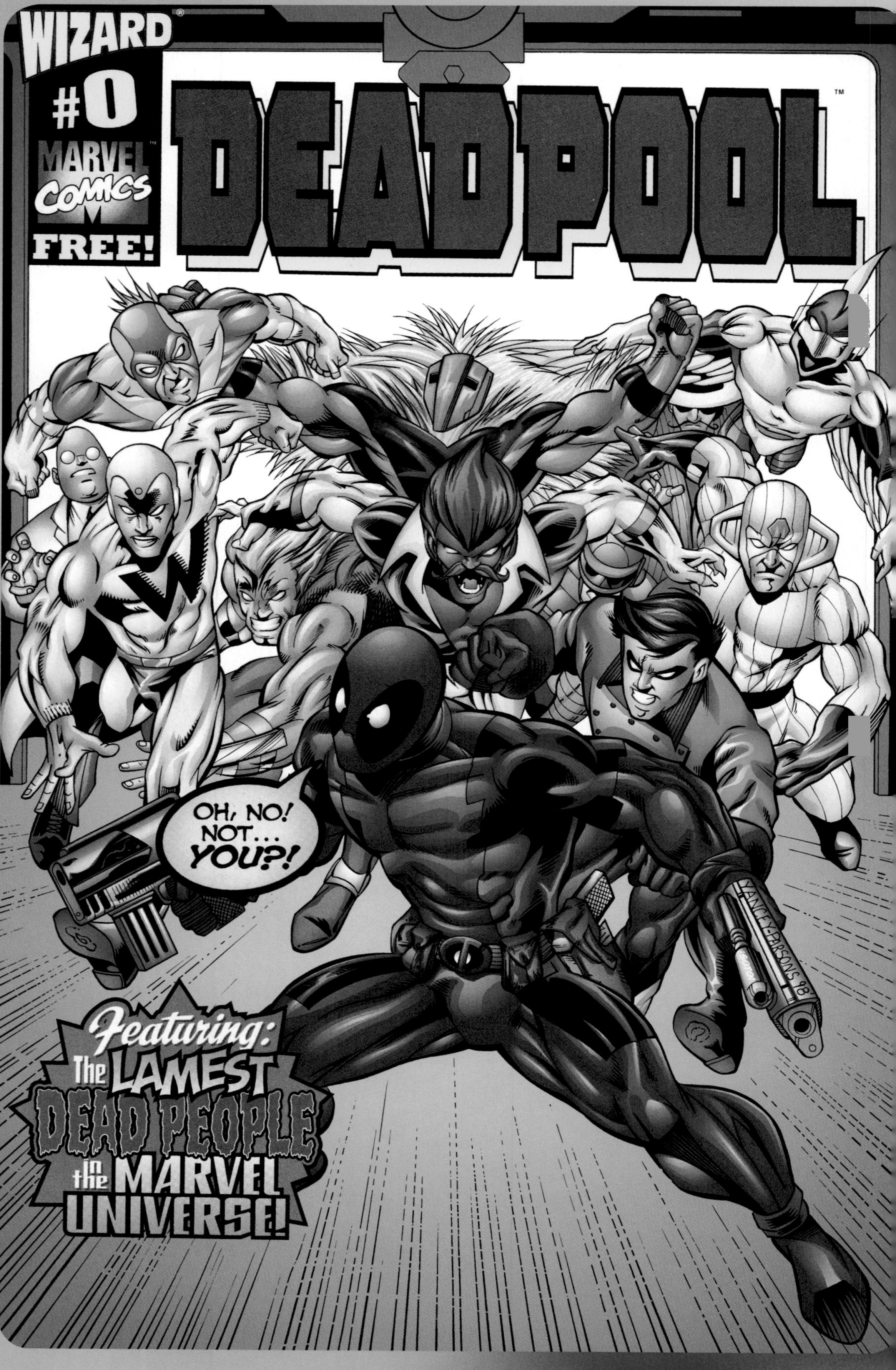
WIZARD®
#0
MARVEL COMICS
FREE!
DEADPOOL™
OH, NO! NOT... YOU?!
YANCEY-PARSONS '98
Featuring: The LAMEST DEAD PEOPLE in the MARVEL UNIVERSE!

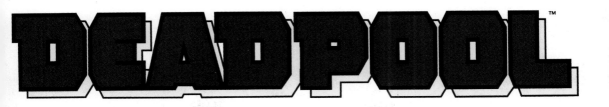

Stan Lee presents
A DEADPOOL TAKES A WIZARD SPECIAL
"YOU ONLY DIE TWICE"

MARVEL COMICS

Writer by day... Whizzer by night
JOE KELLY

Pencils with Porcupine quills
YANCEY LABAT

Mild-mannered inker a.k.a. the Ringer
SEAN PARSONS

Colors/Separates by night...in a Cheetah suit
**SOTO with help from
COLORGRAPHIX and JAMES BROWN**

The Salem's Seven with a steno pad
**RICHARD STARKINGS and
COMICRAFT/EM**

Bucky the Assistant Editor
PAUL TUTRONE

Editor D. Century
MATT IDELSON

Body model for Arnim Zola
BOB HARRAS

WIZARD ENTERTAINMENT

President/Publisher
GAREB S. SHAMUS

Executive VP
FRED PIERCE

Editor-in-Chief
PATRICK McCALLUM

Promotions Manager
IAN M. FELLER

Design Manager
STEVE BLACKWELL

Production Director
DARREN SANCHEZ

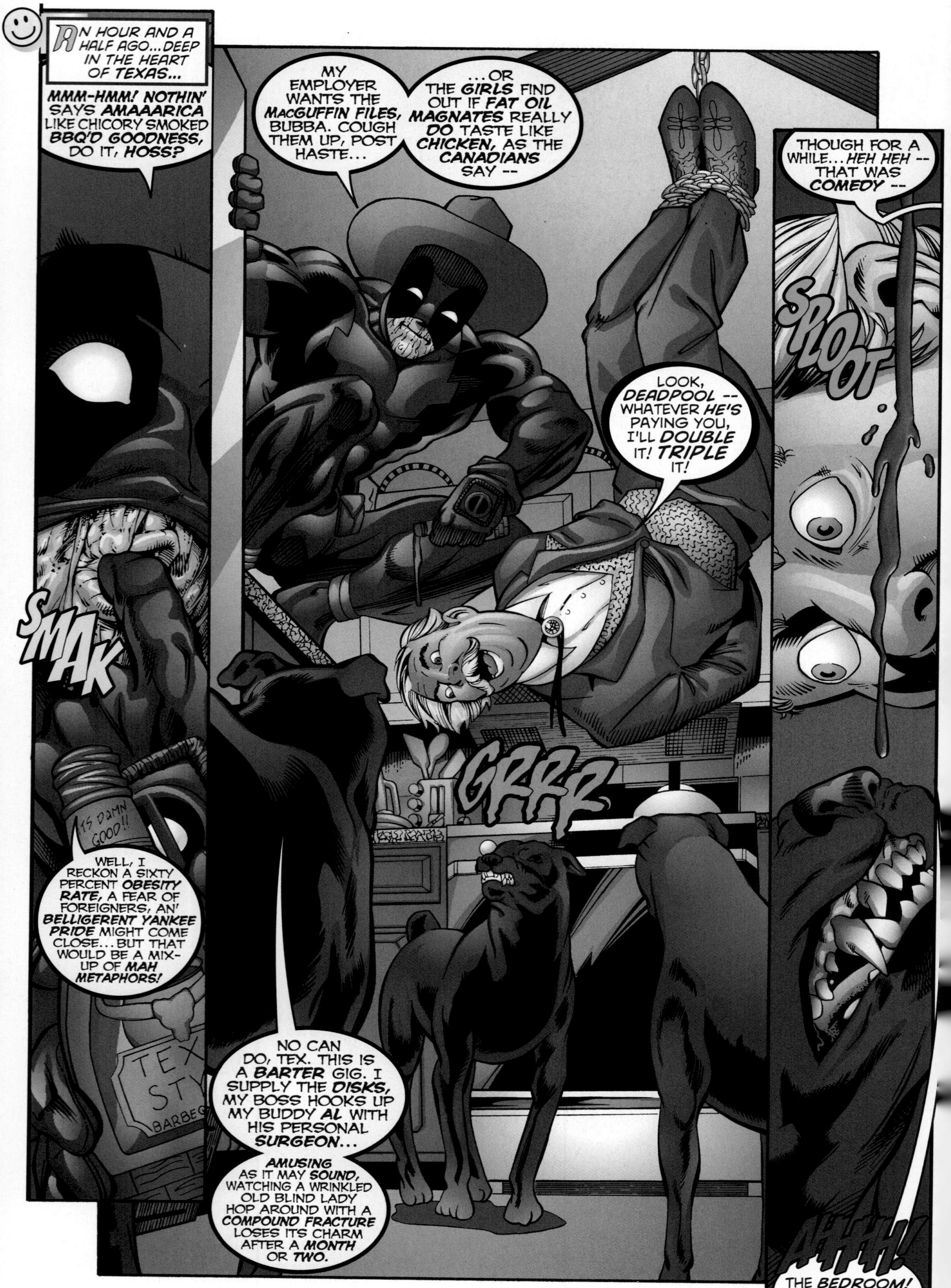

AN HOUR AND A HALF AGO...DEEP IN THE HEART OF TEXAS...
MMM-HMM! NOTHIN' SAYS AMAAARICA LIKE CHICORY SMOKED BBQ'D GOODNESS, DO IT, HOSS?
SMAK
ITS DAMN GOOD!!
WELL, I RECKON A SIXTY PERCENT OBESITY RATE, A FEAR OF FOREIGNERS, AN' BELLIGERENT YANKEE PRIDE MIGHT COME CLOSE... BUT THAT WOULD BE A MIX-UP OF MAH METAPHORS!
MY EMPLOYER WANTS THE MacGUFFIN FILES, BUBBA. COUGH THEM UP, POST HASTE...
...OR THE GIRLS FIND OUT IF FAT OIL MAGNATES REALLY DO TASTE LIKE CHICKEN, AS THE CANADIANS SAY --
LOOK, DEADPOOL -- WHATEVER HE'S PAYING YOU, I'LL DOUBLE IT! TRIPLE IT!
GRRR
NO CAN DO, TEX. THIS IS A BARTER GIG. I SUPPLY THE DISKS, MY BOSS HOOKS UP MY BUDDY AL WITH HIS PERSONAL SURGEON...
AMUSING AS IT MAY SOUND, WATCHING A WRINKLED OLD BLIND LADY HOP AROUND WITH A COMPOUND FRACTURE LOSES ITS CHARM AFTER A MONTH OR TWO.
THOUGH FOR A WHILE... HEH HEH -- THAT WAS COMEDY --
SPLOOT
AHHH!
THE BEDROOM! THE WALL SAFE IN THE BEDROOM!

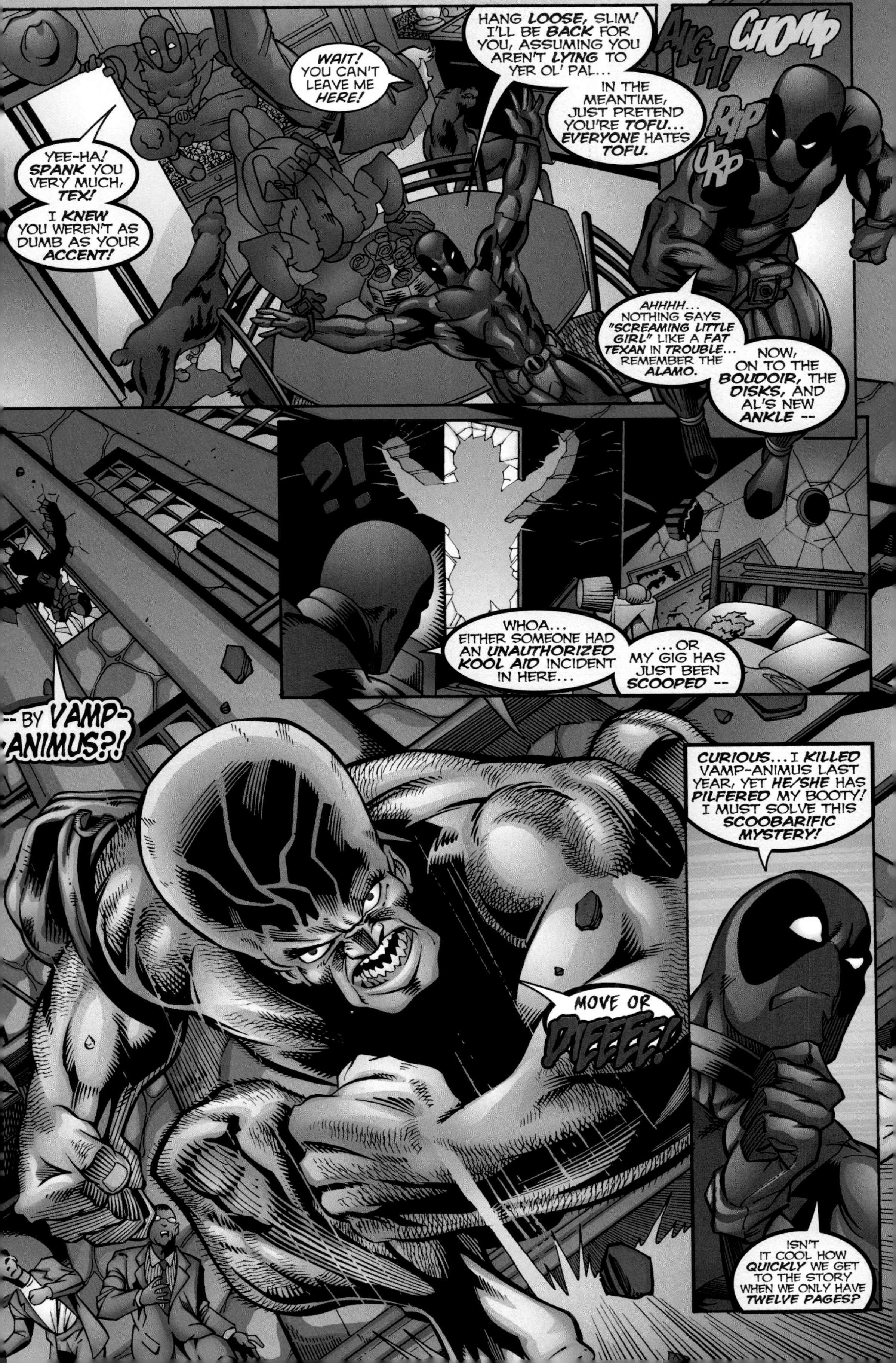
WAIT! YOU CAN'T LEAVE ME HERE!
HANG LOOSE, SLIM! I'LL BE BACK FOR YOU, ASSUMING YOU AREN'T LYING TO YER OL' PAL...
IN THE MEANTIME, JUST PRETEND YOU'RE TOFU... EVERYONE HATES TOFU.
YEE-HA! SPANK YOU VERY MUCH, TEX!
I KNEW YOU WEREN'T AS DUMB AS YOUR ACCENT!
AAGH!
CHOMP
RIP
URP
AHHHH... NOTHING SAYS "SCREAMING LITTLE GIRL" LIKE A FAT TEXAN IN TROUBLE... REMEMBER THE ALAMO.
NOW, ON TO THE BOUDOIR, THE DISKS, AND AL'S NEW ANKLE --
?!
WHOA... EITHER SOMEONE HAD AN UNAUTHORIZED KOOL AID INCIDENT IN HERE...
...OR MY GIG HAS JUST BEEN SCOOPED --
-- BY VAMP-ANIMUS?!
CURIOUS... I KILLED VAMP-ANIMUS LAST YEAR, YET HE/SHE HAS PILFERED MY BOOTY! I MUST SOLVE THIS SCOOBARIFIC MYSTERY!
MOVE OR DIEEEE!
ISN'T IT COOL HOW QUICKLY WE GET TO THE STORY WHEN WE ONLY HAVE TWELVE PAGES?

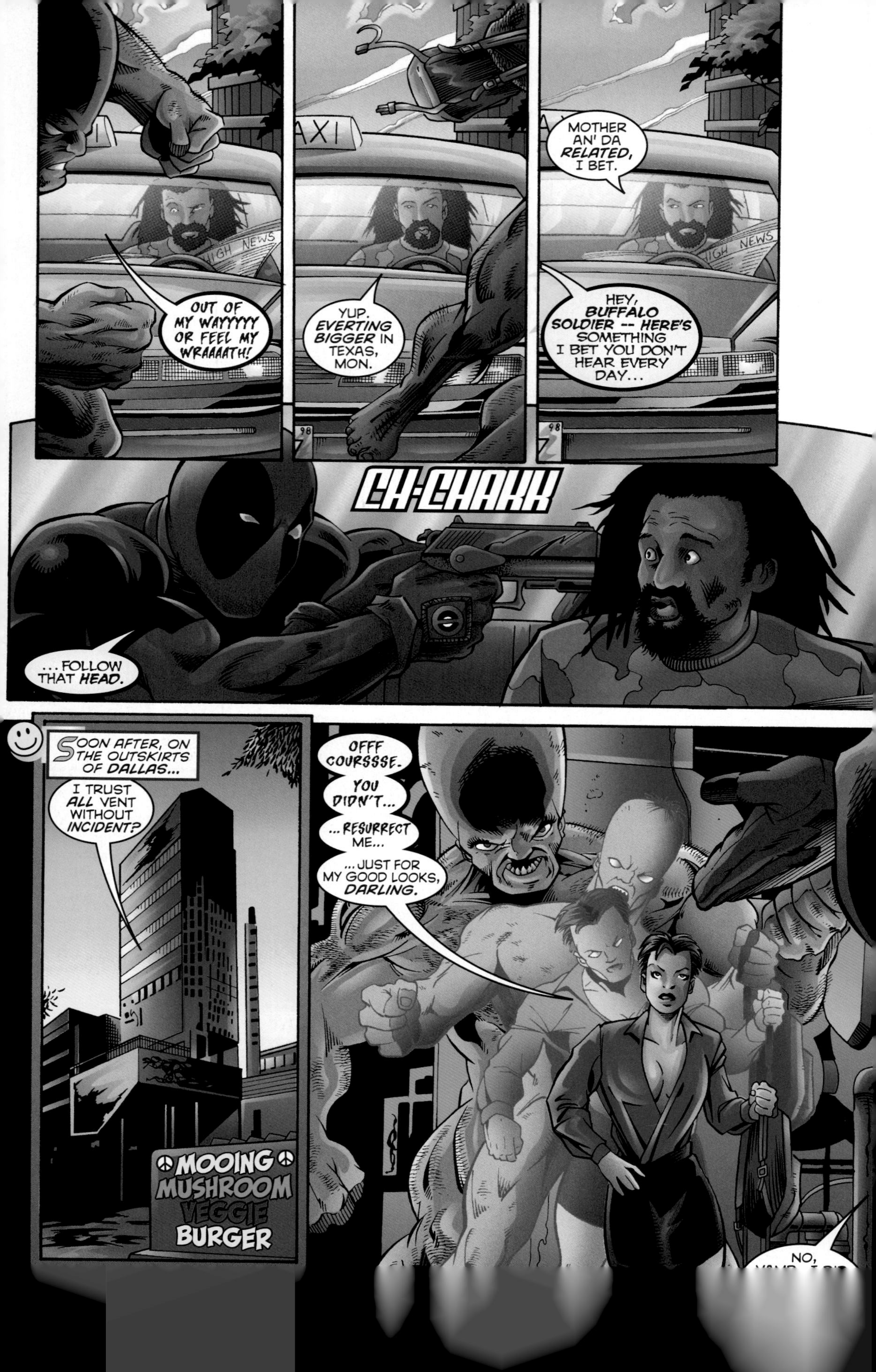

OUT OF MY WAYYYYY OR FEEL MY WRAAAATH!
YUP. EVERTING BIGGER IN TEXAS, MON.
MOTHER AN' DA RELATED, I BET.
HEY, BUFFALO SOLDIER -- HERE'S SOMETHING I BET YOU DON'T HEAR EVERY DAY...
CH-CHAKK
...FOLLOW THAT HEAD.
SOON AFTER, ON THE OUTSKIRTS OF DALLAS...
I TRUST ALL VENT WITHOUT INCIDENT?
MOOING MUSHROOM VEGGIE BURGER
OFFF COURSSSE.
YOU DIDN'T...
...RESURRECT ME...
...JUST FOR MY GOOD LOOKS, DARLING.
NO,

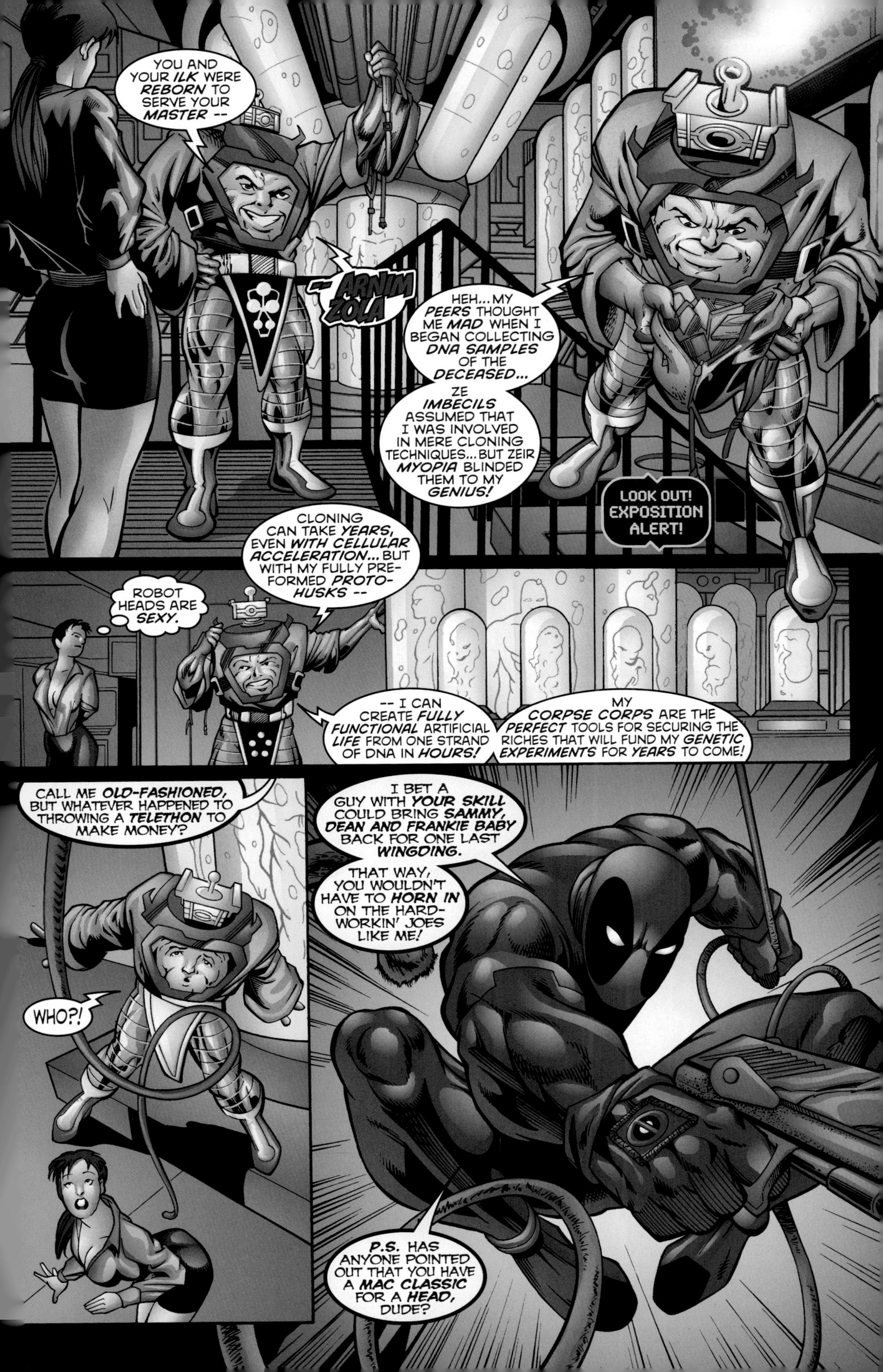
YOU AND YOUR ILK WERE REBORN TO SERVE YOUR MASTER --
-- ARNIM ZOLA
HEH... MY PEERS THOUGHT ME MAD WHEN I BEGAN COLLECTING DNA SAMPLES OF THE DECEASED...
ZE IMBECILS ASSUMED THAT I WAS INVOLVED IN MERE CLONING TECHNIQUES... BUT ZEIR MYOPIA BLINDED THEM TO MY GENIUS!
LOOK OUT! EXPOSITION ALERT!
CLONING CAN TAKE YEARS, EVEN WITH CELLULAR ACCELERATION... BUT WITH MY FULLY PRE-FORMED PROTO-HUSKS --
ROBOT HEADS ARE SEXY.
-- I CAN CREATE FULLY FUNCTIONAL ARTIFICIAL LIFE FROM ONE STRAND OF DNA IN HOURS!
MY CORPSE CORPS ARE THE PERFECT TOOLS FOR SECURING THE RICHES THAT WILL FUND MY GENETIC EXPERIMENTS FOR YEARS TO COME!
CALL ME OLD-FASHIONED, BUT WHATEVER HAPPENED TO THROWING A TELETHON TO MAKE MONEY?
I BET A GUY WITH YOUR SKILL COULD BRING SAMMY, DEAN AND FRANKIE BABY BACK FOR ONE LAST WINGDING.
THAT WAY, YOU WOULDN'T HAVE TO HORN IN ON THE HARD-WORKIN' JOES LIKE ME!
WHO?!
P.S. HAS ANYONE POINTED OUT THAT YOU HAVE A MAC CLASSIC FOR A HEAD, DUDE?

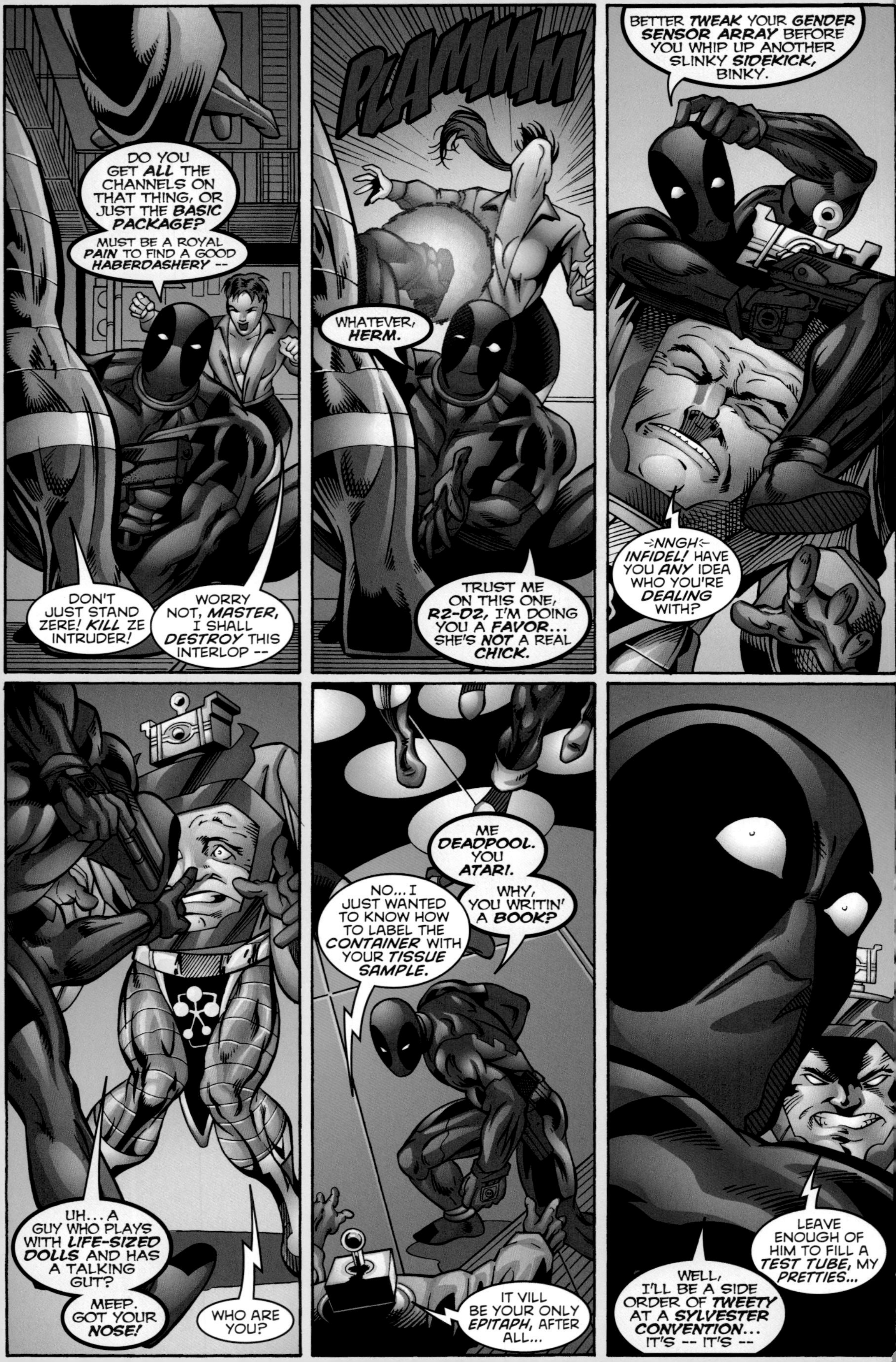
DO YOU GET ALL THE CHANNELS ON THAT THING, OR JUST THE BASIC PACKAGE?
MUST BE A ROYAL PAIN TO FIND A GOOD HABERDASHERY --
DON'T JUST STAND ZERE! KILL ZE INTRUDER!
WORRY NOT, MASTER, I SHALL DESTROY THIS INTERLOP --
PLAMMMM
WHATEVER, HERM.
TRUST ME ON THIS ONE, R2-D2, I'M DOING YOU A FAVOR... SHE'S NOT A REAL CHICK.
BETTER TWEAK YOUR GENDER SENSOR ARRAY BEFORE YOU WHIP UP ANOTHER SLINKY SIDEKICK, BINKY.
-NNGH- INFIDEL! HAVE YOU ANY IDEA WHO YOU'RE DEALING WITH?
UH... A GUY WHO PLAYS WITH LIFE-SIZED DOLLS AND HAS A TALKING GUT?
MEEP. GOT YOUR NOSE!
WHO ARE YOU?
ME DEADPOOL. YOU ATARI.
WHY, YOU WRITIN' A BOOK?
NO... I JUST WANTED TO KNOW HOW TO LABEL THE CONTAINER WITH YOUR TISSUE SAMPLE.
IT VILL BE YOUR ONLY EPITAPH, AFTER ALL...
LEAVE ENOUGH OF HIM TO FILL A TEST TUBE, MY PRETTIES...
WELL, I'LL BE A SIDE ORDER OF TWEETY AT A SYLVESTER CONVENTION... IT'S -- IT'S --

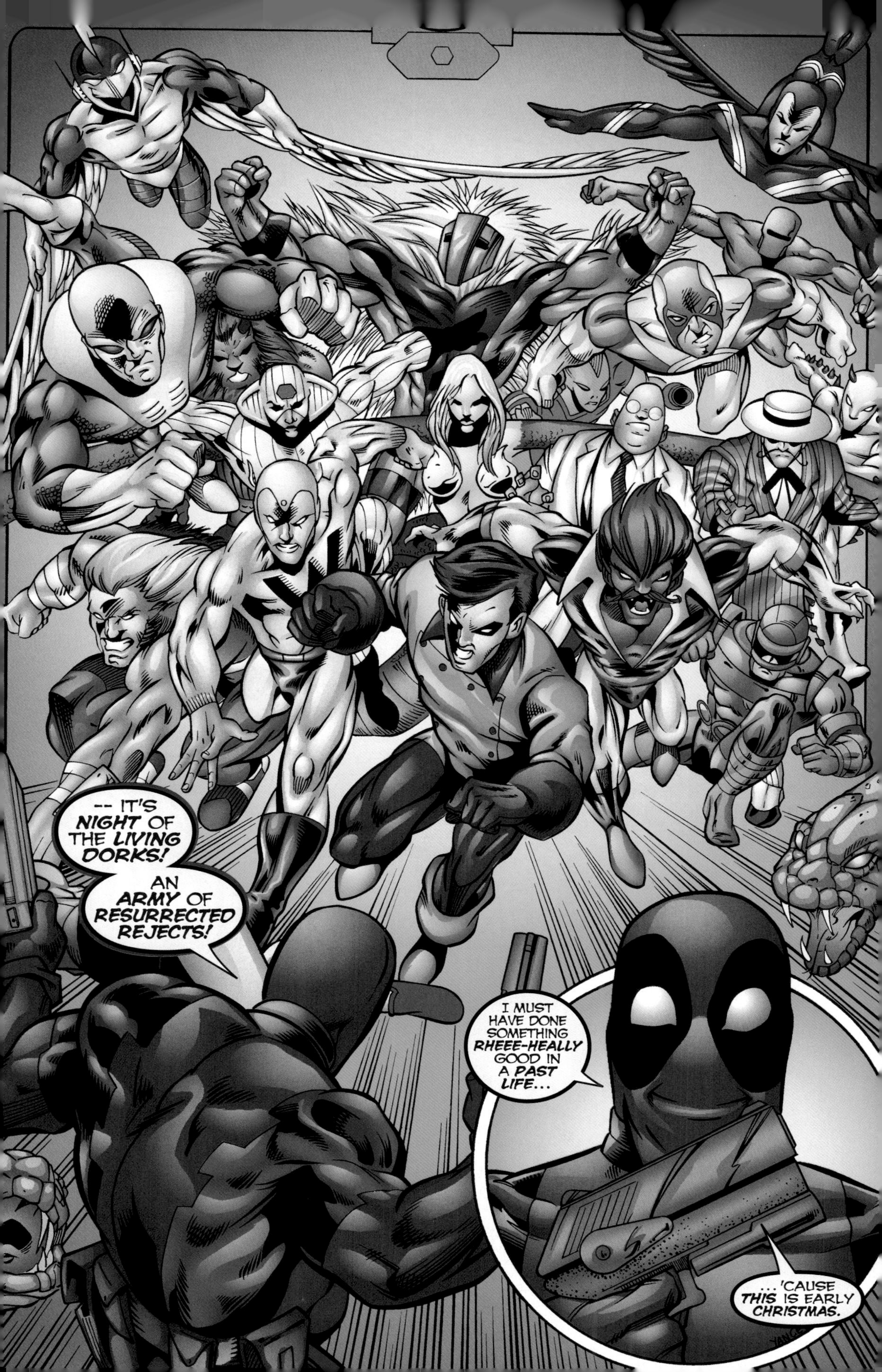
-- IT'S NIGHT OF THE LIVING DORKS!
AN ARMY OF RESURRECTED REJECTS!
I MUST HAVE DONE SOMETHING RHEEE-HEALLY GOOD IN A PAST LIFE...
...'CAUSE THIS IS EARLY CHRISTMAS.

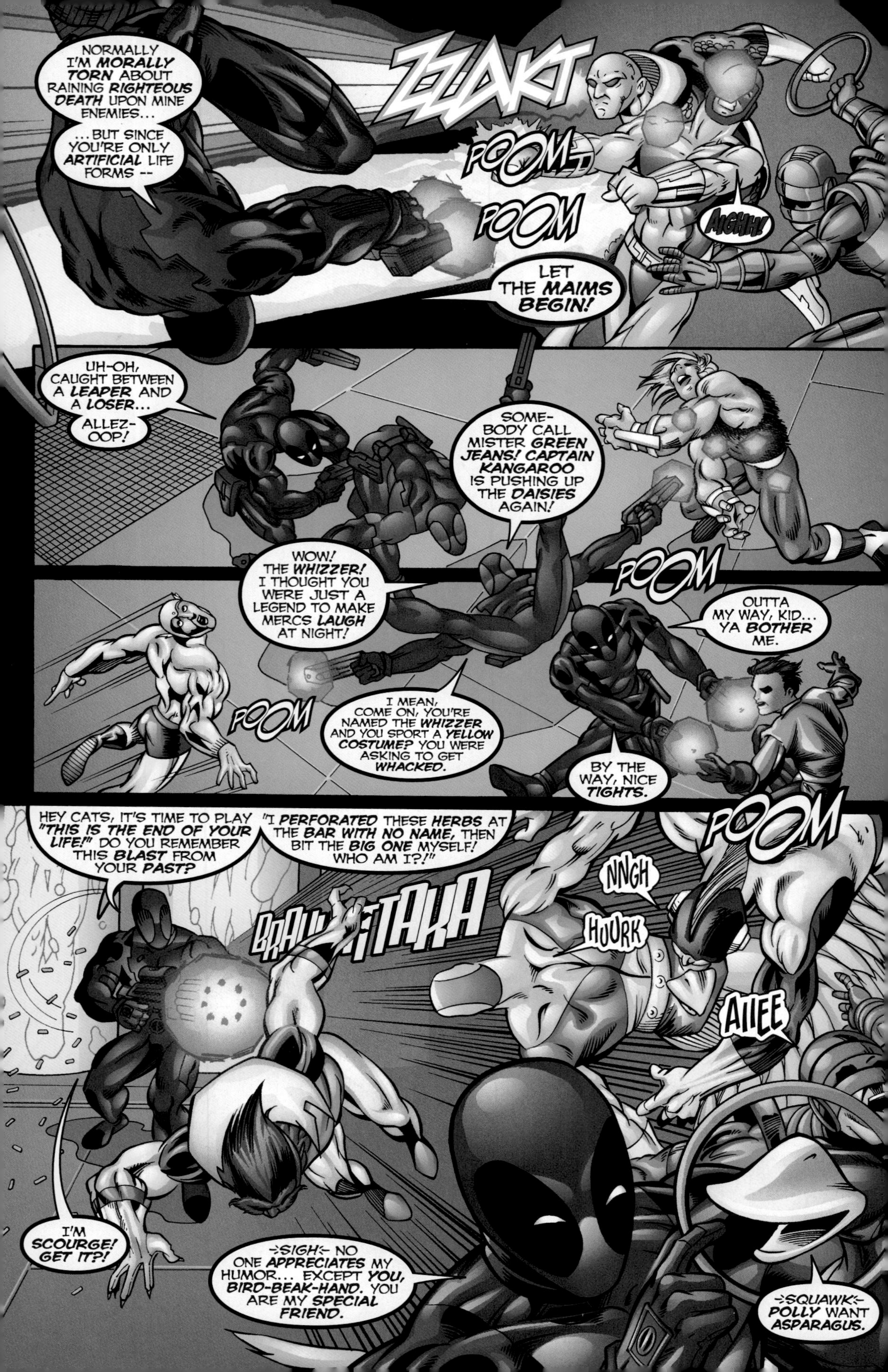
NORMALLY I'M MORALLY TORN ABOUT RAINING RIGHTEOUS DEATH UPON MINE ENEMIES...
...BUT SINCE YOU'RE ONLY ARTIFICIAL LIFE FORMS --
ZZZAKT
POOOM
POOOM
AIGHH!
LET THE MAIMS BEGIN!
UH-OH, CAUGHT BETWEEN A LEAPER AND A LOSER...
ALLEZ-OOP!
SOME-BODY CALL MISTER GREEN JEANS! CAPTAIN KANGAROO IS PUSHING UP THE DAISIES AGAIN!
WOW! THE WHIZZER! I THOUGHT YOU WERE JUST A LEGEND TO MAKE MERCS LAUGH AT NIGHT!
POOM
POOM
I MEAN, COME ON, YOU'RE NAMED THE WHIZZER AND YOU SPORT A YELLOW COSTUME? YOU WERE ASKING TO GET WHACKED.
OUTTA MY WAY, KID... YA BOTHER ME.
BY THE WAY, NICE TIGHTS.
HEY CATS, IT'S TIME TO PLAY "THIS IS THE END OF YOUR LIFE!" DO YOU REMEMBER THIS BLAST FROM YOUR PAST?
"I PERFORATED THESE HERBS AT THE BAR WITH NO NAME, THEN BIT THE BIG ONE MYSELF! WHO AM I?!"
POOM
NNGH
HUURK
AIIEE
I'M SCOURGE! GET IT?!
-SIGH- NO ONE APPRECIATES MY HUMOR... EXCEPT YOU, BIRD-BEAK-HAND. YOU ARE MY SPECIAL FRIEND.
-SQUAWK- POLLY WANT ASPARAGUS.

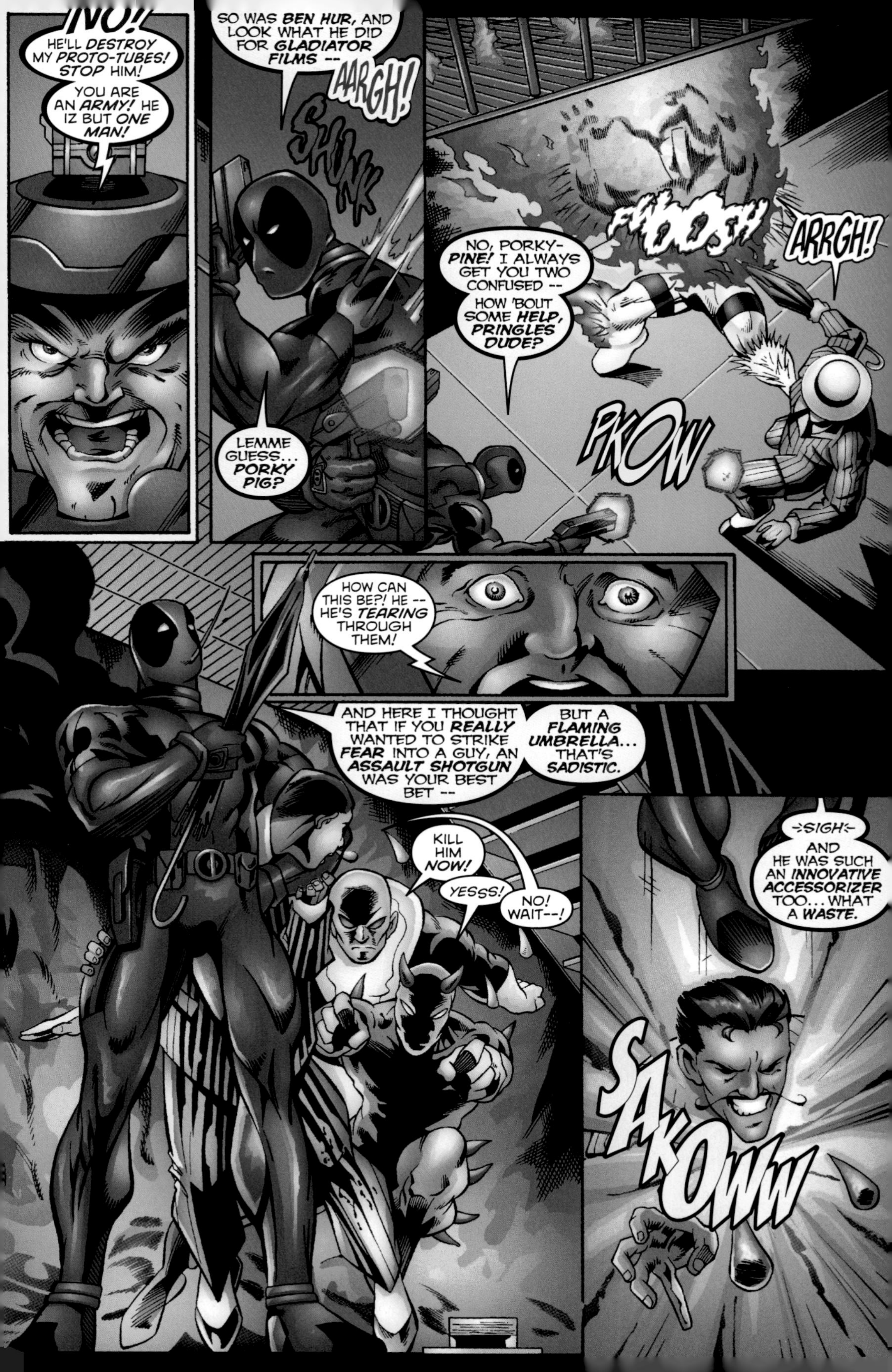
NO!
HE'LL DESTROY MY PROTO-TUBES! STOP HIM!
YOU ARE AN ARMY! HE IZ BUT ONE MAN!
SO WAS BEN HUR, AND LOOK WHAT HE DID FOR GLADIATOR FILMS --
AARGH!
SHUNK
LEMME GUESS... PORKY PIG?
FWOOSH
NO, PORKY-PINE! I ALWAYS GET YOU TWO CONFUSED --
HOW 'BOUT SOME HELP, PRINGLES DUDE?
ARRGH!
PKOW
HOW CAN THIS BE?! HE -- HE'S TEARING THROUGH THEM!
AND HERE I THOUGHT THAT IF YOU REALLY WANTED TO STRIKE FEAR INTO A GUY, AN ASSAULT SHOTGUN WAS YOUR BEST BET --
BUT A FLAMING UMBRELLA... THAT'S SADISTIC.
KILL HIM NOW!
YESSS!
NO! WAIT--!
-SIGH-
AND HE WAS SUCH AN INNOVATIVE ACCESSORIZER TOO... WHAT A WASTE.
SAKOWW

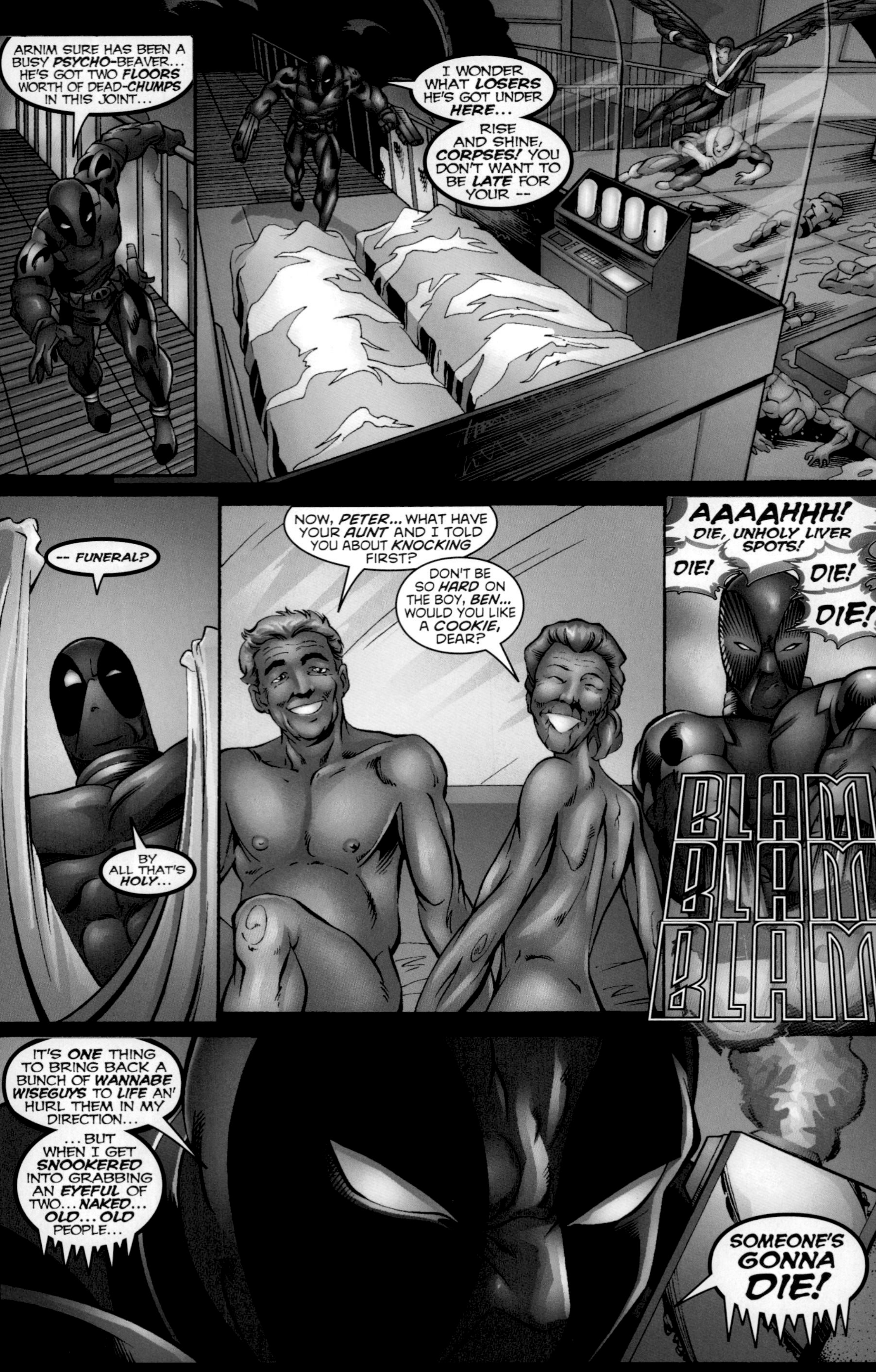
ARNIM SURE HAS BEEN A BUSY PSYCHO-BEAVER... HE'S GOT TWO FLOORS WORTH OF DEAD-CHUMPS IN THIS JOINT...
I WONDER WHAT LOSERS HE'S GOT UNDER HERE...
RISE AND SHINE, CORPSES! YOU DON'T WANT TO BE LATE FOR YOUR --
-- FUNERAL?
BY ALL THAT'S HOLY...
NOW, PETER... WHAT HAVE YOUR AUNT AND I TOLD YOU ABOUT KNOCKING FIRST?
DON'T BE SO HARD ON THE BOY, BEN... WOULD YOU LIKE A COOKIE, DEAR?
AAAAHHH! DIE, UNHOLY LIVER SPOTS!
DIE! DIE! DIE!
BLAM BLAM BLAM
IT'S ONE THING TO BRING BACK A BUNCH OF WANNABE WISEGUYS TO LIFE AN' HURL THEM IN MY DIRECTION...
...BUT WHEN I GET SNOOKERED INTO GRABBING AN EYEFUL OF TWO... NAKED... OLD... OLD PEOPLE...
SOMEONE'S GONNA DIE!

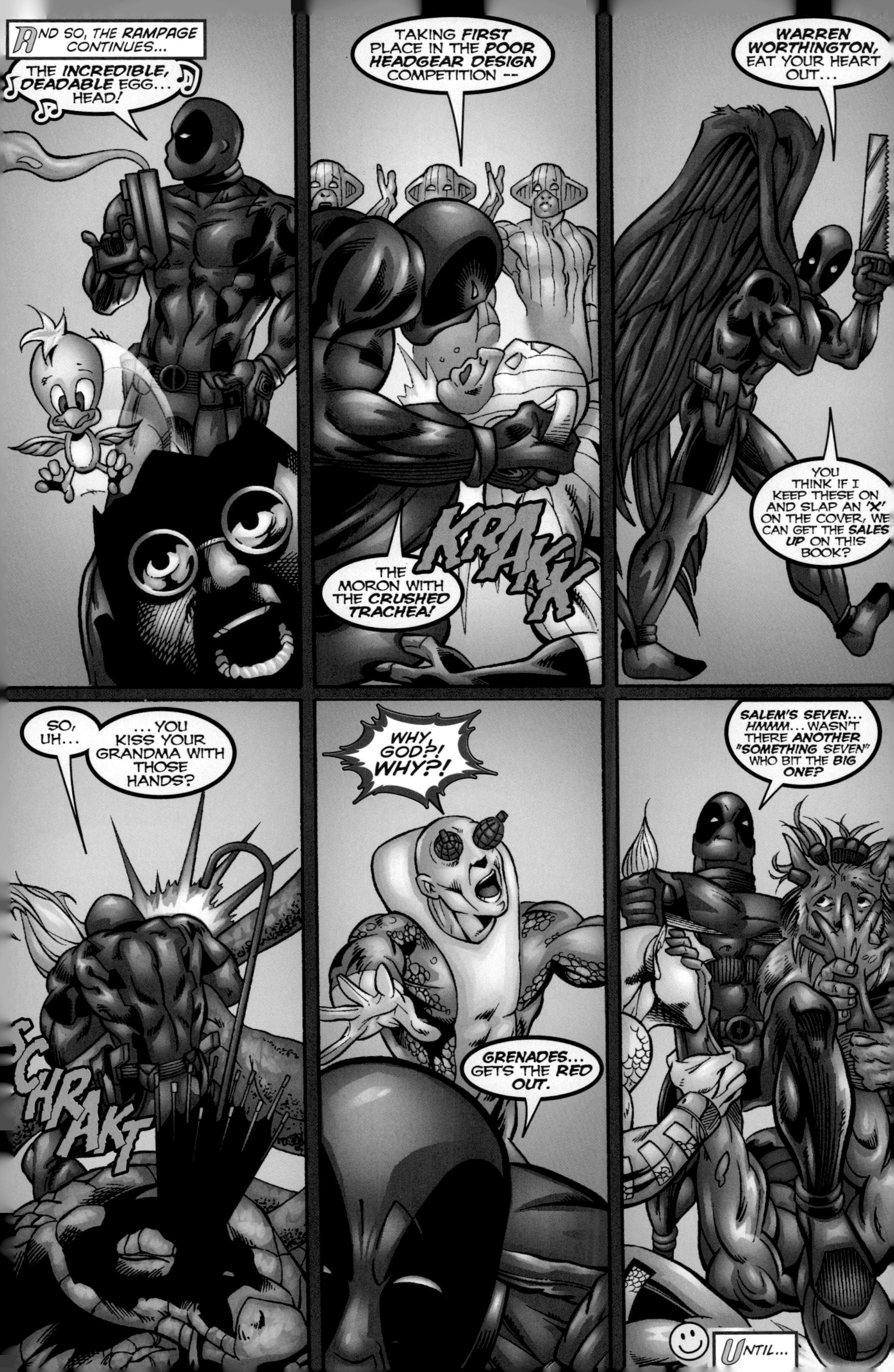
AND SO, THE RAMPAGE CONTINUES...
THE INCREDIBLE, DEADABLE EGG... HEAD!
TAKING FIRST PLACE IN THE POOR HEADGEAR DESIGN COMPETITION --
KRAKK
THE MORON WITH THE CRUSHED TRACHEA!
WARREN WORTHINGTON, EAT YOUR HEART OUT...
YOU THINK IF I KEEP THESE ON AND SLAP AN 'X' ON THE COVER, WE CAN GET THE SALES UP ON THIS BOOK?
SO, UH...
...YOU KISS YOUR GRANDMA WITH THOSE HANDS?
SCHRAKT
WHY, GOD?! WHY?!
GRENADES... GETS THE RED OUT.
SALEM'S SEVEN... HMMM... WASN'T THERE ANOTHER "SOMETHING SEVEN" WHO BIT THE BIG ONE?
UNTIL...

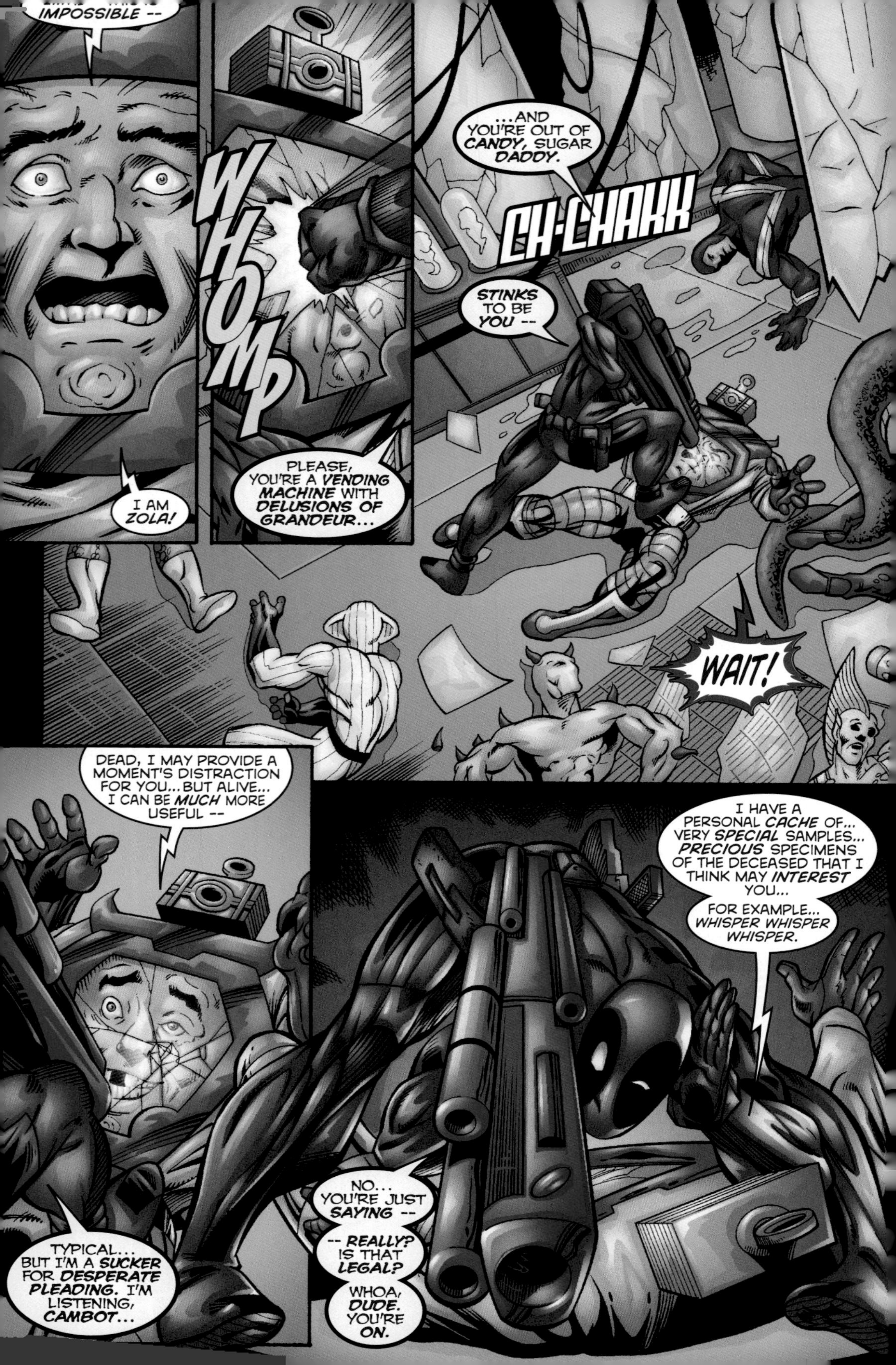
IMPOSSIBLE --
I AM ZOLA!
WHOMP
PLEASE, YOU'RE A VENDING MACHINE WITH DELUSIONS OF GRANDEUR...
...AND YOU'RE OUT OF CANDY, SUGAR DADDY.
CH-CHAKK
STINKS TO BE YOU --
WAIT!
DEAD, I MAY PROVIDE A MOMENT'S DISTRACTION FOR YOU...BUT ALIVE... I CAN BE MUCH MORE USEFUL --
I HAVE A PERSONAL CACHE OF... VERY SPECIAL SAMPLES... PRECIOUS SPECIMENS OF THE DECEASED THAT I THINK MAY INTEREST YOU...
FOR EXAMPLE... WHISPER WHISPER WHISPER.
TYPICAL... BUT I'M A SUCKER FOR DESPERATE PLEADING. I'M LISTENING, CAMBOT...
NO... YOU'RE JUST SAYING --
-- REALLY? IS THAT LEGAL?
WHOA, DUDE. YOU'RE ON.

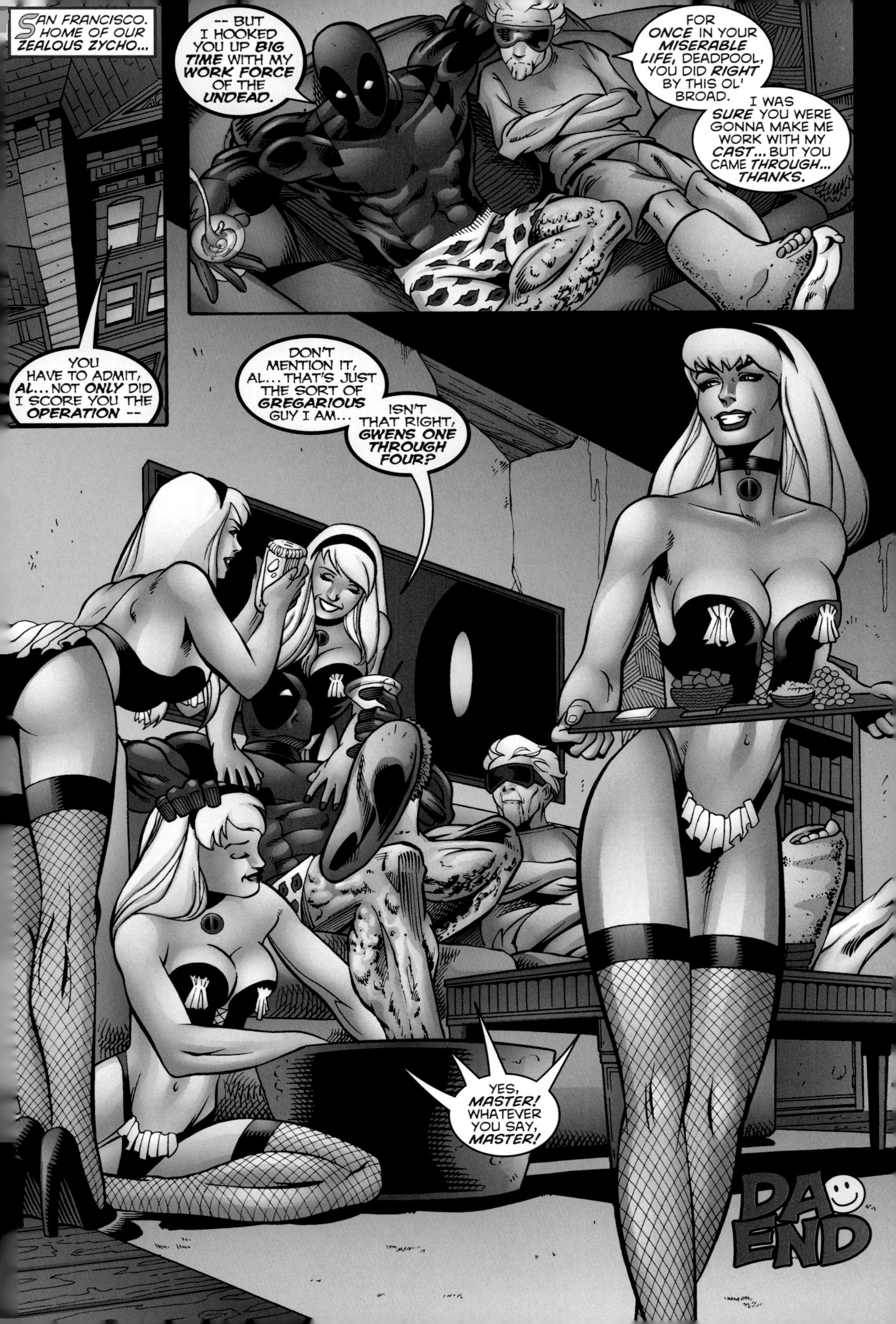
SAN FRANCISCO. HOME OF OUR ZEALOUS ZYCHO...
YOU HAVE TO ADMIT, AL... NOT ONLY DID I SCORE YOU THE OPERATION --
-- BUT I HOOKED YOU UP BIG TIME WITH MY WORK FORCE OF THE UNDEAD.
FOR ONCE IN YOUR MISERABLE LIFE, DEADPOOL, YOU DID RIGHT BY THIS OL' BROAD.
I WAS SURE YOU WERE GONNA MAKE ME WORK WITH MY CAST... BUT YOU CAME THROUGH... THANKS.
DON'T MENTION IT, AL... THAT'S JUST THE SORT OF GREGARIOUS GUY I AM...
ISN'T THAT RIGHT, GWENS ONE THROUGH FOUR?
YES, MASTER! WHATEVER YOU SAY, MASTER!
DA END

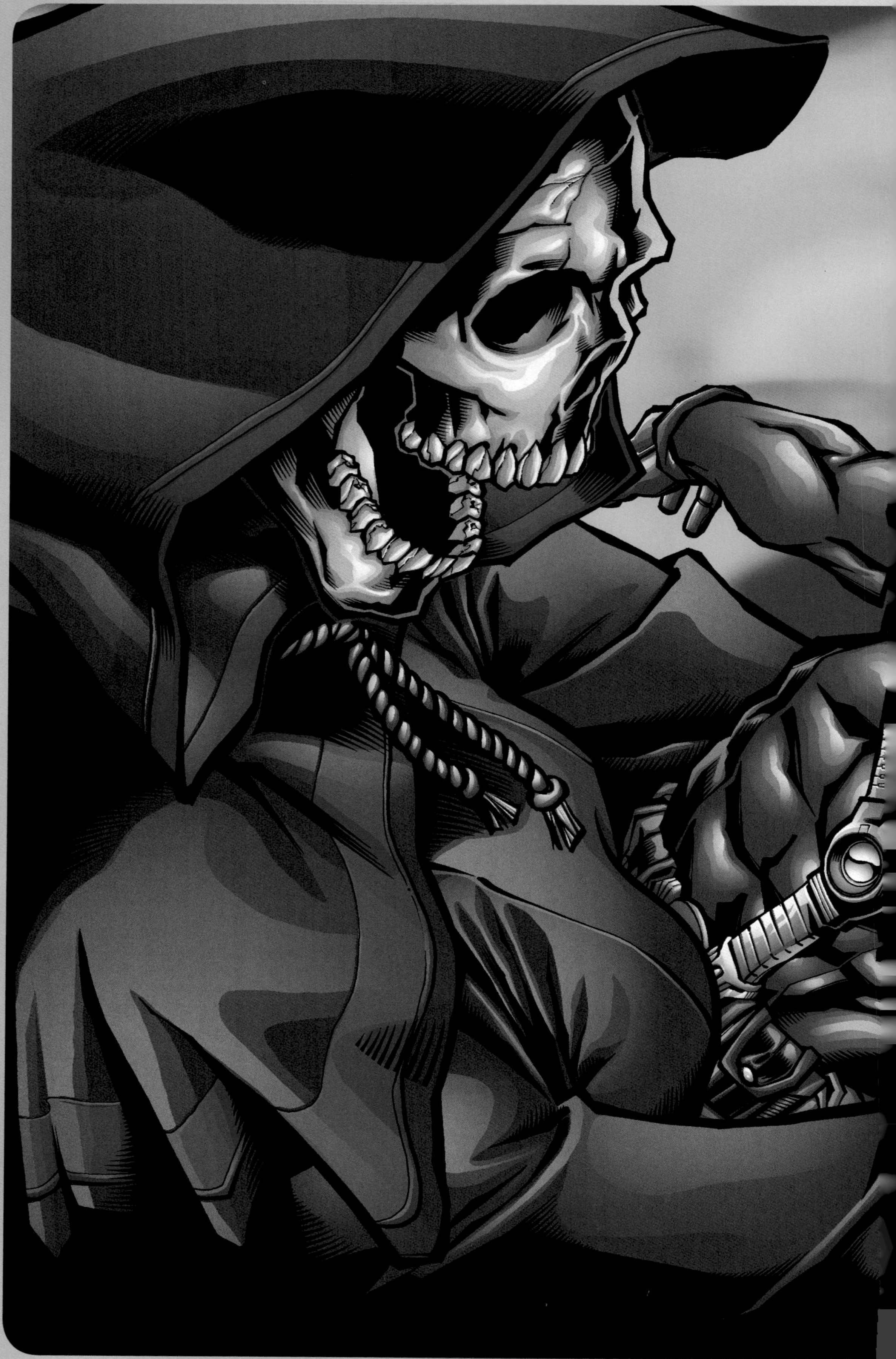

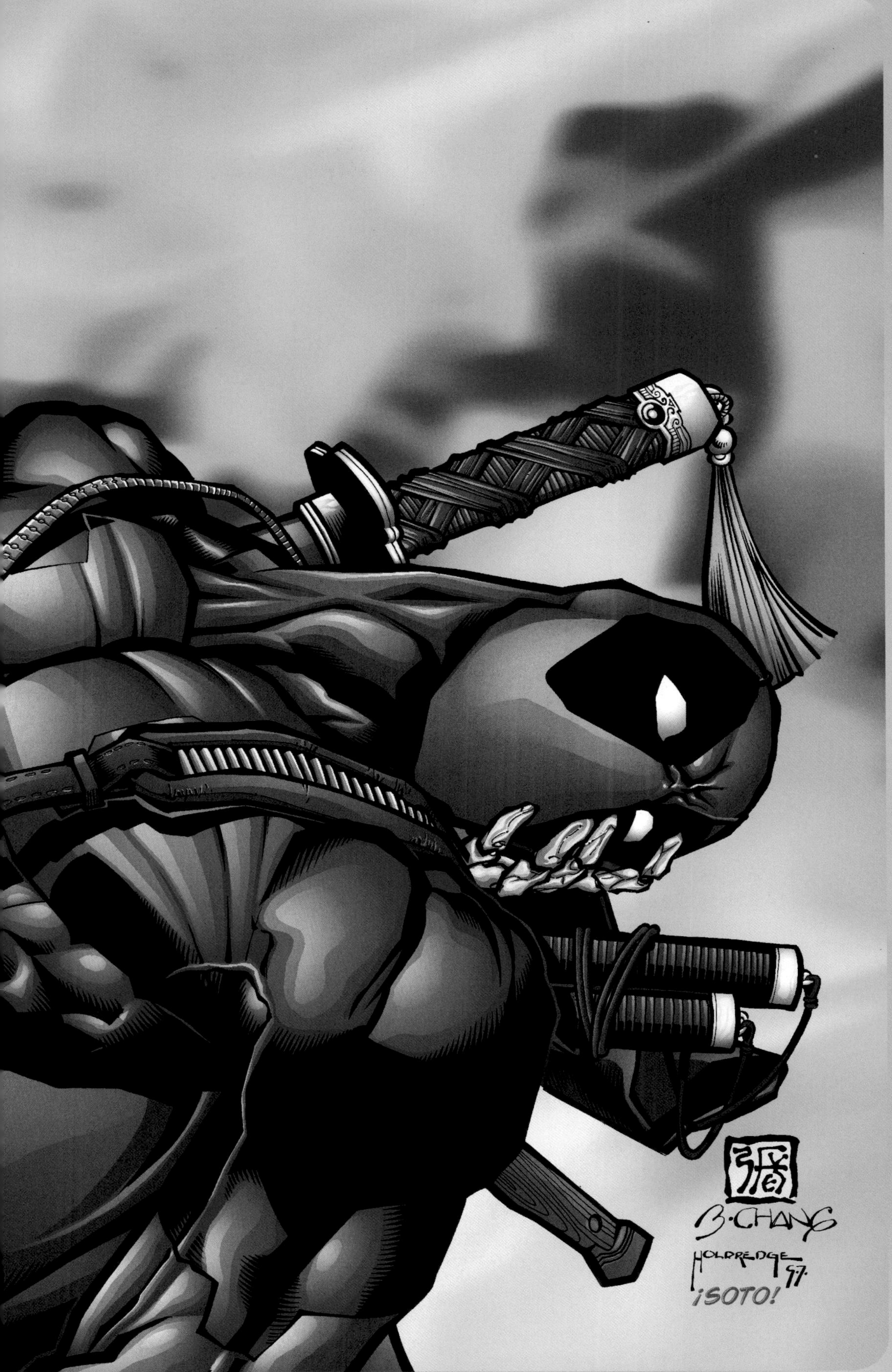
B. CHANG
HOLDREDGE 97.
¡SOTO!

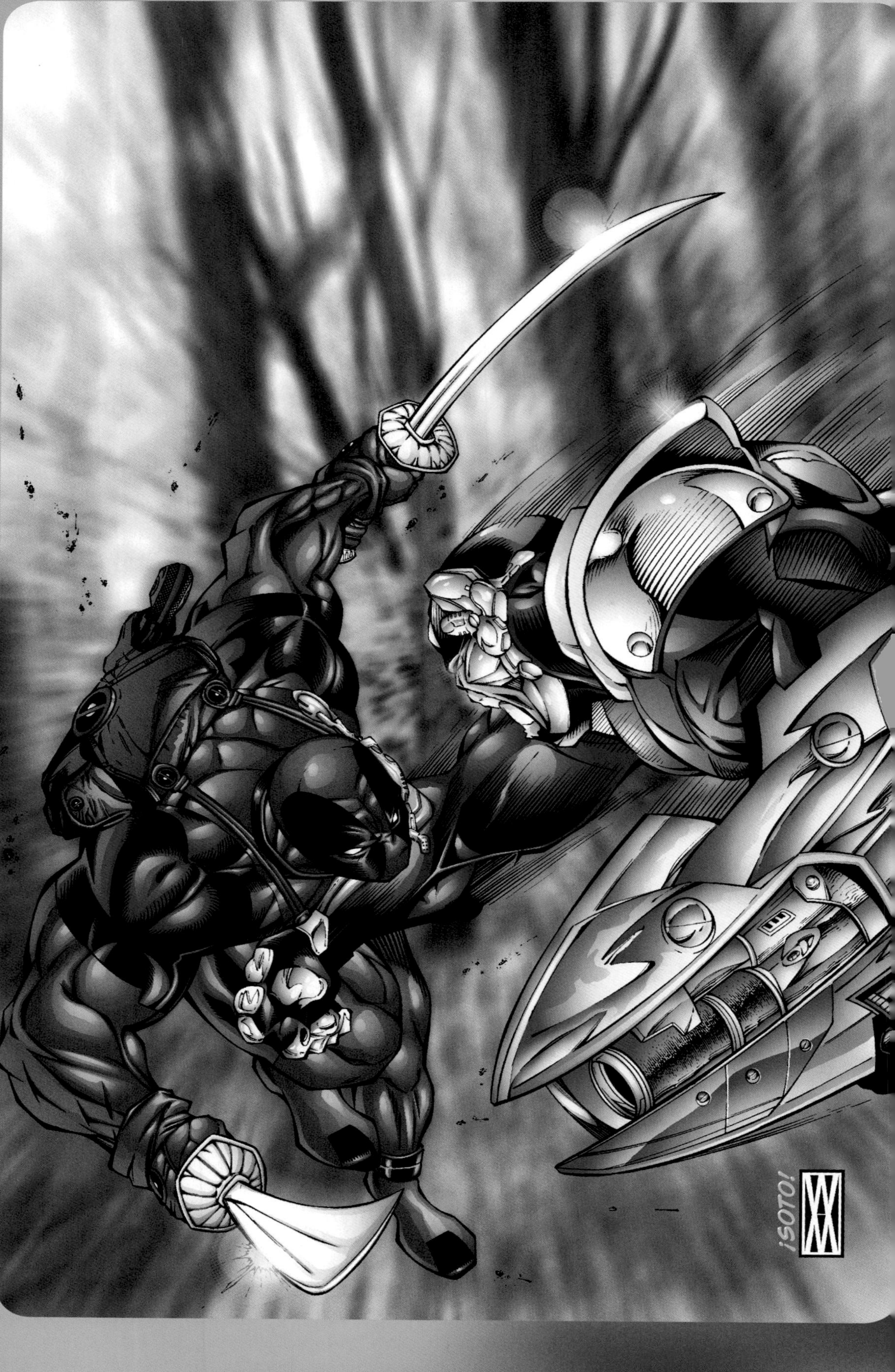
¡SOTO!

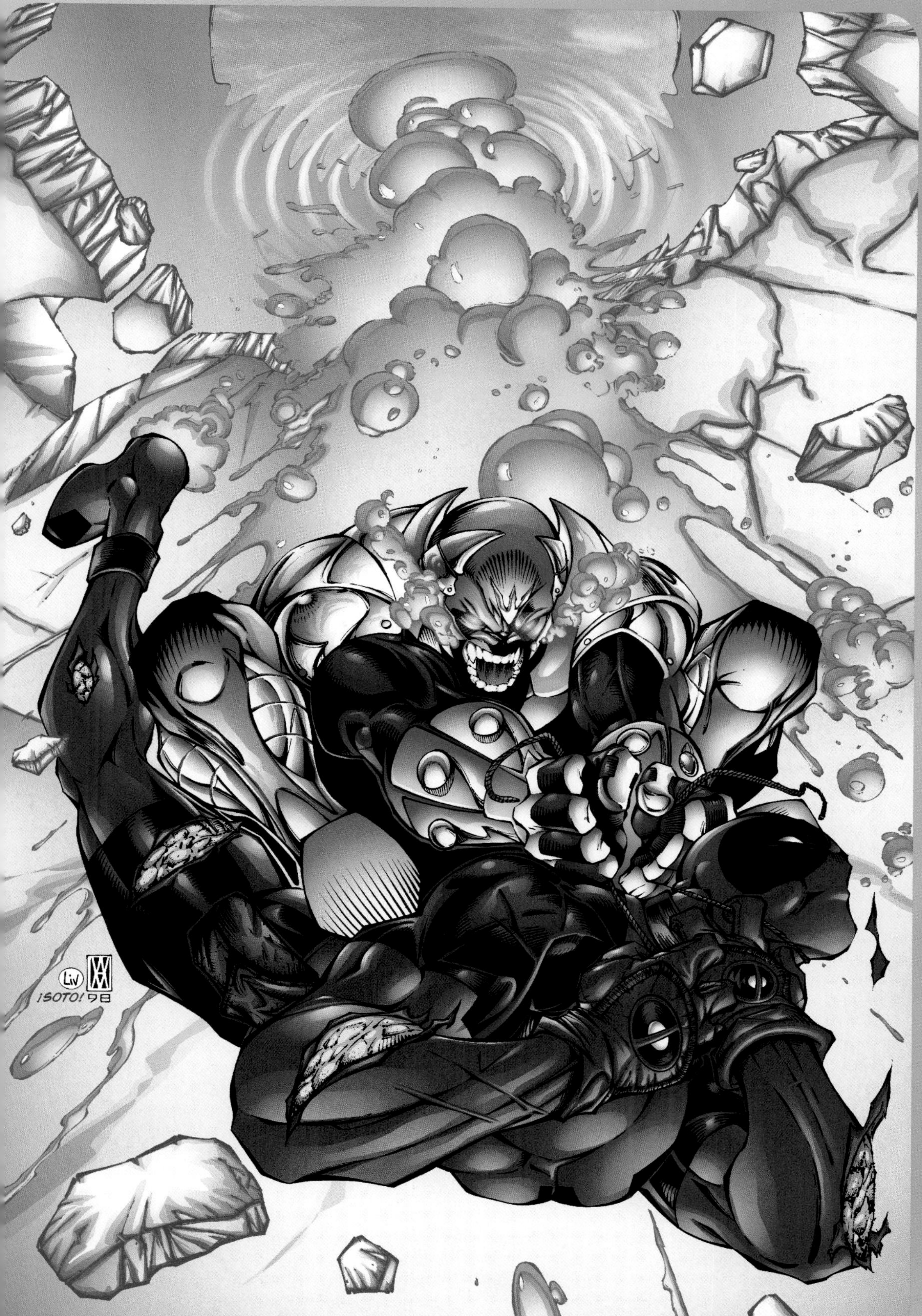
Liv
¡SOTO! 98

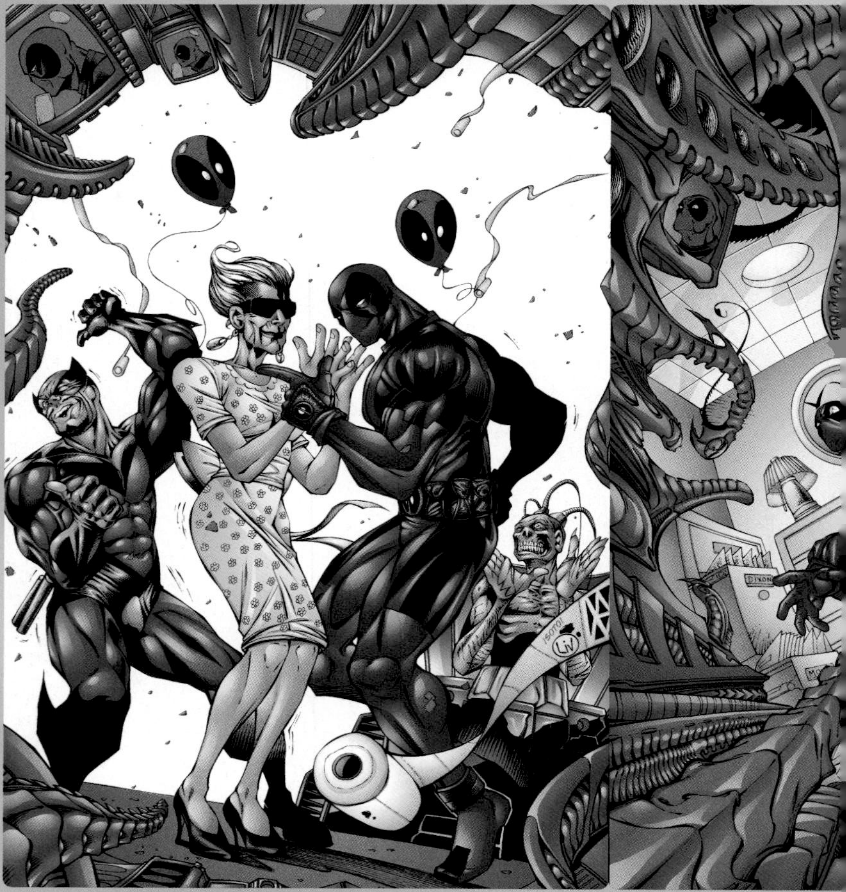

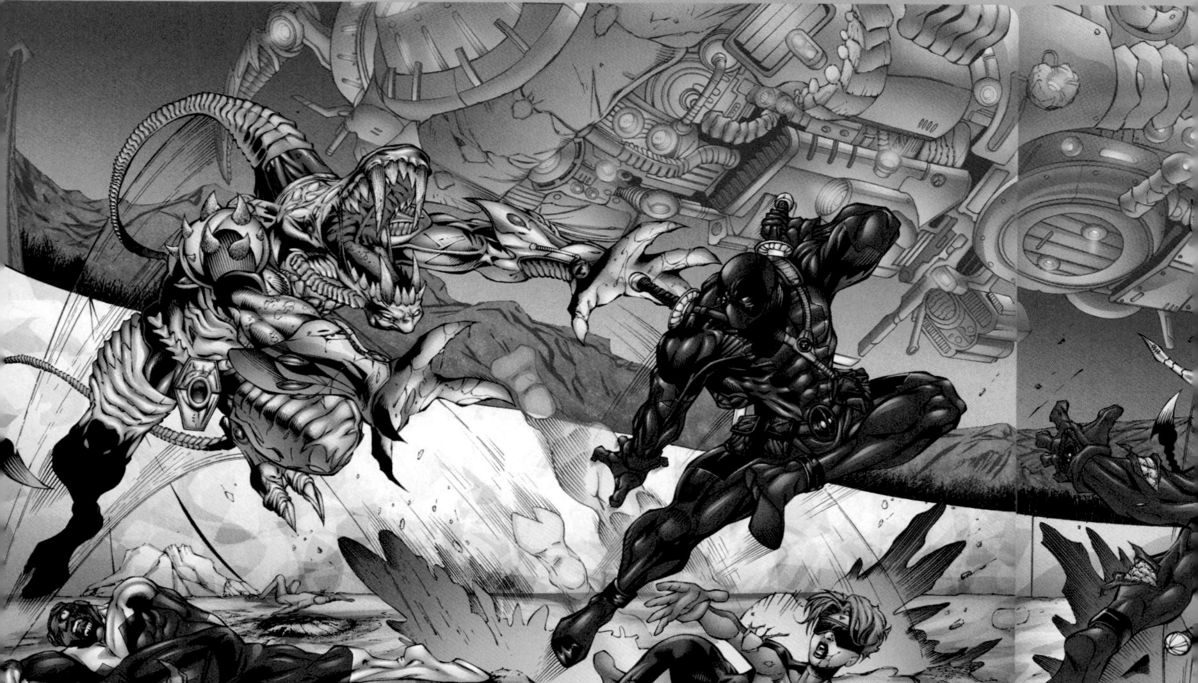

sketchbook

This page was going to be page one of *Deadpool* #22, also drawn by Pete Woods (no conspiracy, honest!). However, after Pete had already finished penciling the page, we decided to assign him to the *Deadpool Team-Up Starring Widdle Wade* one-shot instead. Considering he only did one page, it wasn't a big deal to just start *Deadpool* #22 over with Anthony Williams on penciling duty! We think it worked out pretty well!

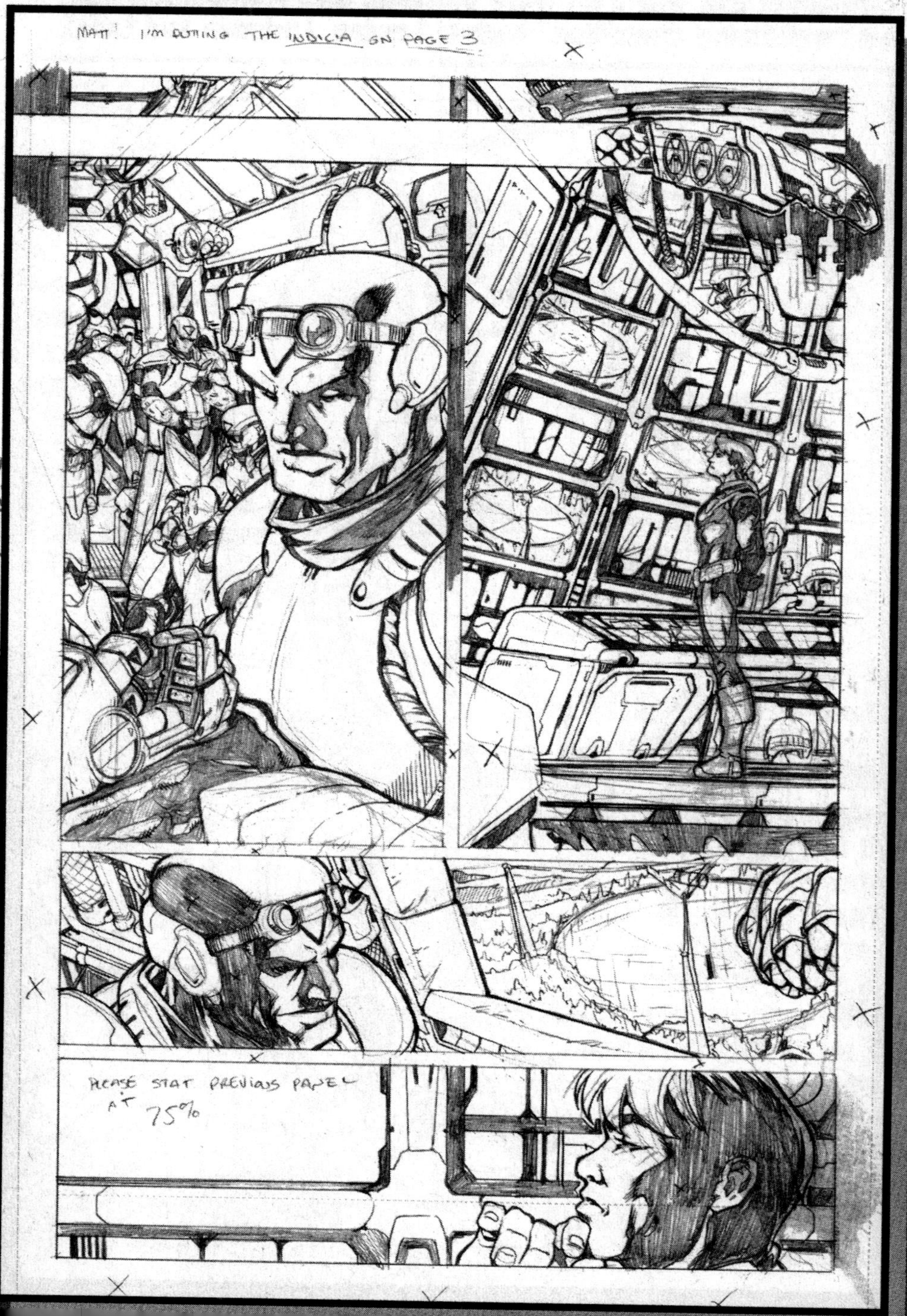
MATT! I'M PUTTING THE INDICIA ON PAGE 3
PLEASE STAT PREVIOUS PANEL AT 75%

Over here we've got an unused page of Pete Woods pencils from issue #20. According to the original plot, the issue was supposed to end with Blind Al setting up a booby trap for our witty mercenary. However, we decided to drop the page (funny as it was) so that we could end the issue with a dramatic, suspenseful cliffhanger that was a lot more powerful (i.e., Montgomery and his "welcoming committee" back at Landau, Luckman and Lake).

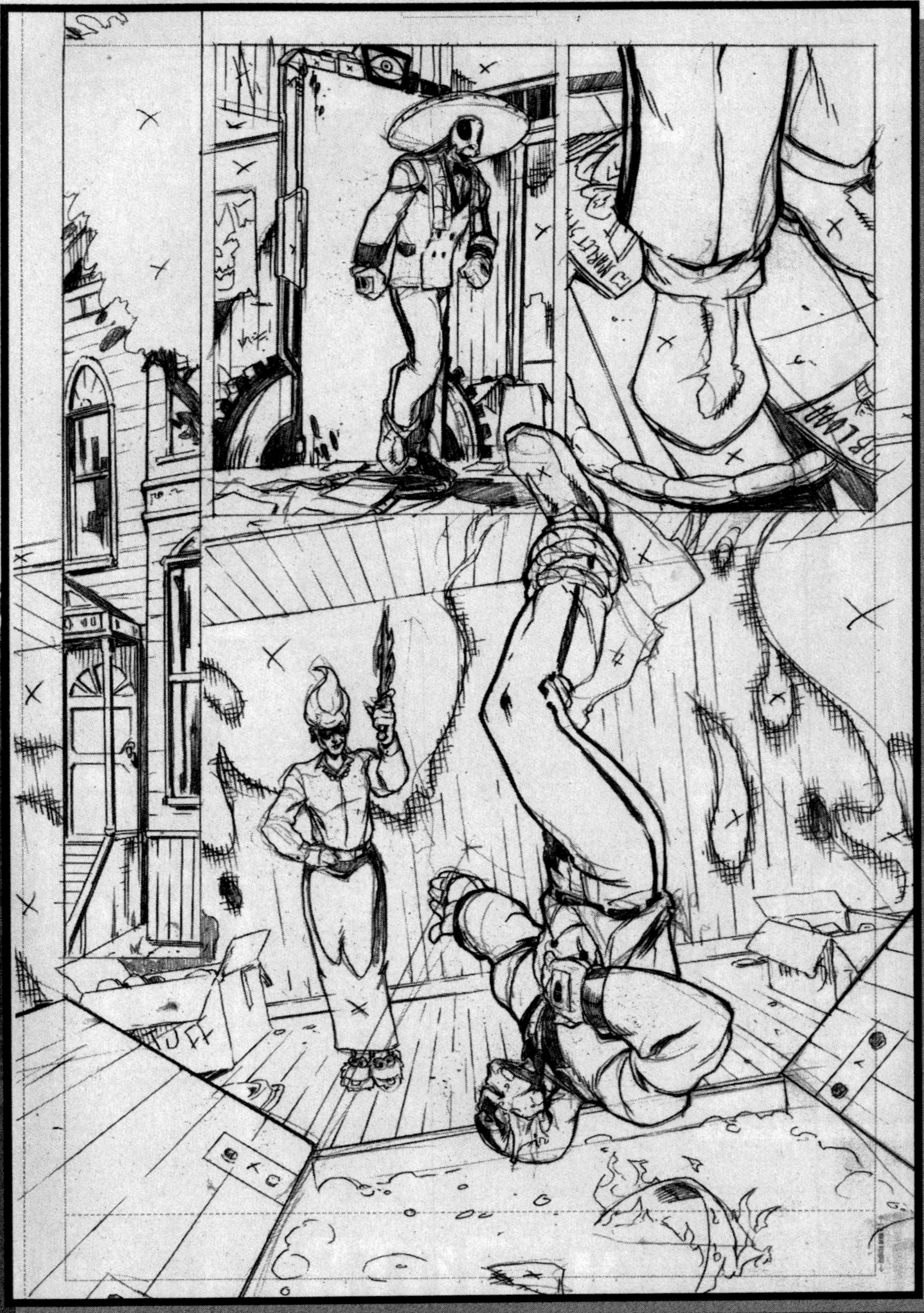
MARKET ST
BLAM

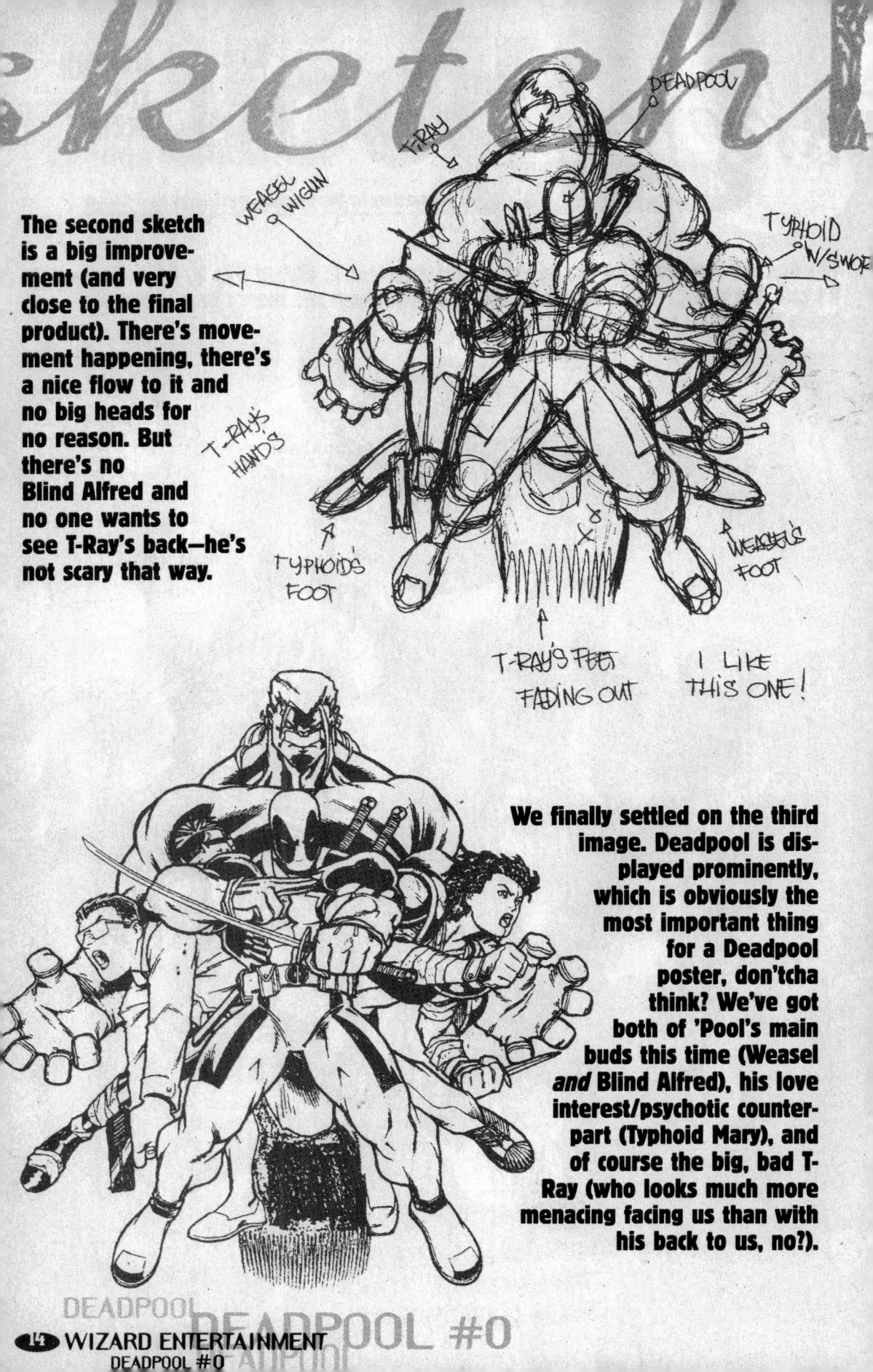

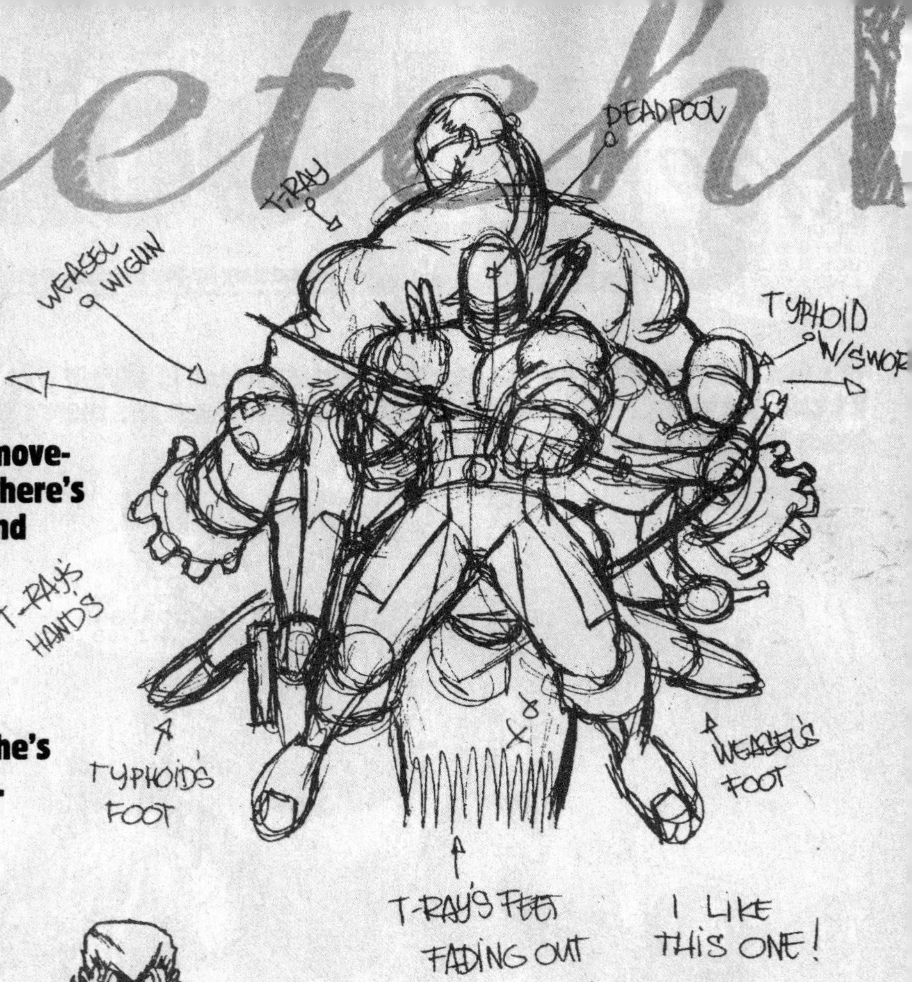
sketch
DEADPOOL
T-RAY
WEASEL W/GUN
TYPHOID W/SWOR
T-RAY'S HANDS
TYPHOID'S FOOT
WEASEL'S FOOT
T-RAY'S FEET FADING OUT
I LIKE THIS ONE!

The second sketch is a big improvement (and very close to the final product). There's movement happening, there's a nice flow to it and no big heads for no reason. But there's no Blind Alfred and no one wants to see T-Ray's back—he's not scary that way.

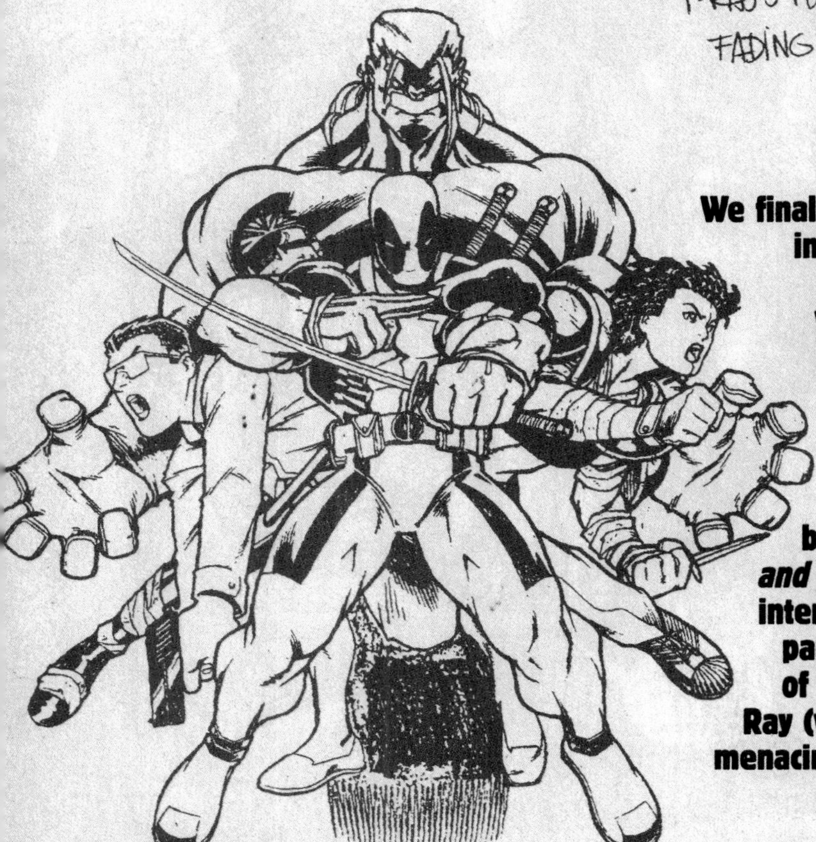

We finally settled on the third image. Deadpool is displayed prominently, which is obviously the most important thing for a Deadpool poster, don'tcha think? We've got both of 'Pool's main buds this time (Weasel *and* Blind Alfred), his love interest/psychotic counterpart (Typhoid Mary), and of course the big, bad T-Ray (who looks much more menacing facing us than with his back to us, no?).

sketchbook deadpool

BEHIND THE SCENES GOODIES

Commentary by Deadpool assistant editor Paul Tutrone

This was the first sketch for the Deadpool poster that ran in *Wizard* #71 by Ed McGuinness. It's cool, but kinda...calm. There's no action, no movement and there's three really big heads for, like, no reason.

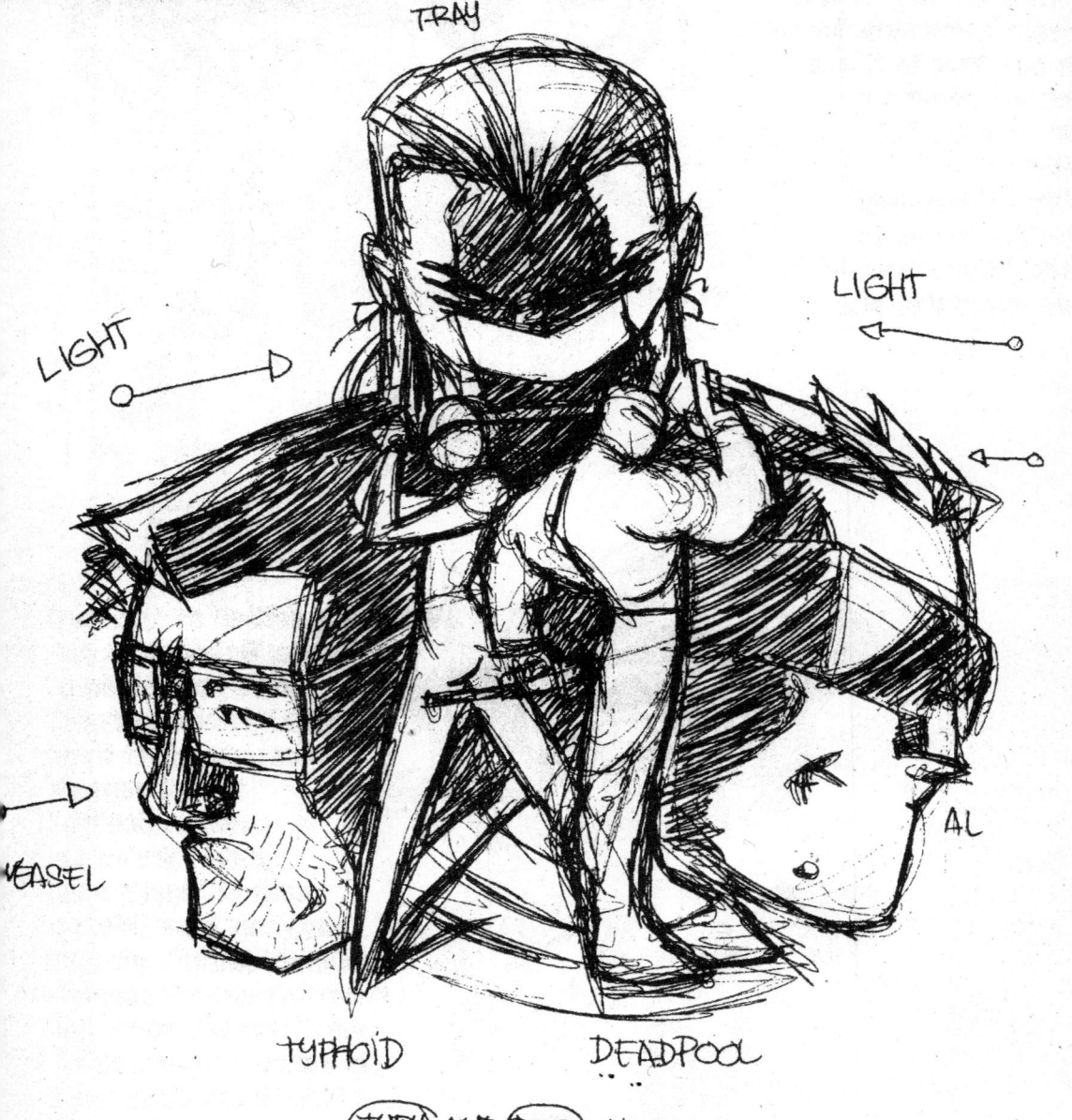

TRAY

LIGHT

LIGHT

WEASEL

AL

TYPHOID

DEADPOOL

TYPH AND DEAD HAVE VIRTUALLY NO DARKS ON THEM TO OFFSET HEAVY BACKGROUND SHADOW.

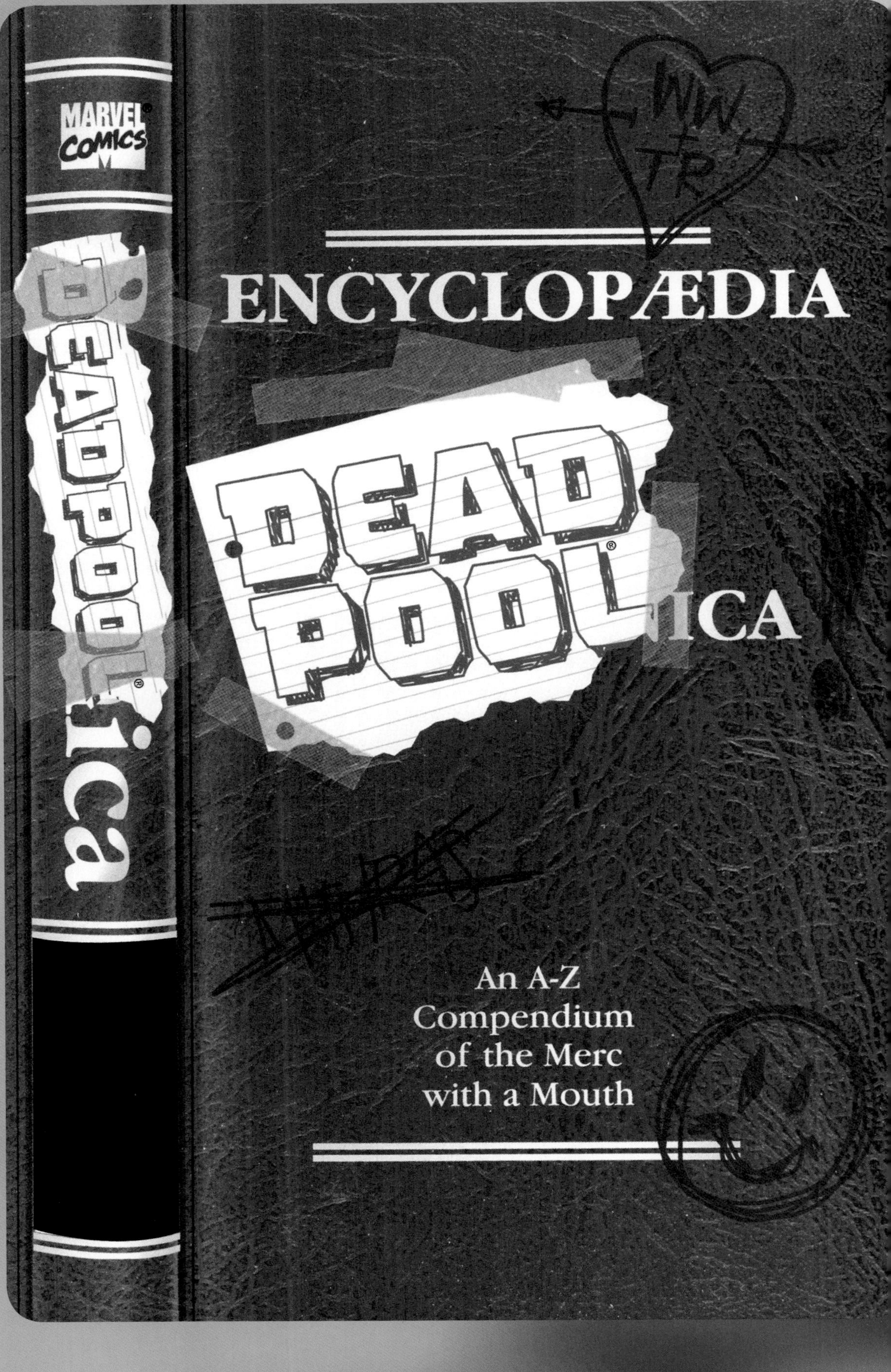
MARVEL COMICS
DEADPOOLica
ENCYCLOPÆDIA
DEADPOOLICA
An A-Z
Compendium
of the Merc
with a Mouth

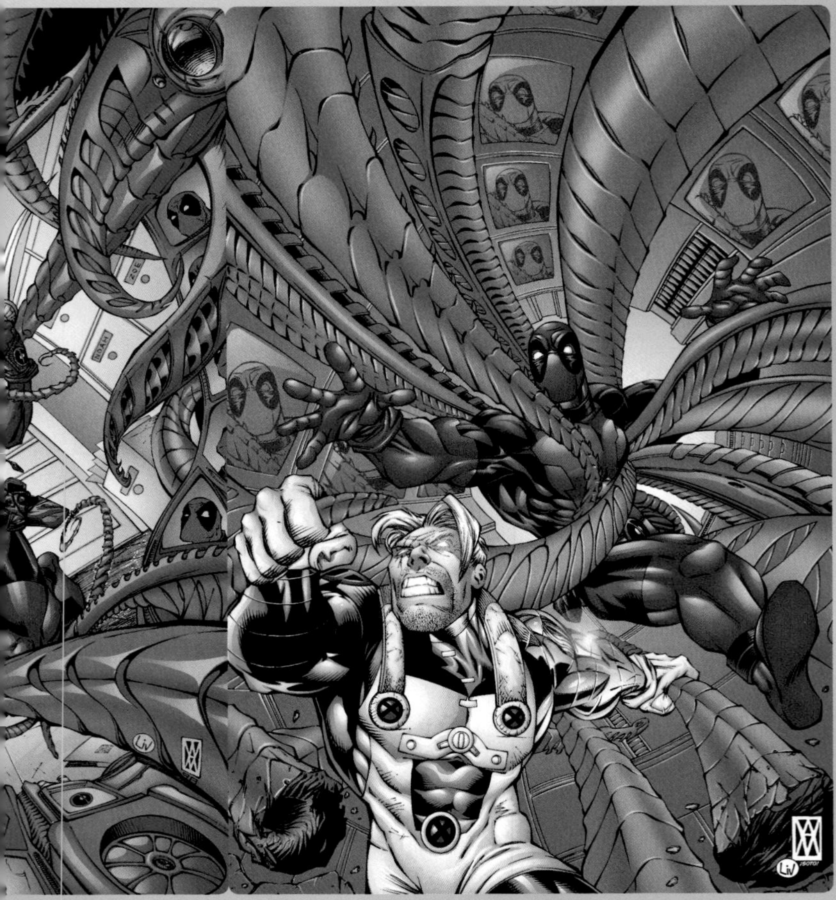

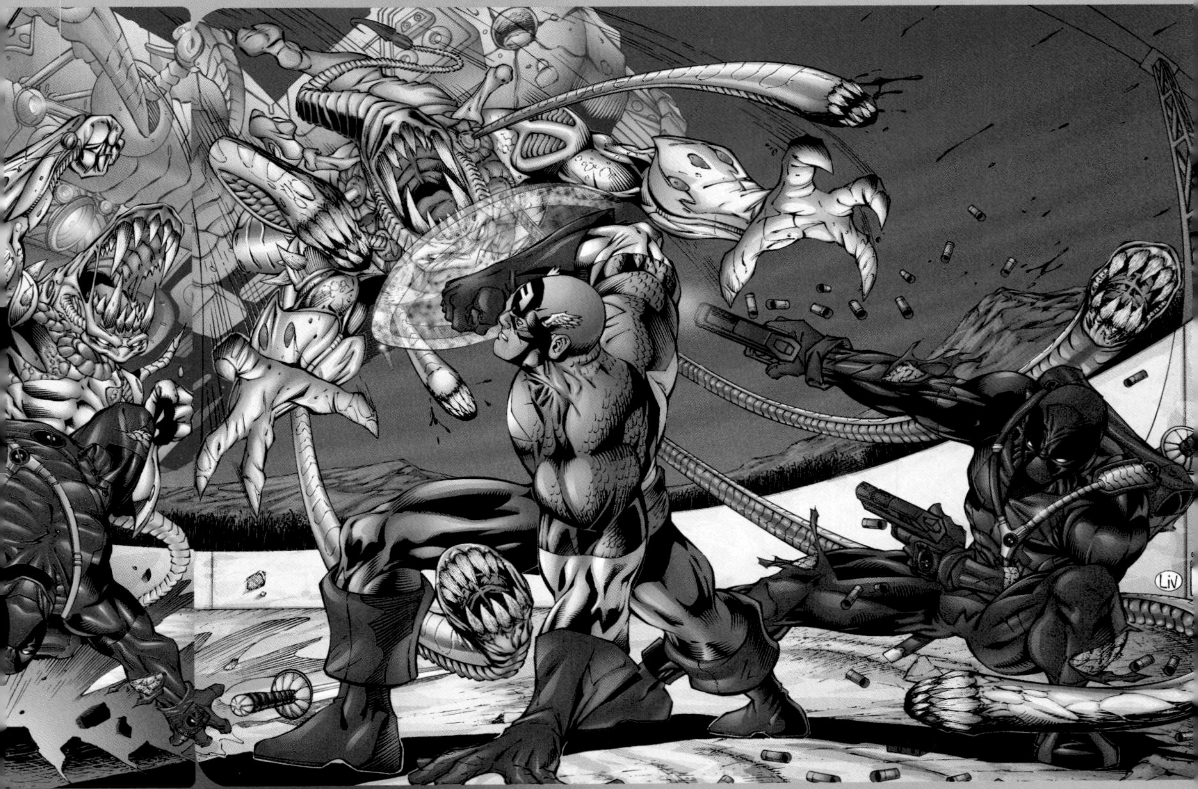